GO-GO to Glory

Edited by Don Zminda
Associate editors: R. J. Lesch, Len Levin & Bill Nowlin

Society for American Baseball Research, Inc.
Phoenix, AZ

Go-Go to Glory: The 1959 Chicago White Sox
Edited by Don Zminda
Associate editors: R. J. Lesch, Len Levin & Bill Nowlin
Copyright © 2019
Society for American Baseball Research, Inc.
All rights reserved. Reproduction in whole or in part without permission is prohibited.
ISBN 978-1-970159-11-0
Ebook ISBN 978-1-970159-10-3
Book design: Jennifer Hron
Chapter fonts: Optima & Baskerville, Cover fonts: Brush Script MT, Arial & Optima
Society for American Baseball Research
Cronkite School at ASU
555 N. Central Ave. #416
Phoenix, AZ 85004
Phone: (602) 496-1460
www.sabr.org
Facebook: Society for American Baseball Research
Twitter: @SABR

Contents

Introduction by Don Zminda vi

Setting the Stage

The Beginning: Frantic Frankie and Popoff Paul by Warren Corbett 1

Comiskey Park by Bob Webster 5

Team Management

Bill Veeck by Warren Corbett 12

Hank Greenberg by Scott Ferkovich 21

Al Lopez by Maxwell Kates 26

Ray Berres by Don Zminda 33

Johnny Cooney by Ray Birch 39

Tony Cuccinello by Barb Mantegani 43

Don Gutteridge by David W. Anderson 47

The Players

Luis Aparicio by Leonte Landino 52

Rodolfo Arias by Jose Ramirez 58

Earl Battey by Jack Herrman 62

Ray Boone by Joe Wancho 66

Johnny Callison b John Rossi 70

Camilo Carreon by Justin Thompson 73

Norm Cash by Maxwell Kates 76

Dick Donovan by Joe Wancho 89

Del Ennis by Edward Veit 93

Sammy Esposito by Justin Murphy 97

Nellie Fox by Robert W. Bigelow & Don Zminda 102

Billy Goodman by Ron Anderson 108

Joe Hicks by Don Zminda 114

Ron Jackson by Bill Nowlin 117

Ted Kluszewski by Paul Ladewski 122

Jim Landis by Mike Richard 126

Barry Latman by Ralph Berger 130

Sherman Lollar by John McMurray 134

Omar "Turk" Lown by Adam Ulrey 138

J.C. Martin by Neal Poloncarz 143

Jim McAnany by Mel Marmer 148

Ken McBride by Peter Gordon 151

Ray Moore by Mel Marmer 154

Don Mueller by J.A. Petterchak 157

Gary Peters by Mark Armour 161

Bubba Phillips by Anthony Basich and Don Zminda 165

Billy Pierce by Rob Neyer 169

Claude Raymond by Alexandre Pratt 175

Jim Rivera by Richard Smiley 179

John Romano by Todd Newville 184

Don Rudolph by Mike Hasse 188

Bob Shaw by Bill Johnson 192

Harry Simpson by Cort Vitty 196

Lou Skizas by Matt Bohn 200

Al Smith by Gary Livacari 204

Jerry Staley by Jim Sargent 208

Joe Stanka by C. Paul Rogers III 213

Earl Torgeson by Mark Armour 220

Early Wynn by David Fleitz 226

The Sox Broadcasters

The 1959 White Sox on the Air by Curt Smith 230

Jack Brickhouse by Tim Wiles 236

Bob Elson by John Gabcik 238

Vince Lloyd by Brian P. Wood 244

Don Wells by Brian P. Wood 248

Memorable 1959 White Sox Games

April 22: Sox Get 11 Runs in an Inning with 1 Hit by Kevin Larkin 251

May 1: Early Wynn Homers Late, Wins One-Hitter by Scott Ferkovich 253

July 25: Walk-Off after 17-Inning Battle by Mike Huber 256

August 30: White Sox Sweep Tribe by Paul Hofmann 258

September 22: White Sox Clinch First American Pennant in 40 Years by Don Zminda 260

October 1: White Sox Clobber Dodgers in Fall Classic Kickoff by Russ Lake 263

October 6: White Sox Beat Dodgers to Stay Alive in World Series by Thomas J. Brown Jr. 266

The Season, the Series and the Aftermath

The 1959 Season by R.J. Lesch 269

The 1959 World Series by R.J. Lesch 285

The '59 White Sox in Literature: Haunted by Ghosts of the Black Sox by Bill Savage 292

Recalling 1959: Sox Fans Remember by Pam Schur 295

Go-Going-Gone: Bill Veeck's Trades and Their Consequences by Don Zminda 300

Thanks and Credits

Contributor Biographies 303

Acknowledgments 310

Photographs 311

Introduction

By Don Zminda

The 1950s were not a great period for most Chicago sports teams. The Chicago Bears, once the NFL's dominant franchise, won no league championships during the decade and were routed by the New York Giants, 47-7, in 1956, when they made their only 1950s appearance in the league championship game. The area's only major college football team, the Northwestern Wildcats, were competitive under coach Ara Parseghian by the end of the decade, but more often overmatched by the Big Ten's bigger schools. The NHL Chicago Blackhawks were on the rise but still no match for the mighty Montreal Canadiens. And Chicago had no NBA franchise at all following the dissolution of the Chicago Stags after the 1949-50 season.

That leaves baseball, still the number-one sport in the 1950s. On the North Side the Cubs hadn't appeared in a World Series since 1945, and would finish in the National League's second division in every season from 1947 to 1966. The days in which the Cubbies would be considered a national team and Wrigley Field a cherished landmark were decades away; in fact the Cubs would draw over a million fans to Wrigley only twice during the '50s, in 1950 and 1952, and wouldn't crack the million mark again until 1968. For Windy City baseball fans, the baseball action for most of the '50s – and well into the 1960s – was on the South Side, with the White Sox.

In 1951, the "Go-Go Sox" began a run of 17 consecutive first division finishes with a team built around pitching, defense, and speed on the bases. The South Siders weren't just successful on the field; they consistently outpaced the Cubs at the box office with colorful teams featuring players like Nellie Fox, Billy Pierce, and Luis Aparicio. To be sure, the Sox often frustrated their fans, playing well but constantly finishing behind the New York Yankees in the American League standings. But in 1959, Bill Veeck took over the team and it all came together: The Sox won their first American League pennant in 40 years. After years of frustration, it was a sweet summer for the city of Chicago.

This book celebrates the 60th anniversary of that memorable Sox team. There have been several books written about the 1959 White Sox, most notably Bob Vanderberg's *'59: Summer of the Sox* and Larry Kalas's *Strength Down the Middle*. Those books cover the details of the 1959 season in chronological fashion, and we won't try to duplicate or expand upon their excellent work. Instead, the focus of *Go-Go to Glory* will be on the *people* who comprised the team.

And what people they were! Both the team president, Bill Veeck, and the general manager, Hank Greenberg, are members of the Baseball Hall of Fame. So are manager, Al Lopez, and four players who performed for the team in 1959 (Luis Aparicio, Larry Doby, Nellie Fox, and Early Wynn). Both the club's radio (Bob Elson) and television (Jack Brickhouse) broadcasters have been honored by the Hall's Ford C. Frick Award. And the '59 White Sox also featured many other longtime major-league stars such as Ted Kluszewski, Del Ennis, and Sherm Lollar, and future stars like Norm Cash, Earl Battey, and Gary Peters.

This book is their story – and not just the big names, either. We tell the life stories of every member of the 1959 club, whether they played in one game or 154. Many of the stories are quite remarkable. There's Joe Stanka, one of the first American-born players to play and star in Japan. There's Joe Hicks, a minor-league batting star who was still umpiring high school games in Virginia at the age of 75. There's Lou Skizas, once described by a baseball scout as "not a thinker," who would go on to earn a Ph.D. in biology. There's Lopez and coaches Ray Berres and Don Gutteridge, all of whom lived well into their 90s. And of course there are the luminous names like Veeck and Doby and Fox.

This book, which was originally published by ACTA Publications in 2009, has been updated and expanded for the 2019 edition to celebrate the 60th anniversary of the Go-Go White Sox. The book is a product of the Society for American Baseball Research, and part of SABR's Baseball Biography Project—an ongoing effort to produce a biography of every person who ever played or managed in the major leagues, as well as any person who touched baseball in a significant way. It is also one of a steadily-increasing series of books celebrating significant teams and events in baseball history. We hope you'll enjoy *Go-Go to Glory: The 1959 Chicago White Sox*. To quote the popular song written by Al Trace and "Li'l Wally" Jagiello:

White Sox! White Sox!
Let's Go-Go White Sox!
Chicago is proud of you!

The Begining:
FRANTIC FRANKIE and POPOFF PAUL

By Warren Corbett

The Go-Go Sox were born on Opening Day at Comiskey Park in 1951, children of a fast-talking general manager and a slow-talking manager.

After the Black Sox were banned, the White Sox recorded only seven winning seasons in the next 30. They had gone 31 years without a pennant, the longest drought of any big-league club.

The deaths of founder Charles A. Comiskey in 1931 and his son J. Louis in 1939 left the franchise in the hands of Louis's widow, Grace. She held most of the stock in trust for her three children. Although she served as the team's president, Mrs. Comiskey spoke up only when it came time to make a decision on spending money. Her usual answer was no.

When her only son, Charles A. Comiskey II, reached his 21st birthday in 1946, he went to work in the White Sox farm system. In 1948 he joined the board of directors as vice president. Young Chuck regarded the team as his birthright. Among his first moves was a critical one that would turn the franchise around.

Frank Lane

Comiskey brought in Frank Lane as general manager. Lane grew up in baseball under the volatile Larry MacPhail, working in the Cincinnati Reds and New York Yankees organizations when MacPhail ran those teams. He came to Chicago from the presidency of the Triple-A American Association. A wavy-haired man who favored expensive, tailored suits, Lane was 52 years old and had been lusting for his chance to run a big-league team.

The 1948 White Sox had lost 101 games and finished last. Lane said, "The first thing we have to think about is trades and purchases."[1] He embarked on a trading frenzy. Within two years he acquired a pair of new catchers, Gus Niarhos and Phil Masi, and a new infield: first baseman Eddie Robinson, second baseman Nellie Fox, third baseman Hank Majeski, and shortstop Chico Carrasquel. He added pitchers Billy Pierce, Ray Scarborough, and Bob Cain. Sportswriters nicknamed him Frantic Frankie, but his deals made little difference in the standings. After the Sox lost more than 90 games in both 1949 and 1950, Lane hired Paul Richards to manage the club.

Richards, a lanky 42-year-old Texan, had been a weak-hitting catcher for the Dodgers, Giants, and Athletics. He was still in his 20s when he realized that his future lay in managing. He led the Atlanta Crackers to two Southern Association pennants in five seasons as player-manager, then returned to the majors in 1943 as a wartime replacement player for Detroit. After the war he managed four years in Triple-A, winning an International League pennant for Buffalo.

Richards was a ferocious umpire-baiter who drew comparisons to the Vesuvian John McGraw. International League writers called him Popoff Paul and Ol' Rant and Rave. He was a Baptist Sunday School teacher who never said anything stronger than "damn" or "hell" at home, but he shocked ballplayers and even hardened umpires with his abusive, obscene tirades on the field.

Go-Go to Glory

Most important, Richards was a teacher. He explained to author Donald Honig, "There are an awful lot of small details that add up to the winning of a ball game, and it's up to the man in charge to see that his players are always drilled in and constantly alert to those things."[2] When his team butchered a play, he would put them back on the field after the game and practice that play "not just eight or ten times, but fifty or a hundred times," Eddie Robinson said.[3] He had earned a reputation as a master teacher of pitchers. His most famous pupil was the Tigers' Hal Newhouser, a wild, hot-tempered young left-hander who blossomed into a two-time Most Valuable Player and four-time 20-game winner under Richards' tutelage.

Many managers believe pitching and defense are keys to a winning team. For Richards, that was a religion, not just a strategy. He told Chicago writers, "The most important thing to me is to get the other fellow out. Almost every game is decided by the loser giving it away rather than the winner winning it. A good defense, inclusive of pitching, is the most vital part of a successful team."[4]

Richards had little to say to the writers, or to his players. Many of the Sox echoed infielder Joe DeMaestri's description: "No conversation. No words of encouragement. Seldom a smile. He never got close to his players. But in a game he was always two, three innings ahead, like he knew what was going to happen."[5]

The team Richards inherited had just four decent players. Twenty-four-year-old lefthander Billy Pierce, who had pitched for Richards in Buffalo, held opposing hitters to a .228 average in 1950, second lowest in the league, but walked more men than he struck out. Eddie Robinson contributed 20 home runs after being acquired from Washington. Chico Carrasquel, purchased from the Dodgers, was a slick shortstop who batted .282 as a rookie. Gus Zernial set a team record with 29 homers, but also led the majors in strikeouts and was a liability in the outfield.

Richards and Lane overhauled the pitching staff, trading journeymen Ray Scarborough and Bill Wight to Boston for veteran Joe Dobson and a .300-hitting outfielder, Al Zarilla. They drafted right-hander Harry Dorish from the minors; he would become the team's top reliever. Another of Richards' makeover projects, right-hander Saul Rogovin, came from Detroit. He had enjoyed his only success under Richards at Buffalo.

Before spring training Richards declared second base "our weakest spot."[6] The tiny incumbent, Nellie Fox, had posted a .608 on-base plus slugging percentage with just 19 extra-base hits. Richards assigned coach Doc Cramer to turn the 23-year-old into a hitter and brought in the recently retired all-star second baseman Joe Gordon to teach him to turn the double play. After many hours of extra batting practice and thousands of groundballs, Fox won the manager over with his grit. "We just gave him a chance, that's all," Richards said. "He took it."[7]

Beginning the season in St. Louis, the White Sox battered the Browns for 19 hits in a 17-3 victory. Three days later they opened at home against Detroit. Rookie center fielder Jim Busby singled in the fourth inning, then stole second and third on consecutive pitches. Richards, coaching at third, told him, "Well, regardless of what happens, Jim, you've got to go home on this next pitch." The manager put on a suicide squeeze. The batter, pitcher Randy Gumpert, laid it down and Busby raced across the plate. Years later Richards recalled, "That was the birth of the Go-Go Sox."[8] Fans began chanting "Go! Go!" whenever a player reached base.

By mid-May the Sox had stolen 20 bases, more than in the entire previous season. With home run totals rising, few teams were running; the stolen base was a surprise play. The Sox finished with 99 steals, the most in the AL since the war, and led the league for the next 10 years. "We've been getting as much benefit from our *reputation* as a running team as from actual running," Richards said. "Sometimes it's better to have one of your speed men *not* run, but stay on first base and upset the pitcher rather than go to second."[9]

The season was two weeks old when Lane pulled off the best trade of his hyperactive career. After 20 hours on the telephone, he swung a three-way deal that brought rookie Orestes Minoso from Cleveland. Minoso had batted .339 in the Pacific Coast League in 1950, with 70 extra-base hits and 30 steals. Richards, who had watched him while managing Seattle, wanted him badly, but Lane protested that Minoso was a poor outfielder and a worse third baseman. Richards replied, "I'll find a place for him. …We'll just let him hit and run."[10] Minoso was a black Cuban; the White Sox were only the third American League team to integrate. He homered in his first time at bat for Chicago and quickly became the engine of the Go-Go Sox.

• FRANTIC FRANKIE and POPOFF PAUL •

The White Sox gave up their leading power threat, Gus Zernial, in the Minoso deal. Richards was building his offense around speedy line-drive hitters. "That's the only way you can win at Comiskey Park," he said. "You're beating your head against a stone wall by trying to pack a lineup with long-ball hitters. With the long fences we have [352 feet down each foul line] and the wind constantly blowing in, a home run hitter is severely handicapped. He just hits long flies that are easy outs."[11]

Richards pulled another trick out of his bag – his most famous one – in a May 15 game at Boston. With Ted Williams due to lead off the ninth, Richards moved right-handed pitcher Harry Dorish to third base and brought in lefty Pierce to face the left-handed slugger. After Pierce got Williams to pop out, Dorish returned to the mound. Veterans of the American League's first season – including Connie Mack and Cy Young – were on hand to celebrate the league's 50th anniversary. None of them could remember seeing such a pitcher switch.

Chicago won the game on Nellie Fox's 11th-inning homer, the first of his career after 804 at-bats. It was the beginning of a 14-game winning streak that lifted the club to first place. An Associated Press reporter wrote that the White Sox had gone "from rags to Richards."[12]

A rare epidemic struck the South Side of Chicago: pennant fever. A June series against the Yankees drew 130,720 fans over three days, a franchise record. The national press took notice, too. *Life* magazine published a five-page photo spread on the "White Hot" Sox. *The Saturday Evening Post* profiled the manager in a piece titled "He Put the White Sox Back in the League."

By the time the *Post* dubbed them "the darlings of baseball," the Sox had begun to droop.[13] Locked in a tight four-way race with the Yankees, Indians and Red Sox, they barely stayed above .500 in June, then fell to 11-21 in July. They lost the lead for good on July 14. But a fourth-place finish and 81-73 record gave the club its first winning season since 1943. The fans kept coming – more than 1.3 million of them, the first time the franchise had topped 1 million in its 51-year history.

The makeshift pitching staff allowed the third-fewest runs in the league. Saul Rogovin, fresh off the scrap heap, led the league in ERA; Pierce was fourth. The young lefty cut his walks in half.

Paul Richards

Minoso and Fox emerged as stars. Minoso led the league with 31 stolen bases and his .922 OPS was third best. Fox batted .313 while striking out only 11 times in 681 plate appearances. They became two of the most popular players ever to wear the White Sox uniform, captivating fans with their all-out hustling style.

Richards and Lane moved the White Sox up to third place for the next three seasons, but they could not catch the powerful Yankees and Indians. Chicago writer John P. Carmichael said they "often thought as one man."[14] While Lane made the deals, many of the players he acquired were Richards' choices.

By the time Richards left in 1954 and Lane was forced out by the Comiskeys a year later, they had resurrected the moribund franchise. They built the foundation for 17 straight winning seasons and the team's first pennant since the Black Sox.

Sources

This article is adapted from *The Wizard of Waxahachie: Paul Richards and the End of Baseball as We Knew It*, by Warren Corbett (Dallas: Southern Methodist University Press, 2009).

Notes

1. *The Sporting News*, October 20, 1948: 22.
2. Donald Honig, *The Man in the Dugout* (Chicago: Follett, 1977), 142.
3. Eddie Robinson, interview by the author, August 18, 2006, Fort Worth, Texas.
4. *The Sporting News*, October 25, 1950: 1, 4.
5. Norman L. Macht, "Turn Back the Clock: Memories from Former Shortstop Joe DeMaestri," *Baseball Digest*, September 2003, 77.
6. Neal R. Gazel, "Nellie Does Right by the White Sox," *Baseball Digest*, August 1950: 5.
7. David Gough and Jim Bard, *Little Nel: The Nellie Fox Story* (Alexandria, Virginia: D.L. Megbeck Publishing, 2000), 76.
8. Paul Richards, interview by Clark Nealon, February 5, 1981. In the collection of the Texas Sports Hall of Fame, Waco.
9. *Chicago Tribune*, May 31, 1951: C5.
10. Jerome Holtzman and George Vass, *Baseball Chicago Style* (Chicago: Bonus Books, 2001), 102.
11. *The Sporting News*, May 9, 1951: 7.
12. Associated Press-*Charleston* (West Virginia) *Daily Mail*, June 19, 1951: 11.
13. William Barry Furlong and Fred Russell, "He Put the White Sox Back in the League," *Saturday Evening Post*, July 21, 1951: 91.
14. *The Sporting News*, November 10, 1951: 11.

Frank Lane's trade for Orestes (Minnie) Minoso in June 1951 helped put the "go" in the Go-Go Sox. The first black player in White Sox history, Minoso led the American League in stolen bases in each of his first three seasons with the team.

COMISKEY PARK

By Bob Webster

In 1890, Charles Comiskey was a member of the Chicago Pirates of the Players' League, a league that only operated for only one season. They played their games at Brotherhood Park on 35th Street between Shields and Wentworth. Comiskey played baseball through the 1894 season, when he retired from playing and bought a Western League team based in Sioux City, Iowa, which he soon moved to St. Paul, Minnesota.

During his playing days, Comiskey knew Bancroft "Ban" Johnson. Johnson was president of the Western League, and they worked together to grow their league into a league that could compete with the National League. Comiskey moved his team from St. Paul to Chicago in 1900 and renamed it the White Stockings, a name discarded by the Chicago National League ball club currently known as the Cubs. A gentlemen's agreement with the National League team would keep the White Stockings south of 35th Street. Comiskey searched in the area that he played in 10 years before and found a former cricket grounds on 39th Street between Princeton and Wentworth, just a few blocks from Brotherhood Park.[1]

Fifty years earlier, in 1850, Comiskey would have seen open prairie in that area, broken only by small outposts on the South Branch of the Chicago River. In 1848 the Illinois and Michigan Canal opened and soon after that the area started to grow rapidly.

Between 1870 and 1900, Chicago's population grew from 300,000 to 1.7 million. By the time Comiskey was looking for a place for his team to play baseball, the area he scouted was pretty much filled in. Residential areas ran from the east of where he was looking to Lake Michigan. A combination of residential and industry areas was to the west, but there was a small area between the two that provided enough room for a ballpark.

The American League was formed for the 1901 season and the White Stockings won the pennant that year. In 1906, the White Sox, as they were now known, won the third-ever World Series. Growing attendance demands forced Comiskey to find a location for a new ballpark with more seating capacity.

In December 1908 Comiskey bought a parcel of land from the daughter of Long John Wentworth, a former two-term mayor of Chicago who also served six terms as a member of the US House of Representatives. Wentworth owned 5000 acres of land that included the land that he sold to Comiskey for the ballpark. The parcel was bordered by 35th Street on the south, Wentworth Avenue on the east, 34th Street on the north, and Shields Avenue on the west. The 15-acre site was large enough for a ballpark, which would be placed on the eastern side of the parcel, with a winter amusement park consisting of an indoor skating rink and gymnasium on the western portion. The ballpark would be built of concrete and steel and was expected to hold 30,000 people. The ballpark would be similar to Shibe Park, then being built in Philadelphia, expecting to cost $500,000. Space for stores that would front Wentworth Avenue would be placed under the stands. Charles Comiskey insisted that none of the parcel not used for baseball would be allowed to go to waste.[2]

Ground was broken for the park in May of 1909. William Steele and Sons, the architects of Shibe Park, were hired to design the structure. Comiskey wanted to design his new concrete and steel ballpark after the new parks in Philadelphia (Shibe Park) and Pittsburgh (Forbes Field). The final design, submitted by Zachary T. Davis of William Steele and Sons, called for a grandstand that would hold 15,000. The exterior would be patterned after the Roman Coliseum. Pavilions down each line and outfield bleacher seats could hold another 15,000. The seats would be designed so that "there will be no occasion for the spectators to rise from their seats at any time in order to watch a play."[3]

A steelworkers strike delayed construction for a while but that was overcome and the ballpark was ready by the planned opening date, July 1, 1910.[4] The White Sox played their last game at South Side Ballpark on June 27.[5]

The gates of Comiskey Park opened on July 1, and 32,000 were present to see the St. Louis Browns defeat the White Sox 2-0. Owners and officers of many major-league clubs were in attendance.

Only the bleachers were made of wood. An electric scoreboard measured about 60 to 80 feet long and 25 to 30 feet high. One oddity of the park was that down each foul line, between the outfield bleachers and the field level pavilion seating down each base line, there was iron fencing and gates that allowed access for equipment onto the field. The fences and gates, which were partially in fair territory, were made of one-inch rods with openings of four to five inches. Since fair batted balls could bounce through or roll under these iron gates, the effective fence height in the left and right-field corners was zero. This arrangement had an unintentional but substantial effect as balls that went through the iron gates and fences were considered home runs.

Depending on which newspaper you read, the dimensions of the park were either 362, 363, or 365 feet down the lines and 420 to center. Foul territory was also large, with a distance of 94 feet from the plate to the backstop.

The first remodeling or expansion of Comiskey Park took place in time for the 1927 season. The architect of the expansion was Zachary T. Davis, the 1910 architect. He also designed the park now known as Wrigley Field. The foul-line pavilions and wooden outfield bleachers were removed and replaced by steel and concrete double-deck stands. The construction was not quite completed by Opening Day of 1927; the upper-deck portions of the outfield stands were not finished. The construction was, however, completed by the time Babe Ruth and the New York Yankees came to town for a series beginning May 7. The plan for the expansion called for a seating capacity of 55,000, but the Chicago Fire Department limited the capacity to 52,000. This expansion made Comiskey Park the third-largest major-league park in terms of capacity, behind Yankee Stadium and the New York Giants' Polo Grounds.

The remodeling and expansion changed the dimensions of the field. The left-field and right-field stands were now at a 90-degree angle to the foul lines, resulting in dead center being 455 feet from home plate. The fences now consisted of a four-foot concrete base topped with a six-foot wire screen. The iron gates and fences that allowed the balls to travel through or under were gone.

The White Sox acquired Al Simmons, Mule Haas, and Jimmy Dykes from the Philadelphia Athletics for the 1933 season. After that season, in an attempt to help Simmons, home plate was moved 14 feet toward center field. This also reduced the dimensions in right and left field from 352 to 342 feet. After the 1935 season, Simmons was traded and the plate was moved back 14 feet, returning to the dimensions that were in place after the 1933 season.

The next big change to Comiskey Park was to add lights. Four years after Crosley Field in Cincinnati became the first major-league park to install lights, the first night game was played at Comiskey Park on August 14, 1939. It drew a crowd of 30,000 as the White Sox beat the Browns, 5-2. Comiskey Park was the third American League ballpark to host a night game, all that season; Cleveland's Municipal Stadium had hosted one on June 27 and Philadelphia's Shibe Park hosted a night game on May 16. The players reported that visibility at the White Sox game was nearly perfect.[6]

In 1941 and 1942 the ballpark's capacity was reduced to 46,550 when the original seats were replaced with wider curved-back seats. More of these seats were added in 1947 and some seats were removed in center field to provide a better batter's background, reducing the capacity by another 2,000 seats.

Throughout the lifespan of Comiskey Park, the field dimensions were changed 13 times from the original 1910 dimensions. The distance to the center-field wall varied between 404 and 449 feet and right and left field varied between 349 and 384 feet.

The Neighborhood

After the ballpark was built in 1910 and with the population of Chicago still growing, the surrounding neighborhood evolved once again. Comiskey Park would become surrounded by people from three continents. The neighborhood to the west of the ballpark, called Bridgeport, was started by people with Irish roots, but grew with the addition of people from all over Europe. Douglas, to the east, was Chicago's port of entry for African-Americans. Chinatown, to the north, was the smallest of the three but the most durable over the years with its identity and culture. The ballpark was built in a small neighborhood between those three that was called Armour Square. The combination of the three cultures attending games created a sense of toughness in each of the groups, a toughness that remains at the new ballpark today. The toughness was created by the neighborhoods' inhabitants going after a common dream of making it and succeeding in life. By 1930, the working-class Bridgeport neighborhood was full of

COMISKEY PARK

Comiskey Park as it looked during the 1959 season.

well-kept homes. The Irish made up only 6 percent of the neighborhood, now joined by Polish, Lithuanians, Germans, and Italians. Bridgeport supplied the now-legendary string of mayors who ran the city from the early 1930s through 2011, that included Ed Kelly, Martin Kennelly, Richard J. Daley, Michael Bilandic, and Richard M. Daley.

Special Events at Comiskey Park

Comiskey Park hosted three All-Star Games, one American League Championship Series, and four World Series.

The very first All-Star Game, in 1933, was played at Comiskey Park. It was originally called The Game of the Century instead of the All-Star Game and was expected to be a one-time event to coincide with the Century of Progress Exhibition in Chicago. A coin toss decided between Comiskey Park and Wrigley Field as host for the game.[7] The American League won the game before a sold-out crowd. It was broadcast on WGN radio by Bob Elson and also on NBC and CBS radio, and they raised $46,506 for charity. It was announced immediately after the game that it would become a yearly event.

The All-Star Game returned to Comiskey Park in 1950. The St. Louis Cardinals' Red Schoendienst homered in the 14th inning to win the game for the National League, 4-3. Ted Williams suffered a broken elbow when his arm hit the outfield wall while he caught Ralph Kiner's line drive.[8] Williams had surgery and did not return until September 7. The third and final All-Star Game held at Comiskey Park was the 50th Anniversary Game in 1983. The American League won, 13-3.

The first of four World Series with games at Comiskey Park was played between the New York Giants and Chicago White Sox in 1917. The ballpark's capacity at the time was 32,000, and to accommodate fans who could not obtain seats, the Stockyards Pavilion and Arcadia Hall hired semipro baseball players to re-create the plays as they were telegraphed from Comiskey Park. The White Sox won the series in six games, bringing home the White Sox' second World Series championship.

The Chicago Cubs borrowed Comiskey Park for their home games during the 1918 World Series between the Cubs and the Boston Red Sox. The Cubs' Weeghman Field (now known as Wrigley Field) held only 20,000 at the time while Comiskey Park held 32,000. Due to federal travel restrictions imposed by the World War, the first three games of the Series were to be played in Chicago with the remaining games to be played in Boston.[9] Attendance was disappointing for the Series: The regular season ended on Labor Day and bad weather, the lack of the best players, and general concern for the war resulted in crowds being sparse.

The White Sox returned to the World Series in 1919 against the Cincinnati Reds. The Reds won, five games to three, in the Series that went down in history because of the Black Sox Scandal, in which eight White Sox players plotted to throw games. The players were banned from baseball for life. The 1959 World Series, between the White Sox and Los Angeles Dodgers, was the last one to be played at Comiskey Park. The Dodgers beat the White Sox in six games.

The White Sox advanced to the postseason in 1983, playing the Baltimore Orioles in the American League Championship Series. The teams split the first two games in Baltimore before playing the first ALCS ever at Comiskey Park. The Orioles won Game Three, 11-1 before a crowd of 46,635. Down two games to one, the White Sox had to win the next two to get to the World Series, but they lost Game Four, 3-0, and the Orioles advanced to the World Series.

Negro League Baseball at Comiskey Park

Negro League baseball was played at Comiskey Park as soon as the park opened in 1910. The majority of Rube Foster's American Giants games were played at South Side Park, recently vacated by the White Sox. When the White Sox were out of town, the American Giants played an occasional game at Comiskey Park.

The most notable of Negro League games at Comiskey Park were the East-West All-Star Games, held each year from 1933 to 1960. The game brought African-Americans together from across the country and attracted a who's who of African-American society to Comiskey Park. The ballpark was decorated in red, white, and blue banners and a jazz band played between innings. People like Count Basie, Ella Fitzgerald, and Billie Holiday would always make it a point to be in Chicago at that time and entertain at the jazz clubs at night.[10] It was far more than just a game, as Buck O'Neil proclaimed. He said "(The white major leagues' All-Star Game) was, and is, more or less an exhibition. But for black folks, the East-West Game was a matter of racial pride."[11]

Yankee Stadium hosted the classic in 1961, ending the 28-year tradition of Comiskey Park holding at least one of the annual games. Seven men played in both an East-West Game and a major-league All-Star Game: Jackie Robinson, Larry Doby, Roy Campanella, Satchel Paige, Minnie Minoso, Ernie Banks, and Jim Gilliam. Twenty-five men enshrined in the Baseball Hall of Fame appeared in an East-West Game.

As the major leagues were signing more black players, the Negro leagues collapsed, bringing to the forefront the Indianapolis Clowns, a barnstorming team with an emphasis on entertainment as much as competition. The Clowns toured the Midwest and made stops at Comiskey Park into the 1970s.

To honor the tradition of the East-West Games at Comiskey Park, on Monday, July 7, 2008, a collaboration between the Negro Leagues Baseball Museum and the Chicago White Sox resulted in the first Double Duty Classic at US Cellular Field, showcasing the finest inner-city high-school talent throughout the Midwest. Part of the day's festivities included a forum on Negro League history.[12]

The Bill Veeck Years

The White Sox' first 19 years were great. Successful teams, large crowds, and a new ballpark. After the 1919 Black Sox scandal, the White Sox headed downhill for a while. Charles Comiskey died in 1931. The White Sox went through a couple of decades of mediocre baseball until, beginning in 1951, they had a winning record for 17 years in a row. In 1959 the White Sox made it to the World Series.

Bill Veeck came onto the scene in 1959. When Comiskey built the park in 1910, it was a state-of-the-art facility. By 1959 it still looked like a turn-of-the-century ballpark. When Comiskey opened for the 1960 season, it had lost some of its early century association: The ballpark was painted white, from its original dark green. It now looked brighter and cleaner.

That was only the beginning. Veeck installed a scoreboard unlike any others. It was eventually known as the Monster. The scoreboard took up the entire center-field backdrop and rose higher than the right- and left-field upper decks. Ten towers rose from the back, surrounding a large clock that was trimmed in lights. When a White Sox player hit a home run, the scoreboard "exploded." Lights around the clock and beneath the scoreboard turned on and off. Fireworks shot up from the top of the scoreboard and from above the right- and left-field upper decks. Lit-up pinwheels spun. The scoreboard caused controversy and resentment. The players hated it. But the technology outlived Veeck and all of the naysayers and proved the critics wrong.

Another unique addition to Comiskey Park was in place in 1960. Part of the left-field wall was replaced by a chain-link fence and behind the fence at ground level was a picnic area. The view of the entire ballpark was obstructed but the view at field level was unique.

Veeck sold the team to Arthur and John Allyn in 1961 and the name of the ballpark was changed to White Sox Park. Despite the 17 straight winning seasons between 1951 and 1967, attendance dwindled. The neighborhood was labeled a "crime-ridden area" that kept fans from the games. Too many seats were behind poles and concessions were inadequate. Allyn wanted to build a new ballpark, but the funding never materialized. In time for the 1969 season, AstroTurf was installed on the infield and the outfield wall was moved in. The White Sox hit more home runs, but so did their opponents. The '70s weren't any nicer to the White Sox and the financially strapped team had to shut off the scoreboard in 1975. The exploding scoreboard was the only constant throughout Allyn's tenure and it looked as though the White Sox were going to move to Seattle.

When Veeck sold the team in 1961 after owning it for just two years, some fans called him an opportunist who just wanted to make a quick buck. When he reacquired the team in 1975, he was looked upon as a savior. Veeck made some immediate changes. The name was changed back to Comiskey Park and the AstroTurf was removed. The ballpark received a new coat of white paint. The center-field fence was removed, creating a 445-foot canyon in front of the center-field bleachers, making the park more conducive to doubles and triples.

The voice of the White Sox, Harry Caray, and organist Nancy Faust helped Veeck bring the fans back to the ballpark. Veeck urged Carey to sing "Take Me Out to the Ball Game" during the seventh-inning stretch with Faust accompanying him on the organ, a tradition he took with him across town to the Cubs in 1982.

Nancy Faust had been with the White Sox for six seasons by the time Veeck purchased the team in 1975. Faust was one of the first female organists at a major-league ballpark. She performed before small crowds in her first few seasons, but that changed in 1977, when the team was called the South Side Hitmen because they could hit for power. Richie Zisk, Oscar Gamble, and Eric Soderholm combined for 86 home runs. In 1970 the White Sox drew 495,000 fans. In the month of July 1977, they drew 480,000.[13]

Nancy Faust became part of the fun and began playing the 1969 song "Na Na Hey Hey Kiss Him Good-Bye" when opposing pitchers were being removed from the game. The song was also played after the last out of a White Sox victory. Both traditions remained as of 2019.

After the last game of the 1977 season, Faust played the song for the last time of the season. Then, nothing happened. No one moved. Everyone stayed where they were. Nobody wanted this to end. The excitement of the season was so overwhelming to the fans that they did not want the season to come to an end. Fifteen minutes went by. Then, 30, 45, 60 minutes went by and everyone was still there. An hour and a half later, the fans started shaking hands and saying goodbye to one another. They were finally ready to say goodbye to this season.

Probably the biggest promotion at Comiskey Park came on July 12, 1979. Local radio disc jockey Steve Dahl was upset that the radio station he worked for changed its format from rock to disco. The White Sox scheduled Disco Demolition night for a doubleheader between the White Sox and the Detroit Tigers. The fans could get into the ballpark for 98 cents and a disco record. Things got out of hand early as the sold-out crowd and the many more who could not get in were supposed to give up their records at the gate, but attendants quit taking them because of the number of people coming in. Some spectators started throwing the records like Frisbees onto the field. Dahl blew up the records in center field between games of the doubleheader. The blast sent pieces of records high into the sky and parts of the field caught fire. About 7,000 fans charged the field, stole the bases, and tore up the field so badly that the White Sox had to forfeit the second game.[14]

For health reasons, Bill Veeck sold the team to Jerry Reinsdorf and Eddie Einhorn in 1981.[15] It has been said that Veeck owned the White Sox for fewer years than any of the other owners, but his legacy remains long after his death.

Interesting Facts and Records

In the first-ever All-Star Game in 1933, Babe Ruth hit a two-run homer to pace the American League to victory.

- Cleveland's Bob Feller threw the major leagues' only Opening Day no-hitter on April 16, 1940.
- Larry Doby, the first African-American in the American League, made his debut with the Cleveland Indians as a pinch-hitter in a game at Comiskey on July 5, 1947.
- In front of more than 51,000 fans, 42-year-old Indians pitcher Satchel Paige threw a shutout on August 13, 1948.
- Red Schoendienst of the Cardinals hit a 14th-inning home run in the 1950 All-Star Game.
- In 1983, Fred Lynn hit the first All-Star Game grand slam.
- Yankee Andy Hawkins threw a no-hitter against the White Sox on July 1, 1990, but lost the game 4-0 on walks and errors.
- On May 8-9, 1984, the White Sox and Milwaukee Brewers played the longest game by time and innings: 25 innings in 8 hours and 6 minutes. Harold Baines hit a solo walk-off home run to win the game for the White Sox.

Other Sporting Events at Comiskey Park

Baseball was not the only sporting event held at Comiskey Park. Notable boxing matches include the 1937 bout between James Braddock and Joe Louis before a crowd of 55,000, in which Louis won the heavyweight championship. In a heavyweight championship fight in 1962, Sonny Liston defeated Floyd Patterson, in their first fight.

Roller Derby, wrestling, and a sport called auto polo were all played in Comiskey Park.

When Soldier Field was scheduled for renovation in 1978, the Chicago Sting, a member of the North American Soccer League, played their home games at Comiskey Park. The Sting played several more games at Comiskey Park until the league disbanded after the 1984 season. In addition to the Sting, the Chicago Mustangs of the United Soccer League played at Comiskey Park in 1967 and 1968.

Football at Comiskey Park

In 1920 the Chicago Cardinals became a charter member of the American Professional Football Association (which became the National Football League in 1922) after playing in the Chicago area off and on for 20 years. The team, which is now the Arizona Cardinals, played home games at Comiskey Park from 1922 to 1925 and again from 1929 to 1958. The Cardinals played at Soldier Field and Metropolitan Stadium in Minnesota in 1959 before the team was moved to St. Louis for the 1960 season.[16]

Non-Sporting Events and Concerts

Two other nonsporting events at Comiskey Park involve Charles Lindbergh in 1927 and the Jehovah's Witnesses in 1955. After Lindbergh returned to the United States from his solo flight across the Atlantic to Paris, he was awarded the Congressional Medal of Honor and then took a victory tour across the country. In Chicago, Lindbergh stopped at Comiskey Park to be awarded a "gold star" by Chicago Police Chief Michael Hughes. On June 22 and 23, 1955, 20,000 Jehovah's Witnesses attended a convention at Comiskey Park.

Rock concerts that were too large for indoor venues started to play in outdoor sports arenas. On August 20, 1965, the Beatles played afternoon and evening concerts at Comiskey Park. The afternoon concert drew 25,000 fans, and the evening show 37,000. Each show consisted of 10 songs lasting a total of 45 minutes. Ticket prices ranged from $2.50 to $5.50.[17] Apparently, the teenage girls who dominated the audience screamed so much during the two shows that the Beatles were hardly heard.

Bill Veeck wanted to increase the revenue brought in by Comiskey Park, so a number of concerts were held there. Groups including the Police, Journey, Santana, the Beach Boys, Blondie, Aerosmith, AC/DC, Foreigner, Foghat, and South Side Johnny and the Asbury Dukes played concerts or mini-festivals there in front of as many as 70,000 people. A three-night show in October 1984 by Michael Jackson and his brothers drew 40,000 each night.

• COMISKEY PARK •

Demolition of Comiskey Park

In 1990 Chicago had a collection of classic sports arenas. Still in use besides Comiskey Park were Soldier Field (1924), where the Bears played, Chicago Stadium (1929), the home of the Bulls and Blackhawks, and Wrigley Field (1914), the home of the Cubs.

Many fans did not want Comiskey Park to go away. A crowd gathered on that March 1991 morning when the demolition was about to begin. As soon as the wrecking ball started to swing, a few people started to boo. Others joined them until a low, droning "Booooooooooo" continued as the wrecking ball took its first few swings.

Meanwhile, on the opposite side of the ballpark, people started a demolition project of their own. They started to pry the park apart with crowbars and hammers. Mostly just bricks were taken, but one man was spotted carrying a door with "Players Entrance" stenciled on it. Signs were also a popular item to get away with. The police were there, but as long as the people didn't use their tools on one another, they let it go.

Sources

In addition to the sources cited in the Notes, the author also consulted:

Leventhal, Josh. *Take Me Out to the Ballpark* (New York: Black Dog & Leventhal Publishers, 2011).

Lowry, Philip J. *Green Cathedrals* (New York: Walker & Company, 2006).

Sullivan, Floyd. *Old Comiskey Park* (Jefferson, North Carolina: McFarland, 2014).

Notes

1. Warren Brown, The Chicago White Sox (Kent, Ohio: Kent State University Press, 2007), 11.
2. "Comiskey Buys New Grounds for White Sox," Chicago Tribune, December 29, 1908: 4.
3. "Work Is Started on New Sox Park," Chicago Tribune, May 9, 1909: 8.
4. "Ironworkers Back at Park," Chicago Tribune, June 9, 1910: 10.
5. "Sox in 7-2 Defeat Leave Old Home," Chicago Tribune, June 28, 1910: 10.
6. "Night Baseball Inaugurated by Chicago White Sox Club," Logansport (Indiana) Pharos-Tribune, August 15, 1939: 2.
7. Arch Ward, "Comiskey Park Awarded Game of the Century: White Sox to Accept Ticket Orders June 1," Chicago Tribune, May 27, 1933: 19.
8. "Operate on Ted Williams' Elbow Today: Boston Ace's Arm Broken as All-Star," Chicago Tribune, July 13, 1950: 21 (Part 4, 1).
9. James Crusinberry, "World Series Opens Here on Sept. 4: Cubs May Play Red Sox on South Side," Chicago Tribune, August 25, 1918: 17.
10. Larry Lester, Black Baseball's National Showcase: The East-West All-Star Game 1933-1953 (Lincoln: University of Nebraska Press, 2001), 21-22.
11. Lester, 64-66.
12. Scott Merkin, "White Sox Host Double Duty Classic," mlb.com, mlb.mlb.com/news/print.jsp?ymd=20080707&content_id=2087166&vkey=news_mlb&fext=.jsp&c_id=mlb&affiliateId=CommentWidget.
13. Dan Helpingstein, South Side Hitmen – The Story of the 1977 Chicago White Sox (Charleston, South Carolina: Arcadia, 2005), 76.
14. Derek John, "July 12, 1979: 'The Night Disco Died – Or Didn't,'" National Public Radio, npr.org/2016/07/16/485873750/july-12-1979-the-night-disco-died-or-didnt.
15. Retrieved from: https://www.baseball-reference.com/bullpen/Bill_Veeck.
16. Retrieved from: sportsteamhistory.com/chicago-cardinals.
17. Ibid.

BILL VEECK

By Warren Corbett

Bill Veeck's one-man carnival came blaring into Chicago on March 10, 1959. He and an investor group bought a majority interest in the Chicago White Sox from Dorothy Comiskey Rigney, granddaughter of the franchise's founder, Charles Comiskey.

The 45-year-old Veeck was coming home. He liked to say, "I am the only human being ever raised in a ballpark."[1] The ballpark was Wrigley Field, where his father was president of the Cubs.

Veeck's road to Comiskey Park wound through Cleveland, where he set attendance records and won a World Series; and St. Louis, where he lost his sports shirt trying to save the Browns. Fellow owners ran him out of the game, but they could not stop him from having fun along the way.

Bill Veeck lived a joyously public life and wrote his own legend. Sometimes it is hard to know where the life stops and the legend begins.

William Louis Veeck Jr. was born in Chicago on February 9, 1914, to William L. Veeck Sr. and Grace Greenwood DeForest Veeck. His father was a sportswriter under the pen name Bill Bailey. After Veeck criticized the Cubs in his columns, owner William Wrigley dared him to take over the team and prove he could do better. Veeck did so in 1918, and built pennant winners in 1929, 1932, and 1935.

Young Bill began hanging around the ballpark at the age of 10, working as a vendor and ticket seller. The boy was sent to the exclusive Phillips Academy in Andover, Massachusetts, but lasted only a few weeks. After two years in a public high school in the Chicago suburb of Hinsdale, he was dispatched to the Ranch School in Los Alamos, New Mexico, whose experimental curriculum followed the back-to-nature philosophy of Henry David Thoreau. Bill left without graduating.

He passed an entrance exam at Kenyon College in Ohio. He remembered his brief college career as a nonstop party, but he was elected freshman class president, played football and basketball, and joined the Beta Theta Phi fraternity. He quit in his second year when his father was diagnosed with leukemia. In the last weeks of his life, William Veeck could not digest anything but wine. Prohibition was on, so, his son said, he procured a supply from Al Capone. The father died in 1933, when Bill was 19. Veeck Jr. always referred to his father simply as Daddy, and revered him, but the two could not have been less alike. William Veeck was a starchy, formal gentleman, the perfect picture of establishment dignity. Junior famously never wore a necktie, had wild, kinky, reddish hair that won him the nickname Burrhead, and spent his life tilting at every establishment windmill in sight.

Veeck took an $18-a-week job with the Cubs, who were now owned by William Wrigley's son, Philip K. Like Veeck, P.K. Wrigley was an apple who fell far from the tree. His father was a supersalesman; Philip was painfully shy, happier when tinkering with a car or some other machinery than meeting the public. Young Veeck was brimming with promotional ideas, such as installing lights at the ballpark. Young Wrigley rejected all of them. Veeck's only contribution to the Cubs was planting the ivy on Wrigley Field's outfield walls, but that was Philip Wrigley's idea.

Veeck married Eleanor Raymond on December 18, 1935. She had been an elephant wrangler and horseback rider with the Ringling Brothers and Barnum & Bailey Circus. Bill said her daredeviltry appealed to him, but Eleanor maintained that he exaggerated her feats with the circus.

At 27 Veeck bought his first ballclub, the Milwaukee Brewers of the Double-A American Association, then the highest level of the minors. He sometimes said he paid nothing for the failing franchise while assuming $100,000 in debts, but the Brewers' business manager, Rudie Schaffer, said Veeck put up $40,000. It was mostly other people's money, as it would always be when Veeck bought a team.

The 1941 Brewers were in last place when he took over, bringing along one of his investors, Charlie Grimm, as manager. Grimm, who played first base and the banjo left-handed, had managed the Cubs' 1935 pennant winner. Jolly Cholly was a perfect fit for Veeck.

Milwaukee became Veeck's tryout camp, where he auditioned his promotional schemes. He took the successful ones with him to the majors. He cleaned and painted the Brewers' dilapidated park. He gave away prizes almost every night, showing a fascination for animals: live lobsters, pigeons, chickens, guinea pigs, and a particular favorite, a swaybacked horse. Most of the promotions were not announced in advance; he wanted fans to come to the games anticipating a surprise. He scheduled morning games for overnight workers at war plants, and served a breakfast of cornflakes to all comers. He believed a trip to the ballpark should be fun. But he also built a winning team. Veeck bought players, spending money he did not have, and sold them to raise capital for more purchases. The Brewers nearly won the American Association pennant in 1942, his first full season, then won the next three in a row.

Veeck later wrote that he tried to buy the bankrupt Philadelphia Phillies after the 1942 season, and intended to stock the team with black players, breaking organized baseball's color line three years before Jackie Robinson signed with the Dodgers. In his 1962 autobiography he asserted that he had lined up financing and enlisted the promoter Abe Saperstein, owner of the Harlem Globetrotters, to help sign Negro Leagues stars. Veeck said he informed Commissioner Kenesaw Mountain Landis of his plan as a courtesy, but that Landis and National League president Ford Frick thwarted him by arranging a quick sale of the Phillies to another buyer.

Most histories of baseball integration have repeated the story. It fit Veeck's carefully burnished image as the bane of authority. But in 1998 David M. Jordan, Larry R. Gerlach, and John P. Rossi declared, "[I]t is not true."[2] Although Veeck claimed his bid was "known all over the baseball world," later researchers have found only a handful of references to it before Veeck's autobiography, most of them based on Veeck's statements. When Veeck signed the second black major leaguer, Larry Doby, in 1947, he did not mention that he had tried to integrate baseball five years earlier. However, the historian Jules Tygiel noted that is impossible to prove a negative, and concluded that Jordan, Gerlach, and Rossi may have been too quick with their "blanket dismissal of Veeck's assertions."[3]

In any event, Veeck was not around to celebrate the Brewers' pennants. He joined the Marines after the 1943 season. The next spring he was stationed on the Pacific island of Bougainville when the recoil of an anti-aircraft gun smashed his right leg. He spent the rest of the war in hospitals.

Grimm left the Brewers for another tour as

Veeck was noted for not wearing a tie... and for creating excitement on a daily basis.

manager of the Cubs in 1944, and persuaded his old friend Casey Stengel to take over in Milwaukee. Stengel had been fired after losing records as manager of the Brooklyn Dodgers and Boston Braves. Veeck was furious when the news reached him in the Pacific weeks later. He wrote Grimm a blistering letter, demanding that he fire that clown Stengel forthwith. After Stengel brought home the pennant, Veeck admitted his mistake. He asked Stengel to stay for 1945, but Casey had heard about the letter and went home to California.

Veeck sold the Brewers soon after he returned from military service in 1945. "It was a choice between the club and my marriage," he wrote later.[4] The marriage had been in trouble even before Veeck joined the Marines. He moved Eleanor and their three children to a dude ranch in Arizona that he named The Lazy Vee.

His reconciliation with his wife didn't take. Neither did his divorce from baseball. Within a few months he began looking for a way to get back into action, "a vulture in search of a dying ball club." The Cleveland Indians had not won a pennant since 1920, and had seldom been in the race. Veeck put together a syndicate to buy the team for $2.2 million. He devised what he called a debenture-stock group, which allowed his backers to leverage their investment by paying only a small amount for stock and putting the majority of their money in the form of a loan to the team (the debenture), then leverage it again by borrowing most of the purchase price. He put up just $268,000 in cash for a 30 percent share of the club.

Veeck brought his stunts, fireworks, and giveaways with him. Although other minor-league owners had embraced the value of promotion, such folderol had never befouled a big-league park. New York Yankees public relations director Red Patterson summed up the state of the majors' marketing efforts. He said Yankees general manager George Weiss vetoed a cap giveaway with the disdainful remark, "I don't want every kid in New York walking around in a Yankee cap."[5]

Responding to sneers that his stunts were decidedly lowbrow, Veeck said, "My tastes, I have found, are so average that anything that appeals strongly to me is probably going to appeal to most of the customers."[6] In his philosophy, "every day was Mardi Gras and every fan a king."[7] And a queen: he gave away nylon stockings, which were hard to get soon after the war, and thousands of orchids. After he took over in June 1946, Veeck pushed the Indians' lagging attendance above 1 million for the first time. He moved the games from League Park, which had room for only 22,500 people, to Municipal Stadium, with a capacity of 78,000. (The team had previously used the bigger park only on Sundays, holidays, and for games when a large crowd was anticipated.) He removed the door to his office and listed his home phone number in the public directory.

Veeck tried again to patch up his marriage during the 1946 World Series. He invited Eleanor to join him at the Series – unfortunately, along with dozens of friends and business associates. Veeck spent his time entertaining his guests rather than his wife. The Series lasted seven games. Eleanor did not. She left him for good.

After the Series, Veeck's right leg was amputated below the knee. When his new artificial leg arrived, he threw a party to celebrate. He later endured successive amputations as infections traveled up the stump of his leg, 36 operations in all.

The Indians finished sixth in 1946 and rose only to fourth the next year, although attendance jumped to 1.5 million, second best in the league. Veeck signed the AL's first black player, Doby, in July. The next year he signed Negro Leagues legend Satchel Paige, played up the mystery surrounding Paige's age, and had a new drawing card as well as a useful pitcher.

Veeck also acquired Yankee second baseman Joe Gordon, a former MVP who returned to stardom with Cleveland for a few years, but he had to give up pitcher Allie Reynolds, who became a key man on New York's five straight World Series winners. Finally, he decided to get rid of his shortstop and manager, Lou Boudreau. At 30, Boudreau was a former batting champion and seven-time All-Star, but Veeck derided him as a "hunch" manager.

When word of the plan to trade Boudreau leaked, Veeck faced a hurricane of criticism. There was no sports-talk radio then, but fans made their opinions clear in letters to the papers, and sportswriters lent a megaphone to the outcry. Veeck tried to turn a public-relations disaster into a coup. He announced he would bow to the fans' wishes and keep the manager.

The Boudreau trade was the best deal Veeck never made. Boudreau had the season of his life in 1948, batting .355 with a .453 on-base percentage and a .534 slugging average, and winning the MVP award. Veteran third baseman Ken Keltner turned in a career year, Gordon slugged 32 home runs, and unheralded pitchers Gene Bearden and Bob Lemon each won 20 games while finishing 1-2 in ERA. The Indians fought the Yankees, Red Sox, and the surprising Philadelphia Athletics in a tight pennant race. With a winning team and a thrilling race added to Veeck's nonstop promotions, 2.6 million fans turned out, a major-league record that stood for 14 years. The season ended with Cleveland and Boston tied. In a one-game playoff, Boudreau hit two home runs as the Indians won, 8-3.

Veeck made the World Series an event for the common fan. Series tickets had always been sold in sets for all home games (the middle three were played in Cleveland), but Veeck sold single-game tickets to allow three times as many people to see their team play for the championship. The Indians defeated the Boston Braves in six games.

That 1948 season was the triumph of Veeck's life. After the victory parade, he went home to his empty apartment. He wrote later, "I had never been more lonely in my life."[8]

That may explain why Veeck's years in Cleveland were marked by a desperate quest for excitement. He joined a group of late-night revelers known in the gossip columns as the Jolly Set. When Cleveland's café society proved too tame, he began making overnight commutes to New York, flying into the city to close down the Copacabana nightclub, then flying home the next morning.

Inevitably, the 1949 season was an anticlimax. The Indians dropped to third place as attendance fell by more than 300,000. Veeck continued to rev his promotional engine, but he could not top himself. When the club was eliminated from the pennant race, he staged a funeral at the ballpark and buried the 1948 flag. That stunt outraged some of his players and fans. Before the season was over he was looking to sell.

Although he said the thrill was gone in Cleveland, Veeck sold because he needed cash to settle his divorce and provide trust funds for his and Eleanor's three children. He seldom saw the children after that. His middle child, Peter, met him only twice between the ages of 8 and 23. His daughter Ellen said her mother became withdrawn following the divorce, "so I feel as if I have been raised as an orphan." [9]

While negotiating to sell the team, Veeck was taking instruction to convert to Catholicism. He had fallen in love with Mary Frances Ackerman, a vivacious publicist for the Ice Capades show, and she wanted to be married in her church. The Catholic Church did not recognize divorce; some of Veeck's associates said church authorities granted him a dispensation because his first wedding had been performed in the Episcopal faith. He and Mary Frances were married on April 29, 1950. He had found his life partner. She joined him as a host of radio and television shows, and as an energetic public speaker promoting whatever team he owned. They also produced six children. (His son Mike said later, "My father loved baseball so much he had nine kids. When the DH was introduced, my mom left town." [10])

The couple moved to Veeck's Arizona ranch, but not for long. Civic leaders from Milwaukee, Los Angeles, and other cities wanted him to buy a major-league club and bring it to their area. Veeck set his sights on the St. Louis Browns, the American League's perennial doormats. The team had won its only pennant in the wartime 1944 season, when its draft rejects proved stronger than the competition's. The Browns were poor stepchildren to the Cardinals in the majors' smallest two-team market. Visiting teams complained that their share of the sparse gate receipts did not even cover travel expenses.

When Veeck bought the Browns in July 1951, it was widely predicted that he would move the franchise, but he later insisted that he planned to run the Cardinals out of town. On his first night as owner he served a free beer or soda to everybody in the ballpark. Six weeks later, he pulled his most famous stunt. Three-foot-seven-inch Eddie Gaedel popped out of the Browns' dugout to lead off in the second game of a doubleheader against the Tigers. After manager Zack Taylor showed the umpire that Gaedel had, indeed, signed a contract (Veeck mailed it to the American League office too late to get there before game time), the tiny man squeezed into a deep crouch at home plate, displaying a strike zone slightly larger than a matchbox. Veeck threatened to shoot him if he swung the bat. As the largest crowd in nearly four years whooped with delight, Detroit catcher Bob Swift dropped to his knees and pitcher Bob Cain delivered four high ones. Gaedel trotted to first base, slapped his pinch-runner on the backside, and ran to the dugout waving his cap. Humorist James Thurber had written a story years before about a midget batting in a big-league game, but Veeck said he had never heard of it.

Five days after the Gaedel game, Veeck struck again with Grandstand Manager Night. He handed out placards printed with "Yes" and "No" to fans sitting behind the home dugout, and at key points in the game they were asked to call the plays: Steal? Bunt? Hit-and-run? Manager Taylor watched from a rocking chair, puffing his pipe, while the Browns beat the Athletics.

Veeck had gone too far. He had inserted his stunts into the ballgame – made a mockery of the game, in the eyes of his many critics. But the Browns' attendance improved in the second half of the season, even though the team finished last. In 1952 attendance nearly doubled, but it was still the lowest in the league as the club rose only one slot in the standings.

The Internal Revenue Service brought Veeck down, although it had nothing to do with his own shaky finances. Cardinals owner Fred Saigh was convicted of income-tax evasion and forced to sell his club. At first it looked as if Veeck had won; a Houston group put in a bid. But August A. Busch Jr., owner of the giant Anheuser-Busch brewery, stepped up to keep the Cardinals in St. Louis. Veeck knew his game was over: "I wasn't going to run Gussie Busch out of town."[11]

• Go-Go to Glory •

In a classic Bill Veeck stunt, a group of "Martians" attempt to capture Nellie Fox and Luis Aparicio. One of the men from Mars was Eddie Gaedel, the dwarf who Veeck had sent up to bat for the 1951 St. Louis Browns.

Within weeks he struck a deal to move the Browns to Baltimore. His fellow owners turned him down. He had enraged them not only with his stunts, but by proposing the "socialistic" idea of sharing television revenue. "The vote against me was either silly or malicious," he said, "and I prefer to regard it as malicious."

Now he was a lame duck in St. Louis – "a villain without any money," in his words. He sold Sportsman's Park, where the Cardinals had been his tenants, to Busch for $800,000. During the 1953 season he sold several players, as well as his Arizona ranch, to stay afloat. In their last game the Browns ran out of new baseballs and had to use scuffed warm-up balls. At the end of the season, AL owners again blocked Veeck from moving to Baltimore. Defeated, he sold the club to a Baltimore syndicate, and the league instantly approved the transfer of the franchise. "They didn't care whether they bought him out or froze him out," John P. Carmichael of the *Chicago Daily News* wrote. "Just so they got even with him, after five years, for disturbing the old, established order of things." [12]

Veeck was again searching for a way to get back into the game. He tried to buy the Philadelphia A's and the Detroit Tigers. He worked with the governor of California on bringing major-league ball to the West Coast. He even negotiated to buy the Ringling Brothers and Barnum & Bailey Circus; he said people had been telling him for years that he belonged in a circus. He scouted for the Indians, where his friend Hank Greenberg was general manager, and spent one season running the Triple-A Miami Marlins. He served as a commentator on NBC-TV's *Game of the Week*.

A family feud finally opened a door. When White Sox president Grace Comiskey died in 1956, she left the majority ownership of the club to her oldest child, Dorothy Rigney, rather than her son, Charles Comiskey II. Thirty-one-year-old Chuck Comiskey, who was running the team, was now a minority owner and bitterly resented it. The club's board of directors was deadlocked, with two votes controlled by Chuck and two by Dorothy. She owned 54 percent of the stock, not enough to appoint a fifth member.

• BILL VEECK •

Worn down by two years of squabbling, Mrs. Rigney told her lawyers to find a buyer. Veeck put together a group of local and out-of-town financiers to acquire an option on her shares. Although he had sold the Browns for a small profit, Veeck had no money, but he never had a shortage of willing investors. He offered $2.7 million for her 54 percent, valuing the franchise at $5 million. Mrs. Rigney's lawyers told him that Chuck would be given a chance to match the price, but Veeck said young Comiskey submitted a lowball offer.

The Veeck group exercised its option in February 1959. Chuck Comiskey sued to block the sale. In the coming months he would paper the courthouses with lawsuits. He lost them all. Veeck said later, "Chuck had grown up firmly convinced that the divine order of the universe called for the earth to spin on its axis, the sun to rise in the east, and Charles Comiskey II to preside over the fortunes of the White Sox."[13]

Comiskey vented his resentment in pettiness. Since he was the highest-ranking officer of the corporation, he declared that Veeck and his partner Hank Greenberg "can't be on the payroll unless I sign the checks." When Veeck came to Comiskey Park on the day after the sale closed, Comiskey left the building. "I won't talk to Veeck as far as business is concerned," he huffed.[14] Veeck invited sportswriters to "have 54 percent of a cup of coffee."[15]

Comiskey's petulance was more than an annoyance. Veeck structured the deal so that most of the purchase price went to buy the players' contracts. Players were assets just like the ballpark and the groundskeepers' rakes and shovels. Since a player's value declined as he got older, he was an asset that could be depreciated to reduce the corporation's taxes. Under IRS rules, Veeck and his partners needed to own 80 percent of the stock to take advantage of the depreciation scheme. He claimed they could save $2 million in taxes – if Chuck would sell. Chuck would not. Veeck never got his tax break, but other sports-team owners did, for decades afterward.

Veeck and Comiskey put aside their differences to appear together at the 1959 home opener. Left-hander Veeck threw out the first ball, and Comiskey caught it. Then a fusillade of fireworks erupted in left field. At the seventh-inning stretch, each of the 19,303 fans was invited to have a free beer. Bill Veeck was back. But the front-office truce was strictly for public consumption. Comiskey continued his court fights, while Veeck mostly ignored him. Greenberg became the unwilling go-between.

Veeck threw his frenetic energy into filling Comiskey Park, making as many as three speeches a day and appearing on radio and television shows from morning till midnight. One morning he showed up at his office at 5 A.M., startling the night watchman. He spent a reported $150,000 painting and scrubbing the old ballpark.

He gave away orchids on Mother's Day. In the same game, the "lucky chair" prize was 36 live lobsters. Other fans received 1,000 cans of beer, 1,000 pies, 1,000 bottles of root beer, 1,000 cupcakes, and 100 free restaurant dinners. "You give a thousand people a can of beer and each of them will drink it, smack his lips and go back to watching the game," he wrote. "You give a thousand cans to one guy, and there is always an outside possibility that 50,000 people will talk about it."[16] He also staged free days for cab drivers and bartenders, believing they were valuable public-relations boosters for the club. After fans booed left fielder Al Smith, Veeck let everyone named Smith (or Smythe or Schmidt) in free as Al's guests. Comiskey Park attendance reached a franchise-record 1,423,144, but it fell just short of the Chicago record set by Veeck's father's Cubs in 1929.

Veeck's assessment of his new team: "I spent the first two-thirds of the season predicting that we didn't have enough power to beat the Yankees."[17] But manager Al Lopez assured him the White Sox could win. As a result, Veeck made few changes in the roster. His only additions were three over-the-hill veterans. Two-time All-Star outfielder Del Ennis lasted seven weeks before he was released. Outfielder Suitcase Simpson batted only .187 before he was traded to Pittsburgh on August 25 for 34-year-old first baseman Ted Kluszewski. Big Klu had been a slugging star for Cincinnati, but chronic back problems had sapped his power. He managed just two homers in 31 games for the White Sox, but slammed three in the World Series.

The White Sox took over first place for good on July 28. Veeck remarked, "Who ever thought that a team could win a pennant strictly on pitching, defense, and speed on the bases? Certainly I didn't. This is contrary to everything I've learned about baseball."[18] He gave all the credit to Lopez. Preparing for the Sox' first Series since the infamous Black Sox, Veeck again sold tickets on an individual-game basis after collecting the names and addresses of fans who had supported the club for years. "These are our vvvvips," he said. "Our very, very, very, very important persons."[19]

Go-Go to Glory

After Chicago battered the Dodgers 11-0 in Game One, it looked as if Lopez's assessment of the team was correct. But when Los Angeles claimed the championship, Veeck said ruefully, "We got licked by the one thing we didn't have in common: power."[20] A joke made the rounds: the White Sox would change their name to White Nylons, because nylons get more runs.

Veeck set out to fix that. In his search for power, he traded away much of his club's future. Six young players went out the door: catchers Earl Battey and John Romano; first basemen Norm Cash and Don Mincher; 20-year-old outfielder John Callison; and pitcher Barry Latman. Every one was a future All-Star. The deals brought in two of Veeck's favorites, both past their primes. Thirty-three-year-old first baseman Roy Sievers had played for him with the Browns. He had signed outfielder Minnie Minoso for Cleveland, but traded the Cuban Comet to the White Sox before he became a star. Minoso was somewhere in his mid-30s; his exact age remains in dispute. Veeck also acquired some younger talent, 26-year-old third baseman Gene Freese and 25-year-old pitcher Frank Baumann.

Defending the deals, Veeck said, "It has been my impression that Youth Plans and Five-Year Plans lead not to pennants, but only to new Five-Year Plans."[21] The impatient Veeck simply refused to wait for prospects to develop. The White Sox fell to third, fourth, and fifth over the next three years. They did not reach the postseason again until 1983.

In 1960 Veeck introduced his most lasting innovations. He put players' names on the backs of their road uniforms (names were added to home uniforms the next year) and built an exploding scoreboard to celebrate the home team's home runs. "It shrieks, wiggles, burps, whines and twinkles," *The Sporting News* marveled. "Fireworks explode beneath the scoreboard while tape recordings give out virtually every sound imaginable ... a cavalry charge, machine-gun fire, two trains crashing head-on, subway screechings, jet bombers, and a woman screaming, 'Fireman, save my child.'"[22] The cacophony delighted fans and infuriated opponents. Cleveland outfielder Jimmy Piersall threw a baseball at the board. Casey Stengel orchestrated a puckish response: After Mickey Mantle hit a homer, Stengel and the Yankees paraded in front of the visitors' dugout waving sparklers. Most other teams eventually added names to their uniforms and sound-and-light shows to their scoreboards.

The 1960 White Sox broke the Chicago attendance record with more than 1.6 million, but Veeck was suffering frightening health problems. The chain smoker broke down in coughing fits that sometimes caused him to pass out. In April 1961 he went to the Mayo Clinic for tests. Doctors diagnosed a variety of ailments, and prescribed retirement. Veeck sold his share of the team to one of his partners, Arthur Allyn Jr.

The 47-year-old Veeck moved his family to a Maryland farm on the shore of Chesapeake Bay. He called the place Tranquility. In 1962 he published his autobiography, *Veeck as in Wreck*, co-authored by sportswriter Ed Linn. The book is both joyful and bitter. He settled some old scores and lobbed new grenades at the baseball establishment. The final lines read: "Sometime, somewhere, there will be a club no one really wants. And Ole Will will come wandering along to laugh some more.

"Look for me under the arc-lights, boys. I'll be back."[23]

Over the next few years Veeck wrote a newspaper column, captivated the many sportswriters who made the pilgrimage to Tranquility, and recovered his health. Reflecting on his many hospital stays, he said, "Suffering is overrated." While watching local Little League games, he discovered a 12-year-old with a sweet swing, Harold Baines. He and Linn wrote another book, *The Hustler's Handbook*. He tried to revive a failing Boston racetrack, Suffolk Downs, and wrote a book about the experience, *Thirty Tons a Day* — the horses' major output.

By 1970 he was ready to scratch his baseball itch. He tried to buy Washington's struggling expansion team before owner Bob Short moved it to Texas. His friend Jerry Hoffberger put the Baltimore Orioles up for sale, and Veeck thought he had a deal, but Hoffberger backed out. *Baltimore Sun* writer Bob Maisel believed Hoffberger was afraid Veeck would sell the team after a few years, and would not care if the next owner took the Orioles away from Baltimore.

For a man lusting to get back into baseball's club, Veeck did himself no good when he testified in support of Curt Flood's court challenge to the reserve clause. He described a ballplayer's condition as "human bondage," but said the reserve clause should be phased out gradually to avoid chaos.[24] Veeck, Hank Greenberg, and Jackie Robinson were the only other baseball men to testify on Flood's behalf.

In 1975 Veeck learned that the White Sox were for sale. Owner John Allyn, who had bought control of the team from his brother Arthur, was near bankruptcy. Attendance had sagged as fans stayed away from the deteriorating neighborhood around Comiskey Park. The franchise was on the verge of being transferred to Seattle. The 61-year-old Veeck put together a group of more than 40 investors, including Greenberg and onetime White Sox manager Paul Richards, but American League owners rejected the bid. They said Veeck's deal was too dependent on borrowed money. That was the public explanation. Several owners acknowledged their distaste for a man who had ridiculed and criticized them for years. After Veeck raised additional cash, they voted him down again. It wasn't the deal they disliked, it was the dealer. Then Detroit Tigers owner John Fetzer told his colleagues that Veeck had done everything they asked: "Look, I don't like it any more than you do that we're allowing a guy in here who has called me a son-of-a-bitch over and over. But, gentlemen, we've got to take another vote."[25] Many of them may have been biting their tongues, but they approved him by 10-2 – one more than the three-fourths majority necessary.

Veeck greeted the vote by kicking his wooden leg high above his head. Then he put up a sign saying "Open for Business" in the hotel lobby where the winter meeting was being held, and spent 14 hours making trades in public. On his first day after being re-admitted to the club, he was already horrifying his fellow owners. Milwaukee's Bud Selig fumed, "This is a meat market."[26]

Veeck had only 13 days to celebrate his comeback. On December 23 arbitrator Peter Seitz abolished the reserve clause that bound players to their teams for life. Ruling on grievances by pitchers Andy Messersmith and Dave McNally, Seitz said the clause allowed a team to renew a player's contract for one year, not over and over forever, as the owners had maintained and players had long believed. The decision opened the door to free agency and the spiraling salaries that came with it. Veeck was short of working capital, with no margin for error. As soon as he got back into the game, he was on his way out.

He would not go quietly. The party started on opening day. To celebrate America's Bicentennial, he re-enacted Archibald McNeal Willard's famous painting of "The Spirit of '76." Wearing bandages and uniforms of the Revolutionary army, Veeck wore a peg leg and played a fife; his longtime sidekick Rudie Schaffer beat a drum; and manager Paul Richards carried the American flag as the trio marched across the field. The stunts continued nonstop throughout the season: a bevy of belly dancers, parades of horses and cattle, nightly prizes for random fans. He outfitted the players in Bermuda shorts for a few games. He put coach Minnie Minoso, who was said to be 53 years old, in the lineup as a designated hitter. Comiskey Park attendance jumped by 20 percent, to 915,000, but it was only 10th highest in the league. The White Sox finished last.

Veeck told general manager Roland Hemond, "Don't bother drawing up a budget. We don't have any money. We'll think of something."[27] But he still worked and played for 20 hours a day, drinking two dozen beers and smoking up to four packs of Salem Longs, stubbing out the butts in an ashtray built into his prosthetic leg. Hemond said, "I tell people I worked for Bill Veeck five years, but it was really ten because I never slept."[28]

In 1977 Veeck found an angle and nearly rode it to glory. His plan was "rent a player." He acquired players who were a year away from free agency, knowing he could not afford to keep them. With sluggers Richie Zisk and Oscar Gamble, the "Go-Go Sox" were transformed into the "South Side Hit Men." The team belted 192 homers, second-most in the majors, and won 90 games. They contended for the Western Division championship for much of the season before sinking to third place. Veeck broke his own Comiskey Park attendance record with more than 1.6 million and was named Major League Executive of the Year by *The Sporting News*.

It was downhill from there. He told the fans, "We will scheme, connive, steal, do everything possible to win the pennant – except pay big salaries."[29] The average player's paycheck more than doubled in just three years, driven by free agency and salary arbitration. Veeck could not keep up. He hired Larry Doby as the majors' second black manager, but fired him after less than a full season. The next year he hired Tony La Russa, a 34-year-old career minor leaguer, to run the club.

Veeck's doomed second time around in Chicago hit bottom on July 12, 1979, Disco Demolition Night. It was an ill-begotten attempt to attract young people and show that the Sox were "hip." Bring a disco record, buy a ticket for 98 cents, and watch as the records were blasted to smithereens between games of the doubleheader. An overflow crowd crashed the gates, and they soon began sailing their discs onto the field. Fueled by beer and marijuana, thousands spilled out of the stands and ran amok. The second game was forfeited to visiting Detroit.

By 1980 Veeck's luck, money, and health had run out. The 66-year-old's hearing and eyesight were failing; he suffered from emphysema and underwent an operation on his remaining leg. But he could not even leave the game without controversy. When he agreed to sell the White Sox to shopping-mall magnate Edward J. DeBartolo, the American League refused to approve the deal on the grounds that DeBartolo would be an absentee owner who also owned racetracks. DeBartolo suspected the real reason was his Italian heritage, with its stereotype of Mafia connections. Veeck said, "I've never been ashamed to be a member of the American League – but I am now."[30]

Chicago real-estate developer Jerry Reinsdorf and television entrepreneur Eddie Einhorn bought the club. At their first press conference, Einhorn promised to run a high-class operation. Veeck was insulted, and never again went to Comiskey Park. Einhorn later insisted he meant no offense, but did not back away from his criticism of Veeck's operation. "He called his ballpark the world's largest outdoor saloon, and was proud of it," Einhorn said. "We came in immediately and tried to change that image. And we succeeded in making it a family place to be." [31]

Veeck returned to his roots as a Cubs fan, and became a regular in the raucous Wrigley Field bleachers. In 1984 he contracted lung cancer. He died at the age of 71 on January 2, 1986. His cremated remains were interred at Oak Woods Cemetery in Chicago. He and Mary Frances had been married for 35 years. She said, "It was a romance from beginning to end."[32] She continued to live in Chicago, and when the White Sox won the 2005 World Series, the club gave championship rings to her and members of the Comiskey family.

Besides Wrigley Field's ivy, Bill Veeck's baseball legacy is his son Mike, part-owner and flamboyant promoter of several minor-league teams. Mike's most infamous stunt was Vasectomy Day – a fan would get a free one on Father's Day – but that was aborted by religious opposition. He said of his father, "He had this tremendous sense of the absurd, and he gave that to me."

Veeck was inducted into the Baseball Hall of Fame in 1991. His enemies on the Veterans Committee kept him out until he was dead, as they did with Leo Durocher. His plaque at Cooperstown reads, "A Champion of the Little Guy."

Notes

1. Gerald Eskenazi, *Bill Veeck: A Baseball Legend* (New York: McGraw-Hill Book Company, 1988), 5.
2. David M. Jordan, Larry R. Gerlach, and John P. Rossi, "The Truth About Bill Veeck and the '43 Phillies," SABR's *The National Pastime*, No. 18, 1998.
3. Jules Tygiel, "Revisiting Bill Veeck and the 1943 Phillies," *Baseball Research Journal 35*, 2007.
4. Bill Veeck with Ed Linn, *Veeck As In Wreck* (Chicago: The University of Chicago Press, 2001; originally published 1962), 80.
5. Ross Newhan, "Red Patterson Dies of Cancer," *Los Angeles Times*, February 11, 1992.
6. Veeck, 105.
7. Ibid.
8. Veeck, 208.
9. Eskenazi, 55.
10. http://thepastime.net/, accessed on June 28, 2008. An account of Mike Veeck's speech at the 2008 SABR convention in Cleveland.
11. Veeck, 229.
12. Eskenazi, 113.
13. Veeck, 318.
14. "No Meetings for Comiskey," *Baltimore Sun*, March 12, 1959.
15. *Baltimore Sun*, March 12, 1959.
16. Veeck, 340.
17. Veeck, 334.
18. Jerry Holtzman, "Pale Hose Kicking Up Heels in Steps of Hitless Wonders," *The Sporting News*, August 19, 1959.
19. Veeck, 351.
20. John Carmichael, "World Series Post Mortems: Sox Too Daring on Bases," *The Sporting News*, October 21, 1959.
21. Veeck, 141.
22. Jerry Holtzman, "Dykes Blasts Veeck's 'Pin-Ball' Scoreboard," *The Sporting News*, May 11, 1960.
23. Veeck, 379.
24. Eskenazi, 148-49.
25. Veeck, 382.
26. Veeck, 383.
27. Roland Hemond, interview with the author, October 18, 2006.
28. Hemond.
29. Wayne Stewart, editor, *The Gigantic Book of Baseball Quotations* (New York: Skyhorse Publishing, 2007), 105.
30. Dick Kaegel, "Dealer Herzog – Where Action Is," *The Sporting News*, December 27, 1980.
31. Eskenazi, 177.
32. Ira Berkow, "When Baseball's Circus Came to Town," *New York Times*, October 20, 2005.

HANK GREENBERG

By Scott Ferkovich

Any list of the greatest sluggers ever to wear a Detroit Tigers uniform has to include Hank Greenberg. Despite losing four years of his physical prime to World War II, he still put together a 13-year career (all but one with the Tigers) that included 331 home runs with 1,276 RBIs. A .313 hitter, he also drew a high number of walks, contributing to his .412 lifetime on-base percentage. Add to that a slugging average of .605, and his career OPS (on-base plus slugging) is an exceptional 1.017, a figure topped by only four other players at the time of his retirement (Babe Ruth, Ted Williams, Lou Gehrig, and Jimmie Foxx). Greenberg made a serious run at Babe Ruth's single-season home-run mark in 1938. His Tigers teams went to four World Series, winning two of them. He did all this while enduring anti-Semitic slurs that were part and parcel of baseball at the time.

His parents were both Jewish immigrants from Romania. David Greenberg and Sarah Schwartz met in America, and married in 1906. Henry Benjamin Greenberg, who would later be known throughout baseball as "Hammerin' Hank," was born on January 1, 1911. He was originally supposed to be named Hyman, but apparently the man filling out his birth certificate had never heard of such a name. Henry had an older brother, Ben, an older sister, Lillian, and a younger brother, Joe.

In time, David Greenberg moved his family from their Greenwich Village home to more spacious living quarters in the Bronx, across the street from the municipal baseball fields of Crotona Park. It was there that the young Henry Greenberg fell in love with the game that was to make up his livelihood. He spent hours hitting the ball in the park, getting the neighborhood kids to shag for him.

Greenberg was a multisport star at James Monroe High, and his best sport wasn't baseball, but basketball. He also excelled at soccer and track and field, and while he wasn't a particular fan of football, he tried out nonetheless just to prove that he could play it, and wound up catching a touchdown pass in the season's final game. The Yankees, along with the Washington Senators and Pittsburgh Pirates, were hot on the prospect's trail. Yankees scout Paul Krichell even took Greenberg to a game at The Stadium. From his front-row box seat, Greenberg was impressed by the power of Lou Gehrig, but Krichell leaned over to the teenager and whispered, "He's all washed up. In a few years, you'll be the Yankee first baseman."[1]

It didn't materialize that way, as Tigers scout Jean Dubuc got Greenberg to sign with Detroit in September of 1929.

Greenberg's first year in professional baseball was with the Raleigh (North Carolina) Capitals of the Class-C Piedmont League in 1930. Only 19, Greenberg put in a very good season in Class-C ball, hitting .314 with 19 homers in 122 games as a first baseman. He also spent part of the summer with the Hartford (Connecticut) Senators of the Class-A Eastern League, getting into 17 games. Meanwhile the second-division Tigers wanted to get a look at the powerful kid, and called Greenberg up for the season's final three weeks. He got into one game, on September 14 at Navin Field against the Yankees, popping up to second base.

It had been a lonely first year for Greenberg, as he was the victim of Jew-baiting, even from some of his own teammates. During batting practice one afternoon, pitcher Phil Page reportedly called Greenberg a "goddamn Jew" after Greenberg had lined a pitch that struck Page in the knee. But other teammates, like Schoolboy Rowe and Billy Rogell, were an encouragement to the youngster. "Go out and outplay the bastards," Rogell told him.[2]

Solid seasons for the Evansville Hubs (Class B) and the Beaumont Exporters (Class A) the next two seasons led to Greenberg's finally making the Tigers for good in 1933. Under manager Bucky Harris, Detroit sputtered along at 75-79, good for fifth place in the American League. Greenberg's first big-league home run came in Detroit, off Washington's Earl Whitehill, on May 6. He was beginning to find a consistent stroke, hitting .301 with 12 home runs and 87 RBIs. He was also filling out physically, at 6-feet-4 and 215 pounds of muscle.

The next season, 1934, was Greenberg's (and the Tigers') breakthrough season. Under new player-manager Mickey Cochrane, Detroit won its first

American League pennant since 1909. Greenberg, with a league-topping 63 doubles, 26 home runs, 139 RBIs, and .339 batting average, was now a feared slugger in a lineup that also featured Charlie Gehringer and Goose Goslin.

That year Greenberg was first faced with the dilemma of whether or not to play on Rosh Hashanah, which fell on September 10. In the past, Greenberg had never hesitated to play baseball on the Sabbath, but the High Holy Days were another matter. In 1933 he had abstained from playing both on Rosh Hashanah and Yom Kippur. As the calendar turned to September 1934, the Tigers were in first place, but could feel the Yankees breathing down their necks. Many fans wanted Greenberg to make an exception and play on Rosh Hashanah.

After much reflection (even consulting a rabbi), Greenberg decided to play in the game that day. It was one of the defining moments of his career, as he homered twice, helping the Tigers win 2-1. Ten days later, with the pennant all but wrapped up, Greenberg declined to play on Yom Kippur. The popular nationally syndicated newspaper poet Edgar Guest penned an ode to Greenberg, ending with the lines: "We shall miss him on the infield and shall miss him at the bat, But he's true to his religion – and I honor him for that!"[3]

Greenberg was the first to admit that he never strongly identified himself as a Jew. But every day opposing bench jockeys, and a certain element of abusive fans, never let him forget his Jewishness. "Sure, there was added pressure being Jewish," he recalled. "How the hell could you get up to home plate every day and have some son of a bitch call you a Jew bastard and a kike and a sheenie and get on your ass without feeling the pressure. If the ballplayers weren't doing it, the fans were. I used to get frustrated as hell. Sometimes I wanted to go up in the stands and beat the shit out of them."[4]

In the World Series the Tigers squared off against the St. Louis Cardinals. It was a tough Series for Detroit, as they fell in seven games. Greenberg, however, boasted solid numbers, with nine hits, one home run, seven RBIs, and a .321 average.

With equal parts power at the plate and crowd appeal at the gate, Greenberg was one of the biggest sports stars in Detroit, in spite of all he had to endure. Affectionate nicknames abounded: "Greenie," "King Kong," "The Big Moose," "Lanky." Baseball was experiencing a resurgence in the Motor City, and Greenberg was leading the way.

The Tigers finally won their first World Series in 1935, although they did it without the services of their star first baseman. Greenberg led the league in home runs (36) and RBIs (170), but he injured his wrist sliding into home plate in Game Two of the Series, and played no more. Detroit overcame the loss, however, to defeat the Chicago Cubs in six games.

Any chances the Tigers had of reaching the World Series again in 1936 went down the drain when Greenberg reinjured his wrist early in the season, and Cochrane, the heart and soul of the club, suffered a nervous breakdown. But Greenberg had a fine comeback in 1937, as he banged 40 home runs and knocked in 183 runs, coming within two of Lou Gehrig's American League mark of 185. (Hack Wilson holds the major-league record with 191.)

It was 1938, however, that truly put Greenberg in the national consciousness. All summer long he chased Babe Ruth's single-season home run record of 60. After a two-homer game in the second half of a doubleheader at St. Louis on September 27, Greenberg entered the final five games needing only two to tie the Babe.

The pressure had been mounting, and Greenberg was both physically and mentally spent. He didn't hit another home run, finishing at 58. The final game of the season was played in Cleveland's cavernous Municipal Stadium. He almost hit one out, but instead it banged off the fence in faraway left-center field. As twilight set in, umpire George Moriarty reluctantly called the game because of darkness. Turning to Hank, he said, "I'm sorry, Hank, this is as far as I can go." An exhausted Greenberg replied, "That's all right, George, this is as far as I can go too."[5]

Greenberg thrived despite the raging anti-Semitism that surrounded him at times. "It was 1938 and I was now making good as a ballplayer. Nobody expected war, least of all the ballplayers. I didn't pay much attention to Hitler at first or any of the political goings-on at the time. I was too stupid to read the front pages, and I just went ahead and played. Of course, as time went by, I came to feel that if I, as a Jew, hit a home run, I was hitting one against Hitler."[6]

Another fine season ensued in 1939, and, despite a switch to the outfield (to accommodate new first baseman Rudy York), Greenberg continued to put up spectacular numbers in 1940. Detroit reached the World Series again, falling in seven games, this time to the Cincinnati Reds. Greenberg slugged 41 home runs, drove in 150 runs, and batted .340 for the year.

• HANK GREENBERG •

And then, like so many other diamond stars of the time, Greenberg was off to war. Whether or not he would be drafted was an open question for several months, mainly because of his flat feet. Finally told that he would have to report for duty on May 7, 1941, Greenberg began the season with Detroit. In his final game before entering the service, he rose to the occasion by slamming two home runs as the Tigers beat New York 7-4 at the recently renamed Briggs Stadium on May 6.

The following morning, Greenberg was inducted into the Army at Fort Custer, Michigan (Fifth Division, Second Infantry Anti-Tank Company). About three months after he went into the service, Congress passed a law dictating that men over 28 years old were not to be drafted. On December 5, 1941, 30-year-old Sergeant Greenberg was given his discharge. He headed home to Detroit to begin getting ready for the 1942 season.

But things changed only a few days later, on December 7, when the Japanese attacked Pearl Harbor. Greenberg decided his country still needed him, and enlisted in the Air Corps. With all the uncertainty in the world, he wasn't sure when he would ever put on a big-league uniform again. "We are in trouble and there is only one thing to do – return to service," he said. "I have not been called back. I am going back of my own accord. Baseball is out the window as far as I'm concerned. I don't know if I'll ever return to baseball."[7]

Greenberg was sent to Officer Candidate School, and commissioned as a first lieutenant on graduation. He later spent time in the China-Burma-India Theater. He received his discharge – again – on June 14, 1945.

For Greenberg, his time spent defending his country in World War II was life-changing. By the time he returned to the States, he realized that there

Hank Greenberg

were more important things in life than baseball. He had matured as a man. "It was a long hitch and it was a wonderful experience," he wrote later. "I can't say it was enjoyable insofar as we were deprived of our liberties, but considering that so many men had suffered much greater hardships than I had, and quite a few of them had lost their lives, I guess I was just lucky to come back in one piece."[8]

Still, he wasn't through playing yet. He rejoined a Tigers team that was in first place, battling for the pennant with the Yankees. In his first game back, on July 1, 1945, before a capacity crowd at Briggs Stadium, he hit a home run to cap a 9-5 Tigers win against Philadelphia.

Greenberg's signature moment as a Tiger, however, came on September 30, the final contest of the 1945 campaign, when he hit a ninth-inning grand slam in the rain at Sportsman's Park in St. Louis, to win the pennant for Detroit. Rounding the bases, even

Greenberg couldn't believe it. "I wasn't sure whether I was awake or dreaming."[9]

By virtue of his memorable poke, the Tigers had the honor of facing the Chicago Cubs in the Series. In a seven-game duel, Detroit won its second World Series title. Greenberg hit the team's only two home runs, and paced the Tigers attack with seven RBIs.

The following season was a mixed bag for Greenberg. While he led the league in home runs with 44, and RBIs with 127, he'd also hit a career-low .277. At age 35, the Tigers felt that his better days were behind him. Greenberg couldn't argue the point, as he spent much of the summer on the trainer's table tending to various aches and pains. "I feel I'm on borrowed time. I don't have the old beans anymore out there, and I'm not the hitter I used to be," he said.[10]

On January 18, 1947, he was sold to the Pittsburgh Pirates for $75,000.

Greenberg contemplated retiring, figuring he was getting too old for the ballplayer's life. And after all, wasn't Forbes Field, the Pirates' home, a death valley for right-handed hitters? But the Pirates agreed to pull in the fences in order to lure Greenberg, naming the section "Greenberg Gardens." They also offered to make him the first $100,000-a-year player in the game's history. Throughout his tenure with the Tigers, Greenberg was a tough negotiator when it came time to talk salary, so the Pirates' overtures were much appreciated.

The biggest beneficiary of Greenberg's move to the National League was young Pirates slugger Ralph Kiner. Kiner had led the circuit in home runs as a rookie, but he was still a raw talent, undisciplined at the plate. Upon joining the Pirates in spring training, Greenberg immediately took Kiner under his wing, teaching him the finer points of what it takes to be a consistent slugger in the major leagues. "He was the most astute student of hitting I ever knew," Kiner remembered about Greenberg later.[11] Kiner went on to a Hall of Fame career, with 369 home runs. "Hank was the biggest influence on my life," he recalled. "The biggest thing Hank taught me was that hard work is the most important thing."[12]

The 1947 season was Jackie Robinson's first year in the big leagues, and the Brooklyn Dodgers came into Pittsburgh for a series in May. Greenberg gave some heartfelt advice to the young African American trailblazer. "Listen, I know it's plenty tough. You're a good ballplayer, however, and you'll do all right. Just stay in there and fight back. Always remember to keep your head up."[13]

As for Greenberg, he hit 25 home runs in 125 games in 1947, with an unspectacular .249 batting average. His league-leading 104 walks contributed to his fine .408 on-base percentage. The Pirates were awful, at 62-92. "At the end of the season that year he couldn't wait to get out of Pittsburgh," Kiner noted. "Not the city but the way the ballclub was being run. There was no direction for the players, and we were at the bottom of the National League."[14] Greenberg's final hit in the major leagues was a home run on September 15 in Pittsburgh, off Philadelphia's Charley Shanz.

After retiring as a player, Greenberg hooked up with his best friend in baseball, Bill Veeck, who at the time owned the Cleveland Indians. Greenberg became the team's general manager, helping to put together the nucleus of the team that won 111 games, but lost the World Series in 1954. But his marriage to Caral Gimbel (whose family owned the New York department store of the same name) was turning sour. The two had been husband and wife since 1946, but their paths always seemed to diverge. Greenberg was a company man, interested in the business of baseball, while Caral appreciated art and music, and kept fine show horses. The marriage benefited both financially, but there didn't seem to be much else there.

Baseball's highest honor came to Greenberg in 1956, when he was elected to the National Baseball Hall of Fame, along with Joe Cronin, the Red Sox' All-Star shortstop and manager. "I've had many thrills in baseball," Greenberg told the Cooperstown crowd. "This, though, is the greatest. Today I have the same butterflies in my stomach that I used to have when I came to the plate with the bases full with Grove or Gomez or Ruffing pitching."[15]

When Veeck sold his interest in the Indians and became the owner of the Chicago White Sox, Greenberg followed him, becoming a part-owner and vice president. But his marriage continued to have problems, and by 1959 he and Caral were divorced. Together, they had three children: Glenn (also known as "Little Hank"), Steve, and Alva, along with eight grandchildren.

Always an astute investor, Greenberg plunged into the stock market and made millions on Wall Street in the 1960s. He sold his stake in the White Sox (for a neat profit), left his Manhattan home for sunny Beverly Hills, and lived the life of Reilly. He married Mary Jo Tarola, a minor movie actress, in 1966.

• HANK GREENBERG •

In 1983 Greenberg made it back to Detroit for one of the few times since he'd been let go after the 1946 season. The occasion warranted it: The Tigers planned a ceremony at Tiger Stadium to retire his uniform number 5, along with Charlie Gehringer's number 2. Both players were able to make it, smiling and waving to the large stadium crowd. It was the final time Greenberg put in an appearance at the site of his greatest glories as a player. "I am very proud," he told the throng, "of the fact that my name and uniform number will be remembered as long as baseball is played in Detroit."[16]

On September 4, 1986, Greenberg died after a lengthy battle with cancer. He is buried in Hillside Memorial Park in Los Angeles. Greenberg's is the classic American success story: With hard work, brains, and a little good fortune, a man can overcome his humble beginnings to be the master of his own destiny. Shirley Povich, the longtime sports columnist for the *Washington Post*, once wrote: "He was the perfect standard-bearer for Jews. Hank was smart, he was proud, and he was big."[17]

Notes

1. William Kashatus, *Lou Gehrig: A Biography* (Westport, Connecticut: Greenwood Press, 2004), 50.
2. John Rosengren, *Hank Greenberg: The Hero of Heroes* (New York: New American Library, 2013), 37.
3. Hank Greenberg with Ira Berkow, *The Story of My Life* (Chicago: Ivan Dee Publishers, 2001), 58.
4. Richard Bak, *Cobb Would Have Caught It* (Detroit: Wayne State University Press, 1993), 85.
5. Terry Foster, *100 Things Tigers Fans Should Know and Do Before They Die* (Chicago: Triumph Books, 2009), 9.
6. Greenberg, 111.
7. Greenberg, 142.
8. Greenberg, 144.
9. Rosengren, 268.
10. Greenberg, 160.
11. Rosengren, 306.
12. Greenberg, 184.
13. Rosengren, 309.
14. Greenberg, 186.
15. Ira Berkow, *Hank Greenberg: Hall of Fame Slugger* (Philadelphia: The Jewish Publication Society, 2001), 85.
16. Associated Press, "Tigers Retire Numbers of Gehringer and Greenberg," *Daytona Beach Morning Journal*, June 12, 1983.
17. Greenberg, xii.

AL LOPEZ
By Maxwell Kates

He was equally as adept at coordinating pitchers and throwing out baserunners as he was as a leader and strategist in the dugout. However, Alfonso Ramon Lopez chose to credit his supporting cast of players for his successes rather than himself. Much like his mentor Casey Stengel, Lopez knew that he could not have won the American League pennants in 1954 or 1959 without his players. Although disappointed that he never played or managed for a World Champion, he received countless honors from his peers on the diamond, his community, the Baseball Hall of Fame, and fans spanning four generations. Lopez was the son of Spanish immigrants. His father, Modesto, was attracted to employment offers in the cigar trade in Cuba. After convincing his bride to abandon their Castilian roots, they spent "eight or nine years" in Cuba; they migrated yet again to the United States in 1906, settling in the Ybor City section of Tampa.[1] The Lopez family settled in a modest four-bedroom house which lacked running water. It was here that their seventh of nine children, Alfonso, was born on August 20, 1908. At the time, Ybor City was hardly the popular nightclub district that it is today. Lopez encapsulated his neighborhood living conditions with the following anecdote told to Tom McEwen: "Tough place, Ybor City was, once. I went to work one day and had to step around a couple of guys who had been murdered in the streets."[2] Among Lopez' earliest memories was the stench of his father's cigar-stained clothing upon returning from the factory where he worked as a tobacco selector. He vowed to work diligently to avoid having to follow in his father's footsteps.[3]

In the days before the ubiquity of the automobile, Lopez remembered no traffic in the unpaved streets of Ybor City. The beach was a source of leisure for Lopez and his friends for crabbing, fishing, and swimming. It was an older brother who introduced him to a second childhood pastime, baseball. Throughout his youth, Lopez played the game with friends on weekends at local sandlots. Dominoes and gin rummy were two additional lifelong hobbies. A member of the Catholic faith, Lopez attended the Jesuit High School of Tampa, but dropped out after his freshman year to support his family.[4]

Lopez accepted a job working for La Joven Francesca Bakery. Nearly nine decades later, he still remembered delivering bread by horse and buggy for the factory workers; "we would hang it in a paper bag, on a nail, by their front door!"[5] Lopez' introduction to professional baseball was nothing short of unorthodox. In 1925, still five years short of the age of majority, he was hired by the Washington Senators to catch batting practice in spring training.

"For some reason," he told Bill Madden, "they didn't want to use their regular catchers, Muddy Ruel and Pinky Hargrave, and I was playing sandlot ball when they called and offered me $45 a week. Heck, I'd have done it for nothing, but that was my start in professional baseball."[6] The young catcher impressed a veteran righthander fresh from recording six shutouts among 23 victories for the defending World Series champions. After practice had concluded, Walter Johnson congratulated Lopez, offering, "Nice game, kid. You're going to be a great catcher someday"[7] Lopez never forgot the experience of catching the Big Train: "Johnson threw hard, maybe the hardest of all, but he was easy to catch because he was always around the plate."[8]

Lopez took his experience catching the Washington Senators to a tryout with the Tampa Smokers of the Florida State League. He made the team, adding an extra $150 every month towards his family's budget throughout the 1925 season. Lopez was later promoted to Jacksonville, and on August 26, 1927, his contract was purchased by the Brooklyn Robins for $10,000. He spent most of the 1928 season playing for Macon, where he earned a spot on the South Atlantic Association All-Star team. Brooklyn manager Wilbert Robinson was sufficiently impressed with reports on his catching prospect to recall him to "the show" in September. Lopez made his debut at Ebbets Field against the Pittsburgh Pirates in the first game of a doubleheader on September 27, 1928.

The first pitcher Lopez faced in the majors was legendary spitball artist Burleigh Grimes. Although the pull-hitting rookie made contact with Grimes, none of the balls he hit evaded the glove work of third baseman Pie Traynor or shortstop Glen Wright.

• AL LOPEZ •

The Robins beat the Pirates 7-6, an extra inning victory for Jesse Petty. Although Lopez failed to hit safely in a dozen official at-bats during his National League initiation, he remembered the experience as "my greatest thrill as a player."[9]

After another year of seasoning in the minors, Lopez had returned to Brooklyn in 1930. He established an offensive personal best for himself as a rookie, batting .309 and driving in 57 runs; meanwhile, his fielding average was .983 in 126 games behind the plate. Compared to other catchers around the league, Lopez was considered small, standing 5-feet11 and weighing a mere 180 pounds. As Arthur Daley chronicled in the *New York Times*, "what he lacked in bulk, he compensated for in agility, speed, intelligence, and class."[10] As a rookie, Lopez was responsible for a change in the rulebook. A fly ball out of Bob Meusel's reach bounced over the Cincinnati outfielder's head and into the stands and was ruled a home run. After the season, this type of play was reclassified as a ground rule double.[11]

After five consecutive sixth-place finishes, the Robins leapt to challenge the St. Louis Cardinals and the New York Giants for the National League pennant. Although the Robins fell to fourth place by September, they won 86 games and set a franchise attendance record by drawing over a million for the first time. As one of the catalysts in the Robins' turnaround, Lopez was offered a raise, no questions asked.[12] The man Daley called "Happy Hidalgo" enhanced his reputation as a dependable catcher, fielding .977 in 1931 and .976 a year later for the rechristened Brooklyn Dodgers.

As a young player, Lopez carried a reputation of an umpire baiter. On one instance, he found himself ejected from a game at the Baker Bowl in Philadelphia. En route to the visitors' clubhouse in center field, Lopez paused at the pitcher's mound to drop his glove, mask, and chest protector. Infuriated, the umpire ordered him to leave the field. Lopez ignored him, continuing his mock burlesque act by

In his 19-year playing career, Al Lopez caught 1,918 games, a major league record that lasted until 1987, 40 years after his retirement.

removing one shinguard, then another, and tossing them gingerly beside him. At that point, he collected his belongings and moved towards center field slower than a Studebaker with a flat tire.[13]

In 1933, Lopez tested the patience of another authority figure, Dodgers general manager Robert Quinn. When training camp opened, Lopez was nowhere to be found – he was holding out for a better contract. Manager Max Carey called him, urging him to reconsider, as his job was threatened by "a young catcher who looks pretty good."[14] That "young catcher" was actually a year older than Lopez, but the two backstops would emerge as lifelong friends. Ray Berres later served as Lopez' pitching coach for over a decade with the Chicago White Sox. Meanwhile, in 1932, the Dodgers acquired another of Lopez' future coaches, shortstop Tony Cuccinello.

On the heels of batting .301 in 1933, Lopez was assigned to represent the Dodgers at the 1934 All-Star

Game at the Polo Grounds. Among the thousands of spectators who "happened to be at that game" was Evelyn Kearney. Known to all as "Connie," the Broadway chorus girl met Lopez after the game. Five years later, on October 7, 1939, the pair was wed. They welcomed a son, Al Jr., in 1942. Over the years, the Lopez family would expand to include three grandchildren and nine great grandchildren.[15]

The 1934 season also introduced Lopez to new Brooklyn manager Casey Stengel. Despite his later successes with the Yankees, Stengel led the Dodgers to pedestrian records of 71-81 in 1934 and 70-83 in 1935. Rumors began to circulate that several star players would soon be traded. Stengel attempted to placate any apprehension Lopez might have by assuring him that "it's going to be to a good club."[16] Instead, on December 12, 1935 Lopez and Cuccinello were traded to the Boston Braves. Lopez was understandably offended at Stengel's false reassurance. In 1935, the Braves won 38 and lost 115, established themselves as the worst team in baseball. As Lopez recalled, "then [in 1938], he comes over to Boston to manage and trades me to Pittsburgh."[17]

Lopez played for the Pirates through the 1946 season when he was traded to Cleveland for outfielder Gene Woodling on December 7. He was well-respected enough in the latter stages of his career that even superstars from opposing teams asked him for advice. In March 1939, when legendary Yankee Lou Gehrig suddenly stopped hitting with alacrity, he turned to Lopez for advice on his swing.

"So I told him, 'the only thing I can think is that you're not slapping the ball, you're pushing at it.'"[18] At the time, Gehrig's diagnosis of ALS was undetected.

Lopez' arrival in Cleveland coincided with the inception of the Indians' golden age. Bill Veeck was the owner, Lou Boudreau the manager, Bob Feller and Bob Lemon anchored the rotation, and on July 5, 1947, the trailblazing Indians integrated the American League with the emergence of Larry Doby. Lopez caught for one season for the Indians as Jim Hegan's backup and then retired. Nineteen seasons in the major leagues yielded 1,547 hits, 206 doubles, 43 triples, 51 home runs, 652 runs batted in, and a lifetime average of .261. Catching 1,918 games, a major league record until 1987, he produced a sterling .985 fielding percentage. In 1941, he caught 114 games with the Pirates without as much as a passed ball. Lopez knew his career as a catcher would not last forever; as a member of the Bees, he invested in Texas land options prior to a real estate boom.[19] Lopez enjoyed the financial freedom to concentrate on his career ambition, managing in the major leagues.

"I always wanted to manage when my playing career was finished, but if that was part of Veeck's plan when he got me, he never told me about it," said Lopez."[20] Not offered a position with the Indians, Lopez was assigned in 1948 to manage the Indianapolis Indians of the American Association. The baby Indians flourished under Lopez' tutelage, winning 12 of their first 15. Led by Les Fleming's .323 batting average and Bob Malloy's record of 21-7, they finished with a record of 100-54. Lopez even caught in 42 games for the Indians. They finished ahead of the Milwaukee Brewers by 11 games to garner the American Association pennant. Was this a sign of big-league accomplishments for Lopez?

After two more years at Indianapolis, Lopez was hired on November 10, 1950 to manage the Cleveland Indians. One of the keys to his success in Cleveland was his rapport with chief operating officer Hank Greenberg.

"We worked well together," said Lopez. "Hank picked up some good players, guys who were especially important to us in 1954 when we had a lot of injuries. The club in those days didn't spend a lot of money… but Hank was able to do some things that didn't cost a lot because we did so well."[21]

The Indians were consistent if not spectacular under Lopez, winning 93 games in 1951, 93 in 1952, and 92 in 1953. Yet, it was not enough to unseat the New York Yankees from the apex of the American League. Managed by Lopez' nemesis Casey Stengel, the Bronx Bombers were completing their sweep of five successive World Series titles. Without the financial wealth or the farm system resources of the Yankees, the Indians left their fans frustrated. Lopez retained a personal respect for Stengel, describing him as "a great guy and a fine manager [who] loved to teach." He added, "I learned a lot from Stengel – but apparently not enough."[22]

Fate would be kinder to the Cleveland Indians in 1954. Although the Yankees won 103 games, their highest total under Stengel, they were relegated to listening to the World Series on the radio. The Indians, meanwhile, played evenly against the Yankees and the White Sox while posting a torrid 89-21 record against the other five clubs. Posting an overall record of 111-43, the Tribe vaulted to the American League pennant. As Lopez later reported

• AL LOPEZ •

to veteran sportswriter Russell Schneider, the Indians "had a lot of leaders, which is one of the reasons we did so well. I've got to say that (Al) Rosen was the number one guy. I had great respect for the way he played the game and the way he demanded that others play the game."[23]

The Indians were leaders on the mound. Bob Lemon and Early Wynn earned league titles with 23 wins apiece, while the club converted 19 victories from Mike Garcia, 15 from Art Houtteman, and 13 from Bob Feller. Lopez described his pitching staff as "the greatest ever assembled."[24]

The Indians were leaders at the plate as well. Second baseman Bobby Avila captured a batting crown hitting .341, while Larry Doby led the American League with 32 home runs and 126 runs batted in. The Indians were tops in the American League with 156 dingers.

Lopez credited the Indians' bench and bullpen as integral components to the team's success. Without contributions from acquisitions Sam Dente, Hank Majeski, Vic Wertz, and Wally Westlake, he maintained that the Tribe "probably could not have won." Credit should also be given for converting pitchers Don Mossi and Ray Narleski into relievers – "a big factor in beating the Yankees."[25]

They fell into a slump against the New York Giants during the World Series. In the eighth inning of Game One, Vic Wertz hit a line drive which travelled 460 feet deep into the Polo Grounds before landing in Willie Mays' glove. After Dusty Rhodes delivered a pinch home run for a 10th inning Giants' victory, momentum remained on their side. The Giants swept the Indians in four straight. Lopez insisted that the Indians would have fared better had they opened the series at Municipal Stadium, where Wertz' line drive would have been a home run.

Losing the 1954 World Series did not prevent the City of Tampa from dedicating its new spring training facility in Lopez' honor.[26] For better than three decades, Al Lopez Field was the winter home of the Cincinnati Reds. It did not take long for Lopez to make history in "his" stadium. On the very first play of the 1955 spring opener, he argued the call with umpire John Stevens. The arbiter warned the manager that "one more word and you're gone." Lopez protested: "You can't throw me out of this ballpark. This is my ballpark – Al Lopez Field." Stevens said, "Get out of here." Years later, Lopez reflected with perplexity that anyone would throw him "out of [his] own ballpark."[27] Lopez also had the distinction of outliving the use of his stadium, which was destroyed in 1989.

After two more second-place finishes in Cleveland, Lopez resigned as the Indians manager in 1956. Chronic stomach ailments brought forth by years of anxiety suggested it was time for a change in scenery.[28] He took his managerial acumen to Chicago, where he replaced Marty Marion as the manager of the White Sox. Though he assumed control of a talented roster, the White Sox were notorious for their "June swoon" and as "hitless wonders." Marion advised Lopez that "he better bring his pitchers with him."[29]

Playing in spacious Comiskey Park, the White Sox under Lopez' stewardship focused their game around pitching, speed, and defense. Importing his philosophy from another cavernous ballpark, Cleveland, Lopez stressed the stolen base, the hit and run, and run manufacturing to get ahead of the opposition. A player and coach for Lopez in Indianapolis, Don Gutteridge was the Senor's second in command for better than a decade in Chicago. Gutteridge remembered: "As an organization, the White Sox were trying everything they could to win." He also recalls Lopez advising his players, "If you don't let them score that run and you score that *run* – you win."[30] Lopez inherited an outfield of Minnie Minoso, Larry Doby, and Jim Rivera. His middle infielders, Nellie Fox and Luis Aparicio, were both defensive stalwarts destined for Cooperstown. Doby was not the only Cleveland personality with whom Lopez reunited in Chicago. Bill Veeck and Hank Greenberg joined the club as executives a year later.

The White Sox opened the 1957 season by winning 11 of their first 13 games. On June 8, the Sox enjoyed a six-game lead in the junior circuit, their largest advantage since Buck Weaver was permitted to play third base. But when the dust cleared on 1957, Lopez found his White Sox in a familiar position, in second place behind the Yankees. However, true to his word, Lopez relied upon pitching, speed and defense to win 90 games. The Sox led the American League with 109 stolen bases. On the mound, Billy Pierce (20-12, 3.26) and Dick Donovan (16-6, 2.77) led the rotation which was coordinated by veteran receiver Sherm Lollar. Observed Don Gutteridge from his view in the dugout: "Of course, Al Lopez was excellent with pitchers, too. He was a great catcher for so many years that he really knew what was going on with his pitchers. Between Lopez and Berres, they really knew pitching and always got the most out of our staff."[31]

The city and the uniform had changed for Lopez, but after managing in the American League since 1951, his club still finished second to the New York Yankees. The 1958 season marked the seventh year out of eight that a Lopez club played bridesmaid to the Bronx Bombers. Although the White Sox won 90 games in 1957 and 82 in 1958, it was not enough to stop Casey Stengel's juggernaut from adding to their surplus of American League titles. Lopez' critics, particularly those in the New York media, accused him of being anti-Yankee. Defending himself, he argued, "I'm anti any club that wins all the time."[32]

Jim Rivera has fond memories of playing for Al Lopez. The outfielder described his manager as "very fair," adding, "if you did something good, he would compliment you. If you struck out or made an error, he wouldn't say a word as long as you hustled and worked hard."[33] However, broadcaster Milo Hamilton insisted that Lopez was a disciplinarian as the situation warranted. If a player made a mental mistake, he reprimanded the poor soul behind closed doors rather than before his teammates or the media. Hamilton also remembered Lopez for his sense of fashion. Always dressed in a suit and tie when not in uniform, the manager "had a presence you couldn't forget." Hamilton added that when Lopez travelled, "he just looked the part of somebody *important*."[34]

And important he was. In 1959, Al Lopez accomplished something no White Sox manager had in done four decades. He led his club to an American League pennant. Despite hitting only 97 aggregate home runs, fewest of any team, the "Go-Go Sox" led the American League with 113 stolen bases, 46 triples, and a 3.29 earned run average. Early Wynn won 22 games and the Cy Young Award while Nellie Fox batted .306 as the league's Most Valuable Player. Fastest on the basepaths was Aparicio who led the league with 56 steals. The Sox won 35 of 50 one-run decisions, winning their first season series over the Yankees since 1925 by posting a 13-9 record against New York.

White Sox fans knew that 1959 would be an unusual season on April 22, when they scored 11 runs in one inning on 10 walks, a hit batsman, three errors, and only one hit. The Sox battled the Indians for control of first place for most of the summer when in July, Chicago raced ahead by winning 11 games of a

Between 1949 and 1964, Al Lopez was the only American League manager to disrupt the Yankees' run of World Series appearances. Lopez took home pennants with the 1954 Indians and 1959 White Sox.

12-game homestand. Although Cleveland recovered to within a game in the standings by late August, the Sox reaffirmed their dominance over the Indians with a four-game sweep at Cleveland. When the Sox clinched the pennant on September 22, Mayor Richard J. Daley activated air raid sirens throughout Chicago. A White Sox fan, Hizzoner had no idea of the extent of the terror he instilled in his citizenry. As Harold Rosenthal later reported, "everyone wanted to know how far up Michigan Avenue the Russians had advanced."[35]

Contrary to the 1954 World Series, the White Sox opened the 1959 Fall Classic with an 11-0 victory at home. Early Wynn threw seven scoreless innings against the Los Angeles Dodgers as Ted Kluszewski drove in five runs on two homers and a single. Although they led 2-1 in the sixth inning of Game Two, the Sox lost the game and ultimately the Series, four games to two.

Although the White Sox remained competitive in the early 1960s, they did not return to the World

• AL LOPEZ •

Series under Lopez' tutelage. Managing pennant races for 15 consecutive summers took their toll on his well-being. Managing was no longer fun for a man in his fifties who spent many late nights pacing the clubhouse floor due to an insomniac condition.[36] Not even Lopez' gin rummy marathons with broadcaster Bob Elson were enough to lift his spirits. As was reported in *Time*, the insecurity of having never won a World Series "kept him melancholy." Few were aware of his stomach condition, let alone its severity, which prevented him from digesting fruit or vegetables and forced him to drink milk – a beverage he detested.[37] After leading the Sox to a 95-67 record in 1965, good for another second-place finish, Lopez' illness forced him to step down as manager in favor of Eddie Stanky. While the White Sox prospered initially under Stanky, they floundered in 1968. Mired in eighth place on July 11, the Sox fired Stanky; as Lopez was healthy enough to return to work, he was hired to his second tour of duty with the Sox. Although the Pale Hose won 21 and lost 26 under Lopez, it was not enough to salvage the season. The 1968 Chicago White Sox went 67-95, finishing 36 games behind Detroit tied for eighth place.

The White Sox began the 1969 season with promise as Carlos May belted two home runs in a 5-2 victory in the home opener against the expansion Kansas City Royals. However, the early season heroics were a false hope. A respectable record of 8-9 through May 2 was not enough to prevent Lopez' insomnia from returning. As he told Hal Bodley decades later, "That's when I knew it was time to get out."[38] Announcing his retirement to coaches Berres, Gutteridge, Kerby Farrell, and Johnny Cooney, Lopez wanted "one of you four to take over from me."[39] Gutteridge reluctantly accepted. Dressed in one of his trademark suits, Lopez returned to Comiskey Park in 1970 to watch an Opening Day loss to Minnesota before departing the Chicago sports scene for good.

Lopez returned to Tampa where he enjoyed his retirement. He played cards regularly with lifelong friends, watched *The Price is Right* religiously, and golfed his age well into his 70s. In 1977, he was inducted into the Baseball Hall of Fame. His baseball interest peaked during the 1990 World Series between clubs managed by Tony La Russa and Lou Piniella, both Tampa natives.

Even in his 90s, Lopez showed few signs of slowing down. He was one of four Hall of Famers invited to throw the ceremonial first pitch to welcome the Tampa Bay Devil Rays into the American League on March 31, 1998.[40] At his 95th birthday party, a gala event at Tampa's Columbia Restaurant, Lopez was awarded an honorary doctorate from the University of South Florida.[41] Then on October 26, 2005, he "stayed up past his bedtime" to watch the Chicago White Sox finally win the World Series.[42]

"They have a darn good ballclub," he told sportswriter Hal Bodley. "I was so happy to see it. Chicago's a real fine city, and that manager [Ozzie Guillen] is doing a great job."[43]

Four days after watching the White Sox sweep the Houston Astros for the 2005 World Championship, Al Lopez was gone. Hospitalized after suffering a massive heart attack, Lopez died on October 30, age 97. He was buried beside his wife Connie, whom he widowed in 1983. As Tom McEwen wrote in his obituary of El Senor, his heart "would have to be massive" because "he had given so much of his heart away."[44]

Lopez may have been a humble man in life, but after his death he continued to receive honors and accolades. In 2006, he was enshrined into the Cleveland Indians Hall of Fame. The Devil Rays now offer the Al Lopez Award to the organization's top rookie in spring training. Meanwhile, the Rays invited his son, grandson, and great grandson to throw the ceremonial first pitch in 2006 – each of them named Alfonso Ramon Lopez.[45]

As a catcher and as a manager, Al Lopez was undoubtedly a baseball legend. He earned the respect and acclaim of teammates and adversaries alike, and became an inspiration to thousands of athletes and spectators in Tampa. Lopez returned to his hometown each winter, watching his community expand over the course of the 20th century. Though modest about his accomplishments, he left an indelible mark in the minds of fans from Ybor City to Brooklyn, from Cleveland to Chicago, and all points in between.

Sources

In addition to the sources cited in the Notes, the author also consulted www.baseball-reference.com, retrosheet.org, and:

"Un-Covering the Past – Hall of Fame Manager Al Lopez," *Baseball Digest*, May 2001.

Operation White Sox (Chicago: The Chicago White Sox, 1964).

The Exciting Story of the White Sox (Chicago: The Chicago White Sox, 1965).

Dewey, Donald and Acocella Nicholas. *Total Ballclubs: The Ultimate Book of Baseball Teams* (Toronto: Sport Media Publishing Inc., 2005).

Helpingstine, Dan. *Chicago White Sox: 1959 and Beyond* (Charleston, South Carolina: Arcadia Publishing, 2004).

Johnson, Lloyd and Wolff, Miles. *The Encyclopedia of Minor League Baseball*, 2nd ed. (Durham, North Carolina: Baseball America, 1997).

Murr, Chuck. "Broussard's Homer Helps Top Tribe, 3-1." Indians Ink (July 30, 2006). Available from http://indians.scout.com/2/550918.html.

Weiss, Bill and Wright, Marshall. "Team #85: 1948 Indianapolis Indians" (2001): 15 pars. [Journal Online]. Available from http://web.minorleaguebaseball.com/milb.history/top100.jsp?idx=85.

Acknowledgments: Arthur Kates, Len Levin, Herb Moss

Notes

1. Keith Niebuhr, "He's the Hall's 'Senor' Citizen," *St. Petersburg Times*, July 25, 2005.
2. Tom McEwen, "El Senor Gave So Much of His Big Heart Away," *Tampa Bay Online*, October 31, 2005.
3. Richard Goldstein, "Al Lopez, a Hall of Fame Manager, Is Dead at 97," *New York Times*, October, 31 2005.
4. Niebuhr.
5. McEwen.
6. Bill Madden, "Reminiscing with Al Lopez," *Baseball Digest*, August 2004.
7. Arthur Daley, "The Two Managers," *New York Times*, September 26, 1954.
8. Madden.
9. *The Exciting Story of the White Sox* (Chicago: The Chicago White Sox, 1965), 65.
10. Daley.
11. Madden.
12. Donald Dewey, and Nicholas Acocella. *Total Ballclubs: The Ultimate Book of Baseball Teams* (Toronto: Sport Media Publishing Inc., 2005), 110.
13. Daley.
14. John Kuenster, "Oldest Hall of Fame Member Revives Some Baseball Memories," *Baseball Digest*, July 2003).
15. Niebuhr.
16. Goldstein.
17. Goldstein.
18. Niebuhr.
19. Harold Rosenthal, *Baseball's Best Managers*, (New York: Bartholomew House, 1961), 152.
20. Russell Schneider, *The Cleveland Indians Encyclopedia*, (Champaign, Illinois: Sports Publishing LLC, 2001), 513.
21. Schneider, 513.
22. Schneider, 514.
23. Schneider, 512.
24. Schneider, 67.
25. Schneider, 513.
26. Raymond Arsenault, "Our Roots Run Deep," *Tampa Bay Devil Rays Magazine*, Volume 1, Number 1 (April 1998).
27. Jennifer Kay, "Al Lopez, Who Led ChiSox to '59 Series, Dies at 97," *USA Today* (October 30, 2005).
28. Schneider, 517.
29. Rosenthal, 152.
30. Don Gutteridge, Ronnie Joyner, and Bill Bozman, *Don Gutteridge In Words and Pictures* (Dunkirk, Maryland: Pepperpot Productions Inc., 2002), 174-75.
31. Gutteridge, 175.
32. Goldstein, 4.
33. Goldstein, 9.
34. Milo Hamilton and Dan Schlossberg, *Making Airwaves: 60 Years at Milo's Microphone* (Champaign, Illinois: Sports Publishing LLC, 2006), 55-56.
35. Rosenthal, 155.
36. "The Garter on the Sox," *Time*, May 28, 1965.
37. *Time*.
38. Hal Bodley, "Lopez – The Senor – Has Wonderful Memories of '59 Series," *USA Today*, October 18, 2005.
39. Gutteridge, 182.
40. "Son, Grandson, Great Grandson of Al Lopez to Throw Out First Pitch At Rays' Home Opener" on Devil Rays Homepage (March 7, 2006) www.devilrays.com.
41. McEwen.
42. Bodley.
43. Ibid.
44. McEwen.
45. www.devilrays.com.

RAY BERRES

By Don Zminda

As pitching coach for the White Sox in the 1950s and '60s, Ray Berres was noted for two things: developing quality pitching staffs year after year, and not wanting to draw attention to himself. Quiet and unassuming, he once said, "I attribute my longevity in baseball to the fact that I do not give interviews to reporters."[1] But Ray Berres couldn't avoid the limelight completely, for one reason: his work – as one of the most successful pitching coaches of all time – was simply too good.

Raymond Frederick Berres was born in Kenosha, Wisconsin, on August 31, 1907 (according to Berres' son John, Ray's name on his baptismal certificate was listed as "Reimann"[2]). "I thought it was wonderful," Berres said about growing up in Kenosha. "The streets weren't paved and we could play ball in the streets morning, noon and night."[3] Ray's father, a carpenter and repairman, had immigrated to the U.S. from Germany and had no interest in baseball. He died when Ray was 14; his mother was not a baseball fan, either, but his two brothers and four sisters encouraged his baseball ambitions (Ray was the youngest of the seven children).

In his late teens, Berres caught for sandlot teams in the Kenosha area, traveling as far as Chicago on occasion to play ball. He caught the attention of former major-league pitcher Dick Crutcher, who was managing a semipro team for Nash Motors in Kenosha. With Crutcher's help, Berres was offered a professional contract with the Oklahoma City club of the Class A Western League. He went to spring training with Oklahoma City in 1929, but in his eagerness to show the team his throwing ability, he developed a sore arm. Rather than take a chance on waiting for the untried youngster's arm to heal, the club handed Berres his release at the train station just before departing for its opening game. "Here I was, suitcase in hand, proud as heck," Berres remembered years later. "I was really broken-hearted."[4]

Lacking the money to return home after his abrupt release, Berres began hitchhiking back to Kenosha. When he reached Waterloo, Iowa, he remembered that an old teammate of his from Kenosha was trying out for the Waterloo Hawks of the Class D Mississippi Valley League. He found the hotel where his friend was staying, met the manager, and was given an opportunity to try out for the team. His arm was still sore at first, but the club showed patience with him and offered him a contract (ironically, to make room for Berres, the team released his friend). Berres rewarded the club's patience by hitting .300 in his debut season, but was limited to 64 games after spraining his ankle and hurting his knee sliding into second base. With the club threatening to release him, he returned to action with the ankle still in a cast, and came up with a sore arm again. But he soldiered on, grateful to have a job playing baseball. "I was making $75 a month," he recalled.[5]

Ray Berres

After that season Berres' contract was purchased by the Birmingham Barons of the Class A Southern Association for $7,500. "The Birmingham owner, Bill Curtis, kept calling me all winter about the ankle, telling me to do a lot of dancing to strengthen it," he recalled.[6] The Barons were loaded with catchers in 1930, and sent Berres to Montgomery of the Class B Southeastern League for that season. He was recalled to Birmingham in 1931 and spent three seasons there under manager Clyde Milan. "He was like a godfather to me," Berres said of the former Washington Senators outfielder. "I asked him if he thought I would make it to the major leagues – I was a comparatively small man (5'9"). He said, 'Your enthusiasm and your work and your ability will get you there. You'll never be a good big-league hitter, but observant as you are and as cooperative as you are, you'll always have a job.'"[7] However, injuries continued to hold Berres back; played in only 69 games in 1930 and 36 in 1931. "I suffered a lot of broken fingers," he recalled.[8]

Berres was healthy and productive in 1932 and '33, hitting over .280 for Birmingham both years, and after the 1933 season, he was drafted by the Brooklyn Dodgers. He made his major-league debut for the Dodgers in 1934, playing for manager Casey Stengel, and got into 39 games, hitting .215 while backing up veteran catcher Al Lopez, who became his roommate and lifelong friend. However, Berres' arm began acting up again and he spent the 1935 season back in the minors with Sacramento of the Class AA Pacific Coast League. It proved to be a break for Berres. He developed a new way of throwing while in Sacramento that was less taxing on his arm. "The warm weather in Sacramento helped my arm also," he said.[9]

In December 1935 the Dodgers traded Lopez to the Braves and brought Berres back to Brooklyn. Sharing the club's catching chores with Babe Phelps in 1936, he caught 105 games on a mostly veteran staff led by colorful right-hander Van Lingle Mungo. Phelps was by far the better hitter, but Berres' throwing ability and his knack for working with pitchers helped him get playing time. His knowledge of hitters' strengths and weaknesses was encyclopedic; even when he was in his late 80s, Berres could tell an interviewer what pitches were best to throw to Ernie Lombardi, Mel Ott, or the Waner brothers.

But while Berres was proving Clyde Milan correct when he told Ray that his knowledge and ability would get him to the majors, he was also living up to Milan's prediction that he'd never be a good major-league hitter. Berres batted .240 for the Dodgers in 1936, a good season with the stick by Ray's modest standards; however, Phelps, batted .367, and the next year Berres was back in the minors with Louisville of the Class AA American Association. "Burleigh Grimes (the Dodgers' new manager) had never seen me play," recalled Berres. "He had an outfielder in Louisville that he wanted, and Louisville needed a catcher." So a trade was worked out. "I was really despondent; I was going to quit," said Berres. "I thought my chances were going to run out."[10] But Berres was told that other major-league teams were interested in him, so he reported to the Colonels.

The Pittsburgh Pirates brought Berres back to the majors late in the 1937 season, but a broken toe limited him to two major league games that year. He spent 1938 and '39 with the Bucs as a backup receiver ("I was brought back primarily to catch the curveball pitchers, like Cy Blanton and Russ Bauers," said Ray[11]). In June of 1940, he recalled, "We blew a game in the Polo Grounds, and (Pirates manager) Frankie Frisch was going from one locker to the other, giving everybody hell. When he came to me, he said, 'And you… get your ass up to Boston. I just dumped you.'"[12] The Pirates traded him – for Al Lopez, of all people. (Pittsburgh also gave the cash-poor Braves $40,000.)

Reunited with his former Dodgers manager, Casey Stengel, in Boston, Berres earned playing time with his solid defensive work but continued to struggle mightily at bat – hitting .192 in 1940 and .201 in 1941. And according to Ray, he did not get along as well with Stengel as he had when the two had been together in Brooklyn. Despite that and despite his weak hitting, Berres got into 106 games in 1940 (85 of them after the trade to Boston) and a career-high 120 games in 1941. "My whole pride was in defense," Berres said about his playing career. "I think one year I picked more men off the bases than one (regular) catcher threw out stealing. Somebody said I was included in the top 10 defensive catchers in the history of baseball."[13]

One of Berres' best memories of his years in Boston was his marriage to the former Irma Ludwig in July, 1940. "Our families had known each other for years," Ray said.[14] The couple had a son, John, and remained together for 62 years, until Irma's death in 2003.

When the U.S. entered World War II in December of 1941, Berres was physically unable to serve in the military; Berres' son John said that this was primarily due to injuries requiring reconstructive surgery that Ray had suffered in a home-plate collision with the Cardinals' Pepper Martin. As a result, Berres was able to keep playing baseball during the war years, while working during the offseasons assembling engines for USAAF bombers at the Nash Motors plant in Kenosha.

The Pirates sold Berres to the Giants before the 1942 season. According to Ray, Bill Terry, the Giants' general manager, had made the trade with the thought of sending Berres to New York's Jersey City farm team to work with the team's young pitchers, but Ray refused to go back to the minors. He did agree to spend spring training with Jersey City, then spent the 1942-45 wartime years with the Giants as a seldom-used backup catcher, getting a total of 107 at-bats in the four seasons. (Harry Danning, Gus Mancuso, and Ernie Lombardi were ahead of him on the depth chart). The Giants released Berres after the 1945 season, and he finished his major-league career with a lifetime average of .216 and only 78 RBIs and just three home runs in 561 games. (One of those home runs was inside-the-park.) He wasn't quite through playing. He spent the 1946 a player-manager for Richmond of the Piedmont League, but decided, "I hated managing."[15] Though he never played professionally again, Ray Berres was far from through with baseball. The career that would win him lasting fame – as a pitching coach – was about to begin.

Ray began that second career in modest fashion as a bullpen coach (and possible emergency catcher, though he never got into a game) under Billy Southworth with the 1947 Boston Braves. Aware of Ray's ability to impart his knowledge to young pitchers, the Braves arranged for him to room with Warren Spahn, who was then in his second full major-league season. It was probably no coincidence that Spahn improved from eight wins in 1946 to 21 wins in 1947, with a league-leading 2.33 ERA.

In 1948, the Braves sent Berres down to coach with their Milwaukee club in the American Association; while there he worked extensively in spring training with future major-league catching star Del Crandall. Then in 1949, Berres returned to the majors with the Chicago White Sox. "I got a call one day from (White Sox general manager) Frank Lane, asking me to be his pitching coach," Ray recalled.[16] Lane had been president of the American Association while Berres was coaching at Milwaukee, and was familiar with Ray's reputation as someone who had a knack for working with pitchers.

Berres remained a coach with the White Sox for the next 18 seasons. The Sox team he joined had been the worst in the American League in 1948, losing 101 games and ranking next-to-last in team ERA with a 4.89 ERA. The White Sox moved up to sixth place in '49, and the Berres touch was immediately evident as the club improved its team ERA by more than half a run, to 4.30. Berres had his first major success that year with left-hander Bill Wight, who went from 9-20 with a 4.80 ERA in 1948 to 15-13 with a 3.31 ERA in 1949.

After one more bad season (94 losses) in 1950, the White Sox in 1951 began a streak of 17 consecutive seasons with winning records – one of the longest such streaks in major-league history. Berres, who was the pitching coach for all but the last of those 17 years, was a major factor in the White Sox' success. Under his guidance, the White Sox posted an overall team ERA of 3.33 in the years from 1951 through 1966 – the top mark for any major-league team over that time span.

One of Berres' trademarks during his years as White Sox pitching coach was his ability to take pitchers who had struggled with other teams and turn them into winners with the White Sox. Among the pitchers who had the best seasons of their careers after hooking up with Berres were Saul Rogovin, who won the American League ERA title after being traded to the Sox in 1951; Sandy Consuegra, who went 16-3 with a 2.69 ERA in 1954; converted first baseman Jack Harshman, who won 40 games for the White Sox from 1954 through 1956; Ray Herbert, who had his only 20-win season for Berres and the Sox in 1962; and Juan Pizarro, who had several good years in White Sox pinstripes, including a 19-9 season in 1964. There were many others.

"I always went to the ballpark early," said Berres about his ability to notice pitchers on other clubs who had the potential to help the White Sox. "I loved to watch teams work out, and I'd see pitchers getting their work in. I'd see a pitcher and think, 'I believe if I could get him to go my way, he could help us.'"[17] With Berres, it happened again and again.

"I owe a great deal to Ray Berres," said Bob Shaw, who blossomed into an 18-game winner for the pennant-winning 1959 Sox club under Berres' tutelage. "What he basically taught me was quite simple: you've got to break your hands, get the hand out of the glove, keep your weight back, get your arm up. It wasn't all that elaborate. Just basic fundamentals and he knew 'em and there are really very few people in the country who know what they are."[18]

"He was the reason I got to the big leagues," former White Sox pitcher Gary Peters said of Berres. "He had a knack for spotting mechanical problems and he could cure you pretty easily."[19] As with many pitchers, success came quickly to Peters once he was able to grasp Berres' concepts. After several frustrating seasons in which he pitched well for Sox farm teams

• Go-Go to Glory •

The 1959 White Sox braintrust: coaches Ray Berres and Tony Cuccinello, manager Al Lopez, coaches Don Gutteridge and Johnny Cooney.

but could never stick with the big club, Peters won 19 games and the American League Rookie of the Year Award in 1963, then became a 20-game winner the next season.

"He was a quiet fellow, a very, very good coach," Billy Pierce, the ace of the White Sox pitching staff during the 1950s, said of Berres. "Ray's main theory was that a pitcher's arm would drop down as he began to tire. He would watch that intently."[20]

Unlike most other pitching coaches, Berres preferred to spend the game in the bullpen rather than the dugout. "I was never on the bench. … I was always in the bullpen working with pitchers," he said. "We worked on the phone between me in the bullpen and Richards or Lopez or whoever was in the dugout. I'd probably see things from the back of the pitcher that they couldn't see from their angle."[21]

"He keeps a running stream of chatter all during the game," said Bob Locker, a successful relief pitcher for White Sox in the 1960s. "Two of the things he's always looking for are getting the arm up and not rushing the delivery. He thinks the pitcher's motion is the key to everything."[22]

Along with helping the careers of numerous pitchers, Berres played a key crucial role in convincing the White Sox to keep Nellie Fox when the club was about to send Nellie to the minors early in Fox's career. As he told David Gough and Jim Bard, authors of *Little Nel: The Nellie Fox Story*:

> In 1951 Paul Richards came in as manager. In spring training Paul didn't think Nellie was the answer at second base. They wanted someone who could hit the ball long. They were all set to send him to the minors…. We had a meeting with Frank Lane, Paul and the other coaches. They wanted a consensus of opinion on what to do. I told them that I had seen Nellie in all of 1950 and that \he had hit the toughest .250 that I had ever seen. Lots of line drives. I told them "He can play."[23]

The Sox wound up keeping Fox, in good part due to Berres' strong support. And when Fox was posthumously inducted into the Baseball Hall of Fame in 1997, Nellie's widow, Joanne, said, "It is with great appreciation that I remember his mentors, especially coach Ray Berres. I know that he is watching today."[24]

The high point of Berres' years with the White Sox was the pennant-winning season of 1959 – a club managed by Ray's good friend Al Lopez and led on the field by Fox, who was named the American League's Most Valuable Player that year. On the mound, staff ace Early Wynn won 22 games; Bob Shaw was a career-best 18-6; dual bullpen aces Jerry Staley and Turk Lown combined to go 17-7 with 29 saves; and the White Sox led the major leagues with a 3.29 ERA. It was a typically excellent performance from a Berres-coached pitching staff. During the 16-season period from 1951 to 1966, Berres' staffs finished first or second in the American League in team ERA 10 times and never ranked lower than fourth.

Berres was such an unquestioned master at working with pitchers that he was able to keep his position with the White Sox despite frequent changes in managers, front offices, and even owners. From 1949 through 1966 the Sox had six managers (Jack Onslow, Red Corriden, Paul Richards, Marty Marion, Al Lopez, and Eddie Stanky); four vice presidents/general managers (Frank Lane, Chuck Comiskey, Hank Greenberg, and Ed Short); three ownership groups (the Comiskey family, Bill Veeck, and Arthur Allyn) … and one pitching coach (Berres). It was an almost unmatched display of loyalty to a modest man who always preferred to stay in the background. "He'll answer all questions, frankly and courteously, and then he'll poke his broken catcher's finger at his interviewer and say, '…OK, but don't quote me,'" wrote Jerome Holtzman.[25] Toward the end of a long 1996 interview for the SABR Oral History Committee, he commented, "I probably talked more today than I did in 44 years in baseball."[26]

When Lopez retired as White Sox manager after the 1965 season, new skipper Eddie Stanky agreed to keep Lopez's entire coaching staff (Berres, Don Gutteridge, Tony Cuccinello, and Kerby Farrell). After a year at the helm, Stanky decided that he wanted to select some of his own coaches, and Berres and Gutteridge were out of a job. The club nearly won a pennant under Stanky in 1967, but when the Sox got off to a terrible start in 1968, Stanky was fired and Lopez came out of retirement to take over the team. He brought Berres and Gutteridge back with him. Ill health forced Lopez to retire again early in the 1969 season, and Gutteridge took over as manager, with Berres continuing to serve as his pitching coach.

After the 1969 season, the White Sox gave Berres a new role as a minor-league pitching instructor. "That drove me nuts," he said. "Those kids wanted to do things their own way."[27] After a couple of years, Berres finally retired for good, settling down with Irma in the home in Silver Lake, Wisconsin, which they had bought when their son, John, was born in 1947. Eventually they moved to the resort community of Twin Lakes, a few miles away. Both towns are in Kenosha County, where Ray was born.

Berres stayed active well into his 90s, though the aches and pains from years of catching and coaching occasionally caught up with him. "I had 18 pieces of chips taken out of my elbow just from working with pitchers," he told an interviewer.[28] And though he remained a quiet man, he loved telling a story about his first spring training as a professional player with the Oklahoma City Indians back in 1929. As Ray told it, the New York Yankees came to town to play an exhibition game against Oklahoma City, and young Berres was behind the plate when Babe Ruth came to bat.

"Babe came up with the bases loaded and two outs and the count went to 3 and 2, which meant that everybody was on the move," Berres told Pete Jackel. *"He hit the damnedest, highest pop fly that I had ever seen up to that time and the wind was spinning the ball. I started back-pedaling all the way to the mound … and fell on my butt. The ball bounced on the rubber and I happened to look up and I said, 'Good God, that's almost as high as the one he hit!'*

I felt terrible. Everyone scored and the fans booed something awful. When the inning was over, I was depressed, of course, and was walking slowly to the dugout. I thought I was going to get bawled out and, all of a sudden, I felt an arm go around my shoulders and it was the Babe. He said, 'Kid, don't let that bother you. That has happened to a lot of big-league catchers.'[29]

Several years later, when he reached the major leagues with the Dodgers, Berres was behind the plate for another exhibition game against the Yankees. And up came Ruth. "He had a habit of walking up to the plate and tapping it," Berres related. "And as he did, he saw me down there and said, 'Hey, kid! I'm glad to see you made it!'"[30]

Ray Berres passed away from heart failure and pneumonia in his hometown of Kenosha on February 1, 2007, four years after the death of his beloved wife, Irma. He was 99 years old; at the time of his death only one former major leaguer,

Rollie Stiles, was older. He had enjoyed a long and remarkable life; as a long list of people whom Berres had helped could attest, Ray Berres most certainly had "made it."

Special thanks to Warren Corbett for his assistance with this piece, and to Dave Anderson for the material he contributed.

Sources

Ray Berres Interviews, March 8 and 19, 1996, SABR Oral History Committee.
www.retrosheet.org
The SABR Minor Leagues Database.

Notes

1. Dave Nightingale, "He's the Berres," *Chicago Daily News*, July 20, 1968.
2. Letter from John Berres, February 2012
3. Ray Berres SABR Oral History interviews, 1996.
4. Ibid.
5. Ibid.
6. Ibid.,
7. Ibid.
8. Ibid.
9. Ibid.
10. Ibid.
11. Ibid.
12. Ibid.
13. Pete Jackel, "Reluctant Legend," *Racine (WI) Journal Times*, October 13, 2005.
14. Ray Berres.
15. Ibid.
16. Ibid.
17. Ibid.
18. Bob Vanderberg, *Sox: From Lane and Fain to Fisk and Zisk* (Chicago: Chicago Review Press, 1982), 211.
19. "Former Major-Leaguer, White Sox pitching coach Berres dies at 99," *Kenosha News*, February 6, 2007.
20. Telephone interview with Billy Pierce, September 9, 2008.
21. Berres.
22. Nightingale.
23. David Gough and Jim Bard, *Little Nel: The Nellie Fox Story* (Alexandria VA: D.L. Megbec Publishing, 2000), 73.
24. Gough and Bard, 9.
25. Jerome Holtzman, "Horn Tootin' Not For Sox Tutor Berres," *Chicago Sun-Times*, July 8, 1966.
26. Ibid.
27. Ibid.
28. Ibid.
29. Jackel.
30. Ibid.

JOHNNY COONEY

By Ray Birch

John Walter Cooney, the son as well as the brother of major-league baseball players, competed as a major-league pitcher, infielder, and outfielder for 20 seasons, primarily in the National League with the Boston Braves. Known as a fine defensive outfielder, he compiled a .286 career batting average, briefly managed the Braves, and even umpired a game in 1941. He was one of Al Lopez's coaches for the White Sox in the 1959 World Series. Cooney threw left-handed and batted right-handed, a rarity in baseball circles. Including time in the minor leagues and coaching jobs after he retired as a player, his baseball career lasted from 1922 through 1964.

Cooney could boast that he was the only man to have played in both the National League and the American League, coached in both leagues, managed in both, and umpired in one. He conceded that the managing part was a technicality; he filled in for manager Billy Southworth with the Braves while Southworth was sick and for Al Lopez with the White Sox when Lopez attended his mother's funeral.

Johnny Cooney was born on March 18, 1901, in Cranston, Rhode Island, the son of Jimmy Cooney Sr., a shortstop on the Chicago White Stockings, and Ella (Dunham) Cooney. Johnny was only two years old when his father died. His brother, Jimmy Jr., played with the Red Sox, Braves, Giants, Cardinals, Cubs, and Phillies during a seven-year major-league career in the Teens and '20s. An older brother, Harry, played in the New England and New York State leagues.

When Cooney was in high school in Cranston, he threw a one-hitter, which attracted the attention of baseball scouts. In 1920, at the age of 19, Cooney became a pitcher for the Willimantic team of the American Thread Athletic Association, an industrial league, hurling a 1-0 perfect game on August 20 against Rockville.[1] Cooney pitched his gem under most unusual circumstances, according to a 1949 article in *The Sporting News*. On his way to the game, the train on which he was traveling struck an automobile and killed four people. Johnny tried to help get the victims out of the car, but couldn't, and became physically sick. But he took a few sniffs of ammonia to overcome the experience, then went out and pitched the perfect game. After that performance, a scout for the Boston Red Sox, Paul Krichell, remarked that Cooney "had the goods" to become a major-league player. As the story goes, Red Sox manager Ed Barrow offered Cooney a $500 check to sign with them. But his manager at Willimantic, Ed McGinley, wanted the money in cash, fearful that the check would bounce, and an incensed Barrow threw them both out of the office; as a result, the deal with the Red Sox was not consummated. The Boston Braves then offered Cooney the same $500 – in cash – and he signed a contract.

Cooney reported for 1921 spring training in Galveston, Texas, and although he showed great promise, he was still quite young and in need of further physical development. Despite this, he made his major-league debut on April 19, 1921, and pitched in eight games that season. On May 8, 1922, he was optioned to New Haven of the Eastern League, where he starred, posting a 19-3 record that included nine victories in a row. He also stepped in at times to play the infield and outfield. He was so popular in New Haven that the fans took up a collection for him and presented him with $200. Cooney was recalled by the Braves at the end of the season.

In 1923 Cooney made some appearances in the Braves rotation. Despite concerns that his light weight (around 165 pounds) would be a handicap throughout the rigors of a long season, Cooney started eight games and compiled a 3-5 record with a 3.31 ERA, while displaying an effective change-of-pace pitch. On May 24, he was admitted to St. Joseph's Hospital in Providence for an emergency operation for appendicitis, but he was able to return later in the season, at one point hurling 15 consecutive scoreless innings; of note also was his .379 batting average in 66 at-bats.

Johnny followed that up with an 8-9 record and a 3.18 ERA in 19 starts in 1924, and in 1925 he had his best season pitching with the Braves when he started 29 games and completed 20 of them, winning 14 and losing 14 with a 3.48 ERA. During this time, Cooney also developed a "hesitation" pitch that served to baffle opposing batters. As described in the *Washington Post*:

> …the pitch is a "hesitation" delivery. When the batter is all set for the ball, Johnny winds up, comes down with his foot and then lets the ball go. Usually the foot comes down as the ball is leaving the pitcher's hand. This delay throws the batter off his stride as the ball comes up to the plate after the batter is ready for it.[2]

Toward the end of the 1925 season, Cooney also appeared in a number of games at first base and in left field, coinciding with the development of a stiff left arm that limited his pitching appearances in 1926 and 1927. He had a locked elbow; it prevented him from doing simple things such as scratching a mosquito bite. In the fall of 1927, he underwent an operation on his left arm in which 13 pieces of bone were removed, leaving it shorter than his right arm. After being used sparingly by the Braves in 1928 and 1929, and following a holdout over salary issues which did not endear Cooney to the Braves management, he was sent to Jersey City of the International League in 1930 for a 20-day trial, which turned out to be 2½ months. Returned to the Braves, he was optioned to Newark of the same league. Between Jersey City and Newark, he had an 0-1 pitching record but batted .269 with 10 RBIs. He returned to the Braves at the end of the season and eventually was sold to Toledo of the American Association, managed by Casey Stengel, a former teammate of Cooney's on the Braves; this began a four-year absence from the major leagues for Cooney.

Knowing that his days as a pitcher were over, Cooney continued the process of reinventing himself as a major-league player. Using his intelligence and speed, under Stengel's tutelage he developed into a fine outfielder. True to his reputation as a jack-of-all-trades, he even played second base for a game despite the fact that he was left-handed. But the Toledo franchise was having financial problems and sold Cooney to the New York Giants, who used him in a trade with Indianapolis, also of the American Association. Cooney played for Indianapolis for four years, both as a pitcher and as an outfielder, and played in the 1935 American Association All-Star Game.

Despite his success at Indianapolis, major-league teams were reluctant to take a chance on Cooney because of his age. But on September 10, 1935, the 34-year-old outfielder was sold to the Brooklyn Dodgers, due at least in part to the efforts of Stengel, who was then managing the Brooklyn nine; at the time, Cooney was leading the American Association in batting average and eventually won the title with a .375 average. Showing speed, a great throwing arm, and the ability to track fly balls with little apparent effort, he came to spring training in 1936 to vie for a regular outfield spot with the Dodgers.[3] But after securing the starting nod in center field for the season-opening series against the Giants, Cooney was benched after a poor start. Upon being reinserted into the lineup, his hitting, although short on power, picked up, and that, combined with his steady and at times spectacular outfield play, kept him in the Dodgers' starting lineup.[4] Speaking of Cooney's defensive prowess, teammate Van Lingle Mungo said, "I think Cooney is the best outfielder I ever saw in my life or ever heard of. He's not fast, but he doesn't have to be. He's just always there when a ball has to be caught."[5]

Cooney batted .282 and .293 in 1936 and 1937 and was highly popular with the Brooklyn fans. After the latter season, the Dodgers traded Cooney with three other players to the St. Louis Cardinals for Leo Durocher in a deal deplored by Brooklyn fandom because Cooney was leaving.[6] The Cardinals wanted to send Cooney to their Columbus farm club in the American Association, but he resisted and was given his unconditional release in April. He immediately signed with the Boston Bees, again joining Stengel, by now the manager of the Bees. Cooney showed his versatility by playing all three outfield positions as well as first base, and sharing pinch-hitting duties, while batting .271 in 120 games. In 1939, on the way to batting .274, Cooney, by now 38 years old, hit the only two home runs he would have in the major leagues – in consecutive days on September 24 and 25. Both were hit in the Polo Grounds, both hit in the third inning, and both were two-run homers.

While beginning to prepare for life after baseball, Cooney signed with the Bees as a player-coach for the 1940 season; he finished third in hitting in the National League with a .318 average. To acknowledge his great popularity with fans for his hustle and considerable baseball skills, Cooney was honored in September on Johnny Cooney Day; in addition, Cooney received the Walter S. Barnes Trophy at the annual Boston baseball writers' dinner, as the most valuable Boston player of 1940.[7]

• JOHNNY COONEY •

During the 1941 season, Cooney made an unexpected appearance as a major-league umpire, behind the plate, on June 28 against Brooklyn when the regular umpiring crew was fogged in off the Cape Cod Canal after a boating trip. Cooney's stint as arbiter was short, as the regular crew returned to the ballpark in the second inning.[8] Slated to be a backup center fielder in 1941, Cooney continued to impress on the field with a .319 batting average, second best in the National League, and compiling a league-leading .996 fielding average in the outfield. *The Sporting News* selected him as Veteran Player of the Year for 1941.

Asked about his longevity, Cooney said that by keeping his legs strong, he was able to avoid charley horses, muscle pulls, and other nagging leg injuries that frequently hamper athletes. He also embraced a lifestyle that included no alcohol or tobacco and focused on physical fitness, including nine to ten hours of sleep each night.[9]

The 1942 season was not a successful one for Cooney. The 41-year-old appeared in only 74 games and slumped to a .207 average. The Braves released him outright in January 1943. Feeling that he could still play, Cooney rejected a Double-A coaching offer from the Braves. Branch Rickey of the Dodgers, who referred to Cooney as a "coconut snatcher," his preferred pet name for a utility player, signed him as a free agent and Cooney played sparingly with Brooklyn in 1943 and 1944. Displaying his usual team play and detailed preparation, but plagued by neuritis in his shoulder, he played in only 44 games for the Dodgers in the two seasons. He was released by Brooklyn in June 1944 and quickly signed with the Yankees, coincidentally by team president Ed Barrow, who had been unable to sign him for the Red Sox at the start of his career. Released by the Yankees in August, he spent the rest of the 1944 season with Toronto of the International League and in 1945 became a player-coach for the Kansas City Blues of the American Association, managed by his old friend, Casey Stengel, before his playing days came to an end.

After compiling a .286 lifetime batting average, Cooney was asked about his success as a hitter. He replied that "Casey (Stengel) showed me the advantage of hitting down the foul lines, first and third. He pointed out that there is only one man to get the ball by at third and first, whereas if you hit through the middle there are three men who

Johnny Cooney had a unique career in major league history. After breaking in as a pitcher, he hurt his arm but returned as an outfielder, compiling a .286 lifetime batting average.

have a chance to retire you -- the pitcher, shortstop and second baseman."[10] Not only was Stengel a positive influence on Cooney in baseball matters, but the Perfesser also encouraged him to invest in some oil land in Texas that provided considerable money in royalties.

The 1946 season found Cooney employed by the Boston Braves as a coach, after he turned down a chance to coach again for Stengel, this time in Oakland. Cooney remained in Boston as a coach through the 1952 season, at one point assuming the managerial reins when besieged manager Billy Southworth was forced to step down temporarily due to "failing health." Cooney's previous experience as a major-league pitcher was extremely helpful with the Braves pitching staff and he also gave invaluable help to the outfielders. Although reports from the Braves clubhouse were favorable regarding Cooney's leadership style, Johnny himself was very content to remain a coach, citing a desire to steer clear of the pressures of managing. When the Braves franchise moved to Milwaukee in 1953, Cooney followed and remained in Milwaukee as a coach through the 1955 season.

After sitting out the 1956 season, Cooney became a coach with the White Sox in 1957, retiring after the 1964 season; he was a part of the 1959 White Sox team that went to the World Series against the Los Angeles Dodgers.

Cooney died in Sarasota, Florida, in 1986 at the age of 85, leaving behind his wife, Alice, and a son, John.

Notes

1. "Cooney Hurls Another No Hit, No Run Contest," *Hartford Courant*, August 29, 1920.
2. "Notes of the Nationals," *Washington Post*, March 20, 1925.
3. Tommy Holmes, "Cooney Adds Style To Dodger Outfield," *The Sporting News*, September 25, 1936.
4. Ed Rumill, "Johnny Cooney Returns To Boston in Dodger Uniform," *Christian Science Monitor*, May 9, 1936.
5. Roscoe McGowen, "Mungo Nominates Randy Moore As Preferred Dodger Catcher," *New York Times*, April 7, 1937: 31.
6. Tommy Holmes, "Flatbush Chilled by Durocher Deal," *The Sporting News*, October 14, 1937.
7. "In The Press Box," "Boston Dinner, January 30," *The Sporting News*, January 2, 1941.
8. International News Service, "Umpires in Fog, Players Drafted To Conduct Game," *Washington Post*, June 29, 1941.
9. Dick Farrington, "Cooney, Bees' Perpetual Youth, Lost Hurling Arm in '27, Found Outfield Success in '35 and Reached Peak in '40," *The Sporting News*, November 28, 1940.
10. "Letter from Johnny Cooney," *Christian Science Monitor*, December 1, 1944.

TONY CUCCINELLO

by Barb Mantegani

A diminutive Italian-American (5 feet 7, 160 pounds) from Queens, New York, Tony Cuccinello lost out in the closest batting race in major-league history. Serving as the regular third baseman for the Chicago White Sox in 1945—oddly enough, his last season in the majors (but more on that later)—Cuccinello finished the season .000087 behind Yankee second baseman Snuffy Stirnweiss: .3084577 to 3085443 (.000086 rounds up to .000087).

Anthony Francis Cuccinello—Cooch or, more commonly, Tony—was born on November 8, 1907, in the Long Island City section of Queens. Tony played in a semipro league in New York City and, spotted there by a neighbor who happened to play for the International League's Syracuse Stars, signed a contract with Syracuse while still a teenager. After two months of the 1926 season, Cuccinello was sent to play for the Lawrence Merry Macks in the Class-B New England League, where he batted .283 with two home runs. In 1927 he returned to Lawrence and batted .310. In 1928 he was assigned to the Danville Veterans of the Three-I League, a St. Louis Cardinals affiliate. After another .310 season, Cuccinello caught the attention of Cardinals general manager Branch Rickey, who bought his contract for the Columbus Senators in the American Association, one of the three toughest minor leagues of the time.

Cuccinello took the Association by storm. In addition to batting .358 with 20 homers and 111 RBIs in 1929, he topped the league with 56 doubles and 227 hits. Not bad for a 21-year-old infielder. As he later told interviewer Rich Westcott, "I was pretty much a line drive hitter. . . . I watched the way the big guys hit, and because I was small, I figured the best thing for me to do was just meet the ball. So that's how I hit my whole career."[1] After that '29 season, Cuccinello's contract was purchased by the Cincinnati Reds, and he made his major-league debut on Opening Day of 1930, playing third base against Pittsburgh.

Cuccinello enjoyed a solid rookie campaign, batting .312 with 10 home runs and 78 RBIs. In 1931 the Reds shifted Tony to second base and he responded with a .315 average and 93 RBIs (the latter a club record for second basemen that stood for 44 years). In his best game that year he hit safely in six straight at-bats, including two doubles and a triple. He also led National League second basemen in putouts, assists, double plays, and (it should be said) errors.

The following winter, the Reds didn't offer Cuccinello the raise he thought he deserved. He held out, and the Reds shipped him to Brooklyn: home (or close enough). He played in all 154 games for the Dodgers in 1932 and turned in solid numbers for a second baseman (.281 batting average, 12 home runs, 77 RBIs). Just as importantly, he began a lifelong friendship with Dodgers catcher (and future Hall of Fame manager) Al Lopez; the two wound up being teammates for seven seasons.

After the season Cuccinello married Clara Caroselli; they produced three children: Anthony Jr., born in 1936; Darlene Ann, 1938; and Alan Joseph, 1945. Cuccinello's performance in 1933 earned him a spot on the National League's roster in the first All-Star Game; he pinch-hit for Carl Hubbell in the ninth inning and struck out to end the game.

In 1934, Cuccinello's younger brother, Al Cuccinnello, debuted in professional baseball with a .320 season for Nashville in the Southern Association. In 1935 (his only major-league season), Al played in 54 games with the New York Giants, and on July 5, Al and Tony, on opposite sides, homered in the same game.

After that 1935 season, his fourth with the Dodgers, Tony was on the move again when Brooklyn traded him and three others, including Lopez, to the Boston Braves. In 1936, his first season with the Braves, Cuccinello batted .308 and drove in 86 runs. Tony's excellent defensive performances continued as well, as he teamed with a new double-play partner, Eddie Miller (whom Cuccinello later described as the best shortstop he ever played with).

Cuccinello lasted four full seasons and part of a fifth with the Braves. In 1939, he suffered a serious knee injury on May 10 when Cubs shortstop Dick Bartell ran into him at second base. Though the Braves' team physician initially believed Cuccinello

After a 15-year playing career, Tony Cuccinello coached in the big leagues for 21 seasons, 14 of them under Al Lopez in Cleveland and Chicago.

would miss just a few games, he didn't play again until late July, and the damaged knee troubled him for the rest of his life.

On June 15, 1940, the Braves traded Cuccinello to the New York Giants. He didn't hit much as a Giant, but he must have impressed someone, because after the season the Giants hired Cuccinello as player-manager of their farm team in Jersey City (also called the Giants). In 1941 he batted .277 in 86 games, Jersey City finished fifth in the International League, and Cuccinello figured on performing the same double duties in 1942.

But he couldn't resist an offer from Casey Stengel, his old skipper in Brooklyn. Now managing the Braves, Stengel asked Cuccinello to join his staff as a player-coach. So Cuccinello returned to the National League, played some infield and batted .202 in 40 games while also coaching third base and throwing batting practice. In the middle of the '43 season, hardly playing at all (he was hitless in 19 official at-bats), Cuccinello drew his release from the Braves and signed as a free agent with the White Sox, who were, like most of the teams during the war years, desperate for players with any sort of experience. Cuccinello, who suffered from chronic laryngitis—some years earlier he'd essentially lost his voice for three years—had been classified 4-F and was thus exempt from the draft.

Cuccinello still didn't play much, though, in 1943 or '44, and he later said that if not for the war he likely would have retired. But in 1945 Cuccinello went to the White Sox' spring training in French Lick, Indiana, where every day he took a mineral bath, followed by a rubdown and a nap, and he entered the season feeling the best he had ever felt. Whether it was the baths and the naps or the war-ravaged pitching staffs of the time, Cuccinello followed up spring training with one of the finest seasons of his career.

Cuccinello got off to a fast start in 1945, keeping his average in the .380-.390 range for the first few months of the season. The heat of the Chicago summer eventually wore Tony down, however. At 37—then considered practically ancient for a ballplayer—Cuccinello played irregularly, and in fact had to play more often in September to pile up enough plate appearances to qualify for the batting title. His manager, Jimmy Dykes, he later recalled, "would play me seven innings every day, then take me out."[2]

On the last day of the season, Stirnweiss edged Cuccinello when a White Sox doubleheader was rained out and Stirnweiss went 3-for-4 against the Boston Red Sox. One of those three hits, however, was initially ruled an error, and then changed to a hit by the official scorer. According to Cuccinello, he was told at the time that the official scorer changed the call only after he was informed that the White Sox had been rained out and Cuccinello's season was over. Cuccinello later coached Stirnweiss with the Cleveland Indians, and Snuffy confirmed the shenanigans when he said of the scorer, a writer for the Bronx Home News, "He gave it to me."[3]

Batting title or not, it was a fine season. Nevertheless, with the sport flooded by younger players coming out of the service, Cuccinello retired when the 1945 season ended. As he told interviewer Rich Westcott, "My legs were bothering me. Before the season ended, I already had my release in my pocket. Mr. Comiskey thanked me for the job I did, and I moved on."[4] Cuccinello finished his 15-year major-league career with a .280 batting average, 94

• TONY CUCCINELLO •

home runs and 884 RBIs. He batted over .300 in five of those 15 seasons.

Out of baseball in 1946, Cuccinello returned to the game in 1947 to manage the Class-C Florida International League's Tampa Smokers to 104 wins and a strong second-place finish; the Smokers were swept by first-place Havana in the league's championship series. The following year, Cuccinello reunited with Al Lopez, who had been hired to manage the Indianapolis Indians. With Cuccinello serving as Lopez's top lieutenant, the Indians went 100-54 and cruised to the 1948 American Association flag.

In 1949, Cuccinello returned to the majors as a coach with the Reds and stayed for three years. It was the beginning of a 21-year-stint as a major-league coach for Cuccinello. After three years with the Reds, he rejoined Lopez, who had taken over as Cleveland Indians manager the previous year (coincidentally, in '52 one of Cuccinello's charges was Snuffy Stirnweiss, in the last season of his major-league career). Cuccinello's first postseason experience in the majors came in 1954, when he coached for the heavily favored Indians in their loss to the New York Giants. When Lopez left the Indians to manage the White Sox in 1957, Cuccinello went with him.

Their first two seasons in Chicago were relatively uneventful, but 1959 saw the ascension of the Go-Go Sox … and the most famous incident in Cuccinello's post-playing career. It happened in Game Two of the World Series against the Los Angeles Dodgers. In the bottom of the eighth, with the Dodgers leading 4-2, the White Sox had a rally going: Sherm Lollar on first base, Earl Torgeson on second, and nobody out. Al Smith ripped a double to left-center. Torgeson scored easily. Cuccinello, coaching at third, also waved Lollar, a lumbering catcher, home – where he was out by a mile. Smith wound up on third base, but was stranded when Billy Goodman struck out and Jim Rivera fouled out. The White Sox lost that game 4-3, and eventually the Series in six games.

Cuccinello was the No. 1 scapegoat in some quarters, but Lopez defended his friend, telling a Chicago Daily News reporter that the play was fine and, more importantly, was not the key to the Series; instead it was the Sox' inability to run in the Los Angeles Coliseum that led to their demise. Lopez repeated that opinion in an interview published in The Sporting News, noting that it took a perfect play by the Dodgers defense to nail Lollar at the plate.[5] One of the Dodgers involved in the play, outfielder Wally Moon, said after the Series that if he'd been coaching third base he might have sent Lollar, too.[6]

In 1967, an article in The Sporting News, based on an anonymous source, included the claim that Cuccinello had been the middle-man in a long-running scheme for stealing signs. Coaching at third base, Cuccinello had received opposing teams' signs, stolen from Comiskey Park's center-field scoreboard, from manager Lopez, or perhaps even from an electronic receiver hidden under his uniform jersey. For a fastball, Cuccinello would stand perfectly still. For a curveball—or, presumably, any other sort of off-speed pitch—he would "start jumping around." All this seems credible enough; pitcher Al Worthington, a staunch Christian who joined the White Sox late in the 1960 season, soon quit the team, saying he couldn't countenance the club's cheating.[7]

In any event, Cuccinello survived the controversy and continued coaching in Chicago into Eddie Stanky's managerial tenure, which started in 1966. In 1967 Cuccinello joined the staff of new Detroit Tigers manager Mayo Smith, and at the beginning of the season Cuccinello took on Dick McAuliffe as a private project, to help McAuliffe make the switch from shortstop to second base. At the time Cuccinello said McAuliffe had to work on slowing himself down, and in 1968 the work bore fruit, as McAuliffe's defensive improvement was cited by Cleveland Indians manager Alvin Dark and Tigers coach Hal Naragon as a key factor in the Tigers' success.[8] And that fall, more than 38 years after first reaching the majors, Cuccinello enjoyed his first and only World Series championship when the Tigers beat the Cardinals.

Cuccinello left the Tigers in 1969 to once again join Lopez, then managing the White Sox (Stanky had been fired). But Lopez's last stint lasted only 17 games into the season; on May 2 he retired due to ill health. Don Gutteridge took over as manager, and Cuccinello remained on the coaching staff. But after the season he went home to Florida, where he worked as a Yankees scout in the area—brother Al also scouted for the Yankees—before finally retiring from baseball in 1985. Cuccinello lived until 1995, when his heart failed in a Tampa hospital. He was a few weeks short of his 88th birthday, and for years had lived right down the street from his old friend Lopez.

Sources

In addition to the sources cited in the Notes, the author also consulted baseball-reference.com, retrosheet.org, and the following:

Carmichael, J. "Lollar Play Not Series Key -- Lopez," Baseball Digest, Vol. 19 p. 71 (February 1960).

Daniel, Dan. "Over the Fence: Two Big Breaks Influenced Outcome of Series," The Sporting News, October 21, 1959: 10.

"'Dodgers Reeled Off Perfect Play To Nail Lollar' -- Lopez." The Sporting News, January 20, 1960: 4.

Holmes, T. "Carey Experiments With Dodger Infield," The Sporting News, March 31, 1932: 1.

"Majors' All-Stars Meet In 'Game of the Century,'" The Sporting News, July 6, 1933: 1.

http://web.minorleaguebaseball.com/milb/history/top_about.jsp for top 100 minor league teams (accessed September 16, 2007)

Notes

1. Rich Westcott, "Tony Cuccinello-A Great Way to Spend a Lifetime," *Diamond Greats: Profiles and Interviews with 65 of Baseball's History Maker* (Westport, Connecticut: Meckler Books, 1988), 94.
2. Ibid.
3. B. Chastain, "This was the Closest Race Ever for A Batting Title," *Baseball Digest*, December. 1993.
4. Westcott.
5. "'Dodgers Reeled Off Perfect Play To Nail Lollar' – Lopez," *The Sporting News*, January 20, 1960.
6. Bob Oates, "It Took Five Perfect Plays to Get Lollar at Plate!," *Baseball Digest*, February 1960. See also *The Sporting News*, October 21, 1959: 12. The play was also included in a summary of the worst coaching blunders in *The Baseball Hall of Shame*, written by Bruce Nash and Allan Zullo and published in 1985 by Pocket Books, New York.
7. Joe Falls, "Doctored Baseballs – How White Sox Did It," *The Sporting News*, September 30, 1967.
8. Watson Spoelstra, "Relaxed McAuliffe Gave Tigers Their Flag Spark," *The Sporting News*, October 5, 1968.

DON GUTTERIDGE

By David W. Anderson

Don Gutteridge always said he had a wonderful life. He was married to his wife, Helen, for 74 years. In his latter years, she was bedridden, but she was always there for him. "She pushed me on to do well," he said. "She encouraged me and gave me a lot of confidence."[1]

His son, Don Jr., became a successful lawyer in Oklahoma City. Don Jr. and his wife, Sonya, had three sons, who presented Don and Helen with five great-granddaughters and a grandson.

In the offseason during his baseball career, Don did things to, as he put it, "put meat on the table."[2] He taught school, sold cars, worked on the railroad, and refereed football and basketball, but the thing that he was proud of is simple and something many of us would have wanted to say: "I always wanted to be a ballplayer."[3]

Don Gutteridge died on September 7, 2008, at the age of 96, about a month after contracting pneumonia. When he died he was the seventh-oldest living major leaguer and the only surviving member of the 1944 St. Louis Browns, the only pennant-winner in the history of the team.

He was born in Pittsburg, Kansas, on June 19, 1912, to Joe Gutteridge, a foreman for the local railroad, and his wife, Mary. Growing up he would, he said, "bribe" his three brothers to play ball. He began as a mascot on one of the railroad teams in Pittsburg.[4] He began playing in 1928, beginning a career that spanned seven decades in semipro, minor, and major leagues, and coaching and managing in both the minor and major leagues.

In Pittsburg, he played baseball four times a week in a city league. Sometimes they played teams from Wichita and Kansas City. There was no high-school baseball for Gutteridge. He played semipro baseball with a team that promoted the local railroad. There was togetherness in the relationship with his father and his brothers, which helped him a great deal. There was also togetherness with playmates who, Gutteridge said, "played baseball every chance when I was a kid." [5]

He got his break in 1932 when Joe Becker, a scout from Joplin, Missouri who worked for the Brooklyn Dodgers, signed him to a contract. Becker told Gutteridge that if he wanted to play, he could get a spot at third base for the Lincoln club in the Nebraska State League, a Class-D circuit. Becker told him, "If they ask you to play third base, say okay."[6] Gutteridge had been playing second base. He got a railroad pass from his father and began his career. In 1933, his second year in the Nebraska State League, he led the league in hitting with a .360 average.

This was during the Great Depression and times were tough. He began at $75 a month and then in 1933 his salary was cut. Gutteridge and others were making $50 a month. They were glad to have work, but it was getting financially troublesome for the Nebraska State League.[7]

At the close of the 1933 season, Branch Rickey came calling. Rickey, the general manager of the St. Louis Cardinals, had an offer for the Nebraska State League. He would give the league $2,000 if he could take eight players – two from each team in the four-team circuit. Gutteridge was one of them. The league agreed, and Gutteridge was on his way to the major leagues as a St. Louis Cardinal.

As with many other players, Gutteridge's relationship with Rickey was colored by money. He spent seven years in the Cardinals system in the majors and minors (1934-1940) before being let go after the 1940 season. As Gutteridge put it, "When Rickey was done with you, you were out."[8]

He and Helen were married after the 1933 season. He reported to the big-league camp in 1934, but spent the next three seasons in the minor leagues. In 1934 he played with the Houston Buffaloes in the Class-A Texas League; in 1935 he began a two-year stint with the Columbus Red Birds in the Double-A American Association. In September 1936, Gutteridge came up to the Cardinals, playing in his first game on September 7. He got into 23 games and hit .319, driving in 16 runs. He'd made his mark and the next year became the regular third baseman for the Cardinals, but he never hit for as high an average again. During his 12-year career, Gutteridge hit .256 with 1,075 hits and 39 home runs. He remained in the big leagues until 1948.

When Gutteridge broke in with the Cardinals, manager Frank Frisch knew that veteran third baseman Charlie Gelbert was near the end of his career. Gelbert had recovered from a hunting accident in 1933, but he never had the ability he had shown early in his career. After Gutteridge's first couple of games, Frisch told *The Sporting News,* "Did you see that kid? He's really a Gas Houser."[9] Gutteridge knew he had arrived and was in the right place at the right time.

Gutteridge was now a member of the Gas House Gang, a bunch of players who combined shabby appearance with playing excellent baseball and a talent for playing jokes on one another. Gutteridge said, "I wanted to be like Pepper Martin."[10] Third baseman Martin himself said, in Gutteridge's words, "Leave this kid alone, I can go play the outfield."[11]

Gutteridge became friends with Martin and Dizzy Dean. There wasn't a dull moment. They played tricks on each other, and played good baseball. Their style and ability to win made them fan favorites with many around the country. Even though the Cardinals failed to reach the World Series while he was with the club, Gutteridge played well and stuck up for his teammates. Dean often antagonized other teams and at least on six occasions got into fights, Gutteridge would lend a hand and put it this way: when Dean got into a fight, "He NEVER got hurt, but I got hit every damn one of them."[12]

Baseball during the Great Depression was competitive. Gutteridge said, "You look around and know someone could get your job You played and performed because if you didn't someone would be more than willing to take your place."[13] Still, to Gutteridge, it was personal. He said, "I played for the love of the game."[14]

He was dropped from the major-league roster by the Cardinals after the 1940 season, and it seemed that Gutteridge's run in the big leagues was over. But Pepper Martin became manager of the Sacramento farm club for the Cardinals and he wanted Gutteridge to come along as his player-coach. Gutteridge said he was ready to leave baseball, but Pepper talked him out of it. He coached and played 171 games at third base, hitting for a .309 average in the Pacific Coast League.

When World War II broke out, Gutteridge tried three times to enlist in the military. Birdie Tebbetts and Johnny Mize both tried to get him on teams in the armed forces. But he was declared 4-F, not fit for service, each time. As he put it, he would have fallen apart if he had been let into the armed forces. He had a trick knee and a problem with his kidneys; he also had a child and that kept him down the list for the draft.[15]

In 1942, Gutteridge returned to the majors as a member of the St. Louis Browns. He had been released by Rickey, who, he said, told him, "You'll never play major-league baseball again, or be on any winning ballclub."[16]

Gutteridge called the Browns a "bunch of raggedy-assed guys, no college education. They just loved to play baseball."[17] They also liked to drink and have fun. He once told the St. Louis Browns Fan Club, a group dedicated to preserving the memory of the Browns: "You went out there every day and you didn't know if your roommate was going to be there. He might be in the service. He might be in jail."[18]

The Browns also suffered from poor attendance. "Some days the players outnumbered the fans," he told the Browns Fan Club in jest. "Some days I knew everybody in the ballpark on a first-name basis. You could have fired a shotgun into the stands and not hit anyone."[19] Jest or not, the Browns' attendance woes were real, and they resulted in the franchise eventually being sold and moving to Baltimore.

With the Browns, Gutteridge made the transition from third base to second base and had four good seasons. In 1942 he was among the leaders in the league in stolen bases, triples, and runs scored. The next year, his 35 doubles were again among the American League leaders, but 1944 was the year that Gutteridge remembers the best. He was finally in a World Series.

During this time the Cardinals were a dominant team. From 1942 through 1949, they won four pennants and three World Series, and never finished lower than second place. But Gutteridge was now with the Browns, a team that seemed always to take second billing to the Cardinals in St. Louis. However, 1944 saw them play each other in the World Series.

The 1944 Browns won the American League pennant by a single game over the Detroit Tigers. The New York Yankees and Boston Red Sox were in the race until the final weeks of the season. What helped the Browns was that they won the first nine games of the season and then hung on to maintain the lead.

They won first place with an unlikely bunch of players. The manager was Luke Sewell. "He was always an optimist," Gutteridge said. "…If we lost four or five games in a row he'd always say we can we win the next four or five games."[20]

At second base, Gutteridge played beside a valuable shortstop, Junior Stephens. Gutteridge said he believed that if Stephens had played in New York City, "He would have been in the Hall of Fame in a minute."[21] For Gutteridge, it was a pleasure to play with Stephens on defense and it made his job easier at second base. The same could be said of the Browns' first baseman, George McQuinn, who covered a lot of ground on Gutteridge's left.

A problem with the Browns in those wartime days was that you did not know whom you would take the field with. Denny Galehouse, a pitcher, could play when the Browns were at home but if the Browns were out of town, it was tough to use him because of his draft status. That cleared up late in the season when he learned he was not going to be drafted. Chet Laabs, an outfielder, could play only on Sundays or at night because of his job in an armament plant. Many of the other Browns were like Gutteridge, 4-F or subject to being called up only in special circumstances. Among them were Stephens and McQuinn and pitchers Nelson Potter and Bob Muncrief.

The Browns fought hard to win the pennant, while the Cardinals easily won the National League pennant by 14½ games. Playing the Cardinals meant that all the World Series games were played in the ballpark both teams used as a home field but which the Browns owned, Sportsman's Park. In order to have more seats in the stadium, the center-field bleachers, which had been closed during the season, were opened for the Series. Gutteridge said it was tough to hit with center field occupied by fans, a difficult background for a hitter. The Browns took an early lead in the Series but they lost to the Cardinals four games to two. Gutteridge wanted to play well to show the Cardinals that they should have held on to him, but "It was not meant to be."[22] It was a disappointing experience; he hit only .143 during the Series, 3-for-21 without an RBI. He struck out five times and committed three errors.

In 1945, the Browns came in third. Don was the team's third baseman but hit only .238. He knew that it was probably over for him as a big-league player, but Browns general manager Bill DeWitt offered him the opportunity to become player-manager of the Toledo Mud Hens, a Browns Triple-A club. He played in 70 games for Toledo in 1946 and hit .278.

He was settling into his position when the word came that the Boston Red Sox, then running

A baseball lifer, Don Gutteridge managed in the White Sox farm system, spent 14 years as a Sox coach and managed the club in 1969-70.

away with the American League race, needed help. Gutteridge was available, so he returned to the big leagues. He was in nine games at second base, played eight games at third and was in five other games. He stayed with the Red Sox through 1947.

His memories with the Red Sox were good ones. The Sox used him at second base and third base. The team made the World Series in '46, playing the Cardinals. Don got two hits in Game Five, helping give the Red Sox a three-games-to-two lead. He was 2-for-5 in the game, with one RBI. He'd appeared in two earlier games, but these were his only at-bats, leaving him with a .400 average. The Red Sox lost the final two games, and the Series, four games to three. When the Series ended, he was voted a half-share, which Gutteridge thought was fair. The owner of the Red Sox, Tom Yawkey, gave him enough of a bonus to make it a full share.

In 1947, Don hit just .168 in 131 at-bats for Boston. He was sold to the Pirates late in spring training in 1948 and concluded his active career with Pittsburgh with brief appearances in four games that year. The stay with Pittsburgh offered one big thrill, however, as he was on the bench with Pirates legend Honus Wagner. "When I was there he was a coach, and was in uniform every day and came to the bench," related Gutteridge. "Of course, he was always asked questions, and we all carried on conversations with him. He was most pleasant and always available to us." Gutteridge said Wagner would leave about the middle of the game to visit with friends at a bar. He added that Wagner had a great laugh and his only regret was that he never got an autograph from the Hall of Famer.[23]

Summing up his 12-year major-league playing career, Gutteridge said the three teams he played on were distinctive and so different in his experience. "The Cardinals were rough-and-tumble. They would fight you today and love you tomorrow. The Browns were a ragtag pickup team, while the Red Sox were college types and they didn't fight." He added that the Red Sox were very professional and businesslike.[24]

His playing career over, Don almost quit baseball, but an opportunity opened up and he reported to Indianapolis to play under Al Lopez. Lopez needed a third baseman to play for the Indians, a Pittsburgh farm club. Gutteridge was the man. Indianapolis won the pennant and went on to win the 1949 Little World Series from Montreal. Gutteridge worked with Lopez for most of the rest of his career.

From 1949 through 1951, he was a player-coach for Indianapolis. In 1951 Lopez became manager of the Cleveland Indians, and Gutteridge took over as Indianapolis skipper. In 1952 he went to manage Colorado Springs of the Class-A Western League. It was a farm club of the Chicago White Sox, and Gutteridge maintained his affiliation with the White Sox through 1970.

Frank Lane, then general manager of the White Sox, wanted Gutteridge to manage what Lane called his "young kids." Gutteridge managed the Colorado Springs team for two years. They were near the top of their league, losing the 1952 pennant on the last day of the season, but reversing matters in '53 to win the flag on the last day.

In 1954 Don went to Memphis as manager and was promoted back to the big leagues in 1955 when he became the first base coach for the White Sox under new manager Marty Marion. Marion was fired after the 1956 season, and his coaches were in limbo. But Al Lopez, the new manager of the White Sox, said all of the coaches could come back and he wanted them back.

Gutteridge said the combination of Lopez and coaches Johnny Cooney, Ray Berres, Tony Cuccinello, and himself "were envied by quite a few other coaches around the majors."[25] They worked together as a group for eight years with the White Sox (1957-64). They would eat together, went out with their wives, they worked on strategies. Gutteridge said, "These were good years."[26]

Lopez had put together an excellent coaching staff. He finished no lower than second place in his first nine seasons with Cleveland and Chicago. Though he won two pennants, he never won a World Series. He always commanded respect. Dick Donovan said it best, "Lopez was the best manager I ever played for. In fact, he was the best manager in baseball all during my career." Gutteridge added, "Lopez was a great manager. He was always ahead of his game, and he never raised his voice."[27]

Lopez ran the ballclub. John Cooney was his bench coach. Tony Cuccinello was third base coach and Gutteridge was the infield coach and coached at first base. Ray Berres rounded out the staff as pitching coach. Gutteridge called Berres the "best I've ever seen" in working with pitchers.[28]

The culmination of Gutteridge's career came in 1959, when the White Sox won their first pennant in 40 years. Chicago's Mayor Richard Joseph Daley, a longtime Sox fan, set off the air-raid sirens to honor the team. The problem was that some folks thought it was the beginning of World War III, and not the White Sox winning the American League pennant.

The White Sox lost the 1959 World Series to the Los Angeles Dodgers, four games to two, but for Sox fans it was a special season. During that year the team featured five future members of the Hall of Fame: Lopez, Nelson Fox, Luis Aparicio, Early Wynn, and Larry Doby.

In 1966 Lopez retired and Eddie Stanky became the skipper. Tony Cuccinello, Ray Berres, and Don were kept on by the team (Cooney had retired after the 1964 season), but the coaches didn't see eye to eye with Stanky. It was simple: They weren't the coaches that Stanky wanted. At the end of the season, Cuccinello and Berres quit and Gutteridge was fired.[29]

In 1967 the White Sox front office appointed Don manager of the Indianapolis Triple-A team. The Indians finished second in the American Association. He was set to return the next year, but the team was relocated to Honolulu. Helen was dead set against it. But the Kansas City Royals came calling and he became the head scout for the expansion team that would take the field in 1969.

Shortly after the 1968 draft, Gutteridge left the Royals to return to the White Sox as a coach under Lopez, who had had agreed to return as manager when Stanky was fired in midseason. Lopez had retired after the 1965 season because of health problems, and when the problems returned early in the 1969 season, Lopez stepped aside again and the Sox asked Gutteridge to take over as manager. He managed the White Sox until late in the 1970 season. Gutteridge's teams never contended and he ultimately was fired, but his association with baseball did not end. From 1971 to 1974 he scouted for the New York Yankees and from 1975 to 1992 he scouted for the Dodgers.

Gutteridge summed up his career in saying, "I was at the right place at the right time and had a good career."[30] He credited an experience he had when he was 12 years old. "We would have revival meetings. … I went to the preacher after the service and told him how much I wanted to be a ballplayer," Gutteridge said. "He told me to talk to the Lord, and I did. I prayed to spend my life in baseball and my prayers were answered."[31]

In retirement, Gutteridge took an interest in youth baseball in Pittsburg. Just before his death, the JL Hutchinson League renamed its intermediate league (ages 13-15) the Don Gutteridge League. He and a longtime friend, Todd Biggs, wrote a booklet, *Getting Started in Baseball: A Guide to Learning and Teaching Baseball in the Early Years*, and distributed copies to all the players in the league.

"Don had a positive impact on every single person he ever met," Biggs told the *Morning Sun* in Pittsburg. "No matter how long your conversation is, whenever you left his company, you always felt better about yourself."[32]

For someone who was in the right place, Gutteridge won plenty of honors. He is in the Kansas, Missouri, and Columbus (Ohio) Halls of Fame. He is a member of the St. Louis Browns Hall of Fame. A softball and baseball facility in Pittsburg is named in his honor. Early in life, he had set some goals: "I married my wife, Helen. I became a professional baseball player and made it to the World Series."[33] Not bad for somebody who "just wanted to be a ballplayer."

Sources

Interview with Herb Crehan, author of Red Sox histories and player profiles.

------: *The Baseball Encyclopedia, Ninth Edition.*

Cicotello, David, and Angelo J. Louisa, editors. *Forbes Field: Essays and Memories of the Pirates' Historic Ballpark, 1909-1971* (Jefferson, North Carolina: McFarland, 2007).

Gough, David, and Jim Bard. *Little Nel: The Nellie Fox Story* (Alexandria, Virginia: D.L. Megbec Publishing, 2000).

Notes

1. Interviews with Don Gutteridge on November 11, 2006, and May 27, 2008.
2. Gutteridge interviews.
3. Ibid.
4. Don Gutteridge with Ronnie Joyner and Bill Bozman, *From the Gas House Gang to the Go-Go Sox: My 50-Plus Years in Big League Baseball* (Dunkirk, Maryland: Pepperpot Productions, 2007), 376.
5. Gutteridge interviews.
6. Ibid.
7. Gutteridge-Joyner-Bozman, 379.
8. Gutteridge-Joyner-Bozman, 99.
9. Red Byrd, "Gutteridge, Gas House Gang's New Slugger, 'Intends to Lead the N.L. in Thefts This Season," *The Sporting News*, March 25, 1937: 10.
10. Gutteridge interviews.
11. Ibid.
12. Gutteridge-Joyner-Bozman, 33.
13. Gutteridge interviews.
14. Ibid.
15. Gutteridge-Joyner-Bozman, 104.
16. Gutteridge-Joyner-Bozman, 102.
17. Gutteride interviews.
18. Richard Goldstein, "Don Gutteridge, 96, Player for Famed St. Louis Teams, Is Dead," *New York Times*, September 9, 2008.
19. Gutteridge interviews.
20. Ibid.
21. Ibid.
22. Ibid.
23. Ibid.
24. Ibid.
25. Gutteridge-Joyner Bozman, 323.
26. Gutteridge interviews.
27. Ibid.
28. Ibid.
29. Gutteridge-Joyner-Bozman, 325.
30. Gutteridge interviews.
31. Ibid.
32. Don Gutteridge obituary, *Pittsburg* (Kansas) *Morning Sun*, September 13, 2008
33. Gutteridge interviews.

LUIS APARICIO

By Leonte Landino

The name Luis Aparicio is closely linked with Venezuela. Both Luis Aparicio Ortega (Ortega) and his son, Luis Aparicio Montiel (Aparicio), had a significant impact on bringing the game of baseball to new heights in Latin America. For that reason, many say that when talking about one, you can't help but think of the other.

The younger Aparicio was much more than an outstanding baseball player whose endurance, defense, and speed during an 18-year old major-league career earned him a spot in baseball's Hall of Fame. He was a symbol of the growth and development of the game of baseball in Latin America – specifically in Venezuela and in his hometown of Maracaibo. Aparicio's place among the greatest players in baseball signified the climax of a cycle of progress for the game of baseball, which has become the national sport of Venezuela and an intrinsic part of its cultural heritage.

To fully understand the significance, impact, and legacy of Aparicio's career, one needs to take a journey back into the first steps of the game in Maracaibo.

The emergence of baseball in Maracaibo began around the turn of the 20th century when an American businessman, William Phelps (who later became a media mogul and philanthropist), opened the first department store in town, the American Bazaar. While he imported baseball equipment from the United States, he also saw the need for educating local children about the game in order to sell his merchandise. Phelps became a baseball enthusiast and taught schoolkids the rules of the game, which they quickly understood. He served as the first umpire of documented games and built the first baseball field in the coastal city of Maracaibo.

From the sport's inception around 1912, baseball quickly became a favorite pastime of people of all classes. Several fields were created throughout the small urban area, and both adults and children were fascinated with the sport. In just a few years, the game spread throughout the region and it was soon established as a professional game. People fell in love with the game, and were willing to gather and pay to watch the best players and teams. They called it "the game of the four corners." The game of baseball had found its stage in the country.

Through the years, the region had a constant flow of American workers from oil companies who helped shape the identity of the city as well as the influence of American culture. Baseball was no exception. By 1926, a heated rivalry between Vuelvan Caras and Santa Marta was catching the attention of followers and local sports media. In fact, the first big hero of local professional baseball was a shortstop from Vuelvan Caras, Rafael "Anguito" Oliver. Early on, the media shone a spotlight on the role of the shortstop.

Oliver became an icon and two brothers were some of his biggest fans – Luis and Ernesto Aparicio Ortega. The Aparicio Ortega brothers (in the Latin American custom, they used their father's and mother's surname) were also natural athletes; Luis enjoyed soccer but ended up practicing baseball with Ernesto. Both became quality infielders. Luis, however, became the big star, the super athlete, while Ernesto, who had great playing tools, concentrated on learning the game as a science. He became a successful manager, coach, and team owner, transmitting his knowledge over generations.

Luis gained fame for his great plays and intelligence in the position of shortstop. He became a reference, a master, and a key player sought by many teams throughout the country. He played in both professional leagues in the country, in Caracas and Maracaibo. He became the first player "exported" from Venezuela when he signed with Tigres del Licey of the Dominican Republic in 1934.

Also in 1934, Ortega and his homemaker wife, Herminia Montiel, welcomed their son Luis Ernesto Aparicio Montiel. By the time Aparicio was born in Maracaibo on April 29, his father was shining as one of the first baseball superstars of Venezuela and Latin America. Ortega was an All-Star player and one the most famous players ever of Venezuelan baseball. "An artist in the shortstop position," many called him.

Uncle Ernesto became a mentor to Luis. In Gavilanes, where his father also played, little Luis got his first job in baseball: batboy. His father and uncle taught him the secrets of the game. He also had the chance to learn from players of all nationalities, including Cuban, Dominican, and American players.

LUIS APARICIO

Baseball was his life. Aparicio recalls his mother washing baseball uniforms for his team and talking about baseball all day. From the age of 12, when he played shortstop for a team called La Deportiva, Aparicio displayed the grace and elegance he learned from his father. From then on, Aparicio was a member of several teams in Maracaibo, Caracas, and Barquisimeto. He was constantly moving with his family, depending on the time of year and which team his father was playing for.

That was his life: baseball, the stardom of his father, the knowledge of his uncle and whatever the game brought to the family table.

In 1953, Caracas hosted the Baseball Amateur World Series, and Luis Aparicio, then 19 years old, was selected to represent Venezuela. It was his first big tournament, and he played shortstop, third base, and left field. Although Cuba won the tournament, Aparicio was recognized both in the stands and in newspapers as the most electrifying player, who made great plays and showed security and maturity in all positions. Fans waved white handkerchiefs during this tournament, praising the teenager with great speed and a solid glove. All eyes were on him for the first time, but the name of his famous father would always be on his shoulders if he chose to be a professional player.

Soon after the Amateur World Series, the day arrived. Aparicio had to tell his parents he was quitting school to become a professional baseball player. His mother was not happy with the decision. His father, on the other hand, told him something that would stand out in his mind for the rest of his career. "Son, if you are going to play baseball for a living, you will have to be the number one always," said his father. "You will never be a number two of anybody, always be the number one."[1]

That winter, the best four teams in Venezuela played in the country's first national tournament. The teams – Gavilanes and Pastora from Maracaibo, and Caracas and Magallanes from Caracas – rotated their games in four cities and it was the first tournament played under the umbrella of major-league baseball.

Aparicio signed with Gavilanes and his debut was scheduled for November 17, 1953, in Maracaibo. That day it rained, and his debut was postponed until the next day, November 18, which is a special holiday in Maracaibo. The city celebrates the day of its lady patron, the Virgin of Chiquinquirá, and festivities are held all around. Among them is the special baseball game between the crosstown rivals Pastora and Gavilanes.

Aparicio's father, Ortega, who also played for Gavilanes, led off the game against Pastora's Howie Fox, a major-league veteran. After the first pitch, Ortega went back to the dugout and pointed to his son with his bat, signaling it was time for Luis to take his father's bat and replace him at home plate for his first official at-bat.

The crowd of 7,000 gave a 15-minute standing ovation to this simple but magical gesture. They were recognizing Ortega – known as "The Great of Maracaibo" – for his outstanding career, his talent as the best shortstop in Venezuelan baseball, for his dedication on the field, and for more than 20 years of contributing to the development of the game in Maracaibo. At the same time, people were showing Luis the huge burden he had on his shoulders for carrying his father's name, and for the responsibility he had on the field from that moment.

Aparicio Jr., at 19 years old, understood the situation and embraced it with maturity. "I knew the responsibility on me. I knew about the expectations people had everywhere I stepped on a field. I just had to be great as my father, otherwise people would consider me a total deception," he said in later years. "It was destiny."[2]

Panorama, the local newspaper, wrote the next day: "Aparicio´s son's debut was patronized by the Virgin herself." For a very Catholic-religious region, this was a big deal.[3]

Aparicio ended up being named the best shortstop of the tournament. By December, the Cleveland Indians were negotiating with him. Gavilanes manager Red Kress, who was a coach for the Indians, spoke with general manager Hank Greenberg about signing Aparicio, but Greenberg replied that he thought Luis too small to play baseball. Chico Carrasquel, who was playing for Caracas and Chicago at the time, talked to Chicago White Sox general manager Frank Lane and told him about Luis, asking him to sign the youngster before someone else did. Caracas's manager, Luman Harris, also talked to Lane. Soon after, Lane sent an offer and a contract for Aparicio with a $10,000 check. Young Luis became a member of the White Sox.

Aparicio's days in the minor leagues were hard. His English was very limited. He knew he belonged in the majors, but the learning process was strict. Carrasquel was the big-league shortstop. After spring training in 1955, Aparicio was sent to Memphis in the Double-A Southern Association. He thought about going back to Venezuela and quitting the White Sox, but both his father and Carrasquel convinced the novice of his potential and explained to him the process of reaching the majors, a road even tougher for Latinos, especially in those years. Carrasquel, who was the big baseball idol in Caracas, became Aparicio's mentor and a father figure for him. Aparicio also recalls meeting a singer that season in a small bar in Memphis, a young man named Elvis Presley.

In October 1955, the White Sox traded Chico Carrasquel to the Cleveland Indians, leaving the door open for Aparicio. When Lane announced the trade, a Chicago journalist said: "You are trading your All-Star shortstop? You will need a machine to replace Chico." Lane replied, "Yes, that's precisely what we have – a machine, and his name is Luis Aparicio."[4]

Aparicio was named the American League Rookie of the Year in 1956. He was the first Latin American player to win the award. He finished with a .266 batting average and a league-leading 21 stolen bases, and also led the league in sacrifice hits. The stolen base as a strategy was becoming less and less used in baseball in those years. Aparicio revived the essence of the stolen base from the moment he reached the majors. He injected the White Sox with the game of speed, the Caribbean game, where speed is a key. He was praised for his defense but during his first season had 35 errors.

Luis needed work on his throw. Venezuelan journalist Juan Vené, who covered Aparicio's entire career, recalled, "Fans were afraid to sit behind first base and they were really aware of the throw every time Aparicio was fielding a grounder because the ball often ended into the stands."[5]

His debut met everyone's expectations at home, but he knew he needed to do more. After his first season, when he returned home with his wife, Sonia, Aparicio said, "By seeing how so many people have gathered to welcome me at the airport just to say hello and congratulations, it makes me realize that I still have a long way to go and a lot of work to do to go beyond their expectations. I need to put the name of my country and my people up high; I feel my game represents them."[6]

In 1958, Aparicio won his first Gold Glove, was named to his first All-Star Game, hit .266, and led the league in stolen bases for the third consecutive

Hall of Famer Luis Aparicio led the American League in stolen bases for nine straight years (1956-64), won nine Gold Gloves, and retired as the all-time leader in games played at shortstop (2,583).

year, with 29. Chicago ended up in second place for the second year in a row behind the Yankees. The situation in the American League was tough. The Chicago White Sox was an outstanding club but the Yankees were the Yankees, and in those years they simply dominated baseball. There were no playoffs. To go to the World Series they just needed to finish first in the American League. The White Sox needed to reach one more step, and they did it in 1959.

Dámaso Blanco, a former infielder for the San Francisco Giants, remembers 1959: "I went to Chicago in August 1959 with the Venezuelan baseball team for the Pan Am Games and they took us to Comiskey Park to watch the White Sox and Luis Aparicio. It was my first MLB game ever and I was very anxious. Aparicio hit a single on his first at-bat and we all noticed that people started to yell: 'Go! Go! Go!' At first we did not understand what was happening and then our guide explained people were actually rooting for Aparicio to steal second base. I can't really describe how proud we

• LUIS APARICIO •

felt listening to a full Comiskey Park rooting for a fellow Venezuelan and the team leader of the 'Go Go White Sox.' "[7]

That season, the White Sox won 94 games and finally won the pennant. Among the keys to their success were Aparicio's base-stealing skills and his defense along with his double play partner and close friend, Nellie Fox. For Chicago it was a magical era. It was their first trip to the World Series since 1919. This team was the complete opposite of the Black Sox. It was fun to watch. Aparicio remembers: "We were so close, like a family. We enjoyed our game and the fans of Chicago so much during 1959. Having guys in the team like Ted Kluszewski, Jim Rivera, Sherm Lollar, and Early Wynn was just amazing. We just had to win the league because we were good, having fun in the field, and playing very seriously."[8]

Aparicio ended up second to his double-play partner Fox in the voting for the American League's Most Valuable Player. He stole a career-high 56 bases that year. He realized no one in baseball was better than him at stealing. His speed was a key to victory. He led the team in runs with 98. "Before the season Al Lopez, our manager, told me he wanted me to focus on my base stealing," Aparicio said long after his career ended. "They wanted me to spice things up in the club and that was going to be our key to win games that season."[9]

After their great season, the White Sox lost the World Series to the Dodgers in six games. Aparicio hit .308 (8-for-26), and although he was thrilled to participate in the fall classic, he was deeply frustrated in not winning the Series. "The people were very excited in the city, because they waited 40 years to see their team in a World Series. They were disappointed, but at the same time they treated us like winners,"[10] he recalled. This first trip to the Series made Aparicio realize how important it was to be a winner and how hard a team needed to work to win it all.

Hoping to return to the World Series in 1960, the White Sox instead slipped to third place. They fell to fourth place in 1961 and fifth in 1962. The Sox wanted to rebuild their team, and in January of 1963, Aparicio and veteran outfielder Al Smith were traded to the Baltimore Orioles for Ron Hansen, Pete Ward, Dave Nicholson, and Hoyt Wilhelm.

The trade was a jolt to Luis, but he was moving to a contending team built around a foundation of power and pitching. Aparicio added speed to the Baltimore lineup, winning two more stolen base titles in 1963-64 to give him nine consecutive seasons as the American League stolen base champion, an all-time record. More importantly, he helped solidify the Oriole defense. Luis and future Hall of Famer Brooks Robinson formed one of the best shortstop-third base combinations of all time.

In 1966, the Orioles won the American League pennant, and Aparicio once again faced the Dodgers in the World Series. Although his offense was not as solid as it was in 1959, he still contributed with four hits and great defense during the series, which the Orioles swept in four games. It was first and only championship ring of his career. He came back to Maracaibo as a hero, dedicating his part of the title to his parents, who were his biggest supporters.

In November of 1967, Luis was traded back to the White Sox. As a veteran player, he became the team leader and mentor. During his second stint in Chicago, his glove was still his great tool, though his speed was not the same. He worked on his offense and in 1970, at the age of 36, batted a career-high .313.

Before the 1971 season, Aparicio was traded to the Boston Red Sox and played with them for three more seasons. In two of them was he was selected to the All-Star Game. In 1973, at the age of 39, he batted .271 in 132 games and stole 13 bases in 14 attempts.

Vené remembers March 26, 1974: "Luis was in the Red Sox spring camp when he got the notice that he was being released. He wanted to play one more season; he was 40 and still felt he had it. When he went back to the hotel he had a letter from Yankees owner George Steinbrenner. It was an open contract that had a note saying: "You put in the amount to play for the New York Yankees."

Aparicio sent the envelope back with a note that said: "Dear Mr. Steinbrenner, thank you very much for your offer but I just get released once in my lifetime."[11] That was the end of Aparicio's playing career. He went back to Maracaibo that day with his family.

From 1956 to 1973, no other shortstop was more dominant in his position than Luis Aparicio, who won nine Gold Gloves. He was a profound influence on the game during his era with his speed, helping to revive the stolen base as an offensive weapon. He was selected to 10 All-Star teams. He played in two World Series and won one, and he set the most significant personal record for himself: No player had played more games at his beloved position in the major leagues than he (2,583). (The record has since been broken by Omar

Vizquel.) He finished his career with 2,677 hits, a .262 batting average and 506 stolen bases.

After 10 years of eligibility and a huge crusade by many Hispanic journalists pushing his candidacy for the Hall of Fame, he was elected to the Hall in 1984, becoming the first Venezuelan to ever receive this form of baseball immortality. "This is a triumph of Venezuela for all Venezuelans," said Aparicio when he heard of his election.[12]

His biggest regret is that his father didn't live long enough to see his son elected to the Hall of Fame. Luis Aparicio Ortega died on January 1, 1971. After his death he was honored with his election to the Hall of Fame of Venezuelan Sports. The Maracaibo baseball stadium was officially named Luis Aparicio Ortega "El Grande de Maracaibo." After the creation of the Venezuelan Baseball Hall of Fame and Museum, the Aparicio Ortega brothers, Ernesto and Luis, were also inducted.

After retirement, Luis moved back to Venezuela and worked during the Venezuelan league in winter as manager. He managed Caracas, Zulia, Lara, La Guaira, Magallanes, and Cabimas. He was a celebrity and his retirement was not easy for him. They were hard times, not economically because he was very organized financially, but emotionally. He spent more time with his family and was part of many local projects of many kinds.

In the early 1980s he became a television commentator for Radio Caracas Television during the Venezuelan League. In fact, when he got the notice about his selection to Cooperstown, he was working with RCTV. Although he enjoyed it for a while, television was not his passion, but at least something to stay close to the game, if he was not managing.

In the 1990s Luis was back to the field with Tiburones de La Guaira in the winter league as a manager and coach. Aparicio moved to Barquisimeto. He enjoyed spending time with his family and especially his grandchildren and great-grandchildren. His family suffered a big setback when his daughter Sharon was the victim of a crime in Venezuela. After this incident, he concentrated even more on his family. He continued to enjoy and follow baseball and kept his participation in baseball and Hall of Fame events with the help of his son Nelson.

After his election to the National Baseball Hall of Fame, Aparicio's status of celebrity increased greatly. He became known as the most important and influential Venezuelan athlete of all time, the most revered and followed. He also made several trips a year to the US to participate in autograph sessions, fan festivals and former player activities. He was a constant supporter of Hall of Fame gatherings, including All-Star games and Cooperstown induction weekends.

His solid and impeccable image and personality caught the attention of ESPN International and ESPN Deportes who invited him as a special color analyst for the international broadcasts of Venezuelan baseball from 2011 to 2013, alongside veteran and famed Spanish-broadcasters such as Emmy-award winning Ernesto Jerez.

Aparicio has since become an active baseball follower and his voice is present through his social media accounts, where he has provided opinions and personals perspective of issues around baseball. Most notably in 2017 he was invited to participate in a ceremony honoring the Latino members of the Baseball Hall of Fame prior to the 2017 All-Star Game in Miami, Florida. Aparicio respectfully declined the invitation and publicly stated: "Thank you for the honor @mlb, but I cannot celebrate while the young people of my country are dying while fighting for freedom"[13]

Aparicio did not attend the 2017 Hall of Fame induction for the same reasons and actively became a strong opponent of Venezuelan dictator Nicolás Maduro and the regime that has ruled Venezuela since 1998.

Maracaibo still remembers every November 18 as part of the festivities around the Virgin holiday, the anniversary of Luis Aparicio's debut. At the Aguilas del Zulia game, Aparicio has made the ceremonial first pitch. Every year the Luis Aparicio Award is given to the best Venezuelan player of the major-league baseball season. It was a tribute to his career and to the memory of his father.

In 2006 the Chicago White Sox unveiled the Luis Aparicio statue at the U.S. Cellular Field in the center-field concourse and created by artist Gary Tillery. Aparicio attended the event with Sonia celebrating 52 years of marriage and with his son Luis Jr and daughter Karen. The sculpture is part of a two-player series depicting Aparicio waiting to catch a ball from his longtime double-play partner Nelly Fox, whose widow, Joanne, also attended the ceremony. "This is my biggest moment in baseball. I thank the White Sox organization for giving me the opportunity to play baseball, and I thank God for giving me the ability to play this game. The only thing I can say is baseball is so much of me, I even met my wife playing baseball."[14]

The 2014 season of the Venezuelan Winter League was played in honor to the 30th anniversary of Aparicio's induction to Cooperstown and he was honored at every ballpark of the league and the league reinforced and emphasized the biggest honor ever made to a Venezuelan baseball player: the retirement of his number 11 from every team in the country.

Much more than a great player, Aparicio was recognized as a great human being. Most people knew Luis for his playing feats, but ignored his great heart and family values. During his career the integrity he brought to the game was one of his strongest assets. He gave everything he had to win and help his teams. He played simultaneously for 19 years in Venezuelan baseball, doubling the amount of work year round. As a major-league player he played fewer than 130 games in a season only once.

Maybe his greater value was how he embraced and understood his position and his significance on and off the field for the people of Venezuela, a country filled with social problems that universally celebrates the achievements of its people. He was much more than an icon.

People always expected the best from him, and he gave nothing but the best both as a player and as a human being, working hard enough and using his abilities to be among the greatest players of all time. He had huge shoes to fill under the shadow of his father and he never let this issue pressure him during his life. Luis Aparicio assumed a social responsibility and went beyond expectations.

Aparicio was named the Athlete of the 20th Century in Venezuela. Beyond his recognition for being the best player ever born in the country, his integrity and family values always accompanied him. Moreover, he is the role model for future generations and the "godfather" of the dynasty of Venezuelan shortstops in the history of the major leagues. *Panorama* published a letter Aparicio sent to his mother in March 1956: "To Herminia de Aparicio, Maracaibo. Dear Mom: You are finally the mother of a big leaguer. Try to figure out what it means to me to become 'a big leaguer.' Today I've cried alone, when they told me they were sending my luggage to Chicago because I had made the big league team. Tears came out by themselves and I just thought about Dad. Mom, please tell Dad that my debt with him is finally paid. Kisses, your son, Luis."[15]

Luis has said: "When my father asked me to be always a number one, I always kept that on my mind. I think I didn't disappoint him. I wanted him to be proud of me, and I know he definitely was. That's the achievement of my life."[16]

Sources

In addition to the sources in the Notes, the author also consulted:

Verde, Luis. *The History of Baseball in Zulia* (Maracaibo: Editorial Maracaibo SRL, 1999).

Perfiles: Luis Aparicio. ESPN International. 2002-2007.

Author interviews with Luis Aparicio, Juan Vené, Dámaso Blanco, Angel Bravo. Luis Verde, Nelson Aparicio, and Rafael Aparicio.

¡A La Carga! Tripleplay Sports Productions, Maracaibo, Venezuela. Various televisión episodes 1998-2002.

www.eljuegoperfecto.com

www.baseball-reference.com

Notes

1. Author interview with Luis Aparicio, July 2008.
2. Aparicio interview.
3. *Diario Panorama* (Maracaibo, Venezuela), November 19, 1953.
4. Carlos Cárdenas Lares, *Venezolanos en las Grandes Ligas* (Caracas: Fondo editorial Cárdenas Lares, 1990), 78.
5. Author interview with Juan Vené, Cincinnati, August 2007.
6. *Diario Panorama*, October 10, 1956.
7. Author interview with Dámaso Blanco, Cincinnati, August 2007.
8. Aparicio interview.
9. Ibid.
10. Ibid..
11. Vené interview.
12. *Revista IND*, Instituto Nacional de Deportes, Caracas, Venezuela. August 1984.
13. Luis Aparicio, via Twitter, July 11, 2017.
14. Scott Merkin, "Aparicio, Fox honored with statues," MLB.com, July 23, 2006.
15. *Diario Panorama*, March 2, 1956.
16. Aparicio interview.

RODOLFO ARIAS

by Jose Ramirez

Rodolfo Arias's professional baseball career as a left-handed pitcher spanned a total of 23 years in three countries: his native Cuba, the United States, and Mexico, where he made his final farewell to the game he loved. As a member of the Chicago White Sox in 1959, his one year in the majors, he made 34 appearances.

Arias was born in Ciboney's Sugar Mill in Camaguey Province on June 6, 1931. His father, Arturo Arias, managed a railroad station and his mother, Zoila Martinez, was a housewife who never worked outside of the home. The young Rodolfo was a rebellious child and before too long got himself expelled from school and sent to an educational facility sponsored by the courts; his education fell short of high school equivalency.

Baseball in Cuba started in the 1860s and it was frowned upon by the Spanish colonial government, considered a repudiation of everything from Spain and supportive of the new revolutionary mentality of the locals. It was and is the national sport of Cuba. Arias's love for the game started very early and he took every opportunity to play the game with his friends. The equipment he had was crude indeed. The "ball" was a sphere tightly wound with black electrical tape until it took the shape and consistency of a baseball; the bat was simply a branch cut from a local hardwood tree, the guira, which was typically used to make the Latin American musical instrument known as the maracas. Rodolfo had no other real interests; it was, as he recalls, "what we kids did all day long."[1]

Young Rodolfo was so good as a left-handed teenage pitcher that many of his friends wouldn't play against him unless he played first base rather than pitch.

In the early '50s, he played in the Habana Amateur League for a club formed by the Customs office, but the team was not that successful on the field. However, an opening in an amateur tournament on the island allowed him to join the Oriente Province San German club in the Pedro Betancourt League. The team finished in first place and continued on to take first place in the Popular National Amateur League, too. Winning that league enabled Rodolfo and his teammates to travel to the United States in 1953 to play in a double-elimination tournament in Michigan against U.S. amateur teams.

Before the team left Cuba for the United States, Joe Cambria, the Washington Senators' legendary Cuban scout, tried to sign Arias, but Arias, after talking to Popular League president Pedro Tibanier, took Tibanier's advice not to sign with anyone until he got to the United States. If he pitched well, perhaps he could command a better price. He left for the United States, but covered his bases by telling Joe Cambria that he would sign upon his return from the tournament.

From Habana the team traveled to Miami, where they got on a bus for the long ride to Michigan. In 16 days of baseball, they won just two games, both pitched by Arias. Although there were a couple of good players on the team, they were deemed too short by the scouts; Rodolfo, at 5-feet-10 and 155 pounds, cut the right figure to go along with his pitching abilities. Chicago White Sox scout Doug Minor signed him for $3,000. It's his recollection that pitchers like Camilo Pascual and Pedro Ramos were each signed for only $75. Tibanier's advice and his own decision had been correct.

Upon returning to Cuba, Arias was called by Miguel Angel Gonzalez (a former major-league player and coach with 17 seasons mostly as a catcher) of the Habana Lions for a tryout; they had heard of his pitching performance in Michigan. As he entered the park, he slipped on wet stairs and fractured his left arm. Rodolfo is still pained to recall how depressed he felt at the time.

During this period, he traveled to Las Villas Province, where he met his future wife, Olga; the couple fell in love and they were married in February 1954. Though Arias was from Camaguey, both his father and wife were from Las Villas. (Many sources say Rodolfo was from Las Villas, too, but he has not bothered to request a correction.)

During his professional career he alternated between playing in Cuba's winter league, which began in late fall/winter, and the United States, where

RODOLFO ARIAS

the seasons began in the spring. He never thought of or wanted to do anything but to play ball. He recalls thinking, "Why get a job when you can play ball?"[2]

Arias began his minor-league career in the United States in 1953 with the Madisonville (Kentucky) Miners of the Class-D Kitty League, appearing in 37 games, winning 16 and losing 10, and hitting .299. The White Sox advanced him to Class B the following year, and he pitched for the Waterloo White Hawks and had a record of 5-7 in 33 games.

His first year in the Cuban League was with the Habana Lions in '54, playing for Adolfo Luque (who had pitched in the majors for 23 years, compiling a record of 194 wins and 179 losses). He describes Luque as a "warrior" who seemed to care for nothing more than winning baseball games, a demanding manager, perfectionist in his demeanor. Luque died three years later. Arias's teammates included Don Blasingame at second and Ken Boyer at third. He pitched in six games with no wins or losses. He recalls with glee striking out the three "Americanos" of the Almendares team: Rocky Nelson, Gus Triandos, and Earl Rapp.

During 1955-57, Arias played for the Amarillo Gold Sox, the Colorado Springs Sky Sox, and the Toronto Maple Leafs with a combined record of 34 wins and 24 losses. In 1956, he played in the winter league for the Marianao team, winning two games. His son, Rodolfo ("Rudy"), was born during that year. He improved his record in 1957 with nine wins and five losses and in the winter played for the Caribbean Series championship representing Cuba (Marianao), which had five wins and only one loss. Their opponents were Mayaguez (Puerto Rico), Balboa (Panama), and Caracas (Venezuela). Arias was able to pitch in only one game for a total of one inning, giving up three hits with one strikeout.

The year 1958 had Rodolfo pitching in his homeland during the regular season. He was playing Triple-A ball in the International League for the Habana Cuban Sugar Kings with a record of 7-7 and a 3.80 ERA. One of his wins was the only no-hit, no-run game in the history of the team, on August 17 against the Rochester Red Wings. The only Rochester player to reach base was shortstop Roy Smalley, who drew a sixth-inning walk. Arias received $1,000 from Cuba's *Bohemia* magazine for his feat that day. That winter, he returned to Cuba and played for Marianao again (3-7), returning to the Caribbean Series, where he made another brief appearance, giving up one hit and a walk. Marianao once again won the Series with a 4-2 record against the teams from Caguas (Puerto Rico), Carta Vieja (Panama), and Valencia (Venezuela).

During the 1959 season, at the age of 28, Arias was promoted to the Chicago White Sox. His first game saw him come on in the bottom of the ninth in the April 10 game against the Tigers in Detroit. The score was tied, with two outs and a runner on first. He gave up a single, but then recorded the third out, sending the game into extra innings. He was pinch-hit for in the top of the 10th. Arias was used exclusively in relief by the White Sox in 1959, throwing 44 innings in all. He was 2-0, and allowed 49 hits and 23 runs, while walking 20 and striking out 28 batters. During the 34 games in which he appeared, he came to bat only four times, without a hit and striking out twice.

Rudy finished 13 games, his two wins coming on April 17 against the Tigers and on May 12, when he pitched the 11th and 12th innings of a 4-3 win over the Boston Red Sox in Fenway Park.

Arias's last game in the majors was on August 26, 1959. He wound up with an ERA of 4.09, above the team's collective 3.29 ERA. Arias was with the team the entire season and was a member of the Sox' World Series roster. He received a full World Series share, though he saw no action in the Series.

Two hitters he feared the most were Ted Williams and Mickey Mantle. As he remembers, when pitching to Mantle in a spring training game he ran the count to 2 and 1, followed by a second strike with the count now at 2 and 2. The catcher asked for a changeup and Mickey took a mighty swing. According to Arias, who laughs as he tells the story, "That ball almost hit the sun."[3]

Another time, Ryne Duren beaned Nellie Fox and when Arias took the mound, it was Duren's turn to come up to bat. White Sox manager Alfonso Lopez called a time out and approached the mound. His message to Arias was "metele un pelotazo" or "bean him." Arias said that is what you did in those days; there was no choice in the matter - you had to do it. So he reared back and threw at Duren who, knowing what was coming, jumped back and eluded the throw. Arias got him in the stomach with his next pitch. As a fight was about to break out, Earl Torgeson ran from first base and stood between Arias and everybody else. Torgeson was known to be handy with his fists, and nobody touched Arias that day.

His daughter Olga Cristina was born while he was pitching in Chicago. In fact, the White Sox were scheduled to be on a road trip to Washington when the daughter was about to be born but he was allowed to stay back in order to be with his wife. After the birth, he was driven to the airport by Bill Veeck himself, a gesture he appreciates to this day.

Arias returned to Cuba for its 1959 winter league and played for Marianao, where he had a record of 4-8, pitching 118 innings in 29 games with a 3.29 ERA.

He went back to Triple A in 1960, playing for the White Sox' San Diego affiliate in the Pacific Coast League and the Miami Marlins, a Baltimore affiliate in the International League. He had a total of 10 wins and 10 losses in 174 innings. After the season, he pitched for Marianao, where he won 10 games and lost 9 during 150 innings of pitching with 93 strikeouts and 50 walks, and was selected for the All-Star team. On January 17, 1961, Arias set a Cuban League record by pitching a complete 18-inning game against the first team he had played for, the Habana Lions. He lost that game when Dan Morejon hit a single with a runner on second. Who was the winning pitcher in relief? Luis Tiant (Red Sox hurler of fame), who went on to win the Rookie of the Year award for his 10 victories. With the Castro regime fully in power, 1961 was the last season of professional baseball in Cuba.

In the spring of 1961, Arias pitched for the Jersey City Jerseys of the Cincinnati organization in the International League where his record was 8-9 in 157 innings. He returned later in the year to Cuba when he heard a rumor that the new government was starting the baseball league again. While there, he threw without practicing properly and without proper supervision and tore a tendon in his arm. Soon after, he learned that the rumors he had heard about baseball in Cuba were incorrect. Wanting to continue to play ball at the professional level, he left Cuba once more.

The 1959 season was Rodolfo Arias's only major-league campaign, but the left-hander pitched successfully in the minor leagues and his native Cuba for more than a decade.

Arias pitched in 1962 for the Columbus Jets, a Pittsburgh affiliate in the International League, and San Diego, now part of the Cincinnati organization, but he threw only 15 innings because of his bad shoulder and didn't record a win. The Cincinnati medical staff gave him a cortisone injection and the team sent him to the Macon Peaches, a Single-A affiliate in the South Atlantic League. He was 2-1 in 26 innings of work, but his arm was no longer able to respond to the demands of the game and the rigors of pitching, and so he retired.

It was hard to get baseball out of his blood, though, and after a few years, feeling his arm was better, he pitched in the Mexican League for the

RODOLFO ARIAS

Poza Rica team in 1965 and 1966 and was able to put together a record of three wins and three losses, but a slide play at second base left him with a severe leg injury which became infected and prevented him from pitching any more. As he recalls, he was hardly able to walk but had also heard there were rumors that US teams might have an interest in him again. He returned to Mexico in 1967, but his arm had gone bad again. He stayed but one week before he was cut and retired for the last time from professional baseball.

Arias worked in construction in the Miami area but it proved to be too physically hard for him. He was playing softball in a Miami league for the Barnett Bank when a bank official offered him a job in security. He promptly accepted and worked security for 18 years until his retirement in 1995.

In addition to their two children, Arias and his wife Olga, who died in 2010, had four grandchildren and one great-grandchild. Their son, Rudy, was signed by Seattle in 1977 as a catcher but retired after suffering a broken jaw. Later he was a bullpen catcher in three major-league organizations for 11 years.

As for Rudy the elder: Living in the Miami area during his later years, his life was filled spending time with his family. He continued to receive mail from fans and collectors looking for autographs. After being hospitalized with respiratory problems, Rodolfo Arias died on January 12, 2018. He was buried alongside Olga at Woodland Cemetery in Miami.

Sources

Interviews with Rodolfo and Olga Arias, July 6, 20, and 23, 2008

Echevarria, Roberto Gonzalez. *The Pride of Habana* (New York: Oxford University Press, 1999).

Figueredo, Jorge S. *Cuban Baseball A Statistical History, 1878-1961* (Jefferson: McFarland & Company Inc., 2003).

Figueredo, Jorge S. *Who's Who in Cuban Baseball, 1878-1961* (Jefferson: McFarland & Company Inc., 2003).

Torres, Angel. *La Leyenda del Beisbol Cubano, 1878-1997* (Review Printers, 1996).

Notes

1 Interviews with Rudy Arias, 2008.
2 Arias interviews.
3 Arias interviews.

EARL BATTEY

By Jack Herrman

Earl Jesse Battey, Jr. was one of the top defensive catchers in the American League in the early 1960s. His Twins teams were in contention for the pennant in 1962 and 1967, and won the pennant in 1965, losing the World Series to Sandy Koufax and the Los Angeles Dodgers in seven games. Battey was also a part-time player for the pennant-winning 1959 White Sox, though he did not appear in the World Series.

Battey was born in Los Angeles on January 5, 1935, to Earl and Esther Battey. In his own words, "I was the oldest of three brothers and seven sisters. My father was a construction foreman in Whittier, just outside metropolitan Los Angeles. He pitched for the Seventh-Day Adventist Church, and my mother, believe it or not, caught for the Nine-O ladies team that played at church outings."[1] Battey attended Jordan High School in the Watts neighborhood of Los Angeles. There he was scouted by the White Sox. According to Bob Vanderberg, *Chicago Tribune* assistant sports editor, "Billy Pierce told me the story that when the Sox were in California training, Paul Richards after practice asked Billy to go with him to see a high-school game. When Billy asked why, Richards told him about a great young catcher [Battey] who supposedly was the best in the country."[2] White Sox scout Hollis Thurston signed Battey to a $3,999 contract. His mother was ill and his family needed the money. At that time, a player signing for a bonus of $4,000 or more had to be kept on the major-league roster for at least two years.

After high school the White Sox sent Battey to play for Colorado Springs in the Western League in 1953, and then to Waterloo in the Three-I League in 1954, where he hit .292, played in 129 of Waterloo's 135 games and was the league's rookie of the year. He spent most of 1955 in Triple-A, with Charleston, West Virginia, of the American Association. In a 1964 book that Jackie Robinson put together concerning integration in baseball, Battey said he encountered segregation for the first time playing in the minors. His Los Angeles neighborhood had a mix of races and no segregation. In the minors there was no problem at the ballpark, but he was forced to eat and sleep apart from his white teammates in some of the road cities, including Wichita and Louisville, as well as at home during the year he played for Charleston.[3] He was a late-season callup to the White Sox when the roster expanded and made his first appearance in September of 1955. He also played in Chicago briefly at the beginning and end of 1956, but spent most of that year with Toronto of the International League, where he hit .178 in 101 at-bats. Of that season, Battey explained: "I was knocked out in a play at home plate. I suffered a knee injury that kept bothering me when I finally got back in the lineup."[4]

Healthier, Battey hit .331 in winter ball in Venezuela and impressed new manager and former catcher Al Lopez during spring training with the White Sox in 1957. When the major-league roster was cut to 28 on Opening Day and then 25 a month into the season, Battey stayed with the team. He continued to impress defensively as a fill-in when regular catcher Sherman Lollar needed a rest. On June 4 the White Sox were in first place with a five-game lead, and Battey was one of a number of bright spots. Manager Lopez said, "I've tried to rest Sherman Lollar as often as possible. Having a good young catcher like Earl Battey gives us the chance to rest Sherman, of course. The development of Battey has been one of my pleasant surprises."[5] Battey's hitting didn't hold up, however. Later in June Lollar broke his wrist in a game against the Orioles and Battey and Les Moss shared the catching duties as Lollar missed 41 games. Lopez said: "Neither can measure up to Lollar. Lollar would have won one more game against the Yankees. Battey was up with the bases loaded and he struck out. We went on to lose, 6-5."[6] Battey hit only .174 in 48 games with the White Sox that year and in August he was optioned to the Los Angeles Angels of the Pacific Coast League. His hitting improved at that level and in winter ball in Venezuela he again hit over .300. He hit well in spring training of 1958 ("I now have the confidence that I can hit major-league pitching."[7]) and made the major-league roster again. He showed more power (eight home runs in 68 games) and spent the whole season in the majors for the first time, but still hit only .226.

• EARL BATTEY •

Earl Battey saw little playing time with the 1959 White Sox as a third-string catcher behind Sherm Lollar and John Romano. Traded to the Senators prior to the 1960 season, he developed into an All-Star and three-time Gold Glove winner.

The 1959 season was catcher John Romano's first full season with the White Sox, and his presence limited Battey's playing time. In a preseason article, the *Chicago Tribune* speculated about moving Lollar to first if Battey or Romano began to hit with power.[8] Romano did, and caught 38 games while hitting .294. Battey appeared in only 26 games, catching in 20, as he hit .219. Lollar won his third consecutive Gold Glove as the No. 1 backstop. Battey made the White Sox World Series roster in 1959, but saw no action as Lopez relied on the veteran Lollar to start all six games. (John Romano didn't do much better; he got one at-bat in the Series.)

The 1959 team had been built on pitching, speed, and defense. Before the 1960 season began, the White Sox traded some of their young players in order to get some established power. The management wanted 1957 American League home-run champion Roy Sievers from the Washington Senators. The Senators asked for Battey and infielder Sammy Esposito, but Lopez opposed that trade, saying he was "reluctant to give up 'two players who figure to be regulars for the Senators.'"[9] In early April 1960, however, the White Sox offered Battey, minor-league first baseman Don Mincher, and cash for Sievers, and the Senators accepted.

Lopez was right; Battey became a regular for the Senators in 1960. No longer in the shadow of Sherm Lollar, he blossomed into an American League star. He led the league in games caught by a catcher (136), putouts, and assists, but also in errors and passed balls, and he won the first of three consecutive Gold Gloves. Washington won more than 70 games for the first time since 1953 and Battey was voted the team MVP. The right-handed batter drove in 60 runs and hit .270. He finished eighth in AL MVP voting.

The Senators moved to Minnesota and were renamed the Twins for the 1961 campaign. Battey hit over .300 for the only time in his career (.302) and hit 17 homers as he caught in 131 games. He asked for a $1,300 raise from the Twins' owner, Calvin Griffith, but Griffith was noted for being tight with a dollar. "I was quite elated with my season," Battey recalled. "I had never hit over .300 in the majors. But he said, 'We finished in seventh even with you hitting .302,' and he didn't see any reason for a raise."[10]

Metropolitan Stadium was an exciting place for the Twins in the next couple of years. Both the Twins and the Los Angeles Angels challenged the Yankees in 1962 before falling back. The Twins finished second by five games. Battey made the All-Star team for the first time, getting 150 votes from the players and coaches to Romano's 84. Both the AP and UPI postseason polls voted him the best catcher in baseball. He had 17 home runs at the All-Star break the next year and was again voted the starter for the American League, outpolling eventual league MVP Elston Howard, 196 to 70, in the vote among players and coaches. Despite 26 homers, he was fourth in homers for the power-laden Twins. Harmon Killebrew had 45, Bob Allison, 35, and rookie Jimmie Hall, 33. Killebrew finished fourth in league MVP voting and Battey was seventh. The Twins led the league in homers (225), runs (767), and batting average (.255), but were eighth in defense. They won 91 games, but finished third behind the Yankees and White Sox.

The Twins dropped below .500 in 1964 for the first time since 1961. Battey was injured several times, but still caught 125 games. His most spectacular injury occurred when he was knocked out hitting his head against a chair after making a diving catch over a railing on May 10.[11] He had reported to spring training at 260 pounds, a fact that caused the Twins to make $1,000 of his salary dependent on reporting at no more than 230 pounds the following spring. He also reinjured his right knee and was batting .220 at the end of June, but rallied to finish with .272. He did not make the All-Star team in 1964.

In 1965 the Twins, behind great pitching from starters Jim Grant, Jim Kaat, and Jim Perry, excellent relief work from veteran Al Worthington, and an excellent offense led by batting champion Tony Oliva, won 102 games and took the American League pennant by seven games over the White Sox. Always known for his great arm, Battey threw out 26 of the 54 runners who attempted to steal with him behind the plate that year, according to Retrosheet data. Earl hit .297 and was selected to start the All-Star Game. Though he struck out only 23 times all season, he fanned five times in the World Series against the Dodgers, including twice against Koufax, with two runners on in the first inning and with one runner on in the ninth inning of Sandy's three-hit shutout in Game Seven. A factor in Battey's .120 hitting performance in the Series was an injury he sustained in the seventh inning of Game Three. He hit his throat against a dugout railing in Dodger Stadium while chasing a foul pop hit by Willie Davis. He left the game, but returned to start every game in the Series. Nonetheless, the Dodgers stole nine bases in winning the three games played in Los Angeles after losing the first two in Minneapolis.

The Twins kept essentially the same lineup in the following year, 1966, and won 89 games, but couldn't keep pace with the Baltimore Orioles and finished in second place, nine games out. Battey's batting average dropped to .255, but he made the All-Star team as a reserve after Bill Freehan outpointed him among votes from the players and coaches, 111 to 95. Over the first six years of the Twins' residence in Minneapolis, Battey had, despite frequent injuries, played in 805 of the Twins' 972 games.

The 1967 season was Battey's last as a player. It was the year of the exciting four-team race for the pennant among the Twins, White Sox, Tigers, and Red Sox, but Earl was frequently injured and lost his starting job to Jerry Zimmerman. On May 18, after Jim Kaat was knocked out of the box for his eighth consecutive start, manager Sam Mele sent Kaat to the bullpen temporarily and benched Battey. Zimmerman injured his finger on July 17 and Battey played for a while, but then he was placed on the 21-day disabled list on August 9 after a foul ball dislocated his thumb. He ended up playing in only 48 games that year, catching in 41, and hitting .165. The Twins finished in a tie for second place, one game out. He announced his retirement on November 3 after a season "plagued by injuries."[12]

In April of 1968, Battey "accepted a job as baseball consultant to Consolidated Edison … to help run the [NYC] power company's part of a baseball-community relations program."[13] It was known as the Con-Ed Answer Man program. Con-Ed would buy Yankees tickets and give them free to inner-city kids. The youngsters attended the game with Battey, "combination chaperone and the Con-Ed Answer Man (He answered their baseball questions)."[14]

In 1980 Battey enrolled at Bethune-Cookman University in Daytona Beach, Florida. He finished his undergraduate studies in 2½ years. After graduating he taught high school and coached baseball in Ocala, Florida.

Battey was named the catcher on the Twins' 40th-anniversary all-time team in 2000, and attended a reunion ceremony. He died of cancer on November 15, 2003. He and his wife, Sonia, had five children (Earl, Corey, Darren, Brenda, and Barbara) and, at the time of his death, four grandchildren.

Since his death a number of Twins teammates have recognized Battey's contribution during the 1960s. "Earl was a great storyteller, and he could tell them both in Spanish and English," second baseman Frank Quilici said. "He had the biggest personality on the team. That was as close a group of players as I've been around, and Earl was probably the main reason." Harmon Killebrew said, "Earl had two very important things going for him. He was a fun guy in the clubhouse. More importantly, he had everyone's respect, because he had sore knees, sore hands, sore everything, but he stayed in the lineup. I didn't realize how good of a catcher Earl was until he was gone."[15] Sam Mele, his manager from midway through 1961 to midway through 1967, said, "He was one of the best catchers I had in my life. He ran the pitching staff, I don't mind telling you: He was the leader of my ballclub."[16]

• EARL BATTEY •

Earl Battey had a great career with the Twins, and one can only wonder if the White Sox would have been better off keeping him. As one White Sox blogger has noted, the Sox came close in 1964, and if they had kept one or two their young nucleus of future All-Stars — Battey, Johnny Callison, Norm Cash, Barry Latman, or John Romano — they might have won a pennant in the 1960s.[17] In an interview with the *Chicago Tribune* in 1968, farm director Glen Miller shook his head, "as if to say 'never again,' when he [thought] of John Callison, Earl Battey, and Norm Cash, all of whom were Sox property."[18]

Notes

1. Jack R. Robinson and Charles Dexter, *Baseball Has Done It* (New York: J.P. Lippincott Company, 1964), 183.
2. Mark Liptak, "Remembering Earl Battey," Whitesoxintereactive.com aka FlyingSock.com, 2004.
3. Robinson and Dexter, 184.
4. "Battey to Stay with Sox," *Chicago Defender*, April 27, 1957
5. David Condon, "In the Wake of the News," *Chicago Tribune*, June 4, 1957.
6. Edward Prell, *Chicago Tribune*, August 2, 1957.
7. Russ J. Cowens, "Lopez Lauds Battey," *Chicago Defender*, March 18, 1958.
8. Edward Prell, *Chicago Tribune*, January 20, 1959.
9. Edward Prell, "Lopez Opposes Sox Deal for Sievers," *Chicago Tribune*, March 30, 1960.
10. Jon Roe, LaVelle E. Neal III, and John Millea, "Memories of Calvin," *Minneapolis Star Tribune*, October 21, 1999.
11. A Smashing Catch," UPI Telephoto, *Chicago Tribune*, May 11, 1964.
12. *Chicago Tribune*, November 4, 1967.
13. *Chicago Tribune*, April 23, 1968.
14. Blog posted by "Tim" on March 21, 2007, in response to "Absence of African-Americans in Baseball: Crisis or Fact of Life?", "Extra Bases" section of 108 magazine, 108mag.typepad.com/extra_bases/2007/03/absence_of_afri.html.
15. Patrick Reusse, " '65 in 05: A Twins Reunion," *Minneapolis Star Tribune*, August 19, 2005.
16. Jim Souhan, "Twins Notes: Battey joins team Hall," *Minneapolis Star Tribune*, June 6, 2004.
17. Mark Liptak, "Remembering Earl Battey."
18. Richard Dozer, "Meetings May Determine 'Untouchables'," *Chicago Tribune*, September 19, 1968.

RAY BOONE
By Joe Wancho

On July 15, 2003, Ray Boone was taking in the scene at the All-Star Game at Chicago's U.S. Cellular Field. "Anybody that's not proud in this situation," he said, "there's something wrong with them."[1] As the patriarch of the first three-generation family in the major leagues, Boone had reason to beam with pride. His son Bob spent 19 years as a catcher, primarily with Philadelphia and California. His two grandsons, Aaron, an infielder with Cincinnati, and Bret, a second baseman with Seattle, were both participating in the 2003 Midsummer Classic. The Boone family was not only the first family to have three generations play in the majors but also the first and only family to have all members in each generation participate in the All-Star Game. Ray was a two-time All-Star for Detroit, in 1954 and 1956; Bob was a four-time All-Star, in 1976, '78, '79, and '83. Another son, Rod, played in the Kansas City Royals and Houston Colts minor-league systems, and Ray's daughter, Terry, was a champion swimmer.

Boone played in 89 games, batting a solid .306 with Wausau, but put his baseball career on hold by enlisting in the Navy in 1942. He missed the 1943, '44, and '45 seasons. After his discharge, in 1946, the Indians assigned Boone to Wilkes-Barre, Pennsylvania, of the Class-A Eastern League. He split catching duties with Ralph Weigel and hit .258. On October 12, 1946, Boone married his high school sweetheart, Patsy Brown. In 1947 Boone was assigned to Oklahoma City of the Class-AA Texas League, where he began the season splitting catching duties with Ray Murray. When injuries struck the club, manager Pat Ankenman asked Boone to finish the season at shortstop. He brought his average up slightly, to .264.

As spring training opened in 1948, Cleveland player-manager Lou Boudreau kept Boone as the third-string catcher and also had him take infield practice as a possible backup to Boudreau at shortstop. With defensive stalwart Jim Hegan behind the plate, the Indians had no room for Boone, who wanted to play every day. Boone asked Boudreau if he could be sent to Hollywood of the Pacific Coast League. Boudreau granted Boone's request, but three weeks later, hitting .250 for Hollywood, Boone was returned to Oklahoma City. There, his bat caught fire, and he was leading the league with a .355 batting average when the Indians recalled him on August 27. Because Boone played in only 87 games at Oklahoma City, he fell short of the 100-game minimum needed to qualify for the batting title. He did, however, make the Texas League All-Star team.

Boone made his debut for the Indians on September 3, 1948, in St. Louis. He relieved Boudreau at shortstop midway through the first game of a doubleheader and doubled in a run in the eighth inning. For the month, Boone appeared in six games and had five plate appearances. Because he had been called up in August, he was eligible to play in the World Series, in which the Indians faced the Boston Braves. In Game Five, Boone faced Braves great Warren Spahn as he pinch-hit for right fielder Walt Judnich in the eighth inning. Spahn, who was working in relief of Boston starting pitcher Nels Potter, struck Boone out on the way to an 11-5 victory. It was Boone's only appearance in the World Series. The Tribe came back to win Game Six behind starter Bob Lemon, and Cleveland won its first World Series since 1920.

On June 6, 1949, Boudreau named Boone his starting shortstop when the player-manager took over at third base to replace the slumping Ken Keltner. Boone responded by hitting the first two home runs of his career on June 15 at Fenway Park, belting the first off Walt Masterson and the second off Ellis Kinder. Boone played in 76 games at shortstop for the Tribe, and committed 21 errors. His batting average was a modest .252. Boone struggled in learning a new position and replacing the popular Boudreau who, while nearing the end of his playing career, had starred for nearly a decade. Boone had a pep talk with himself. "Raymond, what now?", Boone said. "You have been a catcher all your baseball life. Now you are told you could be a good shortstop. You belong to Cleveland and the Indians have the greatest shortstop the American League has ever seen. Connie Mack says so."[2]

• RAY BOONE •

The Tribe faced major changes with the approach of the 1950 season. Al Rosen took over at third base for Ken Keltner, who was released on the first day of the season and signed the same day with the Red Sox. Boone replaced Boudreau at shortstop on a full-time basis, and Bobby Avila was splitting second base duties with Joe Gordon. Luke Easter became the first baseman when the Tribe shipped Mickey Vernon to Washington on June 14.

Out of options, neither Avila nor Rosen nor Boone could be sent to the minors again without the Indians risking losing them. Given every chance to make good, Boone batted .301 in 106 games, third best on the team behind Larry Doby and Dale Mitchell. Cleveland finished a close fourth, six games behind the eventual world champion Yankees.

Released on November 21, Boudreau signed with the Red Sox (as a player) six days later. Al Lopez replaced Boudreau as Cleveland's manager. Boone now had the shortstop position all to himself. Nevertheless, he could never quite seem secure in the shortstop spot, having so-so seasons in 1951 and 1952, during which he hit .233 and .263 respectively and made 26 and a league-leading 33 errors.

In 1952, the Indians finished only two games behind the Yankees, and Boone received much of the criticism for his team's falling short. Late in the season, Lopez benched Boone in favor of George Strickland, who had come to the Tribe in a trade with Pittsburgh in August. Boone alone did not experience defensive lapses, as Rosen, Boone, Avila, and Easter combined for 94 errors, the most of any infield in 1952.

General manager Hank Greenberg continued to back Boone. "I will tell you something about Boone," said Greenberg. "Many people in Cleveland think we ought to get rid of him. If we do, I know of at least four American League clubs that would be happy to have him. It's easy for someone to see that a player has had a bad season. It isn't so easy to find a fellow who is certain to do better. If Boone is not a big-league shortstop, why are those four other clubs anxious to get him?"[3]

Boone beat out Strickland for the starting shortstop position in 1953, but by June, the Indians had kept Strickland while unloading Boone. After the Yankees swept the Indians in a four-game series just before the June 15 trading deadline, Greenberg traded Boone (hitting .241 in 34 games) and pitchers Al Aber, Steve Gromek, and Dick Weik to Detroit for pitchers Art Houtteman and Bill Wight, infielder Owen Friend, and catcher Joe Ginsberg. Initially, Cleveland was thought to have gotten the better of the deal since Houtteman was considered to have great potential, although he had struggled since winning 19 games in 1950 for Detroit.

Detroit manager Fred Hutchinson immediately inserted Boone at third base, and Ray responded by going 3-for-3 with a home run to lead the Tigers to a 5-3 victory over the Red Sox at Fenway Park on June 16. Hutchinson liked the left side of his infield now that Boone manned third base alongside rookie shortstop Harvey Kuenn. "With Boone and Kuenn," Hutchinson said, "I believe we can figure that the left side of the infield is in good hands for at least five years."[4]

Boone's offense and defense improved dramatically as a result of his relocation to third base after joining the Tigers. In 31 games at shortstop with Cleveland that season, he had made eight errors for a .952 fielding percentage. After the trade, Boone played in 97 games at third base for Detroit, making

Prior to joining the White Sox at the tail-end of his career, Ray Boone was a two-time All-Star who tied for the American League RBI crown in 1955.

14 errors with a fielding percentage of .958. He hit .312 with 22 home runs and 93 runs batted in only 101 games for the Tigers. Boone tied a major-league record since broken by hitting four grand slams in a season. Tigers general manager Charlie Gehringer was impressed. "He found himself at third at Detroit and gained confidence in the field. That helped his batting," Gehringer said. "I always considered him a sound hitter. He isn't fooled often. Have you noticed how he guards the plate and tries to hit to right field when the count is two strikes? Other hitters would profit if they did this instead of taking that last wild swing."[5]

While Boone became a fan favorite in Detroit, the Tigers were a second-division team for most of his time there, always appearing to lack both pitching and power hitting. During Boone's five years with the Tigers, only he, Al Kaline, and Charlie Maxwell hit more than 20 home runs in a season, and no one hit more than 30.

Fans voted Boone the starting third baseman for the 1954 All-Star Game. The game took place in Cleveland, and Avila started at second base and Rosen at first. Rosen hit a three-run home run off Robin Roberts of the Phillies in the bottom of the third inning, and Boone followed his old roommate with a solo shot off Roberts. Boone ended the 1954 season hitting .295 with 20 home runs and 85 runs batted in. New York Yankees manager Casey Stengel said, "In my book, that Ray Boone of the Tigers is the best clutch hitter we face in the course of the season. There's a guy who makes you give him good pitches. Then, when you give them to him, he's apt to belt 'em a mile." [6]

In 1955, Bucky Harris replaced Hutchinson as the Tigers' manager in a year that saw Boone develop injury issues, a problem that plagued him for the rest of his career. Boone suffered from aching knees, which worsened the more he played. Doctors discovered that he had calcium deposits in his knees, a condition he had suffered from since boyhood. But he overcame both a slow start and the injuries to tie Boston outfielder Jackie Jensen for the American League RBI crown at 116, and batted .284. In 1956 he hit .308 with 25 home runs, and again made the All-Star Team, appearing as a pinch-hitter at the game in Griffith Stadium in Washington.

In 1957, new Detroit manager Jack Tighe moved Boone to first base to minimize the wear and tear on his knees, which required regular cortisone injections. The Tigers had acquired Jim Finigan from Kansas City to play third base, and Boone approved of his new position. "I believe I can play more games there," he said. "If my knee acts up later in the season like it did last year, I feel I can stay in the lineup at first base. I couldn't do that at third base."[7] But his batting average dropped off to .273 and his RBIs fell to 65.

In 1958, the Tigers added some veterans by bringing in Billy Martin to play shortstop (Kuenn moved to center field) and Boone's former teammate Jim Hegan from Cleveland to help the young pitching staff. Boone started the season manning first base for the Tigers, but finished the year playing the same position for the White Sox. On June 15, 1958, five years to the day after Detroit had traded for Boone, he was sent along with pitcher Bob Shaw to Chicago for outfielder Tito Francona and pitcher Bill Fischer.

Boone performed steadily for the White Sox. His former manager at Cleveland, Al Lopez, inserted him at cleanup as part of a revamped batting order. Shortstop Luis Aparicio was dropped from leadoff to eighth. The leadoff spot and the third position were rotated between third baseman Billy Goodman and center fielder Jim Landis. Second baseman Nellie Fox batting second and catcher Sherm Lollar batting cleanup were for the most part the only constants in the batting order. The White Sox finished in second place, 10 games over .500, but 10 games behind New York. Between Cleveland and Chicago, Boone finished with a .242 average with 61 RBIs.

Relegated to the bench when the 1959 season started, Boone played sparingly in the early weeks. His best day came on April 24 in Cleveland, when he went 2-for-3 with a home run, had two RBIs, and scored a run. He had appeared in only nine games, going 5 for 21 (.238) with one home run and five RBIs, when the White Sox, looking for added power from the left side of the plate, dealt Boone to Kansas City for Harry Simpson on May 2. In spite of rumors that Boone, stilled plagued by his knee problems as well as bursitis, might retire rather than play with the Athletics, after a conversation with White Sox president Bill Veeck, Ray reported to Kansas City. After playing in 61 games for Kansas City and hitting .273, Boone was claimed on waivers in late August by the Milwaukee Braves, who were involved in a tight pennant race with the Los Angeles Dodgers and San Francisco Giants. Appearing mostly as a pinch-hitter, Boone got into only 13 games for Milwaukee in 1959 and in seven more in 1960 before being dealt again, this time to the Boston Red Sox. Released by the Red Sox on September 14 after batting just .205 in 34 games, Boone didn't think he could be of much value to any team given his knee pain, so he decided to retire. He had a lifetime batting average of .275 with 151 home runs and 737 RBIs.

Boone began a second career with the Red Sox, signing on as a scout to work in the San Diego area, a role he fulfilled for more than 30 years. He also served as an extra coach at spring training. He signed many players for the Red Sox, including Curt Schilling, Gary Allenson, Sam Horn, Marty Barrett, Phil Plantier, and Kevin Romine. Even after retiring as a full-time scout, Boone maintained an association with the Red Sox.

Ray Boone died on October 17, 2004, at the age of 81. He suffered a heart attack after being hospitalized after experiencing complications from intestinal surgery. Boone had also suffered from diabetes for many years. He was survived by his wife, Patsy, sons Bob and Rod, and daughter Terry. He also left nine grandchildren and five great-grandchildren.

Boone's memorial service was held on October 24, 2004. At the same time that his family and many friends were paying their last respects, Curt Schilling of the Red Sox was throwing the first pitch to start Game Two of the World Series at Fenway Park. The symbolism was not lost on those who were celebrating Ray Boone's life, for Boone had signed Schilling to his first major-league contract, in 1986 with Boston.

Bret Boone told the gathering at the memorial service, "All the stories I saw referred to (Ray) as the patriarch of the Boone family," Bret told the funeral assembly. "I looked up the word 'patriarch' to see exactly what that meant. It said a patriarch was the father and ruler of the family. That's what Gramps was."[8]

Notes

1 "Great Grandfather," *Sports Illustrated*, October 25, 2003.
2 Dan Daniel, "Converted Catcher Subs for Lou at Shortstop," *The Sporting News*, June 29, 1949.
3 Ed McAuley, "Trade Talks Bring High Henry Nothing But a Battered Ear," *The Sporting News,* October 15, 1952.
4 Watson Spoelstra, "Aber, Branca Join Hoeft in High Spots in Tiger Hill Plans," *The Sporting News,* August 26, 1953.
5 Watson Spoelstra, "Tigers First Division Club Since June," *The Sporting News,* September 23, 1953.
6 "Stengel Calls Ray Boone 'Mr. Clutch' of the Majors," *The Sporting News,* July 14, 1954.
7 Watson Spoelstra, "Boone Experiment Success, Feels at Home at First Base," *The Sporting News,* April 10, 1957.
8 Chris Jenkins, "Boones eulogize their patriarch at El Cajon services, *San Diego Union-Tribune*, October 25, 2004.

JOHNNY CALLISON

By John Rossi

Early in his 16-year major-league career, Johnny Callison was labeled "the next Mickey Mantle." His manager with the Phillies, Gene Mauch, said Callison could "run, throw, field, and hit with power. There's nothing he can't do well on the ball field."[1] These encomiums proved burdens that the always sensitive Callison found difficult to live up to. His career, spent briefly with the Chicago White Sox and then for 10 years with the Phillies before finishing with short stays with the Chicago Cubs and New York Yankees, was marked by what-ifs and what might-have-beens.

John Wesley Callison was born in Qualls, Oklahoma, on March 12, 1939, the son of Virgil (sometimes spelled Vergil) and Wilda (Faddis) Callison. The family supposedly had Native American roots. The Callisons were poor and his father worked odd jobs in and around Qualls in the dying days of the Great Depression. When Virgil joined the Army during World War II, Callison's mother traveled the path of many "Okies" before her and in 1944 took young Johnny, his brother, and his two sisters and settled in Bakersfield, California.

The quiet and shy Callison discovered that he had exceptional athletic skills. One of his teachers noted that he could run faster backward than most of his classmates could run forward. Sports became his way out of a life of poverty and hardscrabble work. He said later in life that he "found my refuge in baseball" because only on the ballfield did he feel "worthy of measuring up."[2]

Callison was a star athlete at East Bakersfield High School and especially stood out in baseball. The scouts were on his trail before he graduated from school, with the White Sox eventually signing him in 1957 for a bonus of $7,000 plus another $3,000 under the table. To ease his way into professional baseball, the White Sox assigned the 18-year-old Callison to his hometown team, the Bakersfield Bears of the Class C California League.

Callison made an impressive debut in 1957, hitting .340, rapping out 41 extra-base hits, and stealing 31 bases in just 86 games in a league that included such future major leaguers as third baseman Charlie Smith, pitcher Chuck Estrada, and outfielder Vada Pinson. Callison was named the league's outstanding rookie. The White Sox brass believed they had a superstar in the making and the next season jumped him all the way to their Indianapolis Indians team in the fast-paced Triple-A American Association. At 19, Callison was one step from the majors.

Callison's sophomore season saw the first comparison to his fellow Oklahoman, Mickey Mantle.[3] While Callison's average dipped to .283, he led the league with 29 home runs and drove in 93 runs while showing for the first time a cannon-like throwing arm. In September the White Sox brought Callison up for a taste of major-league life. He showed signs that he was ready for the big time by hitting .297 while driving in 12 runs in 18 games. The pitching-strong White Sox, who finished 10 games behind the Yankees in 1958, believed that they had a chance to win the pennant the next season. They brought Callison to spring training hoping that he would add some punch to their weak offense.

Callison made the team out of spring training but was a major disappointment, hitting just .173 with three homers in 49 games. He was sent back to Indianapolis in midseason. The always-competitive Callison was disgusted with himself and felt he had let the White Sox down. The White Sox brass decided that they needed to add offense to continue to compete with the Yankees; despite winning the pennant, they had finished last in the American League in home runs and sixth in batting in 1959. Callison became expendable.

In the offseason, the White Sox made two major trades to add power to their lineup. They got former home run champ Roy Sievers from Washington to play first base and exchanged Callison for third baseman Gene Freese, who had hit 23 home runs for the last-place Philadelphia Phillies.

The trade proved the making of Callison. Going to a developing team where there was no pressure to perform and especially coming under the tutelage of Gene Mauch, he blossomed into one of the premier players in the National League.

Callison's best years were with the Phillies from

JOHNNY CALLISON

1960 to 1969. His first two seasons were a learning process. Mauch loved his potential and made him a special project. In some ways, Mauch saw Callison as the kind of ballplayer he would have liked to be. Callison was not only Mauch's special project but also his pet. Mauch worked on smoothing out the 5-foot-10, 175-pound Callison's left-handed swing and getting him to hit to left field. Mauch also encouraged the speedy Callison to occasionally drag bunt as a way to sharpen his batting eye and upset the defense. By 1961 Callison was showing signs of brilliance. One-third of his hits that season went for extra bases, including ten triples, the first of five consecutive years in which he reached double figures in that category. He led the league in triples with 16 in 1965. His 84 three-baggers for the Phillies rank him sixth in the team's all-time list through 2012. He also ranked 12th in doubles and 12th in home runs in Phillies history.

Mauch tried Callison in left field but that didn't make the best use of his great throwing arm. Beginning in 1962, Callison became the Phillies' regular right fielder, quickly mastering the tricky bounces off Connie Mack Stadium's 34-foot-high wall. From 1962 through 1965, Callison led all right fielders in the majors with 90 assists – quite a feat when you consider that the great Roberto Clemente, possessor of one of the strongest arms in the major leagues at the time, had 59.

The 1962 campaign proved Callison's breakthrough season. He hit .300 for the first and only time in his career – Mauch benched him on the last day of the season to keep his average over the .300 mark. Callison hit 23 homers, tying the record for the most home runs by a Phillies left-handed hitter since the right-field wall in Connie Mack Stadium was raised in height. Then he broke that mark in each of the next three seasons. His 32 home runs in 1965 were the most for any left-hander in the history of Connie Mack Stadium. The 34-foot-high right-field wall probably cost the pull-hitting Callison a number of homers during his ten years with the Phillies.

Arguably, Callison's greatest season came in 1964, the ill-fated season when the Phillies blew a 6½-game lead with 12 games to play and lost the pennant. Playing in all 162 games, Callison hit .274, scored 101 runs, and drove in 104 while banging out 31 homers. He won the All-Star Game with a dramatic ninth-inning, three-run homer off Dick Radatz. That home run became Callison's most enduring memory. He said he was asked about that

Considered the White Sox' best hitting prospect, Johnny Callison was traded to the Phillies after the 1959 season for journeyman Gene Freese. With Philadelphia, Callison blossomed into an All-Star.

feat so many times that he felt like Bill Murray in the film *Groundhog Day*.[4]

During the Phillies' ten-game losing streak, Callison, along with rookie sensation Dick Allen, was one of the few Phillies players to hold his own, hitting .275 with four home runs. Unlike some others, Callison didn't blame Mauch for the team's late-season collapse: "It wasn't all Gene's fault. We played!"[5]

Callison probably would have won the Most Valuable Player Award that season but for the Phillies' pennant collapse. As it was, he finished second to Ken Boyer of the St. Louis Cardinals.

Callison twice hit three home runs in a game for the Phillies, the first against the Milwaukee Braves during the 10-game losing streak in 1964. The second time came a year later, June 6, 1965, against the Chicago Cubs.

Callison had another solid year for the Phillies in 1965, hitting 32 homers and driving in 101 runs. Then, beginning in 1966, his power numbers dropped precipitously. He hit just 11 home runs in 1966 and never hit more than 20 again. Beginning in 1966, Callison's power numbers continued to decline. His slugging percentage reached a peak of .509 in 1965, but dropped over 100 points two years later.

At 27, Callison effectively was finished as a major-league power hitter. What happened to him isn't clear. He claimed he suffered a number of nagging injuries – to his legs in particular – that destroyed his ability to play. In 1966 he complained of problems with his eyes. He tried wearing glasses and even adopted a vigorous exercise program that Carl Yastrzemski said benefited his own career. But nothing worked. In baseball circles it was believed that Callison had lost his self-confidence. Even at the height of his success in 1964, Callison had admitted that he was "the biggest worrier around" in an article in *Sport* magazine.[6]

After three more undistinguished years with the Phillies, Callison was traded to the Chicago Cubs after the 1969 season with pitcher Larry Colton for pitcher Dick Selma and outfielder Oscar Gamble. He loved playing with Cubs but couldn't stand manager Leo Durocher, whom he blamed for some of his troubles, claiming that Durocher almost drove him out of baseball.[7] Callison stayed with the Cubs for two seasons but clashed with Durocher over playing time. In July 1970, while Callison was in the midst of a good season, he wrote that Durocher "got a wild hair up his ass" and began platooning him. Callison found sitting on the bench "torture."[8] Despite playing in 147 games in the season, Callison got to bat only 477 times, an indication that Durocher was pinch-hitting for him at times. That was Callison's last decent season; he hit .264 with 19 home runs while driving in 68 runs. After the 1971 season, he was traded to the New York Yankees, and he finished his career there in 1973.

After retiring, Callison worked in a variety of jobs including car salesman and bartender, none of which suited his talents. He longed to get back into baseball in some capacity but never found a place. For years he attended the Phillies' fantasy camps in Florida, where he was popular with both the fantasy players and his former teammates.

Callison married his high-school sweetheart, Dianne Hammitt, while still in school. Along with their three daughters, Lori, Cindy, and Sherri, they resided for years in Glenside, a small town outside Philadelphia.

Callison's health was poor after his retirement from baseball. He suffered from a serious case of ulcers, experienced a heart attack, and eventually died from cancer on October 12, 2006, at the age of 67.

Despite the decline of his careers with the Phillies after the 1965 season, Callison still has a significant place in the team's records. Through 2012 he was among the top 10 Phillies in games played in the outfield, triples, and extra-base hits. For five years, from 1962 through 1966, he was the idol of the city and easily the most popular player on the team. All in all, not a bad record to leave.

Sources

In addition to the sources cited in the Notes, the author also consulted:

Rossi, John P. *The 1964 Phillies: The Story of Baseball's Most Memorable Collapse* (Jefferson, North Carolina: McFarland, 2005).

Westcott, Rich. *Philadelphia's Old Ballparks* (Philadelphia: Temple University Press, 1996).

Notes

1. John Wesley Callison with John Austin Sletten, *The Johnny Callison Story* (New York: Vantage Press, 1991), 10.
2. Ibid.
3. Rich Westcott and Frank Bilovsky, *The New Phillies Encyclopedia* (Philadelphia: Temple University Press, 1993).
4. Don Bostrom, "Johnny Callison's Most Memorable Moment," home.onemain.com.
5. Stan Hochman. "The Survivors of '64': Johnny Callison," in Richard Orodenker, *The Phillies Reader* (Philadelphia: Temple University Press, 1996), 172.
6. Johnny Callison, "I'm the Biggest Worrier Around," *Sport*, July 1965.
7. Hochman, 175.
8. Callison with Sletten, 182.

CAMILO CARREON

By Justin Thompson

Even though he preferred the comforts of home, whether in his California birthplace or his eventual hometown of Tucson, Arizona, Cam Carreon's batting stroke never showed signs of homesickness. Reaching the majors at the age of 22, he contributed to a contending White Sox team for several seasons (1959-64) and played briefly for the Indians and Orioles until a shoulder injury and a desire to see his children grow up combined to end his playing career. After leaving the major leagues, Carreon remained involved with the game and made a large impact in his local communities that was still being felt more than 20 years after his passing.

Camilo Garcia Carreon was born in the Southern California town of Colton to Miguel and Socorro (Garcia) Carreon on August 6, 1937. His father had immigrated to Colton from the state of Durango in Mexico and was employed at a cement plant in Colton for 30 years. Camilo was the youngest of five children. The family lived in a home next to a set of railroad tracks. Camilo honed his hitting as a boy by hitting rocks pitched to him, or ones that he tossed in the air to himself and swatted with a bat for hours at a time.

Carreon was a standout athlete at Colton Union High School, competing in football and basketball in addition to catching for the baseball team. As a senior in 1956, he was the captain of the baseball team and was named All-Conference catcher. After graduating from high school in 1956, Carreon played with the semipro Colton Lumbermen and worked for a local honey company. He also gained some experience playing for a semipro outfit in Bandon, Oregon, named the Millers. While playing for the Millers, he worked as a lumberman in Bandon.

While playing for the Lumbermen in June 1956, Carreon drew the attention of a pair of scouts for the Chicago White Sox, Hollis Thurston and Doc Bennett. They signed Cam for the White Sox and he finished out the year in Holdredge of the Class D Nebraska State League, the equivalent at the time of a rookie league. His first full season of professional baseball came with Duluth-Superior of the Class C Northern League. He played at Duluth-Superior for two seasons and moved up to Colorado Springs of the Class-A Western League in 1958. His performance that season drew the attention of the Chicago press, and a *Chicago Sun-Times* article quoted scout Jack Sheehan as saying he believed Carreon was the "most powerful fellow of all" of a group of White Sox farmhands that included Norm Cash, Johnny Callison, and Don Mincher.[1] Carreon validated Sheehan's praise by hitting .342 for Colorado Springs.

For Carreon, 1959 was a banner year. In February, he married his high-school sweetheart, Dolores Atellcio. When the season started, he was assigned to Indianapolis of the Triple-A American Association. He hit .311 for the Indians, and hit for the cycle in a mid-August game. His achievements were enough to earn him the Robert E. Hoey Memorial Award, given to the league's outstanding rookie. To top off 1959, Carreon was called up to Chicago in September and had one at-bat for the American League champions, on the last day of the season in Detroit. He replaced Johnny Romano behind the plate in the bottom of the sixth inning and flied out to left field against Pete Burnside in the eighth. Needless to say, it was Sherm Lollar who caught for the White Sox in the World Series.

But 1960 again found Carreon plying his trade in the minor leagues, this time in San Diego, with another September call-up. On the 18th, he collected his first major-league hit, a single in the second game of a doubleheader in Detroit that he started. He broke camp with the team in 1961 and served as the backup to the 36-year-old Lollar, batting .271 in 229 at-bats. In 1962, roles were reversed and Cam received the majority of the playing time at catcher for the White Sox, with Lollar serving in the reserve role. Carreon played in 103 games, hitting .256 with 37 RBIs. He rebounded to hit .274 in 1963.

As Carreon became established as the starting catcher for the competitive White Sox of the early 1960s, he was approached by the Campbell's Soup Company, which wanted him as a spokesman to appeal to its Mexican market. But according to his wife, Chicago had not affected Cam's homebody tendencies, and even though Campbell's offered to provide him with travel back and forth to Chicago, he declined because of his desire to be back home throughout the offseason.[2]

Colton remained home in his early career. Cam, or Camel, as he had been known to friends in high school in Colton, worked as a car salesman in the offseasons. Over time, he and Dolores took a liking to Arizona and moved to Tucson in the early 1960s. Nonetheless, Colton remained a part of their lives, as many of the family remained there. In 1968, Colton paid tribute to Cam by designating a local roadway as Carreon Drive for its hometown boy who made it to the big leagues.

Once the couple moved to Tucson, Carreon hung up his car salesman shoes and spent his offseasons playing winter ball in Latin America, which included stints in Colombia.

As a major leaguer, the promise in Carreon's bat remained unfulfilled as his career took shape. Some had raved about his power while he was a prospect, but it had not developed in his minor-league career. He hit over .300 three times in the minors, but as the 1963 season approached, he carried a career major-league batting line of .261 with an on-base percentage of .327 and a slugging average of .354. He continued to struggle at the plate until a hot streak beginning in late July and extending into August brought his average to .302. An article by Jerome Holtzman in the *Chicago Sun-Times* quoted Carreon as crediting manager Al Lopez for his success. He said, "Before, I'd raise up and sweep at the ball. I don't move up any more. Instead, I'm stepping and striding into the ball. It's made a big difference. I hit the ball solid now."[3]

Carreon cooled off over the rest of the season but still finished with his best batting average as a major leaguer, .274. There would be limited opportunity in the future to determine if he could carry over the improvement to future seasons. He hit the same .274 in 1964, but in only 37 games, largely because he injured his right shoulder badly while sliding into third base in June. Even before the injury, J.C. Martin had been receiving the majority of the playing time behind the plate, even though his production to that point had been worse than Carreon's. At the time of Carreon's injury, Martin was hitting .203 in 118 at-bats.

The shoulder injury proved to be the beginning of the end for Cam Carreon in the major leagues. In January 1965 he was part of a three-team trade that landed him in Cleveland. A season with the Indians that saw limited playing time (52 at-bats with a .231 batting average) was followed by a trade to Baltimore in March 1966 for (then) minor leaguer Lou Piniella.

Carreon played in only four games for the Orioles in 1966. They were his last major-league appearances. He spent most of the season in Baltimore's Triple-A team at Rochester. The next season was more of the same as he appeared in 62 games for Rochester and Jacksonville and hit a combined .145. As his career took this nomadic turn and he continued to struggle with the effects of his 1964 shoulder injury, he was faced with a decision. Cam had always told Dolores that once their children began school, he wanted to stay home with them in Tucson and help raise them. She didn't believe he would follow through, and told an interviewer in 2008 that she wasn't certain what part the injury may have played in his decision. As their first child, Michael, began school, however, Carreon decided to retire from a playing career and stay home in Tucson with his family rather than try to hang on with a major-league team. A daughter, Camille, and a son, future major leaguer Mark Carreon, were already part of the family and Cam was happy to be home in Tucson to see them grow. Another son, Manuel, and a daughter, Christine, would follow. Mark broke in with the Mets in 1987 and enjoyed a 10-year major-league career.

Cam Carreon ended his time in the majors with a .264 lifetime average, 11 home runs, and 114 runs batted in. He was a good defensive catcher with only 13 errors in 320 games and a .993 fielding average.

Carreon enjoyed being close to his family, but he was not entirely through with professional baseball. When the Tucson Toros franchise joined the Pacific Coast League in 1969, he was persuaded to end his one-year retirement and appeared in 57 games, collecting 31 hits (28 of them singles) in 119 at-bats. He shared catching duties with Jim Napier. (Coincidentally, Carreon's oldest son, Mike, became a Tucson firefighter working in the same station with Napier's son.) Carreon played for the Toros just in that one season but remained with the team as a coach through 1972.

Carreon enjoyed being a family man and being able to watch his children grow up in Tucson. After his time with the Toros, he was able to focus on providing instruction to his children in Little League and was heavily involved in amateur men's leagues in the area. The time spent with his sons bore fruit, as in addition to Mark's professional success, both Mike and Manny were standout players. Mike was a member of the Cactus Little League team that played in the 1973 Little League World Series championship

• CAMILO CARREON •

game, and Manny was a star in high school and played at Emporia State University.

Camilo Carreon's devotion to his children helped turn out a handful of adults that any parent would be proud of and who also revered their father for his guidance. His involvement with his friends and the baseball community in Tucson evoked many similar feelings. After a battle with cancer, Carreon died on September 2, 1987, at the age of 50. Six days later Mark made his debut in the major leagues as a September call-up of the Mets. On that day he pinch-hit for Sid Fernandez in the third inning and hit into a fielder's choice. Memorial services for Cam were well-attended both in Tucson and in Colton, where he is buried. Later, a memorial was dedicated in his honor at the El Rio Golf Course in Tucson, where he spent many afternoons with his closest friends. In 2006, Carreon was posthumously elected to the Colton Hall of Fame, the first Hispanic so honored. His family was present for the induction.

Carreon's memory lives on to this day, as his family and friends gather in Colton every August around the time of his birthday to celebrate his legacy and that of his mother, who also shared an August birthday. His influence is also felt in Tucson, where his son Manny took up Cam's role in the community, becoming involved in the amateur men's leagues in the area. As an employee of the Tucson Parks and Recreation Department he was in charge of preparing the grounds at Hi Corbett Field for the final homestand of the Toros in 1997. Both Manny's commitment to the community and Mark Carreon's 10-year career in the major leagues helped preserve the legacy of Camilo Carreon.[4]

Sources

In addition to the sources cited in the Notes, the author consulted Basbeall-Reference.com and the following sources:

Camilo Carreon spent eight seasons in the major leagues, including six with the White Sox, as a dependable backup catcher and occasional regular.

Burris, Jim. "Camilo Carreon Named A.A.'s No. 1 Freshman Player." American Association Service Bureau press release, August 30, 1959.

Carreon, Camilo. Chicago White Sox questionnaire, June 18, 1956. Chicago White Sox personnel file.

Carreon, Mark. Telephone interview. April 24, 2008.

Munzel, Edgar. "Injury To Carreon Hurt Sox," *Chicago Sun-Times*, September 29, 1964.

Notes

1. "Sox Tab Carrion [sic] For Future Power," *Chicago Sun-Times*, 1958 (exact date unknown).
2. Delores Carreon telephone interview, May 22, 2008.
3. Jerome Holtzman, "Carreon Credits Clouting Spree to Tips by Lopez," *Chicago Sun-Times*, August 20, 1963.
4. Greg Hansen, "Toros of Old Leave Their Mark on Tucson," *Arizona Daily Star*, September 3, 2008.

NORM CASH

By Maxwell Kates

Norm Cash would have loved it. The story drew upon metaphors including baseball, the Old West, and the camaraderie of friends. Its title, *City Slickers*, was evocative of the relationship between the burly cowboy and the legions of brewers, auto manufacturers, and teamsters who became his fans. The director, Billy Crystal, who also played the protagonist Mitch Robbins, later filmed a motion picture about the 1961 American League baseball season at Tiger Stadium. In a poignant scene, an elderly cattle driver named Curly, played by Jack Palance, teaches Mitch the meaning of life. Moments later, "Mitchy the Kid" delivers a calf, who he names Norman. Sadly, Norm Cash never had the opportunity to see *City Slickers*. It was released in theaters in 1991, five years after he drowned in a tragic boat accident. But just who was Norm Cash? He was a larger than life first baseman from Texas who lived, drank, and played hard, sang country and western in the clubhouse, and could be depended upon in clutch situations. This is his story.

Norman Dalton Cash was born on November 10, 1934, in Justiceburg, Texas. A railroad junction located southeast of Lubbock, Justiceburg boasted a population of 25 according to the 1925 population census. Fittingly, its most famous citizen wore 25 as his uniform number for most of his professional baseball career. Cash's most dominant childhood memories were of helping on the family farm: "My dad's life was hard work…he had 250 acres of fertile land and we grew cotton on 200 acres. I drove a tractor from the time I was ten. Sometimes I drove it ten to twelve hours."[1]

Working with a hoe on the farm also allowed him to develop his wrists. Ironically, those who knew Cash during his youth remember his athletic abilities, not on the baseball diamond but on the football gridiron. In 1955, during his senior year at Sul Ross State College in San Angelo, he set the school rushing record with 1,255 yards. Following graduation, Cash was even drafted in the 13th round as a halfback by the Chicago Bears. Instead, he chose baseball, signing with the Chicago White Sox as an outfielder on May 21, 1955. Meanwhile, Cash had married his childhood sweetheart, schoolteacher Myrta Bob Harper, on January 24, 1954.

After two seasons at Ft. Bliss, the left-handed hitter and fielder was promoted to Comiskey Park midway through the 1958 season. Cash was soon converted to a first baseman, and after some seasoning at Indianapolis, he was recalled by the White Sox in 1959. Playing backup to Earl Torgeson, Cash batted only .240 but fielded a stellar .993 in 31 games. The White Sox, led by speedy infielders Luis Aparicio and Nellie Fox, raced to the summit of the American League standings, hitting 46 triples and stealing 113 bases in 94 victories. The "Go-Go Sox" outdistanced second-place Cleveland by five games to capture their first pennant in 40 years. However, the Sox were badly overmatched by the Los Angeles Dodgers, losing the World Series in six games. Much like their 1906 predecessor, the '59 incarnation of the White Sox were, indeed, hitless wonders. Not even late season acquisition Ted Kluszewski could save the Sox from their 97 aggregate home runs and anemic .250 batting average. During the offseason, President Bill Veeck acquired veteran Roy Sievers, Gene Freese, and Minnie Minoso to bolster Chicago's offense. However, he was forced to mortgage his future prospects, including Earl Battey, Don Mincher, Johnny Callison – and Norm Cash. No match for Kluszewski and Torgeson, Cash was sent to Cleveland with Bubba Phillips and Johnny Romano in the seven-player Minoso deal on December 6, 1959.

Although Cash wore a Cleveland cap on his 1960 Topps baseball card, he never played an inning for the Indians. On April 12, as the Tribe headed north from Tucson at the conclusion of spring training, Cash found himself traded yet again. This time, he was dispatched to Detroit in exchange for outfielder Steve Demeter. Detroit general manager Rick Ferrell was dumbfounded when Frank Lane, his Cleveland counterpart, offered Cash for Demeter, unsure if he meant "cold cash or Norm Cash?"[2] While Demeter's career with the Indians consisted of merely four games, Cash became a fixture at first base in Detroit for 15 years. Lane was not through making controversial trades with the Tigers. Five days later, he sent Rocky

• NORM CASH •

Colavito to Michigan for Harvey Kuenn, and later in 1960, the two clubs swapped managers, Joe Gordon for Jimmie Dykes.

Cash's teammates took an immediate liking to him. A comedian both on the field and in the clubhouse, he once tried to call time after being picked off first base. In another instance, Cash was stranded on second base during a thunderstorm. Once play resumed, however, he returned to third base. The umpire was baffled.

"What are you doing over there?"
"I stole third," he answered.
"When did that happen?"
"During the rain."[3]

On several occasions, he gave a muddy infield ball to the pitcher instead of the game ball so the hitters could not see it as well. Al Kaline remembers:

"Whenever you mention Norm Cash, I just smile. He was just a fun guy to be around and a great teammate. He always came ready to play. People don't know this, but he often played injured, like the time he had a broken finger."[4] Sonny Eliot, Detroit's ageless wacky weather man, describes Cash as "just old fashioned likeable," comparing his physical form to a kewpie doll from a state fair. "Whenever he came to bat, I would yell 'Hey kewpie doll,' and he'd turn around and laugh."[5] It was another Southerner and recent transplant to Detroit who presented Cash with his nickname: "I was in Baltimore [for six years] and there was a fellow there named Norman Almony," remembers Ernie Harwell. "Everybody called him Stormin Norman. When Norman Cash lost his temper once in a while, I gave him the nickname Stormin Norman. I don't think he liked it at first, but after a while, he started treasuring it."[6]

After a respectable 1960 season in which he batted .286 with 18 home runs, Cash captured the baseball world by storm in 1961. Although playing in the shadow of Mickey Mantle and Roger Maris, Cash posted one of the most outstanding offensive single season records in American League history. Stormin' Norman led the junior circuit with 193 hits and a .361 batting average. Number 25 also established personal marks of 41 home runs, 132 RBIs, and eight triples. Even more astounding, he hit .388 on the road! Facing Washington's Joe McClain on June 11, Cash became the first Detroit player to clear the Tiger Stadium roof, hitting a home run that landed on Trumbull Avenue. Another against Boston's Don Schwall struck a police tow truck. He was equally skilled at first base, fielding a sterling .993 as he caught dozens of long foul balls before they could fly into the stands. With Kaline's .324 batting average and Colavito's .290 complementing Cash in the lineup, the Tigers, led by Frank Lary and his 23 victories, challenged the Yankees for the American League pennant. The Bengals came within a game and a half of the Bronx Bombers on September 1 before retracting to finish eight behind in the standings with 101 victories.

Was Norm Cash destined to become a one-year wonder? Even at the time, he knew his '61 season was a freak, saying that everything he hit seemed to drop in, even when he didn't make good contact. After Frank Lary injured his leg on Opening Day and Al Kaline broke his shoulder during a nationally televised game in May, it became clear that the Tigers would not again challenge the Yankees in 1962. The season was equally disappointing for Cash, who batted only .243 for the season. The 118 points shaved from his average remains a record of futility among batting champs. Cash ultimately found his swing, batting .342 in an autumn exhibition trip to Japan, but by that point, the regular season was long over. Still the 1962 season was far from a write-off for the affable Texan. Cash hit 39 home runs, including three more roof shots, as the league runner-up to Harmon Killebrew's 48. His .993 fielding percentage was identical to his 1961 average.

Cash never again cracked the .300 plateau. Years later, when Mickey Lolich asked why, he replied that "Jim Campbell pays me to hit home runs."[7] Indeed, Cash's 373 home runs for the Tigers remains second only to Al Kaline's 399 among aggregate team records. However, it soon became evident that other factors besides the maturation of expansion pitching compromised Stormin' Norman's batting average. Cheating in baseball was as much an issue in 1961 as it remains today, and Sonny Eliot remembers why Norm Cash called that season "the Year of the Quick Bat."

"We used to sit in the old Lindell's A.C.," said Eliot, referring to the popular watering hole adjacent to Tiger Stadium. "We'd just rib the hell out of him. 'Did you put cork in the bat? If not cork, was it lead?' Or whatever it was, we'd just rib him."[8] He struck out frequently, and fans expecting another batting title consistently booed cash for the balance of his career. Even his wife joined in the chorus on occasion.[9] Stormin' Norman knew that inherently, they were as good natured as he was. After all, when Mayo Smith

• 77 •

removed Cash from the lineup during a slump, the manager was also booed.[10] Although he was not bothered by the sounds of tens of thousands of boos, "when one or two guys get on your back, they drive you nuts."[11] For their appreciation of his congeniality and humor, the Tigers Fan Club crowned Cash as King Tiger in 1969. George Cantor described Cash as "the most popular man on the team," who knew "all the best watering holes" throughout the American League.[12]

Although Cash stifled the cork in 1962 and thereafter, he sound found himself fighting a much larger battle in alcoholism. Denny McLain described his roommate as "a modern medical miracle," who abused his body so mercilessly that he "should [have turned] it over to the Mayo Clinic."[13] Stormin' Norman violated every curfew rule in the book, but he somehow arrived at the ballpark every day, "not only eager to play, but madder than hell if he didn't."[14] Granted, Cash rarely showed up on time: he "could not make 9:00 am workouts because he threw up until 10:00 am."[15] McLain credited hustle and determination as the secret to Cash's big league longevity, although the bespectacled righthander did admit that he was often bewildered "how he managed to remain upright" when he took the field. Still, McLain admitted that "I always felt better about everything when I looked over and saw Stormin' Norman at first base."[16] Players were rarely unanimously accepted by their peers, but Cash proved an exception. As pitcher Jerry Casale once conveyed, "on a team with so many friends, there was no one nicer than Norm Cash."[17]

Cash was nothing if not consistent for the balance of the 1960s. He was the only American League hitter to slug 20 or better home runs each year from 1961 to 1969. In 1964, he set a record among Detroit first baseman by fielding an outstanding .997. On July 9, 1965, Stormin' Norman hit an inside-the-park home

Norm Cash was the Opening Day first baseman for the 1959 White Sox, but didn't hit his stride until joining the Detroit Tigers a year later. Cash belted 373 home runs for the Tigers and won the 1961 American League batting title with a .361 mark.

run against the A's at Municipal Stadium in Kansas City. The blast must have ignited Cash's non-corked bat, as he decimated American League pitching with 23 home runs and 58 RBIs in 78 games after the All-Star break. His second-half exploits earned him Comeback Player of the Year honors, and in 1966, he was invited to the All-Star Game. Cash, once again, led junior circuit first basemen in fielding with a .997 percentage. Meanwhile, the Cash family was expanding, as Norm and Myrta welcomed son Jay Carl on April 28, 1963, and daughter Julie Lee on December 28, 1964.

Stormin' Norman proved to be the exception on the 1968 Tigers as he was fighting an early season slump. On July 27, the 6-foot-0 Cash was barely hitting

• NORM CASH •

his weight, batting .195 on a team cruising to its first American League pennant in 23 years. In dramatic fashion, he hit a torrid .333 in his last 54 games to finish the season at .263. Included in his 12 home runs and 33 RBIs in August and September was a three-run blast against Oakland on September 14. The winning pitcher of the 5-4 decision was Denny McLain, his 30th of the season. Cash led Tigers batsmen in the World Series, hitting .385 against Cardinals pitching. Setting a dubious October record as Bob Gibson's 16th strikeout in Game One, he redeemed himself the following afternoon, homering off Nellie Briles in an 8-1 complete-game victory for Mickey Lolich. Facing elimination in Game ESix, Cash enjoyed another productive day at the plate, accounting for two of the 13 Detroit runs, tying the Series at three games. This set the stage for an historic Game Seven. The Tigers were unfazed at the prospect of facing a pitcher who specialized in winning Game Sevens, Bob Gibson. In the clubhouse after practice, manager Mayo Smith encouraged his players that Gibson "can be beat, he's not Superman!" To this, Cash chimed "Oh yeah? Just a little while ago, I saw him changing in a phone booth!"[18] Tigers hitters proved to be Kryptonite with two outs and no score in the seventh inning. Cash ignited a Detroit rally with a single off Gibson, and later put the Tigers ahead as the first runner to score on Jim Northrup's triple. The final score was 4-1, and the Detroit Tigers were world champions.

After being relegated to pinch hitting in 1970, Cash enjoyed a renaissance season playing in the Renaissance City in 1971. So torrid was his first half that spectators across Major League ballparks voted him to start the All-Star Game on July 13. Played in Detroit, it drew 53,559 spectators. American League manager Earl Weaver, however, took exception to Cash's assignment, as he was not the reigning MVP playing for the defending World Champions. Boog Powell, Weaver's first baseman in Baltimore, could claim both. Accordingly, Weaver, scrapped Cash from the lineup and replaced him with Powell. The roster move was not kindly received by the Detroit faithful. After public address announcer Joe Gentile introduced the National League All-Stars were announced, he began to present the American League. Starting with Weaver! Again, a cloud of boos rained over Tiger Stadium. Although Rod Carew was the next to be announced, the Twins' second baseman did not take his place when called. Carew was apprehended by Cash and Bobby Murcer to prevent him from leaving the dugout, thereby prolonging the catcalls. Only after a prolonged interval did Carew emerge, breaking up the hecklers.[19]

When the dust cleared on the 1971 season, the Tigers had won 91 games, but finished 10 games behind Earl Weaver and the Orioles. Stormin' Norman clubbed 32 round trippers – one shy of Bill Melton's league lead – while driving in 91 runs, batting a respectable .283. His offensive record was enough to win his second American League Comeback Player of the Year Award. It would have surprised nobody to hear Cash proclaim, after accepting the honor, that he hoped he would win the award again next year. Cash was, however, named to the All-Star team once again in 1972, his fourth and final trip to the midsummer classic. is offensive output may have retracted, but the Tigers vaulted ahead in the standings to win their first American League East Division title.

A player known for his pranks, Cash saved his most famous stunt for the twilight of his career. It occurred on July 15, 1973, as the Tigers entertained the visiting California Angels. Not one Detroit batsman had hit safely off starting pitcher Nolan Ryan. With two away in the bottom of the ninth, the Ryan Express had already fanned 16 as his Angels led, 6-0. Potentially the final hitter of the game, Norm Cash strode to the plate substituting a table leg for a bat. Home plate umpire Ron Luciano forbade Cash's creative use of equipment. Cash protested, "But Ron, I've got as much chance with this as I do with a bat."[20] As Jim Northrup remembered from the third base dugout, Cash reluctantly retrieved a bat and struck out on three pitchers against his fellow

Texan. The no-hitter was Ryan's second in as many months; as Cash returned to the dugout, he turned to Luciano and expressed, "See, I told ya."[21]

The 1974 season was a transitional one for the Tigers and their personnel. For only the second time in franchise history, Detroit finished the season in last place. Stormin' Norman no longer held the nomenclatural monopoly when youthful infielder Ron Cash joined the Tigers in spring training. Equipment manager John Hand wanted to change the name on Norm's uniform, but the first baseman refused. Cash exclaimed in disgust, "If the people can't tell the difference between me and the other guy, something's the matter!"[22] He became even more incensed when he received a telephone call from the general manager on August 7. Batting only .228 with 12 home runs and 12 RBIs, Cash was released. "I thought at least they'd let me finish out the year. Campbell just called and said I didn't have to show up at the park."²³

Norm Cash was a player who knew his baseball career would not last forever. As a player, his offseason occupations included banking, ranching, and auctioning hogs. In the early 1970s, Cash hosted a local variety show in Detroit called "The Norm Cash Show." In 1976, he teamed with former October archrival Bob Gibson as broadcasters for *ABC Monday Night Baseball*. Although Cash continued to display his brand of humor, it was not appreciated by all. On-air remarks such as equating entertainment in Baltimore with going "down to the street and [watching] hubcaps rust" earned Cash his dismissal from the network.²⁴ In 1978, he made his film debut with a cameo appearance in *One in a Million: The Ron LeFlore Story*. In a scene filmed at Lakeland, Cash was standing with Kaline, Freehan, and Northrup to watch LeFlore in first spring training after accepting his release from Jackson State Prison. When the others marveled at his speed, Cash chimed in with "He can't be too fast, the cops caught him."²⁵

Now divorced from Myrta, Cash married his second wife Dorothy on May 22, 1973. They moved upstate from Detroit, first to Union Lakes, where Cash worked as a sales representative for an automobile machinery manufacturer. When asked, Cash remarked that "it's good money…but to tell the truth I'm looking for something else to do."²⁶ Sadly, the good times were short-lived. As Detroit automakers proved to be no competition for Japanese imports, Cash's financial windfall proved to be short term. His health began to deteriorate, suffering a massive stroke in 1979. As Ernie Harwell remembers, Cash was out of commission for quite a while. Fortunately, by 1981 he was healthy enough to broadcast Tigers games for the ON-TV cable network. He and Hank Aguirre provided color commentary alongside Larry Adderly's play-by-play. By 1983, partial paralysis of his face made him slur his words and he could no longer continue. In 1986, Cash returned to Tiger Stadium to participate in the Equitable Old Timers' Game. Fans were shocked to see the first baseman a shadow of his physical self. He could no longer field routine infield balls, as a throw from third base hit him in the head before bouncing away. Cash handled the situation with humor, but privately, he was embarrassed by the incident.²⁷ What nobody realized at the time is that the appearance would be his last at the corner of Michigan and Trumbull.

Scott McKinstry remembers Sunday evening of the Columbus Day weekend being a grey, misty one. "I was standing at the lighthouse…on Lake Michigan looking out over the water to where boats head out from Charlevoix to Beaver Island."²⁸ The weather forecast echoed the somber mood to be shared by Tigers fans in unison. Earlier in the day, Cash left his condominium to meet Dorothy and a friend for dinner at the Shamrock Bar on Beaver Island. Those present could affirm that Cash had been drinking.²⁹ After dinner, he returned to the dock to check on his boat after dinner. Unable to navigate the slippery pier in cowboy boots, he fell into the water and could not pull himself out.³⁰ The next morning, he was found floating in 15 feet of water in St. James Bay.³¹ Norman Dalton Cash was pronounced dead on October 12, 1986. He was 51 years old. Tragedy would hit the Cash family a second time in 1987 when Norm's son Jay committed suicide.³²

Like Buddy Holly before him, the Texas legend of Norm Cash lives on. Ernie Harwell recalls receiving an autographed photo from Cash inscribed with his trademark humor, "to the second-best broadcaster in the big leagues. The other 25 tied for first place."³³ Gary Peters, who broke in with the White Sox concomitantly with Cash, remembers his diverse collection of hobbies which included horseback riding, fencing, waterskiing, dancing, and playing the ukulele.³⁴ Whitey Herzog, Cash's roommate in 1963, once claimed that "there was nothing Norm Cash couldn't do." Describing Cash as his roommate, however, might have been an exaggeration; Herzog recalls the experience as "just like having your own room."³⁵ On April 23, 2005, the sandlot in Post, Texas where Stormin' Norman played Little League, was rededicated in memory of Garza County's most famous athlete as Norm Cash Field.

Perhaps the most vocal and outward posthumous tribute to Norm Cash in the final hours of the ballpark whose first base he called home from the Eisenhower to the Nixon administration. A sellout crowd of 43,556 jammed Tiger Stadium on September 27, 1999 for the final game against the Kansas City Royals. Several Tigers switched uniform numbers to pay homage to players who passed before them. Paying tribute to Ty Cobb, Gabe Kapler did not wear any number at all. Rookie Rob Fick switching his number 18 for 25 to honor Norm Cash. Only Fick went one step further. The Tigers enjoyed a comfortable 4-2 eighth-inning lead when Fick crushed a Jeff Montgomery fastball for a grand slam home run. In true Norm Cash fashion, the ball nearly cleared the right field roof. Tom Stanton reports in The Final Season, a diary which paints Tiger Stadium as a metaphor for the bond between fathers and sons, that Fick "looked up in the sky and thought of my dad," who passed away the year before. "I know that he had something to do with all this."[36]

So did Norm Cash.

Sources

In addition to the sources cited in the Notes, the author also consulted www.baseball-almanac.com, www.baseball-reference.com, www.imdb.com,and the following:

"Lobos Fall in Season Finale; Barber Breaks 1,000 Yard Mark" in The Sul Ross Skyline
(16 November 2006): 18 pars. [Journal Online]. Available from
http://www.sulross.edu/pages/3998.asp. Internet. Accessed 6 April 2007.

"Norm Cash." Brooklyn: Topps Chewing Gum Inc., 1960: 488.

Barnes, Tyler. *Detroit Tigers 1999 Information Guide* (Detroit: Tigers Public Relations
Department, 1999).

Barnes, Tyler. *The Inaugural Season: Detroit Tigers 2000 Information Guide* (Detroit:
Tigers Public Relations Department, 2000).

Cohen, Irwin. *Tiger Stadium* (Charleston, South Carolina: Arcadia Publishing, 2003).

Dewey, Donald, and Nicholas Acocella. *Total Ballclubs: The Ultimate Book of Baseball
Teams* (Toronto: Sport Classic Books, 2005).

Hunt, William. "Justiceburg, Texas" in *The Handbook of Texas Online* (2001): 2 pars.
Available from http://www.tsha.utexas.edu/handbook/online/articles/JJ/hnj13.html. Internet. Accessed 6 April 2007.

Lyons, Jeffrey and Douglas B. *Curveballs and Screwballs: Over 1,286 Incredible
Baseball Facts, Finds, Flukes, and More!* (New York: Random House, 2001).

McMillan, Robin. *Official Major League Baseball 1995 All-Star Game Program* (New
York: Sports Publishing Group Inc., 1995).

Middlesworth, Hal. *Detroit Tigers 1973 Press Radio TV Guide* (Detroit: Tigers Baseball Club, 1973).

Middlesworth, Hal. *Detroit Tigers 1974 Press Radio TV Guide* (Detroit: Tigers Baseball Club, 1974).

Middlesworth, Hal. *Detroit Tigers 1975 Press Radio TV Guide* (Detroit: Tigers Baseball
Club, 1975).

Middlesworth, Hal. *Detroit Tigers 1971 Yearbook* (Detroit: Tigers Baseball Club, 1971).

Middlesworth, Hal. *Detroit Tigers 1974 Yearbook* (Detroit: Tigers Baseball Club, 1974).

Paladino, Larry. *Detroit Tigers 1987 Yearbook* (Detroit: Tigers Baseball Club, 1987).

Russell, Cliff. *Detroit Tigers 2004 Information Guide* (Detroit: Tigers Media Relations
Department, 2004).

Thorn, John, Phil Birnbaum, and Bill Deane. *Total Baseball: The Ultimate
Encyclopedia*, 8th edition. (Toronto: Sport Classic Books, 2004).

Notes

1. Bruce Shlain, "Stormin' Norman" in *Oddballs: Baseball's Greatest Pranksters, Flakes, Hot Dogs, and Hotheads* (New York: Penguin Books, 1989), 134.
2. Shlain, 132.
3. Fred T. Smith, *Tiger S.T.A.T.S.*, (Ann Arbor: Momentum Books Ltd., 1991), 39.
4. Bill Dow, "Former Tiger Norm Cash," *Baseball Digest*, September 2001.
5. Correspondence with Sonny Eliot, April 2007.
6. Correspondence with Ernie Harwell, April 2007.
7. Dow.
8. Eliot.
9. Patrick Harrigan, *Detroit Tigers Club and Community: 1945-1995* (Toronto: University Press, 1997), 103.
10. George Cantor, *The Tigers of '68: Baseball's Last Real Champions* (Dallas: Taylor Trade Publishing, 1997), 10.
11. Shlain, 137.
12. Cantor, 39.
13. Denny McLain and Dave Diles, *Nobody's Perfect* (New York: The Dial Press, 1975), 72.
14. McLain/Diles, 72.
15. Denny McLain and Mike Nahrstept, *Strikeout: The Story of Denny McLain* (St. Louis: The Sporting News, 1988), 34.
16. McLaine/Diles, 72.
17. Correspondence with Jerry Casale, 21 May 2001.
18. Tim DeWalt, "Tribute: Norm Cash" in TigersCentral.com (2001-2005). Available from. http://www.tigerscentral.com/comments.php?id=239_0_1_0_C.
19. DeWalt.
20. Bill Shaikin, "California Strikes Gold in Ryan" in *Nolan Ryan: The Authorized Pictorial History* (Fort Worth: The Summit Group, 1991), 66.
21. Brian Britten, *Detroit Tigers 2006 Information Guide* (Detroit: Tigers Public Relations Department, 2006), 256.

22 "There Are So Many Norm Cash Stories…" in *Detroit Tigers History* (2005). Available from http://www.detroit-tigers-baseball-history.com/cash.html.
23 Chris Stern, *Where Have They Gone?Baseball Stars!* (New York: Grosset & Dunlap, 1979), 137-138.
24 Stern, 138.
25 DeWalt.
26 Stern, 138.
27 Cantor, 215.
28 DeWalt.
29 Harrigan, 103.
30 Schlain, 145.
31 Cantor, 215.
32 Shlain, 145.
33 Ernie Harwell, *Life After Baseball* (Detroit: The Free Press, 2004), 137.
34 Shlain, 139.
35 Shlain, 139-140.
36 Tom Stanton, *The Final Season: Fathers, Sons, and One Last Season in a Classic American Ballpark* (New York: St. Martin's Press, 2001), 236.

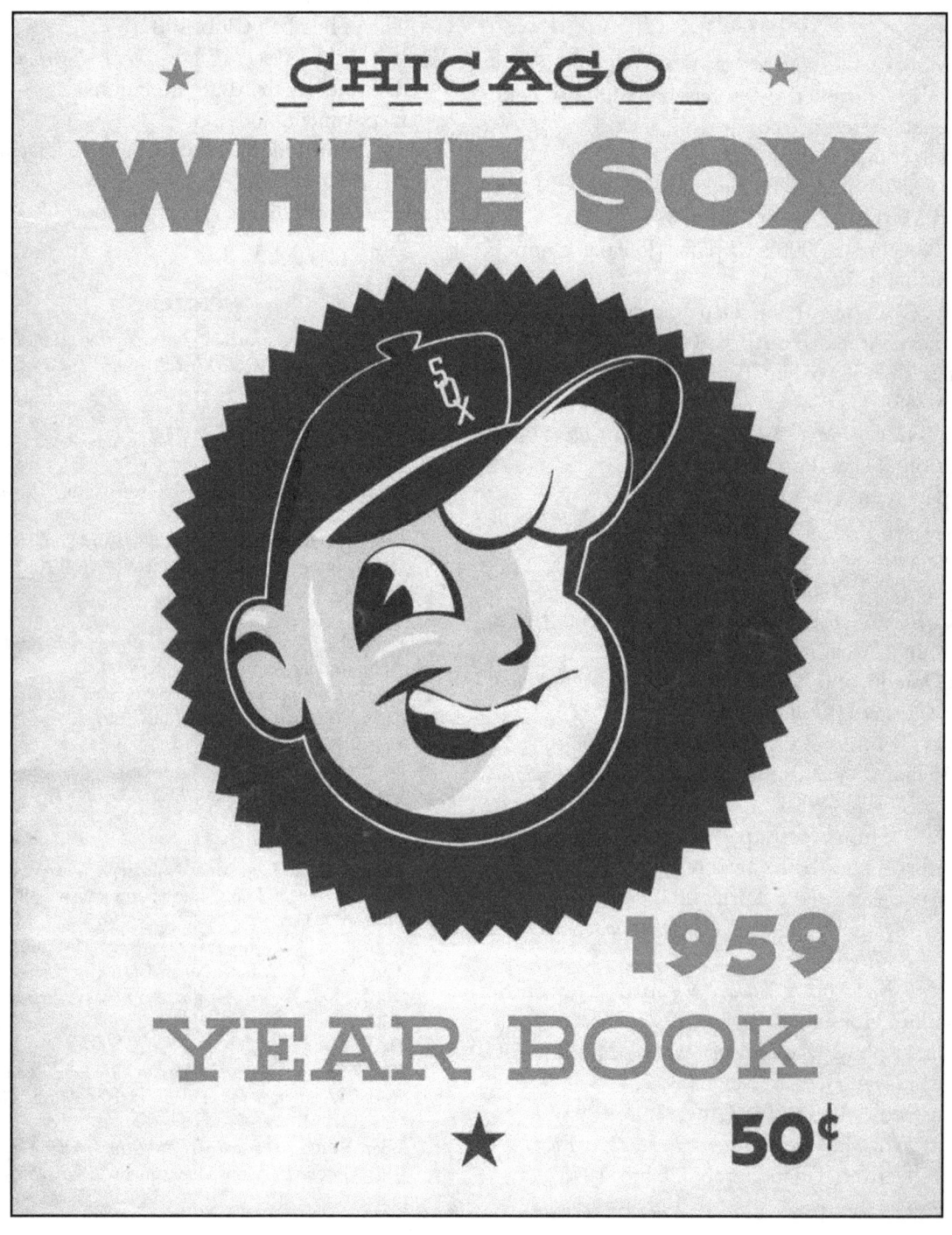

LARRY DOBY

By John McMurray

Larry Doby is best remembered for becoming the first black player in the American League and the second in modern history in major-league baseball. When Doby made his major-league debut for the Cleveland Indians on July 5, 1947, he broke the league's color barrier less than three months after Jackie Robinson first played for the Brooklyn Dodgers.[1] In the face of racial prejudice, Doby remained a superior hitter and outfielder during his 13-season career, with selection to seven American League All-Star teams. "I had to take it," Doby said, "but I fought back by hitting the ball as far as I could. That was my answer."[2]

Lawrence Eugene Doby was born on December 13, 1923, in Camden, South Carolina. Larry's father, David, met his future wife, Etta, while playing baseball on the street in front of her home.[3] Biographer Joseph Thomas Moore wrote that the Dobys were "one of the most prosperous black families in Camden."[4]

David Doby was a stable hand, grooming the horses of many wealthy New Jersey families. The marriage, however, was strained because of David's frequent travel and Etta's strong attachment to her own mother, leaving young Larry often in the care of his grandmother, Augusta Moore. She recounted how Doby said that Augusta "made me go to church with her all the time. I liked what I heard in the Twenty-Third Psalm and the Ten Commandments. Somehow I got the feeling that the church helped black people to be themselves. I liked that feeling."[5]

When Larry was eight years old, his father died in a tragic accident.[6] David had gone fishing on a day off, and he drowned after falling from a boat while fishing on Lake Mohansic, in upstate New York.[7] His death began a tumultuous time for Larry, during which he moved frequently and was cared for by his aunt and uncle.[8] Four years after his father's death, Larry and his mother left South Carolina and moved to Paterson, New Jersey.[9]

It wasn't easy for Doby in Paterson. "I was lonely living alone," he said. "But I just kept trying to be me."[10] In Paterson, Doby began following in the footsteps of his father, who had been a semipro ballplayer. He developed his skills playing sandlot baseball close to home, at the Newman Playground and on Twelfth Avenue. Doby lettered in baseball at Paterson Eastside High School, where he was one of about 25 black students in the school. He won letters in three other sports, a total of 11 in all. Initially, Doby had thoughts of finishing high school and then becoming a physical education teacher or perhaps a coach.[11]

Doby was more introspective than demonstrative, and his personality could confuse his teammates. As recounted by biographer Moore, high-school teammate Al Kachuadurian never felt he could slap Doby on the back, and thought Doby kept his teammates at a distance.[12] "I remember distinctly that if things didn't go just right, he'd sulk. Deep down, he's a warm-hearted guy. But you didn't know if he was sulking at you personally, or whether he was sulking inwardly at himself."[13] Doby, however, later countered that he wasn't sulking at all but had gotten accustomed to being alone based upon the circumstances in his life.[14] In some sense, Doby's self-reliance may have been mistaken for aloofness.

Even before graduating from high school, Doby began playing second base under the assumed name of Larry Walker in the Negro Leagues for the Newark Eagles.[15] He was an immediate star, and team owners offered him $300 to play between high school and college.[16] Although statistics from his first season are inexact, Doby believed he had batted around .400 during that summer.[17]

Doby enrolled at Long Island University. Part of his motivation was to play for renowned basketball coach Clair Bee. Another reason was to be able to visit Helyn Curvy, whom Doby had begun dating at Eastside High School when he was a sophomore.[18] Curvy's father had died, however, and responsibilities for taking care of her siblings prevented Curvy from attending any of Doby's high-school baseball games.[19] "But when I had a game," Doby recalled, "I'd take her brother George to the game with me, then I'd bring him back to her house."[20]

At the time, Doby had concern about being drafted into the military during World War II.[21] He made the difficult decision to transfer from Long Island University to Virginia Union College, where he

• Go-Go to Glory •

The first African-American player in American League history, Larry Doby signed a major league contract with Cleveland Indians president Bill Veeck on July 5, 1947, then made his MLB debut that day.

would play basketball for coach Henry Hucles.[22] Doby believed he could transfer into an ROTC program there.[23] Yet he was drafted into the Navy at the conclusion of the basketball season. The mandated racial segregation of the military at the time left a deep impression on him.[24] He was assigned to Camp Robert Smalls, the black division of the Great Lakes Naval Training Station, outside Chicago.[25]

Due in large part to his outstanding physical condition, Doby was able to become a physical education instructor there.[26] He kept his baseball and basketball skills sharp by playing in the afternoons. Doby got to know future NFL Hall of Famer Marion Motley while on his tour of duty.[27] Later, while stationed in the Pacific, Doby began what became a lifelong friendship with Washington Senators star Mickey Vernon.[28] Vernon wrote to Senators owner Clark Griffith, touting Doby's playing abilities. After their military service was done, "[Vernon] sent me a gift of some bats when I started the 1946 season with the [Newark] Eagles," Doby recalled.[29] "It was a gift I'll never forget."[30]

In 1945, general manager Branch Rickey of the Brooklyn Dodgers signed Jackie Robinson to a contract to play baseball in Montreal. The move made Doby reconsider his options, as playing baseball in the major leagues now seemed a possibility. "My main thing was to become a teacher and coach," Doby said. "But when I heard about Jackie, I decided to concentrate on baseball. I forgot about going back to college."[31]

Doby was honorably discharged from the military in January 1946. After playing two months of winter ball with the San Juan Senators for $500 a month at the invitation of Monte Irvin, a prewar teammate on the Newark Eagles, Doby subsequently rejoined the Eagles. Being close to home also allowed him to date Helyn again. "She told me if we didn't get married that year, 1946, to forget it," Doby said.[32] "We got married on August 10, 1946, in Paterson."[33] The night of their wedding, the couple drove to Trenton, where Doby was scheduled to play.[34] The game was rained out.[35] A few days later, Doby played in a Negro Leagues All-Star game against a team including Josh Gibson.

The Eagles went on to win the Negro Leagues World Series in 1946. Doby batted .272 with one home run in that series against the Kansas City Monarchs of the Negro American League. He tagged a runner out at second base for the second out of the ninth inning of the seventh game, and he caught a popup for the final out of the series. "To play the Monarchs in the World Series!" Doby later exclaimed. "They had Satchel Paige and all those guys. That was a great team. To beat those guys, you were in the upper echelon of baseball."[36]

With Doby's notoriety high after the 1946 championship season, Bill Veeck, the owner of the Cleveland Indians, took notice. Veeck, who had long been eager to racially integrate the American League, hatched a plan for Doby to join Cleveland right after the 1947 All-Star break. Doby had played the first half of the season with the Eagles, and he had hit a home run in his final Newark at-bat. The Cleveland team quietly purchased Doby's contract and brought him to Cleveland. A scoop by local writer Bob Whiting forced the team to move up Doby's first game from July 10, which was the original intention, to July 5.[37]

Teammates, however, did not immediately welcome Doby, averting their eyes and not speaking to him as he made his entry to the clubhouse at Comiskey Park to meet with player-manager Lou Boudreau.[38] "Shrug it off," Boudreau reportedly said.[39] Still, Doby in 2002 recalled, "I knew it was segregated times, but I had never seen anything like that in athletics. I was embarrassed. It was tough." As Bill White later noted, Doby had to go to the Chicago clubhouse to get a first baseman's glove since none of his Cleveland teammates offered him one.[40]

Pinch-hitting for Bryan Stephens against Earl Harrist of the White Sox, Doby struck out in his first major-league at-bat. On July 6, in the second game of that day's doubleheader, Doby made his only start of the season at first base. He got his first major-league hit, a single off Orval Grove in the third inning that also gave him his first RBI.[41] During that difficult first season, Doby batted only .156 in 29 games with two RBIs. "It was 11 weeks between the time Jackie Robinson and I came into the majors. I can't see how things were any different for me than they were for him," Doby said.[42]

He had to wait until the start of the 1948 season to win a starting job in Cleveland's outfield. During his first full season, Doby hit 14 home runs and had 66 RBIs. That fall, Doby became the first black player to hit a home run in the World Series when he connected off the Boston Braves' Johnny Sain in Game Four. His blast helped lead Cleveland to a 2-1 win and a lead of three games to one in the Series. A photo taken after the game showing Doby embracing Cleveland pitcher Steve Gromek has become one of the most famous in baseball history, symbolizing an erosion of racial divisions and Doby's acceptance as a member of his new team.

The 1948 season was the first of 10 consecutive years in which Doby hit at least 14 home runs and drove in at least 50 runs. He was selected to the All-Star team in every year between 1949 and 1955 and finished in the top 10 in the American League MVP voting in 1950 and 1954. Doby's finest statistical season was 1952, when he led the American League in slugging percentage (.541), home runs (32), and runs scored (104). He hit for the cycle that year against Boston on June 4 at Fenway Park. The last time an American Leaguer accomplished that feat until Mickey Mantle did it in 1957.[43]

In 1954, Doby was Cleveland's most dominant offensive player, leading the American League in home runs (32) and runs batted in (126). He also played a stellar center field, committing only two errors in 153 games while finishing second in the league in putouts. Doby's regular season success that year, like that of many of his teammates, did not extend into the World Series, as he was able to manage only two singles in the four games against the New York Giants. Still, for his regular-season efforts, Doby finished second in the 1954 American League Most Valuable Player award voting to Yogi Berra.

After the 1955 season, during which Doby battled a wrist injury, he was traded to the Chicago White Sox for Jim Busby and Chico Carrasquel. At the time, Chicago manager Marty Marion said that Doby's arrival was "the end of the search for a No. 4 hitter."[44] Marion later said, "This guy used to murder us when we played Cleveland. Last year, I definitely felt that, when we could get him out, we could handle the Indians. But we couldn't – and the record shows that they had a season break on us, 12-10."[45]

Doby immediately delivered with Chicago, hitting 24 home runs and knocking in 102 runs. During a nine-game winning streak in June 1956, Doby hit five home runs, leading White Sox owner Charles Comiskey to remark, "Larry Doby, he's our guy. You know, when we dealt for Doby, we weren't worried about Larry. We knew he'd come through."[46]

Doby was involved in one of the bigger melees of the 1957 season. In a game on June 12, Art Ditmar of the Yankees threw a pitch inside, causing Doby to fall to his knees. Both benches emptied, and Doby knocked Ditmar down with a punch to his jaw. Doby also got into an on-field fight with Billy Martin after the umpires had restored order. Doby, teammate Walt Dropo, and the Yankees' Enos Slaughter and Martin were all thrown out of the game. The Yankees, feeling that penalties against their players by the league were unjustified, paid all fines of their players assessed after the incident.[47]

After his power numbers faded a bit during the 1957 season, Doby was traded to Baltimore that December with Jack Harshman, Russ Heman, and Jim Marshall in return for Tito Francona, Ray Moore, and Billy Goodman. Manager Al Lopez explained the deal, saying, "We wouldn't start another season with Doby because the fans are down on him."[48] A contemporary article noted that the fans often booed Doby at Comiskey Park, leading to resentment on Doby's part.[49] Doby never played with the Orioles, being traded again before the season began on April 1. This time he went back to the Cleveland Indians along with Don Ferrarese for Dick Williams, Gene Woodling, and Bud Daley.

By then, however, injuries had taken their toll, and Doby was a part-time player. In 1958, he hit 13 home runs and batted in 45 runs in only 89 games. Just before the 1959 season, Doby was traded to the Detroit Tigers for Tito Francona. Finally, on May 13, 1959, he was purchased from Detroit by the Chicago White Sox for $30,000.

Chicago was Doby's last major-league stop as a player. By then 35 years old, he played in only 21 games, batting .241 with no home runs and only nine runs batted in. His final game in the major leagues was on July 26. Sent down to the White Sox' San Diego farm team in the Pacific Coast League, Doby fractured an ankle sliding into third base on a triple on August 23.[50] Doby finished his major-league career with a .283 batting average, 243 doubles, 253 home runs, and 970 RBIs.

In 1960, Doby signed with the Toronto Maple Leafs of the International League, but because of the lingering effects of his ankle injury, he was released in May without getting into a game. In 1962 he played for the Nagoya Dragons in Japan. He went on to coach with Montreal, Cleveland, and the White Sox.[51] He also owned a lounge and a liquor store in Newark, and he worked in the Essex County prosecutor's office in New Jersey for three years.[52]

During that time, Doby wrote letters to major-league teams seeking the opportunity to be a major-league manager.[53] In 1971, when he was a batting coach for the Montreal Expos, Doby spoke of the possibility of managing in the major leagues in an interview: "The Expos know what I want to do," he said. "But they want me to work my way up. …They want me to wait. I don't mind waiting because right now I'm learning. But I can't wait for the rest of my life."[54] Doby remarked that he enjoyed working with kids in part because he had good training – he had five children of his own.

Doby received the chance to manage in 1978, becoming the second black manager in major-league history when he took over the White Sox. He succeeded Bob Lemon, who was fired, but took over the Yankees and led them to the pennant. Doby's time managing was filled with frustration, however, as he had a record of only 37-50 during the portion of the one season in which he managed during his career. Doby cited injuries for the team's failures, saying, "When you have to use people you hope can play, rather than those you know can play, you are in a bad situation."[55]

He also maintained strong feelings about why he had to wait until the age of 53 to receive the Chicago managerial job: "Why did it take this long? You tell me. I don't mean to sound prejudiced, but you can look at the system and see that, until I was named (to replace Lemon on June 30), there was no black manager in the major leagues."[56]

After the 1978 season, Doby was fired as the team's manager. "I can't truly say what kind of manager I was or could've been because I didn't have enough time," he said.[57] "I thought I could have been successful. I thought I had those intangibles."[58]

After his managerial career was over, Doby remained active with major-league baseball. He was an administrator for the Former Players Licensing Branch of Major League Baseball, helping to license people or companies that wanted to use players or their trademarks for card shows or speaking engagements.[59] In 1995, Doby was named special assistant to American League president Gene Budig, who said at the time, "Few have done more for Major League Baseball than Larry Doby, and we are excited about having him associated with us."[60] Doby later was also named to the Baseball World board.[61]

In 1997, the Indians retired Doby's number 14 on the 50th anniversary of his major-league debut.[62] He became the fifth Cleveland player to be so honored, joining Bob Feller, Earl Averill, Mel Harder, and Lou Boudreau.[63] A banner was displayed in left field on

LARRY DOBY

Larry Doby

July 5, 1997, at Jacobs Field, showing Doby and Jackie Robinson, saying "50 years: 1947-1997."[64] At the ceremony, Hank Aaron said to Doby, "I want to thank you for all that you went through, because if it had not been for you, I wouldn't have been able to have the career that I had."[65] In 1998, Doby was elected to the Baseball Hall of Fame by the Veterans Committee.[66]

Doby's health plagued him in retirement. He battled a cancerous tumor in 1997 and had to have a kidney removed.[67] Helyn, his wife of 55 years, died in 2001 after a six-month battle with cancer.[68] Larry Doby died of cancer in Montclair, New Jersey, on June 18, 2003. More than 300 mourners attended his funeral at Trinity Presbyterian Church.[69] He is buried in Montclair. He was honored posthumously by appearing on a U.S. postage stamp released in July 2012.[70]

Notes

1 Kevin Kernan, "Larry is the stuff of legends: Struggles of Doby a lesson for any time," *New York Post*, July 28, 2002.
2 Kernan.
3 Joseph Thomas Moore, *Pride Against Prejudice: The Biography of Larry Doby* (Westport: Praeger Publishers, 1988), 7.
4 Moore, 6.
5 Moore, 9.
6 Doby, Lawrence Eugene "Larry," in David L. Porter, ed. *Biographical Dictionary of American Sports* (Westport, Connecticut: Greenwood Press, 2000).
7 Ibid.
8 Ibid.
9 Ibid.
10 Moore, 12.
11 Moore, 12-17.
12 Moore, 16.
13 Ibid.
14 Ibid.
15 Moore, 19-20.
16 Moore, 20.
17 Ibid.
18 Moore, 23.
19 Dave Anderson, "A Pioneer's Hall of Fame Wife," *New York Times*, July 26, 2001.
20 Anderson.
21 Moore, 24.
22 Ibid.
23 Ibid.
24 Moore., 24-25.
25 Moore, 25.
26 Ibid.
27 Ibid.
28 Ibid.
29 Ibid.
30 Ibid.
31 Moore, 29.
32 Anderson.
33 Ibid.
34 Ibid.
35 Ibid.
36 Dave Hutchinson, "Doby relives past, the good and the bad: Indians retire his number today." No publication given. Clipping from Doby's file at the Hall of Fame Library.
37 Moore, 41-45.
38 Moore, 47.
39 Ibid.
40 Jerome Holtzman, "Doby's Rightful Recognition," *Chicago Tribune*, March 4, 1998, available at https://chicago.tribune.com/sports/whitesox/article0,1051,ART-4566,00.html.
41 Sam Goldaper and Jack Cavanaugh, "Sports World Specials; Honors for Doby," *New York Times*. July 6, 1987.
42 Dave Hutchinson, "Doby relives past, the good and the bad: Indians retire his number today." No publication given. Clipping from Doby's file at the Hall of Fame Library.
43 Daniel, "Mick Thought Homer Cleared Stadium," July 24, 1957. No publication given. Clipping from Doby's Hall of Fame file.
44 United Press, "Carrasquel, Busby Acquisitions 'Round 1' for Trading Tribe." Clipping from Doby's Hall of Fame file.
45 "Doby Now Tonic to Old Foe: Ex-Indian Esteemed by Chicago Pilot," May 5, 1956. No author or publication given. Clipping from Doby's Hall of Fame file.
46 Doby connects: Jersey Vet 'Finds Range' for Chisox," June 23, 1956." Clipping from Doby's Hall of Fame file.
47 "Police Grab Martin After Fighting Doby: Drysdale and Logan Swap Punches in Brooklyn Free-for-All," June 13, 1957. Clipping from Doby's Hall of Fame file.

48 "Chisox Fans Sour on Doby; Forced Deal with Baltimore," December 11, 1957. Clipping from Doby's Hall of Fame file.
49 Ibid.
50 "Doby to Enter Johns Hopkins, Career in Danger, August 25, 1959." Clipping from Doby's Hall of Fame file.
51 Porter, *Biographical Dictionary of American Sports*.
52 Bob Decker, "Doby's next goal—manage in majors." *Newark Star-Ledger*, January 24, 1971.
53 Ibid.
54 Ibid.
55 Hutchinson, "Doby relives past, the good and the bad: Indians retire his number today."
56 Tom Melody, "Doby's dream now a nightmare," *Akron Beacon Journal*, August 21, 1978.
57 Hutchinson, "Doby relives past, the good and the bad: Indians retire his number today."
58 Ibid.
59 Ibid.
60 American League Press Release, "Doby Named Special Assistant to the American League President," April 17, 1995.
61 "Doby among 3 named to Baseball World board," *Cooperstown Crier*, July 8, 1999. No author or page number given. Clipping from Doby's Hall of Fame file.
62 Kevin Kernan, "Larry is the stuff of legends: Struggles of Doby a lesson for any time," *New York Post*, July 28, 2002, 97.
63 Ibid.
64 Associated Press, "Finally a hankering to honor Doby: Aaron says thanks to barrier-breaker on 50th anniversary of his AL debut," *Newark Star Ledger*, July 6, 1997, Section 5, 8.
65 Ibid.
66 Jerome Holtzman, "Doby's Rightful Recognition," *Chicago Tribune*, March 4, 1998, available at https://chicago.tribune.com/sports/whitesox/article0,1051,ART-4566,00.html.
67 Holtzman.
68 Anderson.
69 Steve Politi, "Doby recalled as a Hall of Famer in Life," *Newark Star Ledger*, June 24, 2003: 53.
70 Baseball Hall of Fame press release, "Postal Service to Unveil New Stamps Depicting Hall of Fame Legends on Friday in Cooperstown," July 16, 2012. Clipping from Doby's Hall of Fame file.

DICK DONOVAN
By Joe Wancho

Ken Coleman, the legendary broadcaster of the Cleveland Indians, Boston Red Sox, and other teams, was truly thrilled when he heard that pitcher Dick Donovan was coming over to Cleveland in a trade with the Washington Senators after the 1961 season. Coleman and Donovan had been teammates on North Quincy (Massachusetts) High School baseball teams - only it was Coleman who was the pitcher; Donovan was the shortstop. Coleman regaled television viewers of Indians games with stories of Donovan when they were coming up together through their boyhood days.

"Dick became such a good pitcher for the CYO [Catholic Youth Organization] that he was invited to pitch for the American Legion All-Star team in an exhibition," recalled Coleman. "Dick put on his uniform and rode his bike to the game. When he got there, they thanked him for coming and told him he would work in the bullpen. He protested, saying that was not the promise that was made. He got on his bike and started to pedal out of the park. On his way, he ran into his dad, who asked him where he was going. Dick told him what happened and his dad began to laugh. Dick then got back on his bike and went home. His dad made no effort to stop him. To me, this incident typified the makeup of Dick. He still has the determination to do what he thinks is right, and has the wonderful ability to see the humor in a situation. This latter quality he obviously gathered from his father."[1]

Richard Edward Donovan was born on December 7, 1927, in Boston, the youngest of five children born to Jeremiah and Gertrude Donovan. Dick attended North Quincy High School and enjoyed success on the baseball diamond, first as a shortstop and then as a pitcher his senior year. He was signed by scout Jeff Jones of the hometown Boston Braves. Jones was overwhelmed by Donovan, calling him "the fire-ballingest pitcher" he'd seen in the scholastic ranks since Bob Feller pitched for the Van Meter, Iowa, High School team in the '30s. Before reporting to the Braves, Donovan served three years in the United States Navy, from 1944 to 1947.

After his discharge, Donovan bounced around in the Braves' minor-league system, making stops in Fort Lauderdale of the Florida International League (1947), Evansville of the Three-I League (1948), and Hartford of the Eastern League (1949), with a brief stint at Milwaukee of the American Association, the Braves' top farm team, in '49. Donovan posted a 12-6 record with an ERA of 2.66 at Hartford, and his ticket was finally punched to break camp with the Braves for the 1950 season.

Donovan made his major-league debut against the Brooklyn Dodgers and Don Newcombe on April 24. The Braves lost, 6-4, and Donovan was lifted in the seventh inning by manager Billy Southworth. Donovan started only seven games for Boston over the next three years, accumulating a record of 0-4. He spent most of his time pitching for Milwaukee, and helped the team claim the American Association flag in 1951. But despite pitching well for the Brewers, he was used sparingly by the parent team in Boston, and he could never find his pitching groove. From 1950 through 1952, he was 0-4 for the Braves and 14-17 for the Brewers.

The Braves moved to Milwaukee for the 1953 season, and sold Donovan outright to Toledo, now the Braves' Triple-A farm. Donovan refused to report, saying that if he went there he would be buried in the Milwaukee organization. He demanded to be traded. "I believed I could win in the major leagues and wanted a chance to prove it,"[2] said Donovan.

At first, his request was denied. Braves general manager John Quinn eventually relented and granted Donovan his wish in principle, but Quinn refused all of the trade offers that were made for Donovan. Unable to work out a deal with Quinn, Donovan got a call from his former roommate with Boston and Milwaukee, Gene Mauch, who was the player-manager of the Atlanta Crackers of the Southern Association. He begged Donovan to come down to Atlanta.

One reason he liked it in Atlanta so much was the relationship he struck up with pitching coach Whitlow Wyatt. "That was the best thing that ever happened to me," said Donovan. "It brought me under the wing of Wyatt. If I make the grade this time, I'll owe it all to Wyatt. It was a slider, you know, that made

• 89 •

him a winner with Brooklyn after he had slid back to the minor leagues. But nobody taught it to Wyatt. He picked it up accidentally.[3]"

Even though Donovan got his wish to play for another organization when he was sold to Detroit after the 1953 season, he was overjoyed when Tigers manager Fred Hutchinson sent him back to Atlanta for the 1954 season. (Wyatt had succeeded Mauch as manager.) The idea of pitching for Wyatt rather than riding the bench for the big-league club was much more appealing. Wyatt had confidence in his young hurler, and showed patience with him. He taught Donovan how to throw the slider, to go along with his tremendous curve and fastball. Donovan responded with an 18-8 record for Atlanta in 1954, after having gone 11-8 in 1953. Considered a good hitter for a pitcher, he socked an astonishing – even in the hitter-friendly Southern Association – 12 home runs and had 32 RBIs for the Crackers, and was the team MVP in 1954.

At the end of the 1954 season, Donovan's contract was sold to the Chicago White Sox. Manager Marty Marion inserted him into the starting rotation to start the 1955 season. Donovan made sure that Marion did not regret it, recording a 15-9 record with a 3.32 ERA. He was named to the American League All-Star team in July, though he didn't get into the Midsummer Classic, played that year at Milwaukee's County Stadium.

Donovan's record was 13-4 on July 30 when he was stricken with appendicitis. After the appendectomy, he made a rapid recovery and resumed workouts in early August. He made his first start back on August 21 against the Tigers and won, giving up only one earned run and raising his record to 14-4 for the year. However, for the rest of the season, Donovan posted just a 1-5 record, raising the question of what might have been if the big Irishman had not had surgery in August. The White Sox finished the season five games behind pennant-winning New York.

A three-time All-Star and the American League ERA champion with the Senators in 1961, Dick Donovan was the one of the White Sox' most dependable pitchers in the 1950s.

The White Sox finished in third place in 1956, and in second place in 1957 and 1958, as the Yankees claimed the American League flag each of those years. Al Lopez replaced Marion as the Sox skipper in 1957. Donovan and Billy Pierce formed a formidable one-two punch of the Sox pitching staff over those three years. But the Sox had little else in the starting rotation and an often unreliable bullpen. Donovan averaged 14 wins against 10 losses, 15 complete games, 234 innings pitched, and 112 strikeouts to 52 walks. His best year was 1957, when he went 16-6 with a 2.77 ERA. Donovan and Pierce led the American League in complete games with 16 apiece in 1957.

• DICK DONOVAN •

As 1959 dawned, Dick made a major change in his life when he married the former Patricia Casey of Quincy on February 7. Dick and Patricia, a stewardess for United Airlines, were married for just short of 38 years.

Another change for Donovan and his White Sox teammates that year was that it was the season Chicago brought home the American League pennant for the first time since 1919. The Chisox, nicknamed the "Go-Go Sox," finished five games ahead of second-place Cleveland. The White Sox teams of the late 1950s were built around pitching, defense, and speed on the basepaths to take advantage of the spacious contours of Comiskey Park. Luis Aparicio led the American League in stolen bases every season from 1956 to 1964, and teammates Jim Landis and Jim Rivera were constantly among the league leaders.

As for Dick Donovan, he suffered from a slow start to the season and later from a sore shoulder, causing him to miss a month. At times he pitched in bad luck. In a game against Detroit on April 17, Donovan had a no-decision (in a game Chicago ultimately won) because a drive by Eddie Yost hit the foul pole for a two-run homer.

As 1959 wore on, it became apparent that New York was not going to stand in the way of the Sox and their first pennant in 40 years; Cleveland proved to be the main competition. The White Sox arrived at Cleveland Stadium for a four-game set in late August holding a slim lead of a game and a half over the Tribe. Cleveland was riding high with an eight-game winning streak and seemed to be building momentum. More than 165,000 turned out for the weekend series as the Sox swept the Tribe and took a commanding 5½-game lead over the Indians. Donovan beat Jim Perry, 2-0, in Saturday's game to improve his record to 8-6. In his only shutout of the season, he scattered five hits and struck out four. After the White Sox won Sunday's doubleheader, they were welcomed home at Chicago's Midway Airport by a reported throng of 10,000 Sox fans. Cleveland never recovered, and the White Sox coasted to the American League title. Donovan finished the season with a 9-10 record and a 3.66 ERA.

In the World Series, Chicago faced the Los Angeles Dodgers, who were making their first postseason appearance since moving from Brooklyn after the 1957 season. White Sox staff ace Early Wynn mowed the Dodgers down in Game One, 11-0. The Dodgers won four out of the next five games, however, to win the world championship. Donovan lost a close Game Three to Don Drysdale, 3-1, giving up two earned runs in 6 2/3 innings, with five strikeouts.

In Game Five, Donovan came out of the bullpen in relief of Bob Shaw and Billy Pierce to earn the save. Bob Burnes of the *St. Louis Globe-Democrat* wrote that the battle between Donovan and the Dodgers' Carl Furillo in the eighth inning was not only one of his top thrills of the Series, but one of the all-time great moments in sports. "In that game, the White Sox had their backs to wall," wrote Burnes. "They were down three games to one, and were nursing a 1-0 lead from the fourth inning. Then the Dodgers loaded the bases with one out as Donovan replaced Bob Shaw and Carl Furillo came in as a pinch-hitter. It was a great duel between two tremendous competitors and it was unbelievable Donovan got him out on a pop fly and kept the Sox alive for another day. It was one of the best jobs of clutch pitching that I have ever seen."[4]

In 1960, the White Sox had high expectations, but New York returned to first place and Chicago slumped to third in the American League, 10 games behind the Yankees. Lopez used Donovan for only 79 innings because he believed the pitcher was nursing a sore arm for much of the season. Donovan went 6-1, but his ERA ballooned to 5.38. He started only eight games, and was primarily used out of the bullpen. After the season, Donovan was left unprotected in the expansion draft, and was claimed by the new Washington Senators franchise for $75,000.

Under Washington manager Mickey Vernon, Donovan bounced back and had a good year for the last-place Senators in 1961. As fate would have it, the Senators opened their home schedule against Chicago. Donovan was pumped up to share Opening Day honors with Washington and new President John F. Kennedy, a fellow native of Massachusetts. But he was unsuccessful, as the White Sox pushed over the go-ahead run in the top of the eighth inning for a 4-3 win.

Still, however, Donovan had a stellar year. His record was only 10-10, but he led the major leagues with a sparking 2.40 ERA, and was the only representative of the Senators to be picked for the All-Star team; he pitched shutout ball for two innings in the year's first of two All-Star Games, at San Francisco's Candlestick Park.

"Donovan is a real professional," Vernon said. "He knows how to pitch and gives you an all-out effort. Dick just doesn't throw the ball -- he has every pitch planned."[5]

Washington finished tied in the American League basement, 47½ games off the pace, which made Donovan's season all the more incredible. He gave up only 138 hits in 169 innings.

So it was shocking that the Senators traded Donovan, catcher-outfielder Gene Green, and infielder Jim Mahoney to Cleveland for outfielder Jimmy Piersall, who had batted .322 in 1961, the third highest average in the American League. The temperamental, sometimes volatile outfielder had just been given a $5,000 bonus for his good behavior during the 1961 season.

One Indian who was thrilled that Donovan was joining the team was outfielder Willie Kirkland. "Donovan alone will help us more than Piersall," said Kirkland. "Piersall may have been a team player at the start when we were winning. But later, he was out for Piersall. Maybe he was out trying to win the batting championship. He'd get two hits and say, 'The hell with it,' and leave the game or start bunting."[6]

Donovan gave manager Mel McGaha and Indians fans something to cheer for when he won the 1962 season opener in Boston, shutting out the Red Sox, 4-0, scattering five hits. A week later, Dick blanked the Red Sox again, 5-0. He had a string of 19 scoreless innings to start the season.

Donovan raced out to an 8-0 start for the Tribe, making general manager Gabe Paul look like a genius. He and catcher John Romano, a former teammate with the White Sox, both were named to the American League All-Star team for the July 10 game in Washington (the first of two All-Star games that year). Donovan surrendered one run in two innings as the National League triumphed, 3-1. He was also named to the second All-Star game, but did not pitch.

The Indians finished sixth in the 10-team American League in 1962, but Donovan was a 20-game winner for the first time. He finished with a record of 20-10 and a 3.59 ERA while pitching 251 innings for the Tribe, who finished with a record of 80-82. He was named by *The Sporting News* as its Pitcher of the Year and to its All-Star Team for the American League. Donovan was also named the Indians' Man of the Year for 1962. He cashed in at contract time, signing for a reported $40,000 for the 1963 season.

When Donovan was toiling in Atlanta, trying to develop his slider to go along with his curve and fastball, he and Whit Wyatt developed a relationship that extended past the baseball diamond. Wyatt got Donovan interested in selling insurance as a way to earn extra money during the offseason. Soon Donovan had his own insurance business, operating out of his home in Quincy. In 1963, he received his stockbroker's license, and was now working for a prestigious firm in Boston.

As good as the 1962 season was for Donovan, 1963 was a down season. He started slowly, and it took a little longer to recapture his winning ways. From August 8 to 24, Donovan posted four complete-game victories, but he still ended the season with an 11-13 record and an ERA of 4.24. For Donovan, 1964 was also a struggle, as he went 7-9 and started to come out of the bullpen in the later stages of the season.

The next season, 1965, was his last in the major leagues. The Indians had some fine prospects that they wanted to see pitch on a regular basis. Sam McDowell, Sonny Siebert, and Luis Tiant were all going to be given a lot of work. Donovan was relegated to bullpen duty, making only three starts for the season. He made his final appearance on June 12 in Kansas City, and he was released on June 15.

Donovan was gracious about his departure. "I figure baseball was good to me," he said. "I was good to a lot of people in baseball too -- the hitters. It will be nice to take it easy if I don't go with another club."[7]

Donovan had a career won-lost record of 122-99 with an ERA of 3.67. He hit 15 career home runs, ranking him one of the top home-run hitters among pitchers in major-league history.

During his baseball career, Donovan had joined Eastman & Dillon in Boston as a stockbroker. Later, he became executive vice president for Bache & Co. in Boston. In 1980, Donovan opened his own real estate appraisal office in Quincy. He retired in 1994. He also worked as a distributor for Earth Care Products of Massachusetts in Quincy, which makes products from recycled plastic.

Dick Donovan died of cancer on January 6, 1997. He was survived by his wife, Patricia, and two children, Peter and Amy.

Notes

1. Hal Lebovitz, "Injuns Blessed With Irish Luck in Grabbing Slab Star Donovan," *The Sporting News*, August 18, 1962.
2. Edgar Munzel, "Donovan Winner on Addition of Slider," *The Sporting News*, July 6, 1955.
3. Edgar Munzel, "Marty Calls Chisox Better Than His '52 Star-Studded Cards," *The Sporting News*, March 9, 1955.
4. Bob Burnes, "Donovan-Furillo Duel," *The Sporting News*, December 30, 1959.
5. Bob Addie, "Hats Off," *The Sporting News*, August 9, 1961.
6. Hal Lebovitz, "Aspromonte Rips 'Reserved' Label Off Keystone Job," *The Sporting News*, February 21, 1962.
7. Bob Addie, "Bob Addie's Atoms," *The Sporting News*, July 3, 1965.

DEL ENNIS

By Edward Veit

Right after the Shibe Park public address system announced, "Now batting for the Philadelphia Phillies, number 14, Del Ennis, left field," either Gene Kelly or later Byrum Saam – both of whom did radio play-by-play for the Phillies – would say, "It's Ding Dong Del" or "Here comes Ennis the Menace." The radio listener could picture Del Ennis with a hand at each end of the bat, raising the bat over his head to stretch or loosen his back and shoulder muscles. Ennis would then stroke two practice swings and step into the batter's box. There was nothing unusual about his stance. He was square to the plate, the bat was still; as the pitcher delivered the ball he would step toward the pitcher and if he liked the pitch, he swung, using shoulders, arms, and wrists that could belong to a blacksmith. And Ennis *was* a menace. Delmer Ennis, born in Philadelphia on June 8, 1925, menaced National League pitchers for 11 years as a member of the Philadelphia Phillies. Signed by the Phillies in 1943, he was a hometown product and the original Whiz Kid.

The Whiz Kids was the name given that group of young Phillies players who in 1950 won the team's first National League pennant in 35 years. Twenty-five-year-old Del Ennis was the power behind the team. The "Kids" included, along with Ennis, Robin Roberts, Curt Simmons, Willie "Puddin' Head" Jones, Granny Hamner, Bubba Church, Richie Ashburn, Stan Lopata, Ralph "Putsy" Caballero, Bob Miller, and Stan Hollmig, all of whom were younger than 25. Ennis had a huge July, which carried the Phillies into first place. He drove in 38 runs during that month.

In 1950 Ennis led the National League with 126 runs batted in; he was fourth in batting (.311), and fifth in home runs (31). He finished fourth in the MVP voting behind teammate Jim Konstanty, Stan Musial of the St. Louis Cardinals, and Eddie Stanky of the New York Giants. It was a memorable and talented team. Roberts and Ashburn were later voted into the Baseball Hall of Fame; first baseman Eddie Waitkus recovered from a 1949 gunshot wound inflicted by a "Baseball Annie" to become the story behind Bernard Malamud's *The Natural*; and Dick Sisler (Hall of Famer George Sisler's son) hit the clinching home run that defeated the Brooklyn Dodgers on the last day of the 1950 season. (George Sisler was scouting for the Dodgers at the time.)

In the spring of 1942 Phillies scout Jocko Collins took a 15-cent trolley ride from Shibe Park to Olney High School; he was anxious to see how a young pitcher named Dick McTough could handle a husky outfielder who played for Olney. That day, Ennis hit three home runs – two shots went onto the tennis court – and a bases-loaded double. Collins immediately lost interest in the pitcher and switched his attention to Ennis, who in high school played outfield, first base, and catcher. Del had also won all-state honors as a fullback for the Olney football team. The young Ennis resisted the scout, telling him he was not good enough for professional baseball. Collins hounded Ennis until Del's father, George, the manager of the straw-hat division of Stetson Hats, sent back a signed contract.

The Phillies assigned Del to their Class-B Trenton team in 1943 and the youngster hit .346 with 18 home runs and 93 runs batted in. Soon after the baseball season ended, the 18-year-old Ennis enlisted in the US Navy. He was sent to the South Pacific, stationed with the rank of warrant officer on Guam. Ennis did not like Guam but he did get to meet and play some baseball with the likes of major leaguers Schoolboy Rowe, Johnny Vander Meer, and Billy Herman. Del developed a reputation and rumors got back to the major leagues about a kid on Guam who was hitting vicious line drives. Phils general manager Herb Pennock received – and refused – trade offers for his "navy kid."

Ennis was discharged in April 1946 and the Phillies planned o give him another season of experience in the minors, but as a war veteran he was allowed to stay with the parent club, so manager Ben Chapman inserted him in left field during their first trip west. During that trip, Ennis hit two home runs at Wrigley Field, the first off Chicago Cubs ace Claude Passeau. He was in the lineup to stay. Ennis was named to the 1946 All-Star team and finished the season with a .313 batting average, 17 home runs, and 73 runs batted in. He was named *The Sporting News* Rookie of the Year. He finished eighth on the National League

Go-Go to Glory

Longtime National League star Del Ennis had seven 100-RBI seasons for the Phillies and Cardinals before finishing his career with the 1959 White Sox.

Most Valuable Player ballot.

Ennis suffered the "sophomore jinx" in 1947. His batting average (.275) and home run (12) totals were down, but after that, he became one of the top run producers in baseball, beginning with a 30-homer, 95-RBI season in 1948. From that point on his numbers were consistent with or even better than those of Mickey Mantle, Ted Williams, Willie Mays, Duke Snider, Gil Hodges, and Stan Musial. For the 10-year span from 1948 through 1957, Ennis batted in 1,075 runs – second only to Musial (1,120) over that period – while maintaining a batting average above .280 and belting, on average, 25 home runs per season.

Much has been said of Ennis's fielding and some of it was not kind. However, he was capable of overcoming his mistakes, sometimes in spectacular fashion. According to Robin Roberts, once in the 1950 season, Ennis overran a shot to right field by Jackie Robinson and though off-stride, reached out and caught the ball barehanded. Robinson ran into right field, yelling at Ennis all the way, "How did you catch that ball?" Richie Ashburn observed, "Ennis reached up and caught the ball barehanded on the dead run, like picking an apple off a tree. He never cracked a smile, just like it was a routine play."[1] In 1952, at the Polo Grounds, the Giants' Willie Mays slugged a ball to deep right-center field, near the 455-foot sign; Ennis was off at the crack of the bat. For Mays this could have been an inside-the-park home run. As Ennis was about to reach for the ball, he tripped over the right-center bullpen mound and as he was falling, reached out and caught the ball, again barehanded.

After the triumph of 1950, Ennis had a down year in 1951. The Philadelphia fans began to jeer and boo, and Ennis, the only Philadelphia native on the team, was their target. It didn't help that the Phillies team never matched the promise the Whiz Kids showed in 1950. They were always finishing behind the Brooklyn Dodgers and their "Boys of Summer" or Durocher's Giants or Musial's Cardinals. In the 1950s New York baseball was in full bloom with the Yankees, Dodgers, and Giants consistently appearing in the World Series; there was no room for the aging Whiz Kids.

Ennis did suffer through a bad season in 1951. His batting average plummeted more than 40 points to .267, home runs fell off to 15, and his runs batted in amounted to only 73 after a league-leading 126 during the pennant-winning year. Ennis bounced from that 1951 slump with four straight seasons of 20-plus homers and 100-plus RBIs, and his 364 RBIs from 1953 through 1955 ranked second in the majors behind Snider's 392. But he remained a target of the fans.

Thirty years or more later, Mike Schmidt received – and in the 2000s Pat Burrell also received – that same booing, but it never matched what Del Ennis endured from 1951 until he was traded to the Cardinals in 1956. Robin Roberts reported in his book *The Whiz Kids and the 1950 Pennant* a comment by one of the Phillies' young pitchers, Steve Ridzik:

> "I had come to a ballgame against the Dodgers in Shibe Park. It was the seventh inning and we were ahead by three runs, but the bases were loaded with two outs. A fly ball goes out to Del and, with two outs, everybody is running. Damn if the ball doesn't hit him on the heel of the glove and he drops it. All three runs score and we have a tie ballgame. We had a packed house and the fans start to boo him unmercifully. It was terrible.

• DEL ENNIS •

The next inning when he went out to left field they booed and booed and booed. They booed him when he ran off the field at the end of the inning. Unmerciful. I looked over at him sitting in the dugout and he's got his hands clenched and he's just white. He's just livid. Here he is a hometown guy and everything… He came to bat in the last of the eighth inning with the score still tied and two outs. The fans just booed and booed and all our guys on the bench are just hotter than a pistol. We were ready to fight the thirty-some thousand. He didn't deserve that. So Del hits one on top of the roof and as he's rounding the bases the crowd goes crazy. They cheered and cheered and cheered. They were standing and wouldn't sit down. They wanted him to come out of the dugout. But he wouldn't move. He just sat there as white as a ghost, mad as hell. When he went out in the ninth inning the fans stood up and applauded again. I had to step back off the rubber a couple of times because they wouldn't sit down.

That was one of the greatest thrills of my career, watching something like that happen to somebody else. It was beautiful."[2]

Another time, in 1955, Ennis took his son to a game on the son's birthday and the Phillies beat the Cardinals, 7-2. Ennis hit home runs in the first, sixth, and seventh innings and drove in all seven runs. He popped out on his other at-bat in the third inning and the fans "liked to boo me out of the park."[3] Several other times he answered the boo-birds with game-winning hits, but much of the booing over a five-year period was harsh. Ennis rationalized that he was from North Philly, and the booing was led by fans from South Philly. Ennis was traded to the Cardinals for Rip Repulski and Bobby Morgan after the 1956 season. When he returned to Philadelphia for the first time, he received a standing ovation that lasted long enough to indicate to Ennis that he had been appreciated.

In 1957 with the Cardinals, Ennis batted .286, with 24 home runs and 105 runs batted in while leaving a void in the middle of the Phillies lineup that wasn't filled until Mike Schmidt arrived in Philadelphia. But the 1957 campaign was the last good season of Ennis's career. In 1958 he hit only three home runs in 329 at-bats while dealing with a family crisis; *The Sporting News* reported that his wife had suffered a nervous breakdown during the season. That October Ennis was again traded, this time to the Cincinnati Reds.

Unfortunately for Ennis, the Reds' new manager in 1959 was Mayo Smith, who Ennis felt had been instrumental in trading him away when Smith managed the Phillies from 1955 through 1957. Ennis said about the 1959 Reds in an interview in *The Major Leaguer*, "We had a good ballclub. We felt we could win. But, here again Mayo Smith had come over to manage the Reds then. I probably had my best spring ever that year too. I hit something like 12 home runs and had about 30 RBIs, but the manager initiated a platoon system in right field with Jerry Lynch."[4] Once the season started, Ennis got only 12 at-bats before being traded to the Chicago White Sox on May 1.

At the age of 34, Ennis finished his 14-season baseball career after playing in 26 games for the White Sox during their 1959 pennant-winning year. He batted .219, had 2 home runs, 6 doubles, and 7 runs batted in; the White Sox released Ennis on June 20. Ennis, however, was anxious to get back to Philadelphia, his family, and his bowling-alley business. He never really wanted to play for any team but the Phillies.

While with the Cardinals, Ennis roomed with Stan Musial, and "Stan the Man" advised him to get into the bowling-alley business. Del Ennis Lanes, a bowling alley owned and operated by Ennis and the Phillies' longtime traveling secretary, John R. Wise, was opened in 1958. Both retired from the bowling-alley business around 1993. Ennis also raised and raced greyhounds; the names of his dogs were those of former teammates from the 1950 Whiz Kids: Granny, Richie, Bubba, Puddin' Head, and so on. Ennis, along with Robin Roberts, was also instrumental in starting "Dream Team" activities – those fantasy-camp activities where men from all walks of life would enjoy a week playing baseball with former major-league stars.

Del and his wife, Liz, raised six children, but only one demonstrated Dad's athletic ability. David Ennis was an infielder for the University of Delaware and became a lawyer in Elkins Park, Pennsylvania.

Del Ennis died on February 8, 1996, in his home in Huntingdon Valley, Pennsylvania, of complications from diabetes. He was survived by his wife, six children, 13 grandchildren, and one great-grandchild.

Sources

Eck, Frank, Associated Press, *Monitor-Index and Democrat* (Mobley, Missouri), November 29, 1946, 8.

Ennis, Liz, Telephone interview, March 10, 2008.

Fitzpatrick, Frank, "Why did they boo Del Ennis?" *Philadelphia Inquirer,* June 29, 2003, D1.

Lawson, Earl, "Redlegs 'Gambling' on Ennis' Return to Old Slugging Form," *The Sporting News*, October 15, 1958.

McKee, Don, "Ennis dies at age 70; starred for the Phils," *Philadelphia Inquirer,* February 10, 1996, C3.

Orodenker, Richard, editor, *The Phillies Reader* (Philadelphia: Temple University Press, 1996).

Roberts, Robin, *My Life in Baseball* (Chicago: Triumph Books, 2003).

Notes

1. Robin Roberts and C. Paul Rogers III, *The Whiz Kids and the 1950 Pennant* (Philadelphia, Temple University Press, 1996), 241.
2. Roberts and Rogers, 239-240.
3. Roberts and Rogers, 240.
4. "The Del Ennis Interview: That Philly Feeling." *The Major Leaguer*, "America's Baseball Newsletter," 1985, 1-2.

SAMMY ESPOSITO

By Justin Murphy

For every 30-home-run hitter and 20-game winner, there is often a role player who, though contributing less, is embraced by the fans and given nearly unconditional support in return for those elusive attributes scrappiness and hustle. For the pennant-winning White Sox of 1959, that player was Sammy Esposito. Despite spending the majority of his career watching Nellie Fox and Luis Aparicio from the bench, the local boy endeared himself to South Side fans with heady play and solid defense. Esposito later made good use of the insight collected during his playing days, becoming one of the most successful coaches in the history of the Atlantic Coast Conference over the course of a long career at North Carolina State.

Samuel D. Esposito was born on December 15, 1931, to Mr. and Mrs. Joseph Esposito on the South Side of Chicago. He first made a name for himself while attending Fenger High School at 112th and Wallace. There, he was a three-sport athlete, starring in basketball and football as well as baseball. In fact, it is debatable which of the three sports he excelled at the most. He began playing football his junior year, when coach Chuck Palmer happened upon him throwing a football in a physical education class. That year, as a 16-year-old, he led Fenger to a tie for the city championship, throwing 12 touchdown passes and running for two. As a point guard on the basketball team, he averaged about 30 points per game in both his junior and senior seasons, leading the city in scoring in the latter despite standing only 5 feet 7 inches tall. In his final game, Esposito set a single-game record for the city of Chicago (since surpassed) by scoring an incredible 81 points. In the spring, he played shortstop and occasionally pitched for coach Harry Dixon, leading Fenger to a 14-8 record in his senior year.

After graduating in 1950, Esposito was offered contracts by several big-league clubs but passed them up in favor of enrolling at Indiana University. There, he continued to play three sports with a great deal of success; he was named IU's outstanding freshman athlete in 1951. Jason Hiner writes in his book *Mac's Boys: Branch McCracken and the Legendary 1953 Hurryin' Hoosiers*:

> Down the stretch of the 1951-52 [basketball] season, Esposito emerged as one of IU's rising stars. He was lightning quick, had great hands, and was very smart with the basketball. He was a terrific passer and could use his athletic ability to break down the defense and create shots for himself and his teammates.[1]

It was on the baseball diamond, however, that Esposito made his biggest mark as a Hoosier. In the 1952 season – his only year of varsity baseball at Indiana – he batted .285 in 26 games, .333 in Big Ten games. He spent that summer playing in the Iowa semipro league, where he batted .450. Esposito's amateur career came to a close on August 29, 1952, as he was signed to a big-league deal by White Sox scout Doug Minor. Minor signed several future major leaguers for the White Sox, including Orval Grove, Bob Kennedy, and Don Kolloway, as well as 1959 White Sox pitcher Rudy Arias. Esposito said in a 1956 interview that he had signed "because I wanted to get into organized ball before he went into the Army."[2] Reports of Esposito's contract differ. A March 24, 1953, *Chicago Tribune* article, which credits Minor, said he signed for $55,000. Jason Hiner wrote that he received $50,000—a $17,000 bonus and $11,000 for each of his first three seasons as a professional. In either case, it was a generous offer for the era, and Esposito was given an immediate opportunity to prove he deserved it.

Sammy's first game in the major leagues came on September 28, 1952, a month after he'd signed, at Comiskey Park. The third-place White Sox were taking on the seventh-place St. Louis Browns in their season finale, and only 10,343 fans turned out to watch. Esposito played shortstop and batted leadoff. He collected his first major-league hit in the game, a single off Dick Littlefield, who had taken over in the fourth inning for injured starter Duane Pillette. Inauspiciously, Esposito was promptly thrown out

Chicago native Sammy Esposito had a 10-year MLB career as a utility infielder before becoming a successful college baseball coach at North Carolina State University.

attempting to steal second. He also struck out twice and made two errors, thereby fitting in well with the lackluster Sox, who lost the game, 12-1. Esposito's hit was one of only five for the team. This brief appearance earned him the distinction of being the youngest player in the major leagues in 1952, as he was several months shy of his 21st birthday. It should be noted that after signing with the White Sox, Esposito continued to work toward his degree in physical education, at Indiana and later at George Williams College in Chicago. He eventually graduated from Indiana several years later.

Esposito attended spring training with the White Sox in El Centro, California, in 1953, but failed to win a roster spot and was optioned on March 24 to the Waterloo, Iowa, White Hawks of the Class B Three-I League. The White Hawks were managed by longtime big-league catcher Zack Taylor, who had also several seasons managing the St. Louis Browns (1946; 1948-51). In Waterloo, Esposito hit .265 in 96 games while playing shortstop. His season was cut short on August 14, 1953, when, as expected, he was inducted into to the Army. He was assigned to the 44th Division in Fort Lewis, Washington, as a private. While stationed at Fort Lewis over the next 18 months, Esposito played on the division's basketball and baseball teams, hitting .390 over 70 games.

The 23-year-old was discharged from the Army in the spring of 1955. He joined the White Sox at the end of May, and was sent to the Memphis Chicks of the Double-A Southern Association. The Chicks played in the peculiarly-shaped Russwood Park, where it was farther to the outfield corners than to straightaway center. Esposito again had the good fortune of playing for a well-known manager, as White Sox Hall of Famer Ted Lyons took over for former Pirate Jack Cassini midway through the year. In 101 games, Esposito rapped out 101 hits. The 1955 campaign also gave the young player his first extended experience at third base, where he had been moved in order to accommodate teammate Luis Aparicio. Esposito later spoke gratefully of manager Cassini's patience with him as he adjusted to the new position. At the end of Memphis' season, he was recalled to Chicago and played two games at third base without collecting a hit.

It was during spring training of 1956 that Esposito finally earned a permanent spot on the club. Manager Marty Marion was enamored with the 24-year-old: "There could be new developments before the season starts," said Marion, "but right now I'd say Esposito will be our third baseman. He's done everything correctly at third. In fact, I don't know what more a kid could do to win a job."[3] George Kell, a future Hall of Famer and the Sox' incumbent third baseman, commented, "I liked Esposito last fall when he played a few games for us. I told [Marion] again this spring that I thought the kid was a very bright prospect."[4]

The season was still several weeks away, however, and by Opening Day, Kell and journeyman Bob Kennedy had moved ahead of Esposito on the depth chart. Sammy made sporadic starts in April and May, but was not rewarded for his success. On May 23, he doubled and drew a bases-loaded walk in a 3-2 victory over the Orioles, but was on the bench the next game as Minnie Minoso played the hot corner.

Five days later, Esposito again made the most of an opportunity, driving in two runs in the ninth inning to tie the game against the Athletics, but again was not in the starting lineup for the next game. The month of May also saw a rather significant shake-up in the Chicago infield as a result of two trades. On May 15, Kennedy, Jim Brideweser, and Harry Byrd were dealt to the Tigers for outfielder Jim Delsing and infielder Fred Hatfield. Six days later, Kell was the centerpiece of a six-player swap with Baltimore, which brought pitcher Jim Wilson and outfielder Dave Philley to Chicago.

Esposito's two spring-training competitors for the third-base position were thus gone just a month into the season. Unfortunately for him, newly-acquired Fred Hatfield stepped into the position; for the season, Esposito appeared in 84 games around the infield. He batted only .228 but had an on-base percentage of .371, walking 41 times against just 19 strikeouts. Three of his eight career home runs also came in 1956; the first was on August 1, off Washington lefty Chuck Stobbs. (Seven of the eight homers were solo shots.)

While Sammy struggled in his rookie season, the White Sox' other young infielder, Aparicio, led the American League with 21 stolen bases and was named the Rookie of the Year, garnering 22 of 24 possible votes. His double-play partner was 28-year-old Nellie Fox, who had already been elected to five All-Star Games. It was perhaps unfortunate timing for Esposito to spend most of his career in the same infield as Aparicio and Fox, both of whom ended up in the Hall of Fame. On many other teams, Sammy might have started, but, talented as he was, he couldn't crack that particular White Sox infield. In a 1959 *Chicago Tribune* feature, he summarized his situation succinctly:

> When I was playing at Fenger High School, I hoped to make the big leagues as a shortstop. So I end up with the White Sox, who have Luis Aparicio, baseball's best shortstop. When I was with the Waterloo club, I figured maybe someday I'd be a major league second baseman. So, how much chance do I have of dislodging Nellie Fox? I played third base at Memphis, alongside Aparicio at short, and when I land in Chicago, where the position is open, I find they don't want .247 hitters at third base.[5]

Marty Marion was replaced as manager after the 1956 season by former Cleveland Indians skipper Al Lopez. Like his predecessor, Lopez was impressed by Esposito's play early on: "When I managed Cleveland, I never thought of him as anything more than a possible reserve infielder. But he really has made me revise my opinion. As a matter of fact, I gained a lot of respect for his ability before we even left spring camp."[6] As in the previous year, however, Sammy failed to convince his manager that he deserved a starting position. He battled Hatfield and rookie Tommy Brown during spring training. When both faltered, Lopez called in outfielder Bubba Phillips to man third base, relegating Esposito to the bench once more.

On June 26, Esposito, who was batting just .171 in limited time, got the start at third base, replacing the struggling Phillips. Over the next five weeks, he started 22 games. In that time, he batted .253, but had an on-base percentage of .357 and committed only three errors. The *Chicago Tribune*, in an a pictorial feature entitled "Sammy's Medicine Show," raved about the young man "who has been performing all sorts of rare fielding tricks for the White Sox at third base"[7]; after a tough loss to New York on July 15, the *Daily Defender* asserted that "Esposito alone must have robbed the Yankees of at least three hits with the brilliant fielding at third base." More significant was the praise of manager Lopez: "Sammy took his lumps and learned a lot while waiting it out, and now it's paid off. … He's young and tough and aggressive, and the kind of third baseman the White Sox have been looking for."[8] As July came to a close, Chicago trailed the Yankees by only 3½ games, while maintaining a healthy 7½-game lead over third-place Boston. Phillips returned to the starting role at the beginning of August. For the season, Esposito hit .205, though with a .344 OBP, in 176 at-bats; it was the last time in his career he had 100 at-bats in a single season.

In 1958, it was newly-acquired Billy Goodman who received the bulk of the playing time at third base, with Phillips chipping in when healthy. Esposito stepped to the plate on 97 times that year, hitting .247 and getting on base at a .358 clip. The high point of the year for Sammy came on September 5, when his seventh-inning double off Cleveland's Don Mossi – one of his three hits that day – moved the tying runs into scoring position in an eventual White Sox victory.

By the start of the 1959 season, Esposito was 27 years old, and had been labeled, not unfairly, as a good-field, no-hit utility infielder. He was no longer seen as competition for a starting position at third base or anywhere else; in 1959 he started three games at third in addition to six starts spelling Aparicio at short. Manager Lopez, however, continued to support him: "Don't underestimate Sam just because he isn't a regular," the skipper said. "Name me any major leaguers who could beat out Little Lu with his glove, or Foxey with his bat!"[9] At the same time, the South Side fans had taken a shine to the local boy, who still lived on Lafayette Avenue with his parents. Indeed, despite appearing at the plate only 81 times in 1959, Esposito was able to deliver some important hits for his team. In the season opener, on April 10, he singled off Detroit's Don Mossi in the 14th inning, allowing Fox to follow with a game-winning home run. On June 21, Esposito hit his only home run of the season, a solo shot that proved to be the difference in Billy Pierce's 3-2 victory over Boston. The game reports added that he "figured in two double plays as well as handling himself with aplomb on defense."[10] In some ways, Esposito was characteristic of the Go-Go Sox of 1959: He played outstanding defense when called upon, and was skilled at drawing walks and sacrificing for teammates. On July 25, when the Sox defeated Baltimore in 17 innings – their 23rd one-run win of the season, and their fourth in a row – it was Esposito who crossed the plate with the game-winner.

Unfortunately for the White Sox and their fans, the euphoria occasioned on September 22, when the Sox clinched the pennant, did not outlive the month of October, as Chicago lost to the Los Angeles Dodgers in six games. Esposito had just two at-bats in the World Series, both in the first game. He entered the game for Goodman in the fourth inning and struck out looking against Clem Labine. In his next at-bat, he tapped a grounder back to reliever Johnny Klippstein. His only other appearance was as a pinch-runner in Game Three.

Esposito played seven full seasons in his career, of which the 1959 campaign was the midpoint. From 1956 to 1958, he amassed 441 official at-bats; from 1960 to 1962, he had just 252. Remaining with the Sox as a utility fielder, he totaled 14, 16, and 19 hits in the first three years of the 1960s, getting most of his appearances as a late-inning pinch-runner or defensive replacement.

Although Esposito's skills were fading, the hometown fans continued to cheer for the scrappy infielder. During one game in 1960, his scrappiness was put to the test. On September 7, in a home match against the Yankees, Esposito was starting at second for the injured Nellie Fox. In the eighth inning, he muffed a double-play ball that would have ended a New York threat. Minutes later, an enraged fan, Willie Harris, charged onto the field and confronted Esposito at his position. "I couldn't make out too well what the guy said," Sammy told the papers. "Something about having money bet on the ball game. I didn't do a thing, and when it looked like he was going to swing, I swung at him. I didn't hit him, I missed him, and then the players and ushers came around and broke it up."[11] After having been escorted off the field, Harris punched a security guard and knocked his front teeth out, earning himself a $25 fine, plus costs, in court the next day.

In 1963, Esposito was bothered by a sore arm and played in only one game with the Sox, appearing as a ninth-inning pinch runner on April 16. He was released on May 9 as the White Sox brought their roster down to 25. The *Tribune* reported that Chicago had offered him a scouting position, but the 31-year-old Esposito opted to pursue his career elsewhere. On May 26, he signed with the Kansas City Athletics. Sammy played in 18 games with Kansas City, starting seven of them and collecting five hits. His final big-league game was a loss to Detroit on August 23, 1963; in this game, he entered the game as a defensive replacement and singled off Frank Lary in his final at-bat. He was released after the end of the season, on October 7.

His playing career over, Esposito began to look toward the future. Since 1959, he had been an assistant basketball coach at East Chicago (Indiana) Washington High School. He returned to Indiana University in 1964 for additional coursework in hopes of becoming a full-time coach.

Esposito's second career began in earnest in 1967, when he was hired as head baseball coach at North Carolina State University in Raleigh. He had almost immediate success, as the Wolfpack won the Atlantic Coast Conference championship in his second season and finished third overall at the College World Series. Among his players that year were future major leaguers Dick Burris, Tommy Smith, and Mike Caldwell, runner-up for the 1978 American League Cy Young award. Esposito also coached the freshman basketball team from 1967 to 1969, then was a varsity assistant under Norm Sloan until 1978.

Twelve of Esposito's college players went on to play in the major leagues, including pitchers Mike

• SAMMY ESPOSITO •

Caldwell, Tim Stoddard, and Dan Plesac, and outfielders Doug Strange and Greg Briley. Besides 1968, his teams also won the ACC crown in 1973, 1974, and 1975. He was named ACC coach of the year in 1984 and 1986, as his teams finished 32-8 and 35-15, respectively. Sam finally retired after the 1987 season at the age of 55. In 21 seasons at the helm, he led the Wolfpack baseball team to an overall record of 513-253-4, making him the winningest coach in school history. His son, Sammy Jr., played baseball at North Carolina State from 1999 to 2002, and in 2008 was an assistant coach for Ray Tanner at the University of South Carolina. Tanner had served as an assistant coach under the elder Esposito at N.C. State, and succeeded him as head coach in 1988 before moving to South Carolina in 1997. Esposito, who spent the last nine years of his life in assisted living in Newland, North Carolina, died at age 86 in on July 10, 2018. His wife Noreen had passed away in January of 2018. The Espositos had a son, Sammy Jr., and a daughter, Toni, along with five grandchildren.

It is often said that mediocre players make the best coaches. For Sammy Esposito, it was certainly educational to spend seven years as a member of a fundamentally sound White Sox team that routinely competed for the pennant. The time he spent on the bench as Luis Aparicio and Nellie Fox took the field may in fact have made him the outstanding coach that he was. Chicagoans will recall Esposito fondly from those Go-Go Sox teams, as a steady if modest contributor, a local boy who made good.

Sources

In addition to the sources cited in the Notes, the author also consulted www.baseball-reference.com, www.thebaseballcube.com, and SABR Minor Leagues Database, http://minors.sabrwebs.com/
2008 N.C. State basketball and baseball media guides.

Archives of the *Chicago Tribune* and *The Sporting News* (contact author for specific issues)

"Wolfpack Baseball: A Century of Achievement" display, North Carolina State library web site. http://www.lib.ncsu.edu/exhibits/baseball/highlights.html.

Samuel Donato Esposito obituary, *Raleigh News & Observer*, July 15, 2018

Thank you to David Vincent, for the home-run information; Eric Hanauer, for his recollections from the period at George Williams College; Dave Goss, for statistics and sources from Indiana University; Lorna Donley of the Special Collections and Preservation Division of Harold Washington Library in Chicago, for locating, photocopying, and mailing things from Fenger High School yearbooks; and readers of the SABR listserve for helpful thoughts and suggestions. Also to the editors and organizers of the 1959 White Sox project, for their patience and encouragement.

Notes

1. Jason Hiner, *Mac's Boys: Branch McCracken and the Legendary 1953 Hurryin' Hoosiers* (Bloomington & Indianapolis: Quarry Books, 2006), 101.
2. John C. Hoffman, "Marion Finds New Sizzler in Esposito at Hot Corner," *The Sporting News*, April 4, 1956.
3. John C. Hoffman, "Chisox Show New Faces in Three Places," *The Sporting News*, April 11, 1956.
4. *Ibid.*
5. David Condon, "Sox Jack of All Trades is Master of One," *Chicago Tribune*, March 5, 1959.
6. Edgar Munzel, "Chisox Find New Third Sacker in 'Forgotten' Sam," *The Sporting News*, July 17, 1957.
7. "Sammy's Medicine Show – Magic Stops and Juggling" (Pictorial Feature), *Chicago Tribune*, July 26, 1957.
8. *Chicago Daily Defender*, July 16, 1957.
9. Condon.
10. Richard Dozer, "Homers Help Pierce Beat Boston, 3-2," *Chicago Tribune*, June 22, 1959.
11. Richard Dozer, "Yanks Beat White Sox, 6-4; Orioles Lose, 3-2," *Chicago Tribune*, September 8, 1960.

NELLIE FOX

By Robert W. Bigelow and Don Zminda

Nellie Fox was the heart of the 1959 Go-Go White Sox, the team that brought Chicago's South Side its first pennant since the tarnished Black Sox season 40 years earlier. The image of Little Nel in his batting stance has become iconic – a choked-up grip on his bottle bat with a wad of chewing tobacco bulging in his cheek. Fox was an unimpressive physical specimen at 5-feet-9 without much innate athletic ability, but determination and opportunity helped a gritty kid with a burning love for the game become a perennial all-star and ultimately a Hall of Famer. Nellie Fox won a Most Valuable Player Award, spent 12 years as an All-Star, won three Gold Glove Awards, and was a dominant force at his position for over a decade.

Jacob Nelson Fox – he was always known by his middle name – was born on Christmas Day 1927 in St. Thomas, Pennsylvania, a small town in Franklin County about 30 miles west of Gettysburg. Nellie's father, Jacob L. Fox, known as Jake, was born on a farm but earned his living as a carpenter. Jake loved baseball and played second base on the St. Thomas town team. He was known as a hard-nosed player and a good bunter, traits he passed on to his son. The Fox family has a picture of young Nelson at the age of 2, holding a homemade bat designed by his father. Even then, Fox was swinging the bat left-handed.

Nelson was the youngest of three brothers. One of them, Frank, died tragically at the age of 3; the other, Wayne, who was seven years Nelson's senior, shared the Fox family's love for baseball. As a boy Nelson was often called by the nickname Pug; he wasn't referred to as Nellie until he began his professional baseball career. Nelson loved all sports, but baseball and soccer were his favorites. "I think I liked soccer better than baseball for a while," Fox told a writer. "I was only about 130 pounds, but I liked the contact. I liked to mix it up."[1]

Fox soon turned most of his attention to baseball, starting out as the mascot and batboy for the St. Thomas town team. He constantly pressured his father and the St. Thomas coach to put him into a game, and when he was given his first opportunity at the age of 10, he amazed everyone by getting a pinch-hit single off a pitcher who was considered the best in the area. Eventually he joined his dad in the St. Thomas lineup, playing first base while Jake manned second. He played ball almost anywhere he could find a team: on the St. Thomas High School team, in American Legion ball, and in the nearby Chambersburg Twilight League. As a teenager he also took on a lifelong habit that would become of his trademarks: chewing tobacco.

Fox was never much of a student: In class he was known to hide sports books or magazines in his notebook and read them when he was supposed to be studying. By the age of 16 he had decided that he wanted to make baseball his career. "I had to be a ballplayer," he said. "I wasn't very good at school and I didn't have any outside hobbies. I played ball. That's what I did."[2] His mother, Mae, was concerned about Nelson's future, and one day early in 1944, she wrote a letter to Connie Mack, owner/manager of the Philadelphia A's. "My boy is baseball crazy," she wrote. "He won't study in school. … He worries me to death. … All he talks about is you and the Athletics."[3] Mack wrote back that if her son actually had talent, it was possible to make a living playing ball. "I may one of these days be able to help him," Mack wrote.[4]

Due to wartime travel restrictions, the A's were holding 1944 spring training in Frederick, Maryland, about 50 miles from St. Thomas, and like most major-league teams, the club was holding open tryouts in an effort to fill its war-depleted farm system. With the encouragement they'd received from Mack's letter, Jake and Mae decided to take Nelson to the camp to try out for the team. Though they didn't tell Nelson, the Foxes hoped that the A's would tell their son that he would be better off staying in school.

So in a story that seems like something out of a 1940s B movie, Jake and Nelson drove to Frederick, found the A's hotel, introduced themselves to Connie Mack, and got a chance to try out for the team. (Fox later squelched the oft-repeated story that he showed up at the A's camp smoking a big cigar.) According to Philadelphia sportswriter Stan Baumgartner, "(Coach) Earle Mack had difficulty finding a small enough uniform to fit the boy."[5] Though he was almost ridiculously short for a first baseman at no more than

• NELLIE FOX •

Few players handled the bat as skillfully as Nellie Fox, the American League's Most Valuable Player in 1959. In over 10,000 major league plate appearances, Fox struck out just 216 times.

5-feet-6, Fox made a good impression on Mack. According to a story in the *Frederick Post*, "Connie Mack liked the way the youth conducted himself at the plate and his technique of handling low throws to the initial sack."[6] To Jake and Mae's surprise, the A's decided to offer the 16-year-old Fox a contract to join their minor-league system. "(Mack) probably thought the boy was good enough for Class D," said Jake, "and that he would get as much education by being around with a baseball team as he would in high school."[7]

After using him in a few exhibition games, the A's sent Fox to the Class-B Interstate League's Lancaster Red Roses, managed by Lena Blackburne. Fox immediately showed some talent, batting .325 while playing both first base and the outfield. It was no surprise that he was not a slugger, with no home runs in 24 games, though he did drive in 12 runs. Nellie was later sent down to the Jamestown Falcons of the Pony League (Class D) for 56 games and hit .304, again with no home runs.

Fox was back with Lancaster in 1945 and hit .314 in 140 games. Moved to second base, the position he would play for the rest of his career, he led the league in hits and runs and hit his first professional home run. However, Fox did not have an opportunity to immediately follow up on this strong showing, as he spent the 1946 season in the military, stationed in Korea. Perhaps the most notable occurrence in his life that year was his engagement to Joanne Statler on Christmas Day 1946. The two had met when both were in high school; "I was a freshman and he was my first date," said Joanne, recalling that they attended a Christmas dance.[8]

Fox was again with Lancaster in 1947, hitting .281 with one home run and 22 RBIs. He was called up to the Athletics very briefly that year and appeared in seven games, going hitless in three at-bats. He spent the 1948 season at Lincoln of the Class-A Western League, hitting .311. He led the league in hits and was named to the All-Star team. He and Joanne were married in Lincoln on June 30; the couple would have two daughters, Bonnie and Tracy. Later in the season, Fox was called up to the big club again and played three games at the end of the season, hitting .154 in 13 at-bats.

In 1949 Fox stayed with the Athletics all year, playing behind Pete Suder, who was in his seventh year with the club and had long had a lock on the second-base job. Fox played 88 games and hit .255 with no homers and only eight extra-base hits. He had desire but there were holes in his game, most significantly the inability to produce consistently at the plate. Connie Mack, often a masterful judge of talent, must have felt that Fox was never going to be more than a journeyman, because the A's put him on the trade market after the season. Connie Mack badly underestimated Nellie Fox.

Shortly after the 1949 season, the A's traded Fox to the White Sox for catcher Joe Tipton. This could not have been terrific news for Fox, who was leaving a Philadelphia team that had a solid, professional second baseman in Suder in front of him to a club that had Cass Michaels, the American League's starting second baseman in the 1949 All-Star Game, patrolling the middle.

After beginning the 1950 season as a backup to Michaels, Fox caught a break when the Sox traded Michaels to Washington on May 31 in a multiplayer deal which netted them slugging first baseman Eddie Robinson. Infielder Al Kozar, who came along with

Robinson as part of the deal, was expected to be Michaels' replacement, but Kozar promptly hurt his back hitting a home run against the Yankees. Given an opportunity to play every day, Fox was a bust, hitting .247 with no home runs and 30 RBIs in 130 games. His most impressive traits continued to be his determination and competitive fire. "Nellie was the greatest competitor I ever played with," recalled Billy Pierce, Fox's longtime teammate as well as his roommate for 11 years. "Baseball, gin rummy, bowling ... whatever he played, he just loved to compete."[9] Getting Fox to hustle and work was never an issue for any man who ever managed him. If anything, those who managed Fox wanted him to take an occasional break.

The White Sox were training in Pasadena, California, in 1951, and Fox was anything but a lock to make the Opening Day roster. "Nellie called me at home from spring training that year," recalled Joanne Fox, "and said, 'I don't think they're going to keep me. It looks they're going to send me back to the minors.'"[10] And in fact the White Sox had already made a tentative decision to sell Fox to the Portland club of the Pacific Coast League. But Fox had a supporter in White Sox coach Ray Berres. Berres told new manager Paul Richards, "He can play. He'll play for you if he has to play on crutches."[11]

Richards adopted Fox as a project. Former Yankee second base great Joe Gordon worked with Fox on his fielding. A particular focus was turning the double play. "It was brutal the way Fox was pivoting," Richards commented later. "I'm surprised he didn't get hurt making the pivot the way he was dragging his foot across the bag."[12] The drills with Gordon paid off, thanks in good part to Fox's determination. "He made himself into a good second baseman just by working so hard," said Billy Pierce.[13]

As a hitter, Fox did have one amazing ability – making contact with the ball. He struck out only once in every 48 plate appearances during his career, and never more than 18 times in a season. But the rest of his offensive game needed work, and White Sox coach Doc Cramer took Fox under his wing. The former Athletics/Red Sox/Tigers outfielder worked with Fox on his hitting, particularly stopping him from lunging at the ball. Cramer also suggested the use of a bottle bat. "Prior to that Nellie had been using a thin-handled bat," said Billy Pierce. "He was pulling the ball too much, but after Cramer gave him a thicker-handled bat, Nellie began spraying the ball all over the field."[14] Richards also worked with Fox on bunting, and before long, according to Pierce, Fox was the best bunter in baseball among left-handed hitters.

The 1951 season was the turning point in Fox's career. One-third of the way through this breakout year, he was hitting .364 and the Sox were in first place. That July he was the American League's starting second basemen in the All-Star Game. He hit only four home runs with 55 RBIs but finished this stellar season with a .313 batting average which was good enough for fifth in the AL. He also tied for second in the league in both hits and triples. His performance helped the club improve to an 81-73 record after seven sub-.500 seasons, finishing in fourth place. This season was the template for the next decade for the Sox and for Nellie Fox – gritty, solid, fundamentally sound baseball. Sox fans had a burgeoning star that they could identify with.

The breakthrough season in 1951 established Fox as a star, and he continued to embellish his reputation over the next decade. Making the American League All-Star team every year from 1951 through 1961, Fox led the league in hits four times during the 1950s and scored 100 or more runs in four straight seasons (1954-57). In the field, Fox led AL second basemen in total chances for nine straight seasons (1952-60), in double plays five times and in fielding percentage four times. In the eight-season span from 1952 through 1959, Fox finished in the top 10 of the American League's Most Valuable Player voting six times.

But while Fox's career continued to flourish, the 1950s were often a maddening time for the White Sox and their fans. The 1954 season was typical. Fox had one of the best years of his career, setting career highs with 201 hits, 111 runs scored, 16 stolen bases, and a .319 batting average. He also led the league in games played with 155 while striking only 12 times in 706 plate appearances. Fox's performance helped the White Sox win 94 games, the most for any Sox club since 1920. But the team still finished a distant third behind the Indians and Yankees.

Paul Richards left the White Sox to take over the Baltimore Orioles at the tail end of the 1954 season, and Marty Marion took over as manager. Neither Richards nor Marion could break the club's streak of third-place finishes, which reached five in a row in 1956, but on August 6, 1955, Marion did break Fox's streak of consecutive games played at 274. Giving Nellie a day off did not sit well with Fox. While Fox referred to it as "the most miserable day I ever spent in baseball," Marion said, "It was the most miserable day of my life too – having to listen to him gripe from the bench."¹⁵ The next day Fox started a new streak that lasted 798 games – an all-time record for second basemen.

The third-place finish under Marion in 1956 marked the arrival of rookie shortstop Luis Aparicio, who took over after Fox's previous double-play partner, Chico Carrasquel, was traded to Cleveland. Though Carrasquel had been a four-time All-Star, it was immediately evident that the Sox had something special in Aparicio. Luis won the Rookie of the Year award in 1956 and stole 21 bases.

Another important man came to the White Sox in 1957, when Al Lopez took over as manager after one pennant and five second-place finishes with Cleveland. Fox celebrated Lopez's South Side debut by leading the league in hits, batting .317, and topping AL second basemen in putouts, assists, and double plays. He also became major-league baseball's first Gold Glove winner at second base and finished fourth in the league's MVP voting behind Mickey Mantle, Ted Williams, and Roy Sievers. Better still, the Sox finally broke out of their third-place rut by moving up a notch to second place.

After another second-place finish in 1958, the Sox added a final key element when a shrewd new owner, Bill Veeck, bought controlling interest in the team. Veeck brought flamboyance, enthusiasm, and a knack for making things happen to a team that was ready to reach the top, and it all came together for the Sox in 1959.

With Veeck and Lopez providing sound management as well as a belief that the mighty Yankees could finally be had, the White Sox broke out of the gate strongly in '59 and never looked back. On the field, the club was led by the determined veteran Fox, the speed of Aparicio and Jim Landis, and the solid catching and power hitting of veteran receiver Sherm Lollar. The pitching staff was excellent with Early Wynn, Billy Pierce, and Bob Shaw leading the starting rotation. The bullpen featured two relief aces in Jerry Staley and Turk Lown.

Fox batted .306 with two homers and 70 RBIs in 1959. He was first in the AL in at-bats and second in both hits and doubles. He batted .383 with runners in scoring position. In the field he led the league in putouts, assists, and fielding average while being voted the league's starting second baseman in the All-Star Game for the fifth straight year. The importance of Fox to this team could not be overstated. Owner Veeck put it well when he wrote that the Sox needed Nellie "no more than your baby needs milk."¹⁶

After beating out the Indians and Yankees for the American League pennant, the Sox faced a Dodgers team making their first World Series appearance since the move to Los Angeles the year before. This was not a dominant Dodgers team of the Brooklyn years but one that took the pennant – barely – with only 88 victories. Two of those wins had come in a best-of-three playoff series with the Milwaukee Braves, who had tied the Dodgers for first place. Sox fans had reason to be hopeful.

The Series began in Comiskey Park, and Game One could not have gone better for the White Sox, who crushed the Dodgers, 11-0, behind the pitching of Early Wynn and two homers from late-season addition Ted Kluszewski. Fox contributed by going 1-for-4 with a walk and two runs scored. But the Dodgers took Game Two by 4-3, then won Games Three and Four as the Series moved to the Los Angeles Memorial Coliseum, a football stadium whose left-field wall was less than ideal for Chicago's pitching-and-defense club. The Sox kept the Series alive by beating Sandy Koufax, 1-0, in Game Five, but back in Chicago, the Dodgers routed Wynn and wrapped up the Series with a 9-3 victory in Game Six. It was a disappointing finish, but the White Sox could hardly blame Fox, who led the team with a .375 World Series batting average. Fox wrapped up a memorable year by winning another Gold Glove, then being selected as the American League's Most Valuable Player.

But 1959 turned out to be a peak for both Fox and the White Sox, who would not reach another World Series for 46 years. Veeck made a flurry of deals prior to the 1960 season, trading away young talent to acquire power hitters Minnie Minoso, Roy Sievers, and Gene Freese, but the Sox dropped back to third place while Fox's average dropped 17 points to .289. In 1961 the Sox fell to fourth place and the 33-year-old Fox was showing signs of age, as his batting average fell to .251. The decline of the Sox continued in 1962, when the team fell to fifth place. Fox raised his batting average to .267, but failed to make the AL All-Star team for the first time since 1950.

In 1963, the White Sox rebounded to a second-place finish, with Fox batting .260 and again leading AL second basemen in fielding average. He was named an All-Star for the 12th and final time. But the White Sox were trying to break in younger players, and Fox's 14-year stint with the club finally came to an end in December of 1963, when he was traded to the Houston Colt .45s for pitcher Jim Golden and outfielder Danny Murphy. There were indications that had Fox remained with the Sox, he might no longer have had his starting position.

In Houston, Fox was reunited with Paul Richards, now general manager of the fledgling Colt .45s. Fox got into 133 games for the ninth-place .45s in 1964 and batted .265, but he was nearing the end of his playing days. In 1965 he lost the second-base job to future Hall of Famer Joe Morgan. Fox played in only 21 games, hitting .268 before being released by Houston (now known as the Astros) on July 31.

Remaining with Houston, Fox coached for the Astros in 1966 and 1967 under manager Grady Hatton. Joe Morgan credited Fox with helping him maximize his potential as a player, and the two remained friends until Fox's death. When Morgan was inducted into the Baseball Hall of Fame in 1990, he said about Fox, "I played with him, and I wouldn't be standing here today if it wasn't for what I learned from him. ... Above all, Fox impressed upon me the importance of going to the park every day bringing something to help the team. ... Nellie Fox was my idol."[17]

After leaving Houston, Fox was offered a chance to manage the Braves' Triple-A farm team at Richmond by Paul Richards, who had become Atlanta's general manager. Fox turned down the offer, instead joining the Washington Senators' staff as a coach under Jim Lemon, a former White Sox teammate. Fox remained a Senators coach when Ted Williams took over as manager in 1969, accompanying Williams to Texas when the club became the Texas Rangers in 1972. Fox was highly regarded by the club and given credit for helping several Senators/Rangers hitters, including Frank Howard and Ed Brinkman. Williams thought so highly of Fox that he recommended that Fox replace him as manager when he resigned after the 1972 season. Instead, the job went to Billy Martin. It wasn't the first time Fox had failed to get an opportunity to manage a major-league club. He had previously been a candidate to manage the White Sox when Don Gutteridge was let go late in the 1970 season, but lost out to Chuck Tanner.

Fox was offered a chance to remain with the Rangers as a minor-league manager, but decided to retire instead. Returning home to St. Thomas, Fox co-owned and operated a bowling center, Nellie Fox Bowl, which he had opened in 1956 in nearby Chambersburg (the bowling center was still in operation with the same name in 2008, long after the Fox family had sold its interest). He also played an occasional round of golf and hunted deer and small game with his beagles, Barney and Nellie. A hometown friend, Clark Gillan, recalled, "Nellie was a dead shot. Man, he could hit anything."[18] Fox also loved Penn State football and frequently attended Nittany Lions' home games.

"I believe that if (Fox) had not gotten sick, that he would have gotten back into baseball after a couple of years," said Joanne Fox.[19] But in the summer of 1975, Nellie was diagnosed with lymphatic cancer. Many former teammates visited him at the University of Maryland's Baltimore Cancer Research Center. After Bill Veeck came home from seeing him, his wife, Mary Frances, said, "That was one of the few times I saw Bill cry."[20] At the time Veeck was involved in negotiations to repurchase the White Sox, and, according to Joanne Fox, he told Fox that he wanted him to manage the team for him.

It wasn't to be; Fox died on December 1, 1975, 24 days before what would have been his 48th birthday. Jim Lemon commented that the cancer "had to be incurable because if it wasn't, Nellie would have beat it."[21] Fox was buried in his hometown at St. Thomas Cemetery.

Nellie Fox's posthumous road to the Hall of Fame was reminiscent of his struggles as a player fighting and scraping for his spot in baseball history. He barely missed election in 1985, his final year of eligibility in the annual BBWAA balloting, finishing with 74.7 percent of the vote and falling just two votes short of the requisite 75 percent, the smallest margin in the history of the Hall of Fame. Veteran Chicago writer Jerome Holtzman argued that, in line with baseball's tradition of rounding off percentages, Fox should have been credited with the necessary total of 75 percent, but Hall of Fame officials disagreed.

Fox's Hall of Fame candidacy then moved to the Veterans Committee, and another lengthy battle ensued. For several years Fox fell short in the committee voting, and there were reports that his former manager Al Lopez, a committee member, was working to block Fox's induction (or at least doing nothing to help it). In 1996, with Lopez now gone from the committee, Fox finally received the necessary 75 percent of the vote, but the committee was allowed to elect only one candidate per year; Jim

Bunning had received one more vote than Fox, so Nellie missed again.

However, Fox's fans never gave up and many people lobbied for his election. In 1997, he finally landed his place in Cooperstown. Speaking at Fox's induction ceremony that August, Joanne Fox said: "He played with all his heart, all his passion, and with every ounce of his being – that was the best way he could show his appreciation to all those who helped him learn the game that became his life."[22] It was never the easy way for Nellie Fox but, as always, determination and grit would get him there.

Sources

http://www.baseball-almanac.com/deaths/nellie_fox_obituary.shtml

http://web.baseballhalloffame.org/hofers/vetcom.jsp

http://www.baseball-reference.com/bullpen/Interstate_League

http://www.baseball-reference.com/bullpen/Nellie_Fox

http://www.jockbio.com/Classic/Fox/Fox_bio.html

http://www.philadelphiaathletics.org/event/fox2001.html

http://www.philadelphiaathletics.org/trail/fox.html

http://www.retrosheet.org/

Alexander, Charles C. *Our Game* (New York: Henry Holt and Company, Inc., 1991).

The Baseball Encyclopedia (Toronto: Macmillan Publishing Company, 1993).

Enders, Eric. *100 Years of the World Series* (New York: Barnes & Noble Publishing, Inc., 2003).

Johnson, Lloyd and Brenda Ward. *Who's Who in Baseball History* (Westport, Connecticut: Brompton Books, 1994).

Johnson, Lloyd and Wolff, Miles. *The Encyclopedia of Minor League Baseball* (Durham NC: Baseball America, Inc., 1997).

Vanderberg, Bob. *From Lane and Fain to Zisk and Fisk* (Chicago: Chicago Review Press, 1982).

Ray Berres interview, March 8 and 19, 1996, SABR Oral History.

Notes

1 David Gough and Jim Bard, *Little Nel: The Nellie Fox Story* (Alexandria Virginia: D.L. Megbec Publishing, 2000), 16.
2 Gough and Bard, 20.
3 Ibid.
4 Gough and Bard, 24.
5 Gough and Bard, 23.
6 Gough and Bard, 25.
7 Gough and Bard, 26.
8 Don Zminda interview with Joanne Fox, July 18, 2008.
9 Don Zminda interview with Billy Pierce, July 18, 2008.
10 Joanne Fox interview.
11 Ibid..
12 Neil R. Gazel, "Nellie Does Right by White Sox," *Baseball Digest*, August 1951.
13 Billy Pierce interview.
14 Ibid.
15 Dave Condon, *The Go-Go Chicago White Sox* (New York: Coward-McCann, 1960), 132.
16 Bill Veeck with Ed Linn, *Veeck As In Wreck* (Chicago: The University of Chicago Press, 2001; originally published 1962), 342.
17 Gough and Bard, 288.
18 Gough and Bard, 271.
19 Joanne Fox interview.
20 Gough and Bard, 277.
21 Associated Press, "Nellie Fox Succumbs of Cancer," *High Point* (North Carolina) *Enterprise*, December 2, 1975.
22 Gough and Bard, 9.

BILLY GOODMAN

By Ron Anderson

The late 1940s Boston Red Sox consisted of larger-than-life, highly paid, talented baseball men who could accomplish just about anything "except win pennants," according to Al Hirshberg in a 1951 *Saturday Evening Post* article on Billy Goodman. Goodman had made his major-league debut in the spring of 1947 and was "not a glamorous slugger, not a colorful, flamboyant personality, not a magnet for autograph hounds." In fact, he was "built like an undernourished ribbon clerk. …. Billy Goodman neither looks nor acts like a baseball star. He just goes out every day and plays the game."[1]

He played the game for 16 major-league seasons with the Red Sox, Baltimore Orioles, Chicago White Sox, and Houston Colt 45s. He finished his major-league playing career with a lifetime .300 batting average.

Goodman is remembered for being extraordinarily versatile, a trait that originated from his very early years; being the youngest and smallest in the neighborhood, "playing regularly" was his goal, which usually meant playing wherever and whenever he was asked to. Billy played every position on his Concord, North Carolina, high-school team. During his senior year he was part of a so-called "reversible battery" with a teammate, pitching one day and catching the next. Earl Kelly, sports editor of the *Concord Tribune*, told Hirshberg that the right-handed-throwing Goodman once pitched a game left-handed and did very well. He was always a left-handed batter.

Hall of Famer Eddie Collins, the Red Sox' general manager in 1947, compared Goodman to Jimmy Dykes, who was considered one of the most versatile players of the 1930s. Collins, a tough critic and perfectionist, described Dykes as "the best until the kid [Goodman] came along."

William Dale "Billy" Goodman was a native of Concord, born on March 22, 1926, the second of three sons born to Fred and Martha Goodman. As a major leaguer, he was listed as 5-feet-11 and 165 pounds, but during the season often fell below 150 pounds. Billy's father was a prosperous dairy farmer, owning more than 300 acres of pastureland, which Billy worked often during his youth. The Goodman roots ran deep there, with an uncle owning comparable farmland nearby, and Billy's grandfather, C.J. Goodman, owning the original family farmstead farther up the street. A few hundred yards from the Goodman homestead was the home of the Littles, who owned a coal and oil business in Concord. Billy and Margaret Little,[2] a childhood sweetheart, were married in October 1947.

Goodman, who was simply known as Bill until he entered major-league baseball, was a three-sport star for Winecoff High School in Concord.[3] He was the high scorer and captain of the high-school basketball team his junior and senior years, and he was a triple-threat halfback star on the football team. But baseball was his real love and his goal was to play professionally. Although Goodman was voted the best all-around athlete at Winecoff High, he was not remembered as a particularly outstanding baseball man. He did not hit for power, even then. Sports editor Kelly, a three-sport star athlete himself, once described Goodman as "steady and dangerous, but … never spectacular."[4] He did the little things, consistently and essentially, when his team needed a key hit and runs to stay in the game. It was just assumed that he would come through for them, and he usually did.

When the North Carolina State League (Class D) suspended its operations in World War II, the semipro four-team Carolina Victory League was formed. After high school in the summer of 1943, Billy joined the Concord Weavers, and helped win the championship that year. Billy played some outfield and was the star second baseman. The manager of the club, former minor-league star Herman "Ginger" Watts, invited young Goodman – who was 17 – to play with them. Hirshberg described the league as being "well covered by the professional scouts."

Claude Dietrich, a scout for the Atlanta Crackers of the Double-A Southern Association, spent the summer of 1943 signing up many of Watts's charges for the Crackers. Dietrich was admonished by Watts for missing the best player on the team, Goodman. It wasn't the first time Goodman was overlooked, and it wouldn't be the last. Larry Woodall, a former coach and later a scout for the Red Sox, observed,

• BILLY GOODMAN •

"Goodman can make a monkey out of a scout. He doesn't look as if he can do anything right when you first see him. You have to watch him for a while before you realize that he can't do anything wrong."[5]

Dietrich signed Goodman to a Crackers contract in December 1943 for $1,200.[6] He joined the Atlanta team in April 1944, playing for manager Kiki Cuyler. Goodman was listed on the roster as an outfielder though he had been mostly a second baseman for the Concord team. Billy made a good start in professional ball, making the league's All-Star team and batting .336 in 137 games, with a league-leading 122 runs scored.

Goodman entered the Navy at the end of the 1944 season and spent his time in the South Pacific, notably the Ulithi Group of the Western Carolines and Guam. He was discharged in June 1946, and promptly went to Atlanta to see if he still had a job with the Crackers. Billy re-signed and "went to work" the very next day. Cuyler was still managing and gave Goodman the first-base job.

A lifetime .300 hitter, Billy Goodman won the American League batting title with the Red Sox in 1950, then helped the White Sox win the 1959 AL pennant.

After a week's trial at first base – where he got a base hit his first time at bat, then failed to hit his next 22 times – Goodman was shifted to the outfield and went on a tear, finishing the season batting .389 in 86 games. The Crackers won the Southern Association pennant and the playoff championship against New Orleans and Memphis, winning both seven-game series four games to three. Atlanta played Dallas of the Texas League in the Dixie Series – resumed after a three-year lapse – and lost four straight. Goodman went 28-for-67 in 18 playoff games (.418).

This performance was convincing enough for the Red Sox to purchase Goodman's contract from the Crackers on February 7, 1947, for $75,000, thought to be the highest amount ever paid for a Southern Association player up to then. Goodman learned of the deal through an *Atlanta Journal* photographer who wanted to take pictures of him for the paper. Billy reported to Red Sox manager Joe Cronin at Sarasota, Florida, in March 1947 for spring training. The Red Sox had a championship team returning for the 1947 season, so little regard was given Goodman that spring. Billy's first look at major-league pitching was in a Red Sox intrasquad game against Boo Ferriss, who had finished 25-6 the previous season. In his first time at bat, as *Boston Globe* reporter Roger Birtwell described it in an April 2, 1947, article in *The Sporting News*, Goodman reached for an outside pitch by Ferriss and with "the ease of a grocer's clerk reaching for a package of biscuits, ripped a line double to left." Interviewed at his Cleveland, Mississippi, home in July 2007, Ferriss exclaimed about Goodman: "Oh, he could hit. You know [he was] a wiry guy, wasn't very big, not a long-ball hitter. He hit very few home runs, but he could swing a bat. And he was versatile. He was playing when I was coaching. I was very close to Billy.... He was like [Johnny] Pesky. He could spray that ball. He could hit.... You looked up and he was on base."

When the 1947 season opened, Goodman was on the bench. He played in just 12 games with two hits – both singles – in 11 at-bats before being optioned in June to the Red Sox' Triple-A Louisville farm club. Goodman started in the outfield for the Colonels, but took over at shortstop on July 15. He hit .340 for the year and finished among the top five American Association hitters. It was at Louisville that Goodman began playing several different positions as team needs arose. As he put it to J.G. Taylor Spink of *The Sporting News*, "Mr. Spink, I used up my paychecks buying myself new gloves for the various positions to which I was shifted."[7]

Goodman's successful season at Louisville brought him back to Sarasota for spring training in 1948, with a new Red Sox manager in place of Cronin. Longtime New York Yankees manager Joe McCarthy had come out of retirement to join the Red Sox for 1948 and faced the dilemma of where to play the versatile Goodman. When the 1948 season opened, Billy was once again perched on the bench.

He saw little action at the start, except for occasional fill-in work for Bobby Doerr and Johnny Pesky at second and third. When the Red Sox spiraled into a nosedive on their first Western trip – winning only one of their first seven games – McCarthy had Goodman take over at first base for the slumping Jake Jones. Billy started at first base against St. Louis on May 25, and remained there for the rest of the season, batting a solid .310 with a .414 on-base percentage and a .993 fielding average (eight errors). He was declared the club's Rookie of the Year by the Boston baseball writers. In the playoff game to decide the league pennant against the Indians, Goodman finished 0-for-3 with a walk.

In spite of Goodman's exceptional rookie year, McCarthy made slugging rookie Walt Dropo the starting first baseman in 1949, and Goodman was riding the bench again. When Dropo slumped to start the season, Goodman again got his job back, and the Red Sox began to improve.

Though the club lost the pennant on the season's final day to the Yankees, Goodman had another good season, batting .298, but missed several games in August because of a fungus condition he had contracted with the Navy that weakened and blistered his hands and legs.[8] Goodman received strong fan support in the All-Star voting, placing second to first baseman Eddie Robinson of the Washington Senators. He substituted for Robinson at first base in the eighth inning of the July 12 game, but he did not have an at-bat.

Based on his solid performance, Billy finally had first base locked up going into the 1950 season. But fate once again struck; in the April 30 game with the Philadelphia Athletics, Goodman sustained a chip fracture to his ankle in a collision with Ferris Fain. He was batting .333 at the time. Walt Dropo was called up from Louisville and performed phenomenally, crushing home runs at a steady pace and hitting for average. Dropo led the league with 144 RBIs and won American League Rookie of the Year honors. Goodman returned after a few weeks but had lost his first-base job.

Goodman's strength – and resiliency – was his ability to play almost anywhere defensively, infield or outfield, which enabled him to be in the lineup more often than was expected of him. When Boston players went down with injuries, Goodman was there to spell them, and he performed well most of the time. On May 24 he began substituting for injured second baseman Bobby Doerr. He played so well there that he remained in the lineup for a while after Doerr had recovered.

When third baseman Johnny Pesky went down, Goodman filled in so admirably that there was speculation that Pesky had lost his job. By mid-June Billy had already played all four infield positions, going counter-clockwise around the diamond as each regular dropped out because of injury.[9] When Pesky returned Goodman went back to his "sub" role as a one-man bench.

On July 11 Red Sox slugger Ted Williams fractured his elbow in the All-Star Game. New Red Sox manager Steve O'Neill first tried Clyde Vollmer in left field, but turned to Goodman on July 16. He had a sensational run and appeared to be made for the left-field job. In one stretch of eight games he was 17-for-32, a .531 pace, and was playing left field "as if to the manner born," wrote Shirley Povich of the *Washington Post*, on July 28, 1950. On August 15 Dropo was beaned by the A's Hank Wyse, knocking him out of the lineup. Goodman took over at first with Vollmer going to left. Dropo did not return to

• BILLY GOODMAN •

first base until the 23rd, and Goodman – who was batting .361 – returned to left field.

Remarkably, Goodman was the league's leading hitter and naturally people began to wonder what to do with him when Williams returned. The rest of the team was hitting well and the Sox were on a roll, winning 44 of 61 games during Ted's absence from the regular lineup, their .721 clip moving them two games behind the league-leading Yankees. There was reportedly some resentment among the players, knowing that temperamental slugger Williams would displace their best-hitting handyman.

But Johnny Pesky came to Goodman's rescue. He went to manager O'Neill a few weeks before Williams' return and offered to sit down in order to keep Goodman in the lineup. It was a selfless gesture, and one that paid off for Goodman. Not only was Billy playing exceptional ball, but he would not obtain the requisite number of at-bats to win a batting title if he did not play regularly for the balance of the season. Goodman went to third base on September 15, replacing Pesky. He went on to win the American League batting title with a .354 average. He is recognized as the only major-league player ever to win a batting title without having a regular position. The Red Sox finished third, four games behind the first-place Yankees.

For his heroics on the diamond, Goodman was recognized as a candidate for the 1950 top male Athlete of the Year by the Associated Press. He finished 11th in the voting – Jim Konstanty of the Philadelphia Phillies won the award – among many sports notables of the day, amateur and professional. Goodman also finished second in the league MVP voting to New York shortstop Phil Rizzuto.

Astonishingly, over the winter there was talk that there might not be everyday room in the lineup for the 1950 batting champion. Manager O'Neill characterized Goodman as a bit of a pleasant dilemma. The Boston press labeled it the "Goodman problem." O'Neill rationalized that Goodman should play every day; yet, when asked what he would do with his other stars, and whom he would sit down, O'Neill countered that Goodman would be his "number one utility man while still playing regularly every day."[10] Only days later, the Red Sox traded right fielder Al Zarilla, a .325 hitter in 1950, to the White Sox. O'Neill confided that this was done to provide steady work for Goodman in the lineup. True to his word, O'Neill started the season with Goodman as a regular in the outfield, batting second.

The Red Sox got off to a bad start, losing their first three games. O'Neill showed no patience and quickly began to juggle his lineup, including sitting down Walt Dropo, who was not hitting, and moving Goodman to first base. Billy again moved between three infield positions – first, second, and third – and some outfield. He received ample playing time in '51, but did not reach the heights of 1950, finishing the season batting .297. The Red Sox finished in third place, 11 games behind the first-place Yankees.

The year 1952 was as a period of change for the Red Sox, with a new manager, core players either leaving or aging, and vacancies needing replacements. Bobby Doerr called it quits at the age of 33 toward the end of the 1951 season, and manager Steve O'Neill was replaced by Lou Boudreau in the offseason. Ted Williams was recalled to military duty because of the Korean War and left the team on May 2. Both Pesky and Dropo were traded away in midseason. There were holes to fill.

The foremost dilemma for Boudreau – "the game's greatest manipulator," wrote Shirley Povich of the *Washington Post* – was whom to call on to replace future Hall of Famer Bobby Doerr.[11] Boudreau juggled his lineup with regularity throughout the year, favoring youth over experience, speed and defense over power, and constant platooning. Goodman played three infield positions – mostly at second base – and some outfield. Billy had more at-bats (513) than any other Red Sox player, and was second on the club with a .306 batting average. The Red Sox had little to cheer about, however, finishing in sixth place, 19 games out of first.

The next season, 1953, was not looking to be a much better year for the Red Sox, but it was a happy one for Billy Goodman because Boudreau made him his full-time second baseman. This was the first time in the major leagues that Billy could call a position his own, and he was doubly pleased because he was taking over from his idol, Bobby Doerr.

Interviewed at his Oregon home years later, Bobby Doerr described Goodman warmly: "He [was] just a very, very fine person and a darn good ballplayer. He was like the perfect guy to be on a ballclub because he could play so many different positions. If he was [playing] utility he was great when he went in [to a game]. … He played a good first base. He didn't have the power that first basemen generally have, but he was always on base and ran the bases good. [He was a] good fielder. …

As a utility player he was perfect in that way, too. He could go in any time and do a good job."[12]

On May 10, 1953, Billy got into a dispute with an umpire over a close call, and became so enraged that he had to be restrained by teammate Jimmy Piersall, who wrapped his arms around the flailing second sacker and bodily carried him from the field. Goodman sustained cartilage damage to his ribs from the "hugging" incident, and was sidelined for nearly a month. Boudreau later remarked that Goodman's absence was a factor in the Red Sox not being a contender in 1953. Casey Stengel agreed, commenting that Goodman's absence "changed the whole complexion of the first division."[13] Boston finished in fourth place, 16 games behind the first-place Yankees. In spite of his injury and long absence, Goodman had a good year, batting .313, tied for third with Minnie Minoso in the American League batting race. He was named to the AL All-Star team as the starting second baseman. He went 0-for-2 with a walk, and was caught stealing.

Goodman played on mediocre Red Sox teams from 1954 to 1956. They finished fourth each year. He continued his steady play, batting .303, .294, and .293, respectively, while often being used in utility roles. In 1957 he was being used sparingly by manager Mike Higgins, and the Red Sox traded him to the Baltimore Orioles for pitcher Mike Fornieles.

Orioles manager Paul Richards regarded Goodman as the team's ultimate utility player, using him at all infield positions – mostly third base – as well as in right field and left field, a total of six fielding slots. Billy stroked a home run – one of 19 he hit for his entire major league career – in his debut with Baltimore, and batted .308 for the Orioles for the season. On December 3 the Orioles traded Goodman, Tito Francona, and Ray Moore to the Chicago White Sox for Larry Doby, Jim Marshall, Jack Harshman, and Russ Heman. Billy played solid baseball in 1958 for manager Al Lopez, mostly at third base, and batting .299. Chicago finished 10 games behind New York, in second place.

The "Go-Go" White Sox were the American League champions in 1959 – their first World Series since the infamous 1919 Black Sox scandal – and were known mostly for their speed, defense, and solid pitching. "Powderpuff hitters," they were called. Goodman, who batted .250 during the regular season, platooned at third base with Bubba Phillips. The White Sox lost the World Series, four games to two, to the Los Angeles Dodgers. Goodman played in five of the six games, starting in three of them, and in pinch-hit roles. He went 3-for-13 – all singles – in the Series.

Chicago used Billy sparingly in 1960 and 1961 as a utility player and pinch-hitter. The White Sox did not equal their success of 1959, finishing third in 1960 and fourth in 1961. Goodman played in just 30 games in 1960 and 41 in '61, hitting .234 and .255, respectively.

Almost 36 years old, Goodman went to spring training with the White Sox in 1962, but he was given his unconditional release on April 3. On May 15, he signed with the expansion Houston Colt .45s of the National League. He played in utility roles once more, appearing in 82 games and batting .255. He was released after the season.

For 1963 Goodman signed on as player-manager of the Durham Bulls of the Class-A Carolina League. He left that assignment toward the end of the 1964 minor-league season, going to Houston's rookie camp in Cocoa, Florida, as manager-instructor, where he remained through '65. In the winter of 1966 Billy caught on with his old team, the Red Sox, who hired him as a "special scout." In 1967 he joined the Kansas City Athletics as an instructor, and then spent four years with the Braves in a similar role.

In 1973 Goodman joined the Kansas City Royals at their Baseball Academy in Sarasota, Florida (by then Goodman's home town), as an infield and hitting instructor. The Royals closed their academy in the spring of 1974, but retained Goodman on the payroll along with a few other instructors. Billy stayed on as manager of one of their rookie league clubs in the Gulf Coast League, the Academy Royals. In May 1976 the Atlanta Braves hired Billy, again, this time as an instructor in their minor-league system. In June he joined the Braves' Triple-A Richmond club as batting instructor.

Goodman's widow, Margaret, said that between 1977 and 1982 Billy was retired from baseball, playing golf, fishing, hunting, and gardening, and doing some occasional work with her in her antiques business – her store was called the Babe Ruth Auxiliary -- and in their other commercial properties. He appeared for an old-timers game, the Cracker Jack Old-Timers Baseball Classic, in July 1982 at RFK Stadium in Washington. Billy and Margaret also owned a 30-acre orange grove which they sold before he died.

Billy became ill with multiple myeloma in 1983, and died on October 1, 1984, in Sarasota. He was 58. He was survived by Margaret, of Sarasota; daughter Kathy Goodman Simpkins of Concord, North Carolina; and son Robert Goodman – named after Goodman's good friend, Bobby Doerr – of Bradenton, Florida. By 2007 Margaret had three grandchildren – all girls – ages 24, 17, and 16. Asked if she ever remarried, Margaret's response was a decided "Oh no. We grew up together and there's one love in a lifetime, and I had him."[14]

Billy Goodman played in 1,623 games in his major-league career, collecting 1,691 base hits and a .300 lifetime batting average. He played in two All-Star Games and one World Series. He ranks 10th all-time for on-base percentage in a season by a rookie, with a .414 percentage in 1948. In 1969, Goodman was honored by his native state, North Carolina, by being inducted into its Sports Hall of Fame. He is also a member of the Boston Red Sox Hall of Fame, inducted in 2004.

Sources

Thanks to Dick Bresciani, Boston Red Sox vice president of publications and archives.

Hirshberg, Al. *Saturday Evening Post*, March 17, 1951, 34, 141-144.

Spatz, Lyle, ed. *The SABR Baseball List & Record Book* (New York: Scribner, 2007), 349.

Notes

1. Al Hirshberg, "That Modest Young Guy in the Outfield," *Saturday Evening Post*, March 17, 1951.
2. Ibid.; J.G. Taylor Spink, "Goodman Proves Right Man at First Base," *The Sporting News*, September 22, 1948. Goodman's wife, Margaret, was known as "Evelyn" – she was born Margaret Evelyn Little – throughout her youth and during Billy's early years in baseball. Billy said in his 1948 interview with J.G. Taylor Spink, "My wife was Evelyn Little." According to Margaret – in interviews in May, September, and October 2007 – her first name took hold when they moved to Sarasota, Florida, and started their businesses there. She used the given name, Margaret, on all formal documents, and it stuck.
3. Hirshberg. Billy Goodman was called "just plain Bill" in Concord, where he played high school and semipro ball, as well as with the Atlanta Crackers. According to Goodman's widow, Margaret, the name Billy took hold while he was with the Red Sox, but she does not remember how it got started.
4. Hirshberg.
5. Hirshberg.
6. Jack Troy, "Goodman, Expert Cook, Gives Hot Plate Service to Crackers," *The Sporting News*, June 22, 1944. Atlanta scout Claude Dietrich tells the tale of the first time he encountered Goodman "wearing an apron" cooking a rabbit in the Goodman home. Dietrich was startled by Billy's slight appearance, accentuated by his donning of an apron. Father Fred Goodman later explained that Billy took over the kitchen duties as "chief cook" after his mother's death that year.
7. Spink.
8. Roger Birtwell, "Whattaman Goodman – and What a Man!" *The Sporting News*, September 13, 1950. Goodman was plagued with a chronic fungus – a so-called "saltsea fungus called 'jungle-rot'," the Birtwell article says. It made him generally weak, and "affected his hands so much he couldn't get a firm grip on his bat." Margaret Goodman recalled the circumstances, saying that Billy "had to wear special things on his feet and he had something on his hands when he batted…. It was always with him."
9. Birtwell, 3, 6; Bill Nowlin, *Mr. Red Sox: The Johnny Pesky Story* (Rounder Books, 2004), 136-138. Goodman briefly filled in for Vern Stephens at shortstop "on one occasion" before he subbed for Pesky, thus effectively playing at every infield position, moving counter-clockwise around the infield.
10. Steve O'Leary, "Goodman Problem Tackled by O'Neill – He'll Be a 'Daily Sub'," *The Sporting News*, November 29, 1950.
11. Shirley Povich, "This Morning, with Shirley Povich," *Washington Post*, April 17, 1952.
12. Bobby Doerr, telephone interview, June 5, 2007.
13. Hy Hurwitz, "Boudreau Bubbles Over Bosox Babes – and His New Pact," *The Sporting News*, October 7, 1953.
14. Margaret Goodman, telephone interviews, May, September, and October 2007; Doerr. Goodman's widow, Margaret, was not entirely certain about the years 1977 and 1982. She did feel that Billy was most likely fully retired at the time and engaged in recreational pursuits along with his occasional assistance in her antiques business. Doerr – who maintained some contact with Goodman – expressed a similar opinion.

JOE HICKS

By Don Zminda

A hitting star for more than a decade in the minor leagues, Joe Hicks batted over .380 twice and compiled a career batting average of .313 while playing in the White Sox, Senators, and Mets farm systems. Hicks's major-league career was brief and a lot less successful (a .221 career average in 416 official at-bats), but the lack of success at the big-league level never diminished Joe's love for the game. Well into his 70s, Hicks was still actively involved in baseball at the amateur level.

William Joseph Hicks (he was known from his early years by his middle name) was born in Ivy, Virginia, on April 7, 1933. Young Joe grew up on a farm, and his father worked as both a part-time farmer and a rural mail carrier in the area near the Hicks's Northern Virginia home. Joe was the fourth of five children, with two brothers and two sisters. He attended Meriwether Lewis High School in nearby Charlottesville and played baseball and basketball there, leading the baseball team in hitting all four years. He also played some American Legion ball.[1]

Despite his success on the ballfield as a prep, Hicks did not did not received any offers to play professional ball, so after finishing high school, he accepted an academic scholarship to the University of Virginia (the school did not award athletic scholarships in baseball). Again he played well, hitting .325 as a collegian and leading the Virginia varsity in RBIs twice. It was his play for the Cavaliers' baseball team that first attracted the attention of major-league scouts.

"We were playing VPI during my junior year (1953)," recalled Hicks in a 2008 interview, "and during a timeout while VPI was having a conference on the mound, the plate umpire took off his mask and said, 'Hey, Joe, how would you like to play pro baseball?'"[2] It turned out that the ump, Ralph Breeden, was a part-time bird-dog (scout) for the Chicago White Sox, and the next day the White Sox sent scout Harry Postove to look Joe over. Postove liked what he saw and offered Hicks a $250-a-month contract to join the Madisonville, Kentucky, team in the Class-D Kitty League. Hicks accepted the offer, but not until the Sox agreed to his mother's stipulation that baseball not interfere with Joe's completing his college education.

Hicks reported to Madisonville when the school year ended in June of 1953. He was an immediate sensation, hitting .389 with 16 homers and 63 RBIs in only 67 games while playing center field. When Madisonville's season ended, the White Sox promoted Hicks to Class-A Colorado Springs, and Hicks finished his first season in pro ball by batting .346 in 12 games for the Sky Sox. That fall Hicks returned to the University of Virginia, graduating the following June with a degree in education. He then returned to Colorado Springs, where the season was well under way. Again he hit very well, posting a .349 average in 41 games, but his season was cut short when he tore some cartilage in his knee while swinging the bat. The injury required surgery, but it had one side benefit for his baseball career: Hicks had received his draft notice, and the bad knee kept him out of the Army, at least temporarily.

In 1955 Hicks, still only 22 years old, was promoted to Memphis in the Double-A Southern Association. At the time the White Sox did not have a Triple-A farm club, and playing for Memphis meant that Hicks was only one stop away from Chicago. Playing against stiffer competition, Hicks was hitting over .300 entering the season's final day, but a 1-for-5 performance dropped his average to .299. A shot with the White Sox was the logical next step, but Uncle Sam intervened: Hicks's knee was now sound enough for him to pass his Army physical, and he spent the 1956 and 1957 seasons in the military. Although Hicks was happy to serve his country, the timing could not have been worse for his baseball career. "It was unfortunate," he commented later. "I was ready to come up in '56. (The White Sox) had positions open then." Hicks spent most of his service time in Frankfurt, Germany, but he was able to play a little baseball on Army teams both in Germany and the US.

After receiving his Army discharge early in 1958, Hicks rejoined the White Sox farm system. The club now had a Triple-A team in Indianapolis and Joe began the 1958 season there, but his

• JOE HICKS •

A consistent .300 hitter in the minors, Joe Hicks made his major league debut with the 1959 White Sox. Unfortunately for Hicks, he failed to produce in the few chances he was given at the MLB level.

bat skills were rusty after two years away from professional ball. After hitting only .153 in 22 games, he was sent back to Colorado Springs. He rebounded immediately, finishing second in the league with a .381 batting average and making the Western League All-Star Team.

After the 1958 season, Hicks went to Nicaragua to play winter ball. The stay in Latin America not only helped him sharpen his batting skills; it led to Hicks's meeting his lifetime partner. The office manager of the hotel where the ballplayers were staying was, in Joe's words, "a pretty señorita" from Nicaragua named Antonia Moody. Joe and Antonia began dating, and they were married in Managua, Nicaragua, on New Year's Eve 1958. Antonia returned to Virginia with Joe when the winter league season ended, and the couple eventually had three daughters.

The White Sox were poised to make a pennant run in 1959, and Hicks was sent back to Indianapolis for his first full year of Triple-A ball. He had another fine year, batting .314 for a club that included future major leaguers Johnny Callison, Jim McAnany, J.C. Martin, Camilo Carreon, Ken McBride, and Gary Peters. When Indianapolis's season ended, most of those players were recalled to Chicago for the September stretch run. The Sox were about to clinch their first pennant in 40 years, and Hicks saw only brief action. He was struck out by the Tigers' Jim Bunning in his first major-league plate appearance, on September 18, but went 3-for-7 (.429) in his first taste of major-league ball.

In the spring of 1960, Hicks was 27 years old with nothing left to prove in the minor leagues. He made the Sox' Opening Day roster for the first time, but there was no chance to play regularly on a championship club that had made an offseason trade for South Side favorite Minnie Minoso to join veterans Jim Landis and Al Smith in the outfield. "I made the team as an extra outfielder, but didn't play much and got really rusty," Hicks recalled. Though he spent most of the year on the White Sox roster, Hicks got only 47 major-league at-bats before being sent to Triple-A San Diego in early August with a .191 batting average. Again he proved he could handle minor-league pitching by batting .303 in 32 games, but Hicks's time as a member of the White Sox system had come to an end. With the American League expanding to 10 teams in 1961, the White Sox left Hicks unprotected in the expansion draft to stock the two new teams, and Hicks was selected by the new Washington Senators.

Though Hicks was now with an expansion club that seemed made to order for a player who'd never been given a real chance at the major-league level, he found himself battling for playing time as badly as when he was with the White Sox. The Senators had three other left-handed-hitting outfielders in veterans Jim King, Marty Keough, and Gene Woodling; though he made the team's Opening Day roster, Hicks played little over the first month (29 at-bats, .172 average) before being sent to Triple-A Indianapolis for the rest of the season. Before the demotion, he managed to gain some revenge on Jim Bunning, belting his first major-league home off the future Hall of Famer at Griffith Stadium on May 2. The 1962 season was better for Hicks, but only to a degree. This time he stayed on the major-league roster for the entire season and played in 102 games, but most of those appearances (65) were as a pinch hitter. It was a role ill-suited for Hicks, who batted just .224. "I needed to play more than sporadically to get into a groove," he commented. "Pinch-hitting's a horrible job."

The 1963 season proved to be Hicks's last as a major leaguer, but it was definitely his most satisfying one. As a result of an offseason deal, he was now with another expansion team, the New York Mets, who had purchased Hicks in preparation for their second major-league season. Hicks began the year back in the minors with Triple-A Buffalo, but after being recalled in mid-July (he'd posted typically good numbers with the Bisons, batting .320), Joe had his first real stretch of success at the major-league level. Inserted into the lineup as a platoon outfielder against right-handed pitchers, Hicks began to pound the ball. In one stretch he homered in three straight games, including an 11th-inning walk-off home run off Don Larsen that beat the San Francisco Giants, 9-7. Though he cooled off after his torrid start, he was still batting .267 with a .455 slugging percentage – good numbers in the pitcher-dominated National League of 1963 – in mid-August before a late slump dropped him to .226 at season's end.

With the Mets, Hicks played under Casey Stengel, a manager he greatly respected. "He really knew the game," Hicks commented about Stengel. "He had a tremendous memory. Now they have all these computers and printouts, but Casey knew in his head what pitchers threw." Hicks also liked the way that Stengel stuck up for him even when he failed. In his Mets debut on July 12, Hicks recalled, Stengel sent him up to pinch-hit against the Dodgers' Sandy Koufax, who would win the Cy Young Award and the National League Most Valuable Player Award that year. Hicks struck out, but as he walked back to the dugout, Stengel shouted, "Don't let it fret you, Hicksie! He's struck out a lot of guys!"

Had he been a little younger, Hicks might have stayed longer with the Mets, but the club moved into Shea Stadium in 1964, and as Joe commented, "They were beginning to have a youth movement." Hicks, 31 in 1964, went back down to Triple-A Buffalo ("a good town"), had two more solid seasons, then retired from baseball after hitting .174 for the Bisons in 1966.

Looking back at Hicks's career, it's obvious that he did not have much success at the major-league level, but it's also easy to imagine how things could have been different for a player with such impressive minor-league numbers. Coming out of college in an era when players generally began their professional careers after high school, he got a late start. When he seemed poised to reach the majors in 1956, the Army came calling. When the White Sox reached down to Indianapolis to recall an outfielder in the middle of their 1959 pennant run, they chose Jim McAnany rather than Hicks because they had more need for a right-handed hitter. When he finally reached Chicago, the club was loaded with outfielders, and the Senators used him primarily in a role (pinch-hitter) in which he always struggled. And he had turned 30 by the time he got his final brief chance with the Mets. Hicks himself commented, "It was a combination of not getting a chance to play when I was *ready* to play, and then being too late when I finally got the chance. I was kind of a victim of circumstances."

After retiring from baseball, Hicks returned to the Northern Virginia area where he grew up and became the athletic director for the city of Charlottesville. He also became an expert on baseball rules, so much so that the state of Virginia hired him to go around the state and hold clinics for coaches and umpires, explaining the intricacies of the rules. He also did some high-school and college umpiring. "I probably could have umpired professionally and I felt I was good enough," Joe said, "but all the traveling didn't appeal to me." Hicks was still active as an umpire on the high-school level in 2008, the year in which he turned 75, and he and Antonia celebrated their 50th wedding anniversary on New Year's Eve that year. Joe Hicks may not have had a successful major-league career, but he certainly has had a successful life.

Notes

1 Chicago White Sox file for Joe Hicks.
2 Interview with Joe Hicks, August 14, 2008. All quotations from Hicks come from this interview.

RON JACKSON

By Bill Nowlin

Ron Jackson was a tall, impressive slugger who debuted in the major leagues the day he was signed. The 6-foot-6¾-inch, 225-pound right-handed hitter held the interest of a number of ballclubs because of the gaudy numbers he put up in the minor leagues, but he never truly stuck in major league ball.

Ronald Harris Jackson was born in Kalamazoo, Michigan, on October 22, 1933. He was a good player from an early age, playing neighborhood ball with 14- or 15-year-old boys when he was just 10 years old. Or perhaps it was because he was the one with a new bat and ball, which he'd bought with money earned from delivering magazines. These were the years before Little League in the era, and the Jaycees started a program with six or eight teams in the city. At the age of 12, he went into American Legion baseball.

Ron's father, William Harris Jackson, was a welder at Sutherland Paper in Kalamazoo. Sutherland had a company team in the local industrial league and one of Ron's earliest memories of baseball was going to the games with his parents. Ron's mother worked, too; Eleanor Lucille (Koenigs) Jackson was a biller for Consumers Power.

At 13, Ron had already grown to be 6 feet tall. He said that working out "morning, afternoon and night" under coach Harold McKee of the American Legion Blues was what really gave him a solid grounding in baseball.[1] While a student at Kalamazoo Central High, he starred in basketball and the team won three consecutive Class-A titles. He played American Legion baseball and – after graduation from high school – for the same Sutherland Paper team he'd enjoyed watching as a boy. Right from the beginning, Ron always played first base exclusively. As early as the age of 15, he was being watched by scouts from a number of teams while he played on the Maroons, the tournament team of the American Legion. He remembered, "Our team won the district and regionals and was always in the state tournament. The state tournament's probably where you got more of your scouts." His Legion team won the National Baseball Congress tournament at Battle Creek, Michigan, twice, in 1949 and 1951.

Ron and his father talked at length with the Phillies a couple of years later but Ron had been accepted to the University of Michigan and so declined their interest. Upon arriving at the Ann Arbor campus, he found the university too large and overwhelming. "I suddenly realized that I was a small-town boy," he told an interviewer. "So I turned right around and went home. At Western Michigan University I could be among my family and friends, so that was for me."[2] There might have been a little tug from baseball, too. Jackson said he was in the Amateur Baseball Congress tournament with Sutherland Paper and that particular year, 1951, they won it. "I was with them until I had to go to school – but the tournament wasn't over yet. I wanted to come home and play baseball!" His father suggested that he look at Western, and he was able to get a scholarship there. "They almost made me play basketball. I didn't know how to say no."

A few months after beginning college, he met a fellow student, Carol Plantefaber, and they were married on January 29, 1953. In late 1953, they had a son, Mark. In 1955, the couple added a daughter, Martha, to the family. In 1958, a second daughter, Teresa, was born, and in 1970, Jennifer. When the couple celebrated their 55th anniversary in January 2008, they enjoyed nine grandchildren and one great-grandchild.

The Detroit Tigers had scouted Jackson for two years but the Chicago White Sox blew him away with an offer he couldn't refuse. White Sox scout Pete Milito of Grand Rapids had been watching him, too, since he graduated from high school in 1951. Milito told *Chicago Tribune* writer Ed Prell that the White Sox had offered to sign Jackson right after he graduated from high school, but that he'd wanted to get a couple of years of college under his belt before he signed anywhere.[3] He made the WMU varsity as a freshman. "That was the one year you could play as a freshman. That was the Korean War and in the '51-52 season, freshmen could play. The next year, they stopped them. I played on the varsity and we won the (Mid-American Conference) – actually tied with Miami of Ohio." Jackson hit .435 in his sophomore year. After finishing his junior year (.340), he decided to go play baseball in Halifax, Nova Scotia, for the summer. He'd been faced with a choice of heading to the Adirondacks in New York state to play basketball or to Halifax to play summer league college baseball, and baseball won out.

As Ron prepared to take the train to Halifax in June, Milito talked him into coming to Comiskey Park for a workout or two.[4] He hit 15 or 20 pitches out of the park and both manager Paul Richards and general manager Frank Lane felt they had a real find. They offered him bonus money sufficient to seal the deal – on the spot. "My dad and wife and Milito and I went over there," Jackson recalled. "The three of them came home and I stayed. They gave me some money to go buy some clothes."

The amount of the bonus has been variously reported as $10,000, $25,000, and $40,000. He never told anyone the amount of the deal, but he was given a three-year contract. A "bonus baby" in those years was someone who was given more than $6,000 to sign. Under the rules of the day, the player had to be kept on the big-league club for two years. Essentially, the team was penalized for signing players for too much money. Jackson was asked if he felt it hurt him to have to forgo the development he might have experienced had he played ball regularly in the high minors. His response was perhaps a bit understated: "Well, it didn't help me."

Jackson signed on June 15, 1954 – and saw action that very same day. "I was in uniform that night. The only ones on the team who even know who I was, was just a few of them that I worked out with." In the bottom of the ninth inning, Jackson pinch-hit for Harry "Fritz" Dorish and fouled out to first.

Jackson next turned up in a White Sox box score after entering the June 27 game as a defensive replacement at first base in the top of the ninth. He saw no action, either at the plate or in the field. His first at-bat was a single, when he took over late in the first June 29 game for first baseman Phil Cavaretta. The White Sox were losing, 9-1, and Paul Richards wanted to have Cavaretta fresher for the day's second game. Jackson was now 1-for-1.

White Sox starting first baseman Ferris Fain suffered a bruised right knee, and then his backup, Cavaretta, suffered both a pulled groin and a charley horse at the same time. Jackson stepped in to start the second game of the July 5 doubleheader and hit a solo home run in the bottom of the seventh to break a scoreless tie with the Orioles. Jackson hit a Duane Pillette pitch into the upper deck in left. The White Sox won the game, 2-1. His wife and his younger brother, Don, were both in the stands to see the home run. The first homer, he said, was his "greatest thrill in sports." He added that it came on his "third time at bat in my third game with the White Sox. It took me three hours to sign with the White Sox." He'd signed at 3 P.M. Two days later he hit another one, again a solo job.[5] It was his fourth game with Chicago, but the third in which he'd batted. Ron's brother Don was born William Donald Jackson, a year younger. He worked in banking in California; Don died in the early 2000s.

Al Wolf, in his column in the *Los Angeles Times*, noted Jackson's height, but added that he was "graceful afield and powerful with the bat."[6] He was making an impression around the league, but the one club he didn't impress sufficiently was his own. First base was up for grabs; by mid-August of 1954, 11 different White Sox had played the bag. After Fain was hurt, Cavaretta, Jackson, and George Kell all put in time at first. By season's end, Jackson had appeared in 40 games, accumulating 93 at-bats, and hit for a .280 average. He'd struck out almost as often as he'd hit safely, though. He had four homers and 10 RBIs to his credit.

A bonus player who joined the WhiteSox in 1954, Ron Jackson showed occasional flashes of power but was never able to land a job in the starting lineup.

• RON JACKSON •

In December, Chicago traded Fain to the Tigers for Walt Dropo as part of a six-player deal. Dropo got the lion's share of the work at first base in 1955. Jackson got even less than he'd had in the half-season of 1954, with just 74 at-bats spread over 40 games. He hit only .203 for the year, with two homers and seven RBIs but, as a bonus baby, the White Sox couldn't send him to the minors until June 15, 1956, the second anniversary of his signing. White Sox owner Chuck Comiskey suggested to a reporter that Jackson might lack sufficient drive. He said he thought some time in the minors might help, saying, "You know, last spring Jackson came to me and said he'd read in the papers about the possibility of the Sox sending him out in 1956, and I told him he'd better worry about what the Sox were going to do with him in '55." [7] They stuck with him, but send him out at the first opportunity to do so without losing rights to his contract was exactly what they did when the date came around. In 1956, he hit .250 during 16 games in May, filling in for manager Marty Marion when Dropo was benched due to his .121 average. Jackson got one hit or more in each of his first 10 games, but then cooled down with a 1-for-12 stretch. He hit one homer and had four RBIs, and was optioned to the Vancouver Mounties in June on the first possible date. It wasn't an unwelcome move. Jackson said he never felt that Marion wasn't in his corner, "but he believed in his heart that you should come up through the minors." Jackson was told it could do him good to have the experience of playing under Mounties manager Lefty O'Doul.

There he had the chance to play more regularly and enjoyed at least one spectacular game, against Los Angeles on September 3. He hit a grand slam, a triple, and two singles, driving in seven runs. In the half-season he played, he hit .304 with nine homers, driving in 49 runs. This earned him a call back up in September after the Pacific Coast League season was over. He went to bat eight more times for Chicago but without connecting safely even once. His year-end major-league average was .214. And he had an operation on the cartilage in his knee.

He'd started slowly in 1957, hitting .250 in eight spring training games, and was disappointed to be sent to the Indianapolis Indians right at the end of spring training. Then again, a *Sporting News* writer survey tagged him as the "most disappointing player" on the White Sox. Marty Marion had said, "I've never seen anyone hit a ball harder that Ron Jackson does." Trouble was, he didn't hit the ball enough, with continued high strikeout totals. Al Lopez had become White Sox manager, and after Jackson got the news, he emerged from Lopez's office saying, "I'm sorry I couldn't stick. It's hard to say I got a fair trial. My personal feeling is that I was the best out there."[8] It looked like the right move, though. He flourished in Indy, playing in 143 games and hitting 21 homers with an average of .310 and 102 runs batted in. His big game for the Indians came on June 23, a two-homer day with four other hits in eight total at-bats. He was the starting first baseman on the American Association All-Star team and was named the game's MVP, with a homer and a single driving in four runs to help beat the Wichita Braves, 5-4. It was the second All-Star game in which he'd excelled. Just the year before, in the Pacific Coast League's game, he'd tripled with the bases loaded. He credited regular play and a shorter grip on the bat with making the difference.

Unlike Richards, who tried to trade for Jackson after taking the managerial reins in Baltimore, Al Lopez and Jackson never clicked. Ron respected Lopez, and remained impressed all his life with the talented way Lopez continually re-positioned fielders to what often seemed to be the perfect spot, "but he was never in my corner."

In 1957, Jackson doubled his 1956 major-league home run and RBI totals, but appeared in only 13 September games. His three-run homer beat Baltimore on September 18, and he hit safely four times on the 24th. All in all, he hit a very strong .317 in 60 at-bats. This seemed to augur well for 1958. Lopez said he hoped for a lot from both Jackson and outfielder Jim Rivera in 1958. "They're the key men," El Señor said at Chicago's annual Diamond Dinner banquet in January. "They have to come through for us. If they do, our offense will be as good as it was last year."[9] Jackson was still only 24 years old, and Lopez praised his defensive work as well, though it was the power the White Sox needed, to help make up for the trades of Minnie Minoso and Larry Doby.

Dropo, Jackson, and Earl Torgeson were all in the running for the first-base post and a January 1958 *Sporting News* photograph of him was captioned "believed ready." He had begun to learn to pull the ball consistently, and was foreseen as the starting first baseman and cleanup hitter. Writer Jerome Holtzman called him "weak in the field and slow on the bases" and in April *The Sporting News* dubbed him the "slowest player afoot" on the White Sox.[10] Jackson was bold enough to ask Ted Williams for some batting tips, and The Splendid Splinter characteristically obliged. That day Jackson pinch-hit once in each game of a doubleheader against the Red Sox, hitting a homer in the first game and driving in a run with a single in the second. Ron hit .233 for the year with a major-league career high 146 at-bats, with seven homers and 21 RBIs. In the offseason, Jackson began to work in the insurance business back home in Kalamazoo. His father-in-law had started the firm and it remains active today as a family business, with son Mark and daughter Jennifer and her husband running the business. The Ron Jackson Insurance Agency building bears a baseball logo. The firm also has a second office in Plainwell, Michigan. "I'm retired," he said in early 2008. "I go into the office now and drink some coffee but that's it."

Jackson showed up for spring training in 1959 carrying 26 fewer pounds on his big frame, and began to take sharpshooting lessons with several other White Sox in a program designed to try to improve their concentration. By April, however, looking back over Jackson's career to his days as a bonus baby, veteran Chicago sportswriter Edgar Munzel declared that he simply "just hasn't made any progress."[11]

Earl Torgeson beat out all the other contenders for the first-base job and Jackson was optioned to Indianapolis again, due perhaps in part to what he calls a "private disagreement with Lopez." The team relied on Ray Boone to back up Torgeson. Jackson got off to a hot start with Indianapolis, but soon started slumping and seeing his fielding suffer as well. In time he recovered, started hitting, and again became the starting first baseman for the American Association All-Star team. He banged out 30 home runs for Indy, and hit .286. He saw very brief duty with the major-league club: six games in April and May, and four hitless games in September. He had but three hits in 14 at-bats and drove in two runs. He was not on the postseason roster, but was given a quarter-share of the proceeds after Chicago lost the World Series to the Dodgers.

Jackson ended up in a sports page headline in the November 3, 1959 *Chicago Tribune*: "Sox Give Up on Ron Jackson." The White Sox had swapped their former bonus baby to the Red Sox for Boston's bonus baby, pitcher Frank Baumann. Neither player had really panned out as hoped for, though Jackson had again done well in the American Association, leading the league with his 30 homers and 99 RBIs in 1959 despite missing 33 games while with the big-league club. The Red Sox were still seeking the elusive right-handed slugging first baseman that they hadn't had since Jimmie Foxx.

Jackson went back to college three different years and in early 1960 finished the course work for his degree at Western Michigan. He majored in teaching, but though he got his degree he never began in that field, instead joining the insurance company.

When mailing in his contract to Boston GM Bucky Harris, Jackson wrote that he believed he'd finally found himself with the great season he'd had with Indianapolis in 1959. He told Boston writers that he hadn't really been happy in Chicago since Paul Richards left town. Ted Williams remained very high on Jackson's potential. The left-field wall at Fenway Park beckoned, and manager Billy Jurges opined, "We're depending a lot on Jackson and I hope he can … give our attack this big right-handed lift. I'm giving him plenty of time to get set and in the groove."[12] Jackson worked closely with Rudy York, who'd been a boyhood hero. "When I was a kid, he was hitting home runs in Detroit," he said. The Tigers were, of course, the closest team to Kalamazoo, and the only team whose radio broadcasts were heard.

Early in 1960 spring training, Jackson was hurt, though it was kept quiet. "After we started playing games, about the second or third game, I went into second base and upended the second baseman and he come down on my elbow, and it popped. It didn't break but I ended up with what you call tennis elbow." He was hampered and required ultrasound to get his arm straightened out each morning. "I played through that, but right away this trainer that they had said, 'You're all done playing baseball, but just keep your mouth shut.'"

As early as April 11, one can find news stories saying that "Jackson … has failed to measure up."[13] Jurges said he was going to use the newly-acquired Bobby Thomson at first base, declaring, "Let's face it. Jackson has been a big disappointment. He looks confused up at the plate. Maybe he's pressing and trying too hard. But we can't stand still."[14] The Bosox actually settled rather quickly on Vic Wertz instead, and Wertz did the trick, driving in 103 runs. Ron Jackson got into only 10 games and was gone by May 17, traded to the Milwaukee Braves for Ray Boone. The trade wasn't perhaps a true case of trading damaged goods; Boone himself was suffering a bit.

Jackson had been hitting .226 at the time of the

trade. He didn't know it yet, but he'd played his last major-league game. For the Red Sox, Hy Hurwitz wrote, the Baumann-for-Jackson trade "turned out to be one of the sourest deals in Boston history and did more to depose Jurges and General Manager Bucky Harris than anything else."[15]

The Braves assigned Ron to the Louisville Colonels farm club, and he hit rather well, with a couple of home runs and a number of RBIs in the very first week. He began to find it hard to hit to the right side, and sought out orthopedic treatment, which did the trick. The Braves sent him to finish out the season with Indianapolis, another American Association ballclub. He hit .290 that year. Doing yard work in the offseason, laying some sod, he reinjured his elbow. He hit .265 for Louisville in 1961, with 25 home runs and helped win the Little World Series, but he knew he wasn't pulling the ball as well anymore and he wasn't hitting the ball as sharply as he had.

The Houston Colt .45s had their first season in 1962 and Jackson was picked up in the draft as they were looking to build their roster. "But they did not think of me in terms of the big leagues. They thought of me in terms of Oklahoma City," Jackson said. No one from the club really called him, and he had the insurance business available to him, so he called it a day after Houston assigned him to their Oklahoma City 89ers club in November. He finished with a career .245 batting average, with 119 strikeouts to 116 hits, 17 homers, and 52 RBIs, and with a very good fielding percentage of .992.

Jackson kept in touch with some former teammates and enjoys receiving alumni mailings from the ballclubs. "When I stopped playing baseball, I stayed away for about 10 years. I didn't follow anybody. But I got it out of my system and I very much enjoy watching it now."

After a bout with pancreatic cancer, Jackson died on July 6, 2008 in his hometown, Kalamazoo. Jack Moss, the former sports editor of the *Kalamazoo Gazette* remembered him as "the epitome of a real sportsman. He was modest, soft-spoken, a really good athlete and a good person. He never bad-mouthed anybody, yet he had a fire within him and was very competitive."[16]

Notes

1. Interview with Ron Jackson by Bill Nowlin on February 5, 2008. All quotations attributed to Jackson are drawn from this interview unless otherwise indicated.
2. Ed Rumill, "Jackson of White Sox Trying Long Jump From Campus to Big Leagues," *Christian Science Monitor*, July 24, 1954: 10.
3. Edward Prell, "Sox Defeat Tigers, 9 to 0," *Chicago Tribune*, July 8, 195: D1.
4. Ed Rumill, "Jackson of White Sox Trying Long Jump From Campus to Big Leagues,"
5. Ed Prell, "Chisox Limp, But Lean On Their Hurling," *The Sporting News*, July 14, 1954: 21.
6. Al Wolf, "Sportraits," *Los Angeles Times*, July 19, 1954: C2.
7. David Condon, "In the Wake of the News," *Chicago Tribune*, March 2, 1956: B1.
8. John Kuenster, *Chicago Daily News*, quoted in *The Sporting News*, April 10, 1957: 14.
9. Edgar Munzel, "Senor Tabs Jackson, Landis as Key Men in Chisox' Chances," *The Sporting News*, January 22, 1958: 19.
10. Oscar Kahan, "Six Rookies Rated Spring "Surprises"," *The Sporting News*, April 16, 1958: 15.
11. Edgar Munzel, "Soft Sox Bats May Result In Shift of Lollar," *The Sporting News*, April 8, 1959: 10.
12. Ed Rumill, "Red Sox Need Hitting From the Right-Handers," *Christian Science Monitor* April 5, 1960: 16.
13. "Jurges Will Try Thomson at First," *Christian Science Monitor* April 11, 1960: 15.
14. "Jurges Will Try Thomson at First," *Boston Globe*, April 12, 1960: 32.
15. Hy Hurwitz, "Hub Howitzer Wertz Ready for Fast Start," *The Sporting News*, February 8, 1961: 4.
16. "Ron Jackson's life was full and rewarding," *Kalamazoo Gazette*'s M.Live.com web site, July 11, 2008.

TED KLUSZEWSKI

By Paul Ladewski

The area known as Argo is located eight miles west of Chicago's old Comiskey Park in Summit, Illinois, a lowdown five-figure village in Cook County known for a corn milling and processing plant that is among the largest of its kind – and has the odor to prove it. It was also home to Ted "Klu" Kluszewski, the 6-foot-2, 225-pound mountain of a man with the famous 15-inch biceps, whose legend in baseball history will live even longer and go farther than the home runs he hit decades ago.

Kluszewski has often been referred to as one of the most underappreciated players of the post-World War II era; one whose accomplishments as a player and a coach have remained under the radar far too long. In the mid-1950s "Klu" was the original "Big Red Machine," a long-ball hitter and run-producer without peer. In the four seasons from 1953 to 1956, he averaged 179 hits, 43 homers, and 116 RBIs, numbers every bit as impressive as those of Eddie Mathews (152-41-109) of the Milwaukee Braves and Duke Snider (180-42-123) of the Brooklyn Dodgers in the same period. It's not a stretch to believe that if Kluszewski had stayed healthy and productive for four or five more seasons, he would have joined Mathews and Snider in the Hall of Fame. Despite an abbreviated career, his 251 homers while he was with rank fifth on the Reds' all-time list.

Born on September 10, 1924, Theodore Bernard Kluszewski attended Argo High School in Summit, where he excelled in football. His father worked in a local factory. As a youth, Klu's baseball experience consisted mostly of sandlot games. Indiana University recruited him primarily as a football player, but he also played baseball there, and his 1945 season ranks as one of the best for a two-sport athlete in the school's history. As a center fielder, Kluszewski hit .443, a school record that stood for 50 years; then the star end and kicker helped lead the Hoosiers to their only outright Big Ten football championship. The squad, which also included future NFL players Pete Pihos and George Taliaferro, finished with a 9-0-1 mark, the only unbeaten Hoosiers football team.

If not for World War II, Kluszewski most likely would have embarked on a professional football career. During that time the Reds held spring training at the Indiana campus in Bloomington because major-league teams were forbidden to train in the South. One day they invited the kid to take some hacks at batting practice. As legend has it, "Big Klu" promptly launched a few rockets over an embankment nearly 400 feet away. After they picked up their jaws off the ground, team officials offered him a $15,000 contract, which he accepted.

With the bonus in hand, Kluszewski married Eleanor Guckel in February 1946. Eleanor was a fine athlete herself, excelling at softball, and Klu later credited her with helping his major-league career by taking films of him at bat and in the field from seats close to the field.

Making his professional debut for the Reds' Columbia (South Carolina) farm team in the Class-A South Atlantic League in 1946, Kluszewski was an immediate sensation, leading the league with a .352 batting average and driving in 87 runs in 90 games. He made his Cincinnati debut in April 1947, but logged only 10 at-bats with the Reds, spending most of the season with Memphis of the Double-A Southern Association. Again he tore up the league, winning the batting crown with a .377 average.

In 1948 Kluszewski returned to Cincinnati to stay for 10 full seasons. It wasn't long before his large biceps prompted Klu to cut off the sleeves of his jersey, one of the boldest fashion statements in baseball history. At first, he did it because the sleeves were restricting his swing, but after a while it became part of his persona. "I remember the first time that I saw Ted in those cut-off sleeves," former White Sox teammate Billy Pierce said of his trademark style nearly a half-century later. "They were good-sized. He was a big man. A big man."[1]

Despite those massive arms, Kluszewski did not immediately become a home-run hitter at the major-league level. He hit only 12 as a rookie in 1948, and just eight in 1949, though he showed overall improvement as a hitter by lifting his batting average 35 points from .274 to .309. He showed his power potential for the first time in 1950, hitting 25 home runs and driving in 111 runs to go along with a .307

TED KLUSZEWSKI

batting average. After a dip in 1951 (.259-13-77), Klu had 16 home runs in 1952 while raising his average to .320. His big breakthrough came a year later.

In 1953 Kluszewski finally blossomed as big-time slugger, as his .316 batting average, 40 home runs, and 108 RBIs translated into a seventh-place finish in the Most Valuable Player vote. A career year followed in 1954, when he led the NL with 49 home runs. He hit .326 (fifth overall), slugged .642

(third), drove home 141 runs (first), and finished a close second to New York Giants outfielder Willie Mays in the MVP vote. In the All-Star Game at Cleveland, he delivered an RBI single and a two-run homer in consecutive innings, the latter of which broke a 5-5 tie in an eventual 11-9 loss. Klu was at his best when the stars came out, as he hit .500 in four midsummer classics.

Kluszewski did the brunt of his damage at the cozy confines of Crosley Field, which produced one of the highest home-run rates of the decade, but he wasn't known for front-row jobs. What separated Kluszewski from the rest of the musclemen was his off-the-charts discipline at the plate. He totaled 31 fewer strikeouts (140) than home runs (171) in his four peak seasons. Of the ten times in major-league history that a player hit at least 40 homers with fewer strikeouts, three were by Kluszewski. The others on the list: Lou Gehrig (twice), Johnny Mize (twice), Mel Ott, Joe DiMaggio, and Barry Bonds.

"Everybody moves at his own pace," Billy Pierce said many years later. "I mean, we had a Nellie Fox who jumped around all the time. Sherm Lollar couldn't move very fast no matter what happened. But both gave you everything they had on the field and Ted was the same way. He worked at his own pace, and he had a pretty good career that way."[2]

Kluszewski didn't make many mistakes in the field, either, although his detractors argued that the low error totals were the result of an inability or reluctance to move more than one step either way. If you believe in range factors, though, Big Klu was well above average in this regard before his achy back came into play. He led the league in fielding percentage in a record five consecutive seasons, largely the result of excellent hands and nimble footwork.

"Everybody knows Ted could hit a baseball," said the late Bill "Moose" Skowron, the former New York Yankees first baseman who crossed paths with Big Klu many times in their careers. "What some people don't know is that he was a hell of a first baseman and a hell of a nice guy, too. And he always played in those short-sleeve shirts. He was built like a rock, you know."[3]

Kluszewski might have had a long run as one of baseball's top sluggers if not for a back injury that resulted from a clubhouse scuffle during the 1956 season. The disc problem proved to be Delilah to Klu's Samson, as he would never be the same power hitter again. After the 1957 season, one in which Klu was limited to a half-dozen homers and 21 RBIs in 69 games, he was dealt by the Reds to Pittsburgh in return for Dee Fondy, another veteran first baseman.

In 1958, his only full season with the Pirates, Kluszewski produced a mere four home runs and 37 RBIs in 100 games, but he had a positive influence on a young, talented team that was on the move. Before he left, Klu made history at Forbes Field on May 9, when he went deep against Philadelphia Phillies pitcher Robin Roberts leading off the 12th inning, the 19th walk-off homer to decide a 1-0 game since the turn of the century.

Big Klu began the 1959 season with the Pirates, but was reduced to part-time status behind Dick Stuart and Rocky Nelson. He had started only 20 games and logged just 122 at-bats by late August when the White Sox, looking to add power for the stretch and (hopefully) the World Series, traded outfielder Harry "Suitcase" Simpson and minor-league pitcher Bob Sagers for Kluszewski on August 25.

While the 34-year-old Kluszewski was deep into the back nine of his career at the time, news of his return to Chicago was well received by South Siders. "Certainly, the attitude of the fans was positive about the trade," said John Kuenster, who covered the 1959 pennant-winners as a *Chicago Daily News* beat writer. "Ted was a nice guy, a popular guy. He was well known in the area and his return was very well received there."[4] At the very least, the consensus went, Klu could do no worse at the position than 35-year-old warhorse Earl Torgeson, a .226 hitter at the time, or 24-year-young prospect Norm Cash, a .231 hitter who was new to the pressure of a pennant race.

Besides, the righty-dominated lineup had been rather "Kluless" for months. The veteran lefty provided a much-needed option for a "Go-Go" Sox team that was overly dependent on speed and defense at the time. "We didn't have a regular first baseman," Pierce recalled. "When we got Ted, we all thought it was a very, very good thing for us, because he gave us a strong left-handed hitter with a good reputation. We never thought he was past his prime but that he would help us. We were very glad to have him on our ballclub."[5]

What Kluszewski lacked in glitzy numbers, he made up for in stature. His mere physical presence gave the Second City a sliver of security, a reason to flex its own muscles for a change. "Ted was a quiet fellow, but he had been with a winner in Cincinnati and had many accomplishments in his career," Pierce said. "A fellow like that is a kind of automatic leader on the team. He gave us stability, which was very good for us."[6]

As it turned out, Kluszewski didn't quite turn back the clock in the final weeks of the regular season, but he had his moments. The most significant took place in Chicago on September 7, when the White Sox defeated the Kansas City Athletics in a Labor Day doubleheader. In the opener Kluszewski contributed a key run-scoring hit in a 2-1 victory; in the nightcap he slugged a pair of homers and drove home five runs in a 13-7 rout. As a result of the sweep, the White Sox maintained a 4½-game lead over the second-place Cleveland Indians, who scored an emotional sweep of the Detroit Tigers by 15-14 and 6-5 scores the same day.

While Kluszewski had rather modest statistics in the final 32 games of the regular season – .297 batting average, 2 homers, 10 RBIs – the hidden numbers suggest the White Sox were deeper and better because of him. "Ted was a great asset for us," Pierce said. "He was an important cog in the middle of the lineup."[7] With Klu as protection in the cleanup spot, outfielder Jim Landis immediately picked up the pace in the third hole. The offense produced more runs (4.5 vs. 4.3 per game) and team won at a higher rate (.625-.607) with Big Klu than without him.

But it was his performance in the 1959 World Series against the Dodgers that made South Side fans forever remember the Kluszewski trade as one of the greatest Brinks jobs in White Sox history; a local boy who made very, very good one unforgettable season. In the six World Series games, Kluszewski hit .391, slugged three home runs and drove in 10 runs. His 1.266 OPS (on base plus slugging) was just plain silly.

Kluszewski smashed two home runs in an 11-0 rout of the Los Angeles Dodgers in the Series opener. "Oh, man, the two home runs that Ted hit…," Pierce smiled at the thought of them. "That was exciting. I mean, there we were in the World Series. … The fans were excited, we were excited, everybody was excited."[8] Witnesses said Comiskey Park never rocked the way it did in the moments after Kluszewski took reliever Chuck Churn for a ride to the upper deck in the fourth inning. The two-run blow not only sealed the victory, but it did much to "chuck" Churn, as it turned out. The pitch was his last in the big leagues.

Until outfielder Scott Podsednik went deep to decide Game One of the 2005 World Series, the monster blast stood as the most memorable home run in team history. "There was a similar feeling with the two home runs," said John Kuenster. "They gave White Sox fans a reason to think, 'Maybe we will win this thing after all,' although in the case of the 1959 team, it didn't turn out that way."[9] Alas, the Dodgers won four of the next five games to become world champions.

Kluszewski left the team for the Los Angeles Angels in the expansion draft after the 1960 season

• TED KLUSZEWSKI •

– he had hit .293 with 5 homers in 81 games – but not before he was involved in the most controversial play of the 1960 campaign. In a game at Baltimore on August 28, Kluszewski hit a dramatic pinch-hit, three-run homer against Orioles starter Milt Pappas in the eighth inning to give his team a 4-3 lead. Or so it seemed. The umpire crew agreed that time had been called before the pitch was thrown and the home run was wiped out. After teammate Nellie Fox was ejected from the game, Kluszewski flied out to end the threat. The White Sox went on to drop a 3-1 decision and fell three games out of first place.

Before Kluszewski retired one year later, he exacted a sliver of payback at the same site. In the first game in Los Angeles Angels history, Big Klu took Pappas deep with a man on base in the first inning, the first home run in franchise history. One inning later he greeted rookie John Papa with a three-run homer to set the wheels in motion for a 7-2 victory. Kluszewski finished his final big-league season with a .243 batting average, 15 home runs, and 39 RBIs in 107 games.

Kluszewski returned to the Reds after retiring as a player, and his impact on the team was no small one. He was the Reds' hitting coach for nine seasons in the 1970s, a decade that the Big Red Machine dominated as few other offenses in NL history had done. In 1986, after he had become a hitting instructor in the Reds' minor-league system, Kluszewski suffered a heart attack and underwent emergency bypass surgery. On March 29, 1988, a massive heart attack took his life. He was 63 years old.

That the funeral service in suburban Cincinnati was a virtual Who's Who said as much about Kluszewski the person as Big Klu the athlete. Rose, Johnny Bench, and Tony Perez were among those who paid their respects. Stan Musial and Joe Nuxhall did, too. During the 1988 season the Reds wore black armbands in memory of their late teammate. There wasn't an arm large enough to do justice to Big Klu, a big man in more ways than one.

Notes

1. Billy Pierce, interview with author, August 2008.
2. Ibid.
3. Bill Skowron, interview with author, August 2008.
4. John Kuenster, interview with author, September 2008.
5. Pierce.
6. Ibid.
7. Ibid.
8. Ibid.
9. Kuenster.

JIM LANDIS
By Mike Richard

Jim Landis had a memorable stint with the Go-Go White Sox of the late 1950s, and is considered to be one of the best defensive center fielders in big-league history. He also played with the Kansas City Athletics, Cleveland Indians, Houston Astros, and Detroit Tigers before finishing his career with a short but memorable stint with the 1967 "Impossible Dream" Red Sox. His .989 career fielding average placed him second only to Jimmy Piersall at the time of his retirement among major-league outfielders.

James Henry Landis Jr. was born on March 9, 1934, in Fresno, California to factory worked James Henry Landis and his wife Maida, a homemaker. He was signed for $2,500 by the Chicago White Sox as an amateur free agent in 1952, out of Contra Costa Junior College in San Pablo.[1] Before that, he had a stellar career as a third baseman at Richmond (California) High School.

He was signed "after playing about four games at the junior college," he recalled. "I was approached by a White Sox scout named Bob Mattick who asked me about signing a big-league contract and I said, 'Let's do it.'"[2]

Landis began as a third baseman and outfielder with Wisconsin Rapids of the Class-D Wisconsin State League in 1952. He batted .274 in 92 games.

The next season he moved up to Colorado Springs of the Class-A Western League, where he hit 14 home runs and posted a career-best .313 batting average. "Don Gutteridge, my manager at Colorado Springs, really encouraged me," said Landis in a 2008 interview. "The Sox also had a former major-league center fielder named Johnny Mostil in their minor-league system who really worked my butt off day in and day out."[3]

Landis then spent 1954 and 1955 in the Army. "I was a lucky guy, I got stationed up in Alaska," he said with a chuckle. "I did get to play some baseball up there, but it wasn't a long season."[4]

He returned to Colorado Springs in 1956, and in the same season was quickly promoted to the Memphis Chicks of the Double-A Southern Association. In 1957, on April 16, he made his debut with the Chicago White Sox. "My first game was horrible," Landis recalled. "I was facing Herb Score and the Indians, and I was just kind of floating on air. I remember saying, 'What am I doing here?' It took a little while but finally I said to myself, 'You belong,' and that's when I started to play better."[5]

Landis's first season was anything but easy, however. He played in 96 games as a rookie in '57, splitting time between right field and center field in an outfield that featured veteran stars Larry Doby and Minnie Minoso. On defense the speedy, sure-handed Landis nicely complemented the veteran outfielders, but he struggled terribly at bat. After a decent first month he slumped, and by the end of June Landis's batting average had dropped to .187. But though the White Sox gave Landis some time on the bench, they never gave up on him. "I got off to a slow start with the bat," he recalled, "but my defense carried me. Al Lopez was great. ... He made up his mind that I was going to be his center fielder, and he stuck with me. And eventually my hitting improved."[6] It didn't improve much in 1957 – Landis hit only .212 for the year -- but in 1958 he was a different player, hitting .277 with 15 home runs and 19 stolen bases. Only 24 years old when the 1958 season ended, Landis had established himself as a budding star.

Then came the memorable 1959 Go-Go Sox season. That year, they became the first American League team since the Cleveland Indians (1948 and 1954) to wrest the pennant from the New York Yankees.

"It was a great year. We had a good ballclub, we had four Hall of Famers on one team," Landis said, rattling off the names of Early Wynn, Luis Aparicio, Nellie Fox, and Larry Doby.[7] The White Sox also featured Earl Torgeson at first base, Bubba Phillips at third and catcher Sherm Lollar. Landis, Al Smith, and a platoon of Jim McAnany and Jim Rivera were in the outfield, while the pitching staff included Wynn, Bob Shaw, and Billy Pierce, with Jerry Staley and Turk Lown keys to the bullpen.

"One of the best things about the White Sox was the terrific group of guys I played with," he said. "Guys like Nellie Fox, Billy Pierce, Bob Shaw, Minnie Miñoso, Jim Rivera. All these guys were true vets and I was the new kid. They were all like fathers to me."[8]

Landis batted .272 for the pennant winners and excelled in center field in '59, leading all American

• JIM LANDIS •

Jim Landis's smooth batting stroke helped the White Sox win the 1959 American League pennant. Landis had even more value as a ball-hawking center fielder who would win five Gold Gloves.

League outfielders in putouts. Although he hit only five home runs that year, he ranked 10th in the American League with a .370 on-base percentage, and his 20 stolen bases were tied for the third highest total in the league. After the season he received 66 points in balloting for the American League's Most Valuable Player award, which was won by teammate Fox.

The White Sox were beaten in six games in the World Series by the Los Angeles Dodgers, who were led by the starting pitching of Johnny Podres and the bullpen work of Series MVP Larry Sherry, who won two games in relief and had two saves. In the Series, Landis batted .292 with seven hits for Chicago. "The Dodgers had a playoff series with the Braves to decide the National League pennant, and that delayed the start of the World Series a little," he recalled. "I think that took a little bit of the edge off us. Also, some of brought our wives out to LA for the games there, and that was a bit of a distraction. But we got beat fair and square, and we were in every game except for the last one."[9]

In 1960, Landis's average slipped to .253 as the White Sox, hoping to repeat as American League champions, fell to third place. It was a disappointing season for the Sox, who had traded youngsters Norm Cash, Johnny Callison, Earl Battey, and John Romano to bring in veteran sluggers Minnie Miñoso, Roy Sievers, and Gene Freese. "We sure asked, 'What the hell is going on?'" Landis told interviewer Mark Liptak. "We knew how good those kids were because we saw them in the spring. Every single one of the guys we traded wound up making the All-Star team in the next few years."[10]

Despite his drop in batting average, Landis had a fine all-around season in 1960, stealing a career-high 23 bases and winning the first of five straight Gold Gloves. A fan favorite in the Windy City, he was known for his many over-the-fence catches stolen from Comiskey Park's center-field bullpen. "I knew how to play the game and I'm proud of my Gold Gloves," he said. "I think fielding was my forte, and I felt I knew the game well."[11]

In 1961, Landis had his best year with the bat when he had career highs of 22 home runs, 85 RBIs, and a .283 average. "It was one of my best years. Everything kind of fell together for me," he said. "For a while I think I was hitting just around .300. I had a shot [at .300], but I blew it with a slump in May."[12] May always seemed to be a difficult month for Landis, who had a career average of just .225 in that month.

Landis was selected to his only All-Star Game in 1962. In his lone All-Star at-bat at Washington's D.C. Stadium in the first of two All-Star games that year, Landis struck out against former White Sox teammate Bob Shaw. "I got a real funny feeling because I didn't want to hit against him," he told Mark Liptak. "He was my friend and teammate for a number of years."[13]

Despite the All-Star appearance, Landis batted only .228 in 1962, and he continued to struggle at bat in 1963 (.225) and 1964, when he batted a career-low .208. The '64 season was particularly disappointing as the White Sox had a chance to once again capture the pennant from the Yankees, but fell one game shy.

After the 1964 season, Landis was involved in a three-team deal between the White Sox, Kansas City, and Cleveland. He was traded with outfielder Mike Hershberger and pitcher Fred Talbot to Kansas City; slugging outfielder Rocky Colavito went from Kansas City to Cleveland. The trade was no surprise to Landis. "I had hardly played in '64 compared to previous seasons," he commented. "One thing that happened that year was that I was the Sox player rep, and when the players wanted to receive $50 for doing radio and

TV interviews, I told that to (Sox general manager) Ed Short. He didn't like it and got mad at me."[14]

After one season, playing in 118 games with a .239 average for the last place A's in 1965, Landis was traded with pitcher Jim Rittwage to Cleveland for catcher Phil Roof and outfielder Joe Rudi. As his number of outfield appearances continued to dwindle with the Indians in 1966, he was once again moved.

He began the 1967 season in Houston, and then went to Detroit in June, playing 25 games with the Tigers filling in for Al Kaline, who had broken his finger jamming his bat into the bat rack. Once the Tigers released him in late August, the Red Sox scooped him up in hopes that he could fill the void when Tony Conigliaro was lost for the season as a result of a tragic beaning on August 18.

Landis's debut with the Red Sox was as a pinch-runner for Norm Siebern in a game against the Washington Senators on August 23. He took Jose Tartabull's place in right field and struck out in the bottom of the ninth to end the game at Fenway.

The next day, Landis came on to play defense late in the game against Washington; it was the day Conigliaro was released from Sancta Maria Hospital. With the Red Sox leading, 6-2, in the eighth inning, Landis homered off Darold Knowles, providing a 7-2 cushion, but he made an even bigger contribution in the top of the ninth.

The Senators scored three runs and had the bases loaded with two outs in the ninth, when Ken McMullen hit a fastball from John Wyatt to deep right. A gust of wind caught the ball and, as Ken Coleman noted in his book *The Impossible Dream Remembered*, "Landis did a Tango under it: 'I nearly lost it in the sun,' Landis said. 'The wind slowed down and started to pull the ball away from me.'"[15]

At the last second, Landis, running all the way, made a one-handed grab to end the game, lunging for the ball as the runners circled the bases. The victory put the Red Sox into virtually a first-place tie with Chicago, just a percentage point behind the White Sox. It was one of the very few times since the 1940s that the Red Sox had been atop the standings this late in the season.

The heroics earned Landis a start the following night in right field against the White Sox in the first game of a doubleheader. He batted leadoff and went hitless in a 7-1 Red Sox victory. In the nightcap, Landis was a late-inning replacement in right field as Chicago scored a run in the last of the ninth to win 2-1.

His final appearance came on August 27, another late-game appearance replacing Thomas in right field of the second game of a doubleheader. Gary Peters outdueled Jose Santiago, 1-0, as the White Sox scored a run in the last of the 11th inning.

The next day, Landis was released when the Red Sox signed Ken Harrelson, who had been released by the Kansas City A's after a well-publicized feud with owner Charlie Finley.

Landis' five-game totals for the Red Sox read seven at-bats, with one hit -- the solo home run -- for a .143 batting average. He was reconciled to retirement and knew that the 1967 season would likely be his last in the majors, and relished his brief moment with the Red Sox.

"For me, knowing that I was going home the next year, it was nice to get to know some of those players," he said. "Being around Yastrzemski that year, even for a short time, was a nice ending to my career. I knew I'd be going out at the end of the year, so it was nice to be in the middle of a pennant race."[16]

Ironically, the frantic 1967 American League pennant race featured three teams that Landis had played with in his career: Chicago, Detroit, and Boston.

"To be honest with you, I was pulling for Boston to win it down the stretch," Landis said. "It was the last team I was with. And to be honest, I didn't leave happily from the White Sox."[17]

Landis finished his 11-year major-league career with a .247 batting average, 1,061 hits, 93 home runs, and 139 stolen bases. His good eye at the plate is reflected in his .344 career on-base percentage.

After he retired from baseball, Landis went into a safety sign business for about 15 years, catching on shortly after the creation of OSHA, the federal Occupational Safety and Health Administration. After he retired, he continued to stay active in baseball as a Babe Ruth League baseball coach in the Napa, California, area for several seasons.

He and his wife, Sandra, had two daughters, Vicky and Michelle, and two sons, Craig and Mike. Craig, a shortstop, was the number one draft pick of the San Francisco Giants in 1977 and remained in the Giants' system through Triple A. He was a standout baseball player and football defensive back at Stanford University. Later he went to work as a as a sports agent, representing Paul Konerko, Randy Winn, and Aaron Rowand.

"Even though I only spent a week in Boston, it was a great place to be," Jim said. "Boston fans are great, and it was a good ending to my career. I had no complaints."[18]

• JIM LANDIS •

But it is for his play with the White Sox that Landis will best be remembered. In 2000, he was selected as one of the outfielders in fan balloting for the 27-player White Sox All-Century team, commemorating 100 years of baseball on the South Side. Former teammates Luis Aparicio, Nellie Fox, Minnie Miñoso, Sherm Lollar, Billy Pierce, Gary Peters, and Hoyt Wilhelm were also selected to the team. "I was very grateful," Landis said. "What I'm most proud of is the number of guys from that team forty years ago who made it. … Nellie, Billy, Louie, myself. We had a real good team then."[19] And Jim Landis was an important member of that "real good team."

Landis died of cancer in Napa, California on October 7, 2017. He was survived by his wife Sandra (Foster), his son Craig (a player agent), son Michael, and two daughers, Vicki Robinson and Michele Stafford.

Don Zminda supplied some additional material to this piece.

Sources

Baseball Encyclopedia (Toronto: The Macmillan Company, Information Concepts Incorporated, 1984).

Marazzi, Rich, and Len Fiorito. *Aaron to Zuverink* (New York: Avon Books, 1982).

20th Century Baseball Chronicle (Lincolnwood, Illinois: Publications International, 1992).

Notes

1. Richard Sandomir, *New York Times*, "Jim Landis, 83, Defensive Star of '59 White Sox," *Boston Globe*, October 14, 2017.
2. Interview with Jim Landis by Mike Richard, March 28, 2006.
3. Interview with Jim Landis by Don Zminda, January 9, 2008.
4. Richard interview.
5. Zminda interview
6. Ibid.
7. Richard interview.
8. Richard interview. Jim Landis interview by Mark Liptak, Baseball-Almanac.com, 2006
9. Zminda interview.
10. Liptak.
11. Richard interview.
12. Ibid.
13. Liptak.
14. Zminda interview.
15. Ken Coleman and Dan Valenti. *The Impossible Dream Remembered* (Lexington, Massachusetts: The Stephen Greene Press, 1987), 164.
16. Richard interview.
17. Ibid.
18. Ibid.
19. Liptak.

BARRY LATMAN

By Ralph Berger

For 40 years, the Chicago White Sox wandered in the wasteland of baseball as the Israelites had once wandered in the Sinai desert. Was it punishment for their sinful dealings in the 1919 World Series? No one can say for sure, but in 1959, absolution was at hand. A member of that 1959 White Sox club was a 6-foot-3 Jewish lad with big shoulders. Barry Latman was neither a Moses nor a major star for the White Sox, but he helped the team atone for those 40 lackluster years and win the American League pennant.

Arnold Barry Latman was born in Los Angeles on May 21, 1936, to a well-to-do couple, Nathan and Elsie (Snitzer) Latman. Nathan was a furniture auctioneer. The Latmans were observant Jews and Barry followed their lead to some extent; he would not pitch on the Jewish High Holidays. Barry had two younger sisters, Ann Lorraine and Carolee.

Latman began playing baseball at the age of six. Also, from the age of seven until he was nine or 10, he appeared on a local weekly television program, singing in a boys choir. When he was 10 years old, his parents made him take a "sabbatical" from baseball for three years so he could study for his bar mitzvah. He started playing again at 13, and, as he put it, "never stopped until I retired from the major leagues." At the age of 15, he tried out for his Fairfax High School baseball team. He made the team as a pitcher; one of his teammates was Larry Sherry, who went on to play for the Los Angeles Dodgers (and star against the White Sox in the 1959 World Series).[1]

In 1954, at the age of 18, Latman hurled a perfect game for Fairfax High, the first one in a decade in the Los Angeles school system. A senior that year, Latman was named the Los Angeles All-City Player by the Helms Athletic Foundation. His impressive pitching landed him a spot in the All-Star High School Game in New York. He also impressed major-league scouts, and was offered bonuses by several clubs. However, he declined these offers and accepted a baseball scholarship from the University of Southern California.

In 1954, Latman began a five-year correspondence with Ty Cobb, who had seen him pitch on TV. After some time the two met and Cobb watched Latman pitch. He told Barry that he had the stuff to pitch in the major leagues, and sent him a series of encouraging letters.[2]

Latman grew to become a broad-shouldered man who was nicknamed "Shoulders." While attending the University of Southern California in 1955, Latman signed a contract with the Chicago White Sox. He was sent to Waterloo, Iowa, in the Class-B Three-I League, where he compiled an 18-5 mark with an earned run average of 4.12. He led the league in innings pitched. The next year, 1956, he was promoted to the Memphis Chicks in the Double-A Southern Association, winning 14 and losing 14 with a 3.85 earned run average. In 1957 he moved up to Indianapolis of the Triple-A American Association, Chicago's top farm club, and went 13-13 with an earned-run average of 3.95. In September of that year, the White Sox called Latman up to Chicago.

Barry's major league debut came against the Boston Red Sox on September 10, 1957. He pitched three innings, giving up two hits, striking out two, walking three, and permitting no earned runs. Latman earned his first major-league victory in relief five days later at Griffith Stadium in Washington. He entered the game in relief of Bob Keegan and tossed two scoreless innings. The White Sox scored three runs in the top of the ninth to win the game, 3-1. In his first taste of major-league action, Latman appeared in seven games, winning one and losing two while posting a high earned-run average of 8.25.

After Latman joined the White Sox, pitching coach Ray Berres taught him to throw a slider to complement his fastball, which he threw 60 to 70 percent of the time. Berres also showed Latman how to put pressure on the seams of the ball in order to give the ball more movement.[3]

Latman began the 1958 season back at Indianapolis and posted a 9-11 record with a 4.62 ERA. Though those numbers weren't very impressive, the White Sox brought him back to Chicago in August, and he pitched well over the final two months of the season. Appearing in 13 games, including three starts, he went 3-0 with an exceptional ERA of 0.76. In his final appearance of the season, on September 26,

• BARRY LATMAN •

After going 8-5 with the pennant-winning 1959 White Sox, Barry Latman was traded to the Indians and made the American League All-Star team in 1961.

Latman shut out the Kansas City Athletics on three hits, 1-0, striking out nine and facing only 30 batters.

Latman's late-season performance in 1958 cemented his reputation as one of the White Sox' top pitching prospects, and he began the 1959 season as a member of the starting rotation. But he quickly pitched himself out of that role, going winless in four starts in April and early May while posting a painfully high 9.19 ERA. Sent to the bullpen, his work improved, and he was given another chance to rejoin the rotation in late June. This time he proved ready; from June 25 to the end of the season, Latman was one of the White Sox' most reliable pitchers, going 8-3 with a 3.22 ERA over 21 appearances, including 17 starts. But with the White Sox closing in on their first pennant in 40 years, manager Al Lopez began to rely more on his veteran pitchers, and Latman finished the season back in the bullpen.

Latman's last start of the 1959 season came on September 11, and it was memorable. In the second game of a twi-night doubleheader at Baltimore's Memorial Stadium, the 23-year-old Latman and 20-year-old Oriole starter Jerry Walker both pitched scoreless ball into the 10th inning. Latman was finally lifted when the Birds put two men on in the bottom of the 10th. Reliever Jerry Staley pitched out of the jam, and Staley and Walker maintained the 0-0 tie until the 16th inning, when the Birds finally broke through with a run to complete a doubleheader sweep. (Young Jerry Walker may have paid a price for that 16-inning shutout; after going 11-10 with 2.97 ERA in '59, he won only 25 games during the remainder of his career, and never posted another winning record.)

Though selected to the White Sox' World Series roster, Latman did not appear in Chicago's Series loss in six games to the Los Angeles Dodgers. He must have felt a little frustrated watching from the bullpen, especially since his old high-school teammate Larry Sherry was the star of the Series, winning Games Four and Six for the Dodgers and capturing the World Series MVP award.

Latman's lack of late-season activity with the '59 White Sox proved a harbinger of the club's future plans for him. During the 1959-60 offseason, team president Bill Veeck made a series of trades in which he dealt away young players for veterans, most of them power hitters. Then, on April 18, 1960 – the day before the White Sox were to start the season – the club traded Latman to the Cleveland Indians for left-handed pitcher Herb Score, a former star who had struggled for several seasons after being struck in the eye by a batted ball. White Sox manager Al Lopez had skippered the Indians when Score was starring for the Tribe before the injury, and, according to Veeck, "I've never seen Al want a player as badly as he wanted Score."[4]

While Score went 6-12 in three seasons with the White Sox, Latman found success in Cleveland. His 1960 season was nothing special – 7-7 with a 4.03 ERA while both starting and relieving – but Barry got off to a tremendous start for the Indians in 1961. Working mostly out of the bullpen, he won his first nine decisions. He tailed off later in the season and wound up with a 13-5 record and a 4.02 earned-run average, along with five saves. Latman's great start to the season earned him a spot on the American League roster for the second of the two All-Star Games that year, but he did not appear in the game.

Along with having his most successful season in 1961, Latman married Lynne Schwab in October of that year. She was the daughter of Leon Schwab, the owner of the famous Schwab drugstore chain in California. The newlyweds spent their honeymoon in Israel. They had two children, Nathan and Richard; the couple divorced in 1980.

In 1962, Latman won 8 and lost 13 for Cleveland with a 4.17 ERA, again working as both a starter and reliever. On July 18 he and teammate Jim Perry made some dubious history when the Minnesota Twins became the first team in the 20th century to hit two grand slams in one inning (one off each pitcher). The sluggers were Bob Allison and Harmon Killebrew. In Latman's final season with the Indians, 1963, he went 7-12 with an ERA of 4.94, again splitting his time between starting and relief roles.

On December 2, 1963, the Indians traded Latman to the Los Angeles Angels for slugging outfielder Leon Wagner. It was reported that when Latman's father-in-law heard about the trade, he said, "It's impossible; is that all they got for Wagner?" Barry defended Mr. Schwab, saying, "The truth is that it was my line. … It's what I said to my father-in-law when I first told him about the trade. But he's getting blamed for it all over town."[5] In actuality the Angels did receive more than just Latman in exchange for the popular Daddy Wags. The deal included a player to be named later, and Tribe first baseman Joe Adcock was sent to the Angels on December 6 to complete the deal.

In 1964, his first season with Los Angeles, Latman had his third straight losing season, going 6-10 with a 3.85 earned run average. He suffered a sore arm in 1965 and pitched in only 18 games for the Angels, all in relief, though his ERA was a fine 2.84. In June the Angels sent him to Seattle in the Pacific Coast League, where he compiled a 7-6 record with a 3.09 ERA. Brought back by the Angels in September, he told Los Angeles management that he would like to be traded. On December 15 the club accommodated, sending him to the Houston Astros for cash and minor-league catcher Ed Pacheco.

In 1966, though still suffering from a sore arm, Latman got into 31 games for the Astros and posted the best earned-run average of his career, 2.71. However, he won only two games while losing seven. In 1967, he was 3-6 for Houston and his earned-run average rose to 4.52. The end had come; Latman, only 31 years old, pitched in his last professional ballgame on August 19, 1967, with Houston.

Latman pitched in the big leagues for 11 years. Appearing in 344 games including 134 starts, he went 59-68 with a career ERA of 3.91. Some baseball analysts felt that Latman, who came up to the White Sox with a "can't miss" tag, should have been a better pitcher than his career totals show. Some players felt that Latman was snake-bit; he kept pitching in bad luck. Latman himself said he felt for too long that he could overpower hitters with his fastball, but the strategy did not work. He said he didn't really learn how to pitch until he was 30 years old, by which time he was near the end of his career. Barry added that he was his own worst enemy by popping off too much.

After his baseball career was over, Latman was faced with what to do with his life. Fortunately, he had learned the home furnishings and drapery business during his playing days and became active in that vocation after retiring from baseball. Latman also worked as a project superintendent in custom-home construction.

Latman was remarried in 1989 to Patti Klein in Los Angeles. Between his two marriages Latman has five children and 13 grandchildren. The Latmans lived in Marina Del Rey, a seaside enclave near Los Angeles, then lived on a golf course in northern San Diego County. In 2006 they moved into a condo they purchased in Puerto Vallarta, Mexico.

Although Barry Latman was a journeyman pitcher., he made an impact on people. One evening after his major-league career had ended, Latman was asked to appear at the Beth-El Synagogue in Indianapolis. A young man with no interest in baseball listened to Latman speak. He was taken with the speech Latman delivered and became an avid baseball fan. The fan recently sent a message to an online spot called the Bulletin Board with the hope that Latman would read his message of how he was inspired by Latman's speech.

After a long illness, Latman died at age 82 in Richmond, Texas on April 28, 2019.

• BARRY LATMAN •

Sources

In addition to the sources cited in the Notes, the author also consulted baseballlibrary.com, baseball-reference.com, and the archives at the National Hall of Fame.

Kalas, Larry. *Strength Down the Middle, The Story of the 1959 Chicago White Sox* (Fort Worth: Mereken Land Production Company, 1999).

Koppett, Leonard. *A Concise History of Major League Baseball* (Philadelphia: Temple University Press, 1998).

Reiss, Steven A., editor. *The American League* (Westport, Connecticut: Greenwood Press, 2006).

Notes

1. Danny Peary, editor, *We Played the Game: 65 Players Remember Baseball's Greatest Era, 1947-1964* (New York: Hyperion, 1994), 314.
2. Peter S. Horvitz, Joachim Horvitz, *The Big Book of Jewish Baseball* (New York: SPI Books, 2001), 101-102.
3. Bill James and Rob Neyer, *The Neyer/James Guide to Pitchers* (New York: Fireside Press, 2004), 275.
4. Jerry Holtzman, "Never Saw Al Seek Player So Badly – Veeck," *The Sporting News*, April 27, 19604.
5. Braven Dyer, "Joining Angels Bigger Thrill Than World Series – Latman," *Los Angeles Times*, December 24, 1963.

SHERMAN LOLLAR

By John McMurray

Soft spoken and self-effacing, Sherman Lollar provided a strong defensive presence behind the plate during his 12 seasons with the Chicago White Sox. An All-Star catcher in seven seasons of his 18-year major-league career, Lollar won the first three American League Gold Glove awards, from 1957 through 1959. Although he was not known as a power hitter, Lollar hit 155 career home runs and collected 1,415 hits. He also produced one of the White Sox' few bright moments in the 1959 World Series apart from their Game One victory, a two-out, three-run homer tied Game Four in the seventh inning. (Unfortunately, the Sox lost that game, 5-4.)

Even though Lollar played well and received awards during the 1950s, he did not receive as much national recognition as fellow catcher Yogi Berra, who won three Most Valuable Player awards. As Red Gleason wrote in *The Saturday Evening Post* in 1957, "It is the fate of some illustrious men to spend a career in the shadow of a contemporary. Adlai Stevenson had his Dwight Eisenhower. Lou Gehrig had his Babe Ruth. Bob Hope had his Bing Crosby. And Sherman Lollar has his Yogi Berra."[1]

John Sherman Lollar Jr. was born on August 23, 1924, in Durham, Arkansas. His father, John Sherman Lollar Sr., had been a semipro baseball player and was a veteran of World War I. When Lollar Jr. was 3 years old, he moved with his family to Fayetteville, Arkansas, where his parents opened a grocery store.

Lollar's interest in baseball began at an early age and he remembered playing catch with his father outside the store at the age of 6. When Lollar was only 8 years old, his father died unexpectedly during surgery. At that early age, Lollar, who was the oldest of four children, including two girls (Bonnie and Pat) and a boy (Jerry, who was born after his father's death), had to take on additional responsibilities at home.

His mother sold the grocery store and began working in a nursing home for the Veterans Administration. She told Gleason, "Sherman took a large share of the responsibility of looking after the younger children. He was both a big brother and father. Our being left alone so soon created a sense of oneness in all of us that remains even now."[2]

Even with his additional responsibilities, Lollar's interest in baseball never waned. In 1936, shortly before he turned 12 years old, Lollar became a batboy for the Fayetteville Bears in the Arkansas-Missouri League. After graduating from Fayetteville High School at 16, a school that had no baseball team, Lollar took a job with J.C. Penney in Pittsburg, Kansas. He played with a team affiliated with the Chamber of Commerce in the Ban Johnson League while also studying at Pittsburg State Teachers College. Two years later, after the Ban Johnson League folded, Lollar both played and managed for the semipro Baxter Springs Miners, working as a brakeman in a local mine when he wasn't playing baseball. With Baxter Springs, Lollar was a teammate of Mickey Mantle.

On the recommendation of teammate Stan West, a pitcher on the Baxter Springs team who was under contract to Baltimore of the Class-AA International League, Lollar was signed by Baltimore in 1943, when he was 18. His pay was $20 a month. He started slowly, batting only .118 in 12 games in his first season. Yet Lollar steadily improved: He batted .250 with 15 home runs for Baltimore in 1944. He also drove in 72 runs, one of the highest totals for any catcher in organized baseball that year.

Lollar won the International League's Most Valuable Player award in 1945, tearing up the league with 34 home runs, 111 runs batted in, and a league-leading batting average of .364. Baltimore had a working agreement with the Cleveland Indians and was soon forced to sell its top slugger to the major-league team for $10,000.

After making his major-league debut on April 20, 1946, Lollar played infrequently behind veterans Frank Hayes and Jim Hegan. Soon he asked to go back to Baltimore so that he could play regularly. Back in the minor leagues, Lollar was unable to duplicate his great batting success from 1945, hitting only .234, but he did hit 20 home runs in only 222 at-bats for Baltimore. His biggest gain that year was meeting his future wife, Connie, whom he married in 1949.

In December 1946, Lollar was traded to the New York Yankees, along with second baseman Ray Mack,

• SHERMAN LOLLAR •

in exchange for outfielder Hal Peck and pitchers Al Gettel and Gene Bearden. In New York he was caught in a catching logjam that included Ralph Houk, Charlie Silvera, Aaron Robinson, and a rookie named Yogi Berra. As a consequence, Lollar spent most of the 1947 season with Newark, the Yankees' farm club in the Triple-A International League. There were also concerns about Lollar's attitude. According to writer Bill Roeder, "The Cleveland complaint was that Lollar displayed insufficient dash and spirit. He had the ability all right, but no inclination to exploit it. Within a month, he was homesick for Baltimore, and [Cleveland manager Lou] Boudreau sent him back. Now Sherman belongs to the Yankees, and they hope he will react favorably to the fresh start."³

Seven-time All-Star Sherm Lollar led the pennant-winning '59 White Sox in home runs (22) and RBIss (84).

Lollar appeared in only 11 regular season games for the Yankees in 1947, but he did play in the World Series, getting three hits in four World Series at-bats, including two doubles. In Game Three, sportswriter Dan Daniel wrote, "A secondary standout was Sherman Lollar, who started the game as a surprise entry. [Manager Bucky] Harris benched Berra in favor of the right-handed Lollar against the southpaw [Joe] Hatten. Lollar got a single which became a run in the third, and in the fourth drove in a run with a double."⁴

A contemporary article called Lollar "a Charley Gehringer type," adding, "He appears a colorless, dispassionate individual, on and off the field, but he gets his job done effectively. If Lollar hits as well as Gehringer did, no one will care if he doesn't say a word all season." ⁵

In parts of two seasons with New York, Lollar saw action in only 33 games. Yogi Berra was on his way to becoming a regular in the major leagues in 1948, and Lollar was also hindered by a hand injury caused by a foul tip off the bat of Bob Elliott, requiring him to get stitches on two fingers of his throwing hand. Writing in August 1948, sportswriter Dan Daniel observed, "Sherman Lollar, right-handed hitting catcher, is another who has possibly had his last big opportunity with the Bombers. Now that Yogi Berra is available again, Gus Niarhos will handle all the receiving duties against left-handed pitching."⁶

Not surprisingly, Lollar was soon traded again, this time to the St. Louis Browns on December 13, 1948, with pitchers Red Embree and Dick Starr and $100,000 in return for catcher Roy Partee and pitcher Fred Sanford. In St. Louis, Lollar took over for Les Moss as the team's regular catcher and batted .261 with 8 home runs and 49 RBIs. For three seasons, Lollar stabilized the catching position for the Browns. He was an All-Star for the first time in 1950, and the primary catcher during Ned Garver's only 20-win season in 1951.

Still, the Browns were regularly a second-division team. After the 1951 season, the Chicago White Sox were looking for a replacement for incumbent catcher Phil Masi, and on November 27, 1951, they received Lollar from the Browns along with infielder Tom Upton and pitcher Al Widmar in return for pitcher Dick Littlefield, shortstop Joe DeMaestri, catcher Gus Niarhos, first baseman-outfielder Gordon Goldsberry, and outfielder Jim Rivera. According to his son, Lollar's salary was increased to about $12,000 when he was traded.

Arriving in Chicago was the break that Sherm Lollar needed. Unlike the Browns, who had won only 52 games in 1951, the White Sox had finished eight games over .500 and were considered a potential World Series contender. Still, the 1952 season was a disappointment for Lollar, who endured additional stress when his wife fell ill after childbirth. But while he batted only .240, his work with manager Paul Richards helped to turn the young catcher's career around. As Gleason recounted in *The Saturday Evening Post*, Lollar later said:

"When I was having that terrible year in 1952, Richards called me into his office late in the season. He told me that my natural style of catching lacked appeal and I would have to be more of a holler guy. Paul said he understood my problem because he had been the same kind of catcher that I was. I feel that I've always hustled in baseball, but until Paul talked to me I probably had a misconception of what 'hustle' meant. I hustled to first base on a batted ball, and I hustled when the ball was around me. Richards made me see that something more was expected.

"Paul told me to show a little more animation. He wanted me to be a little more agile in receiving, and to show more zip in returning the ball to the pitcher. He recommended that I run to and from the catcher's box between innings, instead of just strolling out there."[7]

Gleason wrote that Richards recommended Lollar's distinctive style of catching, with his left knee on the ground, because, according to Richards, "This moved him up – closer to the plate – and down – closer to the ground."[8]

With the White Sox, Lollar regularly caught 100 or more games each season, and he was exceptionally durable during his 12 seasons with the team. In his second year there, Lollar changed from wearing uniform number 45 to the more familiar number 10 that he wore for the rest of his Chicago career.

Lollar was an American League All-Star in six seasons with the White Sox (1954-55-56-58-59-60). As evidenced by his Gold Gloves, he developed into perhaps the best defensive catcher in major-league baseball. In 1957, he played without making an error in his first 89 games (471 chances) before throwing wildly to second base on September 14. Years after trading for Lollar, White Sox general manager Frank Lane said, "It was one of the best trades I ever made. Sherm turned out to be one of the best catchers in the American League, behind only Yogi Berra and maybe Jim Hegan."[9] Paul Richards told Gleason that Lollar was a better handler of pitchers than Berra.

Throughout his time in the American League, Lollar was compared to Berra, whose offensive numbers and championships outshined Lollar's.

Wrote Gleason in *The Saturday Evening Post*, "Where Berra is distinctive looking, to put it mildly, the brown-haired Lollar is a sad-faced, sad-eyed individual. In most of his pictures, he looks as though someone has stolen his favorite catcher's mitt. In his 'smiling' pictures, the smile seems forced. Berra is celebrated for malapropisms. Lollar is seldom quoted. An unobtrusive workman, he is obscured on his own club by crowd-pleasers such as Nellie Fox, Minnie Minoso, Jim Rivera, and Luis Aparicio."[10]

Lollar enjoyed his best offensive seasons with Chicago between 1955 and 1959, regularly hitting over .260 with more than 10 home runs and 70 RBIs. On April 23, 1955, against Kansas City during a 29-6 rout, Lollar accomplished the rare feat of getting two hits in a single inning twice in the same game. In spite of playing in Comiskey Park, which was never favorable to hitters, Lollar had his finest offensive season during Chicago's pennant-winning 1959 season, batting .265 with 22 home runs and 84 RBIs. In both 1958 and 1959, he finished ninth in the American League's Most Valuable Player voting.

Perhaps most importantly, Lollar was instrumental in handling the team's pitching staff in 1959, playing in 122 games behind the plate. Although he batted only .227 in the World Series that year, he hit a three-run homer in Game Four off the Dodgers' Roger Craig with two outs in the seventh inning to tie the game at 4-4. Other than the three home runs hit by Ted Kluszewski, Lollar's home run was the only one hit by a White Sox player in that series. However, a key turning point of the series came in Game Two, when the slow-footed Lollar was thrown out at the plate while trying to score from first base on Al Smith's eighth-inning double to left-center field, which helped cement a 4-3 Chicago loss.

Likely due to the wear and tear of catching so many games, Lollar's offensive performance with the White Sox began to decline in 1960. He played with the team through the 1963 season before being released on October 4, 1963. In his major-league career, Lollar committed only 62 errors in 1,571 games behind the plate, finishing with a .992 fielding percentage. When Lollar was released in 1963, only Jim Landis and Nellie Fox remained with the White Sox from the 1959 pennant-winning team.

After his major-league career ended, Lollar remained in baseball. As he sought a minor-league manager's job, Al Lopez remarked, "[Lollar] had

SHERMAN LOLLAR

tremendous ability with young pitchers. I think he shows great ability at handling men, which is the most important part of managing in the game."[11]

Lollar coached with the Baltimore Orioles from 1964 through 1967; coached with the Oakland Athletics in 1968; managed the Iowa Oaks (Des Moines) of the American Association from 1970 through 1972; and managed the Tucson Toros of the Pacific Coast League in 1973 and 1974. Iowa and Tucson were Oakland farm teams. Lollar's Iowa teams finished in second place in his first two years and in third place in his final season; he led Tucson to first place in the PCL's Eastern Division in 1973 before the team lost in the playoffs to Spokane. Lollar reportedly retired from the Toros after the 1974 season because of a dispute with Charley Finley, the owner of the Oakland A's.

During his managerial career in Des Moines, Lollar barely escaped serious injury. While he sat in his car at a red light after a game in 1970, a nearby building suddenly collapsed. "I was just sitting there listening to the radio when – wham! It was like the sky falling," Lollar related. "What made it worse was that I had no idea what was happening. I couldn't see a thing because of the dust and debris."[12] Fortunately, Lollar was unhurt.

After his baseball career ended, Lollar operated a bowling alley in Springfield, Missouri, and refereed high-school basketball games. After a long battle with cancer, he died in Springfield on September 24, 1977. He was 53 years old. He was survived by his wife, Connie, and a son, Sherman Jr. He is buried in Rivermonte Memorial Gardens in Springfield.

Notes

1. William "Red" Gleason, "Is Lollar Better Than Berra?" *The Saturday Evening Post*, June 16, 1957: 36.
2. Gleason.
3. Bill Roeder, "Yankees Hope Lollar Will Catch Fire," Baseball Hall of Fame Sherman Lollar file; publication and exact date illegible, but from 1947.
4. Dan Daniel, title unknown, *New York World Telegram*, October 3, 1947
5. Baseball Hall of Fame Sherman Lollar file; author and title unknown.
6. Dan Daniel, "Experience Will Swing Flag for Us: Bucky," *New York World Telegram*, August 4, 1948.
7. Gleason.
8. Gleason.
9. "Sherman Lollar, an Ex-Catcher for White Sox, Is Dead at 53," *New York Times*, September 26, 1977.
10. Gleason.
11. Brent Musburger, "Lollar Seeking Minor League Manager's Job," *Chicago American*, September 30, 1963.
12. "Narrow Escape for Lollar," Baseball Hall of Fame Sherman Lollar file; publication unidentified, June 20, 1970.

OMAR "TURK" LOWN

By Adam Ulrey

America has always had great duos. In entertainment it was Laurel and Hardy, Abbott and Costello, George Burns and Gracie Allen. In baseball it was the great Chicago White Sox tag team of Jerry Staley and Turk Lown. Together they formed the best one-two punch out of the bullpen in 1959 for manager Al Lopez.

"That year Lown and (J)erry Staley formed baseball's most brilliant bullpen combination," wrote Edgar Munzel in 1963. "These rescue artists were more responsible than any other single department for the success of the White Sox in capturing their first pennant in 40 years."[1]

He was born Omar Joseph Lown on May 30, 1924, in Brooklyn, New York. He got his nickname because of his fondness for turkey. He came from a hard-working middle-class family led by his parents, Omar and Mae Lown. Omar Sr. was a cook in World War I and throughout his life had many jobs around the New York area. Turk had two older brothers, Carl, who died of a heart attack at the age of 50, and Bill, who was, according to Turk, the better baseball player and all-around better athlete. The Lowns are descended from German immigrants. Turk attended Franklin K. Lane High School, where he was an outstanding baseball and basketball player.

Lown was discovered playing for the Ridgewood Bears of the Queens Alliance League in the summer of 1940. The Queens Alliance League, founded in the early 1930s, was a huge amateur league – more than 125 teams at its peak – consisting of teams primarily from the borough of Queens with a few from Brooklyn and some from Nassau County, farther out on Long Island. Professional baseball scouts thought highly of the Alliance, as it was a fertile ground for young prospects. Its players were generally considered to be the most skilled amateurs in the US. Some of the major-league teams had affiliations with Queens Alliance clubs, helping with uniforms and possibly some equipment.

Turk began playing in the Alliance as a strong-armed catcher and outfielder. He started a game on the mound one day in 1942 because his Ridgewood team had run out of pitchers. Turk fanned 17 batters.

A New York paper said the Dodgers got wind of his performance and moved in quickly to sign him. But he actually was signed after a tryout at Ebbets Field. Ironically, Turk's brother Bill was the one invited to the tryout, but had to work and couldn't make it. Turk went instead, and impressed the Dodgers so much that Brooklyn scout Joe Kleinkauf signed him to a pro contract. Until then, he had no intention of pursuing a career in professional baseball, and he had been pitching for only a little over a year.

His first minor-league season, with Valdosta, Georgia, in the Class-D Georgia-Florida League, was nothing short of amazing. He went 18-8 with a 1.94 ERA. In 232 innings he struck out a league-leading 204 batters, but in what was a problem throughout most of his career, he issued 113 walks. However, Turk won seven in a row during one stretch and just missed the league's single-game strikeout record of 17 by one.

After that first year, Turk didn't have much time to celebrate or even look forward to next year for a while. With World War II raging, Lown was inducted into the Army. He was in the infantry for three years and saw combat when the Germans made their last desperate attack in the Battle of the Bulge. Turk came out of it with his right thigh pierced by shrapnel, and he was awarded the Purple Heart. The war over, he returned to baseball in 1946, beginning with Newport News in the Class-B Piedmont League. Because of lingering arm trouble, he pitched just nine games in 1946, going 2-5 with a 3.60 ERA. He walked 31 and struck out 19 in 50 innings, before undergoing arm surgery at Johns Hopkins Hospital in Baltimore.

Arm trouble or not, Lown was moved up to Class A in 1947, and rebounded nicely over the next two years while pitching for Pueblo in the Western League. In 1947 he pitched in 33 games, most of them as a starter. He went 13-7 with a 4.50 ERA – the highest of his career to this point. He was wild, walking a league-leading 133 batters in 190 innings. In 1948 Lown improved on his previous year in almost every way. He went 17-6, leading the league in winning percentage. He lowered his earned-run average a bit, to 4.08, and his walks somewhat, to 112 (his wildness

• OMAR "TURK" LOWN •

Turk Lown went 9-2 with 15 saves for the 1959 White Sox, teaming with Jerry Staley to give the pennant winners the league's best bullpen duo.

earned him the nickname Omar the Passmaker). He moved up to Montreal and got into two games with an 0-0 record. Lown had an array of pitches: an above-average fastball, a curveball, a slider, a knuckleball, a changeup, and a slow pitch, better described as an eephus or blooper pitch.

Lown started the 1949 season one step away from the big leagues with Montreal, but started off 1-7 with a 3.97 ERA and again had more walks (54) than strikeouts (48). After 19 games he was demoted to Fort Worth in the Texas League. There, his season took a turn for the better. He won eight of his last nine decisions and record a 2.96 ERA. He pitched a no-hitter against Tulsa on August 31 – the day his first son, Craig, was born. It was the only no-hitter of his career. The final score was 14-0, but it wasn't pretty with nine walks. (Craig signed with the White Sox and pitched briefly in the minor leagues in the 1970s.)

In 1950 Turk found himself back with Montreal, and this time he impressed the Dodgers and proved he was a candidate for the big leagues. He started 29 games and went 13-9 with a 3.49 ERA, though again he yielded a high number of walks (122). But his dream of pitching with the Brooklyn Dodgers came to end after the season when he was drafted out of the Dodgers' system by the Chicago Cubs. Wid Matthews, a former aide to Branch Rickey at St. Louis and Brooklyn, had had his eye on Lown ever since 1942. After Matthews left the Dodgers and became the Cubs' director of player personnel, he tried more than once to trade for Turk, but the asking price was always too high. Finally Lown was available for the $10,000 draft price. A November 1950 *Sporting News* article quoted Matthews as saying:

"I was crazy about that kid from the very first time I saw him. That was back in 1942, when Lown was with Valdosta. I happened to see him once when he was pitching against Albany, which was the Cardinal farm club. He struck out 17 of our boys. He had plenty of smoke and a good curveball. I was sold on that youngster from that day on. . . . He's still wild, but that doesn't worry me. His ERA and his 14 complete games with Montreal (in 1950) prove that his wildness is not too damaging."[2]

Turk was always known for his unselfishness and commitment to do whatever it would take to be part of a winner. That was evident by a note he sent Matthews in January 1951. In it Turk said that he had turned down a bundle of cash to pitch in Cuba, which he had done the previous year, in favor of preparing himself for his first venture in the big leagues. "I thought a couple of months' rest would do me more good than the money I would get for pitching in Cuba," Lown wrote. Matthews read that paragraph with a smile. "You don't see enough of that kind of spirit these days," he said.[3]

Lown made his major-league debut with the Cubs in 1951, and it was a tough year for Turk and his team, which finished last in the National League. Turk finished 4-9 with a high ERA of 5.46, but it was the 90 walks in 127 innings that did him in. Yet the praise kept coming in from around the league on how good his arm was. A spring training report from the Cubs on March 28, 1952, said that no one doubted Lown's tremendous potential, and it was agreed that Turk had more giddy-up on his fastball than any other Cubs pitcher, if not any other National League hurler.

In 1952 there was some improvement in Lown's work, but in small increments. Turk still had a losing record, 4-11, but his ERA went down over a run to 4.37 and his strikeouts almost doubled to 73. He still walked 93 but it took 30 more innings than the year before to get there. He almost got a no-hitter against his former team, the Dodgers, but the first hitter in the ninth broke it up and the Dodgers went on to score three runs and beat the Cubs.

Like many ballplayers of that era, Turk had an offseason job. During the winter he worked in sales and service for the Madison Electrical Tool Company on Long Island.

In 1953, his third year with the Cubs, Lown was removed from the starting rotation and assigned to the bullpen by manager Phil Cavarretta. He never started a game again in his major-league career. Turk ended up with a winning record, 8-7, but his ERA shot back up, to 5.16. In 1954, Turk got off to a horrible start, and the Cubs sent him to their Pacific Coast League team in Los Angeles. Lown's failure was an especially tough blow for Wid Matthews, who had prized him so highly. However, Turk had tremendous determination and never allowed a setback to get him down. A few years earlier, pitching against his former club, the Dodgers, Lown drilled Roy Campanella with a fastball and the star catcher was carried off the field to a hospital. Campanella was a vital figure in Brooklyn's drive to the pennant and there might be repercussions if he were out for any length of time. But Turk never wavered. In fact, he got even better as the game went along and handed the Dodgers a stunning defeat. "As far as I'm concerned, Lown that day became a pitcher," said Charley Root, then a Cubs coach. "He never lost his nerve and he seemed to have new confidence thereafter."[4]

In retrospect, the best thing that could have happened to Turk's career was being sent to the minors by the Cubs. They had tried to make him into a reliever at the end of the 1953 season, and Los Angeles kept him in the bullpen. It turned his career around. Posting a 5-3 record for the PCL Angels with a 2.48 ERA, he made up for the 46 walks he issued in 72⅔ innings by surrendering only 54 hits. With the Angels again in 1955, Turk had one his best seasons at any level. He led the PCL with 19 saves to go with his record of 12-5. He led the league with 61 appearances. He vastly improved his control, walking only 49 in 114⅓ innings. Besides his fastball, he came up with a slider to help him improve his control. There was strong belief that if Turk had not been sidelined for three weeks with pneumonia, the Angels would have won the PCL pennant.

Several major-league clubs were eager to get their hands on Turk after his brilliant year with Los Angeles, most notably the Giants, but the Cubs had their own plans for him. When the 1956 season began, Lown was again a member of the Cubs' bullpen. Turk was emotionally perfect for the relief role; he wasn't just resigned to being a relief pitcher, he actually wanted to be one. In the mid-'50s, most pitchers disdained bullpen work; nearly all wanted to be starters. Lown admitted that he felt that way, too, until he had such a bad year in 1954. "Then I took stock of my situation," he said. "My objective was to get back to the majors."[5]

After serving in the minors what seemed to be a lifetime sentence, the 32-year-old right-hander set a modern Cubs record in 1956 with 61 appearances, fifth in the National League. He won nine games and finished third in the league in saves, with 13. In 110⅔ innings, he posted a 3.58 ERA. Lown came back in 1957 to put up similar numbers. Breaking his year-old club record by pitching in 67 games, he went 5-7 with 12 saves, with a slightly higher ERA of 3.77. As in 1956, he led the league in games finished with 47. Turk again finished third in the NL in games saved.

The 1958 season proved to be a very busy one for Lown, as he saw himself a member of three different teams. Just a month into the season, he was traded to the Reds on May 8 for another reliever, Hershel Freeman. He got into 11 games for the Reds with not much success before being sold to the White Sox on June 23. Lown helped his new club by going 3-3 with eight saves in 27 games. In those eight saves he struck out 17 in 11⅔ innings while giving up just two earned runs. He was one of the pieces that manager Al Lopez was looking for to shore up his bullpen.

The 1959 season was not only a pennant-winning season for the White Sox; it was the coming-out party for Lown and his veteran bullpen mate, Jerry Staley, both of whom had been written off as washed up by at least two other clubs. Both were brilliant in 1959, with one or the other consistently closing out games.

OMAR "TURK" LOWN

For Lown it was his finest season. He went 9-2 with a league-leading 15 saves, had a 2.89 ERA in 60 appearances with 63 strikeouts, and more importantly surrendered only 42 walks in 93⅓ innings. Lown and Staley (8 wins, 14 saves, 2.24 ERA) gave the White Sox a dominant bullpen.

Manager Al Lopez said time and time again throughout the year that without Staley and Lown, there would be no pennant. Lopez said Lown's fastball could match that of any pitcher in the league. The first time Lown faced Mickey Mantle he threw three fastballs right by him. He did the same thing the first time he faced Ted Williams. As Lown focused more and more on his fastball, his effectiveness as a reliever grew. There came a turning point early in the 1959 season that changed Turk for the rest of his career. On May 3 against the Orioles, he took the mound with the score tied at 2-2 and, after working a scoreless ninth, lost the game in the 10th by serving up home run balls to the two least likely long-ball candidates in the Baltimore lineup, second baseman Billy Gardner and ex-Sox shortstop Chico Carrasquel. Those two home runs raised Lown's ERA to 4.15, and Lopez's temperature was rising as well. "Lown's best pitch is his fastball, but he insisted on throwing curveballs to two Baltimore hitters," fumed the Señor. "The curves he threw Gardner and Carrasquel hung, and they hit 'em out of the park." Decades later, Lopez' disdain for Lown's throwing anything but his fastball was still fresh in the pitcher's mind.[6]

Two days after the May 3 debacle against Baltimore, Turk had another rocky outing against Washington that saw his ERA climb to 5.59. But Lown became almost unhittable the rest of the year. In July, he was stellar; in 20⅔ innings, he gave up just four earned runs for a 1.78 ERA to go along with a 4-0 record, two saves and 12 strikeouts.

Turk said of Jerry Staley, "He was the best roomie I ever had. We were like brothers. It was like we were one. What I wanted to do, he wanted to do. When one of us wanted to take a walk, the other was there, too. If one of us wanted to eat, the other went."[7] The two combined for 17 wins, 29 saves, and a 2.53 ERA. In an era that was not known for bullpens, Lown and Staley helped organizations learn how important relief pitchers could be.

The clinching game came on September 22, against the Cleveland Indians. Both Staley and Lown wanted to be the pitcher standing on the mound for the final out. With the White Sox leading, 4-2, and one out in the ninth, the call was made to the bullpen and Lown hoped it was for him. "It was a choice between Jerry and me," he said, "and he took Jerry. I would've liked to have gone in. I love those spots. But it was Vic Power who had hit that liner to third that time before off me, and maybe Lopez remembered that and decided to bring Jerry in."[8] Staley's sinkerball could induce groundballs, which was what the White Sox needed, and they got just that as Power hit into a double play to end the game and give the Sox their first pennant in 40 years.

In the World Series, the White Sox faced the Los Angeles Dodgers, but Turk was not much of a factor. He did a fine job in his three appearances, giving up just two hits and no runs and striking out three in 3⅓ innings, but all three games were Sox losses. The club lost the Series to the Dodgers, four games to two.

After the 1959 season, the future looked bright for the White Sox, who added power hitters Minnie Minoso, Roy Sievers, and Gene Freese in an effort to take another run at the pennant. It was the last time in Turk's career that he was involved in a pennant race. In 1960 he took a small step back with only 45 appearances. He won two games, lost three and had five saves. His ERA jumped almost a full run, to 3.88. The White Sox came in third, 10 games out. In 1961 Turk bounced back with seven wins, 11 saves, and an ERA, at 2.76, back to its 1959 levels.

Lown turned 38 in 1962, and it was his last year. He appeared in 42 games, winning four and saving six with a respectable ERA of 3.04. Despite those decent numbers the White Sox released him after the season, and replaced him with future Hall of Famer Hoyt Wilhelm. Lown was invited to join the Cincinnati Reds for the 1963 season, but after pitching a few games in spring training, he decided it was time to go home to Pueblo, Colorado, where he had pitched in the 1940s, and call it a career. For a pitcher who started out as a starter and not a very good one at that, he had rebounded to have a very nice career. He ended his career with a 55-61 record, 73 saves and a 4.12 ERA.

In his later years, Lown still resided in Pueblo with his wife. They had three sons, Craig, Gary, and Terry. After Turk left the game he became a postal carrier for 23 years. He died of leukemia in Pueblo on July 8, 2016, a little over a month after his 92nd birthday. "He never really bragged about baseball," his son Terry told reporter Terry Lester. "A lot of people have said, 'I didn't know your dad played that long.' They didn't know he fought in the Battle of the Bulge and received the Purple Heart, either."⁹ Lown might not be remembered with Staley as a famous duo, but for the 1959 season those two were the best and most famous duo in the city of Chicago.

Sources

In addition to the sources cited in the Notes, the author also consulted: baseball-almanac.com, baseball-reference.com, fretrosheet,org, http:/minors.sabrwebs.com/cgi-bin/player, www.timesnewsweekly.com/archives2003/apr.-jun.2003, the Turk Lown player clipping file at the National Baseball Hall of Fame Library, and the following:

Kalas, Larry. *Strength Down the Middle – The Story of the 1959 Chicago White Sox* (Fort Worth: Mereken Land & Production Co. 1990).

Singletary, Wes. *Al Lopez: The Life of Baseball's El Senor* (Jefferson, North Carolina: McFarland & Company, 1999).

Snyder, John. *Cubs Journal. Year by Year and Day by Day with the Chicago Cubs Since 1876*, second edition (Cincinnati: Clerisy Press, 2008).

Johnson, Lloyd, and Miles Wolff, *The Encyclopedia of Minor League Baseball* (Durham, North Carolina: Baseball America Inc., 1997).

Thanks to Turk Lown for an interview with the author on May 25, 2008.

Notes

1. Edgar Munzel, "Hoyt Pins on Turk's Badge as Chief of Chisox Firemen," *The Sporting News*, February 9, 1963 (note: Staley preferred to be called Jerry rather than Gerry and is referred to as such in this book.)
2. Edgar Munzel, "Tabs Turk 100 Grand Cub Grab," *The Sporting News*, November 29, 1950.
3. John C. Hoffman, "Quotes," *The Sporting News*, January 17, 1951.
4. Edgar Munzel, "Lown Assigned Dutch Leonard's Spot in Bull Pen," *The Sporting News*, February 10, 1954.
5. Edgar Munzel, "Bruins' Bull Pen Pair Gives Hack Heave of Relief," *The Sporting News*, March 14, 1956.
6. Bob Vanderberg, *59: Summer of the Sox* (Champaign Illinois: Sports Publishing, 1999), 49-50.
7. Ibid., 83-84.
8. Ibid., p.139.
9. Kerry Lester, "Sox pitcher key to '59 pennant dies as modestly as he lived," *The Daily Herald*, July 29, 2016.

J. C. MARTIN

By Neal Poloncarz

He delivered big hits on occasion but is still asked most often about a thrown ball that struck him in the wrist while he was running to first base in the 1969 World Series.

> "I kid around with the fans and show them how I swelled up. I just stick my arms out. I don't care what some people say about the play or what I did. The umpire said I was safe so I must have been safe. They show my old play again at first base and I could see that ball bouncing off my wrist. It didn't hurt a bit then and it doesn't hurt now. I just get a kick out of seeing that ball roll away and old Rodney [Gaspar] running around those bases; and getting in for that winning run. That's a satisfying scene, yes sir, it certainly is."[1]

J.C. Martin smiled when he considered the turn of events that made him a participant in the Series rather than a spectator.

Joseph Clifton Martin was born on December 13, 1936, in Axton, Virginia. The town is eight miles north of the North Carolina state line. Both of his grandparents were named Joseph. To avoid confusion (along with the Southern tradition of referring to people by using initials), the family called him by his initials, J.C.

In his youth, Martin was an active outdoorsman. J.C. and his younger brother, Melvin, hunted coon and possum and fished in a river along the family farm. They would take their catch to their grandpa's house. In return, Grandpa would fatten the kids up with their catch along with cornbread and buttermilk.

Martin wanted to be a big-league ballplayer. His parents suggested that to fulfill this dream, he could not drink or smoke. His father was deputy sheriff of the county. After school, J.C. would stop off at the county jail to visit his father. As he saw the inmates, he witnessed first-hand how not to live.

Martin told an interviewer he didn't know where he would be if he were not raised a Christian. His hero was second baseman Bobby Richardson of the New York Yankees. Bobby and his roommate, Tony Kubek, were dubbed the Milkshake Twins for their decorous lifestyle.

At Ridgeway High School, Martin lettered in baseball, football, and basketball, and ran track. Several colleges offered him scholarships. Eight baseball clubs extended offers. In addition, he met a young woman named Barbara Cox.

Harry Postove, a scout for the Chicago White Sox, had watched Martin since his sophomore year. Postove assured Martin he would advance rapidly through the Chicago minor-league system as a first baseman. Martin signed with the White Sox for a $4,000 bonus and reported to the Holdrege White Sox of the Nebraska State League.

In 1956, the Nebraska State League was a Class-D rookie league. Rosters combined local baseball stars with collegiate and high school players. The schedule started on July 1 and concluded on Labor Day so players could return to their studies. The Holdrege White Sox played at Holdrege Fairgrounds Park, a decrepit ballpark without a grass infield. Sand and gravel combined with dirt to create a hazard for the players. The grandstand was unkempt. During the winter, glass windows were broken by vandals.

For the 19-year-old Martin, playing in Holdrege was an awakening. He discovered that many ballplayers were not pure as he envisioned them in his youth. After games, he isolated himself from teammates who attended parties to drink, smoke, and meet women. In addition, the pay was low, travel was by bus, and the ballpark lighting was poor.

Playing first base, Martin hit .276 in 64 games, scored 64 runs and had a .481 slugging average. Teammates and opponents who wound up in the majors included Alan Brice, Jimmy Hall, Camilo Carreon, Gary Peters, Deron Johnson, Jim Perry, Bob Allen, and Hal Reniff. After the season, Martin persuaded Barbara to leave college and get married.

In 1957, Martin was promoted to play in the Class-B Three-I League. Martin played only 19 games for the Davenport DavSox, and his lack of experience produced a .208 batting average. Sent down to the Dubuque Packers in the Class-D Midwest League, he hit a respectable .286 with 14 home runs and 64

RBIs. The next season, Martin was summoned to the Duluth-Superior White Sox of the Class C Northern League. In mid-July, Martin led the league with a .358 batting average, on the strength of an 18-game hitting streak. He finished the season batting .330, with 10 home runs and an impressive 86 RBIs.

Martin was promoted to the Triple-A Indianapolis Indians of the American Association for 1959. He hit a steady .287 with 13 home runs and 57 RBIs. His manager was former major leaguer Walker Cooper. Martin earned a September call-up to the White Sox. This was a perfect time to watch how baseball fundamentals were played. The White Sox relied upon solid pitching, good defense, and aggressiveness on the base paths.

The "Go-Go Sox" were managed by Al Lopez. "He was great. Al was the kind of manager who let you play. He wouldn't run you down by playing you day after day after day. He knew the game. He got me into the big leagues and I have nothing but respect for him. We all did," said Martin.[2]

Martin recalled his initial call-up to the big leagues. "It was pretty exciting. I think six guys came up from Indianapolis. I came up along with Johnny Callison, Joe Hicks, and Ron Jackson. I'm sure there were a few others."[3] The 22-year-old made his debut at Comiskey Park on September 10 against the Washington Senators. Camilo Pascual struck him out in his first major-league at bat.

Martin recalled the game when the Sox clinched the pennant in Cleveland:

> "Talk about exciting. . . . It was a real thrill. I still remember Jerry Staley coming in to pitch to Vic Power. Staley threw one pitch, Power hit into a double play and that was it. It was pandemonium in the locker room. Then we flew right back to Chicago, to Midway Airport. I don't know how many people were there but it was a lot (The *Chicago Sun Times* estimated the crowd at 125,000). I know we had to get on a bus and drive out to where our cars were parked."[4]

Martin recorded his first major-league hit and RBI on the final day of the season in Detroit. It was a single to center field off lefty Pete Burnside. He finished the season with one hit in four at-bats, playing two games at third base. Being a late season call-up, Martin was ineligible for the World Series, which the White Sox lost to the Los Angeles Dodgers in six games.

The next season, Martin played Triple-A ball with the San Diego Padres. His manager, George Metkovich, believed Martin would make it to the majors. He batted .285 with 13 home runs and 73 RBIs, and was recalled to the Pale Hose that fall.

The spring of 1961 was difficult for Martin. At Sarasota, Florida, his fielding was atrocious. His hitting was equally poor. Before an exhibition game, he hurt his back in a game of pepper. Manager Lopez ordered him out of uniform for several days to rest. Known for patience with rookies, Lopez was unruffled by Martin's errors. The skipper believed his glove was the culprit. Baseballs would skid off his fingers. Lopez assigned future Hall of Fame shortstop Luis Aparicio to work with Martin. He let Martin borrow his glove. There was an immediate difference, and the Sox ordered the Aparicio model glove for Martin. During the season, his fielding recovered but he hit only .230, with 5 home runs and 32 RBIs. The White Sox slipped to fourth place. As a consolation prize, Martin was named to the Topps Chewing Gum rookie team chosen by young card collectors.

After the 1961 season, during the White Sox organizational meetings, Martin's name was discussed as a possibility for the catching position. Offensively, he lacked power required for a corner infielder. General manager Ed Short sought a third-string left-handed-hitting catcher and suggested converting Martin to a catcher. Lopez agreed. "(In 1962) I went down to Savannah, Georgia (in the South Atlantic League), for three months to see if I could learn the position," Martin said.[5] His manager there was former White Sox catcher Les Moss, and Moss taught Martin how to catch. Martin had a strong fielding percentage .986, but set a league record with 32 passed balls. However, he progressed as a batter, hitting .328 with 8 home runs and 52 RBIs.

After the season, Martin returned to the White Sox as a reserve catcher. On September 10 at Comiskey Park, Martin started his first major-league game as a catcher, calling signals for Ray Herbert. Martin was excellent as Herbert pitched a complete game 4-3 victory over the Kansas City. Martin singled off Bill Fischer in the sixth.

Eddie Fisher, Hoyt Wilhelm, and Wilbur Wood were Chicago knuckleball pitchers in that era. The challenge for Martin was to handle the baffling serves.

J. C. MARTIN

J.C. Martin was an infielder when he made his major league debut with the 1959 White Sox, but he got a new lease on life when the Sox converted him to catcher several years later.

"It was exciting because you never knew where the ball was going. . . . It could do a 90-degree break and then double back! If you didn't wait, you just couldn't see it. You'd have to snatch it when it was right on top of you. It's the best pitch I've ever seen a relief guy throw." Each threw it differently. "Hoyt had the most consistent pitch. The other guys had good ones but every so often they'd throw one that would spin and then they'd get hit. Hoyt's always worked," recalled Martin.[6] According to Charlie Metro, a White Sox coach under Lopez, the manager would bring in Wilhelm and Martin into the game as a team. "He was the only guy who could catch Hoyt's knuckleball," Metro said.[7]

Martin learned the catching position sufficiently to be inserted as the Sox' Opening Day catcher in 1963, at Tiger Stadium. The Sox won and manager Lopez, impressed with Martin behind the plate, made him the first-string catcher. However, Martin hit a miserable .205 that season. In 1964, catching in 120 games, Martin fell below the Mendoza line at .197 as the White Sox finished second, one game behind the Yankees. The Sox won their last nine games, but the Bronx Bombers won enough to hang on. Martin said the Yankees of that era "just had so much that nobody could compete. ... Their benchwarmers could be regulars on other teams."

In 1965, while handling knuckleballs from Fisher and Wilhelm, Martin set a post-1900 record (subsequently broken by Geno Petralli) with 33 passed balls. However, Martin rebounded for his most productive season as a hitter. His batting average rose to .261 in 119 games.

That November, Lopez resigned as White Sox manager. He was replaced by Eddie Stanky, the combative baseball lifer known as "The Brat." In retrospect, Martin was unimpressed by his new skipper:

"He was tough. He was so different from Al. He intimidated. He'd fine guys for anything. He knew baseball ... no question, but he couldn't manage people. After a little while the players would lose interest and loyalty. He actually pumped up the other team more because he was always getting on them. I'll never forget it was in 1967 we got into Boston and went to bed. The next morning I pick up a Boston paper and see this big headline. 'Yaz an All Star from the neck down.' Stanky ripped him to the press. Man, Yaz wound up hitting everything we threw at him but the rosin bag!"[8]

Martin had had a decent season at the plate in 1966 with a .255 batting average. However, he lost his starting job to John Romano. After the season, Romano was shipped to St. Louis. Martin caught 96 games and hit .234 in the epic 1967 season, in which four teams scrapped for the pennant, eventually won by Boston.

Go-Go to Glory

That 1967 White Sox club was known as the latter-day Hitless Wonders because no regular batted over .250. At one point in mid-August, Martin was leading the team in batting. How did the club stay in contention? "We had pitching (league-leading ERA of 2.45) and defense. If you have that, you'll be in every game and we knew how to manufacture runs. Guys knew how to bunt, hit and run, steal bases. We knew what we had to do to win."[9]

On September 10, Martin was behind the plate as Joe Horlen pitched a 6-0 no-hitter over Detroit in the first game of a doubleheader at Comiskey Park. It was the first White Sox no-hitter since Bob Keegan no-hit the Senators in 1957.

> "Joe was great that day," Martin recalled. "In the ninth inning we got the first two guys out. I called time and went out to the mound. I asked Joe what he wanted to throw to the next hitter, Dick McAuliffe. Joe paid me a great compliment because he said, 'You've called the first 8⅔ innings, you finish it up.' I knew that McAuliffe was both a good pull hitter and a good inside-out opposite-field hitter. I wanted to take something away from him, so I decided we were going to pitch him away. Dick hit one to our shortstop Ron Hansen, who threw him out. . . ."[10]

On November 27, 1967, the New York Mets acquired Martin to complete a deal made during the season. A few weeks later, the Sox sent Al Weis and Tommy Agee to the Mets in another trade. The three players were reunited and played key roles in the Mets' 1969 World Series victory.

In 1968, manager Gil Hodges slated Martin to share the catching chores with Jerry Grote. On Opening Day, Martin caught Tom Seaver at San Francisco. The Giants won the game with three runs in the bottom of the ninth inning; in that inning, Martin's finger was broken when it was struck by a foul ball off the bat of Jim Ray Hart. Martin was placed on the disabled list. He wound up playing only 78 games for the year, hitting .225 with three home runs.

The Mets' catching combination of Grote and Martin had a total of 15 years of big-league experience entering the 1969 season. This was imperative for a pitching staff whose first four starters (Seaver, Jerry Koosman, Jim McAndrew, and Gary Gentry) had only three full seasons among them.

Grote got the bulk of the starts behind the plate that year, but as the dog days of summer ended, manager Hodges skillfully played Martin against right-handed pitchers to provide Grote rest. Increased action down the stretch drive enabled Martin to contribute in the postseason. In Game Three of the National League Championship Series, in Atlanta, in the top of the eighth inning, New York loaded the bases with two outs. Martin pinch-hit for Seaver and lined a clean single to clear the bases and provide the Mets with a four-run lead.

In the World Series, there were many heroes for the upstart Mets. Martin, even though he appeared in only one game and had no official at-bats, may have been the unlikeliest. In the bottom of the 10th inning of the fourth game, with the Mets leading the Series two games to one, Martin pinch hit for Tom Seaver with runners at first and second and nobody out in a 3-3 game. As Orioles pitcher Pete Richert wound up, Martin squared to bunt and laid down a beauty. Richert grabbed the ball and threw to first. The throw appeared to have Martin beat. However, it struck Martin on the left wrist and bounded across the infield dirt between first and second base as pinch-runner Rod Gaspar scored the game-winning run from second base and the Mets swarmed around Martin. The umpires ruled that Martin had not attempted to interfere with the ball.

The next morning, controversy swirled around the play. Press box observers clearly believed Martin was out of the baseline, in fair territory, when the throw hit him, and under the baseball rules should have been out. Later photos indicated conclusively that that was the case. Years later, Martin said he believed getting hit with the throw was "just a coincidence," but he acknowledged that he had done what he could to allow circumstance its best opportunity.

> "You try to do everything you possibly can," he said. "You know from experience that if you run close to the first-base line, the throwing angle is very narrow, particularly if the pitcher is left-handed (as Pete Richert was) and has to turn to make the throw. So you run as close as you can. I wasn't thinking about getting hit or anything. I was just looking to shield the ball from the man covering first. As it turned out, the ball happened to hit me on the left wrist. But there was no argument at the time. All the controversy was in the media the next day."[11]

• J. C. MARTIN •

Even Seaver admitted years later that the films showed Martin ran out of the baselines. But it was too late. If Martin had been called out for interference, Gaspar would not have scored on the play, leading the way for the Mets to win the Series the next day.

Before the 1970 season, Martin returned to the Windy City, this time on the North Side. The Chicago Cubs acquired him for rookie catcher Randy Bobb. Playing behind workhouse Randy Hundley, he caught only 36 games and had but 12 hits all season, for a .156 batting average.

In the winter of 1971, Cubs pitching coach Verlon Walker was hospitalized for a persistent fever. General manager John Holland named Martin the interim pitching coach. When the season began, Mel Wright, a coach in the Cubs organization, replaced Martin. For the 1971 season Martin boosted his offensive production (.264, with 2 home runs and 17 RBIs), and was excellent defensively.

Martin played his final season in 1972. At the age of 35, he batted mostly against right-handers; defensively, his throwing arm had diminished and he committed an abundance of errors. He caught in only 17 games and batted .240 in 50 at-bats. Martin was released before the '73 season. He spent the 1974 campaign as the bullpen coach on the staff of manager Whitey Lockman, who was fired in midseason.

In 1975 Martin worked alongside the legendary Harry Caray on WSNS-TV for the White Sox. It was an unhappy experience.

> "I didn't really fit in with Harry," Martin recalled. "He didn't want to work with me. We didn't hit it off at all. I wasn't used to working with a guy that had that kind of authority and Harry used that against me. I was only there for one year. . . . Harry just left me out to dry. I'll give you an example. We were in Milwaukee doing a game and the Brewers had a pregame activity which saw the Milwaukee wives playing a game before the regularly scheduled one. That game caused the regular game to start late. Harry opened the telecast and then just left the booth. He left me there by myself for it must have been 15 to 20 minutes."[12]

Martin was far from a superstar (a career .222 hitter), but he cherished his time in the major leagues.

"I wouldn't trade it for anything," he said. "I spent 14 years in the big leagues seeing the best players ever, guys like Bob Gibson, Willie Mays, Carl Yastrzemski. Players like that just aren't around anymore. Baseball was better back then. ... they didn't have the DH, which has killed all the suspense in the American League, and the ballparks were fair. You didn't have this emphasis on hitting home runs all the time. It was great."

Martin caught five Hall-of-Fame pitchers: Wynn, Wilhelm, Seaver, Nolan Ryan, and Ferguson Jenkins.

Martin was one of the Amazins' good luck charms. He fulfilled his dreams. While he played in the majors, he traveled first class, and ate in the best restaurants. Yet he never ate a heartier meal than those his Grandpa cooked for him back in his youth in Virginia.

Notes

1. Maury Allen, *After the Miracle: The 1969 Mets Twenty Years Later* (New York: Franklin Watt, 1989), 122-123.
2. http://www.whitesoxinteractive.com; WSI (White Sox Interactive News); Flashing back with J.C. Martin with Mark Liptak.
3. Ibid.
4. Ibid.
5. Ibid.
6. Ibid.
7. Charlie Metro with Tom Altherr, *Safe by a Mile* (Lincoln and London: University of Nebraska Press, 2002), .278.
8. Liptak-Martin.
9. Ibid.
10. Ibid.
11. Stanley Cohen, *A Magic Summer – The '69 Mets* (New York: Harcourt Brace Jonavich Publishers, 1988), 292-293.
12. Liptak-Martin.

JIM McANANY

By Mel Marmer

After starting four different players in right field during the first two months of the 1959 season, the Chicago White Sox recalled 22-year-old Jim McAnany, who was batting .315 at Indianapolis, in hope of providing an offensive spark. To make room for McAnany, 19-year-old outfielder Johnny Callison, hitting .163, was sent down to Indianapolis.

"Mac" did an outstanding job – within three weeks, he was batting .382, with 14 RBIs in 15 games. Jim was a complete player: in addition to his timely hitting, he ran well, and racked up six outfield assists.

New York Yankees manager Casey Stengel addressed the White Sox beat reporters about McAnany after a game:

> "They've been a real ballclub since that McSweeney come up. First time I see him, he throws one of my men out at the plate in Chicago. He makes catches, he runs, he hits good. You ain't had a bit of trouble in right field since he got there. Before that, you had nothing else but trouble."[1]

Five years later, Callison redeemed himself with the Philadelphia Phillies and became an All-Star. Jim McAnany's fate was less kind: his baseball career ended prematurely because of nagging injuries. Jim had few regrets, however; he considered himself fortunate to do what he loved best: play major-league baseball, and to have earned a World Series ring in the process. "Mac" enjoyed a "good life" after baseball.

James McAnany was born September 4, 1936, in Los Angeles and grew up in the city's Westside district. His father, Clifford, was a sales manager for Pictsweet/Swanson Frozen Foods and his mother, Stella, nee Pociask, a housewife. There were four children – two boys and two girls. Jim and his brother Tim first played baseball in nearby Rancho Park. At Loyola High School, Jim played the outfield for the school's baseball team, which became the California Interscholastic Federation champion, and graduated in 1954. He was also a halfback on the football team. Jim followed the Los Angeles Angels of the Pacific Coast League on the radio. The first professional baseball game he saw was between the Angels and the Hollywood Stars.

Jim attended USC and played the outfield on the school's baseball team before leaving during his sophomore year. He was signed to a contract by White Sox scouts Hollis Thurston and Doc Bennett, the same pair who signed Johnny Callison a year later.

McAnany was assigned to Waterloo, Iowa, in the Class-B Three-I League for 1955 and batted .260 in 55 games in his professional debut. Back at Waterloo at the start of the 1956 season he experienced his first serious baseball injury – getting hit in the head. "I almost quit playing baseball then because of vision problems," he said.[2]

McAnany's next stop was Colorado Springs in the Class-A Western League, where he finished the 1956 season. In 1957, he returned to the Three-I League, this time with Davenport (Waterloo was no longer in the league and the White Sox had transferred their affiliation). He batted over .300 for the first time in his professional career, and returned to Colorado Springs for the 1958 season.

"I enjoyed it there because we had super people on that team," says McAnany. "We received strong support from the community and won the pennant in 1958. Personally, I had a terrific season. My manager, Frank Scalzi, was very helpful. Everything went my way. What more could I say? I achieved the highest batting average, .400, in organized baseball that year."

McAnany received the Hillerich & Bradsby Co.'s Louisville Slugger Silver Slugger Award for the highest batting average in the minor leagues in 1958. *The Sporting News* wrote that he had a good chance to make the White Sox because "he also throws and runs well and is a capable outfielder."

In a 2008 interview, McAnany recalled, "I was a line-drive type hitter. I changed my batting stance, opening it up, to adjust to faster and better pitching as I moved up in class. When I hit, I just tried to drive the ball. I really enjoyed hitting. I considered myself a student of the game – very intent to learn. I think I hit left-handed and right-handed pitchers equally well."

• JIM McANANY •

Jim McAnany

McAnany was called up to Chicago at the end of the 1958 season and made his major-league debut in Kansas City's Municipal Stadium on September 19, appearing as a pinch hitter for Early Wynn. He struck out swinging against Ralph Terry. He started three games in right field in 1958, finishing the year with a batting average of .000, having made outs in each of his 13 at-bats. Five of the outs were strikeouts. It was a disappointing finish to the year.

McAnany began 1959 in Indianapolis and found a lot more success when the White Sox called him up late in June. He recalled:

> "I was on a plane to Denver. They notified me to say I was going to Chicago. I got to Chicago and took a cab to Comiskey Park. I got there in the third inning of a Yankee game. The next day, I was in the starting lineup!"

That day, Sunday, June 28, Lopez sat left-handed batter Harry Simpson, who had gotten two hits off right-hander Bob Turley the day before, and started McAnany in right field against lefty Whitey Ford. McAnany responded with the first Sox hit of the game, a single. He hit safely in his first four starts, all of them games in which the opposing team started left-handers.

McAnany's hot streak continued well into July. One example: he had only three triples in his career, but two of them came on the same day, July 12, 1959, one in each game of a doubleheader against Kansas City. Both triples came with the bases loaded. Six of his 27 career RBIs came on that one day.

On July 17, McAnany "returned the favor" to Ralph Terry, who had struck him out in his first major-league at-bat in '58, by breaking up Terry's no-hit bid in the ninth inning with a line single into center field. The White Sox went on to defeat the Yankees, 2-0, before their largest road crowd of the season, 42,168. It was an important win, putting Chicago ahead of Cleveland by a game and 6½ up on the Yankees.

McAnany wound up starting a team-high 58 games in right field for the White Sox in 1959. He also started two games in left field, and played three innings in center field. To take pressure off of MacAnany manager Al Lopez penciled him in the eighth batting position—where he stayed most of the year. In the last month of the season Mac was frequently platooned with Jim Rivera. Rivera batted mostly against right handed pitchers and Mac batted against left handers. He accumulated 210 at-bats with a .276 batting average, driving in 27 runs and doing his part to help Chicago reach the World Series.

After the 1959 fall classic, in which McAnany started three games—he walked once and made five outs in six plate appearances for another .000 batting average, he entered the Army Reserve and completed basic training at Fort Leonard Wood, Missouri. In February, while stationed there, he was able to get leave long enough to come home for a weekend and marry his sweetheart, Rosemary Malloy. Back at Fort Leonard Wood, working in the snow and 10-degree temperatures, he injured his shoulder. As spring approached, Jim tried to work out to prepare for spring training. The shoulder problem recurred and began to nag him. It eventually led to his retirement from baseball.

In a 2008 interview McAnany recalled:

> "I was released from duty late and was late getting to spring training in 1960. It was a big disappointment coming off a World Series 'high.' Then, in 1961, I was recalled to active duty because of the Berlin Crisis and spent most of the year at Fort Lewis, Washington. It was a big disruption to my baseball career. But I have no regrets; I felt that it was my duty to serve my country. I just wish that it

had not played such a large part in ending my baseball career prematurely."

McAnany spent most of the 1960 season with San Diego of the Pacific Coast League. In the December 1960 expansion draft, he was selected by the Los Angeles Angels, but never played a game for the Angels: on April 1, 1961, he was traded to the Chicago Cubs for Lou Johnson.

McAnany missed most of the 1961 season while in the Army, but returned to the Cubs late in the season as a pinch-hitter. The Cubs had a poor record in 1961 (64-90 and a seventh-place finish), but four of their players became Hall of Famers: Richie Ashburn, Ernie Banks, Lou Brock and Billy Williams. McAnany's nagging injuries limited his time in right field to exactly one inning. A .300 batting average (3-for-10) kept his hopes alive for continuing on the next season … if only he could triumph over his injuries. He could not. In 1962, McAnany had only six fruitless at-bats and one walk as a pinch-hitter for the Cubs and retired from baseball.

McAnany recalled:

> "I have great memories. I was on the field when we clinched the pennant in Cleveland, and when the fan spilled beer on Al Smith. I really liked all of my teammates. I still keep in touch with Jim Landis, Barry Latman, and Ken McBride. Playing against the Yankees was like a dream come true. My locker was between Nellie Fox and Sherm Lollar. How cool was that! I learned the most from Jim Rivera. The love of the game I saw in the players – especially the 1959 White Sox team – impressed me the most. After leaving pro baseball, I became an insurance agent. I still own and operate my own business."

On his hitting:

> "I had difficulty hitting fastballs and curves, especially those thrown by Sandy Koufax. Fortunately, no pitcher seemed to have had my number; I didn't strike out that much (38 whiffs in 241 big-league at-bats). I'm glad Early Wynn was on our side; I'd have hated to hit against him in a game. Ryne Duren was a tough pitcher – we thought that he was mean-spirited. In retrospect, he was probably using his control problems – lack of it – to intimidate us."

> "I have always watched sports on television. My favorite hobby now is golf. I have a group of friends, mostly ex-FBI agents that I play with every Saturday. We go to Hilton Head and other venues. I enjoy the friendship as much as the golf."

Jim and Rosemary lived near their children and five grandchildren. Son Jim (James Emmot), played in the College World Series for Loyola Marymount University of Los Angeles and was drafted by the Angels. He played 271 minor-league games before joining his father full time in the insurance business. Daughter Michele, a teacher, played baseball for Phil Niekro's Colorado Silver Bullets.

In addition to golf, McAnany exercised regularly and he and his wife enjoyed attending all of their grandchildren's activities, especially the sports. "Fortunately, all three grandsons are athletic," McAnany said. "And life is pretty good. One of my few regrets is that my father never got to see me play major-league baseball. He died in 1957."

Mac attended virtually all of the 1959 White Sox team reunions. He was at the *Turn Back the Clock* weekend celebration on June 18, 2005. Mac also joined Luis Aparicio, Billy Pierce, Jim Landis and Jim Rivera for a first-pitch ceremony on June 25, 2009 at U.S. Cellular Field before a White Sox- Los Angeles Dodgers game at the 50th anniversary reunion after the White Sox defeated the Dodgers, 6-5.

McAnany died at the age of 79 on December 16, 2015 due to complications from a minor surgery. It was reported he was wearing a White Sox jersey when he passed away.[3] Jim and Rosemary were married 56 years.

Acknowledgments

Thank you to Mac and his wife Rosemary for making me feel like family. Thanks to Bill "Tax Man" Mortell for research assistance.

Notes

1. Bob Vanderberg, *'59 Summer of the Sox, The Year the World Series Came to Chicago* Champaign, Sports Publishing, Inc. 1999), 99.
2. Jim McAnany, telephone interview with the author, May 1, 2008. All quotations attributed to McAnany are from this interview unless otherwise indicated.
3. Mark Gonzales, Obituary, "Services held for 1959 White Sox World Series member Jim McAnany," *Chicago Tribune*, January 11, 2016.

KEN McBRIDE

By Peter Gordon

Ken McBride anchored the pitching rotation for the Los Angeles Angels during their first three years in the American League. He led the staff with 36 wins during those years and was the starting pitcher for the American League in the 1963 All-Star Game.

In that game, in his hometown of Cleveland, Ohio, McBride faced a lineup featuring future Hall of Famers Willie Mays and Hank Aaron, along with longtime stars like Tommy Davis, Bill White, Ken Boyer, and Dick Groat. McBride retired the great Aaron twice, but had trouble with Mays, who had a walk, a hit, and two stolen bases off him. Ken left the game after three innings with the score tied 3-3. He accounted for one of the American League's runs, lining a ball off third baseman Ken Boyer's glove in the second inning to drive in a run. The National League eventually won the game, 5-3. McBride finished 1963 with a 13-12 record and an ERA of 3.26, his lowest for a full major-league season. He was only 28 years old and one of the league's better pitchers, but that was his last winning season in the majors.

Kenneth Faye McBride was born on August 12, 1935, in Huntsville, Alabama, but grew up in Cleveland. He starred in baseball and basketball at the city's West High School. He led his basketball team to the state championship in 1952. Asked the key to his basketball prowess, Ken joked, "I shot a lot."[1]

McBride was big enough – 6-feet-1 and 195 pounds – and might have been talented enough for a professional basketball career. But in the early 1950s, professional baseball offered the best opportunity for an athlete to achieve wealth and fame. After McBride graduated from high school in 1953, he pitched for a semipro team sponsored by Mike's Diner. Later that year he was signed by a Red Sox scout, former pitcher Denny Galehouse, for a $500 bonus.

With only 16 teams in the major leagues in those days, even talented players tended to serve long minor-league apprenticeships. In 1954, his first season in pro ball, McBride dominated the Appalachian League, winning 18 games and losing 8 for Bluefield. He led the league in shutouts with five, struck out 180, and had a 2.53 earned-run average. McBride spent most of the 1955 season with Corning in the Pony League, posting a 10-9 record; that July he married the former Catherine Marie Jane Weir. In Greensboro in 1956, he pitched a no-hitter against Fayetteville on August 30, finishing the season 9-7 with a 2.64 ERA.

McBride appeared on his way to a major-league career until injuries limited him to 19 appearances for Oklahoma City in 1957. At Memphis in the Southern Association in 1958, he had his first losing season, going 9-10, but he came back strong in 1959. He won 11 games and lost only 5 for Indianapolis in the American Association, with a 2.79 ERA. One might have thought that the Red Sox, an organization going nowhere in the 1950s, would have wanted to bring the 24-year-old right-hander up to the majors for a look. Instead, they sold McBride's contract to the first-place Chicago White Sox on August 1. Three days later, Ken McBride made his first major-league start.

White Sox manager Al Lopez made a lot of bold moves during the 1959 pennant run. Eschewing the power game for a running offense and giving starts to cast-off pitchers demonstrated the savvy that made El Señor the most successful manager in the 1950s after Casey Stengel. The White Sox' defensive strengths perfectly suited McBride, who had one of the best sinkerballs of anyone pitching at the time. With a Gold Glove catcher, shortstop, and second baseman, the White Sox could get him plenty of groundball outs.

McBride made his major-league debut at Baltimore on August 4. He pitched hitless ball in the first two innings before giving up a run in the bottom of the third. Johnny Romano's two-run homer in the top of the seventh put the White Sox up 2-1. McBride held the lead through the bottom of the seventh but had thrown a lot of pitches.

In 1959, pitchers didn't routinely leave a game after seven innings, no matter how many pitches they had thrown. Gene Woodling, leading off the eighth for Baltimore, hit a groundball to first baseman Norm Cash, who booted it. McBride got Barry Shetrone to foul out, but gave up a single to Joe Ginsberg and then walked Brooks Robinson, loading the bases. Lopez brought in Turk Lown, who walked in the tying run. Baltimore scored another run before the White Sox

Go-Go to Glory

Ken McBride made his major league debut with the 1959 White Sox, but had his best years with the expansion Los Angeles Angels in the early 1960s. McBride was the starting pitcher in the 1963 All-Star game in his hometown of Cleveland.

could retire the side, then held on for a 3-2 victory. But McBride, who had allowed only one earned run in 7⅓ innings, had pitched very well in his first major-league game.

McBride started again at Washington on August 9. This time his pitching wasn't as sharp, and he was lifted in the fifth inning, when Washington scored three times to take a 3-2 lead. One of the three runs he allowed was unearned and the White Sox came back to win the game, 4-3, but McBride made no more starts for the White Sox that season. Although he had clearly showed promise, the team was in a pennant race and had no time to develop young pitchers. Those two games were McBride's only starts for the White Sox. He made only scattered appearances over the remainder of the season. He did earn a save on September 27, the final day of the regular season, pitching a scoreless ninth inning in a 6-4 win over the Tigers, with the pennant already clinched. The club left McBride off the postseason roster, so his contribution to the 1959 pennant was a 0-1 record with the one save. He gave up 20 hits in 22⅔ innings and had an ERA of 3.18. When asked in 2008 why he didn't pitch more that season, McBride replied, "You'll have to ask Al Lopez." (An impossible task; Lopez died in 2005.)

McBride told his interviewer that he was very grateful for the chance to play for a pennant winner. He said the White Sox were successful that season because their stars were all "great competitors" who would do whatever it took to win. Even years later, Ken could chuckle at how mad Nellie Fox got when an infielder caught one of his line drives. Since McBride was a rookie joining the team in the middle of the season, he didn't make many close friends. In fact, he became friendlier with some of the Sox while pitching against them for the Angels.[2]

The White Sox front office reacted to the World Series loss by trading many of the team's prospects for more established players. This didn't work out too well for the White Sox, who wound up dealing future stars of the 1960s like Norm Cash for veterans who were quickly washed up. The White Sox kept McBride in the minors for most of the 1960 season. He went 11-14 with a respectable 3.23 ERA for San Diego in the Pacific Coast League. He was brought up for five games at the end of the season, and he again posted a 0-1 record. After the season, the White Sox made him eligible for the expansion draft to stock the new American League teams in Los Angeles and Washington, and the Angels selected McBride in the December 14 draft.

McBride said that going to the Angels "was the best break I ever had." He became a pillar of their rotation during his first year in the league, winning 12 games and losing 15, with a 3.65 ERA – not a bad won-loss mark for a first-year expansion club with a losing record. He threw 241⅔ innings and struck out 180. The first-year Angels, managed by Bill Rigney, finished in eighth place in the 10-team league, ahead of the Kansas City Athletics and the expansion Washington Senators.

In 1962 the Angels finished in third place – one of the most impressive feats ever for a second-year expansion team. McBride set a team record that lasted for many years with 10 consecutive victories in the first half of the season. He was 11-3 with a 3.25 ERA in July when he felt a sharp pain in his side one night. The pain persisted, and was eventually diagnosed as a cracked rib, combined with pleurisy. Ken made only two more appearances that season.

In 1963 the Angels returned to the second division, but never fell to the depths of the cellar. McBride's 13-12 record and 3.26 ERA confirmed his status as one of the best right-handers in baseball. On June 9, he demonstrated extraordinary devotion to his team when he took his regular turn on the mound despite learning earlier that day that his younger brother had died in a car accident. McBride beat the Minnesota Twins, 4-2, and then went to Cleveland for the funeral.

McBride pitched particularly well against the New York Yankees, winning five straight games against the league's strongest team from 1961 through 1963. He attributed that success to his competitiveness – he always wanted to beat the best. It helped that after a couple of years in the league he learned to get Yankee sluggers like Yogi Berra out. He learned never to throw Berra a strike, but rather to curve him inside.

Newspaper reports frequently described McBride as one of the "classiest" and "best-liked" players in the American League. He said his secret was to just "be nice to everyone. A lot of ballplayers don't." Just 28 years old going into 1964, he appeared to be on the verge of stardom.

Alas, it was not to be. He won the 1964 opener for the Angels and, in his second start, he was ahead 2-0 against Detroit when rain interrupted the game in the fifth inning. After a long delay, the game resumed. Manager Rigney wanted to take McBride out but he insisted on going back in. After he did, he recalled years later, "I heard something pop" in his arm. His arm hurt so badly that he couldn't even comb his hair. From that time on, McBride's curveball and sinker were never the same. He lost 10 games in a row and finished the year with 4 wins, 13 losses, and a 5.26 ERA.

McBride tried to play in 1965, but his 6.14 ERA in the eight games he pitched (four starts) earned him a demotion to the minors in mid-August. He thought about not reporting, but decided to go ahead in order to ensure that he received the rest of his salary. Curiously, neither the team's beat writers nor Ken himself spoke about his physical problems at that time. Instead, McBride was philosophical about his demotion. He said:

> "I had been expecting this for the last couple of months. ... I wish I had an excuse like a sore arm, but I feel better today than the first day I put on a uniform. The owners have given me every chance. ... They treated me better when I was going bad than when I was going good."[3]

McBride started three games for San Jose in the California League during the remainder of the 1965 season, but finished 0-1 with an 11.57 ERA. In January 1966, just 2½ years after he started the All-Star Game for the American League, Ken McBride retired as a player. He finished his major career with a 40-50 record and a 3.79 ERA, numbers that don't look impressive, but during his three prime seasons with the Angels (1961-63), McBride posted a 36-32 record, a 3.46 ERA, and an excellent .237 opponents' batting average.

McBride tried to stay in baseball. He managed in the minors for a year, and in the 1970s worked as a minor-league instructor and coach for the Milwaukee Brewers. In 1974 and 1975, he was the team's major-league pitching coach. However, McBride said, "There wasn't any money in baseball at the time unless you were a player." After the 1975 season, at the age of 40, he moved back to Cleveland to raise his family. He became the co-owner and CEO of a construction company. As of 2008, he was still married to his high-school sweetheart, had two grown children and two grandchildren, and was still going to work every day at age 73. He remained a big fan of baseball and his hometown Indians, and watched their games every chance he got.

Sources

In addition to the sources cited in the Notes, the author also consulted the Ken McBride file at the National Baseball Hall of Fame which includes numerous newspaper articles spanning his career with the White Sox and Angels. Source newspapers not identified, but most likely are the *Los Angeles Times* and the *Chicago Tribune*.

James, Bill, and Rob Neyer. *The Neyer/James Guide to Pitchers.* New York: Simon & Schuster, 2004.

The Baseball Encyclopedia

Thorn, John, Phil Birnbaum and Bill Deane. *Total Baseball.*

Notes

1 Author interview with Ken McBride, August 19, 2008. All quotations from McBride are taken from this interview.
2 McBride interview.
3 Ross Newhan, "Fallen Angel – McBride Okays Trip to Minors," *The Sporting News*, September 4, 1965.

RAY MOORE

By Mel Marmer

Ray Moore was the long reliever and an occasional starter for the pennant-winning 1959 Chicago White Sox. Control problems that plagued Moore, especially early in his career as a highly-regarded Dodger prospect, resurfaced in 1959, limiting the big right-hander's effectiveness.

Raymond Leroy Moore, the ninth of 10 children of Clarence and Mary "Maggie" Moore, was born on June 1, 1926, in Meadows, Maryland. His parents met while working at an insane asylum. Clarence came from a family of nine children and left the farm to try other occupations, eventually settling as a streetcar conductor in Washington, where the oldest children were born.

As the family grew larger, Clarence returned to his roots in Upper Marlboro, Maryland, and rented a farm. Ray's sister, Mildred Fowler, recounted that it was a decision not regretted. "Our parents provided well for us. We had a lot of fun," she said in an interview. "On Sundays, we enjoyed family baseball games with our extended family. Ray, whom we called "Bud," usually pitched. Equipment was scarce. Our father made baseballs from tightly wrapped strips of old rubber. Our parents encouraged us in whatever we wanted to pursue, on the athletic field, or in life. Ray enjoyed baseball, hunting, fishing, and jogging. I liked playing golf."[1]

As a youngster Ray was a complete baseball player. He could run, field, throw, hit well – and hit with power. Not much is known about his formative years in baseball. Mildred said he played some sandlot baseball. Moore enlisted in the Army in January 1945, in Baltimore. He served in the Philippines and was noticed playing baseball in Manila by Brooklyn Dodgers scout Rex Bowen. Reaching the rank of private first class, he continued his military service after World War II ended, serving at Kalispell, Montana.

Moore signed with the Dodgers before the 1947 season began and reported to the Greenwood, Mississippi, Dodgers in the Class-C Cotton States League, where he was 18-7 with a 2.41 ERA. His next stops were Class-A Greenville, South Carolina; Fort Worth; Montreal; and St. Paul. Apart from a 15-9 season with Fort Worth in 1950, he generally had so-so won-lost records, but his ERAs were respectable – never once exceeding 3.75 - and he moved steadily up the Dodgers farm system. His eight-year minor-league record was 84-80.

In spring training with the Dodgers in 1952, Moore uncorked a wild pitch that sailed over the batter and catcher and pierced a plaster wall some 15 feet beyond. Still, the 6-foot-tall, 195-pounder made his major-league debut with the Dodgers on August 1, 1952.

Moore was up and down between Brooklyn, St. Paul, and Fort Worth in 1952, '53, and '54. However, he never got more than brief major-league trials with the talent-laden Dodgers, throwing just 36 1/3 innings in 1952 and 1953, and no big-league work at all in 1954. He was also set back by a sore arm, which limited his work to 20 games and 112 innings for St. Paul in 1954.

On October 8, 1954, Moore was traded to the Baltimore Orioles for infielder Chico Garcia. It was a break for Ray, who was going from a club with a surplus of talent to a second-division team in dire need of help. Orioles manager Paul Richards, considered an expert in developing pitchers, was happy to obtain the right hander. "In my opinion, Moore has the ability to be either a starter or reliever," said Richards after the trade. "I have always liked him, and he can throw as hard as anybody on the Baltimore staff except Bob Turley."[2]

In Baltimore, Moore finally got a chance to pitch at the major-league level, and had three good years from 1955-57, winning 10, 12, and 11 games as a reliever and spot starter. He turned in some fine stretches of work with the Birds, like the second half of 1956, when he went 6-1 with a 3.26 ERA in 15 appearances (14 starts) after the All-Star break. And though he had a losing record in 1957 (11-13), Moore ranked among the American League's top 10 pitchers in innings pitched (227 1/3), strikeouts (117), and opponents' batting average (.236).

Moore came to the White Sox from the Orioles on December 3, 1957, with Tito Francona and Billy Goodman in a trade for pitcher Jack Harshman,

• RAY MOORE •

A starter/reliever for the pennant-winning White Sox in 1959, Ray Moore had his best years with the Orioles, Senators and Twins before and after joining the South Siders.

outfielder Larry Doby, minor-league pitcher Russ Heman, and first baseman Jim Marshall. In his first season with the Sox, 1958, Moore had a lot to prove, as most considered Harshman a quality pitcher and Moore as more of a journeyman, even though he had averaged 11 wins per year in his three years with the Orioles, along with an overall ERA of 3.93. True, Moore was a hard thrower, but he walked nearly as many batters as he struck out (he led the league in walks allowed in 1957), while Harshman had posted higher strikeout totals and had ranked among the American League leaders in ERA from 1954-56.

Moore had a good season for the White Sox in 1958, though he was not as productive as Harshman was with the Orioles (12-15 with a 2.89 ERA). Initially used in relief by the Sox, Moore proved very effective; converted to a starting role, he started 20 games and completed four, of which two were shutouts. In all, he won nine games and lost seven with an ERA of 3.82. Overall, Moore pitched well and earned acclaim as a "Yankee killer" by beating the Bronx Bombers twice in June. On the 5th, he won a complete game, 3-2; and on the 23rd he threw a three-hit, 2-0 shutout. This was his finest month as a member of the White Sox.

In Chicago's pennant-winning season of 1959, Ray won three and lost six, appearing in 29 games, of which eight were starts. His ERA was 4.12. In the World Series against the Dodgers, he pitched one inning, giving up one earned run. On June 1 of that season, Moore threw perhaps his best game of the year – eight innings of three-hit, three-run ball with four strikeouts and no walks. But the Sox lost to Kansas City, 3-1. Moore had been promised a present by Bill Veeck if he won the game; a blue-tick coonhound puppy. Veeck presented the puppy to Moore anyway for his stellar effort. The pup's name was Young Blue, to go with Moore's favorite hound, Old Blue. Moore himself was nicknamed "Old Blue" by some teammates. He was also called "Farmer." He helped his father grow tobacco until his father passed away in 1970. After his father's passing, Ray grew vegetables, including corn, and watermelon.

Moore began the 1960 season with the White Sox, and was the winning pitcher in the Sox' Opening Day win over Kansas City at Comiskey Park on April 19 – despite throwing only a single pitch. Coming in with the bases loaded and one out in the top of the ninth and the score tied, 9-9, Moore got Bill Tuttle to ground into an inning-ending double play with his first pitch … a play that made Sox fans recall Jerry Staley's one-pitch save on a double play groundout to clinch the 1959 pennant against Cleveland. Unfortunately for Ray, his Opening Day heroics were all but forgotten when Minnie Minoso, making a triumphant return to the South Side after coming back to the Sox in an offseason trade, completed a six-RBI day with a walkoff home run off John Tsitouris to lead off the bottom of the ninth – Minnie's second home run of the day.

That victory proved to be Moore's last in a Sox uniform. After going 1-1 with a 5.66 ERA in 13 games, he was sold to the Washington Senators on June 13. The deal proved beneficial to Moore, who overcame his control problems to become one of the top closers in the American League. With Washington, he was 3-2 with 13 saves over the remainder of the 1960 season. He accompanied the team in its move to Minnesota, where he had effective seasons for the Twins in 1961

(4-4, 14 saves) and 1962 (8-3, 9 saves). In an era when the role of relief ace was still evolving, Moore was one of the American League's best in 1960, when his 13 saves ranked third in the league, and again in 1961, when he had the AL's fourth highest save total (14).

Moore's work began to slip in 1962, when his ERA rose by over a run from 3.67 to 4.73, and he was hit hard in 1963, when he logged only two saves and saw his ERA balloon to a hideous 6.98. He worked in only one game in September of 1963, and it was no surprise when the Twins released him on October 15 of that year. Moore, who was 37, chose to retire from baseball and returned to farm life and his beloved coon-hunting dogs. After he retired from farming, the bachelor moved in with his sister, Mildred Fowler.

Ray loved hunting, fishing, and country music; a 1960 *Sporting News* column noted that he'd given out an invitation to his Senators teammates: "I want all of you to come to my farm to do a little hunting on October 20."[3] He was a lifelong bachelor, though he dated. Through his appreciation of bluegrass music, he became a friend of country singer, musician, and minor-league baseball player (Big State League, East Texas League, 1948-49) Roy Clark.

Ray loved dogs, especially blue-tick coon hounds, prized by hunters for their piercing wails. According to Ray's sister, Mildred, he had as many as eight coon hounds and six beagles at one time. She said that the right-hander "was quiet, even-tempered, and hard-working."[4] Moore died from colon cancer on March 2, 1995.

Acknowledgments

Thanks to SABR member and Chicago White Sox fan Bill Mortell for helping with the genealogy of the of the Moore family and in locating Mildred Fowler. Don Zminda and Bill Nowlin supplied some additional material to this piece.

Sources

In addition to the sources cited in the Notes, the author also consulted retrosheet.org and SABR's Minor League database.

Notes

1. Interview with Moore's sister, Mildred Fowler, by the author, January 15, 2008.
2. Hugh Trader, "Orioles' Miles May Step Out as Club Prexy," *The Sporting News*, October 20, 1954.
3. Bob Addie, "Bob Addie's Atoms," *The Sporting News*, September 14, 1960.
4. Fowler interview.

DON MUELLER

By J.A. Petterchak

Outfielder Don Mueller was a hard man to strike out – in five of the eight years in which he played in at least 120 games for the New York Giants in the 1950s, he led the league in fewest strikeouts per at-bats. He was a two-time All-Star who participated in some of the most memorable games of the era.

Born in the St. Louis suburb of Creve Coeur, Missouri, in 1927, young Donald Frederick Mueller learned hitting from his father, Walter J. Mueller, a backup outfielder for the 1922-1926 Pittsburgh Pirates. "He taught me an awful lot," Don recalled. "He showed me how to grip the bat, to use pressure on one hand or the other to hit where you want to hit. He also had me focus on the ball by pitching corn kernels that I would hit with a broomstick. Concentrating on such a small object improved my depth perception."[1]

Don had a brother, LeRoy, a bit more than three years older. His mother, Caroline Lena Heinrichs, and father were both Missouri natives, Caroline's German-born mother the only one of the four grandparents who wasn't a Missourian. Walter Mueller worked as a hauling contractor after his career in baseball.

Mueller played two years of American Legion baseball, hitting .600 one summer, then won a spot on his Christian Brothers High School team, batting left-handed and throwing right-handed.[2] Developing into the caliber of a professional ballplayer, Don received offers from several teams, including the Chicago Cubs, "except," he said, "my dad didn't like the contract they offered me." Walter's choice was the New York Giants, whose scout Gordon Maguire took Mueller to Sportsman's Park in 1944, when the Cardinals were playing the Giants. Manager Melvin Ott, who had been Don's favorite professional player, approved signing the 17-year-old, still in high school, for the Giants' top farm team, Jersey City, managed by the great Chicago Cubs catcher Gabby Hartnett. Mueller played three games that season, driving in three runs with one hit in seven at-bats.[3]

The following year, as a high-school senior, he was invited to the Giants' spring-training camp. Approaching draft age, he signed up for the Merchant Marine and served two years, playing baseball for Jersey City during shore leaves. After leaving the Merchant Marine in mid-1946, Mueller batted .359 for Jersey City during the final weeks of the season and in 1947 – the year he turned 20 – he was asked to get more seasoning at Single-A Jacksonville. He hit .348.

Mueller was back with Jersey City in 1948. Hitting .328 with ten homes runs, he was called up by the Giants and made his major-league debut on August 2, playing 36 games and posting a .358 average with nine RBIs. The Giants had replaced Ott as manager that year with the fiercely competitive Leo Durocher. Under Ott, the offense had been known as the National League's "lumberjacks," for the big but slow power hitters.

"The team did not have a good won-loss record," Mueller said. "Leo got rid of the home-run hitters. He wanted base hits, with good pitching. I got the job because I was his kind of ballplayer: hit, advance the runner."

In May 1949 the 22-year-old Mueller married his high-school sweetheart, Genevieve Babor, and they took up residence in Creve Coeur and then the Maryland Heights suburb of St. Louis where they lived the rest of their lives. After a successful stint in Minneapolis, Mueller batted a meager .232 in 51 Giants games, all but a handful of them as a pinch-hitter. Then in 1950, he became the team's regular right fielder, after the Giants traded home-run hitter Willard Marshall. Durocher, who on his selection as manager had announced, "I come to win," confidently predicted a pennant that year. Mueller moved around in the order more than most of the Giants, batting third more than any other position, but often hitting second, fourth, sixth, and seventh.

Early in the season, the team played mediocre ball, with poor hitting and worse pitching. But in early August as a pinch-hitter, Mueller began improving, with soft singles and line drives. Again in the lineup, he hit well over .300 during the final two months and ended the season at .291. Sportswriters dubbed him Mandrake the Magician for his ability to stroke the ball through holes in the defense.[4]

The Giants finished third in 1950, five games behind the pennant-winning Philadelphia Phillies. Durocher told reporters in the spring of 1951 that the Giants would "take it all." But after a 2-1 start, his team lost the next 11 games. After one particularly bad outing, Durocher berated each of the players, surprising even veterans with his foul-language tirade.[5] "It was a turning point," recalled one teammate. "From the next day on we played fantastic baseball," a winning stretch that continued through the season, aided by the team's 20-year-old rookie sensation, Willie Mays.

Mueller, who had been among the slumping hitters at the start of the year, hit very well in June and July. Of his 65 career home runs, five came in two consecutive games on September 1 and 2 against the Brooklyn Dodgers at the Polo Grounds, tying a record held by Adrian Anson, Ty Cobb, Tony Lazzeri, and Ralph Kiner.[6]

Trailing the Dodgers by 13 games on August 11, the Giants won 39 of their final 47 games to end the season in a first-place tie with Brooklyn, forcing a three-game playoff for the pennant. With the series tied, 1-1, and the Dodgers leading 4-1 in the bottom of the ninth inning of the final playoff game, the Giants' Alvin Dark singled. Mueller, taking the first pitch for a ball, noticed that first baseman Gil Hodges was holding Dark close to the bag. The Magician hit the next pitch between Hodges and Jackie Robinson at second, out of Hodges' reach, allowing Dark to reach third. Whitey Lockman lined a double into left field, scoring Dark. Mueller, scrambling for third, slid past the bag and tore the tendons on both sides of his ankle. Writhing in pain, he was carried into the clubhouse.

His pinch-runner, Mueller's roommate Clint Hartung, was about to become a footnote in history. Bobby Thomson, a journeyman outfielder in the biggest at-bat of his career, stepped to the plate. Giants players and fans hoped for a single that would tie the game, but Thomson hit an astounding walk-off three-run homer into the left-field stands.[7] "I played the whole game and got a big hit in the ninth inning," Mueller recalled. "When Bobby Thomson hit his home run – The Shot Heard 'Round the World – I was the only one in the clubhouse."

He heard the crowd erupt while lying on a clubhouse table.

"I couldn't be certain that it wasn't something good for the Dodgers because there were plenty of Brooklyn fans in that park," he told author Ray Robinson. "I knew pretty quickly what had happened once the players got back to the clubhouse and started to pour champagne over my injured ankle."[8]

Mueller's injury kept him from the World Series, in which Casey Stengel's Yankees won their third straight championship, four games to two. Some analysts believed that had Mueller been in the lineup, the Giants might have won the Series. Indeed, his right-field replacement, Hank Thompson, hit only .143 in the Series and committed two damaging errors.[9]

With a 17-5 start in 1952, fans anticipated another good season. But the team soon felt the loss of their power hitters. Mays left in May for military service (it was the time of the Korean War), while Monte Irvin was out with a broken ankle. The other hitters, including Mueller, may have felt some pressure to attempt home runs. Mueller hit 12, second-most in his career. The team as a whole hit 28 fewer. Mueller also had to prove his ability in right field, vying with Thompson, Hartung, and others, but played more games than any of them and ended the season with a .281 batting average.

Early in the 1953 season, after being benched again for lack of home-run power, Mueller stopped trying to be a power hitter. "My chance of hitting a single is very good," he said. "My chance of clouting a homer is very poor. It is certainly better for the team this way. If I am on base, I save a chance for Mays, Irvin, Thompson, or somebody to knock me in."[10] As proof of his theory, Mueller finished fifth in the National League with a .333 batting average. And with only 13 strikeouts, he was the most difficult batter to fan that year.

On May 2 Mueller "stood in right field and watched five balls go over my head" at Busch Stadium when Stan Musial hit five homers in a Giants-Cardinals doubleheader, all into the right-field seats. Although Mueller had hit five home runs in two consecutive games in 1951, Musial became the first major leaguer with five in one day. Mueller contributed to the Giants' win in the second game, going 5-for-5, including a double and a triple, driving in two runs, and scoring three. "My 5-for-5 got exactly two lines in the paper the next day," he said, referring to the extensive coverage of Musial's feat.

National League All-Star team manager Walter Alston, the Dodgers' skipper, selected Mueller for the

• DON MUELLER •

1954 team. Pinch-hitting for pitcher Robin Roberts in a five-run fourth inning, Mueller came through with a clutch double that gave the NL the lead, though the American Leaguers ultimately won the game, 11-9.

Nearly all season Mueller made at least one hit per game, and in the first game on July 1, against four Pirates pitchers, he hit for the cycle: a double to left field, a triple to right center, a single to center, and in his final at-bat, a home run into the right-field seats off left-hander Paul LaPalme, his first homer of the season. As a left-handed batter, Mueller said, "Normally, I didn't try to pull left-handers. I took them the other way. But I was a situation hitter and this was a situation. So I pulled him over the right-field wall for the home run."[11] That homer was one of Mueller's four that year, all hit at home. He was the first Giant to hit for the cycle since Harry Danning in 1940 and the only major leaguer to accomplish the feat in 1954.

Willie Mays, who had returned from two years of military service, hit 41 home runs to lead the Giants to the 1954 National League pennant. On the final day of the regular season he and Mueller were tied for the batting title. Mueller singled twice in six at-bats, but Mays had three hits in four at-bats to win the crown at .345, to Mueller's .342. Though runner-up in the batting race, Mueller accumulated 212 base hits, the most in the league that year, and 17 more than Mays had. He placed ninth in the MVP voting.

Entering the 1954 fall classic, the heavily favored Cleveland Indians, with four future Hall of Fame pitchers and a league-record 111 wins, had ended the New York Yankees' five consecutive years as world champions. But Durocher managed a four-game sweep by the Giants. Mueller played right field in all four games and batted a composite .389, with seven singles in 18 at-bats. Although Dusty Rhodes was the acknowledged hero of the Series with two homers and seven RBIs in only six at-bats, some believed that Mueller's hit-and-run single in the third inning of Game Three was the key play of the Series.[12] He lived up to his Mandrake the Magician nickname, pushing a groundball through the left side of the infield as George Strickland, the Cleveland shortstop, raced over to cover the bag. The Giants went on to score

Lifetime .296 hitter Don Mueller starred with the New York Giants from 1948-57 before finishing his career with the White Sox.

three runs in the inning on the way to a 6-2 victory and an insurmountable three games to zero lead.

Named to the 1955 National League All-Star team, Mueller started in right field and garnered one hit in two at-bats as the Nationals won 6-5. He ended the season with 185 hits and a .306 average.[13]

The following years saw steady declines in Mueller's ability. His batting average dropped to .269 in 1956 and .258 in 1957. Mueller looked forward to the Giants' move to San Francisco in 1958, but in March the team sold him to the Chicago White Sox for an estimated $25,000.[14] The White Sox had a strong 82-72 second-place season under manager Al Lopez but Mueller, well past his peak years, saw limited playing time: 42 hits in 166 at-bats, for a .253 average. The following May, appearing in only four games and under treatment for gout and arthritis, the 32-year-old retired from baseball.[15] He enjoyed the memorable 1959 World Series from his St. Louis home.

Mueller is probably best remembered for putting the ball in play (that is, not striking out or walking) in 93 percent of his career plate appearances. "Many 21st--century players have more K's in one season than Mueller's career total of 146," wrote baseball analyst Al Doyle, "but his 164 walks would scare off modern number crunchers."[16] Mueller's career batting average of .296 remains a proud accomplishment. In five different seasons, he was the most difficult batter to strike out in the National League.

An avid outdoorsman, during offseasons, Mueller, his brother, and fellow players often spent time together fishing and hunting. After his playing days, Mueller raised cattle on the family farm and for a few years scouted for the Giants in Missouri and Illinois. Then he began a lengthy career as an insurance company investigator.

In 1992 the New York Baseball Writers awarded him the Casey Stengel Award, and in 2001 he was elected to the Brooklyn Dodgers Hall of Fame. Why the Dodgers? "Well, the Giants didn't have a Hall of Fame, and I guess the Dodgers were acknowledging that I was a pain in their butts."

Mueller and his wife settled in suburban St. Louis, where they could enjoy activities with the families of their three sons, Mark, Jurt, and Doug. When they were youngsters, Mueller taught each of them to hit corn kernels, with a Wiffle Ball bat instead of a broomstick. Mark Mueller was born on September 2, 1951 – the day his father hit the fourth and fifth home runs of his five-in-two-days record.[17] Mark was a 34th-round draft pick of the Cardinals in 1971 and played infield during three seasons in the low minors, batting .253, largely in Single A ball.

Genevieve Mueller died on July 9, 2011, and Don died later that year, on December 28, at a nursing home in Chesterfield, Missouri.

Notes

1. Author interview on February 8, 2007. All otherwise unattributed quotations from Mueller come from this interview.
2. Harold Sheldon, "Don Mueller – Star by Birth," *Baseball Digest*, November 1951.
3. Tom Meany, *The Incredible Giants* (New York: A.S. Barnes & Co., 1955), 93.
4. Thomas Kiernan, *The Miracle at Coogan's Bluff* (New York: Thomas Y. Crowell, 1975), 57.
5. Kiernan, 65-66.
6. Meany, 90; *The Sporting News*, May 10, 1961.
7. David S. Neft and Richard M. Cohen, *The Sports Encyclopedia: Baseball* (New York: St. Martin's/Marek, 1985), 286.
8. New York Times News Service, December 30, 2011.
9. Meany, 94.
10. Meany, 90.
11. John C. Skipper, *Inside Pitch; A Closer Look at Classic Baseball Moments* (Jefferson, North Carolina: McFarland, 1996), 77.
12. Chester R. Smith, "Key Plays in the Series," *Baseball Digest*, November-December 1954.
13. *New York Times Book of Baseball History* (New York: Quadrangle, 1975), 182.
14. *Chicago Daily News*, March 22, 1958.
15. Larry Kalas, *Strength Down the Middle: The Story of the 1959 Chicago White Sox* (Chicago: R.R. Donnelley & Sons, 1999), 215.
16. *Past Times*, December 13, 2007.
17. According to one report, Mueller was in the batter's box when on-deck hitter Monte Irvin handed Don a rosin bag and told him to smile, that he had a new baby boy. Mueller then reportedly socked the next pitch over the Polo Grounds roof for his fifth home run in two days. Sheldon, 67.

GARY PETERS

By Mark Armour

He took a long time to find his place in the major leagues. After four brief callups, a successful emergency start in 1963 gave Gary Peters a job with the White Sox on his fifth and final trial. He still managed to put up a few big seasons and 124 wins, coming agonizingly close to the World Series a few times. He was also a remarkably good hitter – 19 home runs in his career made him a frequent pinch-hitter.

Gary Charles Peters was born on April 21, 1937, in Grove City, Pennsylvania, about 50 miles north of Pittsburgh, to Thomas Peters, a gas heater plant foreman and longtime semipro baseball player, and Elizabeth Rowe Peters. Gary grew up in nearby Mercer, and starred in basketball at Mercer High School, being named All-State in his senior year of 1955. His school did not field a baseball team, and Gary's only Organized Baseball experience was a year of American Legion ball and several years on the sandlots playing semipro ball. Peters was mainly a first baseman, occasionally a pitcher, and a great left-handed hitter. He played for several years with his father, who played ball for 30 years in the area.

After Peters' high-school graduation White Sox scout Fred Shaffer took him to Chicago for a tryout at Comiskey Park. Suitably impressed, the White Sox signed Peters to a contract that would pay for him to attend college and allow him to report to play baseball after his spring classes were over. Gary enrolled at Grove City College, majoring in mathematics, with a basketball scholarship.

When Gary arrived in Holdredge, Nebraska, to begin his professional career in the Nebraska State League (Class D but comparable to later rookie leagues), he discovered that the team already had a first baseman – future major-league catcher J.C. Martin. Peters played the outfield for a while before turning to pitching. He had a fine debut, finishing 10-5 with a 2.81 ERA, leading the league in innings pitched (128) and strikeouts (142) and being named the league's outstanding left-handed pitcher. He also hit .321 in 84 at-bats.

The next season the White Sox promoted Peters to Dubuque, Iowa, of the Class-D Midwest League, and he had a very similar season – 10-6 and a 2.75 ERA. He again did not report until June, after the finish of his college year. After the season Gary had the pleasure of going on a brief barnstorming tour of Pennsylvania with the Nellie Fox All-Stars, a group of Pennsylvania residents including Fox, Dick Groat, Roy Face, and others. The tour was mostly for fun and laughs, but Peters got to spend time with big-leaguers for a few weeks.

The 6-foot-2, 202-pound left-hander started the 1958 season with Colorado Springs of the Class-A Western League. After a rocky start – a 7.43 ERA in 23 innings – Peters was reassigned to Davenport in the Class-B Three-I League, and had another good year there, winning 12 of 20 decisions in 25 games. He was selected to the league's All-Star second team. "When I started," Peters later recalled, "all I could do was throw hard. That got me by all right in the low minors. But as I moved up, I found out I had to have something else, too."[1] He added a slider, which came quickly, and a curve, which he struggled with for a few years. As his repertoire was broadened, he learned better control of all his pitches.

For 1959 Chicago sent Peters to its top farm club, Indianapolis of the Triple-A American Association. Gary won 13 games while losing 11, and posting a 3.56 ERA. The highlight was his no-hit, no-run game on July 24 against Minneapolis. At the end of the season he was recalled to the pennant-bound White Sox and pitched in two games. On September 10 in Washington he threw the bottom of the eighth inning in an 8-2 loss, allowing two hits and no runs. Four days later he pitched in Boston, walking both batters he faced in an 8-3 loss.

Over the next few years Peters built a reputation as a decent Triple-A pitcher who might not have the talent to stick with the White Sox. He pitched both the 1960 and 1961 seasons with San Diego of the Pacific Coast League, finishing with 12-9 and 13-10 records, and joined the White Sox in September both seasons. In 1960 he pitched twice, allowing one run in 3⅓ innings. The next year his three appearances netted two runs in 10⅓ innings.

In 1962 Peters made the club in the spring for the first time. After a few solid appearances, he had two rough outings and was demoted to Indianapolis in early May. Back in Triple A, he finished only 8-10 for the season, his first losing record in his seven-year professional career. The White Sox were concerned that he wasn't throwing as hard as he had earlier in

• Go-Go to Glory •

Gary Peters made his major league debut with the 1959 White Sox, but he was still several years away from establishing himself as one of the American League's best pitchers.

his career. "He'd throw hard in some games, but not in others," said manager Al Lopez. "He was trying to pinpoint his pitches too much."[2]

Heading into the 1963 season, Peters was getting his last shot. He was out of options, meaning that the White Sox had to either keep him on the club or place him on waivers. He spent the winter pitching in Puerto Rico, but being used as a relief pitcher – which Peters understood to suggest that his prospects were fading away. He reacted to this disappointment by deciding to reach back and fire his fastball as hard as he could at all times. Suddenly, his ball was harder and livelier.

After a decent spring, Peters again made the White Sox club in 1963, although in those years major-league teams could carry 28 men until May 15, when rosters were further reduced to 25. Peters was surely vulnerable to be one of the three players cut. In the opening weeks of the season he was a situational reliever, not pitching particularly well. Through May 2 he had pitched in six games, losing twice, with a 4.63 ERA in 11⅔ innings. On the 6th he was handed an emergency start because Juan Pizzaro had the flu,

and he beat the Athletics 5-1, allowing just four hits in eight innings, and helping his own cause with a third-inning home run off Ted Bowsfield.

Sometimes in life you are handed an opportunity when you least expect it, and the story told of Peters in later years was that he was an overnight sensation. But he had worked very hard for several years in the minor leagues and every winter – hardly "overnight." He had not pitched much before signing with the White Sox, and it took him six years to become a pitcher worthy of the major leagues. When it came together, it came together quickly.

Although he was still used occasionally in the bullpen for the few weeks after his first start, by early June 1963, Peters was in the rotation to stay. On June 30 he shut out the Indians to bring his record to 5-4. After losing to Whitey Ford in Yankee Stadium on July 4, Peters won his next 11 decisions, including two more shutouts. On July 15, he one-hit the Orioles, striking out 13. The only Baltimore hit was a single by opposing starter Robin Roberts in the third inning.

Through September 18, Peters had run his record to 19-6, but he lost his two bids for his 20th victory. He finished the season 19-8, with a league-leading 2.33 earned-run average and 189 strikeouts in 243 innings. After the season he garnered the league's Rookie of the Year award, beating out teammate Pete Ward, who hit 22 home runs and batted .295 in his debut as the team's third baseman.

By this time Peters had relocated his winter home to Sarasota, where the White Sox trained. He spent the winter there working on his curveball, making it harder and snappier. In 1964 he got through a rough patch early in the season, allowing eight home runs in his first 41 innings, before settling down to another big year. Making up for the disappointment in 1963, he ran off four straight wins in September to get his 20th win on the 26th. He had to be relieved in the seventh, but Hoyt Wilhelm threw 2⅓ one-hit innings to nail down the win. The White Sox lost a torrid three-team race for the pennant in 1964, winning their last nine games but finishing one game behind the New York Yankees.

For the 1964 season, Peters finished 20-8, tying Dean Chance for the most wins in the American League. His 205 strikeouts and 2.50 ERA were both good for fourth in the league and, though Chance won the Cy Young Award, Gary did finish seventh in the voting for league MVP award. He was named to the league's All-Star team, but did not play in the game.

Peters had also developed a reputation as a good hitter by this point, slamming seven home runs in his

• GARY PETERS •

first two seasons. He was used 18 times as a pinch-hitter and eight more times as a pinch-runner in these two years. On July 19, 1964, against the Athletics, he pinch-hit for Hoyt Wilhelm in the bottom of the 13th inning, with the White Sox down 3-2 and a runner on first. After twice failing to lay a bunt down in fair territory, he ended the game with a home run into the right-field stands. After that dramatic game-winner, he was the White Sox' primary left-handed pinch-hitter the rest of the season. As the White Sox had difficulty scoring runs, there was some talk of letting Peters play a position on occasion when not pitching, a notion that Lopez quickly dismissed.

Peters struggled a bit in 1965, slowed by a groin injury that bothered him all season. He finished 10-12 with a 3.63 ERA, a far cry from his great averages his first two seasons. The next season he came back nicely with a 1.98 ERA to again lead the league, though he managed only a 12-10 record. The White Sox were a notoriously poor-hitting team, finishing ninth in the league (of 10) in runs per game while boasting a league-leading 2.68 ERA. Among Peters's 10 losses were three shutouts at the hands of Denny McLain (1-0), Jim Kaat (1-0), and Sam McDowell (2-0), three of the better pitchers in the league. In a 6-0 three-hitter over the Yankees on July 30, Peters threw just 75 pitches, only 25 of which were called balls. He walked no one and struck out just three in a game that took just 1 hour, 57 minutes to play.

After trailing well behind the Orioles in 1966, in the following season the White Sox engaged in a four-way pennant fight with the Boston Red Sox, Minnesota Twins, and Detroit Tigers. Chicago led for two months in midsummer and stayed within a game of the lead all through September before finally succumbing and finishing three games behind the Red Sox. Peters' season highlight may have been pitching three perfect innings in the All-Star Game (won by the NL in the 15th inning), striking out four pretty good hitters: Willie Mays, Roberto Clemente, Orlando Cepeda, and Dick Allen.

The 1967 club was again led by its pitching, especially Joel Horlen and Peters, who finished first and second, respectively, in the league in ERA. Peters put up a 16-11 record and 2.28 ERA, but fell victim to his club's lack of hitting all season, especially down the stretch. In September Peters won only one of his eight starts despite a 2.48 ERA for the month – his monthly ERA's for the season were all between 2.05 and 2.51. On September 27, trailing the Twins by a single game, the White Sox dropped a doubleheader to the lowly Athletics in Kansas City, as both Peters and Horlen were defeated. Though they were still just 1½ games behind, they were now in fourth place, making their task nearly impossible.

After 17 consecutive seasons over .500, the White Sox finally collapsed in 1968, and Peters did his part, dropping all the way to 4-13, with a 3.76 ERA. Peters suffered a back injury early in the season that still bothered him decades later. One highlight came on May 5 when he six-hit the Yankees, 5-1, and hit a grand slam off Al Downing to provide more than enough offense for his own cause. Three weeks later, playing the Yankees in New York, manager Eddie Stanky hit Peters sixth in the batting order, ahead of Duane Josephson, Luis Aparicio, and Tim Cullen. Peters was hitless in two at-bats as the club only managed four hits in a loss to Mel Stottlemyre.

The next season, 1969, Peters hurt his arm in spring training -- it was diagnosed as a rotator cuff injury long after he had retired -- and finished just 10-15 with a 4.53 ERA, easily the worst of his career. After the season, he was traded with catcher Don Pavletich to the Red Sox for infielder Syd O'Brien and pitcher Billy Farmer. When Farmer chose to retire instead, the Red Sox substituted Jerry Janeski.

It was a productive change for Peters, as he went from a team that struggled to score runs to one of the better offenses in the league. After a wonderful spring in which he gave up no runs in 32 innings, Peters started on Opening Day for the Red Sox in Yankee Stadium, and earned the 4-3 victory. He had a terrible May, losing all five of his decisions and posting an 8.04 ERA, but had four solid months the rest of the way. He finished 16-11, with a 4.05 ERA, thanks in part to an offense that led the league with 203 home runs.

In 1971 the 34-year-old Peters had another decent but unspectacular season, putting up a 14-11 record and a 4.37 ERA. Manager Eddie Kasko used him frequently as a pinch-hitter, and he hit .271 with three home runs and 19 RBIs in 96 at-bats. The next season the club acquired or promoted a number of new starting pitchers, and Peters lost his job in the rotation. Although he stayed with the team all year, he had just four starts among his 33 games, splitting six decisions and posting a 4.32 ERA. After the season he was released by the Red Sox. He tried out with the Kansas City Royals the next March but retired when he did not make the club.

Peters was very active in the fledgling Players Association in those years. He was the player representative in Chicago and Boston, and in his last season he was the American League representative, attending high-level meetings with owners' representatives, including those that led to the first players' strike in 1972.

In January 1958, Gary married Jean A. Jackal and soon afterward the couple began making their winter home in Sarasota, Florida, where the White Sox trained for many years. Gary and Jean raised two daughters. After his retirement he went to work for a construction company in Sarasota as a general superintendent, in charge of field work and quality control.

In 2000 Peters was named to the White Sox All-Century Team, one of nine pitchers representing the first 100 years of their existence. He still kept in touch with the team through old-timers events or celebrations on the field, though it became harder when the club left its longtime spring home of Sarasota for Tucson in 1998.

Sources

In addition to the sources cited in the Notes, the author also consulted:

Appel, Marty. *Yesterday's Heroes* (New York: William Morrow, 1998).

Heiman, Lee, Dave Weiner, and Bill Gutman. *When the Cheering Stops* (New York: Macmillan, 1990).

Furlong, Bill. "Gary Peters & Juan Pizzaro—Southpaw Sorcery," in *Baseball Stars of 1965* (Ray Robinson, ed.). Pyramid, 1965.

Notes

1 Bill Furlong, "Gary Peters & Pete Ward—Chisox Wonder Boys," in *Baseball Stars of 1964* (Ray Robinson, ed.) (New York: Pyramid Publications, 1964), 140.
2 Ibid.

The Dodgers' victory over the White Sox in the 1959 World Series was followed by baseball fans across the nation—including these young fans outside Brooklyn's Ebbets Field, the Dodgers' home before moving to Los Angeles in 1958.

BUBBA PHILLIPS

by Anthony Basich and Don Zminda

Noted for his versatility, John Melvin "Bubba" Phillips started games at third base and all three outfield positions for the 1959 American League champion White Sox. That year, he played 117 games and had 379 at-bats with five home runs, 40 RBIs, and a .264 average while batting anywhere from the second to the eighth slot in manager Al Lopez's lineup. Phillips provided some key hits during the season, including a 3-for-10 performance in the World Series. The '59 campaign was one of the most satisfying of Bubba's 10-year major-league career, which included stints with the Tigers and Indians along with the four years he spent with the White Sox.

Phillips was born in West Point, Mississippi, on February 24, 1928 (during his playing career his birth year was listed as 1930); his nickname was a childhood one bestowed by his brother. Bubba prided himself on his Southern heritage; Cleveland writer Hal Lebovitz observed in 1961 that Phillips referred to himself as "The Rebel" and liked to tease his Northern teammates, saying, "You Yankees don't know how to live. Come on down to my place. I'll show you how to enjoy life. We'll hunt and fish and take it easy."[1]

At Macon High School, where he was a standout in football, Phillips became the top prep scorer in the country with 235 points in only nine games, according to an article in the *Hattiesburg American*.[2] Phillips later downplayed that remarkable average of 26 points per game, telling Chicago scribe Bill Gleason, "We played small schools in our own class, and I had a lot of chances to carry the ball because I was the tailback. I kicked the extra points, too."[3]

Awarded a football scholarship to Southern Mississippi University (then known as Mississippi Southern College), Phillips ultimately excelled at both baseball and football. Though relatively inexperienced in baseball – back home in Macon, he had mostly played softball – Phillips led the Mississippi Southern baseball team in hits with 36 in 1948[4] and began drawing the interest of major-league scouts.

At the time, however, Phillips was still known primarily for his football prowess. Playing both cornerback and running back in his four-year college career, Phillips served as a team captain in his senior year of 1950 and was selected a second team Little All-American. He led the team with eight interceptions in 1949, and his Southern Mississippi record of 25 career interceptions from 1947 to 1950 still stands today. As a running back, Phillips rushed for 2,527 yards and 22 touchdowns in the 32 games he played for the Golden Eagles.[5] He loved the sport so much, he even once dreamed of becoming a football coach, according his 1958 Topps baseball card. And Hal Lebovitz commented during his major-league career that Phillips "keeps his recruiting eye open for his alma mater."[6]

"He was one of the greatest running backs I ever saw," Reed Green, former Southern Mississippi athletic director and football coach, told the *Hattiesburg American*. "He was so quick. He had ample speed, but he wasn't the fastest person. You just couldn't hit him." Green also said that it was he who introduced Phillips to the national pastime.[7]

Though Phillips was courted extensively by the San Francisco 49ers of the All America Football Conference – according to Bill Gleason, he actually signed a contract with the Niners but then never reported – baseball was the sport Bubba chose to play professionally. Due to the looser eligibility rules of the time, he began his pro baseball while still in college. Signing a contract with the Detroit Tigers organization in 1948, Phillips got into 11 games for the Stroudsburg (Pennsylvania) Poconos in the North Atlantic League, hitting .302. The following year, Phillips moved up to Thomasville, a Tigers farm club in the Class-D Georgia-Florida League, appearing in 138 games and hitting .329. He led the league with 29 outfield assists.

As he moved steadily through the Tigers' minor-league system, Phillips developed a reputation as the Detroit farm system's most promising player. A 1952 article by the Associated Press speculated that Phillips would certainly be a major leaguer the following year. The Tigers manager at the time, Red Rolfe, was so impressed by Phillips' abilities in spring training in '52 that he was tempted to keep the young outfield prospect up with the big-league club that season. However, Rolfe eventually decided that Phillips would be better served by playing one more season in the minors rather than wasting his talents as a bench player in the majors.

As it turned out, it would be three more years before Phillips made his Tigers debut. After a solid season (.291 with 14 homers) with the Tigers' International League farm team at Buffalo in 1952, Phillips was drafted and spent the next two years in the Army. He married the former Martha Green on December 1 of that year, and would remain with Martha until his death in 1993.

Phillips returned to Detroit for the 1955 season, and finally made his first major-league appearance on Opening Day against the Athletics, going 0-for-3 as the Tigers' starting left fielder in the first American League game ever played in Kansas City. During what would become his rookie season, Phillips was used primarily as a bench player, appearing in 95 games and accumulating 184 at-bats. His overall numbers didn't exactly impress – three home runs, 23 RBIs and a .234 batting average. His .304 slugging percentage showed less than promising power, especially for an outfielder. Among the 69 games he played in the field were four games at third base, although his two errors in those appearances showed he needed more time to hone his infield skills.

The 1955 Tigers finished fifth in the American League. In the offseason, Phillips was traded to the Chicago White Sox for veteran right-handed pitcher Virgil Trucks. Though Trucks would turn 39 in 1956, he was a 13-game winner for the Sox in '55, so it was apparent that the South Siders regarded Phillips pretty highly.

However, Phillips was again mainly relegated to the bench in his first full season with Chicago. He appeared in 67 games and had only 99 at-bats, although his average improved to .273. As an outfielder, Phillips just didn't hit well enough to play regularly, but his competent fielding skills and an ability to play all three outfield positions made him valuable as a defensive replacement. He made 24 starts in total, most of them in right field; he also started one game was at third base.

The 1957 season turned out to be something of a milestone for Phillips, as he was moved to third base to platoon with Fred Hatfield. Although he provided more offense at the hot corner (Hatfield only managed a .202 average in 1957), Phillips still needed to improve his skills as an infielder, committing 14 errors that season. Manager Al Lopez felt Phillips' fielding at third was quite adequate, given his initial unfamiliarity with the position. "He can do the job in the field," Lopez told the United Press in an April article. "He's proved that. He's got a good arm and can throw the ball across there fast."[8]

Phillips finished the year with 393 at-bats, hitting seven home runs and knocking in 42 runs. He also demonstrated that he could be a competent hitter as a full-time position player with his .270 average. He finished the season on a high note, batting .312 (49 for 157) in August and September.

Asked during the '57 season if Bubba was exceeding Chicago's expectations, Sox coach Don Gutteridge, a former major-league infielder who had helped Phillips make the transition from the outfield, told Bill Gleason, "He has done very well, but he didn't surprise me. I had confidence in him all along." Along with his improved play, the Sox admired the hard-nosed football mentality that Phillips brought to the game. "His football training made him a better competitor," Gutteridge commented. "He's the kind of kid who accepts coaching, and he's a kid who loves to play. Back in June he played every day with a very bad ankle that was bruised by a foul."[9] Sox vice president John Rigney added, "Remember that he's a fellow who played football as his major sport and picked up baseball as it came along. On certain plays that a kid who had played baseball all his life would make instinctively, Phillips doesn't know what to do. But he's learning all the time and he has a lot of guts. He gives us the strongest arm we've had at third base since Bob Kennedy's younger days."[10]

But after that breakthrough in '57, the 1958 season was not quite as favorable to Phillips. After getting off to a slow start at bat, Phillips was rounding into his 1957 hitting form when he broke his right foot tripping over first base at Fenway Park on June 8. The injury kept him out of the lineup for six weeks and cut down on his overall playing time, resulting in only 260 at-bats and 72 starts. Phillips also had a challenger at third base in veteran Billy Goodman, who took over at third while Phillips was out and batted .299 in 116 games.

In 1959, Phillips split time with Goodman, starting 86 games at third while also getting 17 starts in the outfield. He had a fine season, highlighted by some big hits for the pennant-winning Sox. On May 10 against Cleveland, in the first game of a doubleheader at home, Phillips tied the score with a home run in the bottom of the eighth inning. With the score tied 4-4 in the bottom of the 11th, Phillips singled to center and brought the winning run home with his third RBI of the game. Phillips also batted in the game-winning run against the Senators on consecutive days (August 21 and 22). The White Sox went on to win the American League flag by five games over the Indians and faced the Los Angeles Dodgers in the World Series.

Splitting time with Goodman, Phillips started Games Two, Five, and Six of the Series and had one hit in all three starts. However, he neither scored nor drove in any runs as Chicago fell to the Dodgers in six games.

Despite the fact that the White Sox had just won their first pennant in 40 years, team president Bill Veeck felt that the club needed an infusion of power in order to repeat, and also wanted to bring longtime Sox favorite Minnie Minoso back to the South Side. On December 6 Phillips was traded to Cleveland along with Norm Cash and Johnny Romano for Minoso, Dick Brown, Don Ferrarese, and Jake Striker. Three days later, the Sox found their replacement at the hot corner by acquiring Gene Freese from the Philadelphia Phillies for outfield prospect Johnny Callison.

During his time in Cleveland, Phillips enjoyed his most productive years as a professional ballplayer, although the success was not immediate. In 1960, Phillips had a difficult year with the Indians, hitting only .207 in 304 at-bats. It was the lowest batting average in his 10-year career, and resulted in Phillips losing starts at third to Ken Aspromonte, whom Cleveland acquired on May 15 of that year. On that very day, Phillips saw his batting average sink to .175.

Yet Phillips rebounded significantly in 1961, putting together his best major-league season. He led all American League third basemen with 18 home runs and collected 72 RBIs in 546 at-bats. His slugging percentage was .408 -- the only year he would ever surpass the .400 mark. The season was highlighted by the only two grand slams of Phillips' career. The first came on April 24 against Milt Pappas of the Baltimore Orioles, propelling the Indians to a 5-1 victory. On August 3 he got some sweet revenge against the White Sox, clearing the bases against Frank Baumann in the bottom of the first in a game the Sox eventually came back to win, 8-6. Phillips also won praise for his defensive work. Sizing up a crop of American League third sackers who included glove wizards Brooks Robinson and Clete Boyer, Mel McGaha, a Tribe coach in 1961 who was promoted to manager the next year, asserted that "Bubba Phillips is as good as any third baseman, if not better."[11]

For a time in '61, Phillips even served as the Tribe's cleanup hitter. "Nothing bothers the boy," Indians

Versatile Bubba Phillips was the White Sox' primary third baseman for most of the 1959 season, but he could also handle all three outfield positions.

manager Jimmy Dykes said of him. "Just watch him between games of a doubleheader. He lays back on the bench, eating an ice-cream stick. He can relax."[12]

Though his success in 1961 won him a lot of praise, Phillips remained the same unassuming player he had always been. "You can write anything about me you want. Just don't ask me for quotes," he told Hal Lebovitz. "I don't like to pop off. If I tell you what's going through my mind and you print it, I might go zero-for-four the next day and I'd sound like a pop-off." Despite his quiet demeanor, Phillips had a reputation as a bit of a practical joker. Lebovitz described how Phillips hid a rookie reporter's typewriter, then enjoyed watching the scribe searching desperately for his machine.[13]

In 1962, Phillips had another good year, though he could not match the power surge of the previous season, hitting only 10 home runs while knocking in 54 runs. His average also slipped from .264 in 1961 to .258. However, he continued to earn praise for his glove work at third base. Despite the two solid years as the Indians' third baseman, Cleveland decided to go in another direction by trading Phillips to his original major-league team, the Detroit Tigers, on November 27, 1962, in exchange for pitchers Ron Nischwitz and Gordon Seyfried. Cleveland was making room on the roster for rookie third baseman Max Alvis.

To add insult to injury, Phillips was publicly humiliated in the Cleveland press when the Indians' former vice president, Nate Dolin, told a newspaper that Bubba "doesn't have the ability you want from your third baseman. Phillips is just good enough to lose with."[14] However, the Tigers seemed happy to acquire Phillips. Detroit general manager Jim Campbell, who was being criticized for adding too many older players, responded by saying, "Take Bubba Phillips at 32. He's in better shape than a lot of players at 27 or 28."[15] Of course, Phillips was actually 34, not 32, but veteran baseball executive Paul Richards praised the deal, saying he'd like to have Phillips.

In 1963, his first season back in Detroit, Phillips shared time at third base with rookie Don Wert. Bubba replicated his offensive production from his pre-Cleveland days, hitting five home runs with 45 RBIs in 128 games. His .310 slugging percentage was the lowest since 1960, although he did achieve a career-best six stolen bases and led the league with 10 sacrifice flies.

Writer Charlie Haeffner, who was a teenager growing up in the Detroit suburb of Bloomfield Hills, often spent time with Phillips during that summer of 1963, learning the finer points of baseball from the veteran major leaguer. "He was a grown boy," Haeffner wrote about Phillips, who befriended Charlie after Haeffner's parents met Bubba and his wife during a trip to Mississippi. "He loved to play with me and my friends in our lake, especially when we played ball-tag with a tennis ball. Man, you didn't want to be hit by that thing when Bubba threw it. It was like a rifle-shot."[16]

With Wert taking over at third in 1964, Phillips was relegated to the bench again, stepping up to the plate only 99 times in 46 games. "I must say that while I and my friends really disliked Don Wert for taking over the Tigers' starting third-base job," said, Charlie Haeffner. ". . . Bubba was accepting of it. He said Wert was a nice young fellow, and wished him well."[17] Phillips' last major-league game was on September 18, 1964, when he came in as a pinch-runner against the Indians during the bottom of the ninth with two out. The next batter flied out as the Tigers lost 3-1. This last appearance came 12 days after his final at-bat – a pinch-hit strikeout against Washington.

After retiring from the game, Phillips worked in real estate, leasing apartment buildings, and selling property throughout southern Mississippi. He also worked as a tennis instructor, teaching classes at his alma mater as well as for the city of Hattiesburg. In his spare time, Phillips took up golf.

Phillips even had a brief stint in the movies, playing Coach Hardy for a 1981 biopic on Satchel Paige. The film was entitled, *Don't Look Back* and starred Louis Gossett Jr. as the legendary pitcher.

In the fall of 1992, Phillips had open-heart surgery. The following summer, he collapsed while loading his pickup truck at home, and subsequently died of a heart attack, on June 22, 1993. He was 65 years old and a man warmly regarded by those who knew men. Wrote Cleveland sportswriter Franklin Gibbons back in 1962, "I have always been an admirer of Bubba Phillips, who was one of the men they had in mind when they invented that red-blooded sports phrase, 'He came to play.'"

Notes

1. Hal Lebovitz, "Blasting Bubba: A Hubba-Hubba Guy With Mace," *The Sporting News*, July 19, 1961.
2. Bubba Phillips file, National Baseball Hall of Fame library
3. William (Red) Gleason, "The Hubba Bubba Boy and the Sudden Sox," *Baseball Digest*, August 1957.
4. University of Southern Mississippi Alumni website: http://www.southernmissalumni.com/s/995indexaspx?sid=995&gid=1&pgid=623&cid=1232&ecid=1232&ciid=1210&crid=0
5. "Ex-White Sox Bubba Phillips Dies," *Chicago Tribune*, June 23, 1993.
6. Lebovitz.
7. Phillips Baseball Hall of Fame file.
8. "Phillips Now Clicking for Chisox at Bat," United Press article, April 27, 1957.
9. Gleason.
10. Ibid.
11. Bob Dolgan, "McGaha Rates Injun Infield Best in A.L. – With Gloves," *The Sporting News*, April 25, 1962.
12. Lebovitz,
13. Lebovitz.
14. "Dolin Would Deal Phillips at Once If He Were Boss," *The Sporting News*, December 1, 1961.
15. Watson Spoelstra, "Plenty of Mileage in Aging Bengals, Campbell Claims," *The Sporting News*, December 15, 1962.
16. E-Mail from Charlie Haeffner to Don Zminda, May 27, 2008.
17. Haeffner.

BILLY PIERCE

By Rob Neyer

Talk about your quick-starting careers.

Billy Pierce didn't play organized baseball until he was 15. Born in Detroit on April 2, 1927, Pierce attended Highland Park (Michigan) High School, but originally he was not a pitcher. As he recalled to Mark Liptak, "I was a first baseman when I was 14, and the kid who was a pitcher on our team left and went to another club because they had better looking uniforms. We were only about a week from starting play in our league and I threw hard, so I became the pitcher. I was wild in those days!"[1]

In 1944, still only 17, Pierce (whose full name is Walter William Pierce) was chosen as Detroit's representative in the inaugural All American Boys Game, sponsored by *Esquire* magazine and played at the Polo Grounds in New York. The two teams were managed by Connie Mack and Carl Hubbell. Also among the nearly 18,000 in attendance were Babe Ruth, Joe McCarthy, and former New York Mayor Jimmy Walker.

And the star of the game? Billy Pierce, a/k/a "Mr. Zero." From the account in the next day's *New York Times*:

> In 17-year-old Bill Pierce, a southpaw from Detroit, who, because of the many shutouts credited to him, is called "Mr. Zero," Mack was favored with a young hurler with unlimited potentialities.
>
> Pierce, endowed with respect-demanding speed and a sharp-breaking curve, twirled the first six innings for the winning combination, yielded three hits and fanned six. George Worgul of Richmond Hill High School and Mason Leeper of Dallas, N.C., who finished, also were impressive, but neither won the fancy of the crowd as much as Pierce did.[2]

Pierce picked up the win in the East's 8-0 victory, along with most-valuable-player honors.

Pierce had already signed with his hometown Tigers, and in 1945 he went to spring training and started the season on the major-league roster (in 1945, there were a great number of very young and very old players on major-league rosters). Pierce later recalled, "For the first six weeks of the season I sat on the Tigers' bench and didn't pitch. Then I was sent to Buffalo. I returned to the Tigers before September 1, so I was on Detroit for three-fifths of the year and we won the world championship. I pitched only 10 innings all year and didn't pitch in the World Series – but I was eligible to pitch and received a ring at the age of 18!"[3]

In 1946, with the veterans back from the war, Pierce went back to the minors, but pitched only 10 games for Buffalo before hurting his back in June. "I was in the Ford Hospital for a while," he remembered. "During the winter they would bake me in an oven three days a week. They decided the pain came from my being a boy doing a man's work. So I rested."[4]

In 1947 Pierce returned to Buffalo, where Paul Richards had taken over as catcher-manager. It wasn't the first time they'd met. Richards later told Donald Honig:

> Billy Pierce is quite a pitcher. You know, I first ran into him when I was playing with Detroit in 1945 and he was working out with them. In fact, he got into a few games that year. He was just a kid. His father owned a drugstore about a block from where I was living. I'd go in now and then to buy something, and there was this kid clerking behind the counter. I never paid any attention to him. Then out at the ball park we had this little left-hander who I'd warm up occasionally. One day he walked up to me on the field and said, "You know, you won't even speak to me when you come into our drugstore."
>
> "What are you talking about?" I asked.
>
> "That's my father's drugstore," he said. "You were in there last night."
>
> I took a good hard look at him and, sure enough, he was the clerk.[5]

Pierce pitched well at Buffalo in '47 and later said

of Richards, "Being with Paul Richards in 1947 was one of the greatest things to happen to me. He didn't work me too hard because he was afraid of stirring up a back ailment I had in 1946. He nursed me along carefully and even caught me himself in two games when he had a broken finger."[6] Pierce started only 23 games (and relieved in five more), but his 14-8 record and 3.87 ERA were enough to get him back to the majors in 1948, all of which he spent with the big club. But he rarely pitched, just 55 innings in 22 games. And after the season, the shocking news …

> In November, I went over to my fiancée's house. We turned on the radio and I learned from a disk jockey that I had been traded to the White Sox. I was traded for Aaron Robinson and 10 grand because the Tigers wanted a left-handed-hitting catcher who could take advantage of the short porch in right field. The Tigers wanted to give the Sox Ted Gray instead of me, but Chicago wouldn't go for it. . . . It was a bad shock to be traded from Detroit.[7]

For the first few years he was in the majors, Pierce – all 5 feet 10 inches and 160 pounds of him – just reared back and threw. And he certainly could throw hard. As Joe DiMaggio supposedly said after batting against Pierce, "That little so-and-so is a marvel. So little, and all that speed. And I mean speed! He got me out of there on a fastball in the ninth that I'd have needed a telescope to see."[8]

But early on, the speed was enough only to make Pierce a *good* pitcher. In 1949 and '50 with Chicago, he posted better-than-average ERAs (3.88 and 3.98) and won 19 games for a lousy team. But he also walked more batters than he struck out (granted, in that era such a feat was not particularly uncommon). He wasn't yet a *great* pitcher.

In 1951, Paul Richards entered Billy Pierce's life again, this time as the White Sox' new manager.

Richards got a lot of credit in the 1940s when Hal Newhouser became one of the American League's best pitchers, and likewise he would get a lot of credit for Billy Pierce's becoming one of the league's best pitchers in the 1950s. According to Richards, "I worked a little with him on his windup to help his delivery and convinced him that he had to throw a slider and an occasional change of pace, and that was all he needed."[9]

In Richards' first season in Chicago, Pierce went 15-14 with a 3.03 ERA. The most striking improvement was in his control of the strike zone. In 391 innings over the previous two seasons, Pierce had walked 249 hitters while striking out 213. Under Richards, Pierce's strikeout rate fell slightly (and temporarily, as it turned out), but his walk rate fell significantly, from one walk every two innings to one walk every three.

Forty years later, Pierce said of his transformation,

> "I learned to control my fastball better and, at Richards' request, learned a third pitch to go with my fastball and curve – a slider. Developing the slider helped me tremendously because it gave me a third out pitch. I threw it almost as hard as my fastball, but I could throw it for strikes better than the fastball or good curve. . . . Richards made me work on it, and it took me about two years before it was consistent."[10]

Pierce didn't really begin to refine his slider until near the end of the 1951 season, and the change really showed up in 1952, when he went 15-12 with a 2.57 ERA. Then he got off to a fast start in 1953. He started the All-Star Game that year (and would start in 1955 and '56, too), and in three innings the only blemish was Stan Musial's single to center field. He finished that season with 18 wins, and for the first time he led the American League in something (strikeouts, with 186). It wouldn't be the only time, though. In 1955, he led the league with a 1.97 ERA; he was the only ERA title qualifier from 1947 to 1962 to post an ERA lower than 2.00. In 1957, he led the league with 20 wins. And beginning in 1956, he led the American League in complete games in three straight seasons.

He did all this while pitching for the White Sox. He also threw four one-hitters, and on June 27, 1958, he just missed becoming the first left-handed pitcher in major-league history to twirl a perfect game. Facing the Washington Senators before 11,300 fans at Comiskey Park, Pierce retired the first 26 batters he faced and owned a 3-0 lead with two outs in the top of the ninth inning. But Washington manager Cookie Lavagetto – who, as a pinch-hitter, famously broke up a World Series no-hitter in 1947 – sent up a pinch-hitter, Ed Fitz Gerald, and Fitz Gerald doubled. He then struck out Albie Pearson to end the game.

• BILLY PIERCE •

In 1982 Pierce told sportswriter Bob Vanderberg:

> "Fitz Gerald was a first-ball, fastball hitter. So we threw him a curveball away. And he hit it down rightfield line for a hit. . . . I didn't feel that badly about it – really not that badly. It didn't mean that much – at the moment. In later years, I wished probably that it had happened. It would've been nice if it had happened."[11]

The 1958 season (17-11, 2.68 ERA) would be Pierce's last great one. In '59 his ERA jumped nearly a full run, to 3.62, and he went 14-15. Most disappointingly for Pierce, after starting 33 games during the regular season, he wasn't given a single starting assignment in the World Series, instead pitching four (scoreless) relief innings.

Why didn't Pierce start in the Series? Early Wynn started three games, which made sense because Wynn had won 22 games during the season. Bob Shaw started twice, which made sense because he'd gone 18-6 with a 2.69 ERA during the season. The other start went to Dick Donovan, who'd gone 9-10 with a 3.66 ERA.

There are two obvious questions: 1) Why did Donovan start instead of Pierce; and 2) While starting Wynn three times wasn't odd in those days, why did he make his third start on just two days' rest? Wynn's second start, in Game Four, ended abruptly in the third inning, undone by five consecutive miscues and three errors. When he was yanked by manager Al Lopez, he'd probably thrown between 50 and 60 pitches. Today, you wouldn't see a pitcher come back and start three days later. But things were different 50 years ago, and Wynn was one of the toughest customers around.

As for why Pierce didn't start Game Three in Los Angeles, David Gough and Jim Bard quoted White Sox vice president Chuck Comiskey in their book *Little Nel: The Nellie Fox Story*:

> Charles Comiskey had hoped, and even appealed to Lopez, to give Billy Pierce a start in the Series. "Lopez wanted to pitch

The winningest left-hander in White Sox history, Billy Pierce won 20 games twice and was the starting pitcher in three All-Star games.

> righthanders against the Dodgers in the Coliseum because of their strength from the right side of the plate. I can't deny that, but Pierce had been such a great pitcher for the White Sox for so many years that I felt he deserved a shot. I said, 'Al, please pitch Billy.' He said, 'I can't.' I was disappointed, but I didn't interfere with the field manager."[12]

So Dick Donovan – rather than Pierce – had started Game Three. And he pitched well; when he left with two outs in the seventh, the score was still 0-0. Donovan did get the loss after his relief gave up a two-run single. But considering that the White Sox scored only one run in the game – the final score was 3-1 – it's hard to blame the loss on Donovan.

Many years later, White Sox outfielder Al Smith told interviewer Danny Peary, "I was surprised that

Al Lopez didn't start Billy Pierce. We all knew why Lopez didn't pitch him, but we never told anyone and I won't say now."[13]

Maybe it's not really so complicated. For his part, Pierce blamed a hip injury that cost him three weeks late in the season. "And then, when the World Series came about," Pierce told interviewer Mike Mandel, "Lopez didn't figure that I'd recovered well enough to start, so I just relieved. . . . [H]e didn't figure that the hip would hold up."[14]

(Coincidentally or not, shortly before going on the disabled list with the hip injury, Pierce had pitched 16 innings in a 1-1 tie against the Orioles. He didn't last more than four innings in either of his next two starts, then was out of action for three weeks.)

Al Smith's support isn't surprising, because Pierce was as well-liked as anyone on the team. He didn't drink but once said:

> "If another player wanted to drink, fine. I could go along and have a Coke. I never had problems with other ballplayers, where if I didn't drink I wasn't part of the group. They understood that I'd rather be at the movies."[15]

Pierce and Nellie Fox, his longtime roommate, were considered the leaders on the club, and Pierce was for years the White Sox' union player representative. Later Pierce pitched for San Francisco, and Giants pitching coach Larry Jansen said about him, "Never had a bad word about anybody – the nicest man you'd ever want to meet."[16]

Oddly, after winning 14 games with a 3.62 ERA in 1959, Pierce won 14 games with a 3.62 ERA in 1960. And a worrying trend continued. After leading the American League in complete games in 1956, '57, and '58, Pierce had completed only a dozen of his starts in 1959 (still eighth most in the league), and in '60 he completed only eight starts and his innings fell below 200 for only the second time since 1949. In 1961, he started only 23 games, his fewest since joining the White Sox.

The word around the American League was that Pierce was damaged goods, that his hip injury was chronic and that his sore shoulder wasn't going to get better. On November 30, 1961, the White Sox traded Pierce and Don Larsen to the Giants for pitchers Eddie Fisher and Dom Zanni and outfielder Bob Farley. Pierce, perhaps still hurting from the 1959 Series, said, "I am not surprised. But it's a rotten trick and I will make Al Lopez sorry he did it."[17]

In the spring of 1962, Pierce pitched like a man with a hip injury and a sore shoulder. Nevertheless, he broke camp with a slot in the rotation, and in his first start he beat the Cincinnati Reds, 7-2. Pierce also won his second decision, and his third, and he just kept on winning, running his record to 8-0 in his eighth start, on June 1, before finally losing a close one (4-3) to the Chicago Cubs on June 7. Pierce's luck was even worse in his next start. Pitching against the Reds in Cincinnati, he was spiked in the first inning and wound up taking a dozen (or more) stitches. He next pitched on July 15, got hammered in three-plus innings, and didn't start again until August 2, when he re-assumed his spot in the Giants' rotation.

Maybe all that rest helped him. On September 26, the last scheduled Wednesday of the regular season, Pierce beat the St. Louis Cardinals to keep the Giants two games behind the first-place Los Angeles Dodgers. On Thursday, both contenders lost. On Friday, the Dodgers lost to the Cardinals and the Giants were rained out. On Saturday, the Dodgers lost again and the Giants split a doubleheader with Houston. And finally, on Sunday the Dodgers lost, 1-0, and the Giants won, 2-1, leaving the contenders tied at the conclusion of the schedule. Just as in 1951, the clubs would play a best-of-three playoff series to decide the National League pennant.

The Giants that season had an odd pitching staff. Among the four pitchers who started more than 15 games, nobody had an ERA higher than 3.53 (Billy O'Dell) or lower than 3.36 (future Hall of Famer Juan Marichal). In the middle were Pierce (3.49) and Jack Sanford (3.43). The playoff series would begin on Monday, October 1, the day after the season ended. Sanford and Marichal had started in the Saturday doubleheader, O'Dell on Sunday.

That left Billy Pierce to face Sandy Koufax, who'd missed most of the last two months of the season with a gruesome hand injury but finished with the lowest ERA (2.54) in the National League. Koufax still wasn't really healthy enough to pitch but it probably wouldn't have mattered, as Pierce pitched a three-hitter to shut out the Dodgers, 8-0 (and run his Candlestick Park record to 12-0). By most accounts, Pierce was relying on slow stuff by the time he joined the Giants, but he could still throw hard when he wanted to. Watching that first playoff game from the press box, longtime National League umpire Babe Pinelli exclaimed, "Look at him fire that fast one! He's been in so many clutch games that they're nothing to

• BILLY PIERCE •

him!"[18] (According to Pierce, his fastball was still his best pitch.)

The playoff series moved south to Dodger Stadium for the second game. The Giants were ahead 5-0 in the sixth inning, but the Dodgers exploded for seven runs to take the lead, then scored once in the bottom of the ninth to break a 7-7 tie and force a third game.

What followed was a near-replay of what had happened 11 years earlier between the same two teams (but on the other side of the continent). Just as they had in the third playoff game in 1951, the Dodgers led after eight innings. And just as they had in 1951, the Giants jumped ahead in the ninth. But this time the Giants were the road team, so the Dodgers would have one last chance. Juan Marichal had pitched the first seven innings for the Giants, and was replaced by Don Larsen in the eighth. Larsen was bumped in the top of the ninth for a pinch-hitter.

Pierce had pitched a complete game just two days earlier, but now Giants manager Alvin Dark called on his 35-year-old lefty once more. He retired the Dodgers in order, and the Giants, 6-4 victors, were the National League champions. "It was the biggest thrill of my life, getting those batters 1-2-3,"[19] Pierce told Danny Peary. Lee Walls made the final out, lifting an easy fly ball to center field. Just before making the catch, Willie Mays reminded himself to save the ball for Pierce. But the moment got the better of him and he "changed his mind and heaved it into the center-field bleachers in a cathartic act of pure, unadulterated ecstasy."[20]

Pierce pitched well against the Yankees in the ensuing World Series. He tossed six shutout innings in Game Three before faltering in the seventh, then beat the Yankees 5-2 with a three-hitter in Game Six. The Giants lost Game Seven, of course, but Pierce was one of the big stories that fall. Including the playoff series against the Dodgers, Pierce pitched in four postseason games, won two of them and saved another, posted a 1.44 ERA, and allowed only 11 hits and three walks in 25 innings.

In the Giants' 1963 home opener, Pierce ran his Candlestick Park winning streak to 14 straight (including the World Series), tossing a shutout against Houston. (According to Charles Einstein, Pierce got some help in his home games. In *Willie's Time*, Einstein wrote that Giants groundskeeper Matty Schwab had a habit of "wetting down the grass on the left side of the infield hours before game time on days when Pierce was scheduled to pitch. This had the effect of slowing down ground balls that righthanded batsmen would get off lefthanded pitching, reducing the number of hits that would go through to the outfield."[21])

The streak finally ended four days later with a 4-0 loss to the Cubs. And it was all downhill from there. Pierce finished 1963 with 3 wins, 11 losses, and a 4.27 ERA, his highest since he was a rookie in 1948.

In December the Giants waived Pierce, soon to be 37 years old. He wanted to keep pitching and thought he would, saying, "I'm sure there is at least one big-league team that wants me."[22] There was; Pierce again went to camp with the Giants, earned a roster spot and signed a new contract on Opening Day. But Bobby Bolin was ready for a spot in the rotation and the Giants had traded for Bob Hendley, who had good stuff and was a dozen years younger than Pierce. So the veteran lefty coming off a lousy season went to the bullpen and pitched effectively (2.20 ERA), though rarely in key situations (four saves, two wins, zero losses in relief).

On September 10, he started for the first time in more than a year, and beat the Dodgers with 7⅔ strong innings. Afterward, somebody asked him if he knew how many strikeouts he had. "Right to the dot," he replied. "I had 1,994 going into the game. I added three more and that leaves me three short of the 2,000 mark."[23] But Pierce wouldn't get another start, and in fact would pitch just once more. On October 3, the next-to-last day of the season, he picked up two K's in three innings of relief, which left him just one short of 2,000 career strikeouts (and in 15th place on the all-time list at the time, between Hall of Famers Dazzy Vance and Red Ruffing).

And that's where Pierce's quest ended. Though he'd gone 3-0 with a 2.20 ERA in '64, he announced his retirement on the season's final day. "My children were growing up and I wanted to be with them," Pierce told Mike Mandel. "I didn't want to be traveling all over the country all the time."[24] He finished his 18-year major league career with 211 victories, 169 losses, and an ERA of 3.27.

Billy and his wife, Gloria (known as Goldie), were married in 1949 and had three children, sons William and Robert and daughter Patti. Before his last year with the Giants, Pierce had moved his family back to the Chicago area. He co-owned an Oldsmobile and Cadillac dealership there for two years, worked briefly as a stockbroker, and occasionally served as an unofficial scout for the White Sox (he's been credited with discovering Ron Kittle). In the early 1970s,

Pierce caught on with the Continental Envelope Company, and worked for the company in sales and public relations for 23 years before retiring in 1997.

Also in 1997, the Nellie Fox Society – of which Pierce was a member in good standing – saw its namesake inducted into the Hall of Fame. The organization was promptly renamed the Billy Pierce Society. Ten years later, Pierce was at U.S. Cellular Field for the unveiling of a bronze sculpture in his likeness on the center-field concourse, joining Carlton Fisk, Minnie Minoso, and his 1959 teammates Fox and Luis Aparicio. He died of gallbladder cancer on July 31, 2015. Said White Sox chairman Jerry Reinsdorf in tribute to Pierce: "He epitomized class, not just as a ballplayer on those great Go-Go White Sox teams of the 1950s, but as a gentleman and as a human being who devoted so much of his life to helping others."[25]

Notes

1. Mark Liptak, "Flashing Back with Billy Pierce," http://www.whitesoxinteractive.com/rwas/index.php?category=11&id=1546
2. Louis Effrat, "East's Nine Wins In Boys' Game, 6-0," *New York Times*, August 8, 1944.
3. Danny Peary, editor, *We Played the Game: 65 Players Remember Baseball's Greatest Era, 1947-1964* (New York: Hyperion, 1994), 48.
4. Ibid., 48.
5. Donald Honig, *The Man in the Dugout: Fifteen Big League Managers Speak Their Minds* (Lincoln and London: University of Nebraska Press, 1977), 137-38.
6. Bruce Jacobs, *Baseball Stars of 1957* (New York: Lion Library Editions, 1957), 142.
7. Peary, 81.
8. Bill James and Rob Neyer, *The Neyer-James Guide to Pitchers: An Historical Compendium on Pitching, Pitchers and Pitches* (New York: Fireside, 2004), 104.
9. Honig, 138.
10. Peary, 168.
11. Bob Vanderberg, *Sox: From Lane and Fain to Zisk and Fisk* (Chicago: Chicago Review Press, 1984), 142.
12. David Gough and Jim Bard, *Little Nell: The Nellie Fox Story* (Bend Oregon: Maverick Publications, 2000), 208-09.
13. Peary, 458.
14. Mike Mandel, *SF Giants: An Oral History* (Santa Cruz: Mike Mandel, 1979), 108.
15. Peary, 105.
16. David Plaut, *Chasing October: The Dodgers-Giants Pennant Race of 1962* (South Bend, Indiana: Diamond Communications, 1994), 126.
17. James-Neyer, 106.
18. Ibid., 106.
19. Peary, 540.
20. Ibid., 186.
21. Charles Einstein, *Willie's Time: A Memoir* (New York: J.P. Lippincott Company, 1979), 163-64.
22. "Pierce Let Go By Giants, Certain He Can Still Win," *The Sporting News*, December 14, 1963: 17.
23. "Pierce Knows Exact Major Whiff Total – Just Three Short of 2,000," *The Sporting News*, September 26, 1964: 17.
24. Mandel, 112.
25. Fred Mitchell and Paul Sullivan, "Former White Sox Great Billy Pierce Dies," *Chicago Tribune*, July 31, 2015.

CLAUDE RAYMOND

By Alexandre Pratt

If it is true that every boy born in the United States comes with a baseball glove on his hand, in Quebec children are more likely to enter the world wearing a pair of ice skates. Claude Raymond, the first baseball player from Quebec ever selected for a major-league All-Star Game, was no exception.

Like all young Quebecers in the 1940s, Raymond spent his days on the neighborhood rink, where he would seek to imitate the moves of Maurice (Rocket) Richard, the star of the National Hockey League's Montreal Canadiens. "During the Christmas holidays," he says, "I would leave the house early in the morning with my skates already on my feet. At noon, I didn't even take them off for lunch. My mother would cover the floor with newspapers right to the table. At suppertime, it was the same thing."[1]

As a boy born in Saint-Jean-sur-Richelieu on May 7, 1937, Raymond was nourished on hockey day and night. But he was also realistic: he recognized that he would never score 50 goals in 50 games, as the Rocket did in 1945. On the other hand, there was baseball, where he could literally tear the cover off the ball. He hit with such force that, at a very early age, even though he was right-handed, he was made to bat from the left side, to ensure that his line drives would not break the stained-glass windows in the church next to the playground.[2]

Raymond was fortunate to grow up in a town where baseball, along with hockey, had long been considered a religion. Thanks to its proximity to the U. S. border, Saint-Jean was one of the first municipalities in Quebec to take up baseball. In 1869, the Crescent became the first team to be formed off the Island of Montreal.[3] Saint-Jean later placed a club in the Provincial League, when in 1898 the French-speaking community put together an amateur circuit to counter the professional English-speakers of the Montreal Royals.

But it was in the 1940s that baseball in Saint-Jean experienced its golden age. Following the end of World War II, as military personnel returned home, a surplus of baseball players developed. Many were drawn to the Mexican League, then seeking to become something of another major league. When this venture failed, these players – some of them now banished from Organized Baseball – followed the lead of Roland Gladu and Jean-Pierre Roy and signed on with the Provincial League, which was not part of Organized Baseball's structure at the time. Between 1947 and 1949 Saint-Jean welcomed a number of stars from elsewhere, including Roy, Myron Hayworth of the old St. Louis Browns, the Japanese-Canadian Kaz Suga, and such veterans from the Negro Leagues as Quincy Barbee and Terris McDuffie.

The Braves were the main attraction in town and Claude Raymond was one of their most loyal fans. He says in his autobiography that by the age of 7 he was earning his way into games by returning foul balls that he caught outside the stadium. He soon became a popcorn vendor, then team mascot, and by the time he was 12 was occasionally even asked to pitch batting practice.[4]

It was in this postwar environment, in a town passionate about baseball, that Claude Raymond came into his own. In 1953, while trying out with the Drummondville Royals of the Provincial League, he began to stand out from the others. The Royals tried to sign him on the spot, but were forced to withdraw the offer when they discovered that their brilliant pitcher was not 17, as he had claimed, but 15 years old.[5]

Raymond next tried his chances with a Montreal junior league, regularly hitch-hiking back and forth from Saint-Jean. After he had pitched two no-hit, no-run games, the scouts started to notice him. Following his second season of junior ball, he signed a contract with the Brooklyn Dodgers organization. But the transaction had to be canceled because Raymond was still in school and the Dodgers had forgotten to seek the special permission required to sign him. Finally, Milwaukee Braves and former Provincial League star Roland Gladu succeeded in getting his name on the dotted line.

In March 1955, Raymond struck out for the United States along with several other French-speaking protégés signed by Gladu (Yvan Dubois, Ron Piché, and Bobby Laforest). Raymond, who spoke only French, set himself the goal of learning

• 175 •

10 new English words every day.⁶ Unlike many French-Canadians who, in the 1940s, '50s, and '60s, returned to Quebec because of problems they encountered with the language, Raymond did not experience homesickness.

Soon he was working his way up through the minor leagues and establishing himself as a relief pitcher, a specialization rare for that time. His first assignment was with West Palm Beach in the Class-D Florida State League, where he posted a 13-12 record with a strong 2.60 ERA, starting 27 games and throwing a full 194 innings. Advancing to Class B with Evanston in the Three-I League, in 1956 he was converted to relief and started just four games, but ending the year with a 9-3 mark and a 2.57 ERA. In 1957, at Jacksonville (South Atlantic League, Class A), he set a league record for the number of games pitched (54, only one of which was a start). But in 1958, an inflammation of the shoulder put the brakes on his development and the Braves decided not to protect him from the intra-league draft. "I was so hoping I would be drafted that I spent two hours in prayer at Notre-Dame-Auxiliatrice Church," he recounts in his autobiography.⁷

Raymond was drafted by the Chicago White Sox and soon received a call from owner Chuck Comiskey, welcoming him to the White Sox organization. His prayers now answered, Raymond had every reason to believe that his career was about to receive a new shot in the arm. And a few weeks later he found himself at training camp in Tampa in 1959 with Nellie Fox as his roommate, working under the watchful eye of manager Al Lopez. He remembers that Lopez, "at one time, told everyone that I had the best curveball in the camp. All of a sudden the season started and I was in the major leagues!⁸

"It was a wonderful day for me. I never thought that I would reach the majors so quickly," he relates in his autobiography. "I spent a month with the White Sox. Manager Lopez called on my services three times. The first time was in relief in a lost cause situation against Kansas City. The first batter I faced was Bob Cerv ... and I hit him with my first pitch."⁹

Following the two innings of work in his April 15 debut, by mid-May Raymond had pitched only four innings and had given up four earned runs. "There was a possibility that the White Sox would cut John Callison, but, unfortunately, I was the one they released," he says in his autobiography.

In keeping with the rules governing the major-league draft, the Quebec pitcher was returned to the Braves. "I took comfort from the notion that the White Sox released me because they already possessed an excellent arsenal of pitchers, including Early Wynn, Billy Pierce, Bob Shaw, Dick Donovan, Turk Lown and Gerry Staley," he says.¹⁰

Now back in Triple A, at the Braves' Louisville farm team, the 22-year-old Raymond found himself in the company of three other Canadian players, Ron Piché, Georges Maranda, and Ken McKenzie. However, after only eight innings of work experienced another demotion, to Double-A Atlanta, where he finished the season ... as a right fielder!

After posting a 9-9 record for Sacramento of the Pacific Coast League in 1960, Raymond returned to the majors as a pitcher with the Milwaukee Braves in 1961. There he picked up his first win and also struck out two of his childhood idols, Dodgers Gil Hodges and Duke Snider. Unfortunately for Raymond, though, the Braves acquired veteran hurler Johnny Antonelli and Raymond was handed his ticket to Triple-A Vancouver. "I was so distraught that my parents, who were on holiday, came to Milwaukee to offer me encouragement," he says in his autobiography.¹¹

The return to the minors was difficult to accept. That winter Raymond considered stepping away from the game. "I was disillusioned. I wanted to recover my balance. I spent my time skiing and playing hockey. I was taking great risks. I don't know how many nasty falls I took on the hills that winter!"¹²

Nevertheless, in 1962 he went to spring training with the Braves and was called up in mid-June. He registered an earned run average of 2.74 in 26 games and was selected the organization's Rookie of the Year. However, when Bobby Bragan arrived as manager in 1963, things once again began sliding off the rails. Bragan thought he could win the championship with only eight or nine pitchers and Raymond found himself nailed to the bench for 27 straight days (as did Frank Funk, for 28 days).

"In those days Milwaukee was a superb town, very welcoming," he told a visiting group of Quebec journalists in 1998. "Among other benefits, we would receive a case of beer every week, courtesy of the most important employer in the city (Miller). ... We were supplied an automobile, full of gas, a carton of cigarettes, dairy products. We could even arrange to have our clothing cleaned for free."¹³

• CLAUDE RAYMOND •

At the end of the 1963 season the National League held a special draft to reinforce the feeble New York Mets and Houston Colts. Raymond was drafted by Houston (the price was $30,000) and enjoyed one of his best seasons. (5-5, 2.82). "I was living at Surrey House and Kenny Rogers was my neighbor. At night, he was a singer in a club with the Bobby Doyle trio. You required a key to enter after midnight and the players went there to listen to him. On Sundays, everything was shut down and we would party out by the side of the pool,"[14] recounted Raymond at the 2007 Western Festival in Saint-Tite, Quebec, where he reconnected with Rogers.

In 1965, still with Houston, Raymond started seven games before ending the year in the bullpen with a respectable 7-4, 2.90 record. At midseason in 1966, now serving as a short-relief specialist, he led both leagues in earned–run average (1.35). Dodgers manager Walter Alston selected Raymond for the All-Star Game squad, a first for a Quebec-born player. (At that time, the teams were chosen by the managers, coaches, and players.) "I was not allowed to tell anybody. I did call my parents and they drove to St. Louis," he said in 1992.[15]

However, much like the situation when his parents had driven to Milwaukee, Raymond remained on the sidelines. Alston was content to stick with only four pitchers that day. "I was disappointed but that was the way things were back then. Alston did have me warm up when Koufax threw three consecutive balls in the third inning. It was 117 degrees on the field (in St. Louis), and so that didn't take me very long."[16]

This was the high point of Raymond's career. In 1967, he returned to the Braves, by now in Atlanta, in exchange for Wade Blasingame. This time, changing clubhouses only involved a few steps, as Atlanta was visiting Houston that weekend. Raymond earned a save on the Friday night and was the winning pitcher on Saturday. He ended the season with Atlanta in fine fashion (4-1, 2.65, after going 0-4 for Houston) and was equally outstanding in 1968 (3-5, 2.83).

On February 1, 1969, Raymond married Rita Duval. As was fitting, the wedding cake was shaped to look like a ballpark. On May 16 the Braves sent him into the fray at Jarry Park against the new Montreal Expos. He recalled, "I was nervous when the stadium announcer called out: 'And now, pitching for the Atlanta Braves … number 36 … from Saint-Jean, Quebec … Claude Raymond.'"[17]

Claude Raymond made his major league debut with the White Sox 1959, but he won his greatest fame a decade later as an All-Star reliever with the Montreal Expos in his native Quebec.

"I have never felt more at home than I did that night. I was very nervous. For the very first time, I was shaking on the mound. I actually dropped the ball, my emotions were so powerful." In the end, after the right-handed reliever had earned an 11th-inning save, the spectators gave him a standing ovation. Then, on August 19, Raymond joined the Expos in a cash deal, becoming the first Quebecer to wear the team's multicolored uniform. (He was followed by Denis Boucher and Derek Aucoin in the 1990s.)

Although the Braves were in first place and the Expos in last place, Raymond was all smiles when he heard the news. "I was delighted to change teams. With Atlanta, I hardly pitched at all. And for a relief pitcher there is nothing worse than a lack of action."[18] Further, he would now be living closer to both his and Rita's families. At the time she was five months pregnant with their daughter Natalie.

Following a nondescript end of the season, Raymond dreaded spring training in 1970. He was experiencing arthritis in the index finger on his right hand – his pitching hand – and manager Gene Mauch seldom turned to him. In effect Raymond became the last pitcher called upon during spring training and the last to be utilized in the regular season.

But bit by bit, as other Expos relievers struggled, Raymond's workload increased. At the beginning of June he retired 25 of 27 batters over five games, registering five consecutive saves. "I was in really good shape," he told writer Jim Shearon some years later. "I wanted to prove that if I was in Montreal, it wasn't because I was a French-Canadian, but because I could still pitch. That was my most satisfying season."[19]

Claude Raymond became an idol for young Quebec athletes and was as popular as the best players on hockey's Montreal Canadiens. In January 1971, he benefited from this attention by signing the most lucrative contact of his career, and then took off for Europe with his family. The heavens were aligned for an exceptional 1971 season, but then the pitcher from Saint-Jean slipped on a piece of wet ground at spring training and an ankle infection set in. This injury opened the door for a young Mike Marshall to stake his claim on the role of number one reliever for the Expos, one that he never relinquished.

As for Raymond, everything began collapsing all around him. During one 17-day period in midseason he was credited with five losses. The Expos kept him on for the balance of the season (1-7, 4.66) but released him after the season. During the winter he approached the Mets, Yankees, Cubs, White Sox, and Tigers, but no one was interested. Raymond's playing career was over. He ended with a lifetime record of 46-53 and an earned run average of 3.66 over 449 games.

After a year off, Raymond returned to the Expos as an analyst, first on radio (1973-84) and then on television (1985-2001). During these years he also offered baseball clinics in all corners of Quebec. Thousands of youngsters were given an opportunity to benefit from his knowledge. In February 2002, Omar Minaya, the general manager appointed by Major League Baseball to run the Expos, hired him as a coach.

On September 29, 2004, at the Expos' last game in Montreal, Raymond represented the team and addressed its French-speaking fans for a final time.

"I didn't want to leave the stadium," he said of that night, "I didn't want to take off my uniform. I know how many young people have dreamed of wearing it. I even thought that I would wear it to bed."[20]

"Claude Raymond is the very opposite of today's spoiled stars," wrote André Pratte, editor-in-chief of La Presse, "a modest man, unpretentious, hard-working. Raymond set out for the United States in 1955, at a time when Quebecers still didn't believe they could compete among the best and become successful beyond the local parish. He wasn't even 20 years old.

"Claude Raymond," continued Pratte, "is a pioneer, an athlete of the highest order and above all a gentleman. He has been an outstanding ambassador for the Expos, for Montreal and for Quebec. Thank you, Mr. Raymond."

Translation: William Young

Notes

1. Claude Raymond and Marcel Gaudette, *Le troisième re*trait (Montréal: Éditions de l'homme, 1973, 1973), 20.
2. Raymond and Gaudette, 20.
3. "Baseball," *Montreal Star*, August 23, 1869: 2.
4. Raymond and Gaudette, 21-22.
5. Raymond and Gaudette, 24.
6. Raymond and Gaudette, 30.
7. Raymond and Gaudette, 37.
8. Jim Shearon, *Canada's Baseball Legends* (Kanata, Ontario: Malin Head Press, 1994), 170.
9. Raymond and Gaudette, 39.
10. Raymond and Gaudette, 39.
11. Raymond and Gaudette, 42.
12. Raymond and Gaudette, 44.
13. Robert Duguay, "On pouvait même faire nettoyer nos vêtements gratis!," *La Presse*, April 15, 1998).
14. "La rencontre des grands, " *Le Nouvelliste*, November 13, 2007.
15. Richard Milo, "Le match des étoiles de Claude Raymond," *Presse Canadienne*, November 7, 1992.
16. Milo.
17. Raymond and Gaudette, 62.
18. Raymond and Gaudette, 64.
19. Shearon, 172.
20. André Pratte, "Merci M. Raymond," *La Presse*, October 1, 2004.

JIM RIVERA

By Richard Smiley

Speedy outfielder Jim Rivera was one of the great characters of 1950s baseball. As Chicago White Sox general manager Ed Short put it, "Jungle Jim may not have the fattest average in baseball, but he gives the fans a show with his daredevil running and sliding, his terrific fielding, and clutch hitting."[1] His all-out style made him one of the most popular White Sox, despite his troubled – and sometimes troubling – history.

Manuel Joseph Rivera was born in New York City on July 22, 1921 to a family of six brothers and five sisters.[2] Of Puerto Rican heritage, he was raised near 112th and Madison in the impoverished section of Manhattan known as Spanish Harlem.[3] He lived there until his mother died when he was 6 years old.[4] With his father unable to care for everyone in the family, he was sent to an orphanage in Blauvelt, New York, about 15 miles up the Hudson from the city, run by a congregation of Dominican sisters. He lived at Saint Dominic's for the next 10 years while he received formal education and learned to play various sports, including baseball.[5]

After he turned 16, Rivera returned home to live with his remarried father. With the family on relief, Rivera took various jobs to support them. Construction work helped build his strength, and he joined other friends from the neighborhood in learning how to box.[6] By the time he was 17, he started fighting amateur bouts around New York City along with St. Dominic's classmate Jim Dorso. Since he was constantly hanging around with Dorso, others began calling Rivera "Jim," a name that would stay with him for the rest of his life.[7] During this time he was still playing baseball. He became good enough to join a semipro team representing the Valencia Bakery, and left the world of amateur boxing.[8]

Rivera resumed boxing after joining the Army Air Corps in August 1942, and captured the light-heavyweight title of his outfit in the Third Air Force at Camp Barkley, Texas.[9] He played baseball on the camp team. In the spring of 1944, his life was thrown into turmoil. He was charged with raping and assaulting the daughter of an Army officer after a dance at Barksdale Field, Louisiana. After a medical examination of the accuser, the charge was reduced to attempted rape. Rivera was found guilty and sentenced to life imprisonment. After serving five years in the Atlanta Federal Penitentiary, he was paroled in 1949.[10]

Rivera played baseball on the prison team. His success in games against local teams outside the prison caught the attention of Atlanta Crackers owner Earl Mann. Mann worked with authorities to secure a parole for Rivera. When he was released in March 1949, a contract with the Crackers was waiting for him.[11] Atlanta farmed Rivera out to Class-D Gainesville, where the 27-year-old, 6-foot, 198-pound left-handed outfielder hit .335, stole 55 bases, and scored 142 runs, leading the G-Men to the Florida State League pennant.[12] Promoted to Class-B Pensacola the next year, he hit .338, scored 139 runs, and drove in 135 to spark the Fliers to the Southeastern League pennant.[13]

In the 1950 offseason, Rivera played for the Caguas team in the Puerto Rican winter league. He began to slide head-first into bases, a style that became a trademark during his major-league career. Rogers Hornsby, who was managing an opposing team in the league, took an immediate liking to him and provided the player with advice and coaching. Hornsby would soon refer to Rivera as "the only man I would pay admission to see."[14]

When Hornsby was named manager of the Seattle club in the Pacific Coast League for 1951, he approached Rivera about joining him. Seattle bought him from Pensacola for $2,500.[15] Rivera enjoyed his finest professional season in Seattle, collecting 231 hits, scoring 135 runs, hitting a league-leading .352, and leading the Rainiers to the pennant – his third in three professional seasons. His speed and dazzling play garnered him the league's MVP award.[16] One reporter said, "He runs in the outfield like a deer, on the bases like an express train, and he throws like a rifle."[17] His exceptional play caught the attention of major-league clubs. In July the White Sox exercised their option to purchase his contract for $65,000, instructing him to report at the end of the PCL season.[18]

Go-Go to Glory

In the fall of 1951, Hornsby was named manager of Bill Veeck's St. Louis Browns. Hornsby urged Veeck to acquire Rivera.[19] Veeck sent catcher Sherman Lollar to Chicago in a three-team, eight-player deal that brought Rivera to the Browns.[20] But the deal caused a stir in St. Louis. Local civic and religious groups began a campaign to have Rivera dismissed from the Browns roster and banned from baseball. In response to the pressure, Commissioner Ford Frick stated, "If the purpose is punishment, then he has already been punished. If the purpose is cure or improvement, then this man has a greater chance to make good being allowed to live as others live. Since Rivera came into baseball his conduct has been beyond question. If in the future he shows that he has not profited by his experience, this office will take action."[21]

Although there were high hopes for Rivera and the rookie-laden Browns in 1952, neither started the season well. Rivera did collect a hit in his major-league debut on Opening Day in Detroit, but he fell into a slump. By the start of May he was on the bench. On May 8 he came into a game in Philadelphia as a defensive substitute, made a sensational catch and hit a ninth-inning home run to win the game for the Browns.[22] That put him back in the lineup, although the team's fortunes did not improve. Hornsby, under constant criticism for continuing to play the slumping rookies, was fired in mid-June.[23] Rivera soon followed him, traded back to the White Sox at the end of July.[24]

Rivera's White Sox debut on July 29, 1952, was a memorable one. In front of a crowd of nearly 39,000, he started in center field and picked up hits in his first two at-bats, helping the Sox build a 7-0 lead over the New York Yankees. The Yankees came back to win that game on Mickey Mantle's ninth-inning grand slam. Rivera homered the next day to lead the White Sox to a win over the Bronx Bombers.[25] Soon his speed on the bases and acrobatic catches made him a fan favorite. Big Jim, as he liked to be called, finished the year with a .253 average, but the 13 stolen bases he collected in two months with the White Sox showed signs of promise.

On the last day of the season, Rivera was arrested in the White Sox clubhouse on charges that he had raped the wife of a soldier.[26] He contended that the relationship was consensual, and took a lie detector test. After he passed, a Chicago grand jury declined to indict him.[27] Commissioner Frick placed him on "indefinite probation." Frick put full responsibility for Rivera's future behavior on the White Sox, and prohibited the team from trading or selling him for a year.[28] This generated more controversy in the press from those who opposed and those who supported his right to play.

Rivera responded by enjoying his finest years in the majors.[29] In 1953 he played center field in almost every game and reached double figures in doubles, triples, and home runs. His 16 triples led the American League while his 22 stolen bases trailed only his outfield teammate Minnie Minoso. His efforts helped the White Sox win 89 games, their best record in more than 30 years. Both the White Sox and Rivera did even better in 1954, as the team won 94 games and Rivera hit a career-high .286. He continued to dazzle in the field and on the bases, but was now patrolling right field with Johnny Groth in center. During this year Rivera's habit of flapping his arms to wave his fellow fielders off fly balls led *Chicago Sun-Times* sportswriter John Hoffman to call him Jungle Jim.[30] The nickname quickly became popular and has stayed with him.

In 1955, Rivera led the American League with 25 stolen bases, but his average dropped to .264 as a pronounced hitch in his swing took its toll.[31] The White Sox participated in their first real pennant race in 35 years and were not eliminated until late September. In an effort to become more competitive in 1956, the team swung an offseason deal for slugging outfielder Larry Doby.[32] Deals in May brought veteran outfielders Jim Delsing and Dave Philley.[33] Rivera's playing time was reduced as his average fell to .255.

After the season ended, Rivera married his second wife, Phyllis Crain of Angola, Indiana.[34] This time was the peak of his popularity in Chicago. Sportswriters could always count on him for a good quote or funny story, and he was in constant demand for personal appearances.[35] An avid filmgoer, Rivera would sometimes take in two movies in a day before a night game and developed the reputation as the team's "film critic."[36] Rumors of potential trades never came true, as he was deemed too popular to move.

When the White Sox acquired even more outfielders, Jungle Jim opened the 1957 season at first base, but was shifted back to right field in June after the Sox acquired veteran first baseman Earl Torgeson.[37] Rivera shared the outfield job with rookie Jim Landis, and his 14 home runs tied for the team lead with Larry Doby. In 1958 Rivera competed for playing time with Don Mueller, Tito Francona, and

• JIM RIVERA •

Bubba Phillips as his average plummeted to .225. His days as a regular had ended, and he began the transformation into a solid bench player.[38]

Rivera contributed on the field to the 1959 White Sox pennant-winning team as a late-inning outfielder, pinch-runner, platoon starter, and pinch-hitter. He contributed off the field with his great enthusiasm for the game and energy. He was praised for staying in excellent shape despite being used sparingly, and for being "the first man in uniform before every game."[39]

Rivera's second at-bat of the season, on April 17, produced a victory over the Detroit Tigers as his two-run double in the eighth inning broke a 4-4 tie.[40] Later in the month, he was inserted into the starting lineup for a few games to spell the slumping Johnny Callison.[41] He suffered a broken rib making a tumbling catch in a game against the Yankees and went on the disabled list.[42]

When he came back toward the end of May, Rivera returned to the bench.[43] He made the most of a spot start in a June 7 doubleheader against the Boston Red Sox, contributing a pair of hits in each game.[44] He started in right field for the rest of the month, but a batting slump reduced him to a platoon role.[45] He pulled a muscle on July 5, and went back to the bench when he recovered.[46] Rivera replaced the injured Jim McAnany on August 21, and his leaping catch against the right-field wall preserved a close victory over Washington.[47] He platooned with McAnany for the rest of the season.

On the evening of September 22, the White Sox took on the Cleveland Indians in Cleveland with the opportunity to clinch the pennant. Since right-hander Jim Perry was starting for the Tribe, Rivera was in the lineup. The Sox took an early 2-0 lead, but the Indians battled back for a run in the bottom of the fifth. Mudcat Grant relieved Perry in the top of the sixth and surrendered a one-out home run to Al Smith. Rivera followed with a home run to right-center. The lead held up as the White Sox earned their first title in 40 years.[48] Rivera called the homer in the pennant-clinching game his best moment in baseball.[49]

Rivera continued platooning with McAnany in the World Series, starting games One, Three, and Four while going 0-for-11 at the plate. He made his most memorable impact in a game he did not start. After the Los Angeles Dodgers had gained a three-games-to-one Series lead, left-hander Sandy Koufax pitched Game Five in front of a record crowd in the Los Angeles Coliseum. The White Sox squeaked out a run in the top of the fourth inning on a double play, but the Dodgers constantly threatened to come back against Chicago's Bob Shaw. After two runners reached base in the bottom of the seventh with two outs and the hot-hitting Charlie Neal coming up, White Sox manager Al Lopez inserted Rivera in right field. The move proved prescient as Neal laced a drive toward right-center that looked certain to clear the bases. Rivera raced back and made an over-the-shoulder catch at the fence to preserve the 1-0 lead and the game.[50]

In 1960 Minnie Minoso returned to the White Sox and Rivera's role was reduced to that of a late-inning defensive replacement and pinch-runner.[51] Although he appeared in 48 games, he started only once and collected a mere 17 at-bats. The following year Rivera again made the White Sox as a reserve, but he fractured his thumb in his first pinch-running assignment while sliding head-first into third.[52] That slide proved to be Rivera's last play with the Sox; upon his return from the disabled list in June

A key member of the Go-Go Sox for a decade (1952-61), Jim Rivera led the American League in stolen bases in 1955 and finished second in the league in steals in six other seasons.

he was released.[53] He was picked up by the Kansas City Athletics, who expressed plans to use him as a "general all-around utility man."[54] He actually ended up back in a platoon role, playing mostly right field and finishing 1961 with a .241 batting average. When the Athletics released him at the end of the year his major-league career was over.[55]

After the season, Rivera managed in the Puerto Rican League and signed with the Indianapolis Indians of the American Association to be a player-coach.[56] His stint with the Indians did not last long. By July he was back with Seattle in the Pacific Coast League.[57] He stayed with the Rainiers through June 1963, when he was given his unconditional release. At the time he was batting .259 with two homers.[58] It was the end of his professional baseball career in the US, but he still wasn't done; signing with the Mexico City Tigres of the Mexican League, he finished the 1963 season south of the border and then played in 87 games for the Mexican League Jalisco Charros in 1964 before finally retiring for good.

Residing in his wife's hometown of Angola, Indiana, Rivera bought a restaurant on Crooked Lake known as the Captain's Cabin.[59] There he reigned as proprietor for over 20 years, regaling customers with stories of days past until he retired to Port Charlotte, Florida, in 1990.[60] He remained loyal to the White Sox, and could always be counted on to make appearances in old timers' games and social events.[61] When Bill Veeck announced plans to have his team wear short pants during the 1976 season, Jungle Jim was there to model them.[62] When the White Sox brought out members of the 1959 World Series team before Game One of the 2005 World Series, Jungle Jim was on the field.[63] He died at age 96 in Fort Wayne, Indiana, on November 13, 2017.[64]

Notes

1. David Eskenazi, "Wayback Machine: Rajah, Rivera, '51 Rainiers," *SportsPressNW.com*, March 27, 2012.
2. There has been some confusion about Jim Rivera's year of birth. The date of birth appearing in many 1950's articles, baseball cards, and press releases -- July 22, 1923 – does not match the date of birth Rivera told to friends and personally gave on questionnaires returned to the White Sox -- July 22, 1921. Turkin & Thompson's 1963 version of the *Encyclopedia of Baseball* and subsequent versions of that book show the date as July 22, 1922. The current standard references (such as Baseball-reference.com) give the date as July 22, 1921 and that is what is used here. David Condon made sport of the two-year discrepancy in his *Chicago Tribune* "In the Wake of the News" column printed on June 13, 1963.
3. Milton Gross, "The Jim Rivera Story," *Sport*, June 1952: 17.
4. Bob Vanderberg, *Sox, from Lane and Fain to Zisk and Fisk* (Chicago: Chicago Review Press, 1982), 156.
5. Gross, 74.
6. Gross, 74.
7. Warren Brown, "Jim Rivera Talking …," *Sport*, October 1955: 21.
8. Brown, 34.
9. Gross, 74.
10. Gross, 74-75.
11. Gross, 75.
12. Joe Halberstein, "Jim Rivera recalls G-Men playing days in '49," *Gainesville Daily Sun*, August 11, 1957;
13. Vanderberg, 158.
14. Harry Grayson, "Sport City," *Portsmouth Herald*, August 30, 1955.
15. Eskenazi.
16. Steve Krevisky presentation at SABR 36 in Seattle, Washington, 2006: "Jungle Jim Leads the Way! The Saga of the 1951 PCL Champs, The Seattle Rainiers;" Perpetual Motion Pictures video: *The Seattle Rainiers*, 2006.
17. Eskenazi.
18. Vanderberg, 158.
19. Vanderberg, 158.
20. Irving Vaughan, "Sox Get Lollar, Widmar, and Dente," *Chicago Tribune*, November 28, 1951: C1-C2.
21. Eskenazi.
22. "Rivera Stars as Browns Top Athletics, 9-8," *Chicago Tribune*, May 9, 1952: C3.
23. "Hornsby Fired; Marion Manages Browns," *Chicago Tribune*, June 11, 1952: B1, B3.
24. Irving Vaughan, "White Sox Get Rivera – Again," July 29, 1952: B1.
25. Vanderberg, page 159.
26. "Arrest Jim Rivera, Sox Center Fielder, on Rape Complaint," *Chicago Tribune*, September 29, 1952: 6; "White Sox's Rivera Charged with Rape of Soldier's Wife," *Chicago Tribune*, September 30, 1952: 5.
27. "Jury Refuses to Indict Rivera on Rape Charge," *Chicago Tribune*, October 15, 1952: 4; Vanderberg, 159.
28. "Sox's Rivera Draws Indefinite Probation," *Chicago Tribune*, November 13, 1952: d1.
29. Edward Prell, "That amazing Sox Outfield!" *Chicago Tribune*, September 11, 1955: k27.
30. Brown, 21.
31. Vanderberg, 160.
32. Edward Prell, "Sox Trade Carrasquel, Busby for Doby," *Chicago Tribune*, October 26, 1955: C1, C4.
33. "Trade Winds Blow," *Chicago Tribune*, May 16, 1956: C1, C3; Edward Prell, "Sox Trade Kell, 3 Others for 2 Orioles," *Chicago Tribune*, May 22, 1956: C1, 2.
34. "Sox's Rivera Takes Indiana Girl as Bride," *Chicago Tribune*, October 13, 1956: B3.
35. Brown, 87.
36. Brown, 85-86.
37. "White Sox Get Torgeson for Philley, Cash," *Chicago Tribune*, June 14, 1957: C2.
38. Edward Prell, "White Sox Figures Prove Left Is Right—Sometimes," *Chicago Tribune*, November 20, 1957: C2; Edward Prell, "White Sox Train New Guns on Yank Dynasty," *Chicago Tribune*, February 11, 1958: b2.

• JIM RIVERA •

39 Richard Dozer, "Sox Opener in Boston Called Off by Rain," *Chicago Tribune*, June 20, 1959: A4.
40 Richard Dozer, "Cubs Win, 9 TO 4; Sox Beat Tigers, 6 TO 5," *Chicago Tribune*, April 18, 1959: E1, 2.
41 "Jim Rivera to Move Into Sox Lineup," *Chicago Tribune*, April 19, 1959: A7.
42 "Batting Drill Pitch Puts Mantle Out," *Chicago Tribune*, May 1, 1959: E6; "Sox Get Ennis from Reds for Rudolph," *Chicago Tribune*, May 2, 1959: A2.
43 Richard Dozer, "Sox Win, 2-1; Cards Beat Cubs in 14th, 3-1," *Chicago Tribune*, May 23, 1959: A1, 2; Baseball-reference.com.
44 Richard Dozer, "Beat Boston, 9-4 in 1st; Drop 2d, 4-2," *Chicago Tribune*, June 8, 1959: C1, C4.
45 http://www.baseball-reference.com/players/gl.fcgi?id=riverji01&t=b&year=1959
46 Richard Dozer, "Nellie, Luis Click Again; Smith, too!" *Chicago Tribune*, July 6, 1959: C1, C5.
47 Edward Prell, "White Sox Win Again by One Run, 5-4!" *Chicago Tribune*, August 22, 1959: 1-2; Vanderberg, 160-161.
48 Edward Prell, "White Sox Win Pennant!" *Chicago Tribune*, September 23, 1959: 1-2; Vanderberg, 161.
49 Joe Goddard, "What's Up with Jim Rivera," *Chicago Sun-Times*, August 18, 2002: 98.
50 Edward Prell, "Sox Win; Final at Home," *Chicago Tribune*, October 7, 1959: 1-2; "Alston Lauds Lopez for Rivera Switch," *Chicago Tribune*, October 7, 1959: E13; Vanderberg, 161.
51 Edward Prell, "Sox Acquire Minoso Again; Cubs Get Frank Thomas," *Chicago Tribune*, December 7, 1959: E1; Edward Prell, "Sox Chorus: 'I'm Growing Old'," *Chicago Tribune*, February 24, 1960: C1, 2.
52 "Jim Rivera Is Placed on Disabled List," *Chicago Tribune*, April 24, 1961: C4.
53 "Sox Release Rivera with 'Reluctance'," *Chicago Tribune*, June 7, 1961: C1; David Condon, "In the Wake of the News," *Chicago Tribune*, June 9, 1961: C1.
54 "Rivera Flies to New York, Signs with A's," *Chicago Tribune*, June 10, 1961: C2.
55 Vanderberg, 161.
56 "Joe Horlen, Sox Hurler, OK's Terms," *Chicago Tribune*, January 16, 1962: C3; "Jim Rivera Indianapolis Player-Coach," *Chicago Tribune*, February 20, 1962: B3.
57 "Jim Rivera Returns to Coast League," *Chicago Tribune*, July 6, 1962: C5.
58 "Seattle Club Gives Release to Jim Rivera," *Chicago Tribune*, June 12, 1963: E3.
59 Robert Goldsborough, "Whatever happened?" *Chicago Tribune*, July 16, 1967: E2; Vanderberg, 154.
60 Joe Goddard, "What's Up with Jim Rivera," *Chicago Sun-Times*, August 18, 2002: 98.
61 Richard Dozer, "John Pitches 5-0 Shutout; Horlen Triumphs, 4-1," *Chicago Tribune*, August 1, 1966: C1, C4; David Condon, "In the Wake of the News," *Chicago Tribune*, June 27, 1969: C1; "'Old' Cubs, Sox Meet Today," *Chicago Tribune*, July 25, 1971: B2.
62 Bob Verdi, "Will sexy garb fit Sox knee-ds?" *Chicago Tribune*, March 10, 1976: E3; *Chicago Tribune*, David Condon, "Opinions flow from all sides on Sox outfits," *Chicago Tribune*, March 10, 1976: E3.
63 Melissa Isaacson, "Aparicio, teammates usher in the Series," *Chicago Tribune*, October 23, 2005: 17. An update in 2017: *After the World Series Rivera continued to show up for White Sox events. He came to SoxFest in 2009 where the author had the opportunity to briefly meet him and later that year participated in festivities surrounding the 50th Anniversary celebration of the White Sox 1959 AL Championship. According to David Hughes (a friend of Jim), he has lived in Fort Wayne, Indiana for the past 20 years while still spending winters in Port Charlotte.*
64 'Jungle Jim' Rivera, who played for 'Go-Go' White Sox, dies at age 96, http://www.espn.com/mlb/story/_/id/21415158/jungle-jim-rivera-former-chicago-white-sox-outfielder-dies-96; accessed January 21, 2018.

JOHN ROMANO

By Todd Newville

In retirement, former major leaguer Johnny Romano took up flying radio-controlled model airplanes near his retirement home in Florida. He liked to fly them high and far.

There was a time, though, when those terms – high and far – also referred to his ability as a hard-hitting All-Star catcher for the Cleveland Indians and Chicago White Sox. Romano was pretty good defensively behind the plate and could handle a pitching staff with a deft hand. With a bat, though, he was even better. He liked to hit the baseball high and far, too.

Romano, who was born on August 23, 1934, in Hoboken, New Jersey, always had the ability to hit with power. Nicknamed Honey by his uncle, he had the ideal physique for a catcher, standing 5 feet 11 and weighing a stocky 205 pounds. Romano used his solid build to his advantage when it came to hitting. But according to Romano, his prowess at the plate was probably due more to genetics than anything. His father, John Sr., was a former semipro baseball player and a longshoreman in New Jersey.

"I was a very good power hitter," Romano said. "It was born in me. My father was a catcher. He used to play semipro. At the time, they wanted him to go professional. But back in those days, he was making more money playing semipro and working off the piers than he would playing professional ball.

"Whenever they had exhibition games against Babe Ruth and Lou Gehrig, my father used to catch in those games. They used to call him Cannonball because he had that kind of an arm."[1]

As young John grew older, he also became a local baseball star in Hoboken, which is just over a square mile on most maps. Even though it's a small community, Hoboken has produced a dozen major leaguers including Romano. Along with Hoboken natives Tom Carey, Bill Kunkel, Leo Kiely, and others, Romano was coached and tutored by Tony Calland, who played for 12 semipro teams from 1918 to 1935 and got into two exhibition games with Babe Ruth and Lou Gehrig in 1930. After his playing days ended, Calland coached for 37 years in New Jersey before retiring in 1972. "He helped me quite a bit," Romano said.

Romano attended Demarest High School in Hoboken, where, he says, "My (older) brother Anthony set a record at Demarest by hitting .631 and then I broke it by hitting something like .681 my senior year. I can't remember exactly, but I had good numbers."

By the time he was 19, Romano was playing in the minor leagues after signing with the Chicago White Sox organization. The two Chicago scouts responsible for signing Romano to a contract were Dutch Deurtch and Ed Holley. It was kind of by accident that Romano ended up in the White Sox organization.

"I always thought I was always going to be a bonus baby with the Brooklyn Dodgers," Romano said. That's because he used to work out with the Dodgers at Ebbets Field by invitation of coach Clyde Sukeforth, a former major-league catcher, coach, scout, and manager who is best known for scouting and helping sign Jackie Robinson. After his days with Brooklyn, Sukeforth also played a part in signing Roberto Clemente to a contract with the Pittsburgh Pirates.

Sukeforth, who died in 2000 at the age of 98, was a great boost to Romano's career. He would encourage Romano and his older brother to take batting practice during pregame warm-ups and was a proverbial "mother hen" to the two Jersey boys.

"I used to work out some with the Dodgers starting when I was about 15," Romano said.

"Clyde Sukeforth was a coach and he saw my potential. Anytime we wanted to, my brother would drive us over and we would work out with Cal Abrams and Clem Labine, and other guys. They took us under their wing. We would follow them around because Clyde told us to do so. It was a fantastic experience, I'll tell you that!"

But it was the White Sox, not the Dodgers, who wound up signing Romano. He moved through the Sox system quickly. Making his debut in 1954, Romano batted .355 with six home runs and 29 RBIs in 27 games for Dubuque (Iowa) in the Class-D Mississippi-Ohio Valley League. Promoted to Waterloo (Iowa) in the Class-B Three-I League in 1955, he hit .321, leading the league with 108 runs scored and 124

JOHN ROMANO

RBIs in only 118 games. His 38 homers that year set a league record. In '56, Romano hit .284 in 33 games for Memphis in the Southern League and .241 in 81 games for Vancouver in the Pacific Coast League.

By 1957, Romano was playing for Chicago's Triple-A affiliate at Indianapolis in the American Association. He had another solid year at the plate, hitting .272 with 15 homers and 62 RBIs. But his defensive work still needed some polish. Romano became more of a complete player after the White Sox sent former major-league catcher Walker Cooper to manage Indianapolis in '58. Cooper had caught 18 seasons in the National League, most notably for the St. Louis Cardinals and New York Giants, for whom he hit .305 with 35 homers and 122 RBIs in 1947.

"When I first went down to the minor leagues," Romano said, "I played for about two or three years for former infielders as managers. (Then) the White Sox sent down Walker Cooper to manage their Triple-A team. He was the backup catcher, plus he was the manager. When Cooper came down there [to Indianapolis], he straightened me out. The White Sox said the only thing that was holding me back from not going to the big leagues was not knowing how to catch. Walker Cooper helped me very much in that regard."

With Cooper as his skipper in 1958, Romano continued to carry a big stick as he hit .291 with 25 home runs, 29 doubles, and 89 RBIs. As expected, his catching abilities improved dramatically. Cooper's help that year enabled Romano to punch his ticket to the majors.

Romano played four games for Chicago in late September of '58, and he performed admirably as a rookie off the bench for manager Al Lopez during the 1959 season. As backup to Sherm Lollar, Johnny hit .294 with five home runs and 25 RBIs in 53 games for the White Sox, who won their first American League pennant in 40 years with a 94-60 record. Romano particularly excelled as a pinch-hitter in '59, going 8-for-13.

Lopez is in the Hall of Fame for his managerial record of 1,422 victories and a .581 winning percentage, but, like Cooper, he was a former big-league catcher who caught 1,918 major-league games during his 19-year playing career. "The two guys I attribute my catching success to would be Walker Cooper and Al Lopez," Romano said. "Those two guys were very instrumental in me being a good catcher."

The White Sox faced the Los Angeles Dodgers in the 1959 World Series. Nicknamed the Go-Go

John Romano was a valuable reserve catcher for the 1959 White Sox, hitting .294. Traded to the Indians after the season, he blossomed into an All-Star receiver.

Sox, Chicago relied on great defense, speed, and solid pitching. "We had a great little team," Romano said. "We played good defense and we had the pitching. In the World Series, I was the No. 1 pinch-hitter at the time. The only time I got to play that whole World Series was when I pinch-hit one time, but I helped get them there. That was nice."

The White Sox already had Gold Glove-winning catcher Sherm Lollar firmly established behind the plate. Romano, though, got Lopez to let him play a little as a rookie in '59 by letting his bat do the talking.

"When I came to the big leagues," Romano said, "I had a difficult time getting into the lineup because, at that time, Al Lopez only played veteran ballplayers. . . . It was very difficult for me to get into the games. One night [May 3, 1959] he ran out of pinch-hitters and we were playing Baltimore. He called down to the bullpen and sent me up there to hit against [left-hander] Billy O'Dell. The second pitch I hit into the upper deck." It was Romano's first major-league home run. He did not play for 16 days after that homer, but when he did, it was again against the Orioles and O'Dell. And once more Romano came through with a pinch-hit, this time a single. "From then on," Romano said, "when we played against a left-handed pitcher, Lollar went to first base and I caught. That was great."

Romano was involved in a rare play while catching for the '59 White Sox. In major-league history, there have been only 13 triple plays in which all the outs were tag outs. On September 27, the last day of the season, in the bottom of the third at Detroit's Briggs Stadium, the Tigers had Tom Morgan on third base and Harvey Kuenn on first. Gail Harris grounded to pitcher Bob Shaw, who threw to third baseman Bubba Phillips. Phillips tagged Morgan in a rundown between third and home for the first out, and then raced across the infield and tagged Harris, who had rounded first base during the rundown. Phillips then fired the ball to Romano to prevent Kuenn from scoring. Kuenn had to retreat to third, where shortstop Luis Aparicio slapped the tag on him.

Heading into the 1960 season, the White Sox had a plethora of young talent and not enough room on the roster. In addition to Romano, first baseman Norm Cash, outfielder Johnny Callison, and catcher Earl Battey were all promising youngsters. Before the season started, all four players were traded.

Callison ended up with the Philadelphia Phillies and became an All-Star. Battey went to the Washington Senators and became a three-time Gold Glove winner. Cash and Romano (along with Phillips) were traded to the Cleveland Indians on December 6, 1959, for outfielder Minnie Minoso, catcher Dick Brown, and pitchers Don Ferrarese and Jake Striker. (The Indians then traded Cash to the Tigers, for whom he won a batting championship, hit 373 home runs, and played for 15 years.)

In 1960, Romano, playing regularly for the first time, hit .272 for the Tribe with 16 homers and 52 RBIs. In '61, Romano was named to the American League's All-Star team by hitting a career-high .299 with 21 homers, 29 doubles, and 80 RBIs. He ranked eighth in the AL in hitting and 10th in doubles. Romano's on base-plus-slugging percentage (OPS) of .860 was the 10th highest in the AL. He had a 22-game hitting streak that year, a Cleveland team record for catchers until it was broken by Ray Fosse with 23 games in 1970. Sandy Alomar Jr. now has the club mark for catchers with a 30-game streak in 1997.

"I didn't even know I had a record," Romano said. "I wasn't going for any records when I played. It wasn't important and I didn't put pressure on myself to do those things. We just went out there and played hard every game. I didn't play that last game [during the '61 season] because I didn't know I was hitting that high. Otherwise, I would have tried to hit .300."

In 1962, Romano hit .261 and set career highs with 25 homers and 81 RBIs. His .479 slugging percentage ranked 10th in the American League and his OPS of .842 ranked ninth. He was named an AL All-Star in the player balloting of the time again in '62, an honor he holds very dear to his heart. "It wasn't a popularity contest in those years," Romano said. "Each ballplayer had one vote. Those guys are the ones that voted me in as the catcher. It was the actual baseball players that played against me that voted for me, and getting voted in by your peers was a big honor. You look today and most of it is just a popularity contest."

In 1963, Romano battled injuries and hit just .216 with 10 homers. He broke his hand when he was hit with a pitch against the Baltimore Orioles during the first game of a doubleheader on May 26. At the time of the injury, Romano was hitting .269. He was on the shelf until July 2.

"I was just about to go to the All-Star Game again," Romano said. "It was a fastball at my face. I stuck my hand in front of it to stop it and the ball shattered my hand. They put a cast on it and I was supposed to have it on for six weeks. Two weeks later, they took the cast off because they wanted me to handle our young pitchers."

The Indians evidently figured that a one-handed Romano was a lot better than no Romano at all. They valued his knowledge and his handling of the many promising young pitchers Cleveland had during Romano's tenure with the team. Sam McDowell was 18 when he broke in with the Indians in 1961 and eventually ended up with 2,453 strikeouts in his 15-year career. Tommy John debuted with Cleveland in '63 when he was 20. He ended up winning 288 games in 26 major-league seasons. Both benefited from Romano's experience early in their careers.

"Before each game, we'd go over every batter with the starting pitchers," Romano said. "I would tell our pitchers what I thought and how we should pitch them. If they had any comments, they would jump in. Handling pitchers was the big thing. Our staff was very young with Cleveland. You had to instill in

JOHN ROMANO

them the confidence they would have in you as their catcher. It was difficult sometimes."

Romano rebounded from his fractured hand by hitting .241 with 19 homers in 106 games in 1964. The Indians, though, traded Romano (along with Tommy John and outfielder Tommy Agee) back to the White Sox on January 20, 1965, as part of a three-team deal that also involved the Kansas City Athletics and returned Rocky Colavito to the Indians.

After the unpopular trade in 1960 that sent Colavito to the Detroit Tigers for Harvey Kuenn, the Cleveland front office was anxious to make its fans happy again. "I was tickled pink to be going back to the White Sox," Romano said. "I was going back to Al Lopez and I was getting away from [Indians manager] Birdie Tebbetts. Birdie helped sign a guy named Joe Azcue from Cuba when he was with Cincinnati. He wanted to bring Azcue on board to Cleveland. I was their All-Star catcher and Birdie wanted to put Azcue behind the plate instead of me. I couldn't figure that out."

Much later, Romano learned the reason. "I definitely wasn't Birdie's favorite, but later on, I understood why. A few years ago, we had a Cleveland fantasy camp here in Florida. Joe Azcue told me that Birdie was just looking after him. He had signed him when he was just 16 out of Cuba. I can understand that, now."

In 1965, Romano hit .242 with 18 round-trippers for Chicago and followed that with a .231 average and 15 homers in '66. The White Sox traded Romano with minor leaguer Lee White to the St. Louis Cardinals on December 14, 1966, for outfielder Walt "No Neck" Williams and pitcher Don Dennis.

In 1967, Romano closed out his 10-year major-league career by hitting .121 for the Cards, who released him after they defeated the Boston Red Sox in a seven-game World Series (Romano did not make the Cardinals' World Series roster). For his career, Romano hit .255 with 129 home runs, 417 RBIs, 355 runs scored, and 112 doubles in 905 games.

Romano is one of seven catchers listed among the top 100 Indians in history, selected when the club celebrated its 100th anniversary in 2001. He hit 91 homers as a Cleveland catcher, which was a team record for backstops until Alomar broke it by hitting 92. "There were a lot of great ballplayers for over 100 years in Cleveland," said Romano. "That was a great honor."

Romano and his wife, Irene, were married on November 11, 1956. The union produced three sons: John Richard (born June 6, 1960); Allen (born October 6, 1962); and Robert (born Sept. 23, 1969). The Romanos have six grandsons and one granddaughter.

After retiring from baseball, Romano sold swimming pools for a while and worked for the government in Bergen County, New Jersey. He and Irene moved to Naples, Florida, in September 1998. In April 2008, Romano suffered his second stroke in four years, according to Irene. The effect was mostly to the left side of his body, but he made a rather miraculous recovery during the summer of 2008 and was still able "to get around and do his thing," Irene said.[2]

In an interview in early 2008, Romano said that while not a fisherman, he enjoyed spending time on the water in his two boats. But flying his radio-controlled planes appeared to be his real passion. "I fly them almost every day," Romano said. "I just sold one of my boats because I don't get on them very much anymore. But I really enjoy flying the planes. It just makes me feel happy."[3]

John Romano passed away at age 84 at his home in Naples, Florida on February 24, 2019. He was survived by Irene and his sons.

Sources

Palmer, Pete, and Gary Gillette. *The 2005 ESPN Baseball Encyclopedia* (New York: Sterling Publishing Co., 2005).

Encyclopedia of Baseball Catchers: http://members.tripod.com/bb_catchers

http://whitesoxinteractive.com

www.baseballlibrary.com

www.baseball-reference.com

www.baseball-almanac.com

Hanley, Robert. "Mighty Hoboken At the Bat In Moscow," *New York Times*, July 14, 1988. Online at http://query/nytimes.com

Johnny Romano telephone interviews on May 10, 2006, and February 3, 2008.

Irene Romano telephone interview, August 18, 2008.

Notes

1 John Romano telephone interview, May 10, 2006. All quotations from John Romano are from this 2006 interview unless otherwise noted.

2 Irene Romano telephone interview, August 18, 2008.

3 John Romano telephone interview, February 3, 2008.

DON RUDOLPH
By Mike Hasse

Don Rudolph was known as an eccentric throughout his career but was often overshadowed by the fame of his burlesque-dancer wife. Known as a confident, quick-working hurler, Frederick Don Rudolph pitched everywhere from Jesup, Georgia, and Colorado Springs to Chicago and Washington during his journeyman career before his untimely death at the age of 37.

Rudolph was born in Baltimore on August 16, 1931. At the age of 19, he started his professional baseball career with the Jesup Bees of the Class D Georgia State League. As a left-handed starter for the Bees, Rudolph won a total of 41 games in 1950 and 1951. After he went 28-8 in 1951, recording the most wins by a pitcher in all of Organized Baseball that season, the White Sox purchased Rudolph's contract from the Bees for $1,000 on the recommendation of scouts Harry Postove and Herb Newberry, starting him on the path to his big-league career.

As a reliever for the White Sox' Colorado Springs affiliate in the Class-A Western League, Rudolph excelled in 1952, and compiled a 7-2 record before being inducted into the Army in midseason. The Sky Sox' fans and Rudolph's teammates appreciated his efforts so much that they honored him with gifts and cash between games of the July 13 doubleheader the night before his induction.[1] After spending 21 months in the Army, Rudolph returned to the Sky Sox in 1954, making 21 starts and 21 relief appearances, and finishing with a 9-14 record and a 4.33 ERA.

One night in 1954, Rudolph made a fateful visit to a nightclub that soon changed his life. Performing that night was Patti Waggin, a popular burlesque dancer. Patti, whose real name was Patricia Artae Brownell, was born into a family of vaudeville performers. After dropping out from Chico State College in California, where she was known as the "Coed With the Educated Torso,"[2] she performed burlesque numbers throughout the country. By the time she met Don, she was well-known in her field, appearing on a list of top five strippers in the country.[3] Rudolph said that after sitting through three straight shows that night, it was "love at third sight."[4] However, when he tried to approach Patti after the last show, he was rebuffed. But Don was a persistent man and when he saw an advertisement for another performance in his hometown of Baltimore, he went to see her again. After another initial rebuff, he was able to charm Patti and buy her a soda. From there, their relationship blossomed and in 1955, they were married.[5]

In 1955, when he pitched in relief for the Memphis Chicks of the Southern Association, Rudolph's career also began to blossom. He cut his walk rate nearly in half, though his earned run average rose to 4.77. The following year, he was given another opportunity to start regularly and stepped up to the challenge. He retained his newfound control, walking only 52 in 223 innings, and finished the year 11-10 with a 3.19 ERA, narrowly missing the league ERA title by a hundredth of a point.

Rudolph's performance with Memphis gained the notice of the White Sox, and he was invited to spring training in 1957. It was then that he began to display some of the eccentricities he would continue to display throughout his career. In a letter to the White Sox accompanying his signed contract, Rudolph took exception to his listed height of 5-feet-11 on the roster. He asserted that he had grown an inch and should be listed as 6 feet. He also told the White Sox he threw hard only when pitching – never when warming up.[6] But overshadowing Rudolph's eccentricities and performance was his wife's profession. Articles in the *Chicago Tribune*, *The Sporting News* and other publications compared Don's curves to those of his wife. No one was pleased more by the publicity than Don himself. An avid supporter of Patti's act, Rudolph acted as her manager and publicist during the offseason. Whether waiting in the wings to catch her flung clothes or packing and unpacking props that included a collapsible park bench and a three-part 6-foot-2 mannequin for her "Parisian number," Don was happy to be at his wife's side. He told the *Chicago Tribune*, "I go out into the theater, too, and study the lighting effects, see that Patti's make-up is just right, and listen to the comments of the audience."[7]

Patti was as supportive of Don's career as he was of hers. An athlete herself (the *Indianapolis Star* reported that she had a "collection of ten trophies

• DON RUDOLPH •

won in motorcycle racing"[8], she often donned spikes and a catcher's mitt to warm up her husband on the field.[9] During games, she charted his pitches, offered advice, and cheered him on. The opposing team often had things to say about Patti and her chosen profession, but it did not seem to bother Rudolph. "At first it bothered me, but not anymore," Rudolph told *The Sporting News*. "Don't forget, it usually helps business, both at the ballpark and at Patti's theatre. But when it gets too rough, a high, hard one under the chin usually shuts them up pretty good."[10] Patti, aware of the razzing, held that if her stripping hindered his career in any way, she would quit.[11]

Despite his hard work in camp and what pitching coach Ray Berres called his "rubbery arm,"[12] Rudolph spent the 1957 season in the minors. With a poor defense behind him (it was reported that no double plays were turned behind him all season[13]), he went 8-20 with a 4.72 ERA while pitching for both Louisville and Indianapolis of the American Association. However, he kept his walk rate low and won a late-season promotion to the White Sox, making his major-league debut on September 21, 1957. In his third appearance, on September 24, Rudolph pitched six innings of relief against the Kansas City Athletics to earn his first big-league win. He also stroked his first big-league hit (a double off Tom Morgan) during the game. Overall, Rudolph made five relief appearances for the Sox in 1957 and finished with a 1-0 record and a 2.25 ERA.

Rudolph showed up for spring training of 1958 with great confidence that he would stick with the Sox. In a letter accompanying his signed contract for 1958, Rudolph told owner Chuck Comiskey: "There won't be anyone in camp who will outbattle me for a berth with the White Sox."[14] But despite his confidence, Rudolph was again sent to Indianapolis for more seasoning. With a better defense behind him, his line improved to 11-12 with a 3.05 ERA, earning him another late-season call-up with the White Sox. Used exclusively as a reliever, Rudolph pitched in seven games, finished six of them, and ended the year with a record of 1-0 and an ERA of 2.57.

In 1959, Rudolph finally broke camp with the big club. As a left-handed reliever in the White Sox bullpen, Rudolph appeared in only four games during the first month of the season but did not allow a run in any of those appearances. Still, the White Sox were becoming disenchanted with Rudolph's lack of stuff — especially his substandard curveball. So on May 1 the

Left-hander Don Rudolph had a six-year major league career, but his fame was usually eclipsed by that of his wife, burlesque star Patti Waggin.

White Sox, attempting to fill an early power shortage, included Rudolph, along with outfielder Lou Skizas, in a trade with the Cincinnati Reds for veteran outfielder Del Ennis. Bill Veeck, successor to Chuck Comiskey as principal owner of the White Sox, commented on the trade: "Alas, the wrong Rudolph has the curves."[15] (Ennis hit only .219 with two home runs, and was released on June 20.)

Rudolph bounced between the majors and minors for the rest of 1959 with stints with the Cincinnati Redlegs, the Seattle Rainiers of the Pacific Coast League, and the Havana Sugar Kings of the International League. Although he struggled with the Redlegs and the Sugar Kings, he performed well as a starter for Seattle, finishing 7-4 with a 3.08 ERA in 13 games. Although Rudolph missed out on most of the White Sox' pennant season, his teammates voted him a one-quarter share of the World Series money.

Rudolph did not reach the majors in 1960, but continued to pitch well for the Seattle Rainiers as a starter, leading the PCL with a 2.42 ERA. He moved to Indianapolis for the start of 1961, a year that turned out to be important for him personally as well as professionally. That year, Patti and Don welcomed their daughter, Julena, into the world. While Patti took time off from her burlesque career to raise their daughter, Don won the American Association's Player of the Month award for August,[16] was a member of the Triple-A All-Star team, and finished with an 18-9 record and a 3.54 ERA.

Rudolph wanted to get another shot in the majors and he got his chance the following year, when the Cleveland Indians picked him up in the Rule 5 draft after the 1961 season. He broke camp with Cleveland after 1962 spring training but pitched only one game before being traded to the expansion Washington Senators with pitcher Steve Hamilton for outfielder Willie Tasby on May 3. The Senators gave Rudolph what he wanted most – a spot in the starting rotation. He took full advantage of the opportunity. On May 9, he won his first start with a complete-game victory over his former team, the White Sox. He pitched 31 consecutive scoreless innings between August 18 and September 2, and even made the American League All-Star Team – as a batting-practice pitcher. Even after an ugly September (0-4 with an 8.27 ERA), he was able to finish the year with an 8-10 record and a 3.62 ERA.

Rudolph was widely known as the "instant pitcher" – one of the quickest workers in the league. Seven of his 23 starts in 1962 were completed in less than two hours, including one against the Angels in only one hour and 32 minutes – the fastest game that year. His low walk rate and the low number of warm-up pitches he took between innings (he often took just three or four of the allotted eight[17]) contributed to his quick work. "It should not require three hours to do a two-hour job," he told *The Sporting News*, "Speeding up the games will not only please the fans, but I think the pitchers will find that their teammates make better plays behind them because they are more alert."[18] Rudolph was credited by some with inspiring the "hurry up" rule enacted in 1963 that cut the number of warm-up pitches allowed between innings to five.[19]

Late in the 1962 season, Rudolph was a participant in a bizarre incident at Memorial Stadium in Baltimore. After troubled Senators outfielder Jimmy Piersall was taunted by a heckler who said "You ought to be in Spring Grove State Hospital (a Maryland mental institution)," Piersall jumped into the stands to confront his heckler. Rudolph, who was standing near Piersall during the incident, jumped into the stands to give chase to Piersall. A police officer was able to confront Piersall before he reached the man and Rudolph sat on him to subdue him.[20]

Fresh off his previous year's success, Rudolph was the first Senator to sign his contract for 1963. Don also had some bold predictions to make: He would be the Opening Day starter for the Senators, and would win 20 games.[21] He was in fact the Opening Day starter for the Senators. But in front of President John F. Kennedy (his final Opening Day), the Orioles bested Rudolph, 3-1, behind home runs by Jim Gentile and Boog Powell. It didn't get much better for Rudolph after that. After his seventh win on August 4, he went 0-8 with a 6.93 ERA to finish 7-19 with a 4.55 ERA as the Senators lost 106 games and finished last in the AL.

In 1964, Rudolph had no bold predictions. While he had a 1.38 ERA in spring training, Don was sent to the Senators' minor-league club in Toronto the day before the season started. After pitching well in Toronto (3-1 with a 1.40 ERA in 45 innings pitched), Rudolph was recalled by the Senators on May 21, but he could not capture the magic of 1962. Used primarily as a reliever and spot starter, Rudolph finished with a 1-3 record and a 4.09 ERA.

Rudolph was unhappy with his treatment by the Senators in 1964, claiming he was misused. He was also upset at being sent to the minors to clear the way for "bonus kids" and promised that he would "be around when these morning glories fade."[22] Despite this promise, Rudolph's major-league career was over. The 1965 and 1966 seasons were spent in the minors with San Diego and Buffalo, where he went 20-28 with a 3.26 ERA. Rudolph retired from professional baseball after the 1966 season at the age of 35.

Throughout his career, Don had many plans for life after baseball. He once said he wanted to open a club for his wife named Don Rudolph's Patti Waggin. Later he said he wanted to be an avocado farmer.[23] But Rudolph ended up starting a contracting business called Underground Utility Company. Tragically, he did not have much time to enjoy his post-baseball life. On September 12, 1968, as Rudolph drove his truck up a steep grade near his home in Granada Hills, California, the truck overturned and he was thrown from the vehicle. The truck rolled over and crushed him. Don Rudolph was dead at the age of 37.[24]

• DON RUDOLPH •

The 1959 series of Topps baseball cards, Don's first, had little cartoons on the back to tell something about the player pictured on the front. Rudolph's (#179) reads: "Don's wife is a professional dancer." But even though he was often overshadowed by his wife, Don Rudolph left his mark on the game through his eccentricities and his quick work on the mound.

Notes

1. "Rudolph Leaves with Win, Gifts," *The Sporting News*, July 23, 1952.
2. Walter Johns, "Rookie Pitcher and 'The Dancer,'" *Mansfield (Ohio) News-Journal*, February 24, 1957
3. Lester Koelling, "Patti Hitches Waggin to Baseball Star," *Indianapolis News*, May 17, 1957.
4. Richard Dozer, "He Pitches – She Twitches," *Chicago Tribune*, April 27, 1958.
5. Ibid.
6. "Sox Rookie Will Vie with Wife in Curves," *Chicago Tribune*, January 31, 1957.
7. Dozer.
8. Koelling.
9. "Sox Rookie."
10. Russ Schneider, "Curves? Rookie Don Has a Lot of 'Em – and So Has His Cute Dancer Wife," *The Sporting News*, February 27, 1957.
11. Schneider.
12. David Condon, "White Sox Halted by Rain; Aim to Play 2d Game Today," *Chicago Tribune*, March 5, 1957.
13. Dozer.
14. Robert Cromie, "Cubs' Moryn, Sox' Rudolph Sign for 1958," *The Chicago Tribune*, February 7, 1958.
15. Lew Freedman, *Early Wynn, the Go-Go White Sox and the 1959 World Series* (Jefferson, North Carolina: McFarland & Co., 2009), 104.
16. Lester Koelling, "Carla Keeps Playoffs Here One More Day; Tribe Evens Series," *Indianapolis Star*, September 11, 1961.
17. Bob Addie, "Rudolph Promises to Win 20 Games," *Washington Post*, February 23, 1963.
18. "Faster Games Help Defense," *The Sporting News*, January 26, 1963.
19. Addie.
20. "Piersall Goes Into Stands After Fan, Runs Into Police Block," *Los Angeles Times*, September 14, 1962.
21. Addie.
22. "Rudolph Eyes Big-Time Hill Berth 'When the Morning Glories Fade,'" *The Sporting News*, January 16, 1965.
23. Addie.
24. "Former Senators' Pitcher Don Rudolph, 37, Killed," *Los Angeles Times*, September 13, 1968.

BOB SHAW

By Bill Johnson

Among the many essential cogs in the Go-Go White Sox machine of 1959 was Bob Shaw, a 6-foot-2, 195-pound right-handed pitcher. In just his second full season in the majors, Shaw won 18 regular-season games and finished third in the American League in ERA. He paired with mentor Early Wynn to give the Sox a lethal one-two punch at the front end of the pitching rotation, and proved a touchstone for the team during its wild pennant chase

Robert John Shaw was born in the Bronx, New York, on June 29, 1933,[1] and grew into a talented three-sport athlete during his high-school years in Garden City, Long Island. He spent the winters lettering in basketball, and his springs on the baseball team, but it was football that captured his real loyalty. Shaw wanted to attend college at Dartmouth but had neither the grades nor the money to join the Ivy League, so instead he accepted a football scholarship to St. Lawrence College in upstate New York. While the grant paid Shaw's tuition, there remained the problem of room and board. Despite working at a variety of odd jobs, he often slept on the floor of a buddy's dormitory room. One snowy night the dorm's roof leaked and Shaw woke up soaked in melted snow. That's when he made a life-changing decision: He would play baseball, and shortly thereafter accepted Tigers scout Ray Garland's offer of a $1,000 signing bonus.[2]

Shaw's road to the big leagues began in 1953 with the Jamestown Falcons, the Tigers' affiliate in the Class-D Pony League, under player-manager Danny Carnevale. Shaw posted a 5.58 ERA but still managed a 10-3 record for a superb team that scored seven runs per game and won the pennant by nearly 20 games. Shaw wasn't as fortunate in 1954, going 6-13 with a 5.00 ERA with Durham in the Carolina League, two steps up the ladder at Class B.

But Joe Gordon, the ex-Yankee great, was a coach on that team, and he noticed that Shaw gripped his fastball across the seams. Gordon told Shaw that in his later days with the Indians he'd watched Mike Garcia and others grip their fastballs *with* the seams, and that Shaw should give it a try.[3] This simple suggestion could not have come at a better time, as Shaw was seriously considering quitting the game. Having worked for New York Life Insurance in the offseason, he aspired to a management position. That goal, coupled with his on-the-field struggles, had almost driven Shaw to give up on baseball.

Fortunately for Shaw, Gordon's nudge paid off, as Shaw proceeded to speed up the rungs of the Tigers' farm system. On August 11, 1957, in an inauspicious major-league debut, he gave up five runs in three innings during the second game of a doubleheader against the White Sox. The next season, after a winter pitching for Marianao of the Cuban League and a strong showing in spring training, Shaw made the Tigers' Opening Day roster. May was rough on the young pitcher. In consecutive appearances, he gave up runs that cost Detroit both games, and on June 11 was returned to the minors.

That was the plan, anyway. Shaw refused to report to Charleston of the American Association. In a 2003 interview, Shaw told Joe Goddard of the *Chicago Sun Times*: "There was a clause in my Tigers contract that I'd make $1,000 if I was called up by June 15, but [general manager] John McHale said he wouldn't pay, so I gambled and went home. It was the best decision I ever made because they traded me to the White Sox."[4]

On June 15, 1958, Shaw and infielder Ray Boone joined the Chicago White Sox in exchange for outfielder Tito Francona and pitcher Bill Fischer. Shaw's 4-2 record over the second half of the 1958 season earned him a spot on Chicago's 1959 roster, but no one could have predicted his success in 1959.

It was in Chicago that he met one of the most profound influences of his early life, both in baseball and beyond, in the person of future Hall of Famer Early Wynn. Upon Shaw's move to the White Sox in 1958, he was assigned to room with Wynn on the road.

Shaw liked the way Wynn dressed, so he began buying his suits at the same store where Wynn bought his. Wynn was a pilot, so Shaw earned his own pilot's license. On the diamond, Wynn taught Shaw some of the nuances of pitching. Shaw said, "Wynn didn't use the [rosin] bag, and he'd watch me as my hands went

• BOB SHAW •

from powdery to sticky on hot days. He told me that he had better control without using the rosin bag, so I stopped using it. I also learned from Wynn how to take the up-and-in part of the plate."[5] Those subtle changes, like the one Joe Gordon had suggested to Shaw earlier, paid enormous dividends.

Most importantly, Wynn demonstrated to Shaw that there was life beyond baseball. Naturally predisposed to business, the young, unmarried pitcher was fascinated that a four-time All-Star like Wynn owned a bowling alley, and that the venture did not seem to inhibit his baseball career. On a recommendation from third baseman Billy Goodman, Shaw took his second-place 1958 World Series share of $1,975, borrowed an additional $10,000, and bought a commercial space that he promptly rented to a doctor.

Shaw, 25 years old when the '59 season started, made his season debut on April 10 with two-thirds of an inning in a 9-7 White Sox victory in Detroit. Two days later he earned the save in another win over Detroit. After a few more relief outings, Shaw bailed out his team and his roommate on April 22 with 7 1/3 innings of scoreless relief. Wynn, in an uncharacteristically bad start, allowed five Kansas City runs in the second inning and, after Roger Maris hit a three-run homer, was pulled in favor of Shaw. Bob allowed only three hits the rest of the way and earned the victory in Chicago's 20-6 blowout.

On May 13, Shaw started and finished a 4-0 victory over the Red Sox at Fenway Park, and afterward he usually followed Wynn in the starting rotation. With the help of his manager and his pitching coach, Shaw continued to develop his pitching skills; he later said, "Al Lopez and Ray Berres changed me with simple, basic mechanics. I threw three-quarters, and they moved me to the side to throw my slider from one spot. It worked immediately." He also adapted to the various catchers on staff. "Sherm Lollar liked to mix it up. . . . John Romano liked curves and Earl Battey liked fastballs."[6]

On September 22, Shaw yielded six hits but still tossed 2 2/3 scoreless innings in relief of Wynn as the White Sox defeated Cleveland, 4-2. That game clinched the American League pennant, the franchise's first since 1919, and allowed manager Lopez to begin setting up his pitching staff for the World Series, which began nine days later.

Bob Shaw had a career year for the White Sox in 1959, winning 18 games, posting a 2.69 ERA and finishing third in the voting for the Cy Young Award.

Behind Wynn in Game One, the White Sox thumped the Dodgers, 11-0, but Shaw took the loss in Game Two after giving up eight hits and four runs. The Dodgers followed up with victories in Games Three and Four, leaving the Sox on the brink of elimination.

But on October 6, in front of 92,706 fans at the Los Angeles Coliseum, Shaw atoned for his Game Two loss with scoreless ball into the eighth inning; with help from the bullpen, he earned a thrilling 1-0 win over Sandy Koufax and the Dodgers, a game that still holds the record for the largest World Series crowd ever.[7] What Shaw called his "best moment in baseball" was a close-run thing, though. "There were two outs and two on in the seventh," he recalled, "when Charlie Neal hit one out to right-center field. I was watching

Jim Landis, but Jim Rivera came out of nowhere to make the catch. Lopez had put Jim in right field just before the pitch and moved Al Smith to left. Brilliant move, wasn't it?"[8]

But Chicago's Series dreams died two days later at Comiskey Park when Wynn was knocked out early in Game Six and Dodgers reliever Larry Sherry turned in a brilliant relief outing as Los Angeles wrapped up the series with a 9-3 victory.

Shaw's 1959 statistics were outstanding. He finished third in the American League in wins (18) and ERA (2.69), led all starters with a .750 winning percentage, and fired three shutouts. Toss in his 2.57 ERA in his two Series starts – including that dramatic Game Five triumph – and Shaw obviously ranked as one of the year's most valuable young pitchers. Shaw was fiery. It was reported at the time that when Sox owner Bill Veeck refused to give Shaw a sufficient payraise, he "reportedly stood atop a catwalk outside Comiskey park and shouted down to the fans: "We're not going to win. Why are you people here?'"[9]

But as brilliant as Shaw's 1959 was, his 1960 became . . . well, if not a disaster, certainly a disappointment. His ERA jumped from 2.69 to 4.06 as he went 13-13 for a White Sox squad that finished 10 games behind the first-place Yankees. Shaw got off to a decent start in 1961, but his White Sox career ended on June 10 of that season. After throwing only 71 innings through the first two months of the campaign, he was sent to Kansas City with Wes Covington, Stan Johnson, and Jerry Staley in exchange for Ray Herbert, Don Larsen, Andy Carey, and Al Pilarcik. His four-month career with the Athletics was unspectacular, netting only a 9-10 record and an ERA of 4.31.

That December, Shaw was again on the move, this time to Milwaukee, along with Lou Klimchock, for Joe Azcue, Ed Charles, and Manny Jimenez. His two years with the Braves provided more instructional opportunities, as he developed – presumably with the help of teammate Lew Burdette – a nasty spitball. It has been rumored that later, when Shaw pitched for the Giants, he shared his secrets with a struggling young pitcher named Gaylord Perry, but this has yet to be either confirmed or denied.

It was with the Braves that Shaw enjoyed his finest individual campaign. Complementing the 1962 Braves' pitching staff paced by Warren Spahn and Lew Burdette, Shaw led the team in ERA (2.80) and strikeouts, and finished second in victories (15, against 9 losses) and complete games (12) as Milwaukee finished in fifth place in the 10-team National League. (It was the first year of major-league expansion.) Shaw's performance was recognized in his selection to the National League All Star Team, and in the national spotlight, as in the 1959 World Series, Shaw was exceptional. At Washington's RFK Stadium in the first of two All-Star games that year, he finished off his two-inning save of the NL win by enticing former Chicago teammate Luis Aparicio to fly out to center field to end the game. As it turned out, that save influenced a change in Shaw's career.

But first, following his spectacular 1962 season, Shaw married his fiancée, Asta Scovill of Wyckoff, New Jersey. Their family eventually grew to include two daughters, Karen and Linda, and a son, Glenn. As of 2007, the Shaws had seven grandchildren.

Spring training in 1963 was uneventful for the Braves, and the season opened with Shaw in the starting rotation. He started the second game of the year against the Pirates, but lost, 3-2 on a Donn Clendenon home run. Shaw pitched inconsistently over the next few weeks, and on May 4, against the Cubs, he set a major-league record by balking five times in one game. The balks netted the pitcher a $250 fine from the Braves and a trip to the bullpen. Manager Bobby Bragan was publicly optimistic about the move, so despite getting rocked for two runs in relief in a loss to the Phillies on June 11, Shaw remained in the bullpen even after Lew Burdette was traded on June 15. On June 18, Bragan called on the right-hander to close out a 7-5, 10-inning win over Pittsburgh, and Shaw's effectiveness marked the unofficial start of his new career as a reliever.

He finished the 1963 season with 13 saves by unofficial count (saves were not then an official statistic). The net effect appeared to have been to attract the attention of other NL general managers, because on December 3 Shaw was part of a blockbuster deal with the San Francisco Giants. The Braves sent Shaw, catcher Del Crandall, and pitcher Bob Hendley to San Francisco in exchange for Ernie Bowman, Felipe Alou, Ed Bailey, and Billy Hoeft.

"With him around, you can do a lot of things with your staff," Giants manager Alvin Dark was quoted as saying in the April 13 issue of *Sports Illustrated*.[10] Shaw notched seven wins in 1964 and 11 saves while working out of the San Francisco bullpen; moved into the starting rotation a month into the 1965 season, he wound up trailing only Juan Marichal in team victories with 16. His work helped the Giants push the Dodgers for 160 games before finally being eliminated on October 2.

Despite that success, Shaw was sold to the New York Mets in June 1966, and though he helped the young Mets team escape the cellar, he was dealt again, to Chicago – this time, the Cubs – in July 1967. On September 11, 1967, Shaw allowed three runs in one inning while taking the loss for the Cubs against the Astros. On the 19th, in the city where his major-league career began, he drew his release. He was 34, and never pitched another professional inning.

Shaw remained in the game for a time, working as a major-league pitching coach for the Brewers, albeit a controversial span. A brief entry by Mark Mulvoy in the July 30, 1973 *Sports Illustrated* captured the essence of Bob Shaw: "The Brewers suffered their biggest loss when Pitching Coach Bob Shaw resigned after a verbal squabble with General Manager Jim Wilson, a former pitcher himself. Preferring to forget that Jim Colborn has developed into a 13-game winner already under Shaw's tutelage, Wilson apparently blamed Shaw for the pitching misfortunes of Bill Parsons this season. A 13-game winner each of the last two years, Parsons has won only three this year because, Wilson claimed, Shaw altered his delivery."[11] Despite the setback, Shaw wrote a 1981 instructional manual on pitching[12] and continued to coach amateur baseball.

Shaw then took his knowledge to the American Legion diamonds of West Palm Beach, Florida, where he coached for years, and in 1986, he led the team from Post 126 (Jensen Beach) to the American Legion World Series title. After Shaw died, the plaudits rained down from coaches that he'd mentored. Kevin O'Sullivan, the coach of the University of Florida team, played for Shaw's American Legion team, and later told Jeff Greer: "Everything I teach, to this day, is from (Mr. Shaw); He meant so much to so many people in the coaching profession."[13]

Despite a medical emergency in the early 1980s – he contracted hepatitis from tainted blood he received after a post-operative infection, and nearly bled to death – Shaw's later life was more like 1959 than 1967. Living near Jupiter, Florida, and happily married until he passed away, Shaw stayed in shape, in part due to his 7 handicap on the golf course, while building on the success of his early real-estate venture as co-owner of Shaw Sowden Realty and Management Properties, a venture in which he remained actively engaged until May of 2010. Shaw died in Tequesta, Florida, on September 23, 2010, after a final battle with liver cancer[14] at the age of 77.

Bob Shaw's lifetime record in the majors was 108-98, with 32 saves and a 3.52 ERA over 11 seasons. His brilliant 1959 campaign earned him a key role in White Sox lore, but it's his life after baseball that truly defined the gentleman that he always remained.

Notes

1. Bob Shaw page at http://www.baseball-reference.com/players/s/shawbo01.shtml
2. Interview with Bob Shaw, November 14, 2008.
3. Shaw interview, 2008.
4. Joe Goddard. "Catching Up With Bob Shaw," *Chicago Sun-Times*, July 27, 2003.
5. Bob Shaw Interview, whitesoxinteractive.com
6. Shaw interview, 2008.
7. Jeff Greer "Bob Shaw, pitcher who beat Sandy Koufax in 1959 World Series, dies at age 77," *Palm Beach Post*, September 25, 2010; online: http://www.palmbeachpost.com/news/sports/baseball/bob-shaw-pitcher-who-beat-sandy-koufax-in-1959-wor/nMBHq/
8. Shaw interview, 2008.
9. Steve Dorsey, "Major leaguer Bob Shaw touched lives of many local Palm Beach County baseball players," *Sun Sentinel*, September 27, 2010.
10. "San Francisco Giants," *Sports Illustrated*, April 13, 1964.
11. Mark Mulvoy, "The Week (July 15-21)," *Sports Illustrated*, July 30, 1973.
12. Bob Shaw *Pitching* (New York: Viking, 1972).
13. Greer.
14. Dorsey.

HARRY SIMPSON

by Cort Vitty

Harry Simpson first saw life as a child in the segregated South. He went on to be one of the first black players to break the color line. Born in Atlanta, Georgia on December 3, 1925, (many accounts list his birth year as 1923 or 1924), Harry was the fourth child of Frank and Maggie Simpson; according to the 1930 Census, he had three brothers and two sisters. As a lad around Dalton, Georgia, a carpet-manufacturing city in the northern part of the state, Harry was called "Goody"[1] because of his kind disposition and willingness to help.

In September of 1941, with conflict escalating in Europe, Harry enlisted in the Army; he was assigned to Fort Benning, Georgia, for basic training and served until the war ended in 1945. Discharged from the Army, he married the former Johnnie Cooper on August 15, 1946.

Goose Curry, manager of the Philadelphia Stars of the Negro National League, signed Simpson for his team in 1946. Originally a right-handed pitcher, Simpson moved to the outfield and hit a respectable .333 in 52 games.

With the Stars in 1947, his average slipped to .244 and a dejected Simpson started to second-guess his career choice. Life in the Negro leagues was hard and Simpson became discouraged. He left the Stars and got a sales job outside of baseball. Johnnie, his wife, convinced Harry that his future was in baseball; she pleaded with him to return to the diamond and he abided by her wishes.

Simpson later recalled those days: "It was a tough life" in the old Negro leagues. "Sometimes you'd play in five cities in five nights and never see a bed. We thought nothing of playing three games in the same day. ... We never had a trainer. You carried some liniment and rubbed it on when you hurt."[2] But despite the tough life, there were great players in the Negro Leagues. Simpson recalled Josh Gibson as "the greatest hitter I ever saw. He was dying when I saw him, that last year. He couldn't even stoop down behind the plate, but man, he could still hit."[3]

Simpson played against Satchel Paige and commented, "He wasn't the fastest pitcher in our league. Maybe he had better control, but he wasn't the fastest. Think what these fellows could've done if they'd been given a chance in their prime."[4] Simpson said Negro League stars earned $2,000 a month during the summer, then would play in Mexico or South America for as little as $50 a month. "Many of them, like Gibson, contracted fatal diseases while earning eating money south of the border,"[5] he asserted.

He picked up his nickname during his Negro League days. Harry wore a size 13 shoe, and a sportswriter dubbed him "Suitcase" Simpson, based on a character by that name with feet as large as suitcases, in the comic strip "Toonerville Folks."[6] A cartoon appeared in the paper showing Harry with feet as long as a bed. "At first, I didn't like the name," Simpson said much later, "now I'm used to it."[7]

In 1948, Simpson caught the eye of NBA coach Eddie Gottlieb, who doubled as an unofficial baseball scout. Gottlieb was greatly impressed and began calling him "the tan Ted Williams," making a comparison to the slugging Boston Red Sox star. "He's built like Ted, is faster and can field much better."[8] Gottlieb said. "I am not going to say that he will hit better than Ted, but he has a chance."[9] Simpson was described by writer Doc Young in *Great Negro Baseball Stars* as "a lean, bony, gangly man who was as loose as a dishrag at the plate."[10] In his prime, the trim outfielder stood 6-feet-1 and weighed 180 pounds.

Based on glowing recommendations, eight major league scouts offered a tryout; all declined the opportunity to sign the prospect. At his own expense, Gottlieb financed a trip to Arizona for Simpson to get a look-see by Cleveland Indians general manager Hank Greenberg. The Indians, owned by Bill Veeck, had signed Larry Doby to be the first black player in the American League and were one of the first major league teams to scout and sign black players. During a split-squad game, Harry went 4-for-4, including two home runs, and Greenberg hustled to sign Gottlieb's protégé.

In 1949, Simpson was assigned to the Wilkes-Barre Indians of the Class-A Eastern League. He hit .305, leading the league with 31 home runs, 120 runs batted in, and 125 runs scored. He made the league's all-star squad. His club finished in third place, making the playoffs, but losing the finals.

• HARRY SIMPSON •

In 1950, Simpson was promoted to the San Diego Padres of the Pacific Coast League. He hit .323 and led the loop with 156 RBIs in the 200-game season; he also contributed 19 triples and 33 home runs. After such an impressive season, it appeared the young man was headed to a prominent big-league career. GM Greenberg called Simpson "one of the finest prospects I've ever seen."[11]

Harry reported to the Indians' 1951 training camp in Tucson, Arizona, and manager Al Lopez started with the Ted Williams comparison too. "He cocks that bat like Williams," Lopez told reporters, "and waits until the last moment to uncoil. Simpson lashes with the bat as if it were a buggy whip."[12] But the Indians roster included four black players - Larry Doby, Luke Easter, Minnie Minoso, and Simpson. According to several sources including *The Sporting News*, Indians management wondered if four Negroes on the club were too many. Internally, they decided to keep three.

When it came time to trim the roster, Greenberg decided to stick with Simpson and peddle Minnie Minoso to the Chicago White Sox. Harry hit over .400 during spring training, but wound up having a disappointing season, getting 332 at-bats but hitting only .229, while driving in a measly 24 runs. Simpson split his time between the outfield and first base. Doc Young of the *Pittsburgh Courier* wrote that Simpson "should have been playing minor league ball for experience. The early promotion to the major leagues stunted a potentially promising career."[13] Simpson admitted that the rush to meet expectations left him anxious in the batter's box; he altered his stance daily to try to get untracked. The pressure on Simpson was magnified when Minoso went on to become a big star with the White Sox.

Determined to find himself in 1952, Simpson attended a pre-spring-training batting school conducted by ex-Indian great Tris Speaker. Speaker remarked that Simpson "has got to find his own way." Coincidentally, Simpson located an article authored by Ty Cobb on the subject of hitting. When in a slump, the article said, Cobb concentrated on only one thing – hitting the ball back at the pitcher. Simpson tried it, abandoning the power stroke he used in the Pacific Coast League. "Might as well face it, I'm not strong enough," Simpson said. "Out there a man hits a ball 360 feet and he has himself a home run. Up here, he's just got himself a big out."[14] An early-season high point for Harry came on April 26 when he broke up a no-hitter by Detroit's Art Houtteman with two outs

One of the first black players in the American League, Harry Simpson broke in with the Cleveland Indians in 1951. He played for five major league teams in his eight-year career, including a stint with the 1959 White Sox.

in the ninth inning. But a hot start (.347 by May 10), cooled to just .266 by season's end, with 10 home runs and 65 RBIs. Simpson was durable, though, playing in 146 of Cleveland's 155 games, over 80% of them in the outfield. His .266 average was slightly above the Indians team average of .262.

In spring training of 1953, the Indians changed Simpson's stance, moving him closer to the plate and placing his left foot slightly behind his right. Simpson believed this stance helped him put better wood on the ball and improved his timing. Sure enough, he was banging away at a .541 clip after 11 Grapefruit League contests, but GM Hank Greenberg cautioned against optimism regarding the highly touted outfielder. "To call him the greatest prospect to come out of the Coast league since Joe DiMaggio is silly. He does have ability and could develop into a fine ballplayer."[15]

Simpson ultimately saw his average dip to .227 in 82 games with the Indians.

The 1954 Cleveland Indians won 111 games while claiming the American League flag, but it was without the services of Simpson. On March 24 he broke his wrist on a close play at the plate. Doctors predicted a recovery period of six weeks and the parent club decided to send Simpson back to the minors. The wrist healed and Harry returned to the lineup with the Indianapolis Indians, playing in an even 100 games. The club finished at the top of the American Association and Simpson contributed a .282 average with 12 home runs.

Spring training of 1955 and the arrival of Ralph Kiner proved that room no longer existed on the Indians roster for the trim outfielder. Simpson was sold to the Kansas City Athletics on May 11. When he reported to the A's, manager Lou Boudreau recommended returning to his original loose stance, spraying the ball to all fields. This relaxed approach plus plenty of playing time produced positive results, culminating in a .301 average and making him a fan favorite. He also showed his versatility by playing all three outfield positions as well as first base.

The next year, 1956, was a banner year for Simpson. He hit .293 with 21 homers and 105 RBIs. Naming him to the All-Star team, Yankees manager Casey Stengel took note of his long, smooth stride in the outfield and strong throwing arm, and called him the best right fielder in the league. On June 24, Simpson became a bit of a folk hero by depositing a homer onto Brooklyn Avenue, outside of Kansas City's Municipal Stadium. The ballpark had a concrete wall atop a 40-foot-high embankment in right field, making it appear impossible to ever plant one on the other side. A barnstorming Babe Ruth even had trouble hitting the target during exhibition games. Simpson accomplished the Herculean feat on a pitch served up by Dave Sisler of the Red Sox.

In 1957, Simpson moved to the Yankees in the aftermath of the brawl at the Copacabana nightclub in New York involving some Yankees players. Simpson was hitting .296 when traded to the Yankees on June 15, along with pitcher Ryne Duren and outfielder Jim Pisoni, in exchange for infielder Billy Martin, a participant in the Copacabana fight, pitcher Ralph Terry, infielder-outfielder Woody Held, and outfielder Bob Martyn. The consensus was that the A's got the better of the deal. Simpson was initially pleased to become a Yankee, but came to regret the deal that sent him to the big city. "The worst break I ever got was being traded to the Yankees,"[16] he said later. He sensed something was wrong upon reporting to the Yankee clubhouse and meeting Casey Stengel. "I introduced myself to Casey,"[17] Simpson recalled. "He didn't say he was glad to have me or anything else. Instead he started talking about how he hated to lose Billy Martin. … It made me feel a little funny."[18] Simpson's sense of the situation was pretty much on the mark. He knew he'd platoon with the Yankees and history showed that he wasn't at his best coming off the bench. He ended the season hitting .250 in 75 games. During the 1957 World Series, Simpson and Elston Howard alternated at first base, spelling an injured Moose Skowron. Simpson hit a disappointing .083 in the Fall Classic as the Milwaukee Braves prevailed over the Yankees in seven games.

Simpson was hitting a mere .216 on June 15, 1958, when the Yankees traded him back to Kansas City along with pitcher Bob Grim for A's hurlers Duke Maas and Virgil Trucks. The deal was announced during a Yankees game against the Detroit Tigers, but Casey Stengel decided to send Harry up as a pinch hitter anyway. Back in Kansas City, he posted a .264 average in 78 games.

Simpson's signed contact for the 1959 season was accompanied by a letter to Parke Carroll, general manager of the A's, in which he wrote, "I'm a better ballplayer than I showed you last year. I just hope you will believe in me. I'll prove I'm better. I've just got to vindicate myself."[19] On May 2 Harry was hitting a solid .286, but the A's sent him to the Chicago White Sox in exchange for infielder Ray Boone. Sox owner Bill Veeck and his general manager, Hank Greenberg, had signed Simpson to his first major-league contract and were of course very familiar with him. They hoped that Simpson would add spark to the Sox lineup and wanted to take advantage of Harry's versatility.

But Simpson batted only .187 in 38 games with the White Sox before being dealt to the Pittsburgh Pirates on August 25 for slugging infielder Ted Kluszewski, a 34-year-old veteran of 13 National League seasons. Simpson got into only nine games with the Pirates, hitting .267 in 15 at-bats. Big Klu hit .297 during the balance of the White Sox season and contributed a torrid .391 batting average during the World Series. After all of the hoopla was over, the White Sox eventually bought Simpson back from the Pirates on October 13. Simpson was about the unluckiest player in all of major-league baseball during 1959; his timing in and out of Chicago cost him a World Series check.

In 1960, Simpson saw action with the PCL San Diego Padres, batting .222 in 95 games. Back with the Padres in 1961, he appeared in 146 games, hitting .303 with 24 home runs and 105 RBIs.

In 1962, the veteran was back with the Indianapolis Indians, where he hit .279 in 132 games with 24 home runs. He started 1963 in Indianapolis, hitting .382 in 11 games, before moving onto the Mexican League Diablo Rojos, where he hit .334 with 21 home runs. He continued with the Red Devils in 1964, hitting .306 with 14 homers. On that note, he retired as a player.

Simpson moved to Akron, Ohio, in 1959. He worked as a machinist at Goodyear Aerospace from 1967 until he retired in 1976. He suffered a heart attack and died on April 3, 1979, in Akron. Services were held at the New Trinity Baptist Church, where Harry was a deacon. He is buried at West Hill Cemetery in Dalton, Georgia.

Harry Simpson criticized any ballplayer who didn't give 100 percent and especially black players who didn't hustle. "The important thing as I see it, is that I, as a Negro, have been given a great privilege and I just wish all members of my race felt the same deep gratitude as I do," he once said. "Here I am making more money than a great percentage of the men of my race. Here I am on a ballclub where I've been given every chance in the world to make good. What more could I possibly want? I live as good as anybody could. I get a good salary. I've got a good job. Baseball has given this to me. Where could I have gotten all this? In what other profession could I have been given the same chance?"[20]

All told, Simpson hit a workmanlike .266 in a career spanning 1951 through 1959. In 888 major-league contests, with 2,829 at-bats, his on-base percentage registered a respectable .331. The versatile outfielder/first baseman had a career fielding average of .984. All of these factors certainly contributed to his longevity in the days when each league had eight teams.

Sources

In addition to the sources cited in the Notes, the author also consulted a number of newspapers, baseball-almanac.com, baseballlibrary.com, baseball-reference.com, sabr.org, and the following:

Johnson, Lloyd, and Miles Wolff. *Encyclopedia of Minor League Baseball* (Durham. N.C.: Baseball America, 1997).

Reichler, Joseph L., editor. *The Baseball Encyclopedia* (New York: Macmillan, 1982).

Rosenthal, Harold. "Simpson Made It the Second Time," *Sport Magazine*, September 1957

Notes

1. *Cleveland Indians Sketchbook*, 1951.
2. Dick Mittman, "Old Negro Loop Players Greatest," *News-Palladium* (Benton Harbor, Michigan), May 2, 1963.
3. Ibid.
4. Ibid.
5. Ibid.
6. *Cleveland Indians Sketchbook*, 1951.
7. Ibid.
8. Rick Swaine, *Black Stars Who Made Baseball Whole* (Jefferson, North Carolina: McFarland, 2006), 237.
9. Frank T. Blair, "Simpson Hailed As Second Williams," *Long Beach Press-Telegram*, May 4, 1951.
10. A.S. "Doc" Young. *Great Negro Baseball Stars and How They Made the Major Leagues* (New York: A.S. Barnes, 1953), 67.
11. "Sad-Eyed Suitcase Simpson Unpacks For Stay In Majors," *The Daily Review* (Haywood California), March 8, 1951.
12. *The Sporting News*, January 28, 1951.
13. Doc Young, *Pittsburgh Courier* (undated clipping).
14. "Cobb and Speaker Helped Simpson Find Himself," *Coshocton* (Ohio) *Tribune*, May 11, 1952.
15. Ray McNally, "Sportingly Yours," *Tucson Daily Citizen Sports*, March 21, 1953.
16. Sam Lacy, *Afro-American*, March 25, 1959.
17. Ernest Mehl, "Simpson of Joy for A's," *The Sporting News*, July 18, 1956.
18. Ibid.
19. "Simpson Adds Pledge to A's With His Pact," *The Sporting News*, January 21, 1959.
20. Larry Moffit & Jonathan Kronstadt, *Crossing the Line: Black Major Leaguers, 1947-59* (Iowa City: University of Iowa Press, 1994), 67.

LOU SKIZAS

By Matt Bohn

"I was a character in baseball. I saw it as an interim type of career," Lou Skizas told Bill Gleason.[1] Skizas, known as "The Nervous Greek" during his four-season major-league playing career, was perhaps best known for an unusual ritual that he followed before coming to bat. Before reaching the plate, the right-handed-batting Skizas dropped his bat, covering it with dirt. Then, wiping the bat off by rubbing it between his pants legs, he kissed the end of the bat before reaching into his back pocket at least three times to touch an object that was said to be a good-luck piece. Placing all of his weight on his right leg, Skizas kept his left foot off of the ground until just before the pitch reached the plate. This was the unorthodox style that belonged to the man Casey Stengel once called "the greatest natural-looking hitter I've ever seen."[2]

Born June 2, 1932, in Chicago, to Greek immigrants Peter and Bessie (Stamos) Skizas, young Lou struggled in school in his early years because of a lack of familiarity with English. "We lived in the vicinity of Polk and Kedzie, the only Greek family on the block," Skizas told Bill Gleason. "We spoke Greek in my home, and the first day I went off to school, the teacher sent me home. I couldn't understand her so she thought I was retarded." [3] Skizas eventually graduated in 1948 from Crane Tech in Chicago, where he excelled in baseball.

John Kringas, a businessman who sponsored teams for young athletes in the Chicago area, told the *Chicago News Journal* in 1976 about Skizas's start in major-league baseball. "Our team was playing in Riis Park and a scout came out to look at the opposing pitcher, who was a tall and highly regarded right-hander," Kringas said. "Skizas, only 16 at the time, blasted out four hits against the highly regarded hurler and right then and there got the recognition that led to a professional career."[4] After signing a contract with the New York Yankees in 1949, Skizas began his professional baseball career as a third baseman for Fond du Lac of the Class-D Wisconsin State League. He finished the season with Independence of the Kansas-Oklahoma-Missouri (KOM) League. With Independence, Skizas batted .297 in 102 games, driving in 76 runs.

In 1950, Skizas and three other Yankee prospects (including shortstop Mickey Mantle, who remained a lifelong friend of Lou's) were promoted to Joplin of the Class-C Western Association. Moving to the outfield, Lou hit .273 in 124 games with Joplin with 21 home runs and 87 RBIs. Scout E.H. "Dutch" Zwilling, in a report to the Yankees, said Skizas was a "fair hitter" with power, but was "weak on slow pitches." The scouting report, found in Skizas's file at the National Baseball Hall of Fame in Cooperstown, also said the 18-year-old had a "careless attitude" and "indifferent disposition" and concluded that he "may develop into real good hitter – has power – may be slow in coming but has possibilities." Zwilling ended his report on Skizas by describing him as "not a thinker at present."[5]

The following year, Skizas was moved up to the Class-B Piedmont League, where he played for the Norfolk Tars. Making his debut on April 29, 1951, Lou hit two home runs and three singles, driving in five runs. A month and a half later, on June 16, he had another impressive performance for Norfolk, hitting three home runs and driving in seven runs against Richmond. Hitting .311 for the season, Skizas helped lead Norfolk to the Piedmont League championship.

After spending 1952 and 1953 in the Army, serving overseas in Germany and Italy, Skizas began the 1954 season with the American Association Kansas City Blues. Sent down to the Southern Association Birmingham Barons in late May, Skizas made an impressive debut with the Barons, racking up five hits in seven at-bats during a May 30 doubleheader. His unique batting style entertained the fans, reported sportswriter George K. Leonard: "When he appeared in Nashville's Sulphur Dell for the first time, June 1, Skizas entertained a crowd of 2,847 with his sideshow shuffling and arm waving. After going through a long ritual before each pitch, Lou stuffed his hand in his back pocket as a good luck gesture just before swinging. Occasionally that gimmick backfired when the opposing pitcher quick pitched."[6] Skizas batted .305 during his 69 games in Birmingham.

Moving up to the Yankees' American Association team in Denver in 1955, Skizas had a good, albeit

• LOU SKIZAS •

injury-plagued, season. Sidelined for two weeks after catching a fly ball on the top of his ring finger, Skizas was leading the league in hitting with a .353 average by early August. But a groin injury on August 6 kept him out of the lineup for 10 days. Shortly after returning to the lineup, Lou was ordered to "bed rest" on August 28. Finishing the season with a .348 average, Skizas was 24 at-bats short of the 400 needed to put him in the running for the league's batting championship. He ended the season with 21 home runs and 99 RBIs.

Skizas's excellent year in Denver got the attention of Yankees general manager George Weiss, who was looking for a "solid outfielder" after the team's loss to the Dodgers in the World Series. "Skizas may be our man," Weiss told sportswriter Dan Daniel.[7]

Starting his major-league career with the Yankees in April 1956, Skizas made an impression on manager Casey Stengel. Not only did his manager call him "the greatest natural-looking hitter I've ever seen," he added that "he can hit any pitcher who ever lived."[8] But though impressed with Skizas's hitting skills, he was less impressed with the player's fielding ability, and Skizas made only six pinch-hit appearances with the Yankees, managing just one hit, before being sent down to the Yankees' Triple-A team in Richmond.

Shortly after arriving in Richmond, Skizas was struck with what *The Sporting News* referred to as a "mysterious back ailment" that left him on the bench for most of the month.[9] After playing only 16 games at Richmond, Skizas was traded to the Kansas City A's on June 14 with first baseman Eddie Robinson for pitcher Moe Burtschy, outfielder Bill Renna and cash. Spending most of the season playing left and right field for the A's, Skizas batted .316 with 11 home runs and 39 runs batted in. Summing up Lou's performance at the end of the season, Kansas City sportswriter Joe McGuff wrote, "For the most part his defensive work proved to be a pleasant surprise, although at times he had alarming lapses."[10]

In the offseason, Skizas played winter ball in the Dominican and Puerto Rican leagues, then spent the entire 1957 season with Kansas City. His eccentric batting style had quickly made him a favorite with the Athletics' fans. By this time, he had taken to occupying the batter's box by walking a path between the catcher and the umpire. Asked about his unusual batting practices by reporter Ernest Mehl in March, 1957, Skizas somewhat cryptically insisted that he didn't adopt his batting style out of superstition. "I

Lou Skizas played for four American League teams in a brief 239-game career, then returned to school, eventually earning a PhD. in biology.

definitely am not superstitious," Skizas said. "A lot of players are, I know. I'm not. Of course, I'll admit that I can't see myself as others see me. But what I do seems natural to me."[11]

Again he spent most of the season playing right field, though he did see some games at left field (the position he preferred) and third base. His average dropped dramatically. In 119 games, Skizas batted just .245. On November 20, he was traded to the Detroit Tigers in a 13-player deal.

Playing in left field and at third base, Skizas's place with the Tigers did not appear to be secure early in the season. Skizas was hitting just .242 in just 23 games, and his defensive play may have made up manager Jack Tighe's mind. "Tighe didn't think I could do anything for that matter," Skizas told *Charleston Gazette* reporter A.L. Hardman. "He not only thought I was a terrible third baseman but not a very good outfielder."[12] Skizas and pitcher Bob Shaw were sent to the Tigers' Triple-A team in Charleston on June 5.

Skizas, who had been attending college courses in the offseason for many years, did not report to Charleston until nearly two weeks after he was assigned there. "There comes a time when a man must reevaluate things," he told A.L. Hardman. "That's what I've been doing. It wasn't that I minded playing in Charleston. But I wondered if being sent back to the minors again didn't signify that I might be failing in baseball. I wanted some time to think it over."[13] He belted out three hits in his first game with Charleston, on June 17, but then struggled, hitting just .163 in his 28 games there. Sent down to the Double-A Birmingham Barons in late July, Lou pulled a leg muscle and a tendon in his second game with the Barons, on August 5, and was out for the rest of the season.

In December 1958, Skizas was selected in the Rule 5 draft by the Chicago White Sox. It was a move that intrigued his former manager, Casey Stengel. "You can't figure him out," the Perfessor said in his prolix way. "He's a guy who fires managers. He's got ability, but he scares you because he might not feel like going after a ball hit his way. I know he's smart, but why doesn't he decide to play baseball or get out of it? I hear he's going to the state university in Illinois and is one of the brightest students there. I understand all the boy's kinfolk come out to watch him play. This gives me the idea that's why the White Sox drafted him. He just might be inspired to be a hell of a player in Comiskey Park."[14]

Skizas's tenure with the pennant-winning White Sox was brief. In just 13 at-bats in April, he had only one hit, a single against his former team, the Yankees, on April 30. The next day, Skizas and pitcher Don Rudolph were traded to the Cincinnati Reds for outfielder Del Ennis. The Reds immediately sent Skizas to the International League Havana Sugar Kings. Skizas, still only 27, never played in the major leagues again.

Skizas played 36 games in Havana in 1959, batting .286, but didn't enjoy playing there. Reportedly suffering a "digestive ailment" from eating Cuban food, he asked to be sent to a team in the United States and was sold to the Seattle Rainiers of the Class-AAA Pacific Coast League. Skizas played with Seattle through part of 1960 before being sent down to the Nashville Vols of the Double-A Southern Association. He saw action in the next two seasons with Indianapolis, Macon, Denver, and finally the Mexico City Tigers before ending his playing career in 1962.

Continuing his education had always been a priority for Skizas. "My parents stressed the importance of education and my older brother, Gus [who earned a master's degree in math], motivated me toward college," he told Bill Gleason. "Gus was an outstanding shortstop for the University of Illinois but four years in the Marine Corps put an end to his dream of being a big leaguer." (Gus spent part of the 1950 seasons with Vincennes, Indiana, of the Class D Mississippi-Ohio Valley League.) Lou obtained his bachelor's degree in 1960, a master's in 1962, and a Ph.D. in biology in 1965. "Counting two years of winter ball and two years in the Army, it took me 11 years to get my bachelor's degree. I'd always start the semester about two weeks late and have to leave in the late winter but I was determined to stay with it," he said.[15] The man who had been labeled "not a thinker" by a baseball scout was now a Ph.D., a rarity for a professional ballplayer.

Skizas taught at Illinois State University for five years before taking a position at the University of Illinois in Champaign as an associate professor in the Department of Life Sciences. He also coached the university baseball team for 10 years. Retiring from teaching in 1995, Skizas lived in the Chicago area, spending his spare time visiting family members (including daughter Jane and son Louie Jr. as well as his cousin, actor John Stamos.) However, even in retirement, Skizas kept his hand in baseball. "I do a little scouting for the Cubs," he told Diamantis Zervos in the late 1990s. "I like scouting. It's not a whole lot of pressure on me. I'm just kind of a bird dog in this area and I watch a lot of baseball games. I stay close to baseball. That's my game. I don't have time for any other game. I love the game."[16]

Sources

In addition to the sources cited in the Notes, the author also consulted:

Falkner, David. *The Last Hero The Life of Mickey Mantle* (New York: Simon & Schuster, 1995).

And a number of articles, including:

Haraway, Frank. "Skizas, Bears' Fidgety Slugger, Gives Flingers Fits With His Hits; 'Nervous Greek' Bids for Loop Batting Title and RBI Crown," *The Sporting News*, August 24, 1955: 29.

Hudson, Jim. "Skizas Locates Friends In Hurry With Three Hits; Davie Pitches Tonight After

LOU SKIZAS

Sens Slam 17 Hits," *Charleston Daily Mail* (West Virginia), June 18, 1958: 12.

Hudson, Jim. "Warming Up; Skizas Wins Some Fans In a Hurry," *Charleston Daily Mail* (West Virginia), June 18, 1958: 12.

"Lou Skizas Back With Denver," *The Sporting News*, June 30, 1962: 32.

"Lou Skizas In Flashy Debut," *The Sporting News*, May 9, 1951: 32.

"Yankees Recall Siebern, Deal Robinson and Skizas to A's," *The Sporting News*, June 20, 1956: 9.

Notes

1. Bill Gleason, "Triglycerides Replace Baseball in Skizas' Life," undated article found in Skizas' player file at the National Baseball Hall of Fame, Cooperstown, New York.
2. Milton Richman, United Press, "Greatest Hitter In Baseball Is Skizas," *Huronite and Daily Plainsman* (South Dakota), April 4, 1957: 10.
3. Gleason.
4. Nails Florio, "Ex-area athlete Kringas Hellenic 'Man of Year'," *Chicago News Journal*, February 26, 1976: Sec. 11, 1.
5. Scouting report from Lou Skizas file, National Baseball Hall of Fame.
6. George Leonard, "Chattanooga Joins 1st-Division Battle," *The Sporting News*, August 13, 1958: 39.
7. Dan Daniel, "Shortstop, Outfielder, 'Solid Pitcher' Listed," *The Sporting News*, October 12, 1955: 7.
8. Richman.
9. *The Sporting News*, June 6, 1956: 32.
10. Joe McGuff, "Skizas Is 18th Player To Sign," *Kansas City Star*, January 30, 1957: 28.
11. Ernest Mehl, "A's Skizas Doesn't Fear Jinx; He's Naturally Unpredictable," *The Sporting News*, March 6, 1957: 34.
12. A.L. Hardman, "Lou Took Some Time To Think Things Out," *Charleston Gazette* (West Virginia), June 19, 1958: 20.
13. Ibid.
14. Edgar Munzel, "Golden Greek Skizas Seen as Green Touch in Pale Hose Garden," *The Sporting News*, December 10, 1958: 19.
15. Gleason.
16. Diamantis Zervos, *Baseball's Golden Greeks* (Canton: Aegean Books International, 1998), 180.

AL SMITH
by Gary Livacari

Al Smith was an accomplished ballplayer whose major-league career spanned 12 seasons with four American League teams. Primarily an outfielder, he played six positions as a major leaguer and was a fine defender with a strong arm and good speed. Smith finished with a .272 lifetime batting average, hit 164 home runs, and reached base nearly 36 percent of the time. He also made two All-Star teams and played for two pennant winners (both managed by Al Lopez). He hit a career-best .315 in 1960 and posted his biggest power numbers—28 homers and 93 RBIs—in 1961. But despite his considerable on-field accomplishments, he will always be best remembered as the unwitting subject in one of baseball's most lasting images: the "beer-bath" photo from Game Two of the 1959 World Series. When Smith died in 2002, his obituary in the *New York Times* was headlined, "Al Smith, 73, Dies; Was Doused in Series."[1]

Alphonse Eugene Smith was born on February 7, 1928, in Kirkwood, Missouri, a St. Louis suburb. He grew up a fan of both local big-league teams, the Cardinals and the Browns, and his hero was Cardinals outfielder Joe Medwick. Nicknamed "Fuzzy," Smith was a versatile, multitalented athlete at Douglas High in Webster Groves, Missouri. The MVP of the baseball team, he also starred in football, basketball, and track, and was a Golden Gloves boxing champion in the 160-pound division. Smith scored 33 touchdowns in one football season and was reputed to have scored 10 touchdowns in one game.

Upon his graduation in 1946, Smith signed with the Negro American League's Cleveland Buckeyes. Because he was only 17, his mother had to sign his contract. In his first full season with the Buckeyes, in 1947, Smith was moved from his natural position of third base to shortstop and batted .285. He led the league with 27 doubles and 11 triples, and finished second with 12 home runs. The Buckeyes, managed by Quincy Trouppe, posted a pennant-winning 54-23 record and played in the Negro League World Series (losing to the New York Cubans). Smith changed positions again in 1948, this time to the outfield. That summer, he caught the eye of Cleveland Indians scout Laddie Placek, who had been dispatched to League Park to evaluate pitcher Sam "Toothpick" Jones. On July 11, Placek signed both Jones and Smith to major-league contracts.

Smith was sent to Class-A Wilkes-Barre in the Eastern League, becoming the league's first African-American player. He hit .316 the rest of the way, and then .311 with the same club in 1949. Smith later said of Wilkes-Barre manager Bill Norman, "He was a thoroughbred. He said he was down there to train and get ballplayers ready to go to the big leagues and if anyone didn't like the idea that I was playing they could get up and leave."[2]

For 1950, Smith earned a promotion to San Diego in the Pacific Coast League, where he spent the next two seasons. In 1952 Smith moved once more, this time to Indianapolis in the American Association, where he played under Birdie Tebbetts, another manager who helped Smith integrate the team. "He was *the* man," Smith recalled, "When he'd tell you something you believed it. He's the kind of guy that if he knew you played good, it didn't make no difference what color you were. He threw all that out the window."[3] Smith finally received the call to the Indians after posting a .332 average in the first half of the season, and debuted in the majors on July 10, 1953.

Although Jackie Robinson famously broke the major-league color barrier in 1947, many teams still had no black players. The Indians were a stark exception. In '47, then-owner Bill Veeck had signed Larry Doby as the American League's first black player, and when Al Smith reported to the team in '53—by which point Veeck was gone—it had four black players: Doby, pitcher Dave Hoskins, outfielder Harry Simpson, and first baseman Luke Easter. Al Smith always held Veeck in high regard, calling him "the greatest man I ever met in baseball," and added: "No one ever treated me better than Bill. I observed him closely and he's one of the smartest men you'll meet anywhere in any kind of business. A great human being, too."[4]

In 1954, his first full season with the Indians, Smith beat out veteran Dale Mitchell for the everyday job in left field. Batting leadoff, he hit .281 and scored 101

• AL SMITH •

runs on a team that set an American League record with 111 wins. Game One of the World Series started with Smith being drilled in the ribs by New York Giants ace Sal Maglie. In Game Two, Smith entered the record books by hitting a home run on the very first pitch of the game, thrown by Johnny Antonelli, becoming one of only three players in major-league history to accomplish this feat. Nevertheless, the heavily favored Indians were swept by Leo Durocher's club in four games.

In 1955, Al Smith ranked as one of the American League's best players. His numbers included 22 home runs, 77 RBIs, and 123 runs scored, the latter figure leading the league. He earned his first trip to the All-Star Game. After the season he finished third in the MVP balloting, behind Hall of Famers Yogi Berra and Al Kaline but ahead of Ted Williams and Mickey Mantle.

Al Smith was a solid player for the White Sox and manager Al Lopez. Smith played under Lopez in nine of his 12 MLB seasons, including pennant-winning teams with the Indians in 1954 and White Sox in 1959.

Smith's numbers fell off substantially in 1956 as the Indians won 88 games and finished well behind the Yankees. His offensive decline continued in 1957 (.247 batting average) as the Indians fell into the second division. What's more, Smith was rankled when new manager Kerby Farrell informed him he'd be playing third base in 1958 - rankled enough to ask for a trade.

The Indians honored that request. On December 4, 1957, Smith and star pitcher Early Wynn were sent to the White Sox for Minnie Minoso and Fred Hatfield. White Sox fans were unhappy about the trade that cost them longtime favorite Minoso, and they took out their frustrations on Smith, who was booed continuously throughout that season and the next. Trying to help, White Sox owner Bill Veeck staged an "Al Smith Night" on August 26, 1959, against the Red Sox. Anyone with the name Smith, Smythe, Schmidt, or Smithe was admitted free and given a button that read, "I'm a Smith and I'm for Al". Smith responded with a forgettable game: 1-for-4 with a strikeout, and he dropped a seventh-inning fly ball that led to a couple of unearned runs on the way to a 7-6 loss. Veeck's plan had backfired. . . .

Or had it? The disastrous game seemed to spark Smith. As Veeck recounted in his book *Veeck as in Wreck*: "Over the last six weeks of the season, he led our team in home runs and runs batted in, and won game after game with the clutch hit in the ninth inning or in extra innings."[5] Like many other stories in Veeck's book, this one is perhaps a bit exaggerated; there were only four weeks in the season after Al Smith Night, and over that span Smith batted .255 and drew exactly two walks. But he did hit six homers and drive in 18 runs, and one of those home runs did come in the pennant-clincher, on September 22 (though it was a solo shot in a 4-2 victory).

In the first game of the World Series, the White Sox beat the Dodgers 11-0 behind Early Wynn. They lost Game Two, though, which has forever been remembered for Al Smith's embarrassing "beer bath," a single instant that seemed to epitomize the White Sox' frustrations throughout the fall classic. In the fifth inning, Smith drifted back to Comiskey Park's left-field fence in pursuit of Charlie Neal's deep drive. As Smith watched the ball disappear into the stands, a fan named Melvin Piehl, sitting in the first row, knocked over his beer and thoroughly drenched the startled left fielder. "It hit the bill of my cap and came down the side of my face," Smith recalled. "It was in my nose and everywhere. At first, I thought the guy dumped it on purpose, but the umpire told me he just tipped it over to get the ball. I wouldn't have caught the ball anyhow. It made the third row." [6]

In a 2000 interview, Piehl, a motor oil company executive, said he was sitting next to his wife and his boss's wife along with a group of his company's top salesmen. In the excitement of the moment, Piehl tried to catch the ball, he claimed, so "it wouldn't hit my boss's wife." [7] The incident was captured by *Chicago Tribune* photographer Ray Gora, stationed near the third-base dugout with a new camera developed to shoot rocket launches from Cape Canaveral. The camera was equipped with a 70-millimeter lens, and every picture it took looked like a close-up. Gora's camera captured the mishap in an eight-part sequence that was featured in newspapers nationwide the next day. Al Smith had involuntarily played a memorable role in World Series history.

Smith kept a blow-up of the famous photo in his Chicago home, and once facetiously remarked that he had signed copies of the picture 200,000 times. At the 40th anniversary celebration of the 1959 team, Smith said of the incident that had long overshadowed his fine career, "All these years, I've never made a dime off of it. Everywhere I go, that's all the people bring up. Maybe I should make T-shirts and sell them." [8] (A remorseful Melvin Piehl shunned publicity, and once declined a guest appearance on TV's *I've Got a Secret*.)

In any event, that was not Smith's only memorable moment in Game Two. With the Sox trailing 4-2 in the eighth inning, Smith came up with Earl Torgeson on second base, Sherm Lollar on first, and nobody out. As Smith later told author Bob Vanderberg, "I was up there to bunt. We were trying to get runners over to second and third. I bunted and fouled it off. Bunted again, and fouled it off." [9] With the bunt off, Smith doubled to left-center field. Torgeson scored, but the slow-footed Lollar, waved around by third-base coach Tony Cuccinello, was out at home by a lot. Smith wound up on third base but was stranded there, and the game ended in a 4-3 Sox loss, thanks to perhaps the most infamous coaching decision in franchise history.

Smith rebounded offensively in 1960, hitting .315 (second in the AL) and making his second trip to the All-Star Game. With the return of Minoso to the White Sox that year, Smith willingly moved to right field so that fan favorite Minoso could play left. In 1961, Smith continued his resurgence and hit 28 homers, his career high. But Bill Veeck had sold the team to John Allyn and Smith ran into trouble with new general manager Ed Short. According to White Sox historian Richard Lindberg, Smith balked at yet another (proposed) move to third base, and was also upset when "they asked him to work as an offseason ticket salesman for the ballclub." [10]

These ill feelings eventually resulted in a trade to Baltimore, on January 14, 1963: Smith and Luis Aparicio to the Orioles; Hoyt Wilhelm, Dave Nicholson, Peter Ward, and Ron Hansen to the White Sox. After one season in Baltimore, Smith was traded back to the Indians, his original team, but was released on August 5, 1964, with a .162 batting average in 61 games. Picked up as a free agent shortly afterward by the Red Sox, he still didn't hit, and played his last game in the majors on October 4.

Smith had married Mildred Winston on February 12, 1956, and they remained together until Smith's death, 46 years later. After the end of his baseball career, Smith worked for the city of Chicago, managing the park district's baseball program, with ex-Cub pitcher Dick Drott, from 1966 through 1981. In addition to his baseball duties, he also served as supervisor of recreation at Ogden Park, on the city's South Side, and worked as a part-time community relations representative for the White Sox. Upon retiring, he became an excellent golfer and consistently shot in the low 80s.

Al Smith died on January 5, 2002, at St. Margaret Mary Hospital in Hammond, Indiana. He was 73 and succumbed to cardiac arrest after arterial surgery. In addition to his wife, Mildred, he was survived by two sons, Al Jr. and Dan; two daughters, Deborah Bender and Maria Chalkey; a brother and three sisters; and 11 grandchildren.

At the time of Smith's death, his White Sox teammate Billy Pierce said, "Al was a very good teammate. Al was always quiet. He never said a lot, but with his actions, he did a lot. He helped us tremendously in 1959 to win the pennant. Unfortunately, people remember him for having the beer spilled on him during the World Series, but they forgot that he drove in a lot of runs for us. He was just a very good player and a real gentleman." [11]

White Sox fans will always be grateful to Al Smith for his contributions to the pennant-winning team in 1959. But he is also fondly remembered in Cleveland. In 1993 he was enshrined in the Ohio Baseball Hall of Fame, and in 2001 was honored as one of the "100

• AL SMITH •

Greatest Indians of All Time." A fine ballplayer and a dedicated husband and father, Al Smith deserves a better fate than to be remembered simply for being doused in beer.

Sources

In addition to the sources cited in the Notes, the author also consulted:

Conklin, Mike. "A Wet Sox Memoir," *Chicago Tribune*, April 14, 2000.
Enright, James. obituary, *Chicago American*, January 30, 1962.
Marazzi, Rich. *Sports Collectors Digest*, September 27, 1996.
Munzel, Edgar, *Chicago Daily News*, December 25, 1957, and March 30, 1963.
Pettica, Mike, obituary, *Cleveland Plain Dealer*, January 4, 2002.

Notes

1. Richard Goldstein, "Al Smith, 73, Dies; Was Doused in Series," *New York Times*, January 6, 2002.
2. Rick Hines, *Sports Collectors Digest* (June 1, 1991): 188.
3. Hines.
4. Quote taken from article in Al Smith's Hall of Fame file, publication and author unknown.
5. Bill Veeck and Ed Linn, *Veeck as in Wreck* (Evanston, Illinois: Holtzman Press, 1962), 348.
6. Goldstein.
7. Goldstein.
8. Goldstein.
9. Bob Vanderberg, *Sox: From Lane and Fain to Zisk and Fisk* (Chicago: Chicago Review Press, 1984), 201.
10. Richard Lindberg, *The White Sox Encyclopedia*, (Philadelphia, Pennsylvania: Temple University Press, 1997).
11. Patrick O'Conner, "Obituary: Al Smith Former Outfielder/Third Baseman Passes Away," www.MLB.com (January 3, 2002).

Nothing captured the struggles of the White Sox in the 1959 World Series quite like the "beer shower" that left fielder Al Smith received in Game Two on Dodger second baseman Charlie Neal's fifth-inning home run.

JERRY STALEY

by Jim Sargent

On September 22, 1959, with one out and the bases loaded in the ninth inning at Cleveland's Municipal Stadium, Chicago White Sox manager Al Lopez signaled to the bullpen for his top reliever, Jerry Staley. (Although his first name was Gerald and he was commonly referred to as "Gerry" both during and after his career, Staley preferred to known as Jerry.) With the game and the American League pennant on the line, the White Sox needed a double play. A sinkerball pitcher with good control who also threw a good fastball, a slider, a changeup, and sometimes a knuckler, Staley could get the job done. As he would later recall about pitching for Chicago in 1959, he grew a little fatigued by September. The fatigue caused him to throw the sinker a little slower, making the ball drop better when it reached the batter – the perfect pitch for starting a ground-ball double play.

Staley entered the game to face Cleveland's right-handed batting Vic Power. A good contact hitter, Power swung at Staley's first pitch, the trademark sinkerball, and, sure enough, bounced the ball to smooth-fielding shortstop Luis Aparicio, who started the game-ending double play. With that clutch pitch from Staley, Chicago clinched the AL pennant over second-place Cleveland – its first in 40 years.

A veteran hurler who pitched his first eight years for the St. Louis Cardinals, Staley fashioned a career mark of 134-111 with a solid 3.70 ERA. He enjoyed five double-digit winning seasons for the Cardinals, peaking with 19, 17, and 18 victories from 1951 through 1953. Beginning in 1957, he became a relief specialist. It was a role in which Staley excelled. Between 1957 and 1960, Staley's 2.43 ERA and 30 relief wins led all American League relievers, and his 38 saves during that period ranked second only to Ryne Duren (42).

Born to lumberman Adelbert Randolph Staley and the former Clementine Steelman on August 21, 1920, in Brush Prairie, Washington, Gerald Lee Staley grew up in Clark County outside Vancouver in southern Washington. Like many youths during the 1920s, he played baseball. "Both of my older brothers were better ballplayers than I was," Staley recalled in a 2003 interview. "But they just never got the break that I got."[1]

Staley attended high school in nearby Battle Ground. After graduating in 1938, the young man worked for two years at Alcoa Aluminum in Vancouver. On the weekends he played baseball in a sandlot league against teams from nearby towns and from across the river in Portland, Oregon. Staley, a six-footer with a strong arm, often played shortstop because he could make the long throw to first. In his third season he also pitched. That led to the "break" he mentioned, signing a contract to play minor-league ball in the Class-C Pioneer League in 1941.

"I was working for Alcoa in 1940," Staley remembered in 2003, "and I was working with a fella who had played [Pacific] Coast League ball. And he knew Jim Keesey, who was going to manage the Boise Pilots in the Pioneer League. The two were friends, and they talked over the situation, whether there were any ballplayers in the area that had a chance to go play for them. The fella I was working with asked me if I wanted to go and try out, and I did. Jim Keesey got several fellas together early in the spring of 1941, and we played three or four games. I wasn't old enough to sign a contract, so Jim Keesey talked to my parents. I had two older brothers who had played sandlot ball too, and they all wanted me to go play pro ball. So I quit the aluminum plant and went to spring training with Boise, and I made the club. I played two years with Boise, and I did pretty well."

Staley made an excellent start, going 22-8 with a 2.79 ERA for first-place Boise in 1941. He led the league in games (39), innings pitched (261), and in wins. The right-hander was named as one of two pitchers on the league's All-Star team. Probably because the club's owner wanted too much money to sell Staley, the right-hander returned for the 1942 season, the first year of World War II for the United

JERRY STALEY

States. Again pitching well, he went 20-10 with a 2.73 ERA as Boise finished second.

After the season, Staley was inducted into the Army at Fort Lewis, Washington. "I was in the Army's Medical Corps," Staley recalled. "I spent most of my time in the South Pacific." According to the *New York Times*, Staley pitched five no-hit, no-run games while overseas.

> "After the war, St. Louis had an agreement with Sacramento of the Coast League," said Staley. "St. Louis could take one serviceman who came back from the war in payment for the Sacramento franchise going independent. They had a half-dozen players to choose from, and the Cardinals picked me. That's how I ended up with St. Louis."

Staley pitched for Sacramento in 1946, producing a 13-12 record with a 2.94 ERA. In 1947, he went to spring training with the Cardinals and made the club. But the Redbirds had a veteran ballclub which had defeated the Boston Red Sox in the 1946 World Series, and on July 23 the Redbirds sent the right-hander to Columbus of the American Association. Pitching for fifth-place Columbus, he contributed six wins while losing once. Recalled to St. Louis late in the year, the rookie started once in September, pitching a complete-game victory. Overall, he worked 29⅓ innings in 18 games for the Cardinals, posting a 1-0 mark with a 2.76 ERA.

In 1948 Staley returned for his first full season. The talented Cardinals again fielded a good ballclub, led by National League Most Valuable Player Stan Musial. Staley, big and strong at 190 pounds, appeared in 31 games, starting three times. He finished with a 4-4 mark, losing one of his three starts. While his ERA rose to a career-high 6.92, the sinkerballer enjoyed a highlight day on Monday, July 5. Playing under intermittent rain and sunshine at Sportsman's Park in St. Louis, the Cardinals defeated the Chicago Cubs twice, and the Washington native won both games in relief.

"I didn't become a regular in 1948, because they still had their pitchers from the year before," Staley recalled. "So I pitched mostly in relief. I became a regular in 1949 when they sold Murry Dickson to the Pirates. That deal opened the way for me."[2] Eddie Dyer's veteran club finished in second place for the third straight year in 1949, losing the pennant to the Dodgers by a one-game margin. Staley produced

Relief ace Jerry Staley will always been known by White Sox fans for the one-pitch save against the Indians on September 22, 1959 that put the club in the World Series.

only a 10-10 record, but his 2.73 ERA paced St. Louis pitchers.

In 1950, the Cardinals – the NL's powerhouse team of the 1940s – slipped to fifth place. Staley produced his second season of double-digit wins, going 13-13 and adding three saves, but his ERA rose to 4.99. On May 30 he again won both ends of a twin bill, this time over the Pirates at Forbes Field. Staley's clutch hurling made him the first reliever in the history of baseball to win both ends of a doubleheader twice.

The Cardinals finished third in the NL in 1951 and 1952, and tied for third in 1953, Staley's peak years as a starting pitcher. He came through with records of 19-13 in 1951, 17-14 in 1952, and a career-best 18-9 in 1953. Thanks to those good seasons, he made the NL All-Star team in 1952 and 1953, although he didn't pitch in either game.

Asked about his best pitches, Staley said,

"I always did have a knuckleball, but I just used it once in a while. I'd throw a knuckleball on a good hitter after I got ahead of him by throwing the sinkerball, which was my main pitch. But I'd use the knuckleball for a change-of-pace. Basically, I was a sinkerball pitcher, but you changed speeds on the sinker. You'd also throw a curveball and a slider every now and then, just to let 'em know that you had one. If I got ahead of the batter with two strikes and no balls, I could come in with the knuckleball. But the knuckler breaks so much that you had a hard time getting the darn thing over the plate!"

The Cardinals gave Staley a certain home-field advantage at old Sportsman's Park (renamed Busch Stadium in April 1953 when August Busch purchased the Cardinals, but commonly called Sportsman's Park for years). In the year 2000 Carl Erskine of the Dodgers recalled that in St. Louis the infield was very hard, except on nights when Staley pitched. On those occasions, the grounds crew would wet down the area in front of home plate so opposing batters would beat that sinker into soft turf for easy ground balls.[3]

Another strong suit for Staley was good control. As he explained to Brent Kelley in 1991, he often worked games where he threw less than 100 pitches: "There were a lot of games I was in the 80- to 90-pitch range. I had pretty good control and they were hitting the first pitch or the second pitch all the time, which is a great help for any pitcher."[4]

But fame is fleeting in the major leagues. In 1954 the Cardinals fell to sixth place, and Staley saw his ledger slip to 7-13 and his ERA soar to 5.26. "Three years in a row I had pretty good years," Staley recalled in 2003. "But in 1954 I'm not sure what went wrong. I didn't have any arm trouble, or anything like that. I think it was one of those years where the opposing batters weren't hitting the ball hard, but they were hitting it out of reach of everybody."

Given his performance, Cardinals management figured the 34-year-old sinkerballer was past his prime, and on December 8, 1954, St. Louis swapped Staley and third baseman Ray Jablonski to Cincinnati for reliever Frank Smith. In 1955 Staley finished with a 5-8 record as a starter for Cincinnati, but according to Staley, the way he pitched was no different from when he won big for St. Louis in 1953. Speaking to Brent Kelley in 1991, Staley said, "The year I was in Cincinnati, it seemed that everything they hit – no matter whether they hit it hard or soft or what – was just in a hole. They just weren't hitting the ball at anybody. That can make a heck of a lot of difference."[5]

On September 11 of the 1955 season, the Yankees, looking for bullpen help, bought Staley from the Reds for the waiver price. But the right-hander did not get any decisions for New York and didn't make the club's World Series roster.

The two-time All-Star's career took an unexpected turn for the better on May 28, 1956, when the Yankees waived him to the White Sox. Chicago's manager Marty Marion – formerly the Cardinals' fine shortstop and later the club's manager for the 1951 season – knew Staley's strengths and figured he could still do the job. Marion was right; over the remainder of the season Staley posted an 8-3 record, hurling five complete games in 10 starts and going 1-1 in relief.

In 1957, Al Lopez became manager of the White Sox, and he elected to use the veteran right-hander strictly out of the bullpen. Thereafter, Staley's career enjoyed a major rebirth.

"The year that Marion was there," Staley told Bob Vanderberg for his 1982 book *Sox: From Lane and Fain to Zisk and Fisk*, "I started a lot of times (10 of his 26 Sox appearances were starts). Then the next year, Lopez came and he figured he needed some people in the bullpen. They were loaded with starters – (Billy) Pierce, (Jack) Harshman, (Dick) Donovan, (Jim) Wilson, (Bob) Keegan. He needed to work somebody into the bullpen, and he needed somebody there who wouldn't take too long to warm up, and who wouldn't come up with arm trouble, and – after one or two pitches – I'd be ready to go in."[6]

Speaking in 2003 about the way Chicago employed him, Staley said, "We didn't have 'closers' in those days. How much I pitched depended on the game. If the starter got into trouble in the third, fourth, or fifth inning, I would come in. Several times I finished up a whole game. As long as you were having good luck and holding the other team down, you stayed in the game." In 1957 Staley made 47 appearances, all in relief, and finished with a 5-1 record and a 2.06 ERA. In 1958 the rubber-armed hurler went 4-5 with a 3.16 ERA in 50 games.

Lopez, meanwhile, developed the "Go-Go" White Sox, building his club around base hits, speed, heads-up base running, the hit-and-run, good defense, and solid starting and relief pitching. The whole mixture came together in 1959 when the ChiSox outdistanced the Indians by five games and won the franchise's first pennant in 40 years. The 38-year-old Staley, who led the majors with 67 appearances in 1959 – all from the

• JERRY STALEY •

pen – posted an 8-5 mark with a fine 2.24 ERA and 14 saves. Staley and Turk Lown anchored a bullpen which produced 37 saves and a 2.80 relief ERA, both figures best in the major leagues that season.

Reflecting in 1982 on the Cleveland game in which Chicago clinched the 1959 pennant, Staley observed, "As a reliever, you're coming in to close ballgames with men on base. So you've got to keep the ball low so they don't hit it out of the park. In the spot I came into that night, the situation is that you're gonna try to make the guy hit the ball on the ground." Asked if he threw Vic Power a good sinker, Staley laughed and said, "Well, evidently. When he hit it, I knew it was on the ground. And it was headed in the right direction – to Aparicio. As long as he fielded the ball clean, we were at least gonna get one out and we'd still be one ahead."[7]

The White Sox entered the World Series against the resurgent Dodgers, a club that tied the Milwaukee Braves for first place in the regular season with an 86-68 record, then defeated the Braves in a best-of-three playoff series. At Chicago's Comiskey Park for Game One of the fall classic, the Pale Hose, fueled by Ted Kluszewski's two homers and RBI single, blasted the Dodgers, 11-0. Early Wynn started and pitched seven shutout innings, and Staley blanked LA over the last two frames.

The Dodgers came from behind to win Game Two in Chicago, 4-3. The Series then moved to cavernous Memorial Coliseum in Los Angeles for Game Three. Right-hander Don Drysdale pitched a strong game for the Dodgers, and longtime Dodgers star Carl Furillo delivered a key two-run pinch single off Staley in the seventh inning, and the Dodgers won, 3-1. Dick Donovan started for Chicago and pitched shutout ball for 6⅔ innings. Relieving Donovan with the bases loaded in the seventh, Staley gave up Furillo's game-winning hit. In a disappointing outing, Staley pitched 1⅓ innings, allowing two more hits and another run.

Game Four was a heartbreaker, the White Sox losing, 5-4, when another longtime Dodger hero, Gil Hodges, homered off Staley, clearing the screen in left field – where the distance from home plate to the foul pole was only 251 feet. Hodges' homer broke a 4-4 tie, and Larry Sherry, working two scoreless innings in relief of right-hander Roger Craig, saved the victory. Staley recalled, "Hodges hit a little fly ball to that short left field. It was really a football field. Evidently I made a bad pitch. That hit would have been an out in Comiskey Park." Chicago rebounded and won Game Five, 1-0, but back in Chicago, the Dodgers wrapped up the Series with a 9-3 victory. Staley worked three shutout innings in the finale, but by then the Dodgers held an 8-3 lead.

Undaunted, Staley came back with a fine 1960 season, leading the AL in relief wins with 13 and relief losses with eight. To go with his 13 victories and 2.42 ERA in 64 games, the sinkerballer added 10 saves, after having saved 14 games in 1959. Making the All-Star team in 1960, Staley didn't pitch in the first of two games played that July. In the second contest he worked the sixth and seventh innings, allowing one run in the NL's 6-0 victory – a solo homer by his old teammate, Stan Musial. Still, Chicago slipped to third place in 1960, 10 games behind pennant-winning New York.

By then Staley was nearing the end of his career. On June 10, 1961, the 40-year-old hurler was traded to the Kansas City Athletics, and on August 2 of that year the A's dealt Staley to the Detroit Tigers, who were involved in a tight pennant race with the New York Yankees. Staley pitched respectably for the Tigers of the last two months of the season, going 1-1 with a 3.38 ERA and two saves in 13 games. But his only loss with the Tigers was crucial. It came in the finale of a make-or-break three-game series between the Tigers and first-place Yankees at Yankee Stadium September 1-3. The Tigers entered the series only a game and a half out of the lead, but the Yankees won the first two games of the series to increase their margin to 3½ games.

Detroit desperately needed a win in the September 3 finale to close the gap, and the Tigers called on Staley to hold a 5-4 lead as the Yankees came to bat in the bottom of the ninth. The veteran reliever, who had come through in this sort of situation so many times in the past, couldn't do it one more time. The first batter Staley faced, Mickey Mantle, homered to tie the game, and Yogi Berra followed with a single. Ron Kline then took over for Staley and, with two on and two out, gave up a game-ending three-run homer to Elston Howard to hand the Tigers a crushing 8-5 defeat which put them 4½ games out. The Yankees eventually won the pennant by eight games over Detroit.

Released by the Tigers in October of 1961, Staley went home and served as pitching coach for Triple-A Portland of the Coast League. He also pitched on occasion, posting a 2-4 mark. The sixth-place Beavers played home games at Multnomah Stadium, which stood across the Columbia River about 15 miles from Staley's longtime home.

Staley had married Shirle A. Lockhart in May 1947; they would have two sons and a daughter. Once the season was over, he'd work in his family's lumber mill. Following his baseball career, Staley served as superintendent of the Clark County Parks system for 17 years, retiring in 1982. Recognizing his stellar achievements in baseball, the Washington Sports Hall of Fame inducted him in 1977.

"I was fortunate to play in an era where there was a lot of good ballplayers," Staley reminisced. "They didn't have so many teams, and the teams were all congregated more closely than the teams are today. We had a lot better teams to play with and against than they do today. "I got to play with and against a lot of great-name ballplayers, from Stan Musial and Enos Slaughter to Nellie Fox and Ted Kluszewski, to name a few. I was fortunate enough to be on All-Star teams in both leagues, and I played in a World Series. I couldn't ask for much more."

An underrated pitcher and a modest big leaguer who earned the distinction of being a stellar starter and also an ace reliever, three-time All-Star Jerry Staley enjoyed several first-rate seasons for several very good Cardinal and White Sox clubs.

Jerry Staley died of natural causes in his home in Vancouver, Washington, on January 2, 2008. He was 87 years old.

Sources

This essay about Gerald "Jerry" Staley's baseball career is based on statistics from *The Baseball Encyclopedia* (Macmillan, 9th edition, 1993); minor-league stats from profile furnished by Pat Doyle, creator of the Professional Baseball Player Database (version 6); clippings from the Staley file in the National Baseball Hall of Fame's Library; a variety of newspaper game stories from ProQuest, mainly for his Cardinal seasons; interviews with Jerry Staley, July 2003; letters from Staley, August 10, 2003, January 25, 2007; "Gerry Staley: A Sinker to Vic Power," chapter in Bob Vanderberg's *Sox: From Lane and Fain to Zisk and Fisk* (Chicago: Chicago Review Press, 1982), pp. 203-208; Brent Kelley, "Gerry Staley: Forerunner to Today's Dennis Eckersley," *Sports Collectors Digest*, July 12, 1991; John Lawrence, "Nuggets Galore at [Washington] Hall of Fame Banquet," *Tacoma News Tribune*, February 6, 1977.

Notes

1. Author interview with Jerry Staley, July 2003. All quotations attributed to Staley are from this interview unless otherwise indicated.
2. Staley interview.
3. Clipping from Staley player file, National Baseball Hall of Fame (exact source unknown).
4. Brent Kelley, "Gerry Staley: Forerunner to Today's Dennis Eckersley," *Sports Collectors Digest*, July 12, 1991.
5. Kelley.
6. Bob Vanderberg, *Sox: From Lane and Fain to Zisk and Fisk* (Chicago: Chicago Review Press, 1982), 205.
7. Ibid., 207.

JOE STANKA

By C. Paul Rogers III

Purchased by the Chicago White Sox from the Pacific Coast League near Labor Day of 1959, Joe Stanka was a 28-year-old journeyman in his 10th minor-league campaign. He appeared in just two games for the Go Go Sox, winning one, losing none, and compiling a 3.78 earned run average in 5⅓ innings of pitching. He was not eligible for the World Series and, just like that, his major-league career was over. But that brief fling with the '59 White Sox is only a small part of the Joe Stanka story. The following year, 1960, found Stanka well on his way to becoming the first American pitcher to become a star in Japan as he won 17 games for the Nankai Hawks. He went on to pitch for seven seasons in Japan, win 100 games, and become one of the most popular and recognizable people in that country. His career peaked in 1964 as he put together a 26-7 won-loss record to lead his Hawks to Japan's Pacific League pennant.[1]

That Stanka became a professional baseball player at all, much less an exceptional one, was more accident than design. He was born in Hammon, in western Oklahoma, on July 23, 1931, the youngest of four children of Bill and Tress Stanka. Bill worked for the Santa Fe Railroad as a repairman and moved the family to nearby Carter before Joe's ninth-grade year. Even though he had no baseball experience, Joe joined the high-school baseball team because he was bored and the team needed someone tall to play first base. The small high school had trouble getting nine guys to show up for the games and so Joe played wherever he was needed, mostly first base or the outfield. He also did a little pitching.[2]

By the time Joe was 15 years old he was 6 feet 5 inches tall. His favorite sport was basketball, and he dominated the competition. Baseball was mostly an afterthought and something to do after the basketball season was over.

The family moved to Waynoka, about 60 miles to the north, before Stanka's senior year. Joe, however, spent the summer far from home, in Boston, staying with his older brother Oral, who was a Navy recruiting officer stationed in the area. It was the summer of 1947 and Joe spent his time attending Red Sox and Braves games almost every day. Among others, he watched three Braves players with whom he crossed paths in his own baseball career: utility infielder Sibbi Sisti, who managed Joe at Sacramento in 1958; third sacker Bob Elliot, Joe's manager with Sacramento in 1959 before his call-up to the White Sox; and first baseman Earl Torgeson, a teammate with the White Sox.[3]

Stanka returned to Waynoka for his senior year and went out for the football team, even though he had never played the game. He played in the second game of the season, only the second football game he had ever witnessed, although he did not know the plays. The highlight of the season came when he met Lida Jean McDaniel, the homecoming queen. He was immediately smitten.[4]

Joe made the most of his senior year in basketball as his team ran off 18 straight wins to start the season. They lost two before winning another 10 in a row to propel themselves into the state tournament. They were upset in the first round, but 16-year-old Stanka was the top scorer in Oklahoma and was named to the All-State team.

Stanka's basketball prowess earned him a scholarship to powerful Oklahoma A&M to play for the legendary Hank Iba. The summer before he enrolled, Stanka played baseball for the Waynoka town team on Sundays. A player named Norm Parsons did most of the pitching until he signed for $300 with a Dodgers farm club. From then on Stanka did the pitching. At a state semipro tournament in Enid, a bird-dog scout saw Joe pitch and offered to sign him with the Dodgers' organization. Stanka declined, however, because he was all set to go to college and play basketball, his first love. If you ever change your mind, the scout told him, give me a call.

Joe's stay at Oklahoma A&M was neither a long or happy one. He wasn't particularly fond of his freshman coach, wasn't keen on going to class, and missed his sweetheart Jean, who was still in high school. When Stanka told Coach Iba that he was going home, the venerable coach told him that he would have a four-year scholarship waiting for him if he ever decided to come back to Stillwater.[5]

Go-Go to Glory

Back in Waynoka, Joe hooked on with the Santa Fe Railroad, married Jean, and planned to raise a family and work for the railroad, just as his father had done. He was still just 17 years old. Joe's initial foray into professional baseball occurred because the arrival of their first child, Joey, coincided with a railroad strike. The Stankas owed $300, which they did not have, to the hospital and the obstetrician. Joe remembered that his town team teammate Norm Parsons had gotten a $300 bonus for signing with the Dodgers and thought he might give baseball a try, since he was out of work anyway.[6]

Stanka contacted Bert Wells, the Dodgers' area scout, and was invited to try out with the 1950 Ponca City Dodgers of the Class-D KOM (Kansas, Oklahoma, Missouri) League. After a few days, the 18-year-old Stanka signed for a $750 bonus, $650 of which was contingent upon his staying with the club for at least 30 days. He made his professional debut about a week after signing and did not fare well, balking home a run and exhibiting a lack of command. Joe also managed to anger his manager, Boyd Bartley, by missing the team photo shoot.[7] So after about a month with Ponca City, during which he compiled a 1-3 won-loss record, he was optioned to the Duncan, Oklahoma, Utts of the even lower Class-D Sooner State League. The Duncan franchise soon folded and was transferred to Shawnee.

To say that Joe was raw is an understatement. He finished with a 1-8 record and an eye-popping 8.72 earned run average with Shawnee. He threw 10 wild pitches, walked 69, and was torched for 11 home runs.[8] After that inauspicious beginning, Stanka was ready to walk away from baseball again, especially when he was able to get a job on the railroad as a switchman, a significant upgrade from his earlier track repair position. However, a conversation with the yardmaster made him realize that the ceiling was not very high for a railroad workman. Still only 18, Joe was not ready to settle for that and decided to give baseball another try.

As a result, he reported to the Dodgers' minor-league spring training in Vero Beach, Florida, and was again assigned to Ponca City. There he experienced a complete turnaround, winning 16 games, losing only 5, and compiling a 2.53 earned run average while leading Ponca City (85-39) to the pennant. That record earned Stanka a promotion for 1952 to the Pueblo Dodgers in the Class-A Western League. There he struggled to a 7-11 record. Joe was still just getting by with his fastball and asked his manager, Bill McCahan, who had pitched a no-hitter for the Philadelphia Athletics in the late '40s, to help him develop a curve. McCahan said, "Joe, I've never thrown a curveball in my life. I don't know how to help you."[9]

Stanka had pitched well against the Des Moines Bruins, a Chicago Cubs farm club, and caught the attention of Wid Matthews, the Cubs' director of player personnel. After the season the Cubs drafted Joe from the Dodgers organization for the Los Angeles Angels, the Cubs' top affiliate in the Pacific Coast League. Joe was not ready for the Angels and spent the bulk of the season with the Cedar Rapids Indians in the Class-B Three I League. He again showed real promise, going 12-8 with 155 strikeouts in 180 innings and a league-leading 2.35 earned run average for a fifth-place club. In 1954, Stanka was back in Class A with the Macon Peaches of the South Atlantic League and showed still more progress, winning 16 and losing just 5 with an ERA of 2.99. Stanka was now considered a bona fide prospect and was invited to pitch winter ball in Puerto Rico for the first time.

His stay with the Mayaguez team in Puerto Rico, where his teammates included Tommy Lasorda and Don Zimmer, was brief. He was rusty when the winter season began and had the misfortune of pitching his first two games against the powerful Santurce Crabs featuring reigning National League MVP Willie Mays. As a result, he had a rough start. Winter league clubs, faced with a short season, did not exercise patience with slow-starting pitchers and Joe was released after a couple of weeks.

In 1955, Joe reported to the Cubs' spring training camp in Mesa, Arizona and pitched well, earning another shot with the Los Angeles Angels. Joe thought he had nailed down the fifth starter's spot but then read in the paper that manager Bill Sweeney was going to start Bob Thorpe, up from Class C the year before, in that position. Thorpe was to start on the first Sunday in the season and Stanka was bent out of shape when he arrived at the ballpark for the Saturday game. Sweeney thereupon told Joe he was starting that day's game since the fourth starter was ill, further making Stanka feel like a spare part.

The start did not go well and Sweeney came out to remove Joe from the game in the fourth inning after four earned runs and numerous walks. Sweeney asked for the ball, as is customary, and Stanka refused to put it in his outstretched arm. After some sharp words,

• JOE STANKA •

Joe threw the ball down behind the mound, refused to pick it up, and finally stalked off the field. The next day Stanka was headed back to Des Moines, where he spent the 1955 season.[10]

Still just 24, Stanka found himself in Class A for a third time, this time battling a sore elbow. An orthopedist in Des Moines recommended massage treatments coupled with squeezing a rubber ball, rather than surgery. Joe also had an understanding manager with the Bruins, Pepper Martin of Gashouse Gang fame. Pepper helped baby Stanka through the season, often starting him on the first and last day of homestands, thereby allowing Joe to skip road trips and get his massage treatments. His teammates referred to him as Pepper's Pet but Martin's handling of Joe paid dividends as he won 17 games against 9 losses, leading the league in victories.[11]

During the offseason, the Cubs traded Stanka to the Sacramento Solons of the Pacific Coast League for another pitcher, Johnny Briggs. Still a notoriously slow starter, Stanka struggled to a 5-14 record for the lowly Solons (often called the Sad Sacs) in 1956, but at least he wasn't sent down to a lower classification. He finished 10-14 for Sacramento in both 1957 and 1958 before improving to 12-12 in 1959.

The Solons were in the business of selling their players to major-league teams for cash, and during his time in Sacramento, Stanka came close to being purchased by the Kansas City Athletics and the Cleveland Indians. Finally, with a month to go in the 1959 season, the Chicago White Sox, in a pennant race with the Cleveland Indians, purchased Stanka for a reported $30,000. Joe reported to the White Sox immediately, a 28-year-old rookie in his 10th year of professional baseball.

When Stanka arrived in Chicago, he found a note from White Sox general manager Hank Greenberg telling him to report to Comiskey Park as soon as possible because he was the starting pitcher that night. Joe was dead tired and very nervous because he had never been in a big-league ballpark before. Manager Al Lopez had other ideas about starting Joe, and Billy Pierce took the mound instead. When Pierce got into trouble, Stanka was told to warm up and in doing so strained his groin. As Stanka tells it, he didn't even know what a groin was before the injury. In any event, Pierce got out of trouble and Stanka was not called into the game that night.

Two days later, Joe made his major-league debut and it was a most successful one. He was called into the game in the fifth inning of a game against the Detroit Tigers and gave up only one hit in 3⅓ scoreless innings. He also slapped a base hit and scored a run as the White Sox rallied to win, making Joe the winning pitcher. His next appearance, a few days later, did not go so well. Woody Held of the Cleveland Indians greeted him with a 450-foot home run into the center-field bleachers. Joe's groin pull was bothering him and he ended up walking four batters in a two-inning stint.

Afterward, Stanka went to the White Sox trainer, who told Joe he needed complete rest for at least a week to let his groin heal. Somehow Al Lopez was not informed about the injury and he and Greenberg came to believe that Stanka was a malingerer. Stanka never appeared in another game for the Sox.

Stanka, who had been added to the Sox roster too late to be eligible for the World Series, was not allocated any Series tickets. He visited Hank Greenberg in his

Joe Stanka's major league career consisted of two games with the 1959 White Sox, but he found fame as one of the pioneering Americans to play in Japan. He won 100 games in a seven-year career in the Japanese League.

office and was told that it was just an oversight that would be taken care of. Stanka also mentioned that he hoped for more money next year since he had actually taken a cut from his Sacramento salary (where he had an unauthorized expense account). Greenberg was taken aback and said, "You've got a lot of gall, asking for more money when you refused to pitch."

Joe said, "What do you mean I refused to pitch?" Greenberg related that Lopez had called the bullpen to tell Stanka to warm up and the bullpen coach had said, "He doesn't want to pitch." Stanka explained about his injury and his understanding that the trainer had told Lopez about it. He also told Greenberg that he had never said anything to the pitching coach and would have pitched any time he was asked. Greenberg promised that he would straighten everything out with Lopez but Stanka still felt very uneasy about his future with the White Sox.[12]

During the World Series against the Los Angeles Dodgers, Stanka pitched batting practice and then showered and watched the games in street clothes from the nosebleed seats, where he was one of 90,000 people attending the games in the Los Angeles Coliseum. After the Series, Stanka was pleasantly surprised when his White Sox teammates voted him a $1,000 share from the Series.

Stanka played winter ball in Caracas, Venezuela, for the third time after the 1959 season. While there he read in *The Sporting News* about all the pitchers the White Sox were bringing to spring training, cementing his belief that he would not really get a fair shot at making the team. After 10 years, he had not been able to stick in the majors and his prospects for doing so with the White Sox did not look very good. Further, he had learned that major-league salaries for marginal players were lower than those in the Pacific Coast League. As a result, Stanka decided to seriously consider his options.

In the spring of 1959, Gary Blaylock of the St. Louis Cardinals had told Joe that the Japanese clubs were looking for American players. Blaylock had given Joe the name of Cappy Harada, a Nisei (an American-born Japanese), who was a talent scout for Americans interested in playing in Japan. Stanka's move up to the White Sox had put thoughts of playing in Japan on the back burner, but after his unpleasant experience in 1959 and his doubts about making the White Sox in 1960, Stanka contacted Harada from Venezuela. Harada quickly obtained an offer of a good salary and bonus from the Nankai Hawks, who were looking for a starting pitcher capable of winning 15 games a year.[13]

Thus, after going on the voluntary retired list with the White Sox, Joe moved his wife and two children to Kobe, Japan, very near Osaka, home of the Hawks. His first start was against the Toei Flyers in Tokyo and, if nothing else, revealed some cultural differences. Early in the game the Hawks' left fielder let a base hit go through his legs with runners on base and then turned and jogged after the ball as the runners circled the bases. Joe blew a gasket on the mound. His manager, Kazuto Tsuruoka, did not understand why he was upset.[14] Joe continued to get hit hard and shortly the manager stepped in front of the dugout, waved in a relief pitcher, and gestured Joe to the dugout. Stanka had seen enough Japanese baseball to know that this was the custom, but he still refused to leave the mound. Only when Tsuruoka strode to the mound did Joe relinquish the baseball and leave the field.[15]

After a rough start, Stanka won 17 games while losing 12 and posting a 2.48 era, sixth best in the Pacific League. His Hawks finished in second place in the six-team league, four games behind the pennant winners, the Daimai Orions. Still, some fans were disappointed because they had assumed that a 6-foot-5 American would be invincible and would cement the pennant. Stanka's periodic bouts of wildness led some of the press to call him the Beanball Yank.[16] The Hawks' ace pitcher, Tadashi Sugiura, had compiled an incredible 38-4 record in 1959 and finished at 31-11 in 1960, so Joe's numbers paled by comparison.[17]

At the time, no working agreement existed between Japanese baseball and the major leagues and the White Sox, no doubt influenced by Stanka's 17 wins, claimed he was still their property. U.S. baseball commissioner Ford Frick agreed but the Stankas had just had a baby daughter and buoyed by their fine treatment and good salary, wanted to stay in Japan. The U.S. State Department even became involved, urging a settlement of the dispute before it ripened into an international incident. Joe eventually agreed to buy his own contract back from the White Sox for $30,000, the amount the Sox claimed to have invested in him.

Joe again started slowly in 1961 and was inconsistent during the first half of the season. Manager Tsuruoka lost confidence in him and Stanka did not pitch much from early July into September. Nonetheless, the Hawks were rolling along with a 10-

• JOE STANKA •

game lead over the Toei Flyers when they lost their ace Sugiura to a sore arm. They soon hit a losing streak while the Flyers got hot and won nearly every game. With five games left in the season, the two clubs were not only deadlocked but were to finish the season against each other.

Stanka arrived at the ballpark before the first game of the series and learned that he was starting. He initially refused to pitch. His contract provided for a bonus if he won 15 games and Joe was unhappy that he had not been allowed to pitch for several weeks and would have little chance to earn the bonus. He finally relented after manager Tsuruoka agreed to put in a good word for him with management. It was a good thing Joe gave in; all he did was pitch a one-hit shutout against the Flyers' 30-game winner Masayuki Dobashi to win 1-0. Stanka faced only 27 men and allowed only a scratch hit by Dobashi. Now, instead of the Beanball Yank, the Japanese press was referring to Stanka as "Big Thunder."[18]

Joe followed that performance with a win in Tokyo two games later to clinch the pennant and secure his bonus. He then pitched the opening game of the Japan Series against the Central League champion Yomiuri Giants, throwing another shutout to win 6-0. The Giants won the second game, 6-4, and Stanka started Game Three in Tokyo. He led 4-3 heading into the bottom of the ninth. With two outs and a runner on base, the batter hit a simple popup to the first baseman, Terada. As he reached to catch the ball, he began to extend his right hand to Joe to congratulate him on the victory and, in doing so, took his eye off the ball and dropped it. It was one of the biggest gaffes in Japanese baseball history.

The next batter was the legendary Shigeo Nagashima, one of the two most popular players in Japan (along with home run king Sadaharu Oh). Nagashima topped an easy groundball to third but the third baseman booted it to load the bases. Stanka then got two strikes on the next batter, Andy Miyamoto,[19] and then threw what some have said is the most famous pitch in Japanese baseball history. Stanka threw a forkball that split the heart of the plate; but umpire Enjyoji called it a ball. Stanka stormed to the plate and, with his hands behind him, bumped the umpire with his chest as he railed at him for the horrendous call.

When play resumed, Miyamoto slammed the next pitch into right field for a single, driving in the tying and winning runs in what the Japanese call a sayonara (game-winning or walk-off) hit. Stanka, joined by his Hawks teammates, again charged umpire Enjyoji and bowled him over. The police finally had to break up the riot of Hawks, fans, and umpires at home plate. Stanka later learned that Enjyoji so favored the Giants that he was known throughout the Central League as "the Giants' 10th man."[20]

Stanka was suddenly the ace of the Hawks' staff and won the fifth game of the series, 6-3, before losing the sixth and last game in relief in 10 innings, 3-2. The Hawks lost the series, four games to two. Afterward, Manager Tsuruoka had to appear before the Japanese baseball commissioner and apologize for his team's accosting of Enjyoji.

After the season, Joe and his family, which now included three children, returned to his hometown of Waynoka for the winter. He appeared on the television show *To Tell the Truth* in New York City and won $1,000 when none of the panel guessed the real Joe Stanka. The family returned to Kobe for the 1962 Japanese baseball season but Joe was plagued by a sore arm and won 8 games while losing 10 as the Hawks finished second to the Flyers.

In 1963, Stanka's fourth year in Japan, he improved to 14-7 with a sharp 2.66 ERA in 186 innings. The Hawks lost a tight pennant race, finishing only a scant game behind the Nishitetsu Lions. That set the stage for 1964, when Stanka, now armed with a sinking off-speed forkball to complement his fastball, became the dominant pitcher the Japanese had long expected. He finished the season with 26 wins against 7 defeats in 278 innings as the Hawks swept to the Pacific League pennant by 3½ games over the Hankyu Braves. Stanka was particularly tough during the last month of the season when his team was slumping and trying to hang on to its lead. The Hawks won only five of their final 14 games, and Joe won all five.

Not surprisingly perhaps, Stanka was in the middle of a couple of melees in 1964. What was surprising was that one involved another American, Chuck Essegian of the Kintetsu Buffaloes, also based in Osaka. (Oddly enough, Essegian had starred for the Dodgers, hitting two pinch-hit home runs against Stanka's club, the White Sox, in the 1959 World Series.) Stanka thought the umpire was squeezing him, refusing to give him any calls on the corners, and began shouting at the arbiter with Essegian at bat. Essegian thought that Joe was yelling at him and the two eventually tangled in the middle of the infield before teammates pulled them apart.

Stanka's other fracas was also against the Buffaloes and involved an inside pitch to Akitoshi Kodama that went past the catcher for a wild pitch. Kodama had arched his body to avoid the pitch but he and the entire Kintetsu bench claimed that the ball had nicked him. The umpire ruled otherwise and when Joe finally started into his windup the Buffaloes' manager, Kaoru Betto, again called for time and walked from the dugout to continue his protest. Stanka rushed from the mound, grabbed Betto, and gave him a healthy shove, precipitating the first player free-for-all in the 30-year history of Japanese professional baseball.[21] It took the police 26 minutes to restore order and the game continued without Stanka, who was ejected.[22]

The Hawks faced the Central League champion Hanshin Tigers in the 1964 Japan Series. Both teams were based in Osaka and both had been propelled to their pennants by a star "gaijin" (foreign) pitcher. Gene Bacque, from Lafayette, Louisiana, had won a remarkable 29 games for Hanshin. He had pitched an astounding 353 innings (in a 130-game season) and finished with a sparkling 1.89 era.[23] The Tigers, however, started 22-game winner Minoru Murayama in the first game, avoiding a pitching match-up of American stars. Stanka pitched brilliantly, shutting out Hanshin, 2-0.

Bacque won Game Two for Hanshin, 5-2. Stanka was asked to start Game Three on only two days' rest. He lost, 5-4, although he was aided by home runs by his two gaijin teammates, Kent Hadley and Johnny Logan. The Hawks won Game Four, 4-3, to even the Series, but the Tigers prevailed in Game Five, 6-3, behind another American, Pete Burnside, to take the Series lead, three games to two.[24]

Stanka finally faced fellow American Bacque in Game Six as the Tigers attempted to win their first Japan Series title. But Stanka had his full four days' rest and continued his exceptional pitching, defeating the Tigers, 4-0, for his second shutout of the Series.

The climactic Game Seven was scheduled for the next day, and the unthinkable happened. Manager Tsuruoka asked Joe to start, apparently prompted by Stanka's teammates and coaches, who thought the Hawks' best chance for victory rested with him. There was some logic behind the request since of the last 30 games, including six in the Japan Series, the Hawks had only 13 wins and nine were by Stanka. In their last 15 games, Joe had rung up seven of the Hawks' eight wins.

Incredibly Stanka pitched another complete-game shutout to win 3-0 and clinch the Japan Series for the Hawks. The two shutouts on back-to-back days with his team facing elimination propelled Stanka to almost mythic status in Japan. He was named the Most Valuable Player of the Series and soon was voted the Pacific League's MVP and Outstanding Pitcher awards, the first foreigner to be so honored.[25]

Joe returned for his sixth season in Japan in 1965 a national hero and was often referred to as "the blue-eyed Japanese." He struggled with a sore arm some that season, but still pitched 173 innings and put together a 14-12 record. The Hawks blazed to a second straight Pacific League pennant, by 12 games. They faced the powerful Yomiuri Giants, who had won the Central League pennant by 13 games, in the Japan Series. In a battle of the two dominant teams in Japanese baseball, the Giants won the series, four games to one. Stanka started Game

Three against the Giants' legendary left-hander Masaichi Kaneda[26] but his Japan Series magic was gone and he lost, 9-3.

Joe, his wife, Jean, and their four children (son Jay was born in June, 1965) stayed in Osaka after the 1965 season, as they had in alternate years. Then, shortly before Thanksgiving, tragedy struck. The Stankas' oldest child, Joey was asphyxiated by a faulty gas heater in the bathroom while taking a shower.[27] He was only 15 years old.

After the tragedy, the Stankas returned to Oklahoma to grieve. Joe initially had no intention of returning to play baseball in Japan but in the spring decided that a return to Japan would aid the family's grieving process. Nankai had already signed its allotted two gaijin players but Stanka soon received an offer to pitch for the Tokyo-based Taiyo Whales of the Central League. Joe struggled to a 6-13 record for a team that finished tied for the basement, 37 games out of first place.[28]

The Whales wanted to sign Stanka for the 1967 season, but at 35, Joe was ready to retire from baseball and move back to the U.S. His Whales and former Hawks teammates presented Joe with a traditional Japanese warrior's helmet at the Tokyo airport on their return to the States. The Stankas settled in Waynoka, Oklahoma, far from the bright lights of Tokyo, where Joe purchased a variety store. In 1967 he sold the store and moved to Oklahoma City to sell insurance. He quickly found it not his cup of tea, so he purchased a franchise of an employment agency and moved the family to Houston, where he has lived ever since. In 1970 Joe sold the agency and began selling home study courses in art, writing, and photography. Later, Stanka sold real estate and in 1988 he and son Jim began a very successful duty recovery consulting firm. He retired from that business in 1996 at the age of 65 to travel with Jean.

After their baseball days, the Stankas returned to Japan on a number of occasions, including attending a 20-year reunion of the championship Hawks in 1984. During the 1990s, Joe traveled to Japan several times for gatherings of the Meikyukai[29] when that group invited a number of former Americans who had been Japanese All-Stars during their playing careers.

When the Stankas were asked to reflect about their time in Japan, they pointed to three events: the birth of their two youngest children, Janet in 1961 and Jay in 1965, and the terrible pain of losing their old oldest son Joey.

The Joe Stanka story ultimately is one of perseverance, persistence, and taking the road less traveled. One of the least known members of the 1959 Chicago White Sox became a baseball icon in Japan. Forty-some years later, Joe Stanka's fame in Japan still far exceeded that of any member of the '59 Sox in the US.

Stanka died at age 87 in his home in Katy, Texas, on October 15, 2018. The headline for his obituary in the *Japan Times* referred to him as the "hero of 1964 Japan series."[30]

Notes

1. The Japanese major-league season is 130 games, compared with the 162-game season in the U.S. major leagues.
2. Correspondence with Joe Stanka, on file with author.
3. Ibid.
4. Ibid.
5. Ibid.
6. Rob Trucks, *Cup of Coffee -- the Very Short Careers of Eighteen Major League Pitchers* (Astoria, New York: Smallmouth Press, 2002), 54.
7. Trucks, 56.
8. Donald S. Connery, "A Yank in Japan," *Sports Illustrated*, June 25, 1962.
9. Trucks, 59-60.
10. Trucks, 61.
11. Jean and Joe Stanka, *Coping With Clouters, Culture and Crisis* (Wilmington, Delaware: Dawn Press, 1987), 52-53.
12. Stanka and Stanka, 63-65.
13. Connery, 65. The Hawks had won the Japan Series in 1959 behind their great submarine pitcher Tadashi Sugiura, who had won an astounding 38 games while losing only 4. He then won four more games in the Japan Series. The Hawks hoped to obtain a dependable starter from America to take some of the pressure off Sugiura in 1960, assuming that as good as he was, he could not repeat that performance in 1960. Stanka and Stanka, 70.
14. SABR Nine: "Joe Stanka, First American All-Star in Japanese Baseball." www.sabr.org/sabr.cfm?2=cms,c,1296.
15. The manager thereafter always went to the mound to remove Stanka from the game and gradually began to do so with all his pitchers. Stanka and Stanka, 82.
16. Connery, 66.
17. Daniel E. Johnson, *Japanese Baseball -- A Statistical Handbook* (Jefferson, North Carolina and London: McFarland & Co., 1999) 102, 106.
18. *San Francisco Chronicle* article dated November 3, 1961, in National Baseball Library on Stanka. It is unclear whether Stanka's moniker was more related to his temper or his mound prowess.
19. Miyamoto was a Nisei (second-generation Japanese) from Hawaii who played in Japan for 10 years.
20. Joe Stanka, told to Al Hirshberg, "I'm Big in Tokyo," *Baseball Digest*, August 1962.
21. Stanka/Hirshberg.
22. June 20, 1964, unidentified clipping from the National Baseball Library file on Stanka.
23. Johnson, 123.
24. Johnson, 126-27.
25. Stanka and Stanka, 134-38.
26. Kaneda holds most of the career records for a Japanese pitcher, including wins with 400. He pitched from 1950 through 1969. Thus, he averaged 20 wins a season for 20 years, all the more remarkable when one considers that the Japanese season is only 130 games long.
27. Stanka and Stanka, 159-66; April 9, 1966 unidentified clipping from the National Baseball Library file on Stanka.
28. Johnson, 132-33.
29. Meikyukai stands for "Association of Great Players" or "Golden Players Club" and represents one of two Japanese Baseball Halls of Fame. Players are automatically inducted if they reach 2,000 career hits or 200 wins in Japanese baseball or the same number when Japanese baseball and major-league baseball statistics are combined. No foreign player has been inducted, however. See www.meikyukai.co.jp.
30. Jason Coskrey, "Nankai Hawks ace Joe Stanka, hero of 1964 Japan Series, dies at 87," *Japan Times*, October 19, 2018.

EARL TORGESON

by Mark Armour

In a 15-year major-league career filled with great stories and accomplishments of various stripes, Earl Torgeson was well known for getting in brawls. Even before he reached the major leagues, in the winter before his rookie season, he had faced assault charges for decking two men on a Seattle street who had used vulgar language in front of his wife. The judge threw out the case, telling the assembled, "I would have done the same thing."[1]

Billy Southworth, his first manager in Boston, called him "as fierce a competitor as I've seen in all my years in baseball."[2] Second baseman Roy Hartsfield said, "Torgy is a very humorous fellow – until the ball game starts."[3] In 1948 Torgeson took offense in a preseason "City Series" game at Braves Field when Red Sox infielder Billy Hitchcock got tangled up with him while returning to the first base bag. After it happened again, Torgeson belted Hitchcock in the mouth, causing both benches to empty and a free-for-all to erupt. The skirmish cost Torgeson his glasses, and after this he would always remove them before a pending confrontation.

Then there was the time in 1950 he was hit in the ribs with a pitch thrown by the Pirates' Cliff Chambers. The very next day Chambers threw one at Torgy's head; believing this action had crossed the line, Earl angrily conversed with the pitcher. The conversation did not go well. After removing his glasses, Torgeson charged the mound and started a multi-player melee. Torgeson played the rest of the season with a broken rib, the result of Chambers' first errant fastball. Fortunately, the second one had missed his head.

A few years later, as he batted in the bottom of the first on July 1, 1952, at Braves Field, Torgeson's backswing hit Giants' catcher Sal Yvars on the shinguard. After Torgeson lined a single up the middle, Yvars picked up the bat and slammed the handle on the plate, shattering it. Torgeson was stranded on the bases, so he did not return to the Braves dugout until after the Giants were retired in the top of the second. When he discovered the broken bat, Torgeson removed his glasses, then sprinted across the field to the Giants' dugout and slugged Yvars in the face, leaving the catcher's right eye swollen, discolored, and bloody. "Sal and I always have been good friends. But breaking a guy's bat is like slapping him in the face." Torgeson said after this incident, "We may be in seventh place but we don't have to take that insult."[4] Torgy was fined $100 for the fight, Yvars $25. The good friends brawled again on July 18, 1954, after both players had changed teams.

"If I had to do it all over again I wouldn't have been such a character," Torgeson reflected many years later. "I just regret the fact that I'm labeled a bad boy." The second "Earl of Snohomish," following townsman Earl Averill, wasn't really a bad boy – he was well-liked, even by the people he was socking in the mouth. He loved laughing, joking with his teammates, and going out on the town. He played baseball with a passion, and the brawling, the all-out head-first slides, this was part of how he needed to play the game. He paid the price for this passion with seemingly annual game-related injuries.

He was a tall (6-foot-3), bespectacled left-handed first baseman who smoked several cigars a day. Observers of the time kept waiting for him to break out with the home run totals, to reach his "potential." In the meantime, he was stealing bases, working the pitcher, fielding his position, and otherwise contributing to the cause. Off the field, he was bright and funny, traits which made him successful in several ventures throughout his life. "He just refuses to be dull," is how teammate Gene Mauch once put it. "He won't let himself get in a rut – in his conversation, his actions, or anything else."[5]

Clifford Earl Torgeson was born in the lumber mill town of Snohomish, Washington, on New Years Day of 1924, the second son of Melvin Carl Torgeson and the former Helen Kornelia Gray. Melvin was a carpenter of Norwegian heritage, while Helen was English and Native American. The couple divorced when Earl was very young, but they both remained in Snohomish and stayed involved in Earl's life. Helen was a fun-loving woman who married Harold King, with whom she ran an appliance store in town for many years. Melvin Torgeson remarried as well, to Clara Morris, and built many of the beautiful homes

• EARL TORGESON •

in the Snohomish area. Earl lived off and on with each parent in the small town.

Like many Snohomish boys, Torgeson idolized Earl Averill, the first "Earl of Snohomish," the slugger and centerfielder for the Cleveland Indians during most of Torgeson's youth. Averill would return home every fall and drive around town in his fancy car, causing the boys to stare, vowing that they would follow him to the major leagues one day. Torgeson used to follow his idol around town, staring in the barber's window watching him get his haircut.

Torgeson first played baseball on the aptly-named Averill Field near his home, and he played it as often as he could. Despite needing glasses as a youngster, he also starred in basketball on a team of much older boys. But his prowess on the diamond, along with the public success of Averill, led townsfolk to petition to school board to prohibit Torgeson from playing football for fear of injury. After playing just two varsity games, he was removed from the gridiron team.

After two years of high school baseball, a year of American Legion, and several years playing semiprofessionally in the area, Torgy signed in 1941 with the Seattle Rainiers on the advice of an old scout named George Hokum. Earl trained with Seattle in '41, but the 17-year-old was soon optioned to Wenatchee of the Class-B Western International League. His manager there, Ted Merritt, took one look at the tall, gangly, bespectacled Torgeson and asked, "What in the Lord's name have they sent me now?"[6] His new first sacker hit .332 in 92 games.

In a 1941 late-season recall to the Rainiers, he got to play with the 39-year-old Averill (just retired from the big leagues), and was an impressive 4-for-10 in four games to help the Rainiers win a tough pennant race and capture the Pacific Coast League title. The next year Torgy was farmed out to Spokane (also of the WIL), but a week into the season the Rainiers sold incumbent first baseman Les Scarsella to Oakland and promoted Earl, who had hit .429 in 28 at-bats for Spokane. Now playing in the best league west of St. Louis, he hit .312 with 32 stolen bases in 147 games for Seattle.

Now about those stolen bases. Torgeson was a big man, listed at 6 feet 3 and 180 pounds at the start of his career, and was always expected to hit for more power than he did. Even well into his major league career, Torgeson hit in the power slots of the batting order, as befitting a large first baseman. He never did develop a lot of power, but he had a great batting eye and was very fast on the bases. Had he had a different body but the same skills, he would have been a fine leadoff man.

The 18-year-old Torgy likely would have been sold to a major league team after the 1942 season had he not been about to be drafted. He served in the Army from January 1943 until March 1946. After a year at Fort Lewis and Fort Lawton in Washington State, Earl saw action in the Aleutians, then in France and Germany. He was injured in the Battle of the Bulge by the blast of a shell that landed in his platoon.

Emil Sick, the Rainiers owner, was a friend of

In a 15-year career that included five seasons with the White Sox, Earl Torgeson compiled an excellent .385 on-base percentage.

Go-Go to Glory

New York Yankees' owner Jacob Ruppert, and had promised the Yankees first crack at Torgeson after the war. When the Yankees and Rainiers could not come to an agreement on a deal in 1945, the Braves stepped in and landed Torgeson's option for five players plus the price of exercising the option, believed to be close to $100,000. Torgeson was in France when he learned about the transaction. "He can't miss," said Torchy Torrance, the Rainiers' general manager. "He can hit, run, field, and think, and what else do you have to do? Wait and see what this kid does to big league pitching."[7]

When Earl reported back to the Rainiers in 1946 the season had already begun. Two days before the Braves' option was to expire on August 20, Torgeson dislocated his right (nonthrowing) shoulder. The Rainiers granted an extension, and after the Braves looked him over they made the deal. After 3½ years away from the game, Torgy slumped to .285 in 103 games for Seattle.

When Torgeson reported to spring camp with the Braves in 1947, new teammate Red Barrett called him "the poor man's Ted Williams," as a way of teasing the heralded rookie from the left coast. After a subpar opening series in Brooklyn, Braves' president Lou Perini had to talk manager Billy Southworth out of benching the rookie first baseman. Torgeson responded by driving in 36 runs in his first 30 games, drawing further comparisons to Williams, a fellow left-handed slugger from across town who also wore number 9. "I didn't ask for it," said Torgy. "I didn't know until the City Series that Ted Williams also wore that number."[8]

In one way Torgeson and Williams could not have been more different. While Ted was known for refusing to tip his cap to the fans, after a home run Torgeson would take his hat off and wave it around in the air. His personality personified the differences between the images of the two teams – the Braves being the blue-collar team of the fans, the Red Sox the rich, pampered club of stars. Torgeson became a crowd favorite.

Although he cooled off later in '47 and lost some playing time to Frank McCormick, Torgy ended up hitting .285 with 16 home runs as a rookie – compared with 10 round-trippers total in three minor-league seasons – and 82 walks. Billy Southworth wanted to take it slow with his young player, and generally left him on the bench against left-handed starters.

The tall man with the spectacles could certainly run the bases. "I'll wager today that he's the fastest man in the National League," said Tigers coach Bill Sweeney, who saw Torgeson play in the Pacific Coast League.[9] Braves first base coach Ernie White added: "I see the best runners in our league tear down the line. And take my word for it, Torgy gets down here the quickest."[10]

Even at a young age, Torgeson quickly became a leader on the club, a guy not afraid to hold court in the clubhouse. Platooning with Frank McCormick in 1948, he slumped to .253 with 10 home runs, but added his typical 81 walks (fourth in the league) and 19 stolen bases (fifth) for the pennant-winning Braves. In the World Series he started five of the six games, missing only lefty Gene Bearden's shutout in Game Three. Torgeson, hitting third in the lineup, hit safely seven times in 18 trips, including three doubles. His .389 average led all regulars from both teams in the Series.

Earlier in '48, Torgeson had contributed to another significant event. On May 22, manager Billy Southworth and several members of the team, including Torgeson, visited a local hospital to surprise a young leukemia-stricken boy from New Sweden, Maine, an event which was later broadcast on Ralph Edwards' *Truth or Consequences* national radio show. Named "Jimmy" to protect his privacy, the 12-year-old was presented with a regulation team uniform and a bat from his fellow Swede Earl Torgeson. Money flowed in for Jimmy's treatment, which spawned the "Jimmy Fund" charity of today's Dana-Farber Cancer Institute which was supported by the Braves until their 1953 departure from Boston and has been championed by the Red Sox ever since. For many years, it was assumed that Jimmy had passed away as only 15 percent of the children encountering his type of cancer then survived. But a half-century later, Einar Gustafson, the real Jimmy, emerged from obscurity and became an instant celebrity. He even still possessed his child-sized Braves uniform and Torgeson's bat, and both were put on display at the Baseball Hall of Fame in 1998.

The 1949 season was far less memorable for Earl. In early May, he made an aggressive attempt to take out Jackie Robinson at second base on a double-play ball, slid clumsily and separated his left shoulder. The injury sidelined him for three months. In August he began working out again, but suffered a broken thumb in a fight after curfew involving teammate Jim

EARL TORGESON

Russell and three soldiers – it's not completely clear what happened, and Torgeson would never talk about it. His season was over after just 25 games, in which he hit .260 with four home runs. The following spring he spent several weeks getting his shoulder to learn to throw again – his former overhand motion replaced with a more accurate sidearm toss. His first-rate play around the bag was now that much better.

Torgeson opened up a sporting goods store in Wellesley, a Boston suburb, with Hank Camelli, a 1947 teammate, and worked there in the offseasons. He also had become a popular after-dinner speaker and had his own radio show, and later a television show.

In 1950 Torgeson was a full-time player for the first time, playing all 156 Braves' games, coming through with 23 home runs, 87 RBIs, and a .290 batting average. He also walked 119 times, third in the league, and led the senior circuit by scoring 120 runs. Historian Bill James suggests that Torgeson might have been the best player in the National League in 1950. The next season he again played every game (155 this time), finishing at .263 but with 24 home runs and 92 RBIs. He walked 112 times, and stole 20 bases. Despite his fine play, however, the Braves finished fourth both seasons.

Torgeson had been married in 1946 to the former Norma Syverson, a beautiful woman of Norwegian descent from Twin Valley, Minnesota. Norma and three sisters had gone to Seattle during the war to find employment. There she met Earl, and they married when he returned from the service. The Torgesons had two children: Christine and Andrew, who later played two years in the New York Yankees' organization. In the early years of Earl's career the family would accompany him to spring training and then back to Boston for the season.

In 1951 the Torgesons settled in Anna Maria, a sparsely populated coastal island in the Gulf of Mexico, not far from the Braves' spring training site of Bradenton, Florida. Many baseball players and families owned cottages nearby, including Warren Spahn, and many baseball teammates and friends visited often. Torgeson's great friend Fred Hutchinson was also a neighbor there. Torgeson spent many a winter golfing every day with his baseball friends. He also loved to host barbecues, gatherings of friends and teammates eating ribs, or lobsters shipped from Maine and prepared by Earl himself.

Despite his fairly impressive statistics, in 1952 many fans and writers thought Torgeson would lose the position to George Crowe, a rookie (and one of the first black ballplayers on the Braves) who had hit .339 or better his previous three seasons in the minor leagues. Torgeson ended up getting most of the playing time, but had his worst year in the majors – hitting .230 with just five home runs in 122 games. After the season Earl was dealt to the Philadelphia Phillies in a complex four-team swap also involving the Dodgers and Reds. For the Braves, this sequence netted them Joe Adcock, who held down first base for the next 10 years.

In 1953, his first year in Philadelphia, Torgy took most of the playing time from incumbent and close friend Eddie Waitkus and hit .274 with 11 home runs in 111 games. Once again, however, an injury set Earl back. He dislocated his right shoulder in January of '54 when he tripped over his dog one night on his way to bed, and he supposedly kept the incident a secret from everyone other than the trainer and a few teammates. The injury sapped his power, leading to just five home runs and a .271 batting average in 135 gutty games. Near the end of the season he broke his thumb, and he ended up having surgeries to correct both conditions.

The following June, his power still not recovered (just one home run in 47 games), Torgy was sold to the Tigers at the June 15 trading deadline; a few weeks later, the Tigers released Ferris Fain, who had been playing first base. Torgeson played very well in Detroit, hitting .283 in 300 at bats, with nine home runs and nine stolen bases without being caught. He also continued to walk, drawing 93 in his two stops during 1955.

On July 17, 1955, the Tigers and Yankees were tied 5-5 after nine innings at Tiger Stadium. In the bottom of the tenth, Torgeson led off with a walk against Eddie Lopat, took third on a single by Ray Boone, and two outs later (with Bob Turley now pitching) stole home to end the game. "After I reached third," said Torgeson, "I noticed Turley didn't look at me before going into his first pitch."[11]

In January 1956, the convertible Torgeson was driving flipped over on a curve, pinning him beneath the steering wheel. Torgy suffered cuts and bruises but remarkably broke no bones. He was charged with reckless driving while drinking, and with not having a driver's license. All of this netted him a $50 fine. In the season ahead, he hit .264 with 12 home runs in 117 games.

The Tigers moved third baseman Ray Boone across the diamond to first base in '57, making Torgeson a part-time player and pinch hitter. He had just 50 at-bats (.240 with one home run) on June 14 when he was dealt to the White Sox for Dave Philley. Torgeson took most of the playing time from Walt Dropo in Chicago, and ended up having a fine second half – .295 with seven home runs in 251 at-bats. New manager Al Lopez became an immediate booster, praising Torgeson's ability to get on base: "I definitely believe that by waiting out the pitcher, Torgy becomes a better hitter and generally contributes more to our attack."[12]

Over the next two years, however, Torgeson became more of a part-time player for the White Sox. In June of 1958 Chicago made a deal with Detroit for Ray Boone, who got most of the playing time at first base the rest of that season. Torgeson played 73 games there, including 45 starts, but pinch-hit and pinch-ran enough to get into 96 games, hitting .266 with 10 home runs. In 1959 Boone had moved on, but the White Sox first gave the job to rookie Norm Cash, who failed to hit, then turned to Torgeson for a few months, and finally acquired Ted Kluszewski in late August to take over the rest of the way. Torgeson hit just .220 with nine home runs. In the World Series he managed a groundout and walk in his two plate appearances, as the White Sox were defeated by the Dodgers in six games.

Torgeson was 36 years old entering the 1960 season, and his days as a regular player were over. Nonetheless, he stuck with the White Sox and stayed all year as a pinch-hitter, hitting .263 in 57 at-bats. After going just 1 for 15 through June 15 in 1961, he was sold to the Yankees, for whom he was no better (2 for 18). On September 2, he was released and redeployed as a coach. He was not on the World Series roster as the Yankees defeated the Reds four games to one.

Earl and Norma divorced in 1961 as Earl's baseball career was ending. In 1963 Torgeson married Molly Power from White Bear Lake, Minnesota, and had three more children: Holly, Brad and Tina. Earl is remembered as a supportive father, who attended many of his children's sporting events through the years, sitting quietly in the stands, supporting their wins and losses.

His daughter Christine remembers something else: "He loved to sing. He had a great repertoire of old sentimental ballads which he learned from his mother. He especially loved jazz and the old favorites. All of us kids learned the old songs from hearing him sing them. My mother said that they could go to a club and the next thing you know he had grabbed the mike and was singing a song."[13]

When Torgeson retired from baseball, he briefly worked as a stockbroker with Mitchell Hutchins Brokerage in Chicago. Soon after he owned and operated Camp Forsyte, a sports camp for boys in Westfield, Wisconsin, which sponsored many underprivileged kids from Chicago in addition to the paying campers. In 1965, Earl and Molly moved to Everett, Washington, near where Earl had grown up.

Torgeson took a job as director of parks for Snohomish County. When major league baseball arrived briefly in Seattle in 1969, Torgeson was hired to manage the Newark Co-Pilots in the New York Penn League that summer, and then the Clinton Pilots in the Midwest League in 1970, succeeding Sibby Sisti. (Both ballclubs were Seattle affiliates). He even suited up for the big-league Pilots as a batting coach in the last few weeks of the '69 season. Earl's previous managerial experience had been in Managua, Nicaragua, during a couple of winters in the late 1950s, and this marked the end of his professional career. His Newark team finished 42-34, in third place, while his Clinton club came in at 57-67.

Earl was elected a county commissioner in 1972 and served four years. While in office he fought off several schemes from political enemies. He was also charged and tried for allegedly using county labor and materials to work on his car and summer home, charges which cost him three years and $25,000 to successfully defend. Two later attempts at re-election were unsuccessful. He later worked many years with a timber company, and served as the county's director of emergency management for eight years.

In late September 1990 Torgeson discovered he had leukemia, and he died just six weeks later, on November 8, 1990, at his home in Everett, Washington. He was survived by his second wife, Molly, his five children, and six grandchildren. Edo Vanni, who had played with Torgeson on the 1946 Rainiers, recalled, "He could do everything. He was a happy-go-lucky guy. Nothing worried him. Slumps didn't bother him. He was just a super guy."[14]

• EARL TORGESON •

When the field at Snohomish High School was named after Earl in October 1990, the citation read, in part: "Your contribution to our youth, through your coaching and personal support, is recognized and respected by everyone in the community. Your fans and the citizens of Snohomish will always remember the values, integrity and courage modeled by you for their children."[15]

Notes

1. John Gillooly, "Earl of Snohomish II," *Sportfolio*, September, 1947: 46.
2. Harry T. Paxton, "The Jesting First Baseman of Boston," *Saturday Evening Post*, May 26, 1951: 27.
3. Ibid.
4. John Drohan, "Bat Breaking 'Slap in Face' And Torgy Couldn't Take It," *Boston Traveler*, July 2, 1952.
5. Edward Kiersch, *Where Have You Gone, Vince DiMaggio* (New York: Bantam, 1983), 104.
6. Paxton, 178.
7. Paxton, 176.
8. Royal Brougham, "Seattle Seconds Braves' Raves for GI Torgy, First Base Star," *The Sporting News*, January 17, 1946.
9. Gillooly, 46.
10. Hub Miller, unidentified clipping, dated August 1947, in his Hall of Fame file, 302.
11. Miller, 302.
12. Lou Miller, "Torgy Steals Home to Win—Turley's Face Turns Red," *The Sporting News*, July 27, 1955: 24.
13. Edgar Munzel, "Torgy Rates Added Salvo From Senor for Batting Extras," *The Sporting News*, November 13, 1957.
14. Christine Torgeson, interview with author, September 12, 2006.
15. Obituary, *Seattle Post-Intelligencer*, November 10, 1990.

EARLY WYNN

By David Fleitz

Chicago fans were outraged when the White Sox traded their most popular player, Minnie Miñoso, to Cleveland in December 1957 with Fred Hatfield for Early Wynn and Al Smith. Wynn was a 37-year-old right-handed pitcher who had posted a losing record for the Indians that season, and his best days appeared to be behind him. However, Wynn joined with Billy Pierce to give the White Sox a formidable one-two punch at the top of their rotation, and his Cy Young Award-winning performance in 1959 led the club to its first American League pennant since 1919. Four years later, at age 43, he became the 14th member of baseball's 300-win club.

Early Wynn Jr., whose family claimed Scotch-Irish and Native American descent, was born in Hartford, Alabama, on January 6, 1920, to Early Wynn, Sr. and his wife, Blanche. Hartford is a small town surrounded by peanut and cotton fields in Geneva County, which borders the Florida Panhandle in the southeastern part of the state. Early Sr. was an auto mechanic and a semipro ballplayer. Early Jr. earned ten cents an hour hauling 500-pound bales of cotton after school. He concentrated on baseball after breaking his leg in a high-school football practice, and at age 17 traveled to Sanford, Florida, to attend a baseball camp operated by the Washington Senators. Legend has it that Early, a husky 6-footer who weighed about 200 pounds, arrived at camp in his bare feet. He did not, Early told writer Roger Kahn years later. "[B]ut I was wearing coveralls."[1] A Washington scout, Clyde Milan, was impressed with Wynn's fastball and signed him to a contract. The young pitcher dropped out of high school and began his professional career in 1937 with Sanford, the Senators' farm team in the Class-D Florida State League.

After a 16-11 season, Wynn advanced to the Charlotte Hornets of the Class-B Piedmont League, where he remained for the next three years. The Senators gave him a trial in Washington at the end of the 1939 season, though Wynn was not yet ready for major-league action and went 0-2 in three games. He spent all of 1940 in Charlotte, and then a good season at Springfield in the Class-A Eastern League in 1941 (16-12, 2.56 earned-run average) brought him to Washington to stay. In 1942 he made 28 starts for the Senators, posting a 10-16 mark with a 5.12 ERA as a 22-year-old with little more than a fastball in his arsenal.

In 1939 Early married Mabel Allman, from Morganton, North Carolina, and the couple had a son named Joe Early Wynn. Tragically, the marriage ended prematurely. In December of 1942, Mabel was killed in an automobile accident in Charlotte, where the Wynns lived during the winter months. Early was left with a baby to raise, with the assistance of his relatives. He won 18 games for Washington in 1943, but fell to 8-17 in 1944 as he led the American League in losses. He married Lorraine Follin that September, shortly after entering the US Army. He served in the Tank Corps in the Philippines, spending all of the 1945 season and part of the next in the military before rejoining the Senators.

At this time, Wynn owned an impressive fastball, but had only a mediocre changeup to complement it. He was inconsistent, posting a 17-15 record in 1947 and an 8-19 mark in 1948. Still, he was undeniably talented, and the Cleveland Indians coveted his services. Bill Veeck, the Indians' owner, tried to acquire Wynn in a trade before the 1948 season, but was rebuffed by Washington owner Clark Griffith. In November 1948 Veeck acquired pitcher Joe Haynes, Griffith's son-in-law, from the Chicago White Sox. Veeck then offered Haynes to the Senators for Wynn, and Griffith agreed, sending first baseman Mickey Vernon with Wynn for Haynes, pitcher Ed Klieman, and first baseman Eddie Robinson.

The Indians figured that Wynn would become a big winner if he could develop more pitches, so the club assigned pitching coach Mel Harder to teach him how to throw a curve and a slider. "I could throw the ball when I came here [to Cleveland]," recalled Wynn years later in *The Sporting News*, "but Mel made a pitcher out of me."[2] By mid-1949 he had mastered the curve and slider, and began to use a knuckleball as an offspeed delivery. With a new array of pitches at his command, Wynn joined the ranks of top hurlers in 1950. He won 18 games and led the American League in earned-run average with a 3.20 mark.

• EARLY WYNN •

Early, nicknamed Gus, got along well with his teammates, but was a grim, scowling presence on the mound. "That space between the white lines – that's my office, that's where I conduct my business," he told sportswriter Red Smith. "You take a look at the batter's box, and part of it belongs to the hitter. But when he crowds in just that hair, he's stepping into my office, and nobody comes into my office without an invitation when I'm going to work."[3] With his large frame, grizzled appearance, and willingness to knock down opposing hitters, Wynn stood out as one of the most intimidating pitchers in the game. Roger Kahn, in his book A Season in the Sun, described how the pitcher once brushed back his teenage son during a batting-practice session at Yankee Stadium. "You shouldn't crowd me," snarled the elder Wynn. As he explained to Kahn, "I've got a right to knock down anybody holding a bat."[4]

Wynn hated losing, and was never afraid to throw at batters who got too close to the plate, or hit line drives at him. Some called him a headhunter, but Wynn regarded close pitches as part of the game. "If they are going to outlaw the inside pitch," said Wynn in an article he wrote for *Sport* magazine in 1956, "they ought to eliminate line drives and sharp grounders hit through the pitcher's box." To those who suggested that he would throw at his own mother, Early famously replied, "I would if she were crowding the plate."[5] One day Mickey Mantle drilled a liner through the box for a single. Wynn then fired several pickoff attempts at Mantle's legs. "You'll never be a big winner until you start hating the hitter," he told rookie pitcher Gary Bell. "That guy with the bat is trying to take away your bread and butter. You've got to fight him every second."[6]

His toughness and durability made Wynn part of one of the greatest pitching rotations of all time in Cleveland, with Wynn, Bob Lemon, Bob Feller, and Mike Garcia all posting 20-win seasons during the early 1950s. Under the tutelage of Mel Harder and manager Al Lopez, Wynn won 20 games or more in a season four times for Cleveland, and anchored the rotation that led the Indians to the American League pennant in 1954. In the World Series that year Early lost to the New York Giants 3-1 in the second game, giving up three runs in seven innings. He did not have the chance to pitch again in the Series, as the Giants cruised to the title in four games.

Early and Lorraine made their permanent home in Nokomis, Florida, where they raised his son, Joe,

300-game winner Early Wynn won the Cy Young Award with the 1959 White Sox and finished third in the American League MVP voting. Wynn's 22 victories included the pennant-clincher against the Indians, and he followed up by winning Game One of the World Series.

and their daughter, Sherry. He spent his leisure hours hunting, driving powerboats, and flying his own Cessna 170 single-engine plane. Beginning in 1955, Wynn produced a regular column for the *Cleveland News*, titled "The Wynn Mill," and donated the money he earned from the effort to the Elks Club in Nokomis. Though he had dropped out of high school, Early wrote without the assistance of a ghostwriter, and his frank assessments of umpires, league policies, and his own management rankled Cleveland team officials and strained his relationship with general manager Hank Greenberg.

Wynn notched another 20-win campaign in 1956, but in 1957 he posted his first losing season in Cleveland (14-17, with his ERA leaping from 2.72 to 4.31) despite leading the league in strikeouts. The careers of both Bob Feller and Bob Lemon drew to a close during this time, and perhaps the Indians believed that the 37-year-old Wynn was fading as well. On December 4, 1957, the team traded Early to the Chicago White Sox. The White Sox inserted a clause in his contract that prohibited the pitcher from writing for newspapers, but the team compensated him for the lost income. Reunited with his old Cleveland manager Al Lopez, who had resigned and taken the Chicago job after the 1956 season, Wynn compiled a 14-16 record in 1958, leading the league in strikeouts again.

Wynn was still a tough competitor, sometimes throwing chairs in the locker room after losses. He hated to be taken out of games, though his advancing age often made it necessary to use relievers to finish his wins. In 1992 Al Lopez described Wynn's competitiveness to biographer Wes Singletary. "So this one day Early was arguing with the umpire," said Lopez, "when I came out there and he threw the ball at me, hitting me in the stomach. It was more of a flip/toss but the press played it up. I said give me the goddamned ball and don't be throwing it at me. After the game he came and apologized to me. I said, Early, I know how you feel but the people upstairs, the fans and media, they see that and think you're mad at me. I told him don't get mad at me, get mad at the guys who are hitting."[7]

Wynn had suffered from gout since the 1950 season and pitched in pain for the last half of his career. Still, he kept in good shape, and his fastball remained sharp as he approached his 40th birthday. Lopez kept Early at the top of the Chicago rotation, and in 1959, everything clicked for both Wynn and the White Sox. On May 1 the 39-year-old pitched a one-hit shutout against the Boston Red Sox and hit a home run that provided the only scoring in the 1-0 victory. He led the league in innings pitched, started that season's first All-Star Game for the American League, and won a league-leading 22 games, pitching the White Sox to their first American League flag in 40 years. Early's 21st win of the season, a 4-2 victory over Cleveland on September 22, clinched the pennant and set off a night of celebration on Chicago's South Side. At season's end, Wynn won the major-league Cy Young Award and finished third in the American League Most Valuable Player balloting behind teammates Nellie Fox and Luis Aparicio.

The White Sox faced the Los Angeles Dodgers in the 1959 World Series, and Early pitched seven shutout innings in the opening game, teaming with reliever Jerry Staley to defeat the Dodgers by an 11-0 score. However, he struggled in the fourth contest, played at the Los Angeles Coliseum before 92,650 fans. He failed to complete the third inning of a game that the White Sox eventually lost, 5-4, though Staley was the losing pitcher. In the sixth game, played in Chicago, a six-run Dodger explosion in the fourth inning knocked Wynn out of the game and saddled him with the Series-ending defeat.

Wynn's 13 wins in 1960 left him with 284 career victories, and the pitcher announced his intention of joining the 300-win club before his retirement. He pitched well in 1961, with eight wins in his ten decisions, but arm soreness, caused by gout, ended his season in July. He gave up eating meat in an attempt to control his gout problem, but the pain persisted, causing problems with his legs and right hand. He fell short of his 300th win in 1962, posting a 7-15 record while relying mostly on a slider and a knuckleball. His seventh win, a complete-game effort against the Senators on September 8, was the 299th of his career, but Early failed in three subsequent attempts to gain number 300. The White Sox were convinced that the 42-year-old pitcher had reached the end of the line, and in November the team released him.

The White Sox invited Wynn to their 1963 spring-training camp, but he failed to make the team. He returned home to Florida, where he stayed in shape and waited for a call from another club. A few teams offered Early one-game contracts, seeking to capitalize on his quest for 300 wins, but Wynn held out for a season-long deal. In June his old club, the Cleveland Indians, signed Early for the rest of the season and put him in the starting rotation. On July 13, in his fourth start of 1963, he pitched five innings against the Kansas City Athletics and left the game with a 5-4 lead. Reliever Jerry Walker held the Athletics scoreless the rest of the way, giving Wynn his 300th, and final, win. He was the first man to win 300 games in the American League since Boston's Lefty Grove reached the mark in 1941.

Wynn started only one more game for Cleveland and retired at the end of the season. His career record stood at 300-244 with an ERA of 3.54. Early remained with the Indians, succeeding Mel Harder as Cleveland's pitching coach in 1964. He moved to the Minnesota Twins in 1967, and then managed in the minor leagues for one season. In 1972, in his fourth year of eligibility, Wynn was elected to the Baseball Hall of Fame. He had been disappointed in not gaining the honor earlier, once calling the institution the "Hall of Shame" in an interview. After his

EARLY WYNN

election, he told *The Sporting News*, "I would have been happier if I'd made it the first year. I don't think I'm as thrilled as I would have been if that had happened. But naturally I'm happy. So is my wife. We've had a long wait."[8]

Early Wynn worked as a broadcaster for the Toronto Blue Jays and the Chicago White Sox after his election to the Hall of Fame, and also owned a restaurant and bowling alley for a time. He fully expected to be the last of the 300-game winners, and often referred to himself in such terms in interviews. Nineteen years passed between Wynn's final victory in 1963 and Gaylord Perry's ascension to the 300-win club in 1982. As it was, Early saw six pitchers, including Perry, surpass his total during the 1980s and '90s. By the end of the 2013 season, Wynn was one of 24 pitchers with 300 wins or more.

Wynn retired during the mid-1980s and resided in Nokomis until his health began to fail after the death of his wife, Lorraine, in 1994. He suffered a heart attack and a series of strokes during the final years of his life, and spent his remaining days in an assisted-living center in Venice, Florida, where he died on April 4, 1999, at the age of 79.

Sources

In addition to the sources cited in the Notes, the author consulted a number of other sources including Marty Appel and Burt Goldblatt, *Baseball's Best: The Hall of Fame Gallery* (New York: McGraw-Hill, 1980), 400-401.

Notes

1. Roger Kahn, "Early Wynn: The Story of a Hard Loser," *Sport*, March 1956.
2. *The Sporting News*, June 15, 1963, 7.
3. Red Smith, *Red Smith on Baseball* (New York: Ivan R. Dee, 2000), 325.
4. Roger Kahn, *A Season in the Sun* (Lincoln: University of Nebraska Press, 2000), 108.
5. Early Wynn, "The Four Sides of the Beanball Argument: The Pitcher's Side," *Sport*, January 1956.
6. *The Sporting News*, October 7, 1959.
7. Wes Singletary, "Señor: The Managerial Career of Al Lopez," *The Sunland Tribune* (Journal of the Tampa Historical Society) 19, November 1993, 57-66.
8. *The Sporting News*, February 5, 1972.

THE 1959 WHITE SOX ON THE AIR

By Curt Smith

On May 7, 2000, Dodgers announcer Vin Scully gave Fordham University's 155th commencement speech. "Don't let the winds blow away your dreams or your faith in God," he said. "And remember, sometimes your wildest dreams come true."[1] Airing NBC Television's 1959 World Series, Scully had covered an American League team for whom many of its fandom's wildest dreams already had.

In autumn 1959 I was eight, raised in Upstate New York and a Yankees fan, to the degree I was aware of baseball. In a sense, that fall's Series was my real TV introduction to the game. Scully's partner in my TV introduction was Jack Brickhouse, his trademark cry "Hey-Hey!", the Go-Go White Sox, a tiara of a team.

Some terms need no embroidery: D-Day, Sputnik, 9/11. Teams can be as vivid: Brooklyn, 1951; the Red Sox, 1978. Ibid, 1959: still as vivid as a day behind the rain. The Bible describes 40 years in the wilderness. The Pale Hose had wandered pennant-less since 1919. Retrieve TV's Brickhouse and Vince Lloyd, radio's Bob Elson and Don Wells, and a year in which the cow jumped over the moon. To those of a certain generation, the Go-Go has never gone.

Elson's photo lit *The Sporting News* April 11, 1959 preview issue:[2] balding, bespectacled, like the speed, defense, and pitching Sox, perhaps slightly behind his time. He and Wells buoyed WCFL 1000 AM: The Voice of Labor in Chicago.[3] At the time, Cleveland's Jimmy Dudley sold Carling's "Mabel, Black Label"; Philadelphia's Byrum Saam, Phillies cigars; and Mel Allen, Ballantine beer.[4] One Sox sponsor was fictive: General Finance Company's Friendly Bob Adams. Others were Budweiser Beer, General Cigar, and Butternut Bread: Saukville on parade.[5]

As a boy, Elson sang in Chicago's famed Paulist Chorister Choir, later entered Loyola, transferred to Northwestern, and visited pool whiz Willie Hoppe in St. Louis. His hotel's top floor housed KWK. Touring, Bob found 40 aspirants in line for an announcer's job.[6] "You're the last today [for an audition]," a woman told him.[7] His career soon caromed: a listener vote chose Elson.

Before long the manager of WGN Chicago read about Bob's coup, offering a job. He debuted March 11, 1928, hooked the Cubs and Hose, and became baseball's pre-war network prism.[8] "I was close to [Commissioner] Kenesaw [Mountain] Landis when he made assignments. He'd bellow, 'Don't mention any movie stars attending the World Series even if they slide into second base.'"[9]

Elson's first Series was 1930. In 1939, the Gillette Company began exclusivity. "Bob got the assignment [with Red Barber]," said 1960s Sox Voice Milo Hamilton. "If he did an event, it mattered."[10] Elson aired 1933's first All-Star Game at Comiskey Park: also, 1943-48's Series highlight film. "He had an excitement," Brickhouse recalled. "His voice cut through the air."[11]

Bob interviewed actors, pols, and singers from the Chicago Theatre, Ambassador East Hotel Pump Room, and LaSalle Street Station "Twentieth Century Limited." By day, he patented the on-field interview, noting how "at first players were antsy. Then they got the swing."[12] At night the gin rummy whiz cut the cards. *Chicago Tribune* columnist and later official baseball historian Jerome Holtzman asked about lessons. "That's like asking Jascha Heifetz to play fiddle," Bob snapped. "I give lessons, but they will cost."[13]

In 1943, "The Old Commander," named for wartime Naval service, got leave to call the Series.[14] "Franklin Roosevelt had been in office a decade, and asked that Bob announce," Brickhouse said. "Only time that a president pulled rank to get a uniformed baseball guy home."[15] Listening was a GI who as a boy threw a ball against dad's corn crib. "I'd hear Bob in [Sacramento] California," said Wells. "Such a creative announcer. No one had such energy."[16]

• ON THE AIR •

Wells later entered broadcast school, did play-by-play in Salinas of the old Sunset League, and joined White Sox radio in 1953. One day Don, future CBS Voice Mike Wallace, and 18 others paid a stripper $40 to crash Elson's daily 15-minute program. "I'm reading sports, minding my own business," said Bob, "and this woman takes everything off except her shoes."[17] In the background, roaring, was a lead conspirator and friend.

Brickhouse was born in 1916, as the Cubs debuted at Wrigley Field. The Sox' post-'19 disgrace made Jack a Cubbies' fan. At 18, he "got a job as a $17 a week WMBD Peoria spare announcer and switchboard operator."[18] In 1940, Bob telegrammed: "Expect call from WGN as a staff announcer and sports assistant. Remember, if asked, you know all about baseball."[19] Hired, Jack introduced Les Brown's band, accompanied Kay Kyser, and in 1942 replaced Navy-bound Elson as WGN's bigs Voice. "People called me gee-whiz," he said. "I've never seen a mirror that doesn't smile back if you do first."[20]

Unforeseen: WGN, axing the Cubs after 1943, day baseball costing the station profitable children's shows. The team blew to WIND, Bert Wilson voicing. Elson's post-war return to WJJD also cost Jack the Sox. In 1947, Brickhouse turned not to radio but a rectangular tube, infant television booming in post-war Chicago. A year later WGN Channel 9 turned pioneer: each home game, *live*, from its South and North Side.[21]

"It worked because the Cubs and Sox weren't home at the same time," Jack said. "You aired whichever was."[22] In 1959, the Cubs televised their entire home schedule. The Hose aired all (54) home day games, sponsored by Oklahoma Oil Co. and Theodore Hamm Brewery.[23] "Wrigley didn't have lights, so kids came home from school and turned TV on. You win Chicago by winning kids,"[24] he mused.

Cassandras feared less interest. Instead, "continuity made life-long fans." Brickhouse soon did "a day game, studio, wrestling three nights a week"—precedents including "daily Voice [180 games yearly], WGN mikeman [boxing], and center-field camera [1951]."[25] Jack wed Franklin Roosevelt's inaugural, five political conventions, golf, Notre Dame and Bears football, wrestling, boxing, golf,[26] "Churchill's funeral, one-on-one with numerous U.S. Presidents, and an audience with Leo Durocher and Pope Paul VI – 'alas,' a writer said, 'not simultaneously,'"[27] Jack laughed.

Brickhouse aired three pre-1959 Series. Locally, his calling card "Hey-hey!" upon a homer roused each side of the Second City. Elson patented "*He's out!*" Brickhouse's TV bud cried "Holy Mackerel!" William F. Buckley, Jr. famously said he would rather be governed by the first 400 people in the Boston telephone directory than by the Harvard University faculty.[28] A Soxaphile would rather Vince Lloyd list them than hear most Voices do a game.

Born: 1917, South Dakota. Graduated: Yankton College. Early stops: Sioux City, Bloomington, and Peoria. In 1949, the World War II Marine arrived at WGN. Next year Lloyd joined the Cubs, adding the White Sox from 1954-64. Vince would air the Chicago Bears and Bulls, De Paul basketball, and professional wrestling.[29] Above all, there was 1959 to savor. For South Siders, it began in winter when Bill Veeck announced that he would exercise his option to buy 54 percent of the Sox for $2.7 million from Charles Comiskey's grand-daughter Dorothy. For the first time in 50 years a non-Comiskey owned Comiskey Park. Veeck shocked many merely by his presence.

At one time or another, Barnum Bill had previously signed Satchel Paige, brought midget Eddie Gaedel at bat, and held a funeral service for the 1948 pennant when the Indians failed to encore a year later.[30] On May 26, 1959, the less con than common man ordered a helicopter landed behind second base before a game. Four midgets—again, Gaedel—dressed as spacemen gave tiny Nellie Fox and Luis Aparicio a tandem ray gun.[31] Fox hit a Most Valuable Player .306. Aparicio stole 56 bases. Sherm Lollar had a team-best 22 homers and 84 RBIs. Early Wynn and Bob Shaw finished 22–10 and 18–6, respectively. Turk Lown and Gerry Staley had 30 saves.[32]

"We beat you, 2 to 1," said Elson. "A rally meant a single, steal, passed ball, and sacrifice."[33] The Yankees had won nine of the last 10 pennants and 10 of the last 12. The '59 Hose seemed unlikely to intrude.

The regular season began in Detroit: White Sox, 9–7, on Fox's 14th-inning belt. Only 19,303 specked Chicago's home opener: White Sox 2, Kansas City 0. On April 22 at Kansas City, an 11-run seventh inning mixed one hit, 10 walks, hit batsmen, and three errors. The South Siders nabbed first place for the first time since June 1957, lost five straight, then fell to fourth. The ultimate Cy Younger Wynn, 39, homered and one-hit Boston, 1–0. Even better: the Sox took first for good July 28.[34]

Next month they swept a four-game set at Cleveland. Later a Comiskey-high 45,410 saw Wynn unhorse the Tribe. The '59ers broke their attendance mark (1,423,144), clinching September 22, 4–2. "The Sox are champions!"[35] The Old Commander repeated for the author his call 35 years later of Indian Vic Power's game-ending 6–3. WGN had broadcast from a United charter returning from Ohio, Brickhouse asking if Fox ever swallowed his chewing tobacco. "Remember it!" said the Mighty Mite. "I don't even want to think about it. But it happened once in Kansas City. I thought I'd swallowed a volcano!"[36]

At Midway Airport, a crowd estimated as high as 100,000 howled as the plane arrived after 2 A.M. "And hey, whatever happened to the Yankees?"[37] Jim Rivera taunted. Veeck caught the moment: "The magic number is none!"[38] Mayor Richard Daley errantly activated city air sirens. "Prophetic,"[39] mused Elson, their wail preceding his. From 1947-65, the Commissioner, NBC TV, and sponsor Gillette chose Series mikemen, each team's Voice telecasting half of each set. "With the Sox in, it couldn't be Mel Allen," said NBC's Lindsey Nelson of the usual AL announcer. "The problem was that Tom Gallery didn't think Elson was in Allen's league."[40]

Improbably, The Old Commander and NBC's 1952-63 sports director had grown up loathing each other on the same Chicago block. "Tom'd shout, 'That bastard won't do our [TV] Series,'" said Lindsey, who set to thinking. "'Brickhouse does Sox TV,' Nelson mused. 'You could put him on with Scully.'"[41] Elson seethed as Allen and Saam also aired NBC radio. "Not doing the network Series," he said, still bitter in 1975, "was the biggest hurt of my career."[42] Bob did air the Classic locally on WCFL.

No TV video preserves 1959 Classic play-by-play. "To record, you had to fuzzily shoot the screen," said Brickhouse, etching a process called kinescope. "Even if you succeeded, it was bulky to store."[43] Only audio recalls a Series viewed or heard by a record 120 million, including the final's still-high 90 million. Brooklyn had waited 55 years for a Dodgers title. Los Angeles beat Milwaukee in a best-of-three playoff, hosting the Series in California bigs year two. It began in Sinatra's kind of town. (All play-by-play below heard on NBC's more than 200 radio outlets).

"And so the [opener's] scene is set," Allen said, Chicago taking an early 3–0 lead. Ted Kluszewski then batted in its one-out/on third inning. "Klu hits a long fly to right!" bayed Saam. "[Norm] Larker goes back, back! It ... goes in for a home run!"—5–0. Later, Charlie Neal tried to nab Al Smith at the plate. "There's a bounding ball to the second baseman. They're coming to the plate. [John] Roseboro lets it get by! ... Another run scores!" The Sox led, 8–0, except that eight was not enough.

Thrice hitting 40 or more homers, Kluszewski had become baseball's Christian Dior. "We had these heavy woolies. I'd feel cramped," Ted explained, cutting sleeves at the shoulder. In the fourth, Nature Boy hit again. "Klu lets go another long salvo to right field! It's a home run into the upper deck!" bayed Saam. "Pandemonium breaks loose in Chicago on the South Side as...the White Sox have two more. They're running away from the Dodgers now, 11 to 0!"

"This is quite surprising," Allen said, "in view of the fact the White Sox have been known as a team that beat you with a base hit or a walk, a bunt or sacrifice, a stolen base. Suddenly, they have broken loose with tremendous power."

By replied, prophetically: "Maybe the Sox should have saved some runs."

Readying to run for President, John F. Kennedy next day sat in Mayor Daley's box. Early precincts pleased. "Lollar smacks the ball just out of Neal's reach for a single," said Scully, voicing the Series highlight film,[44] "and [Jim] Landis scores to give the Sox a quick 2–0 lead." Neal later drove to left." Unintentionally, an eager fans knocks over his drink. And in front of 40,000, Al Smith takes a [beer] bath in left field." The photo won an Associated Press award. In the seventh, Chicago lost its 2–1 lead on Chuck Essegian's pinch-dinger. "Neal then rips into the ball again for a long drive to deep center," landing in the Sox bullpen in pitcher Billy Pierce's glove.

Behind, 4–2, the Hose countered. "Smith gets ahold of one and drills it into deep left-center field!" Vin said. "Over goes [Wally] Moon, but it's going to the wall for a double. [Earl] Torgeson scores. Moon plays the rebound to Maury Wills. His relay to Roseboro cuts Lollar down at the plate by a big margin." Sox lose, 4–3. "The World Series is all even!" moving to a place it had never been.

The Los Angeles Memorial Coliseum had a 251-foot left-field pole, bleachers 700 feet from the plate, and grandstand in Orange County. Game Three's record 92,394 record crowd rolled away, row after row. The Sox lost, 3–1.[45] Next day "Norm Larker lines out over second into center for a base hit," Mel said. Jim Landis' throw to third evaded Billy Goodman. "Here comes Moon to the plate, and he scores!" Straightaway Gil Hodges "lofted over short. There's Aparicio out, and it drops for a base hit!" 2–0, Dodgers.

In the seventh, behind, 4–1, Lollar "swings!" said Saam. "There's a fly ball! Is it going to be a home run? Up she goes! It is a home run for Sherm Lollar! The White Sox have tied the ballgame!" Hodges then played screeno. "A long high fly to left. Will it get over the screen? Back she goes! It's a home run!" Los Angeles, 5–4. A tear grew in Brooklyn.

Gillette wanted a seven-game Series. Less would cost it cash. "The question is," Allen said before Game Five, "will the Series be ended or will we move back to Comiskey Park?" Fox scored on a double play. In the seventh, L.A. still trailed, 1–0: two out and on. "And it's swung on [by Neal]. There's a drive to deep right-center!" barked Mel. "Landis digging hard! And the ball is caught by Rivera! A tremendous catch by Jim Rivera as he raced over to right field!"[46]

Next inning Moon arced to center. "Landis moves in —and he loses the ball in the sun!" The Dodgers filled the bases. Two relievers replaced Shaw. A third straight Series record, 92,706, saw ex-Brooks Carl Furillo and Don Zimmer make out. Given Hose desperation, "The last half of the eighth inning was certainly one of the most dramatic in World Series history," said Allen.[47]

Dodging expiration, 1–0, the Sox only postponed the reckoning. At Comiskey, Wynn was shelled, 9–3. Chicago skipper Al Lopez blamed reliever Larry Sherry's 12 2/3 innings, two wins, and 0.71 ERA. Aparicio scored the Coliseum's din, vastness, its burlesque dimensions. Said Fox: "It was a great year." The Hose stranded 43 runners, including 11 in Game Three: Key hits would have made it greater. Solace was each player's then-record losing share: $7,275.17 per man.[48]

Brickhouse, among others, foresaw of slew of flags. "Fox, Aparicio, I couldn't wait."[49] Instead, the Hose began a long list downward. The '60ers finished third. Next year, returning home, Wells became the expansion Angels' radio/TV *duce*. "One reason I left Chicago was because I was getting shell-shocked by Veeck's scoreboard," he said, seriously, of the exploding bells and whistles installed in 1960. "And the word had gone out that his next gimmick would be to blow up the press box."[50] In a cycle of irony, Kluszewski, picked in the expansion draft, hit the first Angels homer in the team's 1961 opener.

That week a photo of Kennedy and aide David Powers at the Kluless Sox opener showed them reading *The Sporting News*. On WGN's *Leadoff Man*, JFK became the first U.S. president interviewed on TV at a baseball game. Another 1961 *Leadoff*er vanished near airtime. "Where's Roger Maris?" Lloyd told Whitey Ford, who nabbed Yogi Berra and Mickey Mantle. Vince gaped: "I've got three great names." Suddenly, Maris made it four. "I just got a call from my wife in Kansas City. She gave birth to a son!" Hair Arranger conditioner sponsored the postgame show. Vince gave a bottle to guest Rivera, who said, "Gee, thanks a lot," thinking it shaving lotion. "I use this every time I shave."[51]

Lloyd left the Sox in 1965. By 1970, attendance was 495,355. "'Try broadcasting,' Bob Elson would tell me," Nelson mused, "'with a lousy team and almost zero interest.'"[52] Increasingly, The Old Commander turned to watering holes, gin rummy, and on-air clientele. "'Ball two,'" Lindsey recalled Elson saying, "'and we had a ball last night at Mama's Restaurant.'" Nelson laughed. "Bob *had* to be on the take. His plugs weren't even sponsors."[53]

Axed in late 1970, Elson braved a year in Oakland, came home, began a never-completed memoir, and died in 1981, at 76.[54] By then, Brickhouse had been gone from 35th and Shields since 1968. Till then, neither Chicago team telecast with the other at home. That year, starting daily coverage, Sox owner Arthur Allyn dumped WGN for Chicago's first UHF (ultra-high frequency) outlet (WFLD). Livid, Cubs owner Philip Wrigley had Jack call the entire schedule. At Comiskey Park, Jack Drees tried vainly to replace his throaty cloud nine voice.

Brickhouse died in 1998, at 82, from cardiac arrest, after surgery to remove a tumor in his brain.[55] Wells died in 2002, at 79.[56] Lloyd retired to South Dakota, dying in 2003 of cancer.[57] Each repeated "our side, "home team," and "us." Ken (Hawk) Harrelson became their kind of guy. In 1982-85 and 1990-2018, the ex-outfielder aired Hose TV, flaunting vim and verve. The Sox are "black shirts." Upon a "good guys'" homer, "*Yes*! Put it on the board!"[58]

In June 2005, the Dodgers visited the South Side for the first time since 1959. Below were Chicago's Ozzie Guillen and Paul Konerko and Jermaine Dye—or were they Klu and Jungle Jim and Little Looie? Jim Landis and Billy Pierce preceded me in Hawk's WGN booth. Watching—as then-NBC TV avatar Jack Paar often said, "I kid you not"—I was again eight years old.

Radio/TV was still my window, retrieving Turk and Señor Al and the Mighty Mite. *He's* out! Hey-hey! Holy Mackerel! The poet Sophocles said, "One must wait until the evening to see how splendid the day has been."[59] Nineteen fifty-nine's day is splendid, even now.

Sources

Grateful appreciation is made to reprint all play-by-play and color radio text courtesy of John Miley's The Miley Collection. In addition to sources cited in the Notes, most especially the Society for American Baseball Research, the author also consulted Baseball-Reference.com and Retrosheet.org websites box scores, player, season, and team pages, batting and pitching logs, and other material relevant to this history. FanGraphs.com provided statistical information. In addition to the sources cited in the Notes, the author also consulted:

Books

Condon, Dave. *The Go-Go Chicago White Sox* (New York: Coward-McCann, 1960).

Patterson, Ted. *The Golden Voices of Baseball* (Champaign, Illinois: Sports Publishing L.L.C., 2002).

Rickey, Branch, and Robert Riger. *The American Diamond* (New York: Simon and Schuster, 1965).

Vanderberg, Bob. *Minnie and The Mick: The Go-Go White Sox Challenge the Fabled Yankee Dynasty, 1951 to 1964* (South Bend, Indiana: Diamond, 1996).

Wood, Gerald C. Wood and Andrew Hazucha. *Northsiders: Essays on the History and Culture of the Chicago Cubs* (Jefferson, North Carolina: McFarland, 2008).

Newspapers

The *Chicago Tribune* was a primary source of information about the 1959 Chicago White Sox team and broadcasters. *The Sporting News* and *Sports Illustrated* also were extremely helpful. Other contemporary sources include Associated Press, *Baseball* Digest, and the *Los Angeles Times*.

Interviews

Jack Brickhouse, with author, May 1981 and June 1988.
Bob Elson, with author, March 1970 and April 1974.
Milo Hamilton, with author, October 1985
Vince Lloyd, with author, July 1998.
Lindsey Nelson, with author, June 1984 and January 1986.
Don Wells, with author, November 1980.

Notes

1. https://news.fordham.edu./university-news-/vin-scully-tells-graduates-dreams-do-come-true/. "Fordham News: Vin Scully Tele Graduates Dreams Do Come True"
2. "Log of Play-by-Play Broadcasts and Telecasts," *The Sporting News*, April 8, 1959: 38.
3. Ibid.
4. Ibid.
5. Ibid.
6. Ted Patterson, *The Golden Voices of Baseball*. (Champaign, Illinois: Sports Publishing, L.L.C., 2002), 41-42.
7. Bob Elson interview with author, March 1970.
8. Patterson, *The Golden Voices*, 42.
9. Bob Elson April 1974 interview.
10. Milo Hamilton interview with author, October 1985.
11. Jack Brickhouse interview with author, June 1988.
12. Elson April 1974 interview.
13. Ibid.
14. Patterson, *The Golden Voices*, 43.
15. Brickhouse June 1988 interview.
16. Don Wells interview with author, November 1980.
17. Elson March 1970 interview.
18. Brickhouse June 1988 interview.
19. Elson March 1970 interview.
20. Brickhouse interview.
21. https://sabr.org/bioproj/person/2945bb7f. Tim Wiles, "Jack Brickhouse." Society for American Baseball Research.
22. Brickhouse May 1981 interview.
23. "Log of Play-by-Play Broadcasts and Telecasts," *The Sporting News*, April 8, 1959: 38.
24. Brickhouse May 1981 interview.
25. Ibid.
26. https://www.nytimes.com/1998/08/07/sports/jack-brickhouse-dies-at-82-colorful-chicago-broadcaster.html. Richard Sandomir, *The New York Times*, "Jack Brickhouse Dies at 82: Colorful Chicago Broadcaster."
27. Brickhouse May 1981 interview.

ON THE AIR

28 https://www.brainyquote.com/quotes/william_f_buckley_jr_400600.
29 https://sabr.org/node/51081. Brian Wood, "Vince Lloyd," Society for American Baseball Research.
30 Dave Condon, *The Co-Go Chicago White Sox* (New York: Coward-McCann, 1960), 28-29.
31 https://sabr.org/node/51081 Brian McKenna, "Eddie Gaedel," Society for American Baseball Research.
32 Statistics in this graph www.baseball-rererence.com and www.retrosheet.org.
33 Elson April 1974 interview.
34 Condon, *The Go-Go White Sox*, 173-178.
35 Elson April 1974 interview.
36 Condon, *The Go-Go White Sox*, 14.
37 Ibid., 15.
38 Ibid., 18.
39 Elson May 1970 interview.
40 Lindsey Nelson interview with author, June 1984.
41 Ibid.
42 Elson, April 1974 interview.
43 Brickhouse, May 1981 interview.
44 From 1959-65, the Voice of the winning World Series team broadcast its official highlight film: Dodgers' Scully (1959), Pirates' Bob Prince (1960), Yankees' Allen (1961-62), Scully (1963), Cardinals' Harry Caray (1964), and Scully again (1965). Thereafter: NBC's Curt Gowdy aired it for almost a decade.
45 Condon, *The Go-Go White Sox*, 193.
46 Ibid, 199.
47 Ibid, 199 and 201.
48 Ibid, 203.
49 Brickhouse June 1988 interview.
50 Wells interview.
51 Vince Lloyd interview with author, July 1998.
52 Lindsey Nelson interview with author, January 1986
53 Ibid.
54 Patterson, 44.
55 https://sabr.org/bioproj/person/2945bb7f.
56 https://articles.latimes.com/2002/Oct/05/sports/sp-wells5.
57 https:///sabr.org/node/51081.
58 https://www.chicagotribune.com/sports/baseball/whitesox/ct-hawk-harrelson-final-year-20170531-story.html. "Ken 'Hawk' Harrelson to Retire In 2018 After 'Greatest Ride of my Life.'" *Chicago Tribune*, May 31, 2017.
59 https://www.goodreads.com/quotes/29214/one-must-wait-until-the-evening-to-see-how-splendid.

JACK BRICKHOUSE

By Tim Wiles

Jack Brickhouse, a broadcaster best known for covering Chicago Cubs baseball, also covered many other sports and teams and did a significant amount of non-sports broadcasting, including coverage of several national political party conventions and interviews with four U.S. presidents and Pope Paul VI.

"My father ran the gamut of the entertainment world," wrote Jack Brickhouse, of his father John William "Will" Brickhouse. "He was a sideshow barker. He was buried alive. He was a carnival man's carnival man."[1] He also was credited with originating "split-week vaudeville," and was a booking agent for motion pictures. Jack's mother, Daisy James Brickhouse, was a Welsh immigrant who worked as a hotel cashier and hostess.

Born January 24, 1916, in Peoria, Illinois an only child, his father died when Jack was just three years old. His mother remarried Gilbert Schultze, but Brickhouse grew up in a household where every penny was needed. After school at Lincoln Grammar School, Brickhouse would often help his grandmother deliver food trays at Proctor Hospital, in order to have access to a little extra food. Brickhouse also demonstrated his entrepreneurial streak as a newspaper vendor and golf caddie.

While attending Peoria Manual Training High School from 1929-33, the gregarious Brickhouse played basketball, served as a reporter and editor for the school paper, was elected senior-class vice president, qualified for the National Honor Society, and played the lead in the senior class play. In the fall of 1933, Brickhouse enrolled at Bradley Polytechnic Institute (now Bradley University) in Peoria, hoping to become a lawyer. The 6-foot-3 youngster played on the freshman basketball team, but he had to leave college late in 1933, due to a lack of funds.

While working at a distillery, Jack entered an announcing contest held by local radio station WMBD. Though he didn't win, he accepted a job as a half-time switchboard operator, and the other half of his time was spent on the radio, announcing news, weather, barn dances, variety shows, and local sports. He became known for his "Man on the Street" interviews, approaching pedestrians for comment on issues of the day.

During the 1937-38 season, Brickhouse convinced WMBD to broadcast Bradley Braves basketball games. The Bradley team was a national contender, and compiled a 52-9 record from 1936-39. Brickhouse accompanied the Braves on the road and broadcast the first two National Invitational Tournaments from New York's Madison Square Garden. He also covered Big Ten football, minor- league baseball, boxing, and initiated shows of his own, such as *"Here's How They Did It,"* a series of interviews with successful businessmen. On August 7, 1939, he married Nelda Teach of Avon, Illinois.

In the Spring of 1940, Brickhouse was hired by Chicago's WGN as an assistant to legendary broadcaster Bob Elson. He helped out on Cubs and White Sox broadcasts, broadcast big band concerts, and continued his "Man on the Street" interviews. That fall he began broadcasting Notre Dame football.

Brickhouse caught a break in midsummer, 1942, when Bob Elson joined the Navy. Brickhouse finished out the baseball season doing both Cubs and White Sox games. When neither team was at home, Brickhouse would recreate the away games from ticker-tape accounts. Brickhouse himself joined the Marines after the 1943 baseball season, but was discharged two months later due to complications of childhood tuberculosis.

In 1944, WGN took a pass on baseball, and Brickhouse found himself covering the first of many Republican and Democratic national conventions. The next January he was in Washington to cover President Roosevelt's inauguration. He covered White Sox games for WJJD in 1945 until Elson returned from the Navy. In 1946, Brickhouse journeyed to New York to broadcast New York Giants baseball on WMCA.

"Anybody who could see beyond his nose knew that television would be important someday," Brickhouse reminisced, and so he returned to Chicago to experiment with baseball coverage on TV station WBKB in 1947.[2] That same year he became the radio voice of the Chicago Cardinals professional football team.

He rejoined WGN in 1948 as sports service manager and broadcaster. The station covered all Cubs and Sox home games, with Brickhouse as the broadcaster. According to historian Curt Smith, Brickhouse and WGN "began a continuum--an intimacy between ball club and viewer--that decades later, in the wake of cable and thus, WGN's intrusion into millions of American households, fostered for the Cubs an enormous national sect."[3] WGN had played

• JACK BRICKHOUSE •

a pioneering role in radio broadcasting of baseball, at a time when team owners worried that broadcasts of games would hurt attendance, and they took the same role with the new medium of television.

During the late 1940s, Brickhouse continued doing Cubs and White Sox baseball and professional and college football. Still a "Jack of all Trades," he also originated a radio show called "*Marriage License Romances*," in which he interviewed couples applying for marriage licenses at City Hall. On the Cubs opening day in 1949, his only child, Jeanne, was born. Starting in 1948, and continuing for nine years, he also broadcast professional wrestling, an assignment he initially disliked, but came to see as theatrical entertainment.

The 1950 season saw Brickhouse cover his first of five baseball All-Star Games, this time as the national announcer for the DuMont network. During that same year, he began publishing the annual *Jack Brickhouse's Major League Record Book*, helped to pioneer televised golf, and was on the national broadcast team for the first of four World Series. From 1953 through 1976, a period of 24 years, Brickhouse was the radio voice of the Chicago Bears NFL franchise.

In 1962, a portion of a Cubs-Phillies game with Brickhouse at the mike was included in the first satellite television broadcast to Europe. In 1963, Brickhouse began several years of writing the "Jack Brickhouse Says" column for the *Chicago's American* newspaper. In 1964, he was elected to the Cubs board of directors, resigning in 1975 to forestall any concerns about his journalistic objectivity. Brickhouse broadcast his last White Sox game in 1967, when the team transferred to another station, and began doing all Cub games, both home and away. In 1971, he narrated the successful "*Great Moments in Cubs Baseball*" record album.

In 1975, with the White Sox in danger of leaving Chicago, Brickhouse helped assemble investors for an ownership group headed by Bill Veeck which kept the team in town. Jack and Nelda Brickhouse divorced in 1978. In 1979, he broadcast his 5,000th baseball game, thought to be many more than any other announcer at the time. He married Patricia Ettelson on March 22, 1980. He retired from Cubs baseball in 1981, though he remained at WGN in a vice-presidential capacity. In 1982, the Wrigley Field broadcasting booth was named in his honor.

Though he was eventually named to 10 Halls of Fame, his selection as the 1983 recipient of the Ford C. Frick Award, given by the National Baseball Hall of Fame for career excellence in broadcasting, was a personal pinnacle. Brickhouse's legacy in baseball broadcasting is of having carried the flag for WGN as it established itself as the first cable superstation and

Though better known for his work with the Cubs, Jack Brickhouse broadcast White Sox games on WGN-TV from 1948 to 1967.

televised almost all Cubs games from the 1950s through the 1990s. His voice was well known in Midwestern households from the mid 1930s to the early 1980s, and his famous home run call of "Back, back, back...Hey Hey!" is still remembered fondly.

The only criticism of Brickhouse is that he was a bit too positive, cheerful, and optimistic for some viewers, sugar-coating a parade of terrible Cub teams throughout his career. "I like some Gee-Whiz enthusiasm in broadcasting sports," Brickhouse said.[4]

Brickhouse died on March 3, 1998, of cardiac arrest, following surgery to remove a tumor in his brain. He was 82 years old.

A version of this biography originally appeared in *Scribner's Encyclopedia of American Lives*.

Notes

1   Jack Brickhouse with Jack Rosenberg and Ned Colletti; *Thanks for Listening!* (South Bend, Indiana: Diamond Communications, Inc., 1996),1 2.

2   Smith, Curt. *Voices of Summer* (New York: Carroll & Graf Publishers, 2005), 81.

3   Smith, Curt. *Voices of the Game: The Acclaimed Chronicle of Baseball Radio and Television Broadcasting-from 1921 to the Present* (New York: Fireside Books, 73.

4   Chicago Cubs. *Media Guide* (Chicago: The Chicago Cubs, 1981), 68.

BOB ELSON
By John Gabcik

At age 25, Bob Elson had the ideal attributes to appeal to a fledgling radio industry. With a clear voice, an engaging personality, and the innate skill to immediately convert the action before him into words, he was able to parlay a radio contest in St. Louis into a broadcasting career in Chicago covering more than 40 years.

Robert Adolph Elson was born in Chicago, Illinois, on March 22, 1904. The second of five children born to Charles and Elizabeth Elson, Bob started making deliveries for the family grocery business at a young age. At the local Catholic school, his voice made enough of an impression on the nuns that he was given an audition for the world-famous Paulist Choir. Headquartered at St. Mary's Church in downtown Chicago, the 65-member choir was directed by Father William Finn, who ruled with an iron hand. Choir members were held to a strict regimen in their personal lives. The boys were expected to excel in school, to be careful about whom they associated with, and to never abuse their voices by shouting. Elson was a member of the choir for five years, participating in tours of Europe. The choir won first place at an international competition at the Singing Contest in Paris on May 25, 1912.[1]

Elson graduated from DePaul Academy in Chicago, then worked for a year or two earning money for tuition before entering Loyola University, Chicago, for two semesters. He transferred to Northwestern University in nearby Evanston where he was listed as a member of the Class of 1927—but never graduated; opportunities in the field of radio had intervened.

Elson took part in a radio announcing contest in Minneapolis over the summer of 1927 and was offered a job at station WCCO. He also worked for a while at station WAMD in Milwaukee. Then, in 1928, he entered another announcing contest in St. Louis, sponsored by radio station KWK. When Elson won the contest, he was offered a position by KWK, accepted and worked there briefly. But when the results of the contest were reported in the Chicago papers, local station WGN decided to pursue the home-grown talent, offering a studio announcing position. Elson returned and debuted there on March 11, 1929.

He was soon doing a variety of assignments at the station: commercials, news summaries, remotes from Chicago ball rooms offering live music, lead-ins for the amazingly popular *Amos 'n' Andy Show*—everything but sports. The station already had a skilled sports announcer, Quin Ryan. Ryan was a former editor of the *Chicago Tribune,* WGN's owner, but, despite his success as an announcer, Ryan was more interested in the station's management than in being behind a mike. So the same year he joined WGN, Elson was invited to assist Ryan in the announcing booth for both Chicago Cubs and Chicago White Sox home games. By 1931, these assignments were entirely Elson's, at least at WGN, where Elson would continue to handle both teams' home games through 1942.

Radio was still in its infancy with a dearth of programming material, but there was baseball in the afternoon for six months of the year. Five Chicago stations –WGN and its four major competitors – were broadcasting the same games that Elson was describing. "There were no soap operas in those days, so the women either had to listen to baseball or shut the radio off. So the women learned their baseball by listening to the radio" said Elson, describing the situation.[2]

On days when there was no game in Chicago due to bad weather, Elson and WGN had to scramble for an alternative. If a game was scheduled elsewhere where the skies were clear, Elson would arrange for Western Union to send an operator to that city's ballpark, with a second telegraph operator joining Elson at the studio. Elson did the games, pitch by pitch, bringing the game to life for his audience. "There I'd be, surrounded by four blank walls, the crowd noise record blaring away....changing that 'OUT CF' notation into 'a great running one-handed catch by the flagpole.' After seven hours of that, everything was a blur."[3]

Elson's career ascended in 1930 when the Ford Motor Company bought the rights to broadcast that year's World Series for $100,000. The offices of baseball Commissioner Kenesaw Mountain Landis were just down the street from the WGN studio in Chicago, and Elson and Landis often met for lunch. They not only were friends; Landis had a keen appreciation for Elson's broadcasting skills—and now he was to appoint an announcer for the Series. Elson was Landis's choice to announce the 1930 Series. He also did the next 11 years, often sharing the assignment with Red Barber. And when, in 1933, *Chicago Tribune* sports editor Arch Ward's promotional efforts resulted in the first major league All-Star Game, Elson was appointed to call it as well. Elson did nine All-Star Games, missing only the 1936 game in Boston due to illness. Asked about his most exciting World Series and All-Star moments as an announcer, Elson cited Babe Ruth's 1932 Series home run against the Chicago Cubs ("He really did point to the spot before he hit the ball there" [4]), Ruth's hitting the first-ever All-Star home run in 1933 ("It was only right"), and Ted Williams' climactic ninth inning home run in the 1941 All-Star game in Detroit ("It was only time I ever saw Ted show emotion; he danced around the bases.").[5]

Having received major-league baseball's most prized assignments, Elson soon became the announcer of choice for other sports. In the mid-1930s he got into professional football and hockey, calling Chicago Cardinals and Chicago Blackhawks games, spots he held into the mid-1950s. He also reported major boxing matches, horse races, and college football games. At times, he shared the announcing chores with the other great radio talents of the day: Ted Husing, Lowell Thomas. Gabriel Heatter, and Red Barber. On the airwaves, his voice was ubiquitous, and he was popular on the banquet circuit. *Sporting News* issues from the 1930s through the 1960s are peppered with announcements of Elson as emcee or main speaker at various sports galas. But Elson didn't stop at being the top sports announcer of the day; he also became the premiere interviewer of the era.

In 1930, Elson suggested a new program format, a "Man in the Dugout" interview before or after

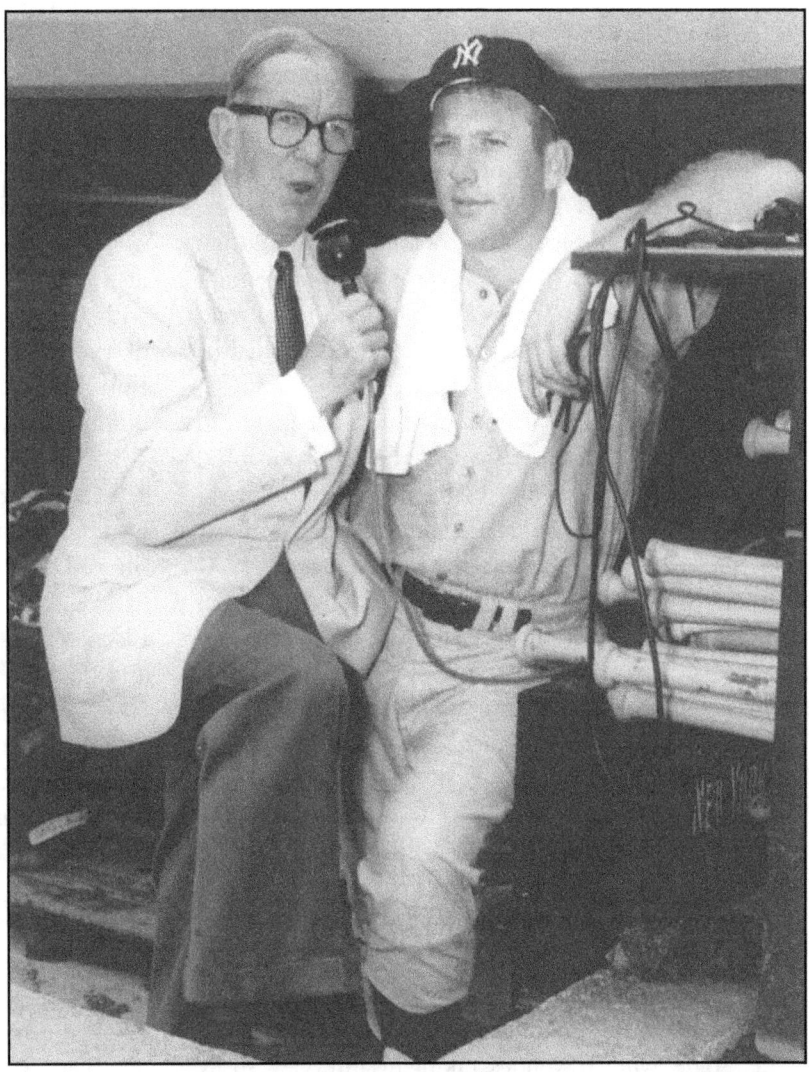

Shown with Mickey Mantle, Bob Elson broadcast White Sox games on radio for over four decades (1929-70).

baseball games. WGN liked the idea, and Elson did his first interview with Connie Mack, the already-legendary owner and manager of the Philadelphia Athletics. Professional athletes were accustomed to interviews by reporters, and to being quoted in print, but Elson provided a new experience for his guests—speaking into a live microphone. Elson developed a positive reputation among the ballplayers by asking good questions, interesting, but not embarrassing, questions. (Elson had one notably bad experience with a ballplayer. On July 29, 1938, he interviewed Jake Powell, a reserve outfielder with the New York Yankees. Elson asked Powell: "How do you keep in trim during the winter months?" Powell responded "Oh, that's easy. I'm a policeman and I beat n----s over the head with my blackjack." Abashed, Elson terminated the interview immediately, and apologized in the next day's issue of the *Chicago Defender*, the local African-American paper.)[6]

Elson soon realized he had interviewing skills that could be expanded. The New York Central Railroad's premier passenger train, the *Twentieth Century Limited*, steamed out of New York City every evening, carrying the rich and famous to Chicago's Union Station, then back. Elson approached the railroad's management about a passenger interview show; when the railroad realized that their famous train would receive a free plug on the radio, they complied. On March 4, 1946, Elson began his 15-minute interview program on WGN, *Bob Elson on Board the Century* sponsored by Krank's Shave Cream. Elson interviewed actors, writers, business leaders, politicians—whomever was making news. The show was broadcast in New York and Hollywood; the stars wanted to be on Elson's program because it upped their prestige. Commissioner Landis had no objection to Elson's interviewing sideline, as long as he didn't mix screen stars up with baseball. Landis warned Elson before one World Series assignment: "Stick to baseball. There's going to be a lot of Hollywood people in the park, and I don't want to hear a thing about them. I don't care if Harpo Marx slides into second base… it better not be mentioned in the broadcast."[7] By the early '50s though, railroad travel was diminishing, and Elson's interviewees were more inclined to fly. He himself was not comfortable with air travel at the time,[8] so he switched venues, taking his interview show to the famous Pump Room in Chicago's Ambassador East Hotel. The program, broadcast on weekday afternoons from one to three, was done whenever Elson was not committed to sporting events.

Elson continued the Twentieth Century interview show for 13 years. He had interviewed such notables as John F. Kennedy, Eleanor Roosevelt, Rita Hayworth, Marilyn Monroe, Richard Nixon, Edgar Bergen, and Jack Benny. Elson had great success at getting VIPs for interviews, even the very private Yankee star, Joe DiMaggio. World famous architect Frank Lloyd Wright was a notable exception. Seeking an interview as Wright brushed by him, Elson fell in step, saying "Mr. Wright, I've always had a great appreciation for your work." Wright then stopped and turned to Elson: "Well, in that case, young man, I've done enough for you already."[9]

As an offshoot to his radio work, in 1940 Elson began doing voice-overs for weekly sports newsreels shown in movie houses. He also teamed up with former major leaguer Lew Fonseca to do the audio for Fonseca's annual season and World Series recap films. And he ventured into television, doing a nightly sports recap around the dinner hour.[10]

Elson encountered a number of changes to his life in 1942. He was attending a fashion show luncheon at the Marshall Field department store's Tea Room with friends in 1941 when he was attracted to one of the models, Jeanne Kuhl, 14 years younger than Bob. They were introduced by friends, a romance bloomed and led to marriage on February 28, 1942. The couple had three children: Barbara (born in 1944), Susan (1946), and Robert Jr. (1957). Elson and his family made their home on Chicago's North Lake Shore Drive until his death.

With the US in World War II since late 1941, Elson felt a commitment to join the armed forces, and on September 14, 1942, he was inducted into the Navy as a lieutenant, senior grade, at the Glenview (Illinois) Naval Station. The Navy didn't need Elson to fly a plane. He was sought for his many connections with show business personalities and his skill in finding quality entertainment for U.S. bases throughout the world. Elson served in this capacity through the end of the war and beyond. Even after his Navy discharge in October 1945, he continued to arrange for groups of entertainers to tour hospitals and service bases.

With the exception of one Series, Elson lost his place as a World Series and All-Star Game announcer while he served. After years of shunning radio, the New York clubs—the Yankees, Giants, and Dodgers—were all broadcasting their games in 1938, and naturally expected their announcers to be assigned to these classics. Elson, however, had been called on to do the 1943 Yankees-Cardinals Series by President Franklin D. Roosevelt, and is still the only announcer to call the Series in uniform.

Perhaps in anticipation of military duty, Elson had sought another sports voice for WGN. He had learned of a fresh new talent calling Bradley Braves college basketball games in Peoria, Illinois. Jack Brickhouse, age 24, received a telegram from Elson on March 14, 1940: "Have recommended you for our announcers' staff and sports assistant. Expect a call. Wire me developments town house Los Angeles. Remember if asked you have a thorough knowledge of baseball. Regards, Bob Elson." Brickhouse successfully interviewed with Quin Ryan, was hired,

• BOB ELSON •

and found himself sitting next to Elson that summer. Brickhouse had the telegram framed and displayed it in his living room for the rest of his life.[11]

In 1947, Elson, now known as "The Commander" due to his service in the Navy, was ready to return to the airwaves. Brickhouse had been able to build a career in Elson's absence, but in post-war euphoria, most major league teams, including the Sox and Cubs, were planning to broadcast all games, both home and away. As a result, broadcasting positions in Chicago were doubled. Elson had his pick of jobs, and chose White Sox radio. The selection was fortuitous, as the Sox embarked on a streak of 17 consecutive winning seasons between 1951 and 1967, while the Cubs remained in the doldrums for 19 years through 1966. But Brickhouse also made a heady career move, becoming WGN television announcer for both the Sox and Cubs.

Elson's postwar White Sox tenure began at Chicago radio station WJJD. He then moved to WCFL ("1000 on your dial"), and finally in the mid-1960s to WMAQ. His Sox broadcasts had a variety of sponsors, including White Owl Cigars, General Finance Company, and Sinclair Oil. Elson gave loyal plugs for his favorite restaurants, tailors, haberdasheries and the like as he described the game, passing on an unsolicited good word for businesses that treated him well.

Elson continued broadcasting the Sox (who futilely pursued the New York Yankees and Cleveland Indians through much of the '50s), and the lackluster football Cardinals (who left Chicago for St. Louis in 1960). And after years of doing games for the subpar Blackhawks, he cut back his workload just in time to miss their ascendency to the Stanley Cup with Bobby Hull and Stan Mikita.

The Sox had hired manager Al Lopez away from the Indians in 1957, giving the franchise renewed hope for a championship, and bringing Elson a gin rummy opponent with reputedly enough skill to challenge The Commander. Elson had long tooted his horn about being the world's greatest gin rummy player. He had a photographic memory which logged all discards, and no one in the Sox organization was willing to play him—until Lopez showed up. (The results between the two men remain unreported).

Both Elson and Lopez were sharp dressers, men who commanded respect in public, but their personalities differed. Lopez was haunted by never having won a World Series. He was a serious man, plagued by chronic insomnia and stomach distress. But Elson had a wicked sense of humor and a reputation as a practical joker; stories written about him usually have an anecdote or two about his antics.[12]

Lopez's competitiveness delivered, and the White Sox finally won the American League pennant in 1959. Chicago fans assumed that Elson, with 12 World Series calls in his portfolio, would be an automatic choice to be the television voice of the Series—but it didn't happen. Tom Gallery, the chief of NBC Sports, had grown up on the same North Side block as Elson, and, out of some childhood or adolescent experience, held a strong animosity against the Sox announcer. So Brickhouse was appointed as the Chicago announcer for the national TV broadcasts of the '59 Series. Elson was relegated to calling the game on Chicago radio only – an outcome that left him "angry" and "bitterly depressed," according to Curt Smith.[13]

Elson had performed quite adequately in the booth without assistance throughout much of his career. Of the 7,000 baseball games he did over a 40-year career, he missed only about half a dozen due to laryngitis or illness. But in 1954, when he was in top form at age 50, the Sox gave him a back-up. Don Wells had gone to announcing school on the G.I. Bill, and with minimal minor league experience, would now complement Elson, calling two innings a game with some between-innings announcements. Wells remained with Elson through 1959, before getting a higher-profile position with Gene Autry's Golden West Broadcasting Company and the expansion Los Angeles Angels. Wells was replaced by Ralph Kiner, a future Hall of Fame slugger who happened to be a close friend of White Sox vice president Hank Greenberg. Kiner and Greenberg had been buddies on the Pittsburgh Pirates at the end of Greenberg's career, and Kiner now wanted to get into broadcasting. Kiner was in Chicago for two years before moving on to the terrible (albeit Amazin') expansion New York Mets.

Milo Hamilton then moved in beside Elson, but he left to take up another mike when the Braves relocated from Milwaukee to Atlanta in 1966. In 1967, Elson was joined in the booth by Red Rush. Rush had built a following in Chicago in the early '60s broadcasting Loyola University basketball games. Loyola's Ramblers were then the highest scoring team in the nation, featuring a pressing defense to go with constant fast-break basketball. The Ramblers were exciting and so was their announcer; Rush brought a flamboyance to the mike which matched the exuberance on the court.

Rush arrived in the Sox booth just in time to assist Elson in describing one of the most exciting pennant races in American League history. Four teams—the Sox, Minnesota Twins, Boston Red Sox, and Detroit Tigers—fought until the last week of the '67 season. Chicago was doing it all with a tremendous pitching staff but very little offense and finally succumbed to Carl Yastrzemski and the Red Sox. Elson's cool delivery combined with Rush's color to match the Sox' fight-to-the-end field mentality.

The White Sox pitching, though stellar again in 1968, couldn't offset the team's chronic weak hitting. Their record plunged, dropping them in eighth place in the 10-team AL. The next year was no better, and in 1970 the Sox hit their nadir, a 106-loss season. The Sox had become a dull, uninteresting club, and it showed at the turnstiles as 1970 attendance plummeted below 500,000.

The White Sox ownership during this period, the Allyn brothers, Art and then John, were businessmen who wanted to be sportsmen but not losers. After the terrible 1970 season, John Allyn frantically searched for a fix, including proposing a move to Milwaukee. Allyn dumped long-time Sox employee and general manager Ed Short, then hired Stu Holcomb to operate the club. Holcomb, a former football coach and athletic director at Northwestern University, found two rising stars in the California Angels organization. He hired Roland Hemond to be the new Sox GM, and Chuck Tanner to be the field manager.

Then, when Charlie Finley of the Oakland A's offered Red Rush a contract to replace his departed announcer, Harry Caray, Holcomb saw no reason not to make a clean sweep. After 34 years as a White Sox announcer, Bob Elson was out of a job at the age of 66. In his place, Holcomb hired the recently-available Caray, who in turn brought in Jimmy Piersall as his booth partner. Holcomb modernized with Caray as the "fan-in-the-booth" and Piersall as the knowledgeable ex-jock. Had Elson's style become passé? Milo Hamilton may have answered the question best: "Hell, no! There was never any doubt he had the talent. It was just that in the sixties, with the world so damn frenetic, laid-back Bob and his slow, sedate style, well, to some he became a relic."[14]

Red Rush pleaded with Finley to hire Elson. Finley conceded, and Elson got a one-year contract for 1971 to do an inning per game and a postgame show. Elson packed his bags and took a hotel room in Oakland, but the arrangement never worked. His contract was not renewed at the end of the season; he was free to return to his beloved Chicago. Elson recalled his Oakland experience: "I never enjoyed it. Finley won't let you enjoy anything. He's a very smart baseball man, and he put together a championship team. But he missed the human equation. People don't mean anything to him. And that's a sad state of affairs."[15]

Elson then gracefully moved into what was for him a form of retirement. He did color as part of the Blackhawks radio team for three years. He was asked by a Chicago bank, Northwest Federal Savings and Loan, to do a live interview show from the bank's lobby on Saturday mornings. Once again, he was doing a work he relished, talking sports with personalities from the Chicago athletic scene, encouraging his guests to reveal a little bit more than they might have intended, yet not enough to cause embarrassment.

On August 5, 1979, Bob Elson was a recipient of the Ford C. Frick Award, the third announcer, after Mel Allen and Red Barber, to be so honored. With his children in attendance, Elson was introduced to the audience by Blake Cullen, a close friend and the Cubs' former traveling secretary. Elson told an anecdote or two, referred to his friendship with Commissioner Landis, and concluded by saying that his only regret was that he had not broadcast more championships for the great fans of Chicago.

Bob Elson passed away from a heart condition on March 10, 1981, at Augustana Hospital in his beloved city, Chicago. He was 76 and had been preceded in death by his wife, Jean, who died of lung cancer in 1975.

Bob Elson is said to have begun a memoir during the last year of his life. His belief was that "a man shouldn't write his life story until he has given up his active career."[16] Had he lived to complete it, his legions of Chicago fans would have loved reading it.

Author's note

In May of 1951, when I was eight years old, the Chicago White Sox had a 14-game winning streak and caught my dad's attention. He started listening to Bob Elson's broadcasts over WCFL radio. Since we didn't have a television and but one radio, Bob Elson's voice became a constant presence in our household and to me as a boy. Elson was a faithful instructor who would mentor me on baseball history, on standings and stats, on strategies and on the Sox' lamentable habit of leaving men on base. There weren't too many "White Owl Wallops" ("and a box of White Owl cigars") for the Sox in those days, and I was too young to hit up "Friendly Bob Adams" at General Finance for a loan. But Bob Elson gave me a passion for baseball, especially good pitching, that I have maintained all my life, and passed on to my son. This one's for you, Bob.

Sources

Barber, Red. *The Broadcasters* (New York: Dial Press, 1970).

Ham, Eldon L. *Broadcasting Baseball* (Jefferson, North Carolina: McFarland and Co., 2011).

Lindberg, Richard C. *Total White Sox* (Chicago: Triumph Books, 2006).

Vincent, Fay. *The Only Game in Town* (New York: Simon and Schuster, 2006).

Wiles, Tim. "Jack Brickhouse," SABR Biography Project, sabr.org.

Baseball-Reference.com.

Retrosheet.com.

Southsidesox.com.dinner

Archives, Loyola (Chicago) University and Northwestern University.

Elson family scrapbook, courtesy Susan Minifie, Bob Elson's younger daughter.

Ed Stone, author's telephone interview, September 23, 2014.

Susan Minifie, author's telephone conversations and email correspondence, 2009.

Notes

1 *The Crisis Magazine*, December 1913, 58.
2 Bob Vanderberg, *SOX: From Lane and Fain to Zisk and Fisk* (Chicago: Chicago Review Press, 1982), 348.
3 Eddie Gold, "Elson Named to Hall of Fame," *Chicago Sun-Times*, February 16, 1979.
4 Jack Craig, "Elson Is Dean of Baseball Announcers," *The Sporting News*, June 13, 1970.
5 Ibid.
6 Larry Lester, *Black Baseball's National Showcase: The East-West All-Star Games 1933-1945* (Lincoln: University of Nebraska Press, 2002), 107.
7 Gold.
8 David Condon wrote in the March 26, 1958, issue of *The Sporting News* "I remember when Elson used to be as white as if he'd just lost a $10 bill at the very mention of airplane travel."
9 John Dunning, *On the Air; the Encyclopedia of Old-Time Radio* (New York: Oxford University Press, 1998), 104.
10 Elson's show, *Sports and Comments*, sponsored by automobile dealer Manhattan Motors, gave game scores and a brief interview. Elson received a 1954 *TV Guide* trophy as Best Sportscaster to go along with his two awards as Best Baseball Announcer from *The Sporting News*. *WBBM Personalities*, March 1957 (Minifie; Elson family scrapbook).
11 Jack Brickhouse, *Thanks for Listening* (South Bend, Indiana: Diamond Communications, 1986), 21.
12 When it comes to practical jokes, what goes around comes around. One evening, Elson was doing his regular sports re-cap show when a group of his friends walked into the studio, accompanied by a beautiful young stripper. Standing in front of Elson, with his audience unaware, the young lady proceeded to do her act—taking off absolutely everything "but her toe nail polish" as Elson did his show. Elson managed to get through the show, sweating bullets and later remarking "Boy, would I like to have a tape of that show. I don't know to this day what I said." Brickhouse, 30.
13 Curt Smith, *Voices of the Game* (South Bend, Indiana: Diamond Communications, 1987), 180.
14 Ibid., 357.
15 Vanderberg, 350.
16 David Condon, "Bob Elson, 76, longtime Cubs, Sox 'voice' dies," *Chicago Tribune*, March 11, 1981.

VINCE LLOYD

By Brian P. Wood

From the mid-1960s to 1980s, Vince Lloyd and Lou Boudreau brought Cubs games to life for legions of fans.

Vince Lloyd Skaff was born June 1, 1917 in Beresford, South Dakota. His parents, Michael T. and Lula (Salem) Skaff, were Lebanese immigrants who owned a family bakery. He had three brothers (Francis, Alfred and John) and a sister (Helen). After graduating from Beresford High School and a stint at South Dakota State University, Skaff transferred to Yankton College on the South Dakota/Nebraska border, a school whose most renowned sports alumnus, along with Lloyd, was NFL All-Pro defensive lineman Lyle Alzado. At Yankton, Vince played tackle on the football team and met his future wife, Miriam (Jacobson). The couple participated in local theater and radio dramas and co-starred in a production of Shakespeare's "Macbeth." They were married on January 2, 1941, in Bloomington, Illinois.

Skaff graduated from Yankton in 1940 with a degree in journalism. (He would later serve as a fundraiser for the college when it was going through financial difficulty. The school closed in 1984 and is now the site of a minimum-security federal prison.) Seeking a career in radio, he successfully auditioned with KTRI in Sioux City, Iowa by describing an imaginary parade in a manner said to be so realistic that the interview was curtailed—the trombones became too noisy. At KTRI, where Lloyd called games for the Sioux City Soos of the Class D Western League, he dropped his surname and became known as Vince Lloyd. He eventually moved to WJBC in Bloomington, Illinois and then to WMBD in Peoria before joining the U.S. Marines in April of 1942.

Serving in World War II, Lloyd advanced from private to lieutenant before being discharged in March of 1946. After returning to WMBD, Lloyd moved to WGN in Chicago in September of 1949, spending the next 38 years there on both radio and television.

From 1954-64 Lloyd partnered with Jack Brickhouse on Cubs and White Sox telecasts, doing some play-by-play and hosting pre-game shows. An impromptu pre-game television interview with President John F. Kennedy on Opening Day 1961 at Washington's Griffith Stadium—the first such interview ever conducted at a baseball game—became Lloyd's defining moment during his years at WGN. The interview almost did not take place, as the Secret Service had not been consulted and would not allow Lloyd access to the president. But after Illinois Senator Everett Dirksen, who was part of the presidential party, waved to him, Lloyd pushed past an agent and started his interview. Hoping for two minutes, he got 15. Lloyd declared, "I was so excited I had to study the tape later to find out what the President had said to me."[1] Asked if Mrs. Kennedy was coming to the game, President Kennedy answered, "No... it's Monday, and she has to stay home and do the laundry."[2]

During spring training 1965, Cubs radio play-by-play man Jack Quinlan died in an automobile accident. Quinlan's partner, Boudreau, encouraged Lloyd to move to the radio booth. He did and they would spend the next 23 years as the radio voices of the Cubs.

Known as "The Voice for all Seasons," Lloyd announced events for the Chicago Bears, DePaul University basketball, professional wrestling, and became the first broadcaster of the Chicago Bulls, teaming with Boudreau. Fans could not get enough of "Vince and Lou." Many would listen to Big 10 football broadcasts just to hear their banter. After Boudreau died in 2001, Lloyd acknowledged, "Most of what I know about baseball I learned from Lou. I can't imagine there's ever been a better baseball analyst."[3]

Lloyd was recognized not only for his deep, distinctive baritone voice, but his vivid descriptions in a "straightforward, concise, and grammatically correct" manner:[4] "Ground ball to short... Kessinger to his left... over to Banks for the out."[5] Lloyd's tone immediately let fans know if the Cubs were winning or not. "Holy mackerel!" became his signature home run call. Lloyd's favorite memories during his Cubs years included Don Cardwell's 1960 no-hitter, Sandy Koufax's 1965 perfect game (in which Cubs pitcher Bob Hendley pitched a one-hitter), and the 1969

• VINCE LLOYD •

Cubs team, which led the National League East for most of the season before slumping late in the year and losing out to New York's Miracle Mets.

Lloyd's career featured some amusing moments.

One night during an interview, Lloyd let Hall of Fame wrestler Vern Gagne use his famed "sleeper hold" on the broadcaster. Lloyd passed out for eight or nine seconds and needed to be carried from the ring.

Before an interview with infielder Connie Ryan, Lloyd suggested he ask how players compare the AL and NL. Ryan readily agreed. However, when asked live, Ryan spouted "That's a very unfair question, Vince!"[6]

When interviewing balding first baseman Vic Wertz, Lloyd offered him a sample of the sponsor's hair product, in a miniature bottle.

Lloyd once ran afoul of White Sox manager Paul Richards during an interview with pitcher Harry Dorish, who revealed details of a secret palm ball/"cosmic" pitch. The camera even showed a tight close-up of it.

Manager Eddie Stanky of the St. Louis Cardinals, given a watch for being interviewed before a game in 1954, professed, "I'm going to put the watch on right now for luck." The Cubs then crushed the Cards, 23-13. Lloyd remarked, "I haven't been within 100 yards of Stanky since." [7]

In 1981: "I'd like to talk about the Cubs' successes, but I'm supposed to talk for more than a couple of minutes. We have a nice bunch of guys, I'll say that. The opposition certainly loves them. The St. Louis Cardinals wanted us to stay over and play another game."[8]

In 1982 there was speculation as to whether or not Lloyd and Boudreau would be rehired. Ray Sons, *Chicago Sun-Times* sports editor, wrote, "Vince and Lou are not plastic media personalities, but people whose gentle warmth has made them seem part of the family to generations of Cubs fans. WGN seems to be getting ready to shove Vince or Lou, or both, out the back door."[9] In the end, however, both returned; Milo Hamilton took over the play-by-play duties while Lloyd delivered radio commentary and hosted pre/post-game shows. He also teamed up with longtime WGN executive director Jack Rosenberg to enlarge WGN's radio network to over 6- stations. "Vince was very effective, especially dealing with managers of smaller stations," said Rosenberg, who had first worked with Lloyd back in Peoria.[10]

Like Jack Brickhouse, Vince Lloyd had a long career broadcasting Cubs games, but he also worked with Brickhouse on Sox telecasts from 1955-64.

Lloyd retired with Miriam to South Dakota in 1987, periodically returning to the booth (including subbing for an ailing Harry Caray in 1994). Miriam passed away in 1999. Lloyd later reconnected with an old friend, Myrtle "Myrt" Giblen. Offering to sell her Miriam's Oldsmobile, he traveled to Tucson where they fell in love and married in June 2000.

In March 2002, Lloyd reflected on his fellow broadcasters, "I cherish the memories of each...and I think I'm as lucky as any can be to have worked with them and to have been friends with them. What more can you ask?"[11] In January 2003, Vince and Myrt drove to Scottsdale, Arizona to be with former Cubs player/broadcaster Ron Santo when the Hall-of-Fame announcements were made.

Lloyd died on July 3, 2003 in Green Valley, Arizona after a battle with stomach cancer. Survivors included son Michael John Lloyd of Deadwood, South Dakota. Jack Rosenberg remembered Lloyd, who had helped entertainer (and fellow Lebanese-American)

Danny Thomas spearhead the effort to support St. Jude Children's Research Hospital in Memphis: "His heart is as warm as the Lebanese sand of his ancestors. Vince was a fantastic man, very compassionate and charitable. Everybody was his friend. Vince did not rip players or managers on the air. That was just not part of his style. And his voice was one of the best."[12] Lloyd's grand-nephew, Rich Williams, arranged for a baseball signed by Lloyd's family to be placed in his casket before his burial.

Pundit Mark Rhoads praised Lloyd's "contagious enthusiasm in his voice no matter what the score or the weather. If the home team was gaining or ahead, the voice became turbo-charged. There was little adversity that could get him down."[13]

The Cubs honored Lloyd on July 4, 2003 with a moment of silence at a Cubs-Cardinals game. It was perhaps appropriate that one who entertained millions with the spoken word should be honored by no words.

In May of 2017, a week before what would been his 100th birthday, Lloyd was enshrined in WGN's Walk of Fame along with longtime colleagues Boudreau and Rosenberg.

Sources

Barber, Doug, "Yankton College: A controversial decision," *Washington County Pilot-Tribune & Enterprise,* September 9, 2010, http://www.enterprisepub.com/news/yankton-college-a-controversial-decision/article_94554636-a022-579e-802a-f8b5ecd3f227.html, retrieved May 26, 2018.

Bechtold, Herb, "Herb Bechtold's Round Robin," *Argus-Leader (Sioux Falls, SD),* September 9, 1964, 18.

Berger, Daniel & Steve Jajkowski, *Chicago Television,* Arcadia Publishing, 2010, 139.

Castle, George, Where Have All Our Cubs Gone? Taylor Trade Publishing, 2013, 334, https://www.amazon.com/Where-Have-All-Cubs-Gone-ebook/dp/B00H8QBUR6, retrieved May 24, 2018.

Charles, Robert, "The Things Ball Players Say on TV!" *Chicago Tribune,* August 2, 1959

Chicago Tribune, TV section, various dates.

Egan, John, "Lloyd returns to S.D. from Chicago sports scene," *Argus-Leader (Sioux Falls, South Dakota),* May 13, 1987, D1 "In the Wake of the News," *Chicago Tribune,* Mar 27, 1965, 2.1.

"John Elias Skaff 1912-2000," iagenweb.com, October 14, 2015, http://iagenweb.org/boards/woodbury/obituaries/index.cgi?read=572788, retrieved May 26, 2018.

Markus, Robert, "They'll be back: WGN keeps Lloyd, Boudreau," *Chicago Tribune,* November 9, 1982, 3.1.

Sherman, Ed. "Ed Sherman on Sports Media: A Cubs fan pays tribute to Vince Lloyd and Lou Boudreau," September 29, 2014, http://www.shermanreport.com/a-cubs-fan-pays-tribute-to-vince-lloyd-and-lou-boudreau/ retrieved May 24, 2018.

"A 'Station Break' for WGN," *Chicago Tribune,* August 15, 1964, 7.

Stolze, Craig, "Counter Punches," *Argus-Leader (Sioux Falls, South Dakota),* April 9, 1954

"Veteran sportscaster Vince Lloyd dead at 86," *Dispatch-Argus (Quad Cities),* via the AP, July 5, 2003, http://qconline.com/sports/veteran-sportscaster-vince-lloyd-dead-at/article_c86e10a3-9cc2-5c79-935a-0d9674b6222b.html, retrieved February 12, 2018.

"Vince Lloyd," Revolvy.com, https://www.revolvy.com/main/index.php?s=Vince%20Lloyd&item_type=topic, retrieved February 12, 2018 "Vince Lloyd: Broadcaster," Variety, August 1, 2003, http://variety.com/2003/scene/people-news/vince-lloyd-1117890305/, retrieved February 12, 2018 "Vince Lloyd: Broadcaster," *Variety,* August 1, 2003, http://variety.com/2003/scene/people-news/vince-lloyd-1117890305/, retrieved February 12, 2018.

"Vince Lloyd (Skaff)," South Dakota Hall of Fame, http://www.sdshof.com/inductees/vince-lloyd-skaff/, retrieved February 12, 2018.

"Vince Lloyd, Sports Announcer, wgngold.com via the internet wayback machine, retrieved May 23, 2018, https://web.archive.org/web/20080705152228/http://wgngold.com/people/lloyd-vince.htm, retrieved May 23, 2018.

• VINCE LLOYD •

"WGN Radio to induct ten honorees into Walk of Fame," WGNRadio.com, March 29, 2017, http://wgnradio.com/2017/03/29/wgn-radio-to-induct-ten-honorees-into-walk-of-fame/ retrieved February 12, 2018.

Yellon, Al. "The Score didn't make much news this week, so here's a look back at a beloved Cubs radio crew from the past," bleedingcubbieblue.com, https://www.bleedcubbieblue.com/2016/3/14/11214132/the-scoreboard-a-nostalgic-look-back-at-vince-lou, retrieved February 12, 2018.

Notes

1 "In the Wake of the News," *Chicago Tribune*, Mar 27, 1965, 2.1, https://www.newspapers.com/image/376466963/?terms=vince+lloyd+white+sox.
2 Cross, Robert, "In Vince and Lou we trust," *Chicago Tribune*, August 28, 1977, 41-42.
3 Jauss, Bill, "Vince Lloyd 1917-2003: Longtime broadcaster 'very compassionate,'" Chicago Tribune, July 5, 2003, http://articles.chicagotribune.com/2003-07-05/sports/0307050093_1_arne-harris-wgn-jack-brickhouse, retrieved February 12, 2018.
4 Boyle, Mary Sandberg, "WGN Radio Walk of Fame: Vince Lloyd," WGNradio.com, March 14, 2016, http://wgnradio.com/2017/05/22/wgn-radio-walk-of-fame-vince-lloyd/, retrieved February 12, 2018.
5 Jauss.
6 Remenih, Anton, "Beachcombers can be envious of Vince Lloyd," *Chicago Tribune*, May 22, 1954, F1
7 Remenih, who reported the score as 23-10. However Retrosheet shows it was 23-13 on April 17, 1954.
8 Fallstrom, Bob, "Cubs: This losing streak is a blessing," *Herald and Review (Decatur, IL)*, April 24, 1981, C1, https://www.newspapers.com/image/76593864/?terms=vince+lloyd+white+sox.
9 Richards, Gary, "Holy mackerel! WGN may ax Vince, Lou," Quad City Times (Davenport, IA), October 27, 1982, 15, https://www.newspapers.com/image/308499130/?terms=vince+lloyd+white+sox.
10 Jauss.
11 Castle, George, "Remembering old friends: Lloyd, 84, last of old WGN crew," The Times (Munster, Indiana), March 10, 2002, C8, https://www.newspapers.com/image/309466075/?terms=vince+lloyd+white+sox
12 Jauss.
13 Rhoads, Mark, "Illinois Hall of Fame: Vince Lloyd," July 30, 2006, http://illinoisreview.typepad.com/illinoisreview/2006/07/illinois_hall_o_29.html, retrieved February 12, 2018

DON WELLS
by Brian P. Wood

In a 20-year major-league broadcasting career with the Chicago White Sox and Los Angeles/California Angels, plus four additional years of professional and college play-by-play, Don Wells worked alongside famed broadcasters Bob Elson, Dick Enberg and Dave Niehaus, all of whom would later win the National Baseball Hall of Fame's Ford C. Frick Award. Although Wells himself never earned such accolades, he had a long career that he could look back on with pride.

California native Wells was born in Sacramento and raised in Salinas, where he listened to the San Francisco Seals and Oakland Oaks of the Pacific Coast League on the family's "aging Kent Radio."[1] After the bombing of Pearl Harbor in December 1941, he worked for the Douglas Aircraft Company in Southern California until he was drafted the following year. He served in World War II as a Corporal in the US Army and attended the Hal Styles School of Radio and Television in Beverly Hills on the GI Bill. Wells recreated play-by-play for a baseball game on an acetate disc for an audition with KSBW (SBW standing for Salad Bowl of the World, a nickname for Salinas due to the large amount of agriculture in the area), where he broadcast Salinas Colts games in the Class C Sunset League in 1949, as well as college and high school football and basketball games in the area. Longtime Salinas native Paul Cahill remembered Wells as a polished broadcaster even at this point in his career. "Wells did a great job of painting the picture when doing the play-by-play. He had a very smooth style which made listening to him a pleasure."[2]

While visiting friends in nearby Carmel, Wells met and courted Jacqueline Anich, who was visiting from San Pedro in the Los Angeles area. They would marry in 1950 and soon welcomed a son, Chris.

In 1951, he broadcast for the Wichita (Kansas) Indians of the Class-A Western League for KWBB.

In 1952, Wells joined Gordon McLendon's Liberty Broadcasting System recreating major league games from tickertape accounts where crowd noise and other ballpark sounds were simulated.

1952 saw the demise of Liberty due to major-league baseball objecting to having its games pirated away from authorized networks. Wells applied for a job with the Chicago White Sox and was selected over future Ford C. Frick Award winner (1992), Milo Hamilton, to work with another futre Frick winner, Bob Elson (1979) beginning in 1953 on WCFL. While there, Wells did play-by-play for Big 10 football and basketball, Southwest and Missouri Valley Conference football, as well as for the NFL Chicago Cardinals. Wells considered Elson to be the "Daddy of them all" when it came to broadcasters.[3] During his time in Chicago he hosted a twice daily one-hour radio show (news, spots, music) on the White Sox home radio station.

After Bill Veeck gained controlling interest from the Comiskey family in 1958, he saw Wells as being a Comiskey man. Never having seen eye-to-eye with Veeck, Wells was terminated following the 1960 season.

After considering an offer from the Minnesota Twins (who had just moved to the Twin Cities from Washington), Wells was hired by Gene Autry in to become of the voices of the expansion Los Angeles Angels for the 1961 season. Wells said he was happy to be out of Chicago, admitting to being "shell-shocked" by Veeck's exploding scoreboard.[4]

He was teamed with Bob Kelley, long-time voice of the Cleveland and Los Angeles Rams (1937-1966), and Steve Bailey, a radio producer for many years (1951-95), broadcasting on KMPC. In the first inning of the Angels' opening game Wells called the team's first home run, a two-run shot by Ted Kluszewski off Orioles starter Milt Pappas with a "Good-bye baseball! Kluszewski hit one!"[5] Kelley departed after one year, and Bailey two.

Wells later recounted in 1963, "We were all tense at the beginning. We belonged to a personal club, sort of holding our meetings in a small place [LA's] (Wrigley Field) downtown. We developed a great favoritism for the Angels. We thought we had to do something to tell the people about this exciting club. So we made it exciting.

"We wanted the Angels to be successful in a hurry and I guess we got pretty tense about it, but tenseness has its rewards. We received criticism and I know I responded to it—although not all of it. My favoritism has never changed. But I'm more relaxed now when I do my job."6

In the mid-1960s, while living in the LA suburb of Brentwood, Wells broadcast UCLA football and basketball contests.

From 1963-68 Wells was partnered with former major leaguer Buddy Blattner, who had been Dizzy Dean's partner on the CBS Game of the Week. Although they were considered to be co-lead announcers, many felt Blattner was brought in as the No. 1 announcer, which hurt Wells. Wells hosted warm-up and wrap-up shows around each televised game. Dick Enberg took over as the lead announcer in 1969 and from 1970-72 Dave Niehaus joined the pair. Both Niehaus (2008) and Enberg (2015) were future Frick Award winners.

Niehaus remembered Wells as a "heck of a broadcaster" who never realized his dream. "He never got that No. 1 job that he always wanted."7 Ironically, Wells had been hired by then- General Manager Fred Haney to be the top announcer because he had wanted a bigger baseball name on the announcing crew. However, he ended up sharing the No. 1 spot with Kelley.

Enberg remembered Wells' advice for broadcasting during the *dog days of summer.* "Think of it as the *Game of the Day.* Imagine that you're broadcasting this game to the entire nation and they don't care what the records are. You have the privilege of being able to call the *Game of the Day.* Do the best you can. Make it interesting. Make them happy they tuned in. *Game of the Day.*"8

Wells' relationship with Enberg was strained, however. Early on, the inexperienced Enberg wanted to quit after an on the air putdown by Wells. And from the other side, in 1972, after the team plane made an emergency landing in Boston, Enberg jumped from his seat next to Wells and said that if he had to die, he "didn't want to go while listening to Wells."9

Wells felt Enberg cost him his job when he was replaced by Don Drysdale. Enberg disagreed and said "there was a lot to like about Don Wells, and I thought he was an outstanding announcer."10

After 12 seasons with the Angels, Wells hung up his baseball broadcasting mic after the 1972 season and became a sports and general news announcer on LA radio station KFWB until 1988. In retirement, Don and his wife Jacque moved to Switzerland where his son, Chris, had settled. They owned a large chalet in their village surrounded by the Alps. On a side note, Wells missed just the second game in his career in August 1971 in order to attend Chris' wedding.

Wells died in Switzerland on October 3, 2002, aged 79 after a long illness as the Angels were preparing for Game Three of the American League Division Series against the New York Yankees. Later that month, when the Angels finally won their first World Series championship, it seemed a shame that the celebration could not be enjoyed by the man who announced the team's first major league homer.

Sources

In addition to the sources cited in the Notes, the author also consulted:

"All-time Owners," http://chicago.whitesox.mlb.com/cws/history/owners.jsp, retrieved November 20, 2017.

"Angels Broadcasters," mlb.com, retrieved 30 Sep 2017.

http://losangeles.angels.mlb.com/ana/history/broadcasters.jsp

"Angels Notebook," *The Sporting News*, August 21, 1971.

Barrett, Don, "Where Are They Now? LARadio.com Los Angeles Radio People, B, Bailey, Steve" http://www.laradio.com/whereb.htm, retrieved February 9, 2018.

Barrett, Don, "Where Are They Now? LARadio.com Los Angeles Radio People, K, Kelley, Bob" http://www.laradio.com/wherek.htm, retrieved February 9, 2018.

"Communications, End of Liberty," *Time*, June 9, 1952. http://www.angelfire.com/ky2/cumberlandgapbc/index61.html, retrieved February 9, 2018.

"[Day of the week] Radio Programs," *Chicago Tribune*, various 1953, 54, 55, 56, 57, 59.

"Don Wells, Anaheim Angels announcer, longtime radio b'caster," *Variety* via AP, Oct 7, 2002, retrieved Sep 30, 2017 http://variety.com/2002/scene/people-news/don-wells-1117873949/

"Ford C. Frick Award," National Baseball Hall of Fame, https://baseballhall.org/awards/ford-c-frick, retrieved October 3, 2017.

Goldsborough, Robert, "Whatever happened?" *Chicago Tribune*, May 21, 1967: sec 5, p4.

Hilliker, Jim, "Celebrating KFWB's 90th Anniversary, Lost Radio History from the Warner Brothers Years 1925 to 1950," 2015, http://jeff560.tripod.com/kfwb.html, retrieved October 2, 2017.

Liptak, Mark, "Flashing Back... ... with MIlo Hamilton," White Sox Interactive, Interview from 2005, http://www.whitesoxinteractive.com/rwas/index.php?category=11&id=3133, retrieved October 1, 2017.

"Los Angeles Angels 7, Baltimore Orioles 2," retrosheet.org, http://www.retrosheet.org/boxesetc/1961/B04110BAL1961.htm retrieved October 2, 2017.

Newhan, Ross. "Wells, Kel, Bailey to Air Angel Tilts," *Independent* (Long Beach, California), Feb 14, 1961, p17

"TV Times" *Los Angeles Times*, various dates, 1964-65.

"Wells To Air Angels' Tilts," UPI (from *Chicago Daily Defender* (Daily Edition), February 14, 1961, 22.

Notes

1. Don Barrett, "Passing Parade of 2002," http://www.laradio.com/2002passingparade.htm, December 30, 2002, retrieved October 2, 2017.
2. Interview with Paul Cahill, February 10, 2018. Mr. Cahill who resides in Durango, Colorado, was a longtime resident of Salinas and is considered an oracle of Salinas sports knowledge by locals in the area.
3. Ross Newhan, "Voice of Angels Glad to Be Back," *Independent* (Long Beach, California), February 27, 1961: 19.
4. Braven Dyer, "Wells Set as Angels' Broadcaster," *Los Angeles Times*, February 16, 1961.
5. Elliott, Helene, "Don Wells 1923-2002, He Was One of First Angels as a Broadcaster" *Los Angeles Times*, October 5, 2002.
6. Don Page, "Call it Madness; Angel Fans Call It Love." *Los Angeles Times*, May 18, 1963, III-3.
7. Ibid.
8. Dick Enberg, with Jim Perry. *Dick Enberg: Oh My!* (New York: Sports Publishing Books, 2012), 97-98.
9. Stuart Shea, *Calling the Game: Baseball Broadcasting from 1920 to the Present* (Phoenix: Society for American Baseball Research, 2015, retrieved Oct 1, 2017, 269.
10. Shea, 267.

Miracle on Brooklyn Avenue
White Sox Score 11 Runs in Seventh Inning on One Hit

By Kevin Larkin

April 22, 1959
White Sox 20, Athletics 6, at Kansas City Municipal Stadium

The 1959 White Sox were noteworthy for getting maximum results out of minimal offensive production. That was never truer than on April 22 against the Kansas City Athletics.

With the season in its infancy, the White Sox entered the game at Kansas City's Municipal Stadium tied for third place in the American League standings with a record of five wins and four losses. They trailed the first-place Cleveland Indians by 2½ games. Kansas City was in sixth place, 3½ games behind Cleveland with a record the opposite of Chicago's, four wins and five losses.

Chicago had finished second in the American League in 1958, 10 games behind the New York Yankees. The White Sox were led by the double-play combination of second baseman Nellie Fox and shortstop Luis Aparicio and a trio of pitchers, Dick Donovan, Billy Pierce, and Early Wynn. Kansas City had finished the 1958 season in seventh place in the American League with a record of 73 wins and 81 losses, 19 games behind New York. On offense the 1958 Athletics were led by outfielder Bob Cerv (.305/38 home runs/104 RBIs). During the '58 season the A's had acquired young slugger Roger Maris (28 home runs, 80 RBIs) from the Cleveland Indians, and the team was hoping to improve in 1959.

To face the A's, White Sox manager Al Lopez chose Early Wynn, (1-1 3.52 ERA), who was making his third start of the 1959 season in year number 19 of his career. Kansas City manager Harry Craft selected Ned Garver, (1-1 1.08 ERA), a veteran in his 12th big-league season. Garver was also making his third 1959 start.

Garver mowed the White Sox down one, two, three to begin the game on a groundout by Billy Goodman and fly outs by Fox and Jim Landis. Wynn gave up a leadoff single to Bill Tuttle, who stole second base with Whitey Herzog at the plate and moved to third when Herzog grounded out. Hector Lopez singled to left field to drive in Tuttle with the first run of the game. After retiring Maris, Wynn walked Kent Hadley but struck out Hal Smith to end the inning.

Chicago quickly tied the game in the top of the second inning on doubles by Sherm Lollar and Jim Rivera. In the bottom half, Kansas City knocked Wynn out of the game with five runs, obtained on run-scoring singles by Garver and Herzog and a three-run home run by Maris. Lopez had seen enough and out came Wynn and in came Bob Shaw, who began what Richard Dozer of the *Chicago Tribune* called "another magnificent relief effort."[1] At that point in his career, Shaw was primarily a reliever, having started only five games in the previous two seasons while pitching in a total of 53 games for the Tigers and then the White Sox.

Chicago narrowed the gap to 6-5 in the third and fourth innings on a run-scoring double by Fox in the third and a three-run homer by Aparicio in the fourth. It was the Chicago shortstop's second home run of the season. The light-hitting Aparicio would have just 29 extra-base hits during the season. After Aparicio's blast, Garver was replaced on the mound by Bud Daley.

Chicago tied the game in the top of the fifth inning. Goodman led off with an infield single and left the game for pinch-runner Sammy Esposito. After Fox had singled, Landis advanced the runners with a sacrifice. The A's then issued an intentional walk to Lollar to load the bases. Ray Boone, pinch-hitting for Cash, brought home Esposito with a fly ball.

Despite giving up a leadoff double to Maris in the fifth inning, Shaw got out of the inning unscathed. The White Sox then went ahead 8-6 in the top of the sixth. An error on a wide throw by second baseman Hector Lopez allowed Aparicio to streak home with the first run, and Fox drove home the eighth run of the game for Chicago with a single to left.

Tom Gorman assumed the pitching duties for Kansas City at the start of the seventh inning, and what followed is a story perhaps worthy of Ripley's "Believe It or Not."

Ray Boone, the first batter, reached first on a throwing error by Joe DeMaestri. Al Smith bunted and was safe when Hal Smith bobbled the ball trying to make a barehanded pickup. Johnny Callison lined a single to right to score Boone, and when Maris fumbled the ball, Smith scored and Callison advanced to third.

Aparicio walked and stole second base and Shaw walked to fill the bases. Gorman was removed from the game after throwing two balls to Earl Torgeson. Mark Freeman took over and walked Torgeson to score Callison.

Fox walked to force in Aparicio with the fourth run of the inning. Landis forced Shaw at the plate, but Freeman passed Lollar and the fifth run strolled home. George Brunet, the sixth Athletics pitcher of the day, then took over. A walk to Boone saw Fox trot home with the sixth run of the inning. Al Smith walked to score Landis, and Callison was hit by a pitch, scoring Lollar with the inning's eighth run. Lou Skizas ran for Callison, who had suffered a bruised arm, but nothing more serious.

Aparicio walked to force home Boone. Shaw struck out, but Brunet passed Bubba Phillips and Fox, pushing across the final two runs of the inning. The 10 walks in one inning fell one short of the major-league record, set by the New York Yankees against the Washington Senators on September 11, 1949. (New York walked 11 times in the third inning of the game.) Brunet got the final out of the inning (which took 45 minutes to complete) when Landis tapped a grounder to the mound. The White Sox now held a 19-6 lead. What was truly remarkable was the scoring of 11 runs in one inning on just one base hit.

Chicago scored another run in the ninth without the benefit of a walk to complete the 20-6 win over Kansas City.

1959 American League Most Valuable Player Nellie Fox starred in the wild 20-6 White Sox victory over Kansas City on April 22. In a game that featured an inning with 11 Sox runs on one hit, Fox went 4-for-5 with two walks and five RBIs.

The White Sox received 13 walks in the game. Wrote Richard Dozer: "The Chicago White Sox proved again Wednesday night that you can score without hitting. But never before were they so forceful in presenting their case."[2] It was a case that the White Sox – who would win the 1959 American League pennant despite ranking sixth in the league in both runs scored and team batting average – continued to present all season long.

Sources

In addition to the game-story and box-score sources cited in the Notes, the author consulted the Baseball-Reference.com and Retrosheet.org websites and the game story by Joe McGuff in the April 23, 1959, *Kansas City Times*.

Notes

1 Richard Dozer, "Sox Win, 20-6: Score 11 Runs on 1 Hit," *Chicago Tribune,* April 23, 1959: 69.
2 Ibid.

Early Wynn Homers Late,
Wins One-Hitter

By Scott Ferkovich

May 1, 1959

Chicago White Sox 1, Boston Red Sox 0, at Comiskey Park

In December 1957 the Chicago White Sox and the Cleveland Indians got together for a headline-making trade. Popular Cuban-born outfielder Minnie Minoso was sent packing to the Tribe, along with utility infielder Fred Hatfield. For Minoso, a five-time All-Star who had turned 32 just days before the deal, it was a homecoming of sorts; he had played a handful of games with the Indians to begin his big-league career. Chicago, meanwhile, landed a couple of All-Stars, one young, the other not so much. Twenty-nine-year-old Al Smith could play all three outfield positions as well as third base. Smith (who had played with the Cleveland Buckeyes of the Negro American League in 1946-48) would bring his solid bat and athleticism to the Windy City. Joining him was another big name, an anchor on one of the greatest pitching staffs the game had ever seen.

Early Wynn was a bulldog on the mound, a take-no-prisoners right-hander who did not hesitate to use the occasional brushback pitch if he felt it gave him an edge. Throughout his career, Wynn struggled with his control, which did not hurt his intimidation factor. He had been a promising, hard-throwing youngster with the lowly Washington Senators, but his fortunes changed when he was traded to the Indians after the 1948 season. In the early 1950s Cleveland abounded in great starting pitchers, but was a perennial bridesmaid to the powerhouse New York Yankees from 1951 to 1953. Finally, in 1954, under skipper Al Lopez, the Tribe won 111 games to capture the American League pennant by eight games over New York. Much of the success came on the strength of its five aces: Wynn (23 wins), Mike Garcia (19), Bob Lemon (23), Art Houtteman (15), and Bob Feller (13). But the Indians were swept by the New York Giants in the World Series.

Wynn won 20 or more games four times with Cleveland (1951, 1953, 1954, 1956). Nevertheless, at the time of his trade to the White Sox, he was fast approaching 38 years of age, coming off an unspectacular campaign in which he had won 14 and lost 17, with an unsightly 4.31 earned-run average. Despite his being reunited with Lopez, who was now skippering the White Sox, Wynn's first summer in Comiskey Park in 1958 was more of the same: 14 wins, 16 losses, and a 4.13 ERA, although he made his fifth All-Star Game appearance.

On the bright side, the 1959 White Sox looked like a team heading in the right direction. After half a decade of being the third-best squad in the AL after New York and Cleveland, Chicago had finished a distant second behind the Yanks each of the previous two seasons. Creating a buzz on Chicago's South Side was new owner Bill Veeck, an iconoclast known as much for his promotional genius as for his eye for talent. The White Sox did not have much offense. They featured solid pitching and fielding, however, and Lopez insisted to Veeck that the team was good enough to win. A lot hinged on what kind of contribution they could get from the geriatric Wynn.

Hoping for a comeback season, Wynn started 1959 well enough, with a complete-game victory against the Tigers in which he gave up only one earned run. He proceeded to get hit hard in his next three starts, including a dreadful game in Kansas City in which he gave up six earned runs in less than two innings to the doormat Athletics (but did not figure in the decision).

By May 1, Wynn's ERA was 6.14. He was scheduled to face the Red Sox that evening at Comiskey. Boston would be without the services of slugger Ted Williams, who was recovering from a

• Go-Go to Glory •

stiff neck suffered in spring training. Although they were playing under .500, the Red Sox lineup still featured Pete Runnels, Vic Wertz, Jackie Jensen, and Frank Malzone. They were no pushovers. Chicago, in second place with a record of 10-6, was only a game behind the Indians.

With one out in the top of the first inning, Wynn stepped off the mound and gestured toward his shortstop, Luis Aparicio. Only two days removed from his 23rd birthday, Aparicio was a slick-fielding Venezuelan, an All-Star in 1958, and one of the rising stars in the game. Apparently, Wynn wanted Aparicio to take a few steps to his right. The positioning struck Aparicio as odd, given that the left-handed-hitting Runnels was due up. A classic singles hitter, Runnels had a great eye at the plate. A two-time .300 hitter, he was also riding a hot bat.

Aparicio, against his better judgment, moved slightly to his right. Moments later, Runnels hit a sharp grounder that eluded Aparicio's outstretched glove just to the left of the second-base bag. As the ball bounded into center field, Aparicio was convinced that had he not listened to Wynn, he would have gobbled up the ball and thrown Runnels out easily.

To the fans still shuffling in, it was just an innocuous-looking base knock. Wynn struck out the next batter, and White Sox catcher Sherm Lollar gunned down Runnels trying to steal second. Runnels' seeing-eye single, however, proved more significant as the game progressed.

Wynn was not at his best. Six times, he walked either the first or the second man in an inning (the second, third, fifth, sixth, and seventh). In the fifth, he issued back-to-back free passes after the first out. Through guile, however, along with a dizzying assortment of sliders, curves, and the occasional knuckleball, Wynn kept the Red Sox off-balance, fending off further trouble.

Wynn's mound opponent, veteran righty Tom Brewer, was pitching a very strong game. At age 27, the South Carolinian was, like Wynn, looking for a bounce-back year. An All-Star in 1956 when he won 19 games, Brewer was coming off a lackluster 12-12 campaign. Both pitchers exchanged zeros, but the Red Sox threatened in the top of the eighth. Don Buddin worked a leadoff walk, advancing to second on a wild pitch. After a fly to deep right, Buddin scampered to third. Wynn settled down, however, striking out the next two batters.

In the bottom of the eighth, Wynn was scheduled to bat leadoff. One of the better-hitting pitchers throughout his career, he had already collected a double in the game. He took two quick balls, then a strike, before lifting a high drive to left field. It was deep, but playable, for Bill Renna. At the base of the wall, Renna timed his leap, reached … and the ball bounced off his glove into the waiting hands of one Bobby Sura, a 16-year-old from the nearby town of Argo.[1] Wynn's home run, his first of the season and the 15th of his career, put Chicago up, 1-0.

Wynn set the Red Sox down in order in the ninth, including a game-ending strikeout of Renna. That gave Wynn 14 K's in the game (a career high), increasing his lifetime total to 1,849, the most among all active pitchers. After the first-inning hit by Runnels, Wynn did not allow another (although he walked seven). It was the second and final one-hitter of his career, the closest he ever came to a no-hitter. Later, in the clubhouse, Wynn admitted that he should never have directed Aparicio to reposition himself. "If I hadn't, he would have fielded it easily,"

In one of the most memorable games of the 1959 White Sox season, Early Wynn defeated the Boston Red Sox 1-0 on May 1, providing the game's only run with an eighth-inning home run. Wynn recorded a career-high 14 strikeouts in the game.

• May 1, 1959 •

he said. "After the game, Looey told me he'd never listen to me again."[2]

Brewer, the Boston pitcher, was equally parsimonious, surrendering only five hits and one walk in going the distance. He wound up with a 10-12 record in 1959, coupled with a 3.76 ERA. Shoulder problems ultimately forced him from the game at 29.

The victory was the 252nd of Wynn's career. Only Warren Spahn had tossed more shutouts among active moundsmen (45 to 38). Wynn would finish out his Hall of Fame career in 1963 with an even 300 victories.

The 13,000-plus in attendance savored the early-season highlight, a rousing start to the Veeck Era. The game helped kick-start a fantastic season for Wynn, who led the majors in wins (22), and the AL in starts (37) and innings pitched (255⅔). He also topped all of baseball in walks (119) for the second time. Wynn won the Cy Young Award in a landslide, back at a time when it was given to the single best pitcher in the major leagues.[3] The White Sox, meanwhile, soon earned the nickname [4]"The Hitless Wonders," riding their strong pitching and fielding all the way to the 1959 World Series, only to fall to the Los Angeles Dodgers in six games.

Sources

In addition to the sources mentioned in the notes, the author consulted baseball-reference.com and retrosheet.org.

Notes

1 Richard Dozer, "Wynn Wins 1-Hitter, 1-0, on Own Homer," *Chicago Tribune*, May 2, 1959.
2 Munzel, "Hats Off…!" *Sporting News*, May 13, 1959.
3 So who got the better of the trade? Wynn went 28-29 for Chicago over the next three seasons before being released, his career win total stuck at 299. He returned to Cleveland to pick up his 300th victory. Al Smith batted .276 in his five seasons in Chicago, including an All-Star Game appearance in 1960. He is most famous for the photograph taken of him in the 1959 World Series: Standing with his back to the Comiskey Park wall on a Charlie Neal home run, Smith is doused on the head when an excited fan accidentally spills a cup of beer on him. Fred Hatfield collected only one hit in his Indians career, and while Minnie Minoso had two fine seasons in Cleveland, his stay was short-lived, as the Tribe dealt him back to the White Sox after the 1959 campaign.
4 The sobriquet was first applied to the 1906 White Sox, who won the AL pennant despite a team batting average of only .230, then captured the World Series from the crosstown Cubs, whose .763 season winning percentage still stands as the best in the majors.

White Sox Prevail Over Orioles,
Walk-Off after 17-Inning Battle

By Mike Huber

July 25, 1959
Chicago White Sox 3, Baltimore Orioles 2, at Comiskey Park

In 1959, it had been 40 years since the Chicago White Sox had won the American League pennant. However, the White Sox were steadily climbing in the final standings, from eighth place in 1948, to sixth in 1949 and 1950, to fourth in 1951, to third from 1952 to 1956, and finally to second in 1957 and 1958. Could 1959 be their year? Edward Prell of the *Chicago Tribune* called the 1959 American League squad "that curious group wearing White Sox uniforms who are trying their best to establish that you can win a pennant without scoring runs."[1] The White Sox played 16 extra-inning games in 1959, (winning 12, tying one). On July 25 Chicago personified Prell's theory by winning a 17-inning game with only three runs.

Lou Hatter of the *Baltimore Sun* described Chicago's battle with Baltimore by writing, "The White Sox taunted the punchless Orioles for 4 hours and 35 minutes."[2] A crowd of 25,782 turned out at Comiskey Park for the game. Only about half (12,562) paid for their tickets. The rest were "striking steel workers, plus idled white collar workers in the industry,"[3] honor students and Pony League ballplayers. It was actually the second time the White Sox and Orioles went 17 rounds in the 1959 season. The first, on June 4 (also in Chicago), consumed 4 hours and 37 minutes and ended with a 6-5 Chicago victory. Both results saw the home team win in walk-off fashion.

Baltimore, seven games out of first place, was in the fifth game of a 15-game road trip, playing the second of a four-game series against Chicago. The Orioles had dropped four games in a row. League-leading Chicago was in a 13-game homestand and owned a three-game winning streak. The night before, Chicago had bested the Orioles, 2-1, with a walk-off homer in the bottom of the ninth by Al Smith off Hoyt Wilhelm. In this Saturday afternoon match on the 25th, All-Star left-hander Billy O'Dell took the mound for the visiting Baltimore, opposed by Chicago's righty Bob Shaw. Shaw was seeking his 10th victory of the season while O'Dell was after win number seven.

Baltimore took the lead in the first frame. Willie Tasby led off with a single to left, then was caught stealing. With two outs, Bob Nieman lifted a fly ball to right that Jim McAnany misplayed for a two-base error. Gene Woodling singled to left, driving in Nieman, and Baltimore was on top, 1-0.

Chicago answered in its half of the second inning. Smith doubled to left. John Romano followed with an RBI single into center field, and the ballgame was tied. O'Dell settled down, allowing just one hit (a two-out single in the third) through the next six innings.

From the second inning until the eighth, Shaw also kept the Baltimore batters in check, allowing just three singles. Then, in the top of the eighth, Tasby led off again, and again he reached on a single up the middle. Bob Boyd's sacrifice advanced Tasby to second. Nieman smacked a double to left, and his "two-bagger sent the Birds ahead."[4] Woodling was intentionally walked by Shaw. Baltimore manager Paul Richards sent Albie Pearson in to run for Nieman. Shaw hunkered down and struck out Brooks Robinson, bringing Billy Klaus to the plate. Klaus singled to left, but the run-scoring opportunity was thwarted when White Sox left fielder Smith fielded the ball and fired to home, nailing Pearson at the plate. However, Baltimore had grabbed the 2-1 lead.

In the top of the ninth, Gus Triandos led off with a single and scooted to second on Shaw's wild pitch. After Billy Gardner flied out, O'Dell sent a grounder to short. Triandos, in a baserunning blunder, tried to

July 25, 1959

advance to third but was easily thrown out by All-Star and Gold Glove-winning shortstop Luis Aparicio.

It was do-or-die for Chicago in the bottom of the ninth. Sherm Lollar sent O'Dell's first-pitch slider over the left-field wall for his 13th home run of the season. The game was tied, but Chicago continued to threaten. Smith worked a walk and Romano bunted him to second. Orioles skipper Richards called for an intentional walk to Bubba Phillips. Then "a gamble by Smith backfired."[5] McAnany bounced a grounder to shortstop Klaus, who threw to second baseman Gardner for the force out. Gardner's relay to first baseman Boyd was not in time to get McAnany. Smith "rounded third and streaked plateward, only to expire at the counting station under Boyd's throw to Triandos on an extremely close play."[6] This now forced extra play.

Chicago had at least two baserunners in each of the 10th, 11th, 12th, 13th, and 14th innings, but the White Sox could not manufacture the winning run. The game kept going. At the end of the 16th inning, the ballpark lights were turned on.

The 17th inning was the deciding, action-packed frame. With one out, Baltimore's Gardner singled to center, and Walt Dropo, who had entered the game in the 15th, singled to left. Both runners were stranded as Turk Lown, the second pitcher for Chicago, retired both Tasby and pitcher Billy Loes.[7] (Loes was sent to the plate because Baltimore had already used 13 position players in the game.)

In the bottom half, Jim Landis started things with a single to left field. Lollar singled to right, sending Landis to third. Sammy Esposito ran for Lollar. Smith was intentionally walked, giving the Orioles a chance for an out at any base. With the bases loaded, Jim Rivera grounded a ball to first, and Boyd threw home to get Landis for the first out. Phillips was due up. Chicago manager Al Lopez held him back in favor of pinch-hitter Harry Simpson. According to the *Chicago Tribune*, Lopez "remembered that Simpson had hit a two-run pinch single against Loes earlier in the year. Simpson also had hit a pinch homer for Kansas City this year to beat Loes in the ninth inning."[8] Simpson lined the knockout blow into right-center "to end the marathon."[9] Chicago had won in a walk-off, 3-2. After the game, Simpson described his success against Loes, saying, "I guess I hit him pretty good. I've made three pinch hits off him this year in four times."[10]

The White Sox marooned 18 runners on the basepaths (to Baltimore's 12). Double plays had choked off the Chicago rallies in each of the 14th and 16th innings. Both starters pitched well enough to win. Shaw stayed on the mound for 11 innings, while O'Dell pitched into the 10th.

Baltimore dropped its fifth straight game, making this the team's longest losing streak of the season.[11] Tasby had the most productive day for Baltimore, with a 3-for-8 performance. Baltimore batters had 12 hits in the game.

Chicago, meanwhile, won its fourth consecutive game (all by one run) and captured its 23rd one-run decision in 28 games. The White Sox finished the season winning 35 of 50 one-run games. The streaking White Sox were winners of 22 out of their last 31 since June 21 and 12 of 16 since the All-Star break.

This extra-inning affair was the second of four matches between Chicago and Baltimore that extended well beyond nine innings. On August 6 the two teams battled for 18 innings (the equivalent of two full games) before the tie game was called "on account of curfew."[12] Then, on September 11, in the second game of a doubleheader, the two teams played 16 innings in a game that ended in a 1-0 walk-off victory for the Orioles.

Sources

In addition to the sources mentioned in the Notes, the author consulted baseball-reference.com, sabr.org, and retrosheet.org.

Notes

1 Edward Prell, "Sox Beat Orioles, 3-2, in 17th Inning!" *Chicago Tribune*, July 26, 1959: 29-30.
2 Lou Hatter, "Chisox Nip Birds, 3-2, on Simpson's Single in 17th," *Baltimore Sun*, July 26, 1959: 41.
3 Prell.
4 Hatter.
5 Ibid.
6 Ibid.
7 Lown relieved Shaw to start the top of the 12th inning.
8 Prell. Simpson had been traded by Kansas City to Chicago in exchange for Ray Boone on May 3, 1959. Then, on August 25, Simpson was traded with Robert Sagers to the Pittsburgh Pirates for Ted Kluszewski.
9 "White Sox Beat Orioles, 3-2, in 17th," *New York Daily News*, July 26, 1959: 191.
10 Edward Prell, " 'Unconcern' Is Game with Winning Sox," *Chicago Tribune*, July 26, 1959: 30.
11 The Orioles fell to the White Sox the next day as well, in the first game of a doubleheader. Baltimore won the nightcap. The six-game losing streak turned out to be their longest of the 1959 campaign.
12 retrosheet.org/boxesetc/1959/B08060BAL1959.htm.

White Sox Sweep Tribe,
Take Commanding Lead

By Paul Hofmann

August 30, 1959 (game 2)
Chicago White Sox 9, Cleveland Indians 4, at Municipal Stadium

The August 28-30 four-game showdown between the Chicago White Sox and Cleveland Indians had been much anticipated for weeks. The peculiarities of the scheduling had kept the two American League contenders apart since July 10.[1] On that date, the Indians finished play with a two-game lead over the second-place Go-Go Sox.

The White Sox arrived in Cleveland with a 76-49 record and 1 1/2 game lead over the Indians. The Tribe, riding an eight-game winning streak, had fans envisaging a return to the top of the standings was imminent. After dropping the first two games of the series, the Indians entered the August 30 doubleheader 3 1/2 games off the pace.

The 1959 White Sox were not an offensive juggernaut. The team finished the season sixth in team batting with a .250 average and dead last with 97 home runs. The team depended on small ball and a strong pitching staff. The Sox finished with a league-leading 3.29 ERA and had one of the strongest bullpens in baseball. The relief corps was led by a pair of right-handers, Jerry Staley and Turk Lown.[2] The roommates combined for 17 wins, 30 saves, and a 2.53 ERA and factored prominently in the doubleheader.[3]

A huge throng of 66,586 fans jammed into cavernous Municipal Stadium on the shores of Lake Erie for the Sunday afternoon twin bill as afternoon temperatures rose to mid-80s under overcast skies. In the opener, right-hander Early Wynn notched his 17th victory of the year when he limited the Indians to three runs over seven-plus innings. He helped his own cause with a sixth-inning 400-foot, one-out home run to right that triggered a five-run rally that gave the Sox a 5-2 lead.[4] Staley came in the eighth and pitched two scoreless innings to nail down the Sox 6-3 come-from-behind victory. The win increased their lead to 4 1/2 games and placed the Indians in a must-win situation heading into the nightcap.

The White Sox sent right-hander Barry Latman to the mound. The 23-year old was making his 18th start of the season and entered the game with a record of 7-5 and 3.61 ERA. The home-standing Indians countered with 22-year-old hard-throwing Gary Bell. The Indians' versatile right-hander, who finished third in the American League Rookie of the Year voting a year earlier, at varying times of the year worked as a starter, long reliever and closer. He entered the game with a record of 14-10 with a 3.78 ERA.

Bell and Latman traded 1-2-3 innings before the White Sox broke through against Bell in the top of the second. Ted Kluszewski, described by a Cleveland writer as a "Percheron among ponies," opened the inning with a single to center.[5] Rookie catcher Johnny Romano drew a walk and with one out Al Smith singled to right-center to score Kluszewski and advance Romano to third. Smith moved up to second when center fielder Jimmy Piersall fumbled the ball in center. Jim Rivera drew an intentional walk to load the bases. Latman followed with a long fly ball that sent Rocky Colavito to the screen to deep right-center for a two-run sacrifice fly. Romano trotted home from third and Smith followed when third baseman George Strickland took the relay throw down the third-base line and started back for the bag at third without realizing Smith had already passed him.[6] Once he realized Smith wasn't there, Strickland pivoted and threw home, but Smith slid in safely ahead of the tag.

The White Sox added to the lead in the top of the third. Second baseman Nellie Fox singled to center to start the inning. Jim Landis grounded into a fielder's choice that forced Fox at second before Kluszewski and Romano walked to load the bases. Fearing the game may be slipping away early, Indians manager

• August 30, 1959 (game 2) •

Joe Gordon summoned 24-year old right-hander Jim "Mudcat" Grant from the bullpen. Grant was greeted with a single off the bat of Billy Goodman that scored Landis and Kluszewski. After Smith was retired on a nubber handled by Indians catcher Ed Fitz Gerald, Grant intentionally walked right fielder Jim Rivera to load the bases and pitch to Latman. Latman flied out to center to end the inning. However, the damage was done and the Sox now had a 5-0 lead.

The Indians finally got on the board in the bottom of the fourth. With two outs Minnie Minoso walked. Tito Francona followed with a single to center before Colavito deposited his league-leading 39th home run into the upper deck down the third-base line to trim the White Sox lead to 5-3.[7]

The inspired White Sox responded quickly with two more runs in the top of the fifth inning. With one out Goodman tripled to center and moments later Smith hit his 12th home run of the year to increase the Sox lead to 7-3. The Indians Woodie Held, who also hit a home run in the opener, trimmed the lead to 7-4 with a lead-off home run in the bottom of the inning. It was Held's 26th of year.

Right-hander Mike Garcia came on in relief in the top of the sixth. The Big Bear, who won 142 games in 12 seasons with the Indians, was nearing the end of his career. After giving up a leadoff single to Luis Aparicio, who was erased when he was caught stealing attempting to steal second, Garcia pitched two scoreless innings.

The hard-throwing Lown came on in relief of Latman in the bottom of the sixth. Lown was in the midst of his best season and entered the game with a 9-2 record with 11 saves and 2.64 ERA. Just as Staley had down in the opener, Lown came in to nail down the victory. Lown scattered five hits and struck out three to earn a four-inning save.

The White Sox added insurance runs in both the eighth and ninth innings. In the eighth, Lown singled to center with one out and advanced to third when Aparicio singled to right. Fox followed with a sacrifice fly to increase the Sox lead to 8-3. In the ninth, Sherm Lollar tripled to right with one out and scored the White Sox ninth and final run of the game when Sammy Esposito, who entered the game in the bottom of the seventh as a defensive replacement at third, sent a sacrifice fly to left.

The victory was the White Sox 13th in 18 games against the Indians that season. Sox players celebrated the four-game sweep by whooping it up in the clubhouse, but when White Sox manager Al Lopez was asked by photographers to pose with a broom to show how the Indians were swept out of the pennant race, he cautioned, "Let's not have any of that. We still have 25 tough games to play."[8] Cleveland manager Joe Gordon acknowledged the White Sox "beat the devil out of us."[9] However, despite being 5 1/2 games off the pace, the Tribe's skipper wasn't ready to concede the race. "Sure the White Sox have a good lead now. You never can tell what's going to happen to a ball club. They might hit a losing streak and we might get hot again and the race is wide open again, Gordon said."[10]

News of the White Sox sweep set off celebrations throughout the South Side of Chicago. It had been 40 years since the Sox had won the American League pennant and their fans were ready to celebrate. When the Sox returned to Midway Airport that evening, thousands of delirious fans were on hand to give the team a hero's welcome. The crowd was so large the players were instructed to collect their bags on the tarmac to avoid a disruption in the terminal due to the large crowd.

Despite the jubilation throughout the Chicago, not everyone was convinced the Sox would hang on to win the pennant. One *Chicago Tribune* reader opined that the White Sox have the fielding and pitching, but lack "the hitting that every pennant winning team must have" and predicted the Indians would win the pennant.[11] On September 22 the Go-Go Sox retuned to Municipal Stadium and clinched the American League pennant with a 4-2 victory over the Indians.

Sources

In addition to the sources cited in the Notes, the author also relied on Baseball-reference.com and Retrosheet.org.

Notes

1 Joe Doyle, "According to Doyle," *South Bend Tribune* (South Bend, Indiana), August 31, 1959: 14.

2 Staley preferred "Jerry" but also appears as Gerry Staley on many baseball reference sites.

3 Adam Ulrey, "Turk Lown," SABR BioProject. Retrieved from https://sabr.org/bioproj/person/9b7e5ac4

4 "Gordon, Lopez Agree: Indians Still In It," *Evening Independent* (Massillon, Ohio), August 31, 1959: 16

5 Edward Prell, "Sox Get Heroes' Welcome: Come Home After Cleveland Sweep 5½ Games Ahead," *Chicago Tribune*, August 31, 1959: 60. A Percheron is a well-muscled breed of draft horse known for its intelligence and willingness to work.

6 Edward Prell.

7 Ibid.

8 "Gordon, Lopez Agree: Indians Still In It."

9 Ibid.

10 Ibid.

11 Thomas Cook, "Says Sox Lack Hitting," *Chicago Tribune*, August 31, 1959: 60.

White Sox Clinch First American Pennant in 40 Years

By Don Zminda

September 22, 1959
Chicago White Sox 4, Cleveland Indians 2, at Cleveland Stadium

As the Chicago White Sox took the field at Cleveland Stadium on the night of September 22, 1959, the city of Chicago was bracing for a celebration. A victory over the Cleveland Indians would clinch the American League pennant for the White Sox—the first AL crown for the Sox since 1919. That 1919 league championship would be tainted forever when eight members of the team were permanently banished from baseball for allegedly throwing the World Series to the Cincinnati Reds; a pennant in 1959 would help put aside some painful memories for the Sox franchise.

The '59 Sox weren't making things easy for their fans. A five-hit 1-0 shutout by right-hander Bob Shaw over the Detroit Tigers on Friday, September 18, had reduced the White Sox "magic number" (the combination of Sox victories and/or Indians losses needed to clinch the pennant) to two. But the magic number had stayed at two on Saturday and Sunday, as the Sox suffered a pair of 5-4 losses to the Tigers while the uncooperative Indians were logging a pair of victories over the Kansas City Athletics (by scores of 13-7 and 4-3). Both teams were idle on Monday, and the Sox entered Tuesday's showdown in Cleveland with a 91-59 record, three and a half games ahead of the Tribe (87-62). Interest in Tuesday night's game was so strong in Chicago that WGN-TV, the club's television outlet, arranged to televise the game "as a public service," with Jack Brickhouse and Lou Boudreau describing the action.[1] Prior to then, WGN had televised only home day games involving the White Sox and Chicago Cubs.

To face the Indians, Sox manager Al Lopez selected staff ace Early Wynn, who entered the game with a league-leading 20 wins (20-10 record). Wynn and Lopez shared a long history, as Lopez had managed the Indians from 1951-56, years in which Wynn had recorded four 20-plus victory seasons for the Tribe. When the White Sox acquired Wynn in a trade with the Indians in December of 1957, Lopez had commented that "If there was one game I had to win, my pitcher would be Early Wynn."[2] Indians manager Joe Gordon countered with rookie right-hander Jim Perry, who entered the contest with a 12-9 record and an excellent 2.61 ERA. Perry was only 23 years old, and his experience paled in comparison to the 39-year-old Wynn, who was in his 19th major-league season and had posted 269 major-league wins. But Indians general manager Frank Lane, who had once held the same job with the White Sox (1949-55) was confident. "He's a great money player," Lane said of Wynn, "but we're going to beat him."[3]

The crowd of 54,293 watched Perry set down the White Sox in order in each of the first two innings. Cleveland threatened in the second when ex-Sox star Minnie Minoso (who had been traded to the Indians in the deal for Wynn) was hit in the left wrist to lead off the frame, and Russ Nixon followed with a single that advanced Minoso to third. Rocky Colavito then lofted a flyball to left field; Sox left fielder Al Smith, who had come to Chicago in the Wynn-Minoso trade (Fred Hatfield had gone to Cleveland along with Minoso), made the catch and "threw on the fly to [catcher John] Romano, who put the ball on the sliding Minoso"[4] for a double play. ("Minnie and I used to have a bet—who could throw out the other guy," Smith would later recall. "That year [1959], he didn't throw me out once. I threw him out three times.")[5] Woodie Held popped out to end the inning. Frank Lane, who was watching the game from the press box, unloaded on his own team for the failure to score: "That guy at third [Coach Jo-Jo White] doesn't think at all. He shouldn't have sent Minnie home. It was only a short fly... That Colavito can't drive in a run except the ones he drives himself in on a homer."[6]

• September 22, 1959 •

The White Sox broke through against Perry in the third. Bubba Phillips singled to center with one out; after Perry retired Wynn, Luis Aparicio doubled home Phillips, and Aparicio raced home on another double by Billy Goodman. Cleveland got a run back in the fifth. Held walked to lead off the inning. After pinch-hitter Chuck Tanner batted for third baseman George Strickland and struck out, another pinch-hitter, Gordy Coleman, singled. Jim Piersall then singled to center to drive in Held, with Coleman advancing to third. As Vic Power stepped to the plate, Lane grumbled: "This'll be a double play. All Power does is hit into double plays."[7] Sure enough, Power grounded to Aparicio, who started a 6-4-3 DP to end the inning, with Lane lamenting that the Tribe should have opted to have Power lay down a squeeze bunt.

Mudcat Grant relieved Perry in the sixth, and after retiring Romano to start the inning, gave up back-to-back home runs to Smith and Jim Rivera to increase the White Sox lead to 4-1. In Cleveland's half of the inning, Tito Francona led off with a single and Russ Nixon hit a one-out single to move Francona to third. After Colavito drove home Francona with a sacrifice fly to center field, Lopez replaced Wynn with Bob Shaw, who retired Held to end the inning. Cleveland threatened again in the seventh when Piersall and Power hit two-out singles, but Shaw got Francona to ground out to end the inning.

Cleveland mounted one last threat in the bottom of the ninth. Shaw retired Held to open the frame, but Jim Baxes singled off the pitcher's glove. Indians manager Joe Gordon then allowed pitcher Jack Harshman, a one-time minor-league slugger as a first baseman, to hit for himself, and Harshman came through with a single that moved pinch-runner Ray Webster to second, and Piersall hit an infield single off Fox's glove to load the bases. With Vic Power due up and Billy Pierce, Turk Lown and Jerry Staley all warming up, Lopez brought in Staley, a sinker-ball specialist. "When the White Sox bought Staley from the Yankees [in May of 1956] he was depending mostly on his knuckle ball," Lopez had commented about Staley. "Over here he throws mostly the sinker, a real good one with great control."[8] Staley was expecting to get the call. "A situation like that, a ground ball gives you a chance to get a double play and get out of the inning," he recalled.[9]

Staley needed only one pitch to bring home a White Sox pennant. Bob Vanderberg recorded Jack Brickhouse's call on WGN-TV. "Here we go. Power is 1-for-4, an infield single—there's a ground ball… Aparicio has it! Steps on second throws to first… The ballgame's over! The White Sox are the champions of 1959! The 40-year wait has now ended!"[10]

According to Vanderberg, the double play was completed at 9:43 PM Chicago time, setting off celebrations both on the field and back in Chicago. "An estimated 20,000 people gathered in the Loop to salute the victory," he wrote. "Thousands more began heading for Midway Airport, where the Sox's planed was scheduled to land around 2 AM."[11] The *Chicago Tribune* estimated the crowd at Midway at 25,000, *The Sporting News* at over 100,000.

Along with the excitement about the White Sox pennant in Chicago, there was confusion and even some panic among many of the city's residents that night. Chicago Fire Commissioner Robert Quinn, a good friend of Mayor Richard J. Daley and a passionate White Sox fan, decided to honor the Sox victory by turning on the city's air-raid sirens. Many citizens feared that the city was under threat of nuclear

Nine-time Gold Glove winner Luis Aparicio starred in the September 22 White Sox win over the Indians that clinched the 1959 American League pennant. Along with recording two hits and driving in the game's first run on offense, Aparicio took part in three double plays in the field, including the game-ending 6-3 twin killing.

attack. "The sirens sounded for about five minutes and brought anything but joyful reaction from thousands of people who thought there was an air raid," wrote Jerry (later known as Jerome) Holtzman. "Television and radio shows had to be interrupted to explain that the sirens were sounded only to signal the first White Sox pennant in 40 years…. The Illinois Bell Telephone Co. said it handled the heaviest deluge of calls since the death of President Franklin D. Roosevelt in 1945."[12]

"The sirens' wail made the night memorable, since there was no way for the people of Chicago to know whether the sirens were announcing the White Sox victory or the imminent arrival of the Russians," wrote Bill Veeck. "I mean, if you were a White Sox fan, you had to figure that it was just your luck for The Bomb to be dropped right after the White Sox won the pennant. What else could follow 1919?"[13]

Sources

Kalas, Larry. *Strength Down the Middle: The Story of the 1959 Chicago White Sox* (Chicago: RR Donnelly & Sons, 1999).

White Sox television schedule information from *The Sporting News Dope Book 1959*.

Notes

1. "WGN-TV Will Televise Sox Game Tonight," *Chicago Tribune*, September 22, 1959: 64.
2. Ed Prell, "Lopez calls on Wynn to Clinch Title," *Chicago Tribune*, September 22, 1959: 61.
3. Robert Cromie, "Indian Fans Dream, Rush for Tickets," *Chicago Tribune*, September 22, 1959: 64.
4. Edward Prell, "White Sox Win Pennant!" *Chicago Tribune*, September 23, 1959: 54.
5. Bob Vanderberg, *'59; Summer of the Sox: The Year the World Series Came to Chicago* (Champaign, Illinois: Sports Publishing, Inc, 1999), 138.
6. David Condon, "In the Wake of the News," *Chicago Tribune*, September 23, 1959: 57.
7. Ibid.
8. Edward Prell, "Castoff Hurlers Aid Lopez's Rise," *Chicago Tribune*, September 22, 1959: 65.
9. Vanderberg, 139.
10. Ibid., 139.
11. Ibid., 140.
12. Jerry Holtzman, "Sirens Sound for Chisox; Calls Flood Switchboards," *The Sporting News*, September 30, 1959: 8.
13. Bill Veeck with Ed Linn, *Veeck—As In Wreck* (New York: G.P. Putnam's Sons, 1962), 350.

Ted Kluszewski (L.) and Early Wynn were the stars of the White Sox' 11-0 rout of the Dodgers in Game One of the 1959 World Series. Kluszewski had three hits, including two home runs, and five RBIs; Wynn pitched seven scoreless innings.

White Sox Clobber Dodgers in Fall Classic Kickoff
Game One of the World Series

By Russ Lake

October 1, 1959

Chicago White Sox 11, Los Angeles Dodgers 0, at Comiskey Park

After a 40-year drought, the Chicago White Sox clinched the American League pennant on September 22, 1959, with a 4-2 victory in Cleveland. Sirens were activated in Chicago to announce the significant baseball happening. The long-wailing scream pierced the night and frightened many sleepy residents who thought the city was under nuclear attack. Mayor Richard Daley dismissed questions of a federal probe for the unintended commotion by explaining that the city council had authorized the sirens. Daly added joyfully, "This is a great night in the history of Chicago."[1] An energetic fandom topping 25,000 apparently agreed with the mayor as they assembled at Midway Airport for the 2:05 A.M. arrival of the team plane. One homemade sign proclaimed that White Sox manager Al Lopez should be considered for president of the USA.[2]

The traditional midweek start of the World Series would have to wait an extra day because the Milwaukee Braves and the Los Angeles Dodgers were engaged in a best-of-three playoff to determine the winner of the National League pennant. The Dodgers swept the series, two games to none. They used eight pitchers during the pair of one-run triumphs, so manager Walter Alston had to sort out his staff before naming a Game One starter.

With a complement of rested hurlers, Lopez enjoyed some luxury as he chose veteran right-hander Early Wynn, who at 39 had led the AL with 22 victories, to start for the White Sox. Alston selected righty Roger Craig, who sported a 5-0 record during the dramatic pennant drive beginning on August 30. The 29-year-old Craig had a World Series record of 1-1 from Dodgers postseasons in 1955 and 1956 when the team represented Brooklyn. Pitching for the Cleveland Indians, Wynn started and lost the second game of the 1954 World Series.

On Thursday, October 1, some White Sox ushers found that their morning coffee routine might bar them from getting to their assigned gates since the entry access was locked to control crowds.[3] Ticket scalpers were plentiful, and one man carrying equipment and dressed in work clothes was turned away as a "gate-crasher" with a phony story that he needed to get to the office of team President Bill Veeck to repair an electrical circuit.[4] Four Chicago policewomen were on duty to watch for female pickpockets in the ballpark.[5]

Outside the ballpark, restaurants and cart suppliers "made a killing" by raising their prices for food and beverages. However, all merchandise costs inside the ballpark remained the same except for the game program which sold for a half-dollar instead of 15 cents.[6] Ever the showman, Veeck had 20,000 red roses handed out to the women in the crowd. The White Sox explained the absence of traditional postseason bunting in the ballpark by saying they wanted the fans to see the interior just as it was during the season. Veeck also decided to have his players wear white stockings with black stripes for the first time in years and added that this had been suggested "by at least 500 letter writers this season."[7] A crowd of 48,013 moved toward their seats to get settled for baseball on a crisp and cool day. Vendors were ordered to peddle their wares without blocking the patrons' view of the game.[8] Singer-actor Tony Martin sang the National Anthem while the crowd gazed

• Go-Go to Glory •

upon an American Flag that had stuck at half-staff because of a pulley problem on the hoist.[9]

The White Sox took the field as the fans roared to encourage their team. The starting battery of Wynn and Sherm Lollar waited while an honorary first pitch was delivered by 1917 White Sox world champion heroes Urban "Red" Faber and Ray Schalk. Dodgers switch-hitter Junior Gilliam stepped into the left-hand batter's box for the symbolic delivery.[10] Faber's "spitter" to Schalk was clearly outside, but plate umpire Bill Summers emphatically signaled a strike.[11] The game begun, Gilliam grounded a 1-and-2 pitch to shortstop Luis Aparicio who fielded the sphere cleanly and fired to first baseman Ted Kluszewski for the out. Charlie Neal knocked a one-out single off the glove of third baseman Billy Goodman. Neal stole second and Duke Snider walked. Wynn escaped the jam when Norm Larker lined out to right fielder Jim Rivera.[12]

Craig started out with a curve for a called strike before Aparicio popped up to shortstop Maury Wills. Nellie Fox walked and took a large lead from first base. During the regular season, the "Go-Go Sox" were tops in the American League in stolen bases. Dodgers catcher Johnny Roseboro called for a pitchout and Fox dived safely back to the bag.[13] Fox raced to third on a single to right-center by Jim Landis. No stranger to the National League and having had great past success versus Craig, the left-handed-batting Kluszewski drilled a groundball single past the lunge of first baseman Gil Hodges. Second baseman Neal dived for the ball, but came up empty; Fox came home and Landis scampered to third. The White Sox tally was the first postseason run recorded by the franchise since October 9, 1919. Landis came across to make it 2-0 after Lollar swatted a long drive to right-center that Larker gloved on the run.[14] (The opening excitement was too much for 62-year-old George Thielmann of Cary, Illinois, who collapsed in his box seat of a heart attack and died.[15])

Both hurlers retired the side in order in the second. Wynn completed another 1-2-3 inning in the top of the third after Neal's long two-out blast to left field barely hooked foul. In the bottom half, Craig retired his fifth consecutive batter before Fox lined a double into the right-field corner. Landis followed with another safety and plated Fox for the White Sox' third run. Kluszewski kept the Chicago fans on their feet by lofting a slider to deep right. The ball, aided by a crosswind, had just enough air under it to drop into

Long-time National League slugger Ted Kluszewski had his greatest day in a White Sox uniform in Game One of the 1959 World Series, homering twice and driving in five runs in an 11-0 Sox victory over the Los Angeles Dodgers.

• October 1, 1959 •

the first row of the stands for a two-run homer and increase the White Sox lead to 5-0.[16] Alston pulled Craig and brought in right-hander Chuck Churn.

Lollar followed with a routine fly ball to left-center. The din of the crowd kept left fielder Wally Moon and Snider from hearing each other,[17] and the outfielders collided. The ball was jarred from Snider's grasp and Lollar slid safely into second.[18] Goodman singled Lollar home, and Al Smith doubled to left-center over Moon's outstretched glove. As Snider chased down the ball. Goodman held up at third, but then he raced home and Smith dashed to third on Snider's errant throw to second. Rivera hit a grounder to second baseman Neal, whose throw home glanced off Rivera's bat in front of the plate and past Roseboro for the Dodgers' third error of the inning.[19] Smith scored and Rivera moved to second. Pitcher Wynn doubled to left-center to drive in Rivera with the seventh run of the inning. The White Sox sent 11 hitters to the plate and turned the opener into a 9-0 laugher.

In the bottom of the fourth, Kluszewski boomed his second home run of the afternoon with Landis on first after his third single for an 11-0 advantage. "Big Klu" sent a hanging curve from Churn down the right-field line, where it hit the façade of the upper deck and dropped to the field.[20] Alston removed Churn for right-hander Clem Labine, and later employed southpaw Sandy Koufax and righty Johnny Klippstein, who all quieted the South Siders' bats and kept the large Chesterfield scoreboard from displaying additional Chicago tallies.

Lopez stayed with Wynn until Gilliam's eighth-inning single. Wynn said his right elbow was stiffening,[21] so right-hander Gerry Staley relieved him and induced Neal to ground into a twin killing. Staley allowed two hits in the ninth, but Kluszewski saved the shutout with a nifty stab of Roseboro's smash and throw to Aparicio for a force play and the second out.[22] Pinch-hitter Carl Furillo then flied out to left to end the game in 2:35. The White Sox had 11 runs, 11 hits, and no errors; for the Dodgers it was no runs, eight hits, and three errors.

The "Main Man" in the victorious clubhouse was Ted Kluszewski, who had three hits, five RBIs, and nine total bases. A sportswriter asked the native of nearby Argo, Illinois, "What's Argo?" Kluszewski laughed and said, "Throw that guy out of here!"[23] Dodgers manager Alston moaned, "We had the Chicago speed figured out, but nobody told us about all this power."[24]

Later in the evening, Broadway odds-makers made the White Sox 9-to-5 favorites to win the World Series.[25]

Sources

In addition to the sources cited in the Notes, the author also accessed Retrosheet.org, Baseball-Reference.com, Newspapers.com, SABR.org/bioproj, and *The Sporting News* archive via Paper of Record.

Notes

1. Edward Prell, "White Sox Win Pennant, Riotous Welcome; Sirens Scare City," *Chicago Tribune*, September 23, 1959: 1.
2. Ibid.
3. "A Tough Cop Guards Gate at Sox Park," *Chicago Tribune*, October 2, 1959: 3.
4. George Bliss, "World Series Usher in 1938 Hits Top in '59," *Chicago Tribune*, October 2, 1959: 2.
5. "A Tough Cop."
6. Ibid.
7. "Veeck Gets Even With Perini," *Chicago Tribune*, October 2, 1959: 55-56.
8. "A Tough Cop."
9. Dave Condon, *The Go Go Chicago White Sox* (New York: Coward-McCann, Inc., 1960), 185.
10. Condon, 182 (photo caption).
11. "Veeck Gets Even."
12. Condon, 185.
13. Video Production, *Baseball Classics, 1959 World Series* (Rare Sportsfilms, Inc., 2000).
14. Ibid.
15. "Executive, 62, Dies at Game as Sox Take Early Lead," *Chicago Tribune*, October 2, 1959: 2.
16. Condon, 187.
17. Richard Dozer, "Losers Await New Day; Winners Too," *Chicago Tribune*, October 2, 1959: 55.
18. Video, *Baseball Classics, 1959 World Series*.
19. Ibid.
20. "Sox Crush Dodgers in Opener, 11-0," *Chicago Tribune*, October 2, 1959: 55.
21. Robert Cromie, "Losers Await New Day; Winners Too," *Chicago Tribune*, October 2, 1959: 55.
22. Video, *Baseball Classics, 1959 World Series*.
23. "Two Homers Klu's Greatest Thrill," *Los Angeles Times*, October 2, 1959: 75.
24. "Losers Await": 57.
25. "Revised Odds Say Sox 9-5 Series Favorites," *Chicago Tribune*, October 2, 1959: 55.

White Sox Beat Dodgers to Stay Alive in World Series
Game Five of the World Series

By Thomas J. Brown Jr.

October 6, 1959

Chicago White Sox 1, Los Angeles Dodgers 0, at Los Angeles Memorial Coliseum

The White Sox needed a win badly. After splitting the first two games of the World Series against the Dodgers in Chicago, they lost the next two games in Los Angeles. Their backs were at the wall and they needed a win to keep their championship hopes alive. *Chicago Tribune* writer David Condon wrote that the White Sox "had experienced only futility since winning the opener 11 to 0 in Chicago."[1]

A crowd of 92,706, the most to ever witness a World Series game, showed up at the Los Angeles Memorial Coliseum hoping to see their team bring home a championship. The White Sox not only faced the Dodgers, but they faced an "expanse of white shirted spectators in the huge oval and a bright sun which made fly balls a hazard for the outfielders."[2]

Sandy Koufax started for the Dodgers. He had pitched two scoreless innings of relief in the Sox blowout back in Game One, and looked sharp from the start as he retired the first six batters on just 13 pitches.[3] The White Sox finally hit Koufax in the third inning when a pair of singles brought Chicago to the verge of scoring. But he got out of the inning without surrendering a run when Luis Aparicio was thrown out at second while trying to stretch his single.

White Sox manager Al Lopez called on Bob Shaw for the start. Shaw had pitched 6⅔ innings in the White Sox' 4-3 loss in the second game of the Series. Shaw surrendered eight hits, three of them home runs, in that game.

Shaw continued to give up hits in this game, surrendering at least one hit in every inning until he was removed after giving up two singles in the eighth. But his solid pitching and the White Sox defense kept Los Angeles from scoring. After Gil Hodges tripled in the fourth inning, Shaw got Don Demeter on a grounder to the mound and John Roseboro on a broken-bat popout to shortstop to snuff out the scoring opportunity.

The White Sox had scored a run in the fourth inning. Nellie Fox led off with a single and raced to third when Jim Landis followed with another single. Koufax got Sherm Lollar to ground into a second-to-first double play and the speedy Fox scored. Little did anyone in attendance, especially the Dodgers, expect Fox to be the only runner to cross home plate that afternoon.

"If our foresight was as good as our hindsight, maybe we would have got out of it by throwing to the plate on Lollar's ball instead of turning it into a double play," Koufax said later. "But at the time, the double play was the logical one."[4]

It looked as though the Dodgers might score in the seventh. Shaw walked pinch-hitter Chuck Essegian, who was replaced by pinch-runner Don Zimmer after a leadoff fly out by Roseboro. Duke Snider batted for Koufax and hit a broken-bat groundball that got Zimmer at second. Johnny Podres ran for Snider. Jim Gilliam followed with a single.

Lopez, in a "stroke of genius," now made a defensive move.[5] He moved Al Smith from right field to left field replacing rookie Jim McAnany and inserted Jim Rivera in right field. Lopez thought that Charlie Neal was likely to hit the ball to the screen in left and wanted the veteran Smith to be there.

Alston hoped that Neal, who had hit two homers in the Dodgers' 4-3 Game Two win, would be able to

• October 6, 1959 •

provide the offensive punch the Dodgers needed. But Shaw was not to be stopped; Neal said later that Shaw threw "almost nothing but sliders away from me."[6]

After Shaw threw a wild pitch that allowed both runners to advance, Neal worked the count to 3-and-2. When he finally hit the ball, it went to right field, not left. The left-handed Rivera, "playing deep after experience with Neal in the Puerto Rican League, sped to his right and made an over-the-shoulder, one-handed catch."[7]

Dodgers manager Walter Alston said: "I'll give Al (Lopez) a helluva lot of credit for that one. He made the right move at the right time."[8] Whether the right-handed Smith would have made the catch can be debated forever, but "Rivera made Lopez look like the smartest guy in the arena."[9]

"I thought for a moment it might give me trouble, but once I was underway I knew I had it," Rivera said. Smith noted that it is "no fun to play [in the Coliseum]. I like baseball but that was nerve wracking."[10]

The Dodgers might have scored on Rivera's catch but third-base coach Pee Wee Reese held up Gilliam at third. "He faked me real good," Reese said. "I thought [Rivera] was going to throw home and not to second. I should have kept Jim coming; I could have stopped him at the last second if necessary."[11]

Koufax left after seven innings, having given up just five hits and the lone run. Dodgers fans had expected the team to score all afternoon so they weren't worried about that one run until late in the game. Alston said of his pitcher, "I can't expect any better pitching than I got today from Koufax."[12]

The bottom of the eighth saw more dramatics as Shaw got himself in trouble again. Wally Moon led off with a single when center fielder Jim Landis lost the ball in the sun. After Norm Larker flied out, Hodges came to bat and hit the first pitch he saw into the left-field stands. The smash brought the crowd to their feet until it was called foul. Reese, coaching at third, said "(I)t was real close, to close to call."[13]

Hodges then drove the ball to center field for a single. Moon beat center fielder Landis's throw to third. The throw allowed Hodges to reach second and suddenly the Dodgers had two runners in scoring position.

A total of 92,706 fans, the most to ever witness a regular or post season game, saw Luis Aparicio stealing a base in the White Sox' 1-0 victory over the Dodgers in Game Five of the 1959 World Series at Los Angeles Memorial Coliseum.

Alston and Lopez tried to outguess each other. Alston sent up Ron Fairly to hit for the left-handed Demeter. Lopez pulled Shaw and brought in lefty Billy Pierce from the bullpen. Alston then Fairly and sent Rip Repulski to the plate. Lopez didn't give him a chance to hit as he called for an intentional walk that loaded the bases.

Alston sent right-handed batter Carl Furillo to hit for Roseboro. Lopez promptly pulled Pierce and sent for right-hander Dick Donovan. When Lopez handed him the ball, his only words were "Get it over and keep it low."[14]

After taking the first two pitches, Furillo hit a high foul pop that bounced off the screen behind home plate, preventing catcher Lollar from grabbing it. As Moon inched down the line, Donovan threw Furillo a low fastball. He connected but popped out to third base as "[a]ll of Dodgerville groaned."[15] Alston had run out of batters on his bench so he was forced to let Zimmer, who hadn't batted since August 24, come to bat. Zimmer lifted an easy fly ball to left field and the inning was over.

Stan Williams set the White Sox down in order in top of the ninth inning. In the bottom of the inning, Donovan returned to the mound, seemingly immune to the "trumpet-tooting Dodger fans and their follow-up throaty 'Charge!'"[16]

Since he had depleted his bench, Alston was forced to use pitcher Larry Sherry as a pinch-hitter for Williams. Sherry, who had just seven hits all season, grounded out to third base. Gilliam, the next batter, already had four singles in the game and Dodgers fans were on their feet hoping to see him get a record fifth. But Donovan got him to ground out to second.

Neal stepped to the plate, the last hope of the Dodgers. From the dugout, Shaw shouted, "Now you've got to go hard, Dick. Go hard!"[17] Donovan got Neal to ground out to Aparicio at short, giving the White Sox the much-needed win and sending the Series back to Chicago.

Donovan said later that "I won't be able to smile for three days. I wish, in all honesty, that I could say that I was completely calm. But I've never been in a spot exactly like that."[18] After the game, Lopez, with a big smile on his face, said, "This was the best played game of the series."[19]

The 1-0 White Sox victory sent the Series back to Chicago, with the team trailing three games to two. Unfortunately for the White Sox, the Dodgers closed out the Series with a 9-3 victory in Game Six.

Sources

In addition to the sources cited in the Notes, the author used Baseball-Reference.com and Retrosheet.org for box-score, player, team, and season information as well as pitching and batting game logs, and other pertinent material.

Notes

1. David Condon, "In the Wake of the News," *Chicago Tribune*, October 7, 1959: 61.
2. Edward Prell, "Sox Win 1-0; Final at Home, *Chicago Tribune*, October 7, 1959: 1.
3. Paul Zimmerman, "Sox Defense Tightens at Crucial Time," *Los Angeles Times*, October 7, 1959: 82.
4. Al Wolf, "Lady Luck Ends Honeymoon With Dodgers," *Los Angeles Times*, October 7, 1959: 85.
5. Edward Prell, "Rivera's Catch in 7th Shares Top Billing," *Chicago Tribune*, October 7, 1959: 1.
6. Wolf.
7. Edward Prell, "Rivera's Catch in 7th Shares Top Billing."
8. "Alston Lauds Lopez for Rivera Switch," *Chicago Tribune*, October 7, 1959: 61.
9. Braven Dyer, "Dodgers Lose Tense Struggle, 1-0, Before Record Throng of 92,706," *Los Angeles Times*, October 7, 1959: 81.
10. Richard Dozer, "We're Going To Win It, Says Lopez," *Chicago Tribune*, October 7, 1959: 61.
11. Wolf.
12. "Alston Lauds Lopez."
13. Wolf.
14. Condon.
15. Dyer: 82.
16. Prell: 62.
17. Condon.
18. Ibid.
19. Zimmerman.

The 1959 Season

By R. J. Lesch

Preseason 1959

True, the White Sox are not a power-laden club. But just as a likable but none-too-handsome man is admired by his friends for his winning personality, so do White Sox fans love their team just for what it is – the fastest team in the majors, a superb fielding team, a hustling team. And if Sox bats occasionally produce the much-overrated home run, why, that makes the team just that much more exciting.

- Letter to the editor
by Cecile B. Conrad, Chicago[1]

As the Chicago White Sox gathered in Tampa, Florida, for spring training, their owners gathered back home to determine the future direction of the franchise. A long custody battle over the Sox, between Dorothy Comiskey Rigney and her brother Charles Comiskey, appeared to end when Rigney agreed to sell her 54 percent interest in the club. When the prospective buyer was announced, however, any illusions of peace and quiet were dashed, although many fans thought that might be a good thing.

Bill Veeck had owned the Cleveland Indians for three and a half years, helping them cross the threshold to a world championship in 1948, and then sold his interest in the club at a profit. He had not had similar success with the St. Louis Browns, and had been out of baseball for several years since then. Veeck shocked his stuffier peers by refusing to wear suits and ties to business and social functions, at a time when businessmen wore such garb as a matter of course. An ex-Marine who had lost his leg, he would routinely remove the wooden replacement during press conferences, and massage the stump while answering questions. He argued baseball with fans in the bleachers, held bizarre promotions at the ballpark, and made waves wherever he went. And now, as part of a five-person syndicate purchasing the Rigney shares, Veeck appeared poised to return to baseball once more.

"Chuck" Comiskey seemed unlikely to withdraw quietly, though, and petitioned to block the sale in court. Manager Al Lopez drilled his charges in Florida, amid the uncertainty. "It would be nice," quipped *Sports Illustrated*, "if Al could know now whether his No. 1 pinch hitter is going to be Ron Jackson or a midget."[2] The picture cleared somewhat when a Chicago court ruled in favor of the sale and against Comiskey's petitions.

More on Lopez's mind, most likely, were his American League rivals. The White Sox had finished a distant second to the New York Yankees in each of the previous two seasons. The Yankees, under manager Casey Stengel, had dominated the league, winning nine of the last 10 pennants. Only Lopez had broken that string, at the helm of the Cleveland Indians in 1954. Those Indians, after a couple of mediocre seasons, appeared to be ready to contend again behind manager Joe Gordon and general manager Frank Lane.

Lopez also pondered whether any of the rookies on his staff were ready to make the jump to big-league ball. Johnny Callison, a 20-year-old outfielder, had led the American Association in home runs the previous year and appeared to have figured out how to hit left-handed pitching. Barry Latman was a tall fireballer who appeared poised to earn a spot in the starting rotation. If either could make an impact in 1959, perhaps the White Sox could close the gap between the Yankees and themselves.

April

Invariably, when a ball takes a bad hop, everybody says the ball hit a pebble. We haven't got a pebble on the diamond. We screen the ball field with one-eighth-inch mesh. There just aren't any pebbles. Sometimes a player will rip up a divot and he won't know it. Then if a ball hits it the ball won't bounce true. But they always say it's a pebble.

- Gene Bossard,
Chicago White Sox groundkeeper[3]

The White Sox started the 1959 season on the road in Detroit, missing the snowstorm that postponed the Cubs opener. On Friday, April 10, at Briggs Stadium, Detroit native Billy Pierce took the mound against fireballer Jim Bunning. Neither was in midseason form. The game went into extra innings tied 7-7, and stayed that way until the top of the 14th inning. Nellie Fox, Chicago's scrappy second baseman, had hit exactly zero home runs in 1958, but with Sammy Esposito on first base, Fox went deep to break the tie. Forty three players got into the game in all, which was one inning shy of the record for longest season opener.

The next day, Early Wynn went to work. Starting his second season with the White Sox, the veteran held the Tigers to seven hits on the way to a 5-3 complete-game win. It was Early's 250th career victory. Not to be outdone by his double-play partner, shortstop Luis Aparicio socked a home run of his own. The Sox posted another 5-3 win the next day to sweep the series, and then went back to Chicago for their own home opener.

Bill Veeck was ready for them. Veeck's role with the club had not yet been formalized, but he had taken the reins firmly. The Opening Day festivities featured fireworks, two Dixieland bands, and unique gifts for the players. Early Wynn received 250 silver dollars, one for each career victory, plus 250 more in anticipation of wins yet to come. Aparicio and Fox received a 25-foot loaf of bread, to "sustain their pep and energy as home run hitters." In the sixth inning, the public address system announced that everyone could "have a drink on the house," and vendors dispensed free beer and soda to everyone in the park. Capping it all, Billy Pierce went the distance to shut out the Kansas City Athletics. In the fifth inning, Johnny Callison bunted his way on base, reached third on a double by Bubba Phillips, and scored ahead of Phillips on Aparicio's single.

The White Sox were off to a hot start with four straight wins, and were 6-4 after one of the unique games of the 1959 season, a 20-6 victory at Kansas City's Municipal Stadium on April 22 that featured an 11-run Sox outburst in the seventh inning – on only one hit! The inning featured 10 Chicago walks, a hit batsman and three Kansas City errors. Talk about doing a lot with a little…[4]

Two days later, the Sox traveled to Cleveland to begin a four-game series with the first-place Indians. Paced by pitcher Herb Score, who appeared to be recovering his 1956 form, and power-hitting infielder Woodie Held, the Tribe had reeled off six wins to start their season, and sported a 9-1 record. Held had hit five home runs in the first seven games while shortstop George Strickland combined with second baseman Billy Martin to tighten up the middle of the infield. Slick-fielding Vic Power teamed with sluggers Rocky Colavito and former Sox favorite Minnie Minoso. Fans were coming back to the ballpark in Cleveland, helping the club lead the majors in attendance early in the season. Over 28,000 Cleveland fans turned out for the series opener, a night game on Friday, April 24. Their team took the honors, 6-4, thanks in part to two unearned runs in the eighth inning when relief pitcher Jerry Staley threw wild to first base.

On Saturday, though, it was Cleveland's turn to give gifts. Strickland booted an apparent double-play ball in the ninth inning, opening the door to five unearned Chicago runs. Earl Torgeson's three-run homer punctuated the 8-6 win. In Sunday's doubleheader, the pitchers took matters into their own hands. Early Wynn socked a two-run double to help himself to an 8-5 win. Billy Pierce topped that in the second game, hitting a two-run double of his own plus a triple in the ninth inning en route to a 5-2 score.

The three wins served notice that the White Sox were going to be in the thick of the pennant race again. Chicago had come close in recent years. The 1955 Sox had been in first place as late as September 3 before falling behind the New York Yankees and Cleveland Indians. They finished in third, five games behind the Yanks and two behind the Indians. The three clubs finished in the same order in 1956, though the Sox were 12 games out that year. The Indians, perennial contenders for a decade, fell back to sixth in 1957 and the White Sox took over bridesmaid status. They finished eight games back of the Yankees that year, and 10 behind in 1958.

Yet the Yankees had played just .500 ball during the last two months of that season and seemed vulnerable in the first month of the new campaign. Their record stood at 6-7 when they arrived in Chicago for the first of two games with the White Sox. It was the Yankees, of course, and no team in their right minds would discount them this early in the season.

Manager Al Lopez and six of his players would miss the Wednesday April 29 game with a flu virus, and coach Tony Cuccinello took the reins of the depleted squad. The Yankees treated the Ladies' Day crowd to a long-ball demonstration, as Mickey Mantle, Hank Bauer and Bill Skowron homered to pace the New Yorkers to a 5-2 win. The next night, though, Billy Pierce and Whitey Ford squared off. Ford appeared to have the edge in this duel, leading 2-1, even though

The 1959 Season

Mantle fractured his right index finger during batting practice and Tony Kubek was in center field instead. In the sixth inning, though, Sox catcher Sherm Lollar led off the inning with a home run, and Bubba Phillips scored on singles by Pierce and Aparicio. Ford left for a pinch-hitter in the seventh, and the Yankees tied it up when Pierce's wild pitch scored Yogi Berra. But Pierce kept dealing through 11 innings, until Al Smith delivered a bases-loaded single to bring the winning run home in the bottom of the 11th. The White Sox raised their record to 10-6, a game behind the Indians, and pushed the defending champs into sixth place.

It was too early to tell where this would lead. Would this be the year? Or would Casey Stengel pull off another miracle and bring the Yankees back into first again?

Standings after April 30

	G	W	L	T	PCT	GB	RS	RA
Cleveland Indians	14	10	4	0	.714	-	92	48
Chicago White Sox	16	10	6	0	.625	1.0	89	80
Baltimore Orioles	16	9	7	0	.563	2.0	63	77
Kansas City Athletics	16	9	7	0	.563	2.0	83	90
Washington Senators	17	8	9	0	.471	3.5	77	77
New York Yankees	15	7	8	0	.467	3.5	72	52
Boston Red Sox	13	6	7	0	.462	3.5	66	65
Detroit Tigers	15	2	13	0	.133	8.5	50	103

May

These [earlier Go-Go Sox] teams, having little besides good leadership, speed and the willingness to give it a 100% try, would play over their heads until the inevitable would happen: other teams with more talent would grind them down. It is a sad commentary on our times that these teams should be remembered, not for playing over their heads for three-quarters of the season, but for failing to provide a miracle for 154 games. Perhaps some people might profit by that corny saying, "Look at the doughnut and not the hole."

- Letter to the editor
by Frank J. Snider, Cedar Rapids, Iowa[5]

On May 1, with one out in the first inning, Boston's Pete Runnels punched a single into center field off Early Wynn. Wynn had moved Aparicio two steps to the right a moment earlier. Later, Aparicio told a reporter, "If I play Runnels where I want, I throw him out easy." It wouldn't have been important, except that Wynn held the Red Sox hitless for the rest of the game, striking out 14. His teammates weren't doing much better, so in the eighth inning, Wynn socked a solo home run off rival pitcher Tom Brewer to break the scoreless tie.[6]

They lost the next four games at home, though. Despite Wynn's example, and the arrival of slugging outfielders Del Ennis and Harry Simpson, the Sox weren't hitting. On May 3, former White Sox shortstop Chico Carrasquel singled and scored a run in the sixth inning, then homered to lead off the tenth, propelling his Baltimore club to a 4-2 win. Then Washington visited for a two-game set and topped Pierce and Wynn to win both games. Now only a game above .500, Chicago played host to the Indians, who had rebounded from the Sox series in Cleveland to win four of six and run their record to 14-6. Behind five-hit pitching by Cal McLish, who was following up a superb 1958 season, the Indians took the first game of the series 3-1

Earlier that day, the reconstituted White Sox board of directors elected Bill Veeck club president, Chuck Comiskey as executive vice president and Hank Greenberg as vice president and treasurer. Perhaps the long-awaited resolution had a positive effect on the clubhouse; for whatever reason, the White Sox found a groove. They jumped on Cleveland for eight runs on only four hits in the second and third innings on Saturday May 9. Herb Score, a week removed from a complete game triumph over the Yankees, walked Al Smith, hit Ron Jackson with a pitch, walked the pitcher, Barry Latman, to load the bases, then walked the uncharacteristically-patient Aparicio to force in a run. Fox singled to bring home two more runs, ending Score's day. Cleveland rookie Jim Perry took the mound and threw one pitch. On it, Aparicio tried to steal home and was tagged out. When Aparicio, protesting the call, threw dirt on home plate umpire Joe Papparella, Papparella gave Aparicio the hook. Cleveland replied with two runs in the top of the third, but Perry walked three of the four batters he faced in the bottom half to help the Sox tally five more runs.

The 9-5 win seemed to jump-start the Sox. Pierce and Wynn teamed up for a Sunday doubleheader sweep, Pierce going the distance in an 11-inning 5-4 contest while Wynn posted a four-hit shutout. Bubba Phillips drove in runs in the opener with a solo homer and each of two singles, including the game-winner. In game two, Aparicio doubled and scored in the first inning; then, in the seventh, he singled to center, stole second, moved to third on a Nellie Fox groundout, and crossed the plate on a Jim Landis bunt single. Taking three of four from the Indians again narrowed the gap between the clubs to a game and a half.

The White Sox continued winning in Boston. Ted Williams, recovering from a pinched nerve in his neck, was in the Red Sox lineup for the first time this season on May 12, but went zero-for-five with a walk. Dick Donovan clouted a two-run homer, and Al Smith, who had batted only .179 in April but whose bat had perked up a little during the home stand, homered in the 12th inning to win the game 4-3. It was Smith's first extra-inning game-winning home run of the season. It would not be his last. Bob Shaw turned in a four-hit shutout the next day to beat the Red Sox 4-0, and Wynn benefited from a 14-6 slugfest in game three.

It was a good start, but nobody was going to get too excited until the White Sox showed they could beat the New York Yankees. The defending champs still struggled, plagued with injuries to Elston Howard, Hank Bauer and Bill Skowron, to say nothing of Mantle's broken finger. Stengel made disparaging comments about "my Jekyll and Hyde pitching staff." The batters went into prolonged slumps and made mental errors in the field. Stengel, apparently forgetting he was a managerial genius, made a series of blunders that had baseball fans everywhere asking whether the Old Professor was losing his touch. "They are beating themselves," Al Lopez told a reporter, "and good ball clubs do not do that." [7]

And yet, the Yankees had been down before. A Cleveland taxi driver, speaking of the Indians' chances, might have been talking about the White Sox as well: "Some of these boobs around here are already talking about the World Series. Well, I'll tell you how I feel. They don't convince me until they beat New York." [8]

On May 15, Billy Pierce did his part. Scattering six hits and striking out seven, Pierce topped Whitey Ford and the Yankees, 6-0. It was the first time Pierce had shut out the Yankees since 1953; in fact, it was the first time any lefty had shut out the Yankees since Herb Score did it on August 21, 1956. Pierce, improving his record to 5-2, including five complete games, seemed to be having another brilliant year. Meanwhile, the White Sox put runs on the board with their special brand of ball. Aparicio led off with a single, moved to second on Fox's single, reached third on a Landis groundout, and scored on a Lollar groundout. They added five more runs, three unearned, capitalizing on Yankee errors.

Meanwhile, Yankee superstar Mickey Mantle was having one of his worst stretches. Against Pierce, he managed only a broken-bat single, and went out three times on the first pitch, earning steady boos from the Yankee Stadium throng. The next day, with two out in the ninth inning, and the Sox down 3-2, Nellie Fox hit a towering fly ball. Mantle misjudged the fly, then scrambled back for an over-the-shoulder catch, and muffed the ball. It was ruled an error on Mantle. Jim Landis walked, moving Nellie to second, and Sherm Lollar singled to bring Fox home with the tying run. In the eleventh inning, Fox singled and scored three batters later on a Del Ennis base hit. Sox reliever Turk Lown retired the side promptly in the home half of the 11th, whiffing Mantle for the final out.

Washington stopped the Sox win streak on May 17. The fourth-place Senators surprised observers with their early-season play, going 11-4 over one stretch. "In Washington," wrote Roy Terrell for *Sports Illustrated*, "it is rumored that Harmon Killebrew is really Joe Hardy and that Mr. Applegate has bought a season box in Griffith Stadium." [9] Back-to-back homers by the nonfictional Jim Lemon and Reno Bertoia chased Dick Donovan in the second inning of the 4-2 loss in game one of a doubleheader. In game two, Killebrew homered twice to extend his league lead in home runs to 14, but the Sox bounced back with 13 hits, only three for extra bases, to take the slugfest by a 10-7 score. The night of May 18, Lollar and Smith homered in the rubber match, and Wynn held the Senators to five hits. The 9-2 victory put the White Sox in first place for a day.

Then it was off to Baltimore for a two-game set with the Orioles. Pitcher Billy O'Dell dealt the Sox a 2-1 loss on May 19. O'Dell helped his cause when he hit a ball down the right-field line. The ball took a freak bounce over Al Smith's head and went for an inside-the-park home run. The next day Dick Donovan went the distance to hold off the Orioles 5-2. The White Sox had won 8 of 10 on their eastern road trip, and 12 of the last 14.

The road trip had one last stop, though, in Kansas City. They won a tough 2-1 decision on May

• The 1959 Season •

22, Bob Shaw running his record to 4-0. The next night, though, Kansas City unloaded on Wynn for eight hits and four runs in four innings, and kept up the bombardment against Latman and Rudy Arias for a 16-0 win. Bud Daley, having his best season, stifled the Sox on four hits. The next day the Athletics shellacked Billy Pierce for seven runs in less than two innings, then held on for the 8-6 win. During the 1959 season, the Athletics, eventual seventh-place finishers, would play the Sox tougher than all but one other team, winning 10 of the 22 contests.

On Tuesday, May 26, the great Deadball-era White Sox pitcher Ed Walsh died in Pompano Beach, Florida, at the age of 78. In Milwaukee, Harvey Haddix of the Pittsburgh Pirates might have been channeling the iron-armed Walsh when he held the Braves at bay for 12 innings. Not one Milwaukee player reached base. It would have gone into the record books as a perfect game if his teammates had managed to score so much as a single run. Milwaukee finally scored in the 13th inning to break up Haddix's perfecto.

Bill Veeck had a different idea of baseball immortality. Eight years earlier, with the St. Louis Browns, Veeck had hired the 3-foot 7-inch Eddie Gaedel as a pinch-hitter and sent him to bat against the Detroit Tigers. Now, in a new city, Veeck brought Gaedel onto the diamond again. Dressed as "Martians," Gaedel and three other little people arrived on the Comiskey Park diamond by helicopter, whereupon they promptly captured Luis Aparicio and Nellie Fox. The double-play combo were listed as being 5-foot-9 and 5-foot-10 respectively, but appeared much smaller in person, and the aliens, in their gold helmets and coveralls, decided instead to make Little Luis and Nellie "honorary Martians" and to aid the duo in their battle against "giant Earthlings." The folks who had showed up early to the ballpark roared with delight.

The honorary Martians did all right in the game that followed, Luis collecting two hits and Nellie one, but their giant Earthling teammates managed only one hit combined off Don Ferrarese and Jim Perry. Ferrarese also hit three doubles, scoring one of Cleveland's runs and driving in the other two.

The White Sox bounced back the next day, in the second game of the two-game series. Wynn held his former team to five hits and Staley got the last two outs to save the 5-1 win.

The Detroit Tigers, a near-.500 club in recent years, had gotten off to a horrible 2-15 start, costing manager Bill Norman his job on May 2. Jimmy Dykes, a long-time American League manager hired to replace Norman, had initially sparked the Tigers to seven wins in his first eight games at the helm. After a week in which Jim Bunning won his fifth complete game in a row, and Tiger batters slugged 11 home runs, Dykes joked, "Gimme a few long balls and a good pitcher and I'm a mastermind." [10] They had cooled off since then, but retained enough heat to beat the White Sox two out of three in Comiskey Park on May 29 and 30.

Kansas City came to town next and rocked Early Wynn for five runs in under two innings en route to a 9-1 win, and then took a 3-1 decision from the Sox on June 1. May ended with the Sox losing six of their last eight games. Yet at 25-19 they were only a game off the pace.

Standings after May 31

	G	W	L	T	PCT	GB	RS	RA
Cleveland Indians	42	25	17	0	.595	-	206	154
Chicago White Sox	44	25	19	0	.568	1.0	203	193
Baltimore Orioles	46	25	21	0	.543	2.0	165	198
Kansas City Athletics	41	20	21	0	.488	4.5	203	184
Detroit Tigers	43	20	23	0	.465	5.5	193	229
New York Yankees	42	19	23	0	.452	6.0	178	174
Washington Senators	37	21	26	0	.447	6.5	207	218
Boston Red Sox	43	19	24	0	.442	6.5	204	209

June

... as Veeck himself said the other day: "We can't always guarantee the ball game is going to be good. But we can guarantee the fan will have fun even if the game isn't so hot."

With that Veeck plunged a hairy fist into a box behind his desk and brought out a can of fried grasshoppers. "What do you think," he asked, "a guy would do with 500 cans of this stuff?" The question was academic at the moment, but before long some lucky White Sox fan will be presented with 500 cans of assorted fried grasshoppers, chocolate-covered Colombian ants and roasted caterpillars.

Go-Go to Glory

One might wonder why Veeck persists in donating doubtfully useful prizes. "You give a radio or a TV set—so what?" he explained. "What does that do for the imagination? Nothing. If I give him 50,000 nuts and bolts, that gives everybody something to talk about."

- *Sports Illustrated*, June 22, 1959[11]

The third-place Baltimore Orioles, managed by Paul Richards, had no superstars but lots of solid players. Brooks Robinson opened the season as the starting third baseman for the second year in a row, but at the moment was in Vancouver working on his hitting. The O's best pitcher was Hoyt Wilhelm, though Milt Pappas was on his way to his first good season, and it was Wilhelm who started the series opener at Comiskey Park on June 2. Baltimore hit Bob Shaw hard but only managed three runs. It was enough, as the Sox could do little with Wilhelm's knuckler, and scored both their runs thanks to walks, an error and a hit batsman. Wednesday afternoon, Billy Pierce turned in a complete game and scored a run to help his team to a 6-1 win.

The June 4 contest gave the White Sox a shot at first place, as Cleveland was idle after dropping five in a row. Baltimore had other ideas, though, and held a 4-3 lead in the bottom of the eighth inning. Bubba Phillips singled and Callison walked to set the table for Larry Doby, who the Sox had purchased from Detroit in mid-May. Doby singled to score Phillips and tie the game. After walking Al Smith on purpose to load the bases, Baltimore pitcher Billy Loes got Earl Torgeson to ground to first baseman Bob Boyd. Boyd threw home to force Callison, then took the throw back from Joe Ginsberg to retire Torgy for the third out.

The teams held each other scoreless in the ninth, and then in the next three innings as well. Chico Carrasquel singled in the top of the 13th inning and came around to score two batters later. Torgeson did the same in the bottom half of the inning, after Oriole third baseman Willie Miranda fielded Aparicio's bunt, then threw the ball into right field. Al Pilarcik hustled the ball back to the plate, too late to catch Torgy, but in time to catch Harry Simpson, who had tried to score from first on the error. Tied again, the game continued until the bottom of the 17th inning, when Torgeson homered with two out off reliever Jerry Walker.

Chicago enjoyed first place for a week and a half. They had to share with Baltimore on June 9 after the Orioles beat Cleveland while the Sox lost to Washington. The O's fell back the next day when Rocky Colavito hit four consecutive home runs to pace Cleveland to an 11-8 win. The White Sox and Orioles met again on June 13 in Baltimore and lost 6-4 to let the Birds within a game of first, but they bounced back to take both ends of a doubleheader on Sunday June 14. Meanwhile, the Indians had won five straight to tie the Sox in the standings on the morning of June 16, the day the Sox opened a three-game set in the Bronx.

Doomsayers who were sure the Yankees would burst the White Sox bubble sooner or later probably felt justified after New York swept the series. On June 18, the Sox managed to send the game into extra innings, but Mickey Mantle homered in the bottom of the 10th. In the same stadium where fans had booed him weeks earlier, the Mick now circled the bases while exuberant youngsters ran onto the field and circled the bases with him.

New York looked better than they had all season, but Cleveland benefited most from the Yankees' victories, regaining first place on June 16. After dropping a doubleheader in Boston on June 20, the White Sox found themselves tied with New York for fourth place, though behind Cleveland by only a game and a half. The White Sox struggled to find hitters for the third and fourth lineup spots. Aparicio had drawn walks at a greater rate than in past seasons during the 12-2 run in May, but had reverted to his old habits. Fox, batting second in the lineup, was hitting well and actually led the club in runs batted in. But nobody was consistently driving in Fox. During the five-game losing streak, the Sox stranded 42 runners. Casey Stengel seemed correct when he said "Keep Fox and Aparicio off the bases and that team is done."[12]

They bounced back a little, Pierce besting the Red Sox 3-2 on June 21, then taking two out of three from the Senators back at Comiskey Park. Then it was time for the Yankees to return the visit. On June 26, the Bronx Bombers picked up where they had left off back home, winning 8-4 to move into a tie with the White Sox for third place, just two games back. After New York reliever Ryne Duren hit Fox with a pitch in the seventh inning, Sox reliever Rudy Arias returned the favor, plunking Duren when he came to bat in the top of the ninth. Duren exchanged words with Arias and the home plate umpire, but rebounded to fan three in the ninth inning and extend his scoreless innings streak to 25.

• The 1959 Season •

On Saturday June 27, the Yankees were up 2-1 after seven innings. Third baseman Hector Lopez had clubbed two solo homers, while the Sox had done little with Bob Turley's pitching. Someone needed to reverse the momentum. With two out in the eighth, Nellie Fox worked Turley for a base on balls. Fox reached third on Torgeson's single, and Turley pitched cautiously to Lollar, walking him. That brought up Harry Simpson.

Turley later insisted that he had thrown Simpson a good pitch. Turley threw inside, wanting Simpson to swing and either miss the ball or hit it on the handle of his bat. Simpson got around on it, though, and jacked it into the upper right field deck. The slam put the White Sox up 5-2.

The Yankees weren't quite done. In the top of the ninth, Rudy Arias took over for Bob Shaw, who had gone eight solid innings before departing for a pinch-hitter. Arias gave up back-to-back homers to Norm Siebern and Bill Skowron, though, bringing the Yankees to within a run. Arias got Berra out and then turned the ball to Staley, who gave up singles to two of the next three batters to put runners at the corners. Then Staley found his groove and fanned Tony Kubek to seal the win.

Simpson's power display was temporarily contagious. During the Sunday doubleheader, a White Sox club that would finish the season with a mere 97 home runs, last in the American League, slugged five of them in one day. They clouted four in the first game, three off Whitey Ford, to coast to a 9-2 win. Meanwhile, Hector Lopez paid for his two home runs the previous day, as Early Wynn plunked him with a pitch in the first inning. Wynn nailed Siebern in the eighth inning too, following Siebern's solo shot in the sixth, and earned a bruiseball of his own from Yankee reliever Jim Coates in the bottom of the eighth for his trouble. Sherm Lollar, who had jacked one in the first game, followed up with a three-run blast off Don Larsen in the second game to pace the Sox to a 4-2 win.

The three losses dropped the Yanks back to fifth place, albeit only four games back of Cleveland, and boosted Chicago to second place, a game back. The White Sox had stuffed the Yankees' magic back into the bottle, for the time being.

Standings after June 30

	G	W	L	T	PCT	GB	RS	RA
Cleveland Indians	70	40	30	0	.571	-	327	278
Chicago White Sox	72	39	33	0	.542	2.0	309	303
Baltimore Orioles	73	38	35	0	.521	3.5	276	316
New York Yankees	72	37	35	0	.514	4.0	336	296
Detroit Tigers	74	38	36	0	.514	4.0	350	373
Washington Senators	72	33	39	0	.458	8.0	324	333
Kansas City Athletics	70	31	39	0	.443	9.0	315	329
Boston Red Sox	71	31	40	0	.437	9.5	324	333

July

The younger White Sox include Bubba Phillips from Mississippi, accent and all, and John Romano from Hoboken, accent and all. Phillips plays third, Romano catches. They room together and can usually be found in the movies. Jim Landis, the fleet center fielder, Bob Shaw, a pitcher with blond wavy hair, a dislike of neckties and a penchant for calling the girls "honey," along with fellow pitchers Barry Latman and Rodolfo Arias, and the incomparable Aparicio, spend their off hours on the road being young, healthy and attractive.

— Walter Bingham, *Sports Illustrated*[13]

The schedule-makers seemed to like the two-game series in 1959. Chicago went on the road to play two in Cleveland, two in Detroit, and three games in two days in Kansas City. They split the games with Cleveland, Pierce dropping a 3-1 decision to Cal McLish on June 30, and Turk Lown saving a 6-5 win for Barry Latman on July 1.

The White Sox also split the two-game set in Detroit, with help from a lucky bat. Al Smith socked a grand slam in the July 2 game, but it wasn't enough as the Tigers outlasted the Sox 9-7. Next day, looking for an edge, Sherm Lollar took up the same bat Al Smith had used to hit his slam. Lollar went deep off Jim Bunning to lead off the second inning. Both clubs battled back and forth, and when the game went into extra innings Al Smith took back the lucky bat, and hit a solo shot to decide the game, 6-5, after 10 innings.

It was off to Kansas City then, for a Fourth of July doubleheader. The White Sox provided the fireworks in the first game, with homers by Romano, Lollar (using the lucky bat again) and Phillips, and Landis putting in a five-for-five day to produce a 7-4 victory. The Athletics returned the favor in the second game, as Jerry Lumpe, Dick Williams and Roger Maris homered to put the A's on top 8-3. The following day, Chicago went back to their old tricks; in the 10th inning, Luis Aparicio singled, stole second and scored on a Nellie Fox single to win the game 4-3.

Most of the White Sox had the next three days off, as July 7 was the All-Star Game in Pittsburgh. This year there would be two All-Star games, actually, with the second set for Los Angeles on August 3. A poll of players, managers and coaches had selected Nellie Fox and Luis Aparicio to start for the American League, and manager Casey Stengel tapped Early Wynn to start the game on the mound. Billy Pierce and Sherm Lollar would also join the squad as reserves. Fox collected two hits and scored a run, but the National League took the game 5-4.

Following the break, the White Sox took four of five at home against Cleveland and Kansas City, then went east for seven games. On July 16, they regained first place briefly after they split a doubleheader in Boston while the Yankees swept their doubleheader against Cleveland. The White Sox jumped out to a 3-0 lead in the first game. Cleveland GM Frank Lane, giving an interview in New York, saw the score appear on the Yankee Stadium scoreboard. "That's a good team," Lane said. "Good speed, good defense and the best manager in baseball."

"Better than the man in Baltimore?" the interviewer asked.

"Richards is good, but he isn't as well rounded as Lopez," Lane explained. "I ought to know. I worked with Richards." [14]

Boston tied the score at three apiece after six innings. In the top of the seventh Lollar broke the tie, doubling to score Landis. Boston took the second game, 5-4, though, thanks to sterling relief work by Mike Fornieles and the bat of Vic Wertz. Wertz doubled twice, then singled to plate the game-winner.

Chicago visited New York for a four-game series, and fared better than they had in their previous trip to Yankee Stadium, winning two of the four. Wynn shut out the Yanks 2-0 on July 17, and then the Sox held on for a nail-biter the next afternoon. Staley relieved Shaw with one out in the ninth, runners at the corners and the Sox ahead by just a run. Staley threw one pitch, which Hector Lopez hit into the ground toward second base. Fox scooped it up and flipped it to Aparicio, who turned the double play.

On the morning of July 1, Al Smith was batting .223, with a .311 on-base percentage and just two home runs. Then Smith got as hot as the weather, batting .306 during July, getting on base at a .410 clip, and clouting seven homers. Three were game-winners, none bigger than the one he hit off Baltimore's Hoyt Wilhelm on Friday July 24. The walkoff ninth-inning blast downed the pesky Orioles, 2-1. Pierce and Wilhelm both went the distance, Pierce yielding just one hit in the last five innings.

The Saturday game was another extra-inning affair. This one ran four hours 35 minutes, just two minutes short of the June 4 game between the same two clubs. Six times a Sox base hit would have won the game, and six time the Baltimore pitchers kept them at bay, helped as Baltimore fielders turned five double plays behind them. Sherm Lollar homered in the bottom of the ninth to tie the score at two apiece, and then Bob Shaw (11 innings) and Turk Lown (six) kept the Orioles off the scoreboard after that. At last, the Sox loaded the bases with none out in the bottom of the 17th. The Orioles threw Landis out at home for one out, but pinch-hitter Simpson came through with a base hit to score Sammy Esposito for the 3-2 win.

The White Sox had captured four in a row, all by one run. "These ball games can really upset a guy," said Lopez. "I wish they'd win some the easy way once in a while. If they get any closer, something's going to snap. Then they'll have to put Old Lopez in a strait-jacket." [15]

The Sox gave Lopez's nerves a break in the first game of the Sunday doubleheader on July 26, taking it from Baltimore, 4-1. Al Smith settled the game with a three-run homer, this one an inside-the-park model. Meanwhile, Wynn posted a two-hitter, and yielded Baltimore's only run in the ninth inning on two walks and two fly balls to center field.

Baltimore regained some respect in the second game, winning 4-0 behind five-hit pitching from Milt Pappas. The loss dropped Chicago back to second place, as Cleveland swept their doubleheader with the Senators. But the three earlier losses took Baltimore out of the race for all practical purposes.

The biggest home crowd in Comiskey Park in two

• The 1959 Season •

years, 43,829, turned out for the first of three games against the Yankees on Tuesday July 28. The Yanks were below .500, though just eight and a half games back. Bill Skowron had returned for one game on July 25 and had promptly dislocated his wrist. He was out for the season. The versatile Elston Howard could handle first, though, and they still had Berra, Mantle, Bauer and the rest of the gang. If the Yankees were ever going to make their move, they had to do it now.

Ralph Terry and Billy Pierce squared off under the lights. The White Sox scored first on a bases-loaded double play in the bottom of the first. The Yankees replied in the fourth, Mantle doubling and scoring on Berra's base hit. It might have led to more. With Hector Lopez at bat, Stengel played the hit-and-run. Anticipating this, Pierce's pitch was high and tight on Lopez, and as Berra broke for second, Lollar fired the ball to Aparicio to catch Berra in a rundown. After Lopez struck out, the next two batters rapped base hits, which would certainly have scored Berra had he been on base.

The Sox regained the lead in the fifth when Pierce singled and scored, and Al Smith homered into the upper tier in left field with Fox on base to make the score 4-1. Pierce went to the mound for the ninth inning. Lopez singled, and Howard grounded to Aparicio. It looked like a double play, but Aparicio booted the ball, and both runners were safe. Shortstop Fritz Brickell singled in Lopez, and two fly balls later, Howard crossed the plate as well. Down 4-3, with Brickell the tying run, Bobby Richardson came to the plate. Richardson had hit Pierce well over the years, but Lopez stuck with his ace. Pierce fanned Richardson to end the game.

In the first inning on Wednesday July 29, Yankee hurler Whitey Ford felt pain in his elbow after throwing a curveball to Sherm Lollar. Ford tried to pitch through the pain, but gave up singles to Landis, Phillips and Shaw, and two Sox runs crossed the plate before Duke Maas relieved him. The teams traded two-run innings until, tied at four apiece after six innings, the light drizzle turned into rain. Bill Veeck kept the fans entertained with fireworks during the delay, but after almost an hour the game was called, and rescheduled for August 24.

The next day two different elements influenced play. With the score tied at 1-1 in the bottom of the seventh inning, Lollar hit a fly ball to short left field. The wind took it away from Siebern and Brickell, and the ball fell in for a double. Billy Goodman singled to score Lollar. The next inning, Tony Kubek lost an Aparicio popup in the sun, and Luis made it to second base. After advancing to third, he scored when Al Smith bounced a single off Ryne Duren's arm. The 3-1 loss spoiled Casey Stengel's birthday, which the Sox had celebrated earlier in the day with a one-hundred-pound cake and a band playing "Happy Birthday," "The Old Gray Mare" and other songs.

The Yankees went to Kansas City the next day and halted the Athletics' surprising 11-game win streak, but it was small comfort. Chicago had posted a 20-7 record in July and had recaptured first place, but the Cleveland Indians had nearly kept pace and were only a game back. Meanwhile, the Sox had dealt vital blows to Baltimore and New York in succession. It seemed clear that, barring a miracle, the race for the American League pennant was now between just two teams: Cleveland and Chicago.

Standings after July 31

	G	W	L	T	PCT	GB	RS	RA
Chicago White Sox	100	59	40	1	.596	-	431	407
Cleveland Indians	101	59	42	0	.584	1.0	489	411
Kansas City Athletics	100	50	50	0	.500	9.5	455	447
Baltimore Orioles	103	51	52	0	.495	10.0	376	431
New York Yankees	101	49	51	0	.490	10.5	456	433
Detroit Tigers	104	50	54	0	.481	11.5	481	501
Boston Red Sox	101	44	57	0	.436	16.0	473	469
Washington Senators	102	43	59	0	.422	17.5	426	488

August

The pennant-chasing White Sox are an anachronism in this era of power batting. Of the 20 teams that have won major league pennants in the last decade, all but one led or were among the leaders in team home runs. The White Sox are different. They are dead last in hitting home runs, and only Baltimore and Washington have scored less often. Lacking home run hitters, the Sox laboriously squeeze out their runs, one by one, and then rely on pitching and defense to hold off the opposition. This formula

• Go-Go to Glory •

has worked well for Chicago this year, because the pitching has been sound and the defense, particularly around second base, has been superb.

- Les Woodcock, *Sports Illustrated*[16]

Washington came to town for a four-game set starting July 31. Nobody was making Joe Hardy jokes any more. The Sox helped the Senators extend their losing streak to 16 games. In the opener, Barry Latman got the start when Dick Donovan's ailing shoulder flared up. Helped by three unearned runs, Latman cruised to a 7-1 win.

On August 1, the Sox shared their dugout with a pup hunting dog. Ray Moore, who had not started since June 17, drew the assignment, and Veeck promised Moore the hunting dog if he won the game. Whether this was the reason or not, Moore held the Senators to four hits over eight innings. Harmon Killebrew scored the lone Senators run after doubling in the fourth. Meanwhile, Camilo Pascual held the Sox hitless until the seventh inning. Billy Goodman doubled with one out to break up the no-no, but the Sox couldn't capitalize, and the Senators kept their 1-0 lead. Pascual's elbow bothered him enough to keep him from going out to the mound for the eighth, and submariner Dick Hyde took over. The Sox struck in the bottom of the ninth after Hyde walked pinch-hitter Norm Cash. Torgeson singled, and Landis doubled to score them both. The win went to reliever Jerry Staley, who was the pitcher of record in the ninth. But Veeck decided Moore had earned the dog anyway.

The second All-Star game, in Los Angeles on August 3, featured Aparicio and Fox as the starting double-play combo. Both played the entire game, Fox going two-for-four with a run and an RBI. Aparicio got on base once, on a walk, and swiped second off Don Drysdale for the game's only stolen base. Sherm Lollar and Early Wynn also played during the 5-3 AL victory.

Unlike the July 7 All-Star contest, the league provided no travel days despite the game being played on the West Coast. The three Sox position players had played the August 2 game against the Senators, and all three were back in the lineup for the Sox when they opened a four-game set in Baltimore on August 4. Perhaps not surprisingly, Fox and Aparicio went hitless that night. In fairness, so did a couple of their teammates, as Billy Hoeft held the Sox to six hits in the 3-2 loss.[17]

The White Sox and Orioles split a day-night doubleheader on Wednesday, August 5, and then squared off for a night game on August 6. Billy Pierce and Billy O'Dell dueled for eight innings. Chicago's Johnny Romano tripled to score Al Smith in the third inning, and the Orioles manufactured a run of their own in the eighth. Hoyt Wilhelm took over for O'Dell, who had given way to a pinch-hitter in the eighth, and dueled Pierce for eight more innings. Wilhelm almost broke the tie himself in the 15th; after reaching on a fielder's choice, he tried to score from second on a Billy Klaus single, but Al Smith threw him out at the plate. Pierce, in 16 innings of work, scattered 11 hits and struck out seven, but left with the score still tied at one apiece. Wilhelm would go two more innings, for a total of ten, until the clock did what neither team could do. In Baltimore, no inning could start after 11:59 p.m., so after both sides went out in the 18th inning, the game was called. The clubs would replay the tie as part of a doubleheader on September 11.

Chicago got back on track in Washington, sweeping a three-game series. An Old-Timer's ceremony preceded the doubleheader on August 9. Fittingly, Early Wynn hurled a shutout in the second game of the twinbill for career victory number 264, tying him for 19th all-time on the career wins list.

The August 10 issue of *Sports Illustrated* featured Nellie Fox and Luis Aparicio on the cover. The accompanying story, "Two for the Pennant" by Les Woodcock, extolled the virtues of the White Sox double play combination. "The double play is doing the job for Chicago," said Detroit Tiger broadcaster George Kell in the article. "Here is a club trying to win on pitching and defense and little power. Their double-play combination of Fox and Aparicio is the most important factor in Chicago's strength. They are the best in baseball. Chicago could hardly win without them." Also boosting Luis and Nellie in the article were Billy Pierce ("It sure is nice to see Fox and Aparicio behind me when I'm on the mound.") and Al Lopez ("The prettiest sight in baseball to a manager is the double play. It means two outs instead of one. It's as simple as that. You seldom win a pennant without good strength up the middle.")[18]

It's interesting, then, that the White Sox were fifth in the league in double plays. Moreover, as Bill James and Jim Henzler would show over 40 years later, in their book *Win Shares*, the White Sox did not turn more double plays than would have been expected given their opportunities. James and Henzler determined that, considering the number of baserunners permitted, the White Sox should have

• The 1959 Season •

turned 150 double plays in 1959. They actually turned 141. By contrast, Baltimore, which would have been expected to turn 142 double plays, actually turned 163, exceeding expectations by three twin killings per month. James and Henzler's study still ranks Fox as the top AL second baseman and Aparicio as the top AL shortstop for 1959, taking into account all aspects of their defense and not merely double plays.

Neither player appeared to suffer from the *Sports Illustrated* jinx. Both batted consistently and played errorless ball while the issue was on the stands. On the other hand, they only turned one double play that week.

The White Sox won two of three in Detroit, and then went to Kansas City. The Athletics had played torrid ball in July, winning 11 straight at one point, and had then cooled off, dropping nine of 10 games before Chicago's arrival. The Sox took the opener, but then the Athletics got healthy again and won the next two, while Chicago appeared to waver in their intensity at key moments.

Down 2-1 in the top of the ninth against the A's, for example, manager Lopez sent Jim Rivera to pinch-run. Rivera reached third base on an error, and Lopez called third-base coach Cuccinello over to the bench.

"Tell Jim to be alive," said Lopez. "Maybe I'll try the squeeze."

With two balls and a strike on rookie Jim McAnany, Lopez flashed the sign. "It isn't a safety squeeze," said Lopez later. "It's a running squeeze, a suicide squeeze." McAnany laid down the bunt, but Rivera, instead of breaking before the pitch, stayed put until after the bunt. He was thrown out by 15 feet, ending Chicago's last best chance to score.

"Did you miss the sign?" Lopez asked Rivera.

"No," said Rivera. "I got the sign, all right. I just forgot to run."[19]

Lyn Daunoras, a reporter for the *Brookfield (IL) Enterprise*, found herself in a tuxedo on a bus to Comiskey Park. Gingiss Formalwear sponsored a ballpark promotion in which a lucky fan would win 500 tuxedo rentals. Brookfield's William Gray won the prize and decided to use them all in one night. He found 482 Brookfield men to attend the ballpark on Tuesday August 18, dressed in white summer tuxedos. Daunoras's paper had sent her along, likewise attired. "Came six o'clock," she wrote, "and out I strode in my black pants, white jacket and matching scotch plaid cummerbund and bow tie, as conspicuous as a jockey at a convention of basketball players and just as uncomfortable. It turned out a to be a beastly night to change sex and if I accomplished nothing else Tuesday night, I found out that I had wasted the better part of my life wishing I had been born a man only to discover how miserably off the poor fellows are." She admitted to her readers that she had worn a sleeveless blouse under the jacket, giving her some respite on the hot August night.

Treated to free sandwiches, pop and beer by Veeck, "ever the perfect host," the boisterous Brookfielders joined over 34,000 fellow fans to watch

Center fielder Jim Landis helped key the White Sox pennant drive by hitting .325 in August, with a .421 on-base percentage.

the White Sox top the Orioles 6-4. The Sox, after blowing a 2-0 lead, won the game on Nellie Fox's two-run double in the eighth inning. While acknowledging the superb play of Fox and Aparicio ("what a pair to watch!"), Daunoras wrote that "it is doubtful whether the Sox could have won without a retired gentleman of Brookfield's south Oak avenue, named Mr. Bermer, whose crossed fingers at the psychological moment always produced Sox hits when they were most needed and snuffed out Oriole rallies." [20]

Sadly, Mr. Bermer was apparently absent the next two nights, as Baltimore won both games.

Friday August 21, was Nellie Fox Night. WCFL Radio handled the logistics and recruited a committee of Chicago businessmen, media personalities and prominent citizens to plan the festivities and solicit gifts for Fox and his family. Committee chairman Harry G. Kipke, the former Michigan football coach turned Chicago business executive, announced that the committee intended to "Out-Veeck" Bill Veeck. The committee was as good as Kipke's word, presenting dozens of tributes and gifts to Fox and his family during a pregame ceremony: a 1959 Cadillac four-door sedan, a Vauxhall station wagon, a sailboat, two round-trip tickets to Hawaii, a year's supply of shoes for the whole Fox family, toys for the Fox children, and much more.

August 21 was also Jerry Staley's 39th birthday, and he was not forgotten. During the festivities Staley received a block of ice with 40 silver dollars embedded in it. The ice was so solid that Staley had to put the block of ice in the clubhouse shower and run hot water over it for a long time to get the money out.

All the pageantry, tributes and gift-giving took place while the Washington Senators cooled their heels in the visitors' dugout. Under the circumstances, Fox, fiercely competitive himself, probably did not blame Washington pitcher Chuck Stobbs for plunking him with a pitch his first time up. Fox made him pay, though, as he worked a double steal with Luis Aparicio. When catcher Clint Courtney's throw went astray, Aparicio scored and Fox reached third base, to cross the plate himself two batters later. The White Sox held on for a 5-4 win, with Rivera and Landis making great catches in the eighth inning to hold the Senators at bay. [21] About the only disappointment of the night was the special fireworks display, which was intended to culminate with a large silhouette of a baseball batter in the night sky above the park. Did it work? "Maybe from another angle," says SABR member Phil Erwin, who attended the game as a youngster. [22]

By now, one loss to the New York Yankees was not enough to make most fans jittery. The Sox themselves seemed to shake it off easily, bouncing back from a Sunday afternoon 7-1 loss to take the next two. They also took two out of three from Boston, to end the homestand on a high note.

The arrival of first baseman Ted Kluszewski buoyed their spirits further. A star with the Cincinnati Redlegs for several years until back trouble hampered his power swing, Klu could still intimidate pitchers with his physique. "Even his muscles have muscles," one of his new teammates remarked after seeing Kluszewski in his trademark nearly-sleeveless jersey. Would "Klu" be the power-hitting RBI man the White Sox had been missing? [23]

He couldn't have arrived at a better time. The White Sox, a mere game and a half ahead of the Tribe, were going to Cleveland for a four-game series. Manager Joe Gordon's pitching, which had suffered collective arm trouble earlier in the month, had rebounded. Cal McLish, Jim Perry and Mudcat Grant were joined by ex-Sox lefty Jack Harshman, who had flopped with the Orioles earlier in the season but had won three straight for the Indians. Cleveland, riding an eight-game win streak, was just a game and a half off the pace. They had a chance to gain some ground, maybe even regain the lead, during this home stand. The Forest City was abuzz, and fans seeking tickets kept the box office phones ringing right up to game time on Friday August 28. That evening, 70,398 fans piled into Cleveland Stadium, the largest paid attendance at a ballgame to date that season.

The Indians tied the score against Bob Shaw, 3-3, in the fifth inning, and had two men on base with one out. Shaw, already sweating heavily, now faced Tito Francona and Rocky Colavito. Francona went out on a pop-up, and then Colavito stopped every heart in the place with a deep drive into the outfield seats – deep enough, but just a few feet foul. Shaw took the ball from the umpire, reared back, and got Colavito swinging on the next pitch. Shaw cruised the rest of the way.

Sherm Lollar's favorite bat had developed a crack, and Lollar had been keeping it together with nails and tape. In the seventh inning, with two men on, Lollar drove a ball to the left field fence. Minnie Minoso gave chase and seemed to catch the ball just as he slammed into the wire fence. The ball popped out of his glove and over the fence. The Sox added one more run, but Lollar's blast was the margin of victory.

• The 1959 Season •

Sadly, the clout was too much for Lollar's poor bat, which cracked irreparably. Lollar, who had hit seven home runs during August, hit only two more the rest of the season. His total of 22 would still lead the team that year.

A Ladies' Day crowd of over 50,000 endured stifling heat on Saturday August 29. A virus shelved scheduled starter Ken McBride, so Lopez started Dick Donovan a day early. Donovan, back from shoulder problems that had sidelined him for almost a month, dueled with Jim Perry. The pitchers posted zeros for six innings, helped by fine defense, such as Vic Power's nice 3-6-3 double play in the third inning to nip a White Sox rally in the bud. In the seventh, with Landis on first base and two out, Earl Torgeson singled to left field. Minnie Minoso wanted to hold the fleet Landis at second, but thinking ahead to his throw to third, didn't get a handle on the ball. By the time he picked it up, Landis was on his way home. He slid across the plate ahead of the throw. Jim Rivera scored an insurance run in the eighth inning, and the Sox held on to win 2-0. "The Cleveland dressing room," reported *Sports Illustrated*, "which had been surprisingly chipper after the Friday night loss, was like the inside of a coffin after Saturday's game. Players sat silently on their stools, talking only in whispers. The situation was critical. Nothing but a double-header victory on Sunday could salvage the series." [24]

The first game of the Sunday twinbill pitted the 16-8 Wynn against the 16-6 McLish. The contest was scoreless until the fifth inning, when Woodie Held led off the inning with his 25th homer of the season, and Ed Fitz Gerald singled and scored to make it 2-0. With one out in the sixth, Wynn homered to deep right field. Luis Aparicio followed with a grounder to Held, whose throw to first base hit Luis in the head. After a five-minute delay, Aparicio shook off the knock and play resumed. Aparicio lost no time swiping second base. Rattled, McLish gave up two walks and two hits and struck a batter with a pitch. The resulting five-run inning put the game in the bag. In the sequel, the Sox pounded Cleveland pitching for nine hits and five runs. Barry Latman made it through five innings, giving up a three-run homer to Rocky Colavito and a solo shot to Held, but Turk Lown iced the game with four innings of shutout ball.

Five and a half games ahead, with 25 games to go, the White Sox had not yet clinched the pennant. But they could see the flag on the horizon, while Cleveland could see it slipping away.

Standings after August 31

	G	W	L	T	PCT	GB	RS	RA
Chicago White Sox	131	80	49	2	.620	-	566	501
Cleveland Indians	130	75	55	0	.577	5.5	620	545
Detroit Tigers	130	65	65	0	.500	15.5	608	610
New York Yankees	131	64	66	1	.492	16.5	584	567
Baltimore Orioles	128	61	66	1	.480	18.0	469	533
Boston Red Sox	131	62	69	0	.473	19.0	624	602
Kansas City Athletics	129	59	70	0	.457	21.0	575	606
Washington Senators	130	52	78	0	.400	28.5	520	602

September

Back home, Chicago took two of three from Detroit, including a bizarre 11-4 win on September 2 in which they scored all 11 runs in one inning. Al Smith homered to lead off the bottom of the fifth. The next 14 batters put up nine more hits, with a walk, a hit-by-pitch and a stolen base thrown in.

After a day off, Chicago hosted Cleveland for a three-game set, starting September 4. Wynn bested Perry 3-2 that night for his 18th victory of the season. Two key defensive plays made the difference, and Minnie Minoso was the victim of each. The first was in the top of the fifth inning. Cleveland second baseman Jim Baxes homered to make the score 2-1 Chicago, and then the Indians put two men on with two out. Jim Landis made a dazzling catch near the 415-foot mark in center field to rob Minoso of an extra-base hit. Wynn must have been relieved, as he forgot to hit Baxes with a pitch next time up.

The score was still 2-1 Sox in the eighth when Minoso, who was playing with a broken toe, doubled with two out. Tito Francona dropped a single in front of Al Smith in left field. Minoso, head down and running at the crack of the bat, rounded third and headed for home. Smith charged the ball and hurled it to the plate. The crowd went silent as Minoso slid, then roared with approval as home plate umpire Frank Umont signaled the out. "It was the biggest out of the week," according to the *Sports Illustrated* correspondent. Minoso protested the call loudly, but it stood. The Sox scored an insurance run in the bottom of the eighth, which helped them survive a scare in the ninth when Rocky Colavito doubled and scored. But Staley recovered to retire the side and preserve the 3-2 win.[25]

The Indians proved they could bounce back, though. They took the next two from Chicago, each by one run. They survived a three-run ninth-inning Sox rally to win 6-5 on Saturday September 5, paced by home runs from Francona and Held. On Sunday, Mudcat Grant bested Dick Donovan in a 2-1 duel. The game was scoreless in the fifth inning when a fan, dressed in Indian garb, leapt from the stands and ran around the field. Bill Veeck, chatting with reporters in the press box, denied that it was one of his stunts. In the ninth inning, down 1-0 with two teammates on base, Cleveland's Vic Power saw what he called the first high pitch he had seen in the whole series. He drilled it to deep right field, just out of Landis's reach, to score both runners.

The White Sox still held a four-and-a-half game lead as Cleveland left for a doubleheader at home against Detroit. The Sox knew they needed to find their game against the Athletics, who had given them trouble all year. They finally solved the A's during a doubleheader on Monday September 7. Pierce went the distance for a 2-1 win, and then Kluszewski hit two of Chicago's four home runs as the White Sox outslugged the A's 13-7. The Sox finished the series sweep the next evening as Early Wynn won a 10-inning duel with Kansas City's Bud Daley, 3-2.

Chicago's last east coast road trip of 1959 started with a two-game split in Washington, and then went to Baltimore for a memorable September 11 doubleheader. Orioles rookie Jack Fisher bested Billy Pierce in the first game, 3-0, for Fisher's first career win. The second game was a replay of the 18-inning 1-1 tie on August 6. Once again, fans attending a Baltimore-Chicago ballgame got their money's worth. For the sixth time this season the White Sox and Orioles went into extra innings, and for the fourth time they made it into the 16th inning. Barry Latman pitched into the 10th inning, scattering five hits and retiring 21 Orioles in a row at one point. Jerry Walker also pitched shutout ball. Brooks Robinson broke the scoreless tie with a base hit off Jerry Staley. Incredibly, Walker went all 16 innings for the Orioles.

The next day Jim Landis singled in the second inning to score Johnny Romano. The run ended two scoreless inning streaks: a 29-inning streak for Chicago and a 19-inning skein for Oriole pitcher Billy O'Dell. Chicago cruised to a 6-1 victory, Early Wynn's 20th of the season.

Back home, Veeck and company felt comfortable enough to plan for an upcoming World Series. A pair of reserved grandstand tickets would cost $14.40, they announced, and a pair of box seats would go for $20.60. Veeck also decided to break tradition and sell tickets for individual games instead of in blocks of four. This would enable the average fan to attend the World Series games.

The Sox split a two-game set in Boston next. The 3-1 win on September 13 featured Goodman's first home run in two years. Things took a frightening turn when Jim Landis ruptured a blood vessel in his leg, reopening a wound incurred in Cleveland three weeks earlier, and spent the night in a Boston hospital. Landis would return on the 22nd, and Bubba Phillips would get the bulk of the playing time in center field during his absence.

In the sixth inning the next day, Turk Lown went to the mound in relief of September call-up Gary Peters. Boston had just scored five runs and loaded the bases for Pumpsie Green. A couple of days later in an interview, Lopez told Arthur Daley that all of Lown's warmup tosses "were this high," gesturing across his own chin. "I give Tony the elbow. 'What goes on here?' I say. 'The bases are full and he can't find the strike zone.'" Lown walked Green to force in the sixth inning, and Lopez trotted out to the mound.

Lopez didn't yank Lown, but, as he told the story, he said "Turk, do me one favor. When you throw the next pitch, bounce it to the plate."

Lown's next pitch, according to Lopez, was "the prettiest low-breaking curve I ever saw." Lown went on to strike out the batter for the second out, and got the next batter on a groundout to end the inning.[26]

The New York Yankees might have been out of the pennant race, but they could still play the unfamiliar role of spoiler. Chicago visited Yankee Stadium and Billy Pierce started against Ralph Terry. Down 2-1 in the eighth, Fox singled off Terry, who then had to leave the game with pain in his side. Whitey Ford relieved, and gave up a walk, a single, a hit batter and a sacrifice fly, good for two runs and a Chicago lead. Aparicio tripled in the ninth inning and scored to add an insurance run. They needed it.

Mantle, leading off the Yankees' ninth inning, launched his second home run of the game halfway

The 1959 Season

up the right-field bleachers. After Berra popped out, McAnany, playing center field for the first time, had trouble with Howard's sinking liner, and it landed for a double. Bobby Shantz pinch-ran for Howard, representing the tying run. Hector Lopez hit a sharp liner to right field. Shantz, certain the ball would get through for a hit, took off with the crack of the bat. But Rivera made a diving catch, just off the top of the grass, then hurled the ball toward second base. Aparicio stretched for the throw, but not enough, and the ball bounced off his glove. Fortunately, it bounced toward Bubba Phillips, who scooped it up and ran it to second himself before Shantz could scramble back. The double play gave the Sox the win.

The Yankees rebounded to win the next day, though, and the White Sox lost two of three to Detroit. Meanwhile, Cleveland had gotten a brief second wind.

Tuesday, September 22

"My neighbors were rushing around the street – they didn't know what was going on!" [27]

After dropping two games to Boston, Cleveland GM Frank Lane had criticized manager Joe Gordon to reporters. Gordon, having had enough of Lane's criticism down the stretch, then announced that he would not remain in Cleveland another season, but would resign as soon as Cleveland was mathematically eliminated. [28] Whereupon Cleveland swept a three-game set in Kansas City while Chicago had dropped two of three to Detroit. (Gordon and Lane would eventually mend fences and agree to a two-year contract. Gordon stayed at the helm until August 3, 1960, when Lane pulled off one of his strangest trades: dealing his manager to Detroit in exchange for Tigers manager Jimmy Dykes.)

Unable to close the deal at home, the White Sox flew to Cleveland for one game. A win would clinch the pennant for Chicago; a loss would keep Cleveland alive for another day.

Bob Kreidler, now a SABR member in Akron, Ohio, was an expatriate Chicagoan attending John Carroll University in September 1959. Kreidler, a former usher, had seen hundreds of games at Comiskey and Wrigley and had suffered through the near-misses of recent years. "We had the sense the White Sox would figure out a way to blow this," remembered Kreidler. He nevertheless convinced three fellow students, also Chicagoans, to make the trip to Cleveland for the September 22 game. They were in Cleveland's Municipal Stadium, on the third base side, in shirtsleeves on that unseasonably-warm September night. Few of the 54,293 vocal fans in the stands that night were Chicago partisans, and the college students found themselves in a boisterous island of their own among an increasingly sullen sea of Indians fans. [29]

In the top of the third, Bubba Phillips singled. With two out, Luis Aparicio socked a double to the right field wall. Rocky Colavito played the carom and fired the ball to home plate. The ball sailed over catcher Russ Nixon's head and immediately bounced back to the infield, but not in time to make a play on Phillips. After Fox walked, Billy Goodman doubled to score Aparicio, giving the Sox a 2-0 lead.

The Indians answered with a run in the fifth, Gordy Coleman and Jimmy Piersall singling in Held, but Aparicio and Fox turned a Vic Power ground ball into a double play to end the potential rally. In the top of the fifth, though, Al Smith and Jim Rivera clouted back-to-back homers to put the Sox up 4-1.

The few intrepid Sox fans in the stands pulled for Early Wynn, formerly of these same Cleveland Indians, to complete the magical night with a complete game victory. Wynn wobbled, though. Earl Battey replaced Johnny Romano behind the plate for the sixth inning, and while Battey and Wynn had worked effectively several times throughout the season, this was not one of those times. Tito Francona and Nixon singled, and Colavito's sacrifice fly plated Francona. With Woodie Held due up next, Battey and Wynn exited, and Lollar and Shaw entered. Shaw got Held to ground to third, forcing Nixon at second and ending the inning.

Shaw held the Indians at bay over the next two innings, but with one out in the ninth, three straight singles loaded the bases for Vic Power. Lopez called for Jerry Staley. Staley threw one pitch. Power hit it hard but, as in the fifth inning, within range of Aparicio's glove. Aparicio snagged the ball, stepped on second, and chucked it to first base. Kluszewski gloved the ball, then ran to the pitcher's mound to embrace Staley. The double play ended the inning, the game, and the 40-year wait.

Like that, the Chicago White Sox were American League champions.

When the last out was made, Kreidler remembers, he and his friends "didn't know how to act." They whooped and hollered as they rushed to catch the train back to school, until they realized that they were the only people celebrating, as far as they could see. They decided to cool it, and managed to restrain themselves until they got back to campus where they went "absolutely bonkers!"[30]

Back in Chicago, their fellow fans did the same thing. The game had been televised in Chicago, and as Jim Rivera started dancing in the clubhouse, the TV cameras picked up the image and shared it with White Sox fans all across the city, who whooped it up themselves. In the excitement, Fire Commissioner Robert J. Quinn ordered the air raid sirens switched on for five minutes. It was intended to be part of the celebration. But as the sirens sounded, alarmed Chicagoans who had not watched the game or heard the news rushed out of their homes in night clothes, or out of their favorite watering holes. Others huddled in air raid shelters, worried about what Cold-War horrors might befall their city. "Damn ignorant," snapped one man later when finding out what had happened. "Pretty stupid."[31]

After the sirens fell silent and word spread, for the most part, all was forgiven. When Al Lopez and his charges arrived at Midway Airport early the next morning, thousands were on hand to greet them. They all knew what was going on. For the first time on 40 years, the Chicago White Sox were going to the World Series.

Final Standings

	G	W	L	T	PCT	GB	RS	RA
Chicago White Sox	156	94	60	2	.610	-	669	588
Cleveland Indians	154	89	65	0	.578	5.0	745	646
New York Yankees	155	79	75	1	.513	15.0	687	647
Detroit Tigers	154	76	78	1	.494	18.0	713	732
Boston Red Sox	154	75	79	0	487	19.0	726	696
Baltimore Orioles	155	74	80	1	.481	20.0	551	621
Kansas City Athletics	154	66	88	0	.429	28.0	681	760
Washington Senators	154	63	91	0	.409	31.0	619	701

Thanks to SABR members Phil Erwin, Bob Kreidler, Paul Ladewski, Richard Smiley and Joe Wancho for their suggestions and recollections.

Notes

1. www.retrosheet.org (box scores, play-by-plays and standings) *Sports Illustrated*, August 10, 1959, 77
2. *Sports Illustrated*, March 2, 1959, 39
3. *Sports Illustrated*, September 13, 1959, 41
4. *Retrosheet* (https://www.retrosheet.org/boxesetc/1959/B04220KC11959.htm)
5. *Sports Illustrated*, August 10, 1959, 77
6. Woodcock, Les. "Baseball's Week." *Sports Illustrated*, May 11, 1959, 10
7. Terrell, Roy. "What's Wrong with the Yanks?" *Sports Illustrated*, May 25 1959, 20-24
8. Terrell, Roy. "Down Went the Yankees." *Sports Illustrated*, May 11, 1959, 70-72
9. Terrell, Roy. "Down Went the Yankees." *Sports Illustrated*, May 11, 1959, 70-72
10. Woodcock, Les. "Baseball's Week." *Sports Illustrated*, June 1, 1959, 13
11. "Cowmanship a la Veeck." *Sports Illustrated*, June 22, 1959, 39
12. Woodcock, Les. "Baseball's Week." *Sports Illustrated*, June 29, 1959, 13
13. Bingham, Walter. "Exquisite Torture in Chicago." *Sports Illustrated*, July 13, 1959, 49-50
14. Bingham, Walter. "The Joys and Agonies of Frank Lane." *Sports Illustrated*, July 27, 1959, 34
15. *Sports Illustrated*, August 3, 1959, 10
16. Woodcock, Les. "Two for the Pennant." *Sports Illustrated*, August 10, 1959, 50-53
17. *Retrosheet* (https://www.retrosheet.org/boxesetc/1959/B08040BAL1959.htm)
18. Woodcock, Les. "Two for the Pennant." *Sports Illustrated*, August 10, 1959, 50-53
19. Daley, Arthur. "Sports of the Times: Listening to Alfonso Ramon." *New York Times*, September 16, 1959, 47
20. Daunoras, Lyn. "In Tuxes All – 483 Men and Lyn." *Brookfield (Illinois) Enterprise*, August 26, 1959, 7. The headline says 483 men, whereas the article says 482.
21. *Retrosheet* (https://www.retrosheet.org/boxesetc/1959/B08210CHA1959.htm)
22. Interview with Phil Erwin
23. Munzel, Edgar. "Klu Takes Cue – Fills Bill as Sox Socker." *The Sporting News*, September 23, 1959, 5
24. Bingham, Walter. "Four Big Games for the Sox." *Sports Illustrated*, September 7, 1959, 33-34
25. *Sports Illustrated*, September 14, 1959, 30-31
26. Daley, Arthur. "Sports of the Times: Listening to Alfonso Ramon." *New York Times*, September 16, 1959, 47
27. Howard M. Tuckner, "White Sox Defeat Indians for Title," *New York Times*, September 23, 1959, 47
28. Tuckner
29. Interview with Bob Kreidler.
30. Kreidler interview.
31. Tuckner

The 1959 World Series

By R.J. Lesch

Next week, somewhere in this great land of ours, a husband will return home from work and his wife will say to him: 'I think Luis Aparicio is cute.' The World Series, you see, reaches everyone. While it is being played, America puts aside stock transactions, algebra lessons and vacuum cleaners. All that can wait. The Series comes first."

- Walter Bingham, *Sports Illustrated*[1]

Before the Series could start, though, the National League had to decide on a pennant winner. A heated three-way race featured the Milwaukee Braves, defending two-time pennant winners, against the Los Angeles Dodgers and San Francisco Giants. The Giants led by two games over the Dodgers and three over the Braves at the end of August, but played 10-13 ball the rest of the way. They were effectively done after the Dodgers swept them in a three-game set at home, September 19 and 20. The Dodgers won eight of their last 10 regular-season games to finish the season with an 86-68 record. The Braves kept pace, going 16-8 in September to finish with an identical record. The Dodgers and Braves would play a best-of-three series to break the tie.

Awaiting an opponent, Al Lopez told an interviewer, "it seems to me that I'm the only one who is tight and nervous. I feel it in my stomach, but I try to keep it to myself. Everybody else seems loose and easy. They joke and whistle. I just don't say anything." Describing his team's play, Lopez explained how the Sox won, depending on pitching, defense and speed instead of the long ball favored by most clubs of the day. "We keep moving and keep the pressure on the other team," he said. "They know they have to rush their plays. The more they rush, the more likely it is they will make an error. With our speed, an error means another base or maybe a run."[2]

Thinking along similar lines, *Sports Illustrated* picked the Sox to beat the Braves or Giants, but the Dodgers to beat the Sox. "In many ways Los Angeles is like Chicago. Each team has depth. Each steals bases. Each led its league in fielding. Los Angeles has better hitting (and the White Sox pitchers have never had to work with that Coliseum screen behind them). The White Sox seem to have trouble beating teams that play White Sox-type baseball. The Dodgers play that type of ball."[3]

The day the *SI* analysis hit the newsstands, Monday September 28, the Dodgers and Braves squared off for game one of their tiebreaker series. The Braves chased Dodger starter Danny McDevitt in the second inning, setting the stage for Larry Sherry to take the ball in relief. The Braves scored the go-ahead run with Sherry on the mound, but Sherry only allowed four hits and no runs the rest of the way, giving the Dodgers a chance to take the game 3-2 on John Roseboro's solo home run in the sixth inning.

Sherry was an unlikely hero. A Los Angeles native who had overcome two club feet as a child, he had signed with the Dodgers in 1953 out of high school. He was unspectacular in the minors and shaky in five appearances with the Dodgers in 1958. While playing winter ball in Venezuela with his brother Norm, a Dodgers catcher, he added a slider to go with his fastball and curve. "By the time the winter season was over," Sherry said later, "I knew I could depend on the slider, even in a jam, and it proved to be the turning point of my career."[4] Sherry rejoined the parent club in July and went 7-2 with a 2.19 ERA and three saves in 23 appearances with the Dodgers down the stretch. His clutch performance against the Braves was his first bow under the national lights. It would not be his last.

Both clubs flew to Los Angeles for Game Two, the very next day. The Braves looked to have evened the series, going into the ninth inning with a 5-2 lead, but Los Angeles exploded for three runs in the bottom of the ninth to tie the score. Carl Furillo singled to score Gil Hodges in the twelfth inning to win the game and the series for the Dodgers.[5]

The Dodgers then climbed onto another plane, this one arriving in Chicago at 4:24 am Wednesday morning. Dodger manager Walter Alston called off morning practice and told his weary players to get some rest.

World Series Game 1:
Thursday, October 1 - 1 p.m. (CT) Comiskey Park, Chicago

For only the second time in a decade, Casey Stengel was not in uniform for the Series. The Yankees' manager was on hand in suit and tie, as a correspondent for *Life* magazine. The regular sportswriters had as much fun covering Ol' Case as ever. He lost his pencil, broke his pen, shrugged and said, "I'm gonna have to keep it all in my head." Casey interviewed Pee Wee Reese, Charlie Dressen, and old friends Al Lopez and Tony Cuccinello, and "never jotted down a note … Casey, in his best Stengelese," wrote one reporter, "asked the questions and provided the answers." [6]

Bill Veeck and the White Sox were ready to greet Stengel the press and the Dodgers, along with thousands of White Sox fans ready for their first World Series in 40 years. Veeck was determined that the Chicago games would be "The World Series of the Common Fan." Rather than selling tickets in blocks on a first-come first-serve basis, a practice which he believed favored large corporate ticket-buyers and left the little guy out on the street looking in, Veeck set up a lottery for the 300,000 fans who applied for the chance to purchase tickets. An 11-person citizens committee drew names. They followed an allocation system which made sure that each area of Chicago would receive tickets in proportion to their support of the Sox to date. "The vvvvips, the very, very, very, very important persons," said Veeck, "are the ones who supported the team all season." Since the South Side, according to Veeck's surveys, made up 65 percent of White Sox fans, they would receive 65 percent of the tickets. [7]

Comiskey Park hosted 48,013 vvvvips on a crisp, sunny autumn afternoon. Their White Sox were 6-5 favorites. Red Faber and Ray Schalk, heroes from the 1917 World Series—the last Series championship for the White Sox—handled the ceremonial first pitch duties to enthusiastic applause.

The Sox lost no time getting on the scoreboard. In the bottom of the first, Nellie Fox drew a walk from Dodger hurler Roger Craig, moved to third on Jim Landis's single, and scored on Ted Kluszewski's base hit to right field. Landis took the extra base, and scored from third on Sherm Lollar's sacrifice fly. The Sox were up 2-0, thanks to the speed and audacity that Lopez had predicted they would need to use to win.

The White Sox left their regular playbook aside in the third inning, though, in an offensive eruption that delighted their fans and shocked everyone else. Fox doubled and scored on Landis's single. Kluszewski sent a high fly ball over the right field wall. The rare home run put the home team up 5-0, chased Craig and brought Chuck Churn out to stop the bleeding. Lollar hit a fly to left-center field, a can of corn that fell to the turf when Duke Snider and Wally Moon collided. Lollar made it to second, then scored on Billy Goodman's single. Al Smith socked a double off the wall in deep left center. Snider, playing with a sore knee, caught up to the ball and threw to Gil Hodges, the cutoff man. A good relay, observers felt, might have caught either Goodman or Smith, as Smith, running hard, was charging toward third base while Goodman was scrambling back to the bag. But the throw went awry and Goodman crossed the plate instead. Snider was charged with the error, but Hodges later took the blame, saying he slipped on the grass and should have had the ball.

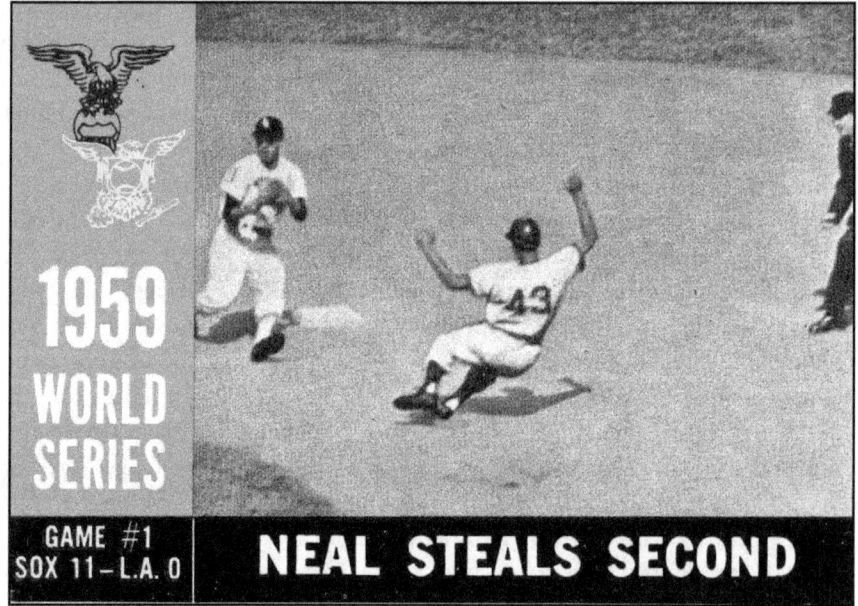

Charlie Neal was signed by the Brooklyn Dodgers as an amateur free agent in 1950 and moved with the team to Los Angeles. He hit two home runs in Game Two of the Series, at Chicago's Comiskey Park.

Jim Rivera grounded to Dodger second baseman Charlie Neal, who threw home in enough time to catch Smith. But Neal's throw bounced off the handle of Rivera's bat, lying in the grass in front of home plate, and past catcher John Roseboro. Smith scored, and Rivera reached second base. Pitcher Early Wynn put the cherry on top of the seven-run inning with a double to score Rivera. The stunned Dodgers, an excellent defensive club, had committed three errors and yielded four unearned runs. "Crimminy, it's just like when I was managin' the Dodgers," growled Casey Stengel. "They is playin' like ribbon clerks." [8]

Big Klu's bat had another surprise left. With Landis aboard again in the fourth inning, Kluszewski smashed Churn's pitch into the upper right-field stands. The score stood at 11-0, and the White Sox faithful were almost delirious.

Meanwhile, Wynn was pitching as he had all season, keeping the Dodgers off balance for seven innings. After Jim Gilliam led off the eighth with a single, Lopez decided to save his ace and called in Jerry Staley. Wynn left to a deafening ovation. When Staley got Neal to ground into a double play, and then pitched out of a jam in the ninth inning to preserve the shutout, no White Sox fan doubted that their club could prevail.

The only rain on the parade was courtesy of commissioner Ford Frick. Local auto dealer Jim Moran had offered a new Ford Falcon to anyone who homered during the World Series. When Klu hit two, Moran announced that he would get two cars. Frick, however, ruled that Kluszewski could not accept the cars, giving no reason for his decision. At the time, though, it seemed low on everyone's list of concerns.

Game 1 Notes[9]

```
LA N    0 0 0   0 0 0   0 0 0  -  0  8  3
CHI A   2 0 7   2 0 0   0 0 x  - 11 11  0
```

WP: Wynn (1–0) LP: Craig (0–1) Sv: Staley (1)
LOB: Los Angeles 8, Chicago 3. 2B: Fox, Smith 2, Wynn. HR: Kluszewski 2. SF: Lollar. SB: Neal. DP: Chicago 1. Errors: Neal, Snider 2.
Umpires: HP Bill Summers, 1B Frank Dascoli, 2B Eddie Hurley, 3B Frank Secory, LF John Rice, RF Hal Dixon.
Time of Game: 2:35
Attendance: 48,013
Gate receipts: $325,757.09

World Series Game 2:
Friday, October 2 - 1 p.m. (CT)
Comiskey Park, Chicago

The TV series "The Twilight Zone" would debut this evening on CBS. White Sox fans might be forgiven for thinking they received a sneak preview that afternoon.

The Sox appeared to pick up where they had left off the day before. Luis Aparicio, whose bat had been silent during Game One, led off the first inning with a double, reached third base on Fox's fly to right, and scored on Klu's hit-and-run grounder to second. Landis, who had walked and moved to second on the grounder, hustled home on Lollar's base hit.

The Dodgers struck for the first time in the fifth inning, with memorable results. With two out, Charlie Neal socked a home run into the left field stands. As bleacherites scrambled for the ball, one fan's beer toppled from atop the nine-foot wall onto the head of Al Smith, standing at the base of the wall. Smith recovered from the shower of suds to snag Wally Moon's fly for the third out. The Sox still led 2-1. They appeared poised to add to the lead when Bubba Phillips doubled in the sixth with one out, but couldn't punch him across the plate.

That set the stage for the Dodgers to take their first lead in the series. Chuck Essegian, pinch-hitting for Johnny Podres, homered into the upper left deck with two out to tie the score. In short order, Bob Shaw walked Junior Gilliam, and then Neal socked his second homer of the game to put the Dodgers up 4-2.

Larry Sherry, the hero of the first playoff game against the Braves, took the mound for the Dodgers. After an uneventful seventh, the White Sox mounted their challenge in the bottom of the eighth. Kluszewski and Lollar singled. Lopez sent in Earl Torgeson to run for Kluszewski, and Smith doubled to left to score Torgeson. Looking for a chance to tie the game, third-base coach Tony Cuccinello waved Sherm Lollar home as well. Wally Moon played the rebound off the wall and threw a perfect strike to shortstop Maury Wills, who relayed the ball to Roseboro. Lollar, out by yards, didn't even slide as Roseboro tagged him out.

The play would be one of the most closely-analyzed of the Series. Cuccinello and Lollar both took the blame, Lollar pointing out that he had hesitated to see whether Moon would catch the ball. Sox coach Don Gutteridge pointed out that this type of aggressiveness had worked in Game One, forcing

Neal's error in the fourth inning. "That is the way we've been playing all year," said Don, "and if we hadn't played it that way I don't think you'd be seeing us in this World Series." [10]

On the other hand, longtime sportswriter Arthur Daley put it this way: "Lollar is an estimable man who is kind to children and helps feeble old ladies at street crossings. But he has about as much speed as a glacier."[11]

Even so, Al Smith had hustled to third on the throw home, and the Sox sent Billy Goodman to pinch-hit for Phillips with just one out. Sherry went to work, fanning Goodman, then getting Rivera out on a foul pop to Roseboro. The Sox went out in order in the bottom of the ninth, and the Dodgers had evened the series at a game apiece with the 4-3 win.

Game 2 Notes [12]

```
LA N   0 0 0   0 1 0   3 0 0  - 4  9  1
CHI A  2 0 0   0 0 0   0 1 0  - 3  8  0
```

WP: Podres (1–0) LP: Shaw (0–1) Sv: Sherry (1)
LOB: Los Angeles 7, Chicago 8. 2B: Aparicio, Phillips, Smith. HR: Neal 2, Essegian. SB: Moon, Gilliam. E: Wills.
Umpires: HP Dascoli, 1B Hurley, 2B Secory, 3B Summers, LF Rice, RF Dixon
Time of Game: 2:21
Attendance: 47,368
Gate receipts: $323,400.27

World Series Game 3:
Sunday, October 4 - 2 p.m. (PT)
Memorial Coliseum, Los Angeles

"WORLD SERIES CITIES 1800 MILES APART ... AND UNITED AIR LINES FLIES BOTH TEAMS"

- United newspaper ad, run during the World Series[13]

The Dodgers were now getting 11-10 odds to win the Series, as the venue shifted to Los Angeles. Game three was the first World Series game on the West Coast and the first set in the cavernous Coliseum. Everyone expected that the combined excitement and capacity would shatter World Series attendance records. 92,394 fans did not disappoint, showing up to see Brooklyn Dodger hero Zack Wheat throw out the first pitch.

The White Sox put Dodgers starter Don Drysdale in a bases-loaded jam in the first inning, but stranded all three runners. It set a pattern. The Sox would outhit the Dodgers 12 to 5 and add four walks, but would only plate one runner. For the first six innings, the Dodgers could do no better against Dick Donovan.

In the seventh, though, Charlie Neal bounced a single off the screen in left field. The screen, forty feet tall and only 250 feet from home plate, was one of the more tantalizing features of play in the Coliseum. A right-handed hitter could pull a high fly over the screen or could bounce hits off of it. Five of the 12 Sox hits would be "Screenos," but none would have the impact of Neal's.

Donovan's control deserted him at this point, as he walked left fielder Norm Larker and Gil Hodges to load the bases. Staley replaced Donovan on the mound while Carl Furillo pinch-hit for Don Demeter. Furillo's grounder hopped over Aparicio's glove and into center field to score Neal and Larker.

The Sox responded with a run in the top of the eighth. Kluszewski and Lollar back-to-back singles chased Drysdale, bringing Larry Sherry in from the bullpen. Sherry hit Goodman with a pitch to load the bases, bringing up Al Smith with nobody out. Sherry got Smith to hit a grounder to Wills for the double play, Klu scoring from third to close the gap to 2-1. The Dodgers got the run back in their half of the inning, Wills scoring on Neal's double.

Sherry closed out the ninth striking out Norm Cash, Aparicio and Landis. He shared hero honors with Roseboro, who had called a solid game while throwing out three would-be basestealers. "It was my most gratifying day in the big leagues," said Roseboro[14]. The gate receipts, topping a half million dollars, must have made for a gratifying day for Dodger brass as well, justifying their move to the West Coast in one stroke.

Game 3 Notes[15]

```
CHI A  0 0 0   0 0 0   0 1 0  - 1  12  0
LA N   0 0 0   0 0 0   2 1 x  - 3   5  0
```

WP: Drysdale (1–0) LP: Donovan (0–1) Sv: Sherry (2)
LOB: Chicago 11, Los Angeles 3. 2B: Neal. SH: Sherry. Double plays: Los Angeles 3, Chicago 1. HBP: Goodman, by Sherry. SB: Landis. CS: Rivera, Aparicio, Fox.

Umpires: HP Hurley, 1B Secory, 2B Summers, 3B Dascoli, LF Dixon, RF Rice
Time of Game: 2:33
Attendance: 92,394
Gate Receipts: $594,071.76

World Series Game 4: Monday, October 5 - 2 p.m. (PT) Memorial Coliseum, Los Angeles

Gate receipts of $551,506.23 for Game Four meant that the total player share for four games would be $892,365.04. At stake now was who would get the winner's share of that pot. To reach that goal, Lopez shuffled his lineup, putting Landis ahead of Aparicio atop the order for the fifth time that season. Landis flied out to lead off the game, but Aparicio walked and stole second. Fox lofted a pop fly to short right field. The ball fell safe and bounced away for a double, but Aparicio, unable to run until he knew the ball would not be caught, could only rach third. Roger Craig passed Kluszewski intentionally, and then got Sherm Lollar to ground into a double play to end the threat.

Craig then held the White Sox scoreless for the next five innings as well. The Dodgers had better luck with Early Wynn, who had stymied them in Game One. In the third inning with two out, Moon and Larker singled. Landis fielded Larker's hit and threw to Goodman at third base to catch Moon. His throw missed Goodman. Wynn, backing up third, recovered the ball too late to keep Moon from scoring. Hodges singled in turn to score Larker. Don Demeter, replacing the hobbled Snider in center, rapped out a hit of his own to put Hodges in position to score on Lollar's passed ball. Roseboro tallied the fifth straight single off Wynn to right field, and Demeter scored when Aparicio dropped Rivera's throw. Turk Lown replaced Wynn and put the inning to bed. The two-out rally put the Dodgers up 4-0.

Chicago hero Billy Pierce made his first appearance of the Series in relief and tossed three innings of scoreless ball, giving the Sox bats time to recover. Recover they did, in the seventh. Landis singled, took second on Aparicio's sac bunt, moved to third when Fox singled off Craig's glove, and scored on Klu's single to center. That set the table for Sherm Lollar, who waited as Alston and Craig conferred on the mound. They wanted to give Lollar a slider away, and that's just what Craig threw, but, as Alston noted, "Lollar got around on it." [16] The ball cleared the left-field screen for a three-run homer, and the game was tied at four apiece.

Jerry Staley replaced Pierce and held the Dodgers off in the seventh. Gil Hodges led off the eighth inning. "When I first went up to the plate," said Hodges after the game, "I thought a little about hitting a homer. But after (G)erry Staley got a strike on me, all I thought about was getting a hit." Hodges grinned. "That's maybe the best time to get a homer." [17] Hodges also cleared the screen in left field, although as Arthur Daley opined, "it probably would have landed in the upper deck at Ebbets Field." [18]

Down 5-4, the White Sox had three outs remaining, but none other than Larry Sherry was on the mound. In his second inning of work Sherry set the Sox down in order to lock down the victory.

Game 4 Notes[19]

```
CHI A   0 0 0   0 0 0   4 0 0  - 4 10 3
LA  N   0 0 4   0 0 0   0 1 x  - 5  9 0
```

WP: Sherry (1–0) LP: Staley (0–1)
LOB: Chicago 9, Los Angeles 6. 2B: Fox. HR: Lollar, Hodges. SH: Aparicio, Roseboro, Craig. DP: Los Angeles 2. E: Landis (1), Aparicio (1), Pierce (1). PB: Lollar (1). SB: Aparicio, Wills.
Umpires: HP Secory, 1B Summers, 2B Dascoli, 3B Hurley, LF Dixon, RF Rice
Time of Game: 2:30
Attendance: 92,650
Gate receipts: $551,506.23

World Series Game 5: Tuesday, October 6 - 2 p.m. (PT) Memorial Coliseum, Los Angeles

Down three games to one, the White Sox needed a win to stave off elimination. Trainer Ed Froehlich suggested the team go back to black stockings. The Sox had switched to white stockings for the series, to help fans forget the 'Black Sox' scandal of 1919. "He thought it would change our luck," Lopez said of the switch back. "And I'm for trying anything to do that." [20]

Bob Shaw got the start against fireballer Sandy Koufax, who had struck out 18 Giants in one game on August 31 to tie Bob Feller's major-league record. Koufax fanned six in seven innings of work on this day. Shaw whiffed only one, but kept the Dodgers off the board in his seven-plus innings of work.

Behind them, both sides played spotless defense. No one was better than Junior Gilliam, whose heady play denied the Sox a run in the third. With Bubba Phillips on second, Aparicio hit a two-out Screeno to left. Seeing no chance to catch Phillips at the plate, Gilliam cut off the throw and caught Aparicio sliding into second for the third out. When the White Sox did score in the fourth, it was on a double play, Fox crossing the plate from third.

The Dodgers had their chances. In the home half of the fourth, Hodges tripled to deep right center with one out, but Demeter grounded out to Shaw and Roseboro popped out to Luis to strand Hodges. Another chance came in the seventh inning. Essegian walked with one out, and with Don Zimmer pinch-running, Snider, batting for Koufax, grounded to shortstop. It could have been a double play, but Snider, gimpy leg and all, ran well enough to reach before Fox's throw. Johnny Podres ran for Snider and Gilliam socked his fourth hit of the game.

With runners on first and second, and the hot hand, Charlie Neal, coming to bat, Lopez made a clairvoyant move. He sent Al Smith from right field to left, and put Jim Rivera in right field. Bob Shaw's wild pitch moved the runners up a base each, and then Neal hit a fly ball toward the wire fence in right field. Rivera, running hard, snared the ball over his shoulder, just feet away from the fence. Rivera's great catch saved at least two runs, and Alston praised it as the play of the game in his post-game interview.

The Dodgers tried again in the eighth. Wally Moon singled to center. Hodges ripped a ball just foul into the left-field stands, then also singled to center, Landis losing the ball in the sun at the last moment. With runners on second and third and one out, Lopez and Alston engaged in some lefty-righty gamesmanship. Lopez sent lefty Billy Pierce into the game to face Ron Fairly, kept him in long enough to give pinch-hitter Rip Repulski a free pass, then replaced him with Dick Donovan when Carl Furillo pitch-hit for John Roseboro. Furillo popped up to Bubba Phillips at third on a fastball, and then Zimmer flied out to left on a Donovan slider for the third out. It was Los Angeles's turn to strand runners, leaving eleven on base in all.

Both clubs showered, changed, and grabbed 6 p.m. flights for Chicago. The Sox would fight another day.

Game 5 Notes[21]

```
CHI A   0 0 0   1 0 0   0 1 0 - 1  5  0
LA  N   0 0 0   0 0 0   0 0 0 - 0  9  0
```

WP: Shaw (1–1) LP: Koufax (0–1) Sv: Donovan (1)
LOB: Chicago 5, Los Angeles 11. DP: Los Angeles 1.
3B: Hodges. SB: Gilliam. SH: Shaw 2.
Umpires: HP Summers, 1B Dascoli, 2B Hurley, 3B Secory, LF Dixon, RF Rice
Time of Game: 2:28
Attendance: 92,706
Receipts: $552,774.77

World Series Game 6: Thursday, October 8 - 1 p.m. (CT) Comiskey Park, Chicago

Music fans mourned the death of Mario Lanza on October 7. Cold War analysts fretted over the significance of the Soviet Union's Luna probe as it sent back the first-ever pictures of the far side of the Moon. White Sox fans had their own concerns. Oddsmakers gave the Sox 11-10 odds to win Game 6, but favored the Dodgers to win the Series, 13-5.

The towering question: Why hasn't Pierce started? "You'll have to ask Al," replied Pierce when questioned. Billy acknowledged that Wynn and Shaw had excellent years, while he had a poor season. He also pointed out that starting a left-hander in the Coliseum, with the short left-field line, would have been a mistake. Pierce still hoped for a Game Seven start, but he would have to wait and see how Early Wynn did in Game Six. The Dodgers sent Johnny Podres to the mound again.

The game started off sunny and bright, with another capacity crowd in the stands. In the third inning, with two out and Wally Moon on base, Duke Snider drove the ball 400 feet to the lower left field stands to put the Dodgers up 2-0. The wheels came off the bus in the fourth inning. Larker singled, and pinch-runner Demeter scored two batters later on Wills's single. Podres doubled to score Wills, and Dick Donovan replaced Wynn. Donovan faced three batters with disastrous results: a walk to Gilliam, a two-run double by Neal and a two-run homer by Wally Moon.

The 1959 World Series

As John Drebinger wrote, "Even the sun went into hiding again."[22]

The Sox got a few back in their half of the inning. Podres hit Landis in the head with a pitch with one out and walked Lollar. He found the strike zone for Kluszewski, who smacked his third home run of the Series. When Podres walked Smith, Alston decided to take no more chances. Enter Larry Sherry, for his fourth Series appearance. Sherry yielded a single to Phillips and walked pinch-hitter Earl Torgeson to load the bases with two out, but got Aparicio to pop out to end the inning. From then on, Sherry was virtually unhittable. Fox doubled in the fifth inning but advanced no further.

By the time Chuck Essegian hit a solo home run in the top of the ninth to put the score at 9-3 Dodgers, a light rain was falling. After Sherry retired the side in the bottom half of the inning, though, the sun emerged again in time to illuminate the Dodgers victory celebration. "It was neat stage direction," wrote Arthur Daley, "almost as if the far-thinking and dramatic-minded Bill Veeck had so ordered it…"[23]

"We hurt ourselves mainly because we didn't hit with men on the bases in the games at Los Angeles," said Lopez after the game. "That hurt us, and our defense was bad in the games there, too."[24]

Meanwhile, Larry Sherry found himself in a world he had never imagined. "I get called to go on 'The Ed Sullivan Show' the following Sunday," the World Series MVP recalled later. "I had to go out and buy a suit. I didn't own one."[25]

Game 6 Notes[26]

LA N 0 0 2 6 0 0 0 0 1 - 9 13 1
CHI A 0 0 0 3 0 0 0 0 0 - 3 6 1

WP: Sherry (2–0) LP: Wynn (1–1)
LOB: Los Angeles 7, Chicago 7. 2B: Podres, Fox, Kluszewski. HR: Snider, Moon, Essegian, Kluszewski. SH: Roseboro. HBP: Landis, by Podres. CS: Demeter. DP: Los Angeles 1. E: Aparicio.
Umpires: HP Dascoli, 1B Hurley, 2B Secory, 3B Summers, LF Rice, RF Dixon
Time of Game: 2:33
Attendance: 47,653
Receipts: $324,463.32

Notes

1. Game stories from *New York Times*, October 1-7, 1959. Bingham, Walter. "Who to Watch and What to Watch For". *Sports Illustrated*, September 28, 1959, 27-28
2. "Nice Guy in First." *Sports Illustrated*, September 28, 1959, 37-38
3. "World Series Critique." *Sports Illustrated*, September 28, 1959, 29-30
4. Goldstein, Richard. "Larry Sherry, 71, M.V.P. of 1959 World Series, Is Dead." *New York Times*, December 20, 2006
5. *Retrosheet* (https://www.retrosheet.org/boxesetc/1959/B09290LAN1959.htm)
6. "Stengelese to Get Innings as Live Language", *New York Times*, October 2, 1959, 32
7. "World Series for VVVVIPs." *Sports Illustrated*, September 28, 1959, 37
8. Daley, Arthur. "Sports of the Times: Fast on the Draw." *New York Times*, October 2, 1959, 32
9. *Retrosheet* (https://www.retrosheet.org/boxesetc/1959/B10010CHA1959.htm)
10. John Drebinger, "White Sox' Donovan to Face Dodgers' Drysdale in 3rd Game," *New York Times*, October 4, 1959, S2
11. Arthur Daley, "Sport of the Times: Reversion to Type," *New York Times*, October 3, 1959, 10
12. *Retrosheet* (https://www.retrosheet.org/boxesetc/1959/B10020CHA1959.htm)
13. *New York Times*, October 6, 1959, 35
14. Bill Becker, "Bad Hop Good for Furillo," *New York Times*, October 5, 1959, 38
15. *Retrosheet* (https://www.retrosheet.org/boxesetc/1959/B10040LAN1959.htm)
16. Bill Becker, "Triumph is Taken in Stride by Team," *New York Times*, October 6, 1959; 47.
17. "After First Strike, Hodges Just Hoped for Hit," *New York Times*, October 6, 1959; 46.
18. Athur Daley, "A Game Called Screeno," *New York Times*, October 6, 1959: 47.
19. *Retrosheet* (https://www.retrosheet.org/boxesetc/1959/B10050LAN1959.htm)
20. *New York Times*, October 7, 1959, 53
21. *Retrosheet* (https://www.retrosheet.org/boxesetc/1959/B10060LAN1959.htm)
22. John Drebinger, "Dodgers Win World Series by Beating White Sox, 9 to 3, in the Sixth Contest," *New York Times*, October 9, 1959; 33
23. Athur Daley, "Sport of the Times: Champions of the World," *New York Times*, October 9, 1959; 33
24. Louis Effrat, "Nearly Every Dodger Has a Theory to Explain Triumph," *New York Times*, October 9, 1959; 34
25. Goldstein
26. *Retrosheet* (https://www.retrosheet.org/boxesetc/1959/B10080CHA1959.htm)

The '59 White Sox in Literature: Haunted by Ghosts of the Black Sox

By Bill Savage

As a franchise, the Chicago White Sox have had a colorful history. With all the organization has endured over the years, some may consider them the most literary of professional baseball teams. Great 20th century writers such as James T. Farrell and Nelson Algren were raised Sox fans on Chicago's South Side, and when writing about the game of baseball, they focused on their childhood heroes. Contemporary Chicago writers including Stuart Dybek and Tony Fitzpatrick also depict the White Sox in their fiction and poetry. But this sunny loyalty has an inevitable shadow: the Black Sox of 1919. Just as any depiction of the New York Yankees evokes the spirits of Babe Ruth and Lou Gehrig, any mention of the White Sox calls forth the troubled ghosts of Shoeless Joe Jackson and Eddie Cicotte.

For baseball fans, as William Faulkner said in a different context, "The past isn't dead. It isn't even past," and no other event in baseball history has generated as many historical investigations and literary representations as the Big Fix and the Black Sox Scandal. Writers and film-makers like Eliot Asinof, John Sayles, W. P. Kinsella, and Phil Alden Robinson have ensured that the Black Sox remain part of the contemporary American baseball narrative, with books and films including *Eight Men Out*, *Shoeless Joe*, and *Field of Dreams* introducing new generations to the story.

Therefore, when the White Sox of 1959 went to the World Series against the Los Angeles Dodgers, it was more than just the second time in a decade that Al Lopez had figured out how to wrest the American League pennant out of the Yankees' grasp. Chicago's first fall classic in 14 years (since Charlie Grimm's '45 Cubs) was haunted by the ghosts of that 1919 team, 40 years gone. After the Sox' pennant-clinching victory in Cleveland, an anonymous scribe in the *Chicago Sun-Times* led his story with the Black Sox:

Forty years of frustration, dating back to the Black Sox scandal, has ended with the White Sox winning the American League pennant. From the time the late Commissioner Kenesaw Mountain Landis banished eight Sox players from baseball for allegedly throwing the 1919 World Series to Cincinnati, the White Sox have struggled through three generations to field another winner.[1]

A few days later, writing about the media coverage of the event, Wilson Fletcher informed his readers in the same paper that two of the men who would be overseeing the Western Union wire services from the series had "worked the keys" as telegraph operators during the 1919 Series. A more physical connection was made as the ceremonial first pitch of Game One was thrown by Red Faber to Ray Schalk, each of whom had played on both the 1917 White Sox World Series championship team, and were among the "Clean Sox" of 1919.[2]

However, as much as baseball tried to clean up its act, the dark side of the game remained. For example, even though Arnold Rothstein was long dead, gambling remained a part of American sporting culture and baseball was still America's premier sport. Chicago reporter Art Petacque kept *Sun-Times* readers up to date with the odds that bookies – both the local mobsters and those from the Chicago Outfit's farm team in Las Vegas – were giving on the '59 Sox.

> Chicago's bookmakers, a notoriously unsentimental fraternity, have picked the White Sox to win the World Series. On the eve of the opening game, the books were laying 6-5 odds that the Sox would win not only the first game but the world championship as well.[3]

The '59 White Sox in Literature: Haunted by Ghosts of the Black Sox

Petacque also reported that scalpers were unhappy with Sox owner Bill Veeck's decision to sell Series tickets by mail order only, preventing them from scooping up large blocks of tickets. "We've waited 40 years for an opportunity like this, and then Veeck had to do this to us," one complained. A Chicago police commander, part of whose job was running scalpers off, told reporter Jack McPhaul, "In 1919 when the Sox last won a pennant, he played hooky from school, got to the bleachers at dawn, and saw the game."[4] And Andy Frain, the legendary usher, had sold seat cushions in 1919, though in 1959 he was mostly worried about keeping people without tickets from getting into the stadium. In another un-bylined article, he listed the strategies his men guarded against. The article ends with a reference to the decades since the Black Sox: "Frain was worried," he said, "that Chicagoans may have dreamed up some gate-crashing techniques unknown even to him. After all, they've had 40 years to think about it."[5]

Chicago writer Nelson Algren had thought about the Black Sox a lot for those 40 years. In his 1951 prose poem, *Chicago: City on the Make*, he recounts the effect of the scandal on his childhood. He was 11 years old when the scandal broke, newly moved from the Far South Side, across the great divide in Chicago identity from White Sox country to "North Troy Street [which] led, like all North side streets – and alleys too – directly to the alien bleachers of Wrigley Field."[6] Algren was a regular book reviewer for the *Sun-Times* and he wrote three stories about the Series, after the first, second and sixth games: "Nelson Algren Writes Impressions of Series," "Algren Writes of Roses and Hits," and "Nelson Algren's Reflections: Hep-Ghosts of the Rain." Throughout these stories, and in their later more literary iteration, Algren returns to the Black Sox to contextualize and understand the events of the '59 Series, both the positive and the negative.

Algren began his first piece with memories of his childhood, when he sneaked into a Sox game, thus acquiring the appropriate nickname – Swede – from the other baseball-crazed boys of the neighborhood. By 1959, he still felt like that child who rooted for Swede Risberg, ignorant of the player's perfidy, yet somehow guilty by association. He wrote, "I had come to the park assuming there would be a roped-off area for Black Sox fans paroled for the series, and really began to enjoy being there right in the middle of the first class citizens." But these first-class citizens, Algren suggests, might not be the best of baseball fans, as he mocks fans ignorant of the game. "One woman asked her husband what the score was and he told her '11 to nothing in the fourth, dear,' he says. I actually heard her ask, 'Does that mean it will be 22 to nothing in the eighth?'" He concludes with a slight jab at Bill Veeck, famous for trying to pack his ballparks: "I left after the Dodger half of the seventh and the attendance hadn't been announced; so I assume they were still selling tickets."[7]

In his second story, the Black Sox played a lesser role. After the Sox routed the Dodgers in the first game, Algren and many other Sox fans thought the series was a lock, and he opened by joking that "the Dodgers might return to Los Angeles, or Brooklyn, or wherever they come from, without playing it out."[8] Shoeless Joe makes a brief appearance, along with Eddie Gaedel, as Algren tells tall tales to distract a female fan from the Dodgers' 4-3 victory. The sense of wistful melancholy from the first story evaporates.

After the Series is over, however, Algren returns to the Black Sox. His own sense of a past began, he writes, when "on the last afternoon of summer I saw Shoeless Joe Jackson leave his glove in left field, walk toward the darkening stands and never come back for his glove."[9] Algren's reflections on the series conclude with an evocation of the ghosts of Chicago's hustlers, haunting the poolrooms and El trains:

> I have seen the ghosts of the blue-moon hustlers leaping drunk below the all-night billboard lights.
>
> Yesterday evening, when the crowd was gone and I stood up at last to leave, I saw the shade of Shoeless Joe.
>
> He was walking toward the darkening stands, and he'd left his glove behind.[10]

For Algren the sadness of a World Series defeat was best expressed by connecting back to the sorrow of not just the defeat, but the betrayal, of 1919. The tragic past isn't dead; it isn't even past.

Yet in his prose and poetry about the Black Sox, Algren may perhaps have begun the rehabilitation of Shoeless Joe Jackson, from criminal to redemptive hero in *Field of Dreams*. Another writer, Daniel Nathan, has written about the transformation of depiction of the Black Sox players from criminals or traitors to tragic victims of greedy gamblers and venal ownership in *Saying It's So: A Cultural History of the Black*

Sox Scandal. Algren was perhaps the first major writer to engage in this shift when he wrote in *Chicago: City on the Make* about his childhood defense of Shoeless Joe: "Out of the welter of accusations, half denials and sudden silences a single fact drifted down: that Shoeless Joe Jackson couldn't play bad baseball even if he were trying to. He hit .375 in that series and played errorless ball, doing everything a major-leaguer could to win."[11] His newspaper stories on the '59 Sox continued to depict the Black Sox as tragic victims rather than criminals.

As a writer, Algren's method always involved reworking old materials. He combined his '59 Series pieces, and revised them into "Go! Go! Forty Years Gone," published in *The Last Carousel*, his 1973 collection of fiction, journalism, and poetry (including "Ballet for Opening Day: Or, the Swede Was a Hard Guy," his retelling of the Black Sox story.) In this revision Algren edits to somewhat de-emphasize the story of being at the game, and to increase the sense of nostalgia and melancholy associated with having been a White Sox fan at a time of scandal leading to a sense of betrayal, a sense of possibilities forever forgone. He depicts the '59 White Sox team almost entirely through the lens of the Black Sox.

Had the '59 Sox beaten the Dodgers, perhaps the Black Sox would have faded further into the past. But instead of erasing 1919, the 1959 season echoed it: another loss, bitter in the mouths of South Siders and Chicago writers. Not a thrown Series, but not a triumph to erase that still-fresh and endlessly rehashed ignominy either.

Finally, in 2005, White Sox manager Ozzie Guillen would follow in the footsteps of Lopez, and then take one step further. Winning the 2005 World Series, the White Sox added another chapter to the long narrative of White Sox and Chicago baseball. However, in all the press coverage of that magical season, local and national media could not help but refer to the Black Sox, nodding only in passing to the '59 squad. Hopefully, with this book, the 1959 team can take its rightful place in the history of this storied franchise.

Sources

Algren, Nelson. *Chicago: City on the Make* (Chicago: University of Chicago Press, 2001). Newly Annotated, Schmittgens and Savage, editors.

——. "Go-Go Forty Years Ago," *The Last Carousel* (New York: Putnam's, 1973).

——. "Ballet for Opening Day: Or, The Swede Was a Hard Guy," *The Last Carousel*. New York: Putnam's, 1973.

Anonymous. "'We'll Win in 4 Games,' Beams Daley," *Chicago Sun-Times*, October 1, 1959.

McPhaul, Jack. "Sox Fans See–And They Believe," *Chicago Sun-Times*. October 2, 1959.

Nathan, Daniel. *Saying It's So: A Cultural History of the Black Sox Scandal* (Chicago: University of Illinois Press, 2003).

Notes

1 "Sox Victory Ends 40-Year Famine," *Chicago Sun-Times*, September 23, 1959.
2 Fletcher Wilson, "600 Writers Here to Cover Classic," *Chicago Sun-Times*, October 1, 1959.
3 Art Petacque, "Who'll Win? Sox, by All Odds," *Chicago Sun-Times*, October 1, 1959.
4 Petacque.
5 "They Shall Not Pass! Frain Stands Guard at the Gates," *Chicago Sun-Times*, October 2, 1959.
6 Nelson Algren, "The Silver-Colored Yesterday," from Charles Einstein, ed. *The Fireside Book of Baseball*, edited by Charles Einstein (New York: Simon and Schuster, 1956), 3.
7 Nelson Algren, "Nelson Algren writes Impressions of Series," *Chicago Sun-Times*, October 2, 1959.
8 Nelson Algren, "Algren Writes of Roses and Hits," *Chicago Sun-Times*, October 3, 1959.
9 Nelson Algren, "Nelson Algren's Reflections: Hep-Ghosts of the Rain," *Chicago Sun-Times*, October 10, 1959
10 Algren, "Nelson Algren's Reflections."
11 Algren, "The Silver-Colored Yesterday," 4.

Recalling 1959: Sox Fans Remember

By Pam Schur

In 1959, I was 27 years old, working for Zimmer, Bergman & Freeman, CPA's as an accountant. I just passed the CPA exam in May, 1959 and I was going to Northwestern University in Chicago at night. My wife was pregnant with our first child, and we were living in Chicago. In that year it wasn't obvious that the Sox were even going to win. I remember when Bill Veeck bought the team, he promised to bring a championship to Chicago the following year. That wasn't good enough for me. I wanted a championship this year, not next year. It looks like I prevailed!

We used to sit in the grandstands, generally in section 20 near the first base dugout. From this angle we got a better view of the Sox dugout. The night they clinched the pennant I was at school. I would run down to the parking lot between classes and turn on the radio for the score. I finished class that night before the game ended. I remember driving home on Lake Shore Dr. when Bob Elson reported "a ground ball to [Luis] Aparicio, he steps on second for one out, and throws to [Ted] Kluszewski at first for the game-ending double play." He screamed, and I screamed and I almost went off the road. I didn't need a car to drive the rest of the way – I was flying. Mayor [Richard J.] Daley joined in and turned on the air raid sirens. The city almost panicked. That was the first time Bob Elson ever showed any emotion. The Sox won that game 4 to 2, and ironically it was a ball hit over Minnie Minoso's head for a home run that won it. Minnie was traded to Cleveland from the Sox earlier in the year. My favorite player was Nellie Fox. Nellie was definitely a self-taught ballplayer. Jungle Jim Rivera was also among my favorites. He probably added more color than quality, but he was ours.

The World Series was a different story. I was truly elated over winning the American League pennant. To me that was the prize. The World Series was just the frosting – and not really the cake. Although after the first game I might have thought different. We scored 11 runs and beat the Los Angeles Dodgers I think 11-0. They wore their old style uniforms with their pure-white sox. Kluszewski drove in five runs in that game. The Sox ended up losing the series four games to two. My brother-in-law promised to get us tickets but he never delivered so we saw the series on TV or listened to it on the radio. It didn't matter. We won the pennant that year. It was an amazing year - 1959. Our first child was born – I passed the CPA exam – THE WHITE SOX WON THE PENNANT. That season: delightful.

- Manny Lubelfeld, Buffalo Grove, IL

I was 23 years old when the White Sox won the 1959 pennant. My wife, Marilyn, and I were living in an apartment building in Rogers Park. I was working for our family business as a salesman in 1959. I really don't remember how or why I became a Sox fan, I think it may have been something I read in the paper when I was six or seven years old. My father had no interest in baseball and I do not think any of my family had strong feelings. I think I attended only one game that season and I drove to the game. We missed a triple play because we were late. On the night the Sox won the pennant, I was home watching the game. Shortly after Early Wynn won the game, the air raid sirens went off; I was very excited. After the big win in the first game of the Series I thought the Sox would take it all. The result: a disappointment.

– Burt Leader, Chicago.

I lived in South Shore with my family in 1959. I was 13 years old and was attending St. Philip Neri grammar school at the time. The school was on the South Side, and also located in South Shore (about 7200 south). We lived in the heart of White Sox country. Everyone was a Sox fan. I did not know one single Cub fan! Unfortunately, I never was able to go to any games that year. The night the Sox won the pennant, I was at home and my dad heard it on the radio. I don't know if the game was televised, but I know the Sox beat Cleveland to clinch. The game I remember most was the first game of the World Series; the Sox won 11-0. My favorite White Sox players were Luis Aparicio, Nellie Fox, [Jim] Landis, "Big Klu" (Kluszewki), and

Go-Go to Glory

Billy Pierce. I remember the Sox usually didn't score many runs (they were known as "hitless wonders") but they had a great defense and good pitching. We were excited that the nuns let us watch the World Series on TV in school; that was unheard of before. It was a big disappointment when LA won the Series in six games. The season: historic!

– Bill Burke, Chicago

Growing up, I was raised as a Cubs fan. But when I met my husband, I had to convert. I was 19 years old and have been a White Sox fan ever since. We used to go to most night games and a few weekend afternoon games. We sat in the lower grandstands along the first base side. I've always loved the friendliness and enthusiasm of the fans. I was home waiting for my husband to come home from school when the Sox clinched. My best friend, Sema, was at our house and we were watching the Sox play Cleveland; Luis Aparicio stepped on second base, threw to first and the double play ended the game. I was pregnant with my oldest child, and started screaming and jumping up and down. My girlfriend told me to stop – she didn't understand how exciting that was! Mayor Daley had sirens going on in the city and it was just great. My favorite players were Luis Aparicio, Nellie Fox, Billy Pierce, Ted Kluszewski, and Sherman Lollar. I loved watching all the games on TV, but really liked Bob Elson the best as the radio announcer; he was the voice of the Sox. The season: fantastic and exciting!

– Reva Lubelfeld, Buffalo Grove, IL.

In 1959, I was 29 years old, living in Skokie, and an accountant (CPA) working for Alexander Grant & Co. (now known as Grant Thornton). I was born and raised on the North Side of Chicago and went to LeMoyne school which was two blocks from Wrigley Field. I went to many Cub games with my dad as a child, with friends or on Sunday school outings. But after the 1945 World Series, the Cubs were habitual losers, having some of the worst players imaginable – Roy Smalley, Lenny Merullo, etc. And when they traded Lou Brock to the Cardinals, who was one of the best Cubs of all time, I gave up on them. At about the same time I had an Army buddy who was a South Sider and Sox fan, and he and I went to then Comiskey Park for some games. I fell for them and the rest is history. I've been a Sox fan ever since. My family is really a house divided. My wife is an ardent Cubs fan and so are my daughter and oldest grandson. I was able to get through to my son to become a Sox fan and his wife and kids are also fans.

In fact, at one of my grandson's Bar Mitzvahs, he thanked me for making him a Sox fan! A summer highlight of the Price family is for me to accompany my son, Neal, and his two sons – AJ and Jake – to a Sox game where we usually have awesome seats. I don't remember how many games I attended during the '59 season. I do know it wasn't many. A most memorable game, just before the Sox clinched the pennant, was watching Early Wynn pitch a 10-inning game in which the Sox won, 1-0. In those days it was not unusual for a pitcher to go the whole game. I heard they clinched on the radio. It was so exciting! My favorite players included Jim Rivera, Minnie Minoso, Nellie Fox, Chico Carrasquel, Early Wynn, and the great pitcher Billy Pierce. I loved listening to the games on the radio; on the days after they lost, I would not read the Sports section of the newspaper. I remember I was fortunate to see the game where the Sox blew out the Dodgers, 11-0. Ted Kluszewski, a late trade from Cincinnati, hit two home runs that day. I got the tickets in an interesting manner: a woman with whom I worked at AG had a husband who was a high official with the City and he knew I loved the Sox. She asked if I wanted to go to a game and that we would go to Comiskey Park to get the tickets. He found a scalper on the street (which was illegal) and took the tickets from him (we did pay him the face value of the tickets). Unfortunately I was unable to see the 2005 World Series. The season: A great ride.

– Selwin Price, Chicago.

Selwyn Price

• Recalling 1959: Sox Fans Remember •

In 1959, I was 34 years old, living in Skokie, and was practicing dentistry. I went to the game with one of my sons who was seven years old. I was never really a Sox fan. When I was young, my foreign-born mother used to take me to see the Cubs on Ladies Day, we both became Cubs fans that way. I did eventually become a Sox fan and my favorite players were Nellie Fox, Sherm Lollar, and Ted Kluszewki. I don't remember where I was when the Sox clinched the pennant but I was at the game when a fan accidentally spilled his beer on Al Smith's head in front of the bleachers! The season: exiting and amazing. – Earl Kuznetsky, Chicago.*** In 1959, my wife and I lived at 2145 E. 97th in Chicago. My father owned a furniture store in those days and I worked for him. Living on the South Side of Chicago, I automatically became a Sox fan. My family wasn't interested but I listened to the games on the radio. I personally do not remember if I went to the ball park. A friend of mine remembers listening to the game between the Sox and Cleveland when the Sox beat the Indians to clinch the American League title. My favorite players at the time were Nellie Fox, Luis Aparicio, Ted Kluszewski, and Early Wynn with Al Lopez as manager. The Sox lost the Series 4-2 but Big Klu hit two homers in Game One and Dick Donovan pitched a 1-0 shutout in Game Five. Dodger reliever Larry Sherry appeared in almost every game and shut down the White Sox. If not for his performance, the Sox could have won. The announcers were excellent.

– Les Klein, Chicago.

In 1959, I was eight years old, lived in South Shore on the South Side of Chicago and went to Horace Mann Elementary School. Being South Siders, there were a lot of Sox fans. My dad knew the White Sox equipment manager so we used to get good tickets and go to games often. I also went a couple of times every summer with my day camp. During the summer of '59, I don't remember how many times I went to games that summer but my guess is 8-10 games and we mostly sat in the grandstands. My whole family went to night games. I don't remember my mother or sister being big baseball fans. But my dad and I used to go to day games together. That's why it was so upsetting when he didn't take me to the World Series game. Instead, my father took the son of a friend of his. Needless to say, I was very disappointed. I remember the park being a fun place to go and I can actually still remember what it felt like being there.

The night the Sox clinched the pennant, I was sitting in my living room. I know my dad was there but not sure about the rest of the family. The game was probably on the radio rather than TV but I just don't recall. I do remember the city sirens going off. We figured out pretty quickly what it was for. My favorite players were Luis Aparicio and Nellie Fox. I remember for sure that a picture of them was on *Sports Illustrated* and the "Go" in "Chicago" was circled on their uniforms. My dad always had the games on when we were driving and I remember boys carrying transistor radios to school when the World Series was on. As for the actual World Series games, I don't remember anything more than the Sox losing and I didn't get to go to a game. It was not the outcome I hoped for. The season: I can't decide between "the best" or "life-changing." Many seasons have gone by in my life and I've watched both the Cubs and Sox get close on occasion and even the Sox winning the World Series. Nothing compares to the excitement of that season and the vivid memories. Yet 1959 was the year I realized that being a girl was a distinct disadvantage and it set me on a path of advocating for women's rights.

– Arlene Mayzel, Deerfield, IL.

In 1959 when the Sox won the American League pennant, I was 37 years old and living in Chicago's Southwest Side. I was working in the furniture business and spent more than 40 years being a manufacturing representative. I became a Sox fan when I was five or six years old. I loved the game of baseball and my next door neighbors (who had nine children) had a significant influence on me to become a loyal Sox fan. Watching the Sox play in the 1959 season was a wonderful experience. I had two season tickets behind third base. This is where the player's wives had their seats. That season I must have seen 60 or 70 games and we always drove to the park. I loved being out in the fresh air and sunshine with the rest of the Sox fans and enjoyed watching the Sox play ball. The most enjoyable memory of that season for me was driving to Cleveland to watch the Sox clinch the pennant on Sunday. I can still see the ball that Vic Power hit into a game-ending double play: Luis Aparicio Nellie Fox to [Earl] Torgeson – that was GREAT! My favorite player was Luis Aparicio for his fielding and base stealing, and his overall baseball instincts. He was the glue that held the team together. I don't believe I had a TV at the time so we always listened to the games on the radio with announcer Bob Elson. I was very disappointed when the Sox lost the World Series to the Los Angeles Dodgers, but Larry Sherry was outstanding for his relief work in the series. The season: Fantastic.

– Frank T. Loftus, Palos Heights, IL

In 1959, I was 10 years old, living in West Rogers Park and attending Boone School in Chicago. Growing up my dad was both a Cubs and Sox fan; the rest of my family was indifferent. My dad and I used to go to Sox games and take the train and sit in the cheap seats. The part I liked best was being with my dad and learning the nuances of the game. The night the Sox clinched, I was at home with my parents, watching the game on our black and white TV set. I recall my mom was actually excited! I was apoplectic with joy. My favorite players were Billy Pierce and Luis Aparicio. Most of the time I would listen to the games on a transistor radio walking down the street using a single earplug mimicking my dad. I thought Bob Elson was OK but my dad loathed the TV broadcaster Jack Brickhouse, so of course I did too. When they were in the World Series, I recall a great graphic in the Chicago paper with a cartoon figure walking along a path with a bunch of markers designating years. The copy in large bold print was "Life begins at 40." Of course the Sox had last been in the Series in 1919. I was very sad about being beaten easily in the series. But I was fascinated by Sandy Koufax. The season: Hypnotic.

– Jeff Urdangen, Evanston, IL

In 1959, I was 12 going on 13. I went to school at St. Mark's, which was staffed by Sinsinawa Dominicans. In September I began eighth grade, which was always taught by the principal. We had a new one that year, Sr. Marie Donald (Hogan), who was Chicago South Side Irish (the significance of which I did not fully realize) and an avid Sox fan. We did not need to worry about whether we would get to watch the World Series. Sr. Marie Donald died just a few months ago, at the Sinsinawa Mound, where my wife and I saw her once or twice a year for the last ten years or so. She very much enjoyed the 2005 season. My dad was a lifelong Cubs fan and took me to some Cubs games. But I found the Cubs really boring. I had an early infatuation with the Yankees, like many boys, but came to love the White Sox, whose brand of baseball seemed far more exciting than the Cubs. We came to Chicago for one game each year and my dad, to his everlasting credit, made that a double-header with the Yankees most of the time, after my allegiance became clear. Due to my mom's illness (cancer) which is the underlying theme of my song, "1959," we did not do a ball game that summer. But I have a clear memory, probably from the previous year, of sitting very near Minnie Minoso, one of my favorite players, who was playing left field. It was a shame Minnie was not around in '59 to enjoy it. Nellie Fox was my favorite but I also loved Luis Aparicio and Billy Pierce. My recollections about the World Series include Sr. Marie Donald letting us watch the games in class; Ted Kluszewski's home run; and the fact Lopez did not pitch Pierce. The season: Lifegiving.

– Jim Croegaert, Chicago

• Recalling 1959: Sox Fans Remember •

1959
Words & Music Jim Croegaert

I remember sleeping on the porch
With my transistor radio
Listening to Bob Elson's voice
Seems like a long time ago
I lay there in my sleeping bag
On that hard wooden floor
While in the background the locusts sang
Sometimes I'd fall asleep before
The game was over

In my mind's eye I could follow
Jim Landis running down a ball
Or Luis stealing second base
I helped the umpire make the call
But something lurked outside the ballpark
Outside the screened-in porch where I lay
I couldn't see it but I could feel it
Sometimes I thought I heard someone say
The game was over

But I found refuge on that diamond
And I hung on every score
The year the White Sox won the pennant
The year my mother lost the war

The close games they were many
One-to-nothing, two-to-one
I couldn't count the big hits by Nellie Fox
He was my favorite oneBut as the summer turned to September
And the Sox bore down for the stretch run
The murmur grew into a tremor
That shook the earth and hid the sun
The game was over

The Sox wrapped it up against Cleveland
And in Chicago the sirens rang
I went looking for something to believe in
And I never did go back again
But I've never seen a team quite like that one
Back in 1959
Every time they hit the field they were battlin'
And they kept on playing past the time
The game was over

But I found refuge on that diamond
And I hung on every score
The year the White Sox won the pennant
The year my mother lost the war

Copyright 1991, Rough Stones Music, 827 Monroe St., Evanston IL 60202. All rights reserved. Used by permission.

Go-Going-Gone:
Bill Veeck's Trades and Their Consequences

By Don Zminda

No book about the 1959 White Sox would be complete without a discussion of what happened *after* the season – in particular, four trades engineered by team president Bill Veeck and general manager Hank Greenberg in an effort to repeat as American League champions in 1960. Each deal featured the same theme: trading young but mostly unproven talent for experienced veterans who were more likely to have an immediate impact. Here are the details of the four trades, along with the ages of the players on Opening Day 1960 (for Minnie Minoso, I am using his current listed date of birth, which is three years younger than his listed DOB during his playing days):

Bill Veeck's 1959-60 Trades
(Player ages as of Opening Day 1960)

December 6, 1959: White Sox trade catcher John Romano (25), third baseman Bubba Phillips (32), and first baseman Norm Cash (25) to the Indians for outfielder Minnie Minoso (34), catcher Dick Brown (25), and pitchers Don Ferrarese (30) and Jake Striker (26).

December 9, 1959: White Sox trade outfielder Johnny Callison (21) to the Phillies for third baseman Gene Freese (26).

April 4, 1960: White Sox trade catcher Earl Battey (25), first baseman Don Mincher (21), and $150,000 to the Senators for first baseman Roy Sievers (33).

April 18, 1960: White Sox trade pitcher Barry Latman (23) to the Indians for pitcher Herb Score (26).

In an article about the four trades in his book *Rob Neyer's Big Book of Baseball Blunders*, the author pulls no punches: "All four trades were absolute disasters," wrote Neyer. Hardly any veteran White Sox fan would disagree. A summary of the aftermath of the four trades:

Brown, Ferrarese and Striker hardly played for the White Sox, but Minnie Minoso gave the White Sox two good years in his return to the team and the town that loved him (.311-20-105 in 1960; .280-14-82 in 1961). As for the men the Sox dealt away, Norm Cash hit 373 home runs after leaving the White Sox (all for the Tigers, who acquired him from Cleveland prior to the start of the 1960 season), with a batting title and four appearances on the AL All-Star team; John Romano became a two-time All-Star catcher for the Indians; and even Bubba Phillips had a couple of serviceable years for the Tribe.

Roy Sievers gave the White Sox two almost identically good seasons (.295-28-93 in 1960; .295-27-92 in 1961). However, Earl Battey became a four-time All-Star and three-time Gold Glove winner for the Senators/Twins; Don Mincher hit 200 home runs, made two All-Star teams and played on two American League pennant-winners (the 1965 Twins and the 1972 Athletics).

Gene Freese had one 17-home-run season for the White Sox before being dealt away. The man he was traded for, Johnny Callison, became a three-time All-Star for the Phillies, was runner-up in the 1964 National League MVP voting and hit 222 home runs after leaving the White Sox.

Herb Score went 6-12 in three seasons with the White Sox; Barry Latman won 47 games after the trade (though with 61 losses) and – of course! – made an All-Star team, in 1961.

The bottom line: the White Sox didn't come close to a pennant in the first few years after the trades, finishing third in 1960, fourth in 1961, and fifth in 1962.

• Go-Going-Gone: Bill Veeck's Trades and Their Consequences •

Ouch! As Bob Vanderberg wrote in his 1982 book *Sox: From Lane and Fain to Zisk and Fisk*, "Many South Side fans have yet to forgive Veeck for mortgaging their future."

In fairness to Bill Veeck, this is looking at the trades from years of hindsight, and in the spring of 1960, a lot of people thought the White Sox had just wrapped up another pennant. Writing in the season-opening issue of *The Sporting News* in April of 1960, Chicago sportswriter Jerry Holtzman (he didn't become known as Jerome until several years later) predicted "a pennant again, possibly breezing." And in the annual poll of baseball writers in the same edition of *The Sporting News*, the Sox were the consensus choice to win the American League pennant, gathering nearly twice as many first-place votes (120) as the Indians (70), who finished second in the balloting.

Even then, though, many people in Chicago were nervous about the trades. When the trades for Minoso and Freese were announced, Holtzman wrote, "The criticism lashed at Veeck and Vice Presidents Chuck Comiskey and Hank Greenberg (who were with him at the winter meetings where both trades were consummated) was that the deals simply were designed for short-term results. There just wasn't enough thought given to the future, the next two or three years, when surely the Sox will need front-line replacements." Prophetic words there.

The reaction to the trade for Sievers the following April was a lot more positive, with Holtzman writing, "The trade was a master stroke for the Sox. ... the Hitless Wonders tag is a thing of the past." However, Holtzman wrote in the same article that the deal had taken a little time to consummate because the Senators wanted light-hitting utilityman Sammy Esposito, who had batted .167 for the '59 pennant winners, as part of the deal instead of Mincher. According to Holtzman, "[Manager Al] Lopez refused. He said he would part with Battey, but that he wouldn't part with Esposito." So to review Veeck and Lopez's winter and spring, their stance toward the club's young talent was:

Sure, Callison's a hot prospect, but that Freese is so Tastee!

Norman Cash? Gone in a dash

Catchers, who needs catchers? Battey and Romano, away they go!

Don Mincha, we'll never miss ya

Barry Latman, Larry Batman, whatever your name is – you're history

But *Sammy Esposito* ... that's where we draw the line!

No wonder the South Side had trouble forgiving Veeck.

So can anyone defend old Will? It's difficult, but let's try to mount at least a semblance of justification for these deals:

Minoso, Freese, and Sievers *did* help improve the Sox offense in 1960, and not just a little. The club, which had scored 669 runs and hit 97 home runs in 1959, scored 741 runs with 112 homers in 1960. The failure to repeat was much more the fault of the pitching staff, as the team ERA rose from 3.29 to 3.60 and no Sox pitcher won more than 14 games.

Veeck may have felt that the Sox had a lot of good fortune in winning the 1959 pennant, and that they were unlikely to repeat without strengthening the roster. That was not an unreasonable position; the Sox outscored their opponents by only 81 runs in 1959, and the pennant was due in good part to their extraordinary success in one-run games (35-15, .700). In 1960 the trades helped the Sox outscore their opponents by 124 runs, but the magic in one-run contests was gone – the club went 22-23 in minimum-margin games.

In the spring of 1960, hardly anyone would have predicted stardom for Norm Cash, who was 25 years and had played very little above the low minors. In fact, the Indians quickly unloaded Cash after acquiring him, trading him to the Tigers for a nobody (Steve Demeter).

Earl Battey had been up with the Sox in for at least part of every season from 1955 through 1959, and hadn't shown much hitting prowess (.209 average in 358 at-bats, though with 13 home runs). He was widely regarded in Chicago as a good defensive catcher but a poor hitter.

Don Mincher had shown power potential in the low minors, but he had yet to play above the Class A Sally League.

Callison, widely considered the star of the group, had lost a bit of his luster by hitting .173 in 104 at-bats for the Sox in '59.

Finally, the Sox *did* receive some more payback out of Freese, Sievers, and Minoso when they dealt them away in three trades that all look pretty astute in retrospect (the first trade was made by Veeck, the latter two by new general manager Ed Short after Veeck sold the team to Arthur Allyn in June of 1961):

White Sox Trades 1961-62
(Players' ages as of Opening Day 1961 or 1962)

December 15, 1960: White Sox trade third baseman Gene Freese (27) to the Reds for pitchers Juan Pizarro (24) and Cal McLish (35).

November 18, 1961: White Sox trade first baseman Roy Sievers (35) to the Phillies for pitcher John Buzhardt (25) and third baseman Charley Smith (24).

November 27, 1961: White Sox trade outfielder Minnie Minoso (36) to the Cardinals for first baseman Joe Cunningham (30).

Gene Freese, the much despise-ed, went to Cincinnati in a deal that brought the Sox left-hander Juan Pizarro, who went 61-38 with a 2.93 ERA from 1961-64 and was a key element in the rebuilding of the club's pitching staff. Similarly, Roy Sievers went to the Phillies in a trade that netted righty John Buzhardt, who was 40-32 with a fine 3.17 ERA from 1962-65. And the Sox traded Minoso, who was reaching the end of the line, to the Cardinals for Joe Cunningham, who had an excellent season for the South Siders in 1962 (.410 OBP) and was having another good year in 1963 (.388 OBP) until he fractured a collarbone. Then in 1964, the Sox dealt Cunningham to the Senators in a trade which netted them useful veteran (and Chicago native) Bill Skowron, a South Side favorite who is still working for the White Sox more than 40 years later.

Even with the caveat that Veeck was gone by the time the Sox dealt away Sievers and Minoso, those three trades make the White Sox look a little better.

But not good enough. Two questions still nag at me:

Why did they get so little for Callison when he was universally regarded as one of the top prospects in baseball? With all due respect for Gene Freese, this looked like a lopsided trade in favor of the Phillies even at the time it was made.

Why trade away *two* power-hitting first-base prospects and *two* good young catchers when the Sox regulars at both positions (Ted Kluszewski and Sherm Lollar) had passed their 35th birthdays?

Like a lot of Sox fans, I still can't get over it.

Contributor Biographies

David W. Anderson (Don Gutteridge) is an admirer of the 1959 White Sox. He went to three games that year and loved Little Looie and Nelson Fox. In 2000 he published *More than Merkle* and has contributed to the SABR *Deadball Stars of the American (and National) League* books, along with submitting articles to *Baseball Research Journal*, presenting at SABR conventions and Seymour Conferences. He lives in Olathe, Kansas. His wife, Judy, teaches in the Olathe Schools. Their three children Karin, Erik, and Julia are succeeding in their chosen careers.

Ron Anderson (Billy Goodman) grew up in the Boston area following their 1950s era major league teams, with loyalty rooted in the cross-town club, the Braves, and then in 1953 morphing allegiance to the vicissitudes of a Red Sox team and its colorful superstar, Ted Williams, upon the Braves departure.) A Purdue University graduate and SABR member since 2005, Ron has been a contributing writer of several SABR biographies and publications, and authored a biography of former Red Sox All-Star first baseman George Scott: *Long Taters: A Baseball Biography of George "Boomer" Scott*, McFarland Publishing, released in the fall of 2011. He lives with his wife, Gail, in Plymouth, Massachusetts.

Mark Armour (Gary Peters and Earl Torgeson) is the author of dozens of articles and six books on baseball. He writes from his home in Corvallis, Oregon.

Anthony Basich (Bubba Phillips) is a lifelong Yankees fan and a resident of New Jersey. He has been a SABR member since 2006 and has been a contributor of book reviews to the Deadball Committee's newsletter, *The Inside Game*. He previously contributed to the BioProject book *Lefty, Double-X, and The Kid*, about the 1939 Boston Red Sox, chronicling the career of infielder Boze Berger.

Ralph Berger (Barry Latman), who passed away in August of 2013, was a writer, poet, teacher, public administrator, an avid baseball historian, and a historian of the World Wars. Ralph was a SABR member since 2000 and contributed dozens of biographies to the SABR BioProject, including stories on Hall of Famers Luke Appling, Lou Boudreau, Jim Bunning, and more.

Robert W. Bigelow (Nellie Fox) Robert W. Bigelow is an attorney and educator practicing law in New York and New Jersey. He has served on the faculty of the School of Business at Capella University since 2004. He contributed to *The Team That Couldn't Hit: The 1972 Texas Rangers (SABR,2019), Deadball Stars of the American League* (Potomac Books, 2006) and SABR's 2004 convention journal *Baseball in the Buckeye State*. Robert lives in New Jersey with his wife Madeline. They have two grown children, Will and Emma.

Ray Birch (Johnny Cooney), a member of SABR since 2000, lives in North Kingstown, RI and is a retired elementary/middle school teacher where he co-taught a class on baseball to students. He has written bios for the 1975 Red Sox book (Rick Burleson), the 1918 Red Sox book (Everett Scott) book, the 1967 Red Sox book (Joe Foy, George Thomas), the 1948 Red Sox and Braves book (Earl Caldwell) and the 1950s Red Sox book (Ike Delock). Ray is a life-long Red Sox fan who attended his first game at Fenway Park in 1961, just missing seeing the great Ted Williams play in person. Ray and his wife recently celebrated the birth of their ninth grandchild, thus covering all positions on the baseball diamond (except DH).

Matthew Bohn (Lou Skizas) is a native of Hemlock, Michigan. A Detroit Tigers fan growing up, he listened to Ernie Harwell and Paul Carey on the radio. Matt currently follows the Tigers and baseball from his home in Milwaukie, Oregon.

Thomas J. Brown Jr. (World Series Game Five game story) is a lifelong Mets fan who became a Durham Bulls fan after moving to North Carolina in the early 1980s. He was a national board-certified high school science teacher for 34 years before retiring in 2016. Tom still volunteers with the ELL students at his former high school, serving as a mentor to ELL students as well as providing support and guidance for former ELL students when they embark on different career paths after graduation. Tom has been a member of SABR since 1995. He has become active in the organization since his retirement and has written numerous biographies and game stories, mostly about the NY Mets.

Warren Corbett (Editorial Assistant, The Beginning) is the author of *The Wizard of Waxahachie: Paul Richards and the End of Baseball as We Knew It* and a past winner of the McFarland-SABR Baseball Research Award. He is a beach bum at Pawleys Island, South Carolina.

Scott Ferkovich (Hank Greenberg, May 1 game story) is the author of *Motor City Champs: Mickey Cochrane and the 1934-1935 Detroit Tigers*. He was the editor of the SABR book, *Tigers by the Tale: Great Games at Michigan and Trumbull*. His work has also appeared in numerous other SABR books.

David Fleitz (Early Wynn), a computer systems analyst and SABR member from Royal Oak, Michigan, has written well-received biographies of Shoeless Joe Jackson, Louis Sockalexis, and Cap Anson, in addition to other works. David is also a baseball trivia expert, having won his third consecutive championship in the individual trivia contest at the annual SABR convention in Cleveland in 2008.

John Gabcik (Bob Elson) was born and raised in Chicago, and has been following the White Sox since 1952. He writes biographies and game stories for SABR, concentrating on under-appreciated White Sox pitchers and other personalities. He also helps Retrosheet develop game play-by-play recreations. He is retired, and lives in Brevard, North Carolina.

Peter Gordon (Ken McBride) is president of the Ernie Banks – Bobby Bragan (Dallas-Fort Worth) SABR Chapter and the co-author of four baseball books, including *The Whiz Kids and the 1950 Pennant* written with his boyhood hero Robin Roberts, and *Lucky Me: My 65 Years in Baseball* authored with Eddie Robinson. He is also co-editor of recent SABR team histories of the 1951 New York Giants and the 1950 Philadelphia Phillies as well as a frequent contributor to the SABR bio project. His real job is as a law professor at SMU where he was dean of the law school for nine years and has served as the university's faculty athletic representative for 32 years.

Mike Hasse (Don Rudolph) studied at the Ross Graduate School of Business at the University of Michigan and is an avid baseball fan. He has attended games at 38 Major League stadiums as well as professional games in Japan and South Korea. He lives in Ann Arbor, Michigan with his wife Amanda.

Jack Herrmann (Earl Battey) is an attorney who lives and works in the Chicago area. He has been a SABR member since the early 1990's. He is originally from Ohio and a life-long Cleveland Indians fan, but has lived in the Chicago area for 30 years. Thus he is married to a Cubs fan and has many friends who are Sox fans, for whom he hopes this book provides some joy.

Paul Hofmann (August 30 game story), a SABR member since 2002, is the Associate Vice President for International Affairs at Sacramento State University and frequent contributor to SABR publications. Paul is a native of Detroit, Michigan and lifelong Detroit Tigers fan. He currently resides in Folsom, California.

Mike Huber (July 25 game story) is a Professor of Mathematics at Muhlenberg College in Allentown, Pennsylvaniia, where he roots for the Lehigh Valley IronPigs. He enjoys contributing to SABR's Games Project and sponsoring undergraduate research in sabermetrics.

William H. (Bill) Johnson (Bo Shaw) and his wife Chris live in central Georgia. Retired from the US Navy, he has written a full-length biography, *Hal Trosky: A Baseball Biography* (McFarland & Co., 2017), along with over two dozen essays for the SABR BioProject, and he is now working on a biography of Negro League star Art "Superman" Pennington.

Maxwell Kates (Norm Cash, Al Lopez) is a chartered accountant who lives and works in Toronto. He has worked in commercial radio and he writes a monthly column for the Houston-based Pecan Park Eagle. He served on the steering committee of Toronto's Hanlan's Point Chapter for twelve years and his speaking credits include the Limmud Conference and the Canadian Baseball History Conference in addition to several SABR conventions and regional meetings. In 2018, he and Bill Nowlin co-edited *Time for Expansion Baseball*. He has attended games in 23 of the 30 current ballparks. This includes Comiskey Park, where he witnessed Frank Thomas hit a home run in 1997 before Blue Jays pitcher Pat Hentgen was serenaded to the showers.

• Contributor Biographies •

Tara Krieger (Assistant Editor) has been an active member of SABR since 2005, attending numerous national conventions and Casey Stengel/Elysian Fields chapter meetings. Although her current day job is as an attorney in New Jersey, she has previously been on staff as a sports writer at *Newsday* and *The Poughkeepsie Journal*. She also worked as an editorial producer at MLB Advanced Media, watched and analyzed baseball games for a living in order to create punchy headlines and clever captions for official team websites. With SABR, she is an editor and contributor to BioProject and has participated in the publication of several SABR books, including *Van Lingle Mungo*, *The Miracle Has Landed*, *Bridging Two Dynasties*, *Go-Go to Glory*, *Minnesotans in Baseball*, and the upcoming collection on no-hitters. She also presented original research, "Andy Coakley vs. the Cubs: Baseball's Forgotten Labor Struggle," at the 2015 SABR national convention in Chicago.

Paul Ladewski (Ted Kluszewski) is the Chicago Baseball Museum communications director and a former sportswriter who covered the Chicago sports scene for the better part of three decades. The Chicago native is a past winner of the prestigious Peter Lisagor Award, and in 2005, the Associated Press named him the top sports columnist in Illinois. In addition to the CBM Web site, his work has appeared in the Daily Southtown and Inside Sports magazine among other publications. He has covered six World Series, six league and division series and five All-Star Games and considers the 1983 White Sox to be the favorite beat in his newspaper career.

Russ Lake (Game One World Series game story) lives in Champaign, IL, and is a retired college professor emeritus. The 1964 St. Louis Cardinals remain his favorite team, and he was distressed to see Sportsman's Park (aka Busch Stadium I) being demolished not long after he had attended the last game there on May 8, 1966. His wife, Carol, deserves an MVP award for watching all of a 13-inning ballgame in Cincinnati with Russ in 1971 – during their honeymoon. In 1994, he was an editor for David Halberstam's baseball book, *October 1964*.

Leonte Landino (Luis Aparicio) is a Venezuelan journalist for ESPN Deportes who has covered baseball in the U.S. and Latin America since 1996. He has extensive experience in the media as a commentator and producer, and as a writer for many print and electronic publications. He has worked for Aguilas del Zulia of the Venezuelan League and the Tampa Bay Rays. He currently produces all baseball properties for the ESPN Deportes Spanish-language network and continues to display his work on ESPNdeportes.com. Landino has done extensive research with SABR on the lives of Luis Castro and Luis Aparicio.

Kevin Larkin (April 22 game story) retired after 24 years as a police officer in his hometown of Great Barrington Massachusetts. He has authored two books on baseball: *Baseball in the BayState (*a history of baseball in the Commonwealth of Massachusetts) and *Gehrig:Game by Game* (an account of all of the major league baseball games played by his hero, Lou Gehrig. He has also co-authored *Baseball in the Berkshires: A County's Common Bond* along with James Tom Daly, James Overmyer, and Larry Moore. He has authored numerous articles for SABR and also recently had published on *Legends On Deck*, a list of who Larkin thinks are the top 100 Black Baseball/Negro League baseball players. He does fact checking and hyperlinking for SABR and according to him, is living the dream of writing and researching about the great sport of baseball.

R. J. Lesch (Associate Editor) is a business analyst living in Carlisle, Pennsylvania, with wife Laura Rumley and two stepchildren. R. J. has been a White Sox fan since the Harry Caray days and a SABR member since 1998. He is delighted to be a member of the Deadball Era and Baseball and the Arts committees, and was a co-founder of the Field of Dreams Chapter. He is also an avid fencer and certified fencing coach, his specialty being sabre. This can be confusing to family and friends.

Len Levin (Associate Editor), a retired newspaper editor, has been the copy editor for all of SABR's recent books. He also has a part-time gig editing the decisions of the Rhode Island Supreme Court. He lives in Providence.

Gary Livacari (Al Smith) is a baseball historian and SABR member. He is the co-editor of the Old-Time Baseball Facebook page (with over 73K followers), and administrator of the Baseball History Comes Alive! web page. He was an editor for the Boston Public Library Leslie Jones Baseball Collection project, helping to identify ball players in almost 3,000 photos from the 1930s and 1940s. He has also written biographies for the SABR BioProject, plus numerous articles and book reviews. He resides in Park Ridge, Illinois.

Barb Mantegani (Tony Cuccinello) grew up in Manchester, New Hampshire, and became a Red Sox fan the summer her (much) older brother broke his leg playing Pony League ball and spent his days in a chaise lounge listening to Red Sox games on the radio, with his adoring 5-year-old baby sister by his side. Barb departed New England for Virginia and a career in tax law in 1980 but has remained a member of Red Sox Nation, and watched the ball settle into Mientkiewicz's glove screaming into the phone with that same big brother who taught her how to love a team no matter what. Barb lives in McLean, VA with her husband, a Tigers fan.

Mel Marmer (Jim McAnany and Ray Moore) lives in Philadelphia, Pennsylvania and Piegaro, Italy with Vickie Schafer Aspinwall and their two dogs, Thatcher and Eli. Mel has two daughters and two grandsons. He is an alumnus of the University of The Arts, Philadelphia, with a degree in Graphic Design. He writes poetry, and short stories. He enjoys literature, history, and baseball, and gets (mostly) down with the Phillies.

John McMurray (Larry Doby, Sherm Lollar) chairs both the Deadball Era Committee and the Oral History Committee of the Society for American Baseball Research (SABR). He is a past chair of SABR's Larry Ritter Award subcommittee, which annually recognizes the best book focused primarily on baseball's Deadball Era.

Justin Murphy (Sammy Esposito) is a reporter for the Democrat and Chronicle newspaper in Rochester, New York. He attended the University of Chicago and the S.I. Newhouse School for Public Communications at Syracuse University.

Todd Newville (John Romano) was born in Norman, Oklahoma and now lives in Plano, Texas, with his wife of 14 years (Melissa) and son Jackson. He is a 1992 graduate from the University of Oklahoma with a bachelor's degree in print journalism. He has worked for two small Oklahoma newspapers in Ardmore and Norman as well as a rodeo publication in Oklahoma City since graduating. He likes all sports, really, but baseball is his forte of knowledge. Currently, he is a free-lance baseball journalist with most of his notable articles (nine to date) appearing in America's oldest baseball publication, *Baseball Digest*, out of Evanston, Illinois. You can view his collection of baseball biographies at his own self-maintained baseball website Baseball Todd's Dugout at www.baseballtoddsdugout.com.

Rob Neyer (Billy Pierce) is a longtime baseball writer and editor for ESPN.com, SB Nation, and FoxSports.com. He began his career as a research assistant for groundbreaking baseball author Bill James and later worked for STATS, Inc. He has also written or co-written seven baseball books, including *The Neyer/James Guide to Pitchers* (with Bill James), winner of the Sporting News/SABR Baseball Research Award; and, most recently, *Power Ball: Anatomy of a Modern Baseball Game*, winner of the 2018 CASEY Award. Rob lives in Oregon with his wife and daughter.

Bill Nowlin (Associate Editor, Ron Jackson) has helped edit a few dozen books for SABR and has been a member of the Board of Directors since 2004. He is a co-founder of Rounder Records and a member of the International Bluegrass Music Hall of Fame.

Emmet Nowlin (Editorial Assistant) co-edited the book *20-Game Losers*. (SABR, 2017). A resident of Cambridge, Massachusetts, he often enjoys cheese omelets on the weekend.

Janice A. Petterchak (Don Mueller) is a researcher and writer of biographies and business histories. Her publications include *The Soldier's General: Omar Bradley and the United States Military in Peace and War*; *Lone Scout: W.D. Boyce and American Boy Scouting*; *Out to Sea Again: A Naval Armed Guard in World War II*; *Jack Brickhouse: A Voice for All Seasons*; and *Illinois History: An Annotated Bibliography*. Ms. Petterchak served as director of the Illinois State Historical Library, assistant executive directory of the Illinois State

Contributor Biographies

Historical Society, and president of the Sangamon County (Illinois) Historical Society. She is a member of the Society of Midland Authors and the St. Louis Writers Guild.

Neal Poloncarz (J.C. Martin), a SABR member since 1997, was raised in the Philadelphia suburbs. His passion for baseball began when his family attended countless games at Veterans Stadium to watch the Philadelphia Phillies. In 1984, cupid slung an arrow through his heart (*or George Steinbrenner signed him for a zillion dollars*) when he attended his first Yankee game, at the Stadium. He hosted a sports-talk radio show at WVOX 1460-AM in New Rochelle, NY. An in-studio guest was devoted SABR member John Vorperian, an ardent Red Sox fan. Neal also interviewed Mr. Arnold Hano, author of *A Day In The Bleachers*; Andy Musser, a retired Philadelphia Phillies Play-by-play announcer; and fellow SABR member, the late Mr. Ernie Harwell. Neal's SABR bios are dedicated in the memory of former SABR member Ross Adell who recommended Neal to write articles for SABR. Neal has written SABR biographies of J.C. Martin, Tim Hosley, Gary Kroll, Gus Triandos, By Saam, Wayne Twitchell, Lee Smith, and Mariano Rivera.

Alexandre Pratt (Claude Raymond) is arts editor for *La Presse* daily, in Montréal. From 1999 to 2001 he covered the Montreal Expos and came to know Claude Raymond. He once benefited from Raymond's advice at a baseball clinic in Saint-Jean, in 1988.

Jose Ramirez (Rodolfo Arias), a native of Cuba and lifelong fan of the Habana Lions (Leones de la Habana), can be seen at the SABR conventions and Fenway Park wearing his red Lions baseball cap. A SABR member since 2001, Jose lives with his wife Judy in Westford, Massachusetts, and Naples, Florida and has two sons, Jose Jr. (also a SABR member) and Jason. Jose has recently published a new book entitled *Cuba and the "Last" Baseball Season* with a Foreword written by his friend and fellow Cuban Luis Tiant Jr. a member of the Red Sox Hall of Fame.

Mike Richard (Jim Landis) spent the "Summer of Love"--1967--falling in love with the Impossible Dream Red Sox. He taught high school English for 26 years, and is now a guidance counselor at Gardner (Massachusetts) High School. He is author of two books: *Glory to Gardner: 100 Years of Football in the Chair City* and *Super Saturdays: The Complete History of the Massachusetts High School Super Bowl, 1972-2002*. He lives in Gardner with his wife Peggy and two college-aged children, Casey and Lindsey.

Paul Rogers (Joe Stanka) is president of the Ernie Banks – Bobby Bragan (Dallas-Fort Worth) SABR Chapter and the co-author of four baseball books, including *The Whiz Kids and the 1950 Pennant* written with his boyhood hero Robin Roberts, and *Lucky Me: My 65 Years in Baseball* authored with Eddie Robinson. He is also co-editor of recent SABR team histories of the 1951 New York Giants and the 1950 Philadelphia Phillies as well as a frequent contributor to the SABR bio project. His real job is as a law professor at SMU where he was dean of the law school for nine years and has served as the university's faculty athletic representative for 32 years.

John Rossi (John Callison) is Professor Emeritus of History at La Salle University in Philadelphia. His most recent book, *Baseball and American Culture: A History, Roman & Littlefield* appeared in September 2018. He has also published sketches on Evelyn Waugh's novel, *Put Out More Flags*, on Kipling's writings and H.L. Mencken for *The American Conservative Magazine*.

Jim Sargent (Jerry Staley), a retired history professor, has written numerous articles about baseball and football players, mostly for SABR BioProject and the Pro Football Researchers Association web sites. Sargent also published two books about the Tigers, *Yesterday's Tiger Heroes* (Wynwidyn, 2014) and *The Tigers and Yankees in '61* (McFarland, 2016). More recently, he has authored two Mickey Mathews mysteries, *Final Secret* (2017), and *The Long Pursuit* (2019).

Bill Savage (The '59 White Sox in Literature) is a Professor of Instruction in the Department of English at Northwestern University, where he teaches the course "Baseball in American Narrative," which focuses on the ways that baseball stories create a sense of American identity. He has co-edited two editions of the work of Nelson Algren: *The 50th Anniversary Critical Edition of The Man with the Golden Arm*, and *Chicago: City on the Make, Newly Annotate*d. A member of the Society for American Baseball Research, he is a lifelong resident of Chicago's North Side, and a die-hard fan and season ticket holder for the Chicago Cubs. But he believes, despite evidence to the contrary, that Cubs and Sox fans can get along, and he acknowledges that the White Sox are the much more literary team. He wrote a column about the 2016 Cubs World Series run for ESPN.com, "The View from Section 416."

Pam Schur (Editorial Assistant) is a Licensed Clinical Professional Counselor (LCPC). She is also a freelance writer and former public relations specialist. This is Pam's first project with SABR, and being a lifelong White Sox fan, has enjoyed it immensely! She is lives in Chicago with her husband, and has 26-year-old twins.

Richard Smiley (Sherm Lollar) lives in Chicago, Illinois where he works as a statistician and demographer. He has been a SABR member for over 30 years and is a member of the Deadball Era, Nineteenth Century, and Ballparks Committees. His article on Heinie Zimmerman's failed pursuit of Eddie Collins in the 1917 World Series appeared in the *The National Pastime* and his biographies of Reb Russell and Matty McIntyre appeared in *Deadball Stars of the American League*. He edited the 1906 chapter in *The World Series in the Deadball Era: A History in the Words and Pictures of the Writers and Photographers*. His current research interests include the history of professional baseball in Chicago prior to the founding of the National League.

Curt Smith (White Sox Broadcasters) is the author of 17 books, the latest 2018's *The Presidents and the Pastime: The History of Baseball and the White House*, the first to chronicle in-depth the tie between two American institutions—baseball and the Presidency. His prior books include *Voices of The Game*, *The Voice*, and *Pull Up a Chair: The Vin Scully Story*. From 1989-93, he wrote more speeches than anyone else for President George H.W. Bush. Smith is a Senior Lecturer of English at the University of Rochester, GateHouse Media columnist, and what *USA Today* calls America's "Voice of authority on baseball broadcasting." He has also been named to the Judson Welliver Society of former Presidential speechwriters.

Justin Thompson (Camilo Carreon) is a student at San Jose State University. Although his window of opportunity working in organized baseball has closed, he appreciates the opportunities SABR provides to be involved with the great game of baseball. He looks forward to honing his skills and continuing to engage in SABR projects.

Adam J. Ulrey (Turk Lown) used to be the featured writer for "Inside Ducks Sports," and spent 10 years on the radio doing a sports talk show in the beautiful Willamette Valley. He enjoys building his own Bamboo Fly rods and has a small catering business. He spends most of his free time in the outdoors doing everything from hiking to fishing in his own stream. But his favorite past time is spending time with his wife Jhody and son Camran. He also has two beautiful dogs named Montana and Behr.

Ed Veit (Del Ennis) grew up in Philadelphia with the Whiz Kids, but his introduction to the major leagues was a 1946 Sunday double-header between the Philadelphia Athletics and the New York. He holds degrees from Johns Hopkins University, Loyola University of Maryland, and West Chester University. He is a former Washington DC policeman and now a retired English teacher from Baltimore County, Maryland; later taught freshman English at York College of Pennsylvania and at one time took tickets at Camden Yards and freelanced for the *York Dispatch*. He coached college soccer at UMBC and has been a SABR member for 20 years.

Cort Vitty (Harry Simpson) is a native of New Jersey, a graduate of Seton Hall University, and a SABR member (Bob Davids Chapter) since 1999. Vitty's work has appeared int the *Baseball Research Journal*; *The National Pastime*; *Bridging Two Dynasties: The 1947 New York Yankees*; and *Pitching to the Pennant: The 1954 Cleveland* Indians. In addition to the essay appearing in this publication, original works are posted at Seamheads.com and PhiladelphiaAthletics.org. For the SABR Biography Project, Vitty has authored biographies of Buzz Arlett, Benny Bengough, James "Ripper" Collins, Mickey Grasso, Billy Johnson, Babe Phelps, and Dave Philley. Although a resident of Maryland, Vitty roots for the New York Yankees.

Contributor Biographies

Joseph Wancho (Ray Boone and Dick Donovan) lives in Brooklyn, Ohio, and is a lifelong Cleveland Indians fan. He has been a SABR member since 2005 and serves as the vice chair of SABR's Baseball Index Project Committee. He was the editor of *Pitching to the Pennant: The 1954 Cleveland Indians* (University of Nebraska Press, 2014) and *The Sleeping Giant Awakes: The 1995 Cleveland Indians* (SABR, 2019). He also authored *So You Think You're a Cleveland Indians Fan?* (Sports Publishing, 2018).

Bob Webster (Comiskey Park) grew up in NW Indiana and has been a Cubs fan since 1963. Now living in Portland, Oregon, Bob spends his time working on baseball research and writing and has contributed to quite a few SABR projects, as well as working as a Stats Stringer on the MLB Gameday app for three years. Bob is a member of the Northwest Chapter of SABR and on the Board of Directors of the Old-Timers Baseball Association of Portland.

Tim Wiles (Jack Brickhouse) is the Director of the Guilderland (NY) Public Library, and was Director of Research at the National Baseball Hall of Fame and Museum from 1995 to 2014. He is the co-author of *Baseball's Greatest Hit: the Story of Take Me Out to the Ball Game* (2008) and co-editor of *Line Drives: 100 Contemporary Baseball Poems* (2002). His primary baseball interests are in baseball culture—music, art, and literature; women in baseball, and the Chicago Cubs. He has performed "Casey at the Bat" in costume a couple of thousand times, starting in 1996.

Brian P. Wood (Vince Lloyd, Don Wells) "Woodie" is a long time San Francisco Giants fan and resides in Pacific Grove, California with his wife Terrise. They have three sons, Daniel, Jack, and Nathan and dog, Bochy. A retired U.S. Navy Commander and F-14 Tomcat Naval Flight Officer, Woodie is a Research Associate on the faculty at the Naval Postgraduate School in Monterey, California specializing in Field Experimentation of new technologies before they are sent to military forces.

Don Zminda (Editor, Ray Berres, Nellie Fox, Joe Hicks, Bubba Phillips, September 22 game story) has been a White Sox fan since attending his first game at Old Comiskey in August of 1954. As Director of Publications for STATS, Inc. (now STATS LLC) from 1988-2000, he co-authored or edited a dozen annual sports publications. Don's book *The Legendary Harry Caray: Baseball's Greatest Salesman* was published by Rowman & Littlefield in April 2019. A SABR member since 1979, he is retired and had lived in Los Angeles with his wife Sharon since 2000.

Acknowledgments

This book on the 1959 White Sox is a product of the Society for American Baseball Research, and an offshoot of the SABR BioProject, an ongoing effort to produce biographies of every player, manager, coach and significant figure in baseball history.

The book was originally published by ACTA Sports in 2009, and is now being reissued in an expanded and updated form as a SABR book and e-book. Our thanks go out to ACTA president Greg Pierce and co-publisher John Dewan of Sports Info Solutions for permission to re-release the book as a SABR publication.

The project began back in 2008 when Mark Armour, the chairman of the BioProject committee, and SABR vice president Bill Nowlin approached me about spearheading the effort to produce this book. Mark and Bill helped round up writers to get the project off the ground, and both provided wisdom and advice throughout the effort. When it became obvious that I needed editorial assistance to edit and manage the manuscripts, Bill volunteered to help edit every biography and asked Len Levin of SABR to join him as an Associate Editor. Our other Associate Editor, R.J. Lesch, helped move the project to completion in a number of ways, most importantly in getting the manuscript in camera-ready condition. Thanks, guys; we could not possibly have finished this project without you.

A number of other people provided editorial assistance in reading through manuscripts, helping round up photos, doing fact-checking and various other tasks: a big tip of the hat to Rich Applegate, Terry Baxter, Warren Corbett, Bob Gregory, Kevin Larkin, Tara Krieger, Rob Neyer, Emmet Nowlin, Mike See, Richard Smiley and Mark Sternman.

This book was written by a large number of writers, all of whom produced outstanding work strictly for the love of the game and the project: many thanks to Dave Anderson, Ron Anderson, Anthony Basich, the late Ralph Berger, Robert Bigelow, Ray Birch, Matt Bohn, Thomas J. Brown Jr., Scott Ferkovich, David Fleitz, Peter Gordon, Mike Hasse, Jack Herrman, Paul Hofman, Bill Johnson, Maxwell Kates, Paul Ladewski, Russ Lake, Leonte Landino, Kevin Larkin, Gary Livacari, Barb Mantegani, Mel Marmer, John McMurray, Justin Murphy, Todd Newville, J.A. Petterchak, Neal Poloncarz, Alexandre Pratt, Jose Ramirez, Mike Richard, C. Paul Rogers, John Rossi, Jim Sargent, Bill Savage, Pam Schur, Richard Smiley, Curt Smith, Justin Thompson, Adam Ulrey, Edward Veit, Cort Vitty, Joe Wancho, Bob Webster, Tim Wiles, and Brian Wood.

Scott Reifert of the Chicago White Sox generously supported the project by helping us contact players and family members from the 1959 team. Scott also let us comb through the White Sox player files for photos and articles, which was a great help to the project. Sox photographer Ron Vesely was extremely helpful in rounding up photos and getting them scanned.

Many of the photos in the book are images of Topps baseball cards from the 1950s and '60s; thanks to the Topps Company Inc. for their generosity in allowing us to use the cards in this book. John Horne of the National Baseball Hall of Fame was of great assistance in helping find rare photos for the book, as was Yvette Reyes of AP Images. Mary Brace of George Brace Photo was a great help in providing some rare photos from the voluminous George Brace collection.

Detailed statistical information is vital to a book of this scope. Many sources were used to gather information, but we as especially grateful to Dave Smith of Retrosheet, Sean Forman of Baseball-Reference.com, Rod Nelson of the SABR Oral History Committee and Kevin McCann of the SABR Minor Leagues Committee.

Finally, many thanks to my wife Sharon and my stepsons Steve and Mike for their patience and support during this long and time-consuming project. We did it!

Don Zminda
Los Angeles, California
February 2019

Photographs

The Topps Company, Inc. — All baseball card images: 4, 30, 54, 67, 71, 87, 90, 98, 123, 131, 135, 152, 162, 185, 199, 201, 209, 227, 267, 286
White Sox Photos: 1, 33, 36, 41, 44, 60, 63, 75, 78, 103, 109, 118, 127, 139, 145, 149, 155, 167, 171, 177, 181, 189, 193, 205, 221, 252, 261, 279, cover
National Baseball Hall of Fame: 7, 13, 23, 27, 49, 94, 115, 164, 197, 237, 239, 245, 254, 262, cover
George Brace Photo: 3, 215
A.P. Images: 16, 84, 207, 264

Aparicio, Luis 16
Aparicio, Luis 54
Aparicio, Luis 261
Aparicio, Luis 267
Arias, Rodolfo 60
Battey, Earl 63
Berres, Ray 33
Berres, Ray 36
Boone, Ray 67
Brickhouse, Jack 237
Brooklyn's Ebbets Field 164
Callison, John 71
Carreon, Camilo 75
Cash, Norm 78
Chicago White Sox Yearbook 82
Comiskey Park 7
Cooney, Johnny 36
Cooney, Johnny 41
Cuccinello, Tony 36
Cuccinello, Tony 44
Doby, Larry 87
Donovan, Dick 90
Elson, Bob 239
Ennis, Del 94
Esposito, Sammy 98
Fox, Nellie 16
Fox, Nellie 103
Fox, Nellie 252
Gaedel, Eddie 16
Game 1, World Series 286
Greenberg, Hank 23
Gutteridge, Don 49
Gutteridge, Don 36
Hicks, Joe 115
Jackson, Ron 118
Kluszewski, Ted 123
Kluszewski, Ted 262
Kluszewski, Ted 264
Landis, Jim 127
Landis, Jim 279
Lane, Frank 1
Latman, Barry 131
Lloyd, Vince 245
Lollar, Sherman 135
Lopez, Al 27
Lopez, Al 30
Lopez, Al 36
Lown, Omar "Turk" 139
Mantle, Mickey 239
Martians stunt 16
Martin, J.C. 145
McAnany, Jim 149
McBride, Ken 152
Minoso, Orestes (Minnie) 4
Moore, Ray 155
Mueller, Don 159
Neal, Charlie 286
Peters, Gary 162
Phillips, Bubba 167
Pierce, Billy 171
Price, Selwin 296
Raymond, Claude 177
Richards, Paul 3
Rivera, Jim 181
Romano, John 185
Rudolph, Don 189
Shaw, Bob 193
Simpson, Harry (Chicago) 199
Simpson, Harry (Cleveland) 197
Skizas, Lou 201
Smith, Al 205
Smith, Al 207
Staley, Jerry 209
Stanka, Joe 215
Torgeson, Earl 221
Veeck, Bill 13
Veeck, Bill 16
Wynn, Early 227
Wynn, Early 254
Wynn, Early 262

New Books from SABR

Part of the mission of the Society for American Baseball Research has always been to disseminate member research. In addition to the *Baseball Research Journal*, SABR publishes books that include player biographies, historical game recaps, and statistical analysis. All SABR books are available in print and ebook formats. SABR members can access the entire SABR Digital Library for free and purchase print copies at significant member discounts of 40 to 50% off cover price.

JEFF BAGWELL IN CONNECTICUT:
A CONSISTENT LAD IN THE LAND OF STEADY HABITS
This volume of articles, interviews, and essays by members of the Connecticut chapter of SABR chronicles the life and career of Connecticut's favorite baseball son, Hall-of-Famer Jeff Bagwell, with special attention on his high school and college years.
Edited by Karl Cicitto, Bill Nowlin, & Len Levin
$19.95 paperback (ISBN 978-1-943816-97-2)
$9.99 ebook (ISBN 978-1-943816-96-5)
7"x10", 246 pages, 45 photos

1995 CLEVELAND INDIANS:
THE SLEEPING GIANT AWAKENS
After almost 40 years of sub-.500 baseball, the Sleeping Giant woke in 1995, the first season the Indians spent in their new home of Jacob's Field. The biographies of all the players, coaches, and broadcasters from that year are here, sprinkled with personal perspectives, as well as game stories from key matchups during the 1995 season, information about Jacob's Field, and other essays.
Edited by Joseph Wancho
$19.95 paperback (ISBN 978-1-943816-95-8)
$9.99 ebook (ISBN 978-1-943816-94-1)
8.5"X11", 410 pages, 76 photos

TIME FOR EXPANSION BASEBALL
The LA Angels and "new" Washington Senators ushered in MLB's 1960 expansion, followed in 1961 by the Houston Colt .45s and New York Mets. By 1998, 10 additional teams had launched: the Kansas City Royals, Seattle Pilots, Toronto Blue Jays, and Tampa Bay Devil Rays in the AL, and the Montreal Expos, San Diego Padres, Colorado Rockies, Florida Marlins, and Arizona Diamondbacks in the NL. *Time for Expansion Baseball* tells each team's origin and includes biographies of key players.
Edited by Maxwell Kates and Bill Nowlin
$24.95 paperback (ISBN 978-1-933599-89-7)
$9.99 ebook (ISBN 978-1-933599-88-0)
8.5"X11", 430 pages, 150 photos

BASE BALL'S 19TH CENTURY "WINTER" MEETINGS 1857-1900
A look at the business meetings of base ball's earliest days (not all of which were in the winter). As John Thorn writes in his Foreword, "This monumental volume traces the development of the game from its birth as an organized institution to its very near suicide at the dawn of the next century."
Edited by Jeremy K. Hodges and Bill Nowlin
$29.95 paperback (ISBN 978-1-943816-91-0)
$9.99 ebook (ISBN978-1-943816-90-3)
8.5"x11", 390 pages, 50 photos

MET-ROSPECTIVES:
A COLLECTION OF THE GREATEST GAMES IN NEW YORK METS HISTORY
This book's 57 game stories—coinciding with the number of Mets years through 2018—are strictly for the eternal optimist. They include the team's very first victory in April 1962 at Forbes Field, Tom Seaver's "Imperfect Game" in July '69, the unforgettable Game Sixes in October '86, the "Grand Slam Single" in the 1999 NLCS, and concludes with the extra-innings heroics in September 2016 at Citi Field that helped ensure a wild-card berth.
edited by Brian Wright and Bill Nowlin
$14.95 paperback (ISBN 978-1-943816-87-3)
$9.99 ebook (ISBN 978-1-943816-86-6)
8.5"X11", 148 pages, 44 photos

CINCINNATI'S CROSLEY FIELD:
A GEM IN THE QUEEN CITY
This book evokes memories of Crosley Field through detailed summaries of more than 85 historic and monumental games played there, and 10 insightful feature essays about the history of the ballpark. Former Reds players Johnny Edwards and Art Shamsky share their memories of the park in introductions.
Edited by Gregory H. Wolf
$19.95 paperback (ISBN 978-1-943816-75-0)
$9.99 ebook (ISBN 978-1-943816-74-3)
8.5"X11", 320 pages, 43 photos

MOMENTS OF JOY AND HEARTBREAK:
66 SIGNIFICANT EPISODES IN THE HISTORY OF THE PITTSBURGH PIRATES
In this book we relive no-hitters, World Series-winning homers, and the last tripleheader ever played in major-league baseball. Famous Pirates like Honus Wagner and Roberto Clemente—and infamous ones like Dock Ellis—make their appearances, as well as recent stars like Andrew McCutcheon.
Edited by Jorge Iber and Bill Nowlin
$19.95 paperback (ISBN 978-1-943816-73-6)
$9.99 ebook (ISBN 978-1-943816-72-9)
8.5"X11", 208 pages, 36 photos

FROM SPRING TRAINING TO SCREEN TEST:
BASEBALL PLAYERS TURNED ACTORS
SABR's book of baseball's "matinee stars," a selection of those who crossed the lines between professional sports and popular entertainment. Included are the famous (Gene Autry, Joe DiMaggio, Jim Thorpe, Bernie Williams) and the forgotten (Al Gettel, Lou Stringer, Wally Hebert, Wally Hood), essays on baseball in TV shows and Coca-Cola commercials, and Jim Bouton's casting as "Jim Barton" in the *Ball Four* TV series.
Edited by Rob Edelman and Bill Nowlin
$19.95 paperback (ISBN 978-1-943816-71-2)
$9.99 ebook (ISBN 978-1-943816-70-5)
8.5"X11", 410 pages, 89 photos

To learn more about how to receive these publications for free or at member discount as a member of SABR, visit the website: sabr.org/join

SABR Publications Patrons

THANK YOU for helping us exceed our goal! We would like to extend our sincere gratitude to all Friends of SABR – our generous donors – for becoming SABR Publications Patrons and supporting our efforts to donate SABR books to libraries, schools, and non-profit organizations. We achieved the $25,000 goal which was matched by SABR Director Bill Nowlin.

Over 100 SABR members have become Publications Patrons and collectively contributed the resources to donate 280 SABR books and a total of nearly $55,000 – in just over a month!

The SABR Publications Patron campaign is ongoing and can be accessed at **sabr.org/publications-patron**. All SABR Publications Patrons receive the SABR commemorative bookmark pictured to the left.

Help SABR Grow

You can become a Friend of SABR by giving as little as $10 per month or by making a one-time gift of $1,000 or more. When you do so, you will be inducted into a community of passionate baseball fans dedicated to supporting SABR's work.

Friends of SABR receive the following benefits:
- ✓ Annual Friends of SABR Commemorative Lapel Pin
- ✓ Recognition in This Week in SABR, SABR.org, and the SABR Annual Report
- ✓ Access to the SABR Annual Convention VIP donor event
- ✓ Invitations to exclusive Friends of SABR events

SABR On-Deck Circle - $10/month, $30/month, $50/month
Get in the SABR On-Deck Circle, and help SABR become the essential community for the world of baseball. Your support will build capacity around all things SABR, including publications, website content, podcast development, and community growth.

A monthly gift is deducted from your bank account or charged to a credit card until you tell us to stop. No more email, mail, or phone reminders.

Join the SABR On-Deck Circle

Payment Info: _____ Visa _____ Mastercard

Name on Card: _____

Card #: _____

Exp. Date: _____ Security Code: _____

Signature: _____

○ $10/month
○ $30/month
○ $50/month
○ Other amount _____

Go to sabr.org/donate to make your gift online

www.ingramcontent.com/pod-product-compliance
Lightning Source LLC
Chambersburg PA
CBHW081353070526
44583CB00020B/2544